WHY WORLD BAND RADIO?

I f you're interested in what's going on and don't listen to world band radio, it's like having one eye closed. You miss a lot of the news, a great deal of the fun—and virtually all the other person's point of view.

So, when *Cosby* and *Murder, She Wrote* begin to wear thin, turn to the BBC for Margaret Thatcher's worldwide phone-in show (yes, she'll take your call). Rather be in Philadelphia? Try the original Philadelphia, in Egypt. Or share in a sunrise guitar concert from the Amazonian rain forest.

German reunification? Hear all about it—from both Germanys. Something lighter for dinner? Dial up songs of love from Paris, or flamencos from Madrid.

There's a whole world just waiting for you, day after day. Dozens of countries with news, world music and sports you can't find anywhere else. It's here—enjoyment has returned to evening entertainment.

Farmer and daughter in Fribourg, Switzerland.

Swiss National Tourist Office

Cheryl Blackerby

Page 21

CONTENTS

WORLD BAND RADIO

Page 109

Page 29

BBC

ISSN 0897-0157

 International Broadcasting Services, Ltd.

PASSPORT TO WORLD BAND RADIO

1991

Editor-in-Chief	Lawrence Magne
Editor	Tony Jones
Features Editor	Rick Booth
Contributing Editors	Jock Elliott, Noel Green (England), Craig Tyson (Australia)
Consulting Editors	John Campbell (England), Don Jensen, Kannon Shanmugam
Special Contributors	James Conrad, Gordon Darling (Papua New Guinea), Antonio Ribeiro da Motta (Brazil), DXFL/ Isao Ugusa (Japan), Kim Elliott, Manosij Guha (India), Ruth Hesch, Konrad Kroszner, Elizabeth Macalaster, Toshimichi Ohtake (Japan), Robert Palmer, RNM/Tetsuya Hirahara (Japan), Jairo Salazar (Venezuela), Don Swampo (Uruguay), David Walcutt
Database Software	Richard Mayell
Laboratory	Robert Sherwood
Marketing & Production	Mary Kroszner
Administration	Jane Brinker
Graphics/Communications	Consultech Communications, Inc.
IBS – North America	Box 300, Penn's Park, Pennsylvania 18943 USA
IBS – Latin America	Casilla de Correo 1844, Asunción, Paraguay
IBS – Japan	5-31-6 Tamanawa, Kamakura 247

COVER: Sangean ATS-803A portable receiver. Photography by Bill Murphy.

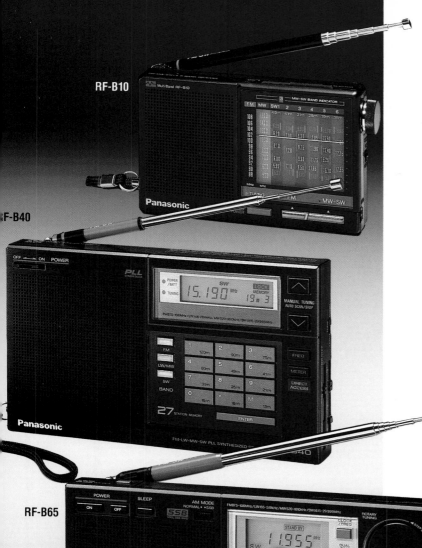

Panasonic presents portable multi-band radios.

You don't have to travel the world to see it. With a Panasonic portable multi-band radio you can see it like never before . . . with your ears.

The complete line is engineered for lightweight portability and heavy-weight performance. Now, if you're just going to the beach, you can hear what's going on in the Gobi Desert.

RF-B10 — Ultra-compact design.
- FM/MW/SW from 5.95 to 17.90 MHz
- Operation Hold switch locks in current function
- DX-local AM sensitivity switch
- High/low tone selector

RF-B40 — Phase-Locked Loop
quartz-synthesized tuner with micro computer control
- FM/MW/LW/SW
- Up-conversion double super-hetrodyne system
- 5-way multi-tuning system
- Multi-function LCD readout

RF-B65 — Receives Single Side Band
- PLL quartz synthesized tuner with MCC
- FM/MW/LW/SW, Single Side Band
- SSB fine tuning
- Up-conversion double super-hetrodyne system
- 1 kHz-step fine tuning for LW/MW/SW
- 6-way multi-tuning system:
- Built-in dual clock/timer keeps time in two zones
- Sleep/standby function
- Multi-function LCD readout with signal strength indicator

So, with a Panasonic compact multi-band radio, when it's tea time, you can take the time to tune in the BBC.

SEE THE WORLD THROUGH YOUR EARS

Panasonic®
just slightly ahead of our time.®

HF-225

Your Gateway to the World

Rugged, reliable, regarded by many as the best receiver they ever used, the HF-225 has shown that there is a new way to provide the listener with all he wants, but without confusing him with a hundred colored buttons and knobs. The HF-225 is technology tamed by the application of common sense. So—what do you get for your money?

High stability, low noise performance, coupled to accurate digital read-out for on-the-nose station location.

<u>All</u> filters fitted for every mode—2.2 kHz, 4 kHz, 7 kHz, 10 kHz, as well as a 200 Hz audio filter for CW. No extras to buy.

30 memory channels for your favorite frequencies, with instant access and instant check facilities.

Hot options include a true synchronous AM detector for combatting those deep fades (it also gives you narrow band FM reception as well); an active whip antenna for portable use, and a handsome, rugged carrying case; a battery pack which fits inside the radio; and a keypad for direct frequency entry, about which Larry Magne had this to say:

". . . there's no fooling around with 'enter' keys, 'kHz' keys, leading zeros, decimals—or any of the time wasters found on other keypads. It is, hands down, the best keypad available on any set, regardless of price."

Chris Williams agreed with Larry when he wrote from Massachusetts:

"As a past owner of receivers such as the Sony ICF-2010 and Grundig Satellit 650 and 500, I must say that none compare to your Lowe HF-225. Without question, for hour after hour listening, nothing compares. I especially like the keypad. Why more receivers do not incorporate such intelligent ergonomics is beyond me."

That just about says it all, but in addition to the praise from users, the HF-225 was voted "Receiver of the Year" by World Radio and TV Handbook.

Write now, and find out how the HF-225 can open your own "Gateway to the World."

LOWE ELECTRONICS LIMITED

Chesterfield Road, Matlock, Derbyshire DE4 5LE England
Telephone 0629 580800 (4 lines)   Fax 0629 580020   Telex 377482

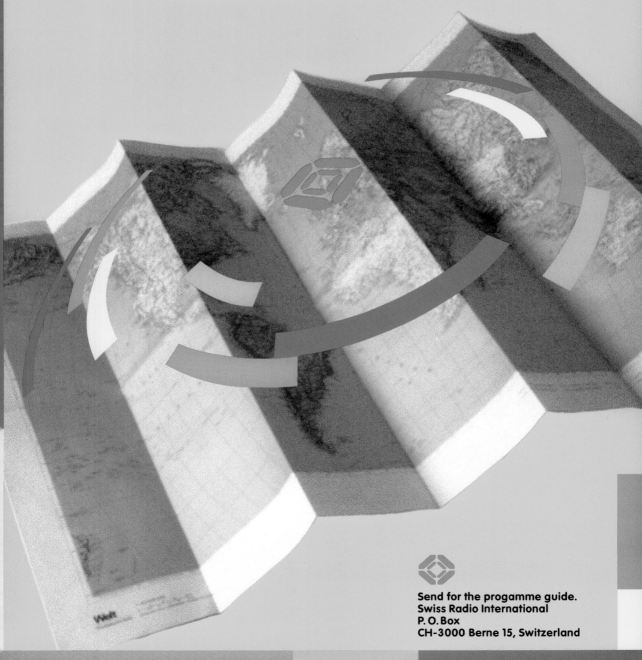

it's Swiss…
it's Radio…
it's International…

Swiss Radio International

news, comment and current affairs
worldwide on shortwave

**Send for the progamme guide.
Swiss Radio International
P. O. Box
CH-3000 Berne 15, Switzerland**

THE WORLD
OF WORLD BAND RADIO

EASY PICKINGS:
20+ BIG SIGNALS

All world band stations are equal, but some—to borrow from George Orwell—are more equal than others. These are the easy ones to hear, and this is so for several reasons.

Power, for one. While the biggest AM and FM stations hardly ever run more than 50,000 watts, world band outlets commonly pump out a quarter—even a half—*million*.

Relaying, for another. Some stations broadcast simultaneously from several spots where they own relay transmission facilities. The BBC World Service, Deutsche Welle, Radio France Internationale and the Voice of America go this route, and they're not the only ones. Not every station can afford such lengths, or even wants to—but those that do certainly make themselves heard.

Trading, for a third. Stations often sign agreements to trade programming. Radio Canada International, for instance, swaps with stations in Austria, China, Japan and South Korea, among others. Listeners who can't hear RCI from its Canadian transmitters might catch its programming elsewhere, and vice versa. In practice, these trades are also referred to as being "relays."

Some of the "lesser equals" enjoy good

Radio Canada International's programs include seafaring—the soul of Canada's rugged maritime provinces and, as here, coastal Quebec.

Industry, Science & Technology Canada

propagation without such elaborate means. When conditions in the upper atmosphere—the *ionosphere*—are right, and more of the signal bounces back to earth than usual, such stations are astonishingly strong. That's particularly true at night, especially if the station is located near the Tropic of Cancer.

All this is good news for you. Strong stations, of course, are the easiest to find. So here are 20-plus world band outlets you're most likely to hear well. All times given are World Time (see *What Is World Time?* on page 106).

EUROPE
Austria

Hardly a "superstation"—**Radio Austria International** never uses more than five transmitters at a time. But they are powerful, beaming reflections of the Austrian character: friendly and independent.

Austria is heard in English to North America at 0130-0200 on 9875 and 13730 kHz; 0530-0600 via the Canadian relay on 6015 kHz; and 1130-1200 on 21475 or 21490 kHz. Europeans can listen at 0530, 0830, 1130 and 1430 on 6155 and 13730 kHz; and at 1730 and 1930 on 5945 and 6155 kHz. Asians and Australians should try 0830 World Time on 15450 and 21490 kHz. If you're in East Asia, best bet is 1130 and 1430 on 15430 kHz.

Belgium

Belgische Radio en Televisie (BRT) is the voice of Belgium's Dutch-speaking population. All broadcasts originate from transmitters located within the country, reaching Europe, Eastern North America and often well beyond.

BRT's 25-minute English broadcasts are a mixture of Belgian news and features, all high-quality. These are heard in Eastern North America at 1330, Monday through Saturday, on 21810 or 21815 kHz; plus daily at 2200 and 0030 on 9925 or 13675 kHz. The 0030 transmission usually provides the best reception.

BRT broadcasts to Europe daily, at 1830 on 5910 (or 5915) and 11695 (or 13675) kHz, and again at 2200 on 5910 (or 5915) kHz.

There is a third transmission at 0730 Monday through Friday on 6035 kHz. This broadcast is also directed to Asia and the

In A.D. 73, Masada, last fortress of Jewish revolt against Romans, was overrun. The millennia of Jewish presence in Israel and its implications for today are offered over Kol Israel, heard clearly throughout Europe and Eastern North America.

Pacific on 11695 or 21815 kHz, and again Monday through Saturday at 1330 on 21810 or 21815 kHz.

All broadcasts are one hour earlier during the summer.

Czechoslovakia

One of Eastern Europe's friendliest stations, **Radio Prague International** has, in the past, leaned heavily on its delightful store of Czech and Slovak music. This has decreased of late in favor of the news, but then Czechoslovakia's march toward democracy is one of the stories of our age.

If you live in North America, tune in at 0000-0015 on 7345, 11680 and 11990 kHz; and 0100-0130, 0300-0330 and 0400-0415 on 5930, 7345 and 11680 kHz. English is beamed to Europe at 0640-0700, possibly 0740-0800 winters; and again at :40 past the hour each hour thereafter until 1200, possibly 1300 winters, on 6055, 7345 and 9505 kHz; 1700-1730 on 5930, 6055, 7345 and 11990 kHz; 1830-1845 on 6055 and 7345 kHz; and at 2000-2030 and 2100-2115 on 5930, 6055, 7345 and 11990 kHz. Listeners in Asia and the Pacific can listen at 0730-0800 on 17840 and 21705 kHz.

France

Radio France Internationale enjoys excellent facilities in continental France, as well as 500 kilowatt transmitters in French Guiana, all of which offer excellent coverage throughout Europe and North

America—especially the U.S. East Coast. Although most of RFI's programs are in French, there are enough in English to make this a station worth chasing down.

RFI's programs in English are not the lightest, but they're quite professional and are usually well-prepared. A 60-minute program in English for Africa at 1600 is as comprehensive as they come, and includes abundant news not easily found elsewhere. Pride of place goes to news concerning the francophone parts of Africa, but that doesn't mean it's not interesting. It is.

There are two daily English programs to Europe and North America, at 0330 and 1230. A second transmission for Africa is broadcast at 1600, and another for Asia and the Pacific is aired at 1400.

The frequency of 9800 kHz is the only one officially in use for North America at 0315-0345, but channels beamed to other parts of the world are also often audible. Try 6045, 7135, 7280, 9550, 9790, 11705 or 11995 kHz. At 1230-1300 you can listen on 17650, 21635 or 21645 kHz. For the 1600-1700 African program, try 11705, 15360, 17620, 17795 or 17850 kHz.

Listeners in Europe can tune in at 0330 on 3965, 6045 or 7280 kHz; at 1230 on 9805, 11670, 15155 or 15195 kHz; and at 1600 on 6175 kHz. The transmission to Asia and the Pacific at 1400-1430 is available on 7125, 11925 and 21770 kHz.

Deutsche Welle, the official station of the Federal Republic of (West) Germany, is easily heard in both Europe and North America. Technically one of the best, and oozing professionalism, this station broadcasts in English to North America evenings at 0100-0150 on 6040, 6085, 6145, 9565, 9735 and 11865 kHz. There are also repeat broadcasts at 0300 on 6085 and 9545 kHz, plus the seasonal frequencies of 6130, 9605 or 15205 kHz, and again at 0500 on 5960, 6120 and 9670 kHz. That last time slot is best for the North American West Coast.

Although not officially broadcasting in English to Europe, Deutsche Welle can still be heard by Europeans. In fact, it's among the best-heard stations in the United Kingdom at 0500-0550 on 6120 kHz. At 0600-0650 try 11765 and 13790 kHz, and in the evening it's 1900-1950 on 11810 or 13790 kHz. Listeners in Asia and the Pacific can try 0900-0950 on 6160, 11945 (or 11740), 17780, 17820, 21650 and 21680 kHz; and again at 2100-2150 on 9670, 9765, 11785, 13780 or 15435 kHz.

You'll almost certainly hear Deutsche Welle loud and clear. Its programs range from the new and excellent *European Journal* to the ever-popular *Random Selection,* which we've praised in the past.

Never heard of *Alphornblowing*? Tune in. Swiss Radio International taps a rich tradition of Alpine music—in this case, from the Canton of Fribourg.

Swiss National Tourist Office

News dominates **Swiss Radio International's** excellent weekday half-hour English broadcasts, but things lighten up on weekends, especially Sundays. *News* and *Dateline* are the weekday backbone—typically thorough Swiss looks at foreign and domestic news. Saturdays feature the long-running *Swiss Shortwave Merry-Go-Round,* while Sunday programs rotate.

North American listeners can tune in at 0200 on 6095, 6135, 9725, 9885, 12035 or 17730 kHz; and again at 0400 on 6135, 9725, 9885 or 12035 kHz. In Europe, hear SRI at 0730, 1300 and 1830—one hour earlier summers—on 6165 or 9535 kHz; and again at 2230 (2130 summers) on 6190 kHz. Best bets for Asia and the Pacific are 0830 on 9560, 13685, 17670 or 21695 kHz; plus 1100 and 1330 on 13635, 15570 or 17830 kHz.

(continued on page 94)

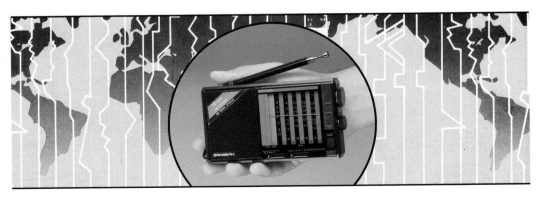

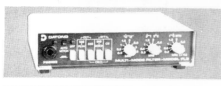

NEW COMRADES ON THE BLOC

by Daniel Lorenzetti

I was a teenage Cold War mutant, and world band was the cause. Thanks to my radio roots, I learned early to listen at a window which lately has been no less than history's panoramic parade.

It's true. Living in Florida, I heard Fidel rave against *el imperialismo yanqui* up and down the AM dial. But we moved during Kennedy's Camelot, and with Fidel out of reach, I needed a radio fix.

I found it in a clunky multi-band shortwave radio, as they were then called—the only appliance in our house stamped "Made in Japan." On cold, clear winter nights, I found all the big world band signals, but my favorites, maybe thanks to Castro, came from the Communist Bloc: Radio Budapest, Radio Prague, and, of course, the Big Throat itself, Radio Moscow. Ah, Radio Moscow, husky voices ripe with anti-U.S. invective.

My country, Moscow told me tirelessly, was filled with "capitalist imperialists, hegemonic oppressors." The Marxist–Leninist world dialectic would, as Mao later would claim, "defeat the U.S. aggressors and all their running dogs."

Vintage stuff, that, reinforced by news from America: Soup kitchens. Riots. Drugs. Prostitution. Bigotry. To lift the spirit, musical favorites like the Red Army's Greatest Hits, and the occasional dirge or anthem. Music for the working masses, Moscow called it. I called it—even then—music for the dead.

The glories of Communism? Naturally: Five Year Plans, the "New Man," unsurpassed collective farming. Every Russian crop, I remember, was a "bumper." They never mentioned dents.

Then came the Mailbag, questions from around the world. I never wrote in myself—not that I didn't have questions. And I never heard any of them asked: "Why build a wall to keep people in East Germany?" "With the wonders of Soviet farming, why buy Canadian and Australian wheat?"

That was then, but hear it now. The Bloc has crumbled, the Wall has tumbled. They only had feet of clay. How now, Chairman Mao?

Change is not only in the air, but on the air. Dialing at random on my newer—and still Japanese—world band radio, I recently heard a well-spoken voice comment on Soviet elections. Most Soviets, the man said, didn't know that "Mikhail Gorbachev is more popular outside the Soviet Union than he is inside."

An amazing message? Hardly, but the source was. I thought I was listening to the BBC, or maybe Deutsche Welle. When I heard "You are listening to Radio Moscow," I checked the dial, and then *Passport's* Blue Pages. Maybe it was frequency drift.

No, it *was* Radio Moscow. The drift was ideological.

Once the Voice of the People, the Tool of the Party, Soviet radio finally spoke that elusive and oft-ignored impediment to the Party, simple truth. So revolutionary has been the change that most citizens of the Bloc haven't quite gotten the hang of hearing straight stories from their own stations.

Cheryl Blackerby

Overjoyed Berliners chip away at the Wall, now reduced to scattered souvenirs. West Germany's Deutsche Welle and East Germany's Radio Berlin International continue to air up-to-the-minute coverage of events as they unfold.

Take East Germany, for example. When its Communist regime announced the opening of the Berlin Wall, few citizens tried to cross. But a few hours later, word from Western stations begat an emigration tidal wave.

I was skeptical myself. Everything I'd ever heard in a lifetime of listening to Radio Moscow said that that election commentator's next beat would be the Gulag Archipelago. But the change is apparently for real. Proclaims Fr. Dominik of Vatican Radio's Russian service, "The Soviet press is extremely reliable, and people no longer have to rely on Western stations."

Not that those Western stations haven't played—and continue to play—a pivotal role, as attested to by no less a person than Lech Walesa. In the United States, at a conference sponsored by Radio Free Europe and Radio Liberty, Walesa was asked how important RFE-RL broadcasts had been to the process of change. For

decades, programs from Western stations gave Eastern Europeans insightful news and juicy features, programming beyond question preferred to the predictable pap of their government. "Would there be land on the earth," the patriotic Pole replied, "without the sun?"

However, real change takes time, which is why Western stations continue to beam heavily to Eastern Europe and the Soviet Union. Ray Heibert, former chairman of the University of Maryland's College of Journalism, is a frequent speaker in Communist Bloc countries. He warns that permanent policy changes, and subsequent programming changes, could take many years. What we are hearing now may be only temporary.

That makes sense, and if it's true we'd better do our listening now, while we can. Should you want to enjoy these short-term benefits, here is a guide to "The New Comrades on the Bloc."

Germany (East)
Radio Berlin International

In 1989, ABC correspondent Gordon Williams tuned into Radio Berlin International, expecting to hear the usual round of propaganda. Instead, what he encountered was the station's program director confessing that he and his colleagues had not always presented the truth. "From now on," he declared, "what you hear on Radio Berlin will be more truthful, accurate and full of reflection of life [here]."

This astonishing admission was a portent of the sweeping events to come. A few days later, the Berlin Wall tumbled into the ash heap of history—and RBI, true to its word, improved its broadcasts.

Most of the station's improvements have centered on news and editorial content. For example, in the old days the station would refer in Newspeak to the "Anti-Fascist Wall" —designed not to keep the population in, but the "fascists" out. RBI's announcers now admit that this was propaganda, and concentrate, instead, on the more positive and unfolding issue of German reunification.

As part of that reunification, Radio Berlin International is scheduled to be merged with the excellent West German station Deutsche Welle. So catch this one before the door slams shut.

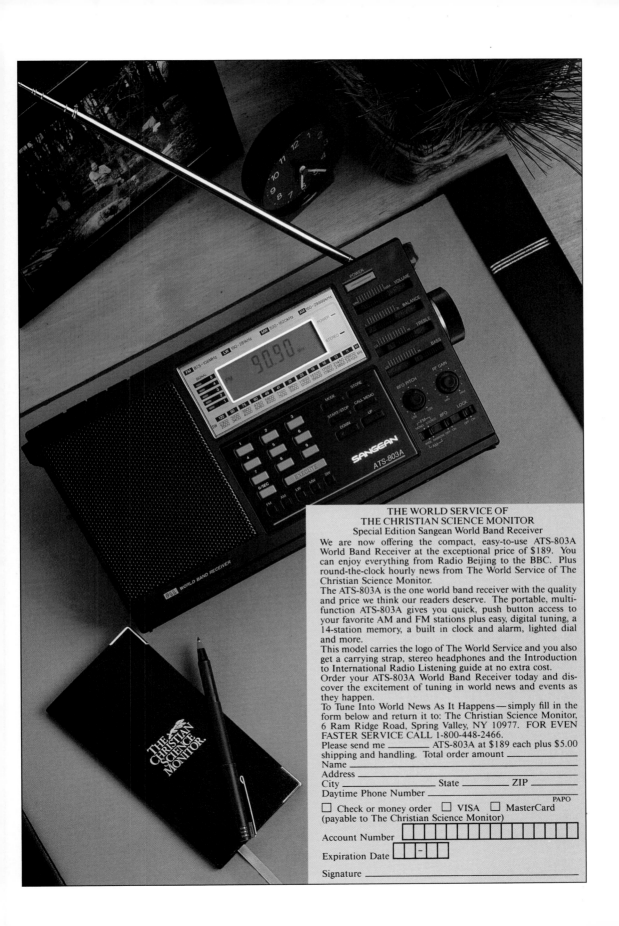

Red Army tanks on patrol.

U.S.S.R.
Radio Moscow

Glasnost has reached new heights, maybe even heaven: A program for believers in the Gospel was heard recently over Radio Moscow.

More-earthly changes have been taking place, too. Radio Moscow's reporting on Lithuania has been excellent by any measure—especially under the circumstances. The station has also done an admirable job of reporting on ethnic disturbances in Armenia and Azerbaijan. Coverage has been open and honest, although the station has steered clear of mentioning the Soviet military's role or casualty counts.

> **Glasnost has reached new heights, maybe even heaven: A program for believers in the Gospel was heard over Radio Moscow.**

Coverage of the Baltic republics, such as Lithuania, has been of a high caliber, as well. In 1990, Radio Moscow reported—accurately—the results of the first Lithuanian election. The station also conducted an interview with a member of the Independent Communist Party who endorsed nothing less than full Lithuanian independence.

Radio Moscow commentators also admit openly that the Soviet economy is in

shambles. They are even asking for assistance from the West to rebuild their economy. One of the ways they reach out is in a program called *Newmarket*. The show is, in essence, free advertising for goods and services from the Soviet Union. You can buy everything from machine parts to tapes of Radio Moscow's Greatest Hits.

Could a Soviet version of the Sears catalog be far behind?

Lithuania
Radio Vilnius

If you've had trouble hearing Radio Vilnius at times in the recent past, here's why.

On the eve of Mr. Gorbachev's first visit to Lithuania, Radio Vilnius informed its listeners that he would be treated not as the leader of their country, but as an alien head of state. Moscow wasn't amused.

Later, Radio Vilnius went over the Kremlin's head and aired an appeal to the governments of all democratic nations. Its patience worn thin, Moscow pulled the plug. Until then, Radio Vilnius had rented air time over Radio Moscow's mighty transmitters to relay its broadcasts to the rest of the world.

As of when *Passport* goes to press, Radio Vilnius is once again being relayed by Moscow. But what is the long-term future for this station, once reduced to near inaudibility?

Muses staff member Vlados Doblias, "Although Lithuania pays for those relay stations, Moscow might just choose to teach us a lesson for being so disobedient." Stay tuned.

Czechoslovakia
Radio Prague International

What Czechs call their "gentle revolution" was given its full voice in May, 1990, following Radio Prague International's purging of its staff of pro-communist elements and others deemed unsuitable.

The new Radio Prague International is gentler, leaner, yet in many ways better. Its former roster of stuffy propaganda shows has been replaced by straight news, especially about Czech political reform, and a scattering of interesting features. Even the interval signal—music played just before the station signs on—is kinder to the ears: a few

(continued on page 99)

Take note of the Republic of China on Taiwan

Listen to the Voice of Free China for music, news, culture and insights into Asia's most dynamic economy.

English ● French ● Spanish ● German ● Japanese ● Korean ● Indonesian ● Thai ● Vietnamese ● Arabic ● Mandarin ● Cantonese ● Amoy ● Chaochow ● Hakka ●

5985KHZ 11740KHZ

For a free program guide, please write to:
P.O. Box 24-38, Taipei,
Taiwan, Republic of China

Voice of Free China 自由中國之聲

Computer Control of ICOM R71A & R7000

Remote Computer Scanning System™

The Remote Computer Scanning System (RCSS™) is designed to enhance your control over the ICOM™ R71A and R7000 receiver. The RCSS™ provides fully automated control over all receiver microprocessor controlled functions including: frequency tuning, mode, band selection, intelligent scanning, and memory.

Just select the frequency on your computer and watch the receiver automatically tune to that channel and update the radio's display. Or set the computer to automatically scan between any two frequencies and watch it quickly find all active channels and store them in it's database for you to use.

Two way communications are sometimes conducted over two separate frequencies. Listening to only one is like listening to half of a conversation. RCSS™ provides the capability for specifying a companion frequency for each stored channel. RCSS™ then scans quickly between the two frequencies so you hear the whole conversation.

You are no longer limited to the channel memory of the receiver since RCSS™ provides unlimited frequency storage banks with additional information on each channel such as: frequency, companion frequency, location, call sign, and your personalized comments for later recall.

Also included is an automatic receive mode for when you can't be present to listen to a specific broadcast. Just set the date and time of day on the computer and when the broadcast is about to begin the computer automatically tunes to the required frequency (and companion frequency) for recording transmissions.

Receiver control is provided by an easy to use graphic interface on the computer screen and operated by either a mouse or keyboard . This approach virtually eliminates the "learning curve" since operation of the computer is the same as operation of the actual receiver.

The RCSS™ runs on both Macintosh and IBM compatible computers with control provided through a standard serial communications port. Package includes software, manual, cables, and interface.

The Remote Computer Scanning System™ (RCSS™) runs on the Macintosh Plus, SE, SE30, II, IIx, and IIcx; and IBM compatible computers running Microsoft Windows.

Scanning Features

- Significantly expands options of control over standard receiver functions.

- Automatic detection and storage of frequencies and other information while scanning.

- Search your frequencies by "Class of Service" or "Type of Unit".

- Scanning resumes upon loss of carrier with user specified delay.

Database Features

- Computer storage and retrieval of unlimited banks of active frequencies.

- Active channels stored with user supplied information like location, call sign, and companion frequency.

- Import and export capability to other applications for custom reports, etc.

- Specify companion frequency for monitoring half-duplex communications.

Ordering Information

To order, receive more information, or join our new-product database, contact us at 4639 Timber Ridge Drive, Dumfries, VA, 22026, USA, (703) 680-3559, Fax (703) 878-1460, Dealer inquiries welcome. Custom versions available.

THE BEST OF BOTH WORLDS.

The pacesetting IC-R9000 truly reflects ICOM's long-term commitment to excellence. This single-cabinet receiver covers both local area VHF/UHF and worldwide MF/HF bands. It's a natural first choice for elaborate communications centers, professional service facilities and serious home setups alike. Test-tune ICOM's IC-R9000 and experience a totally new dimension in top-of-the-line receiver performance!

Complete Communications Receiver. Covers 100KHz to 1999.8MHz, all modes, all frequencies! The general coverage IC-R9000 receiver uses 11 separate bandpass filters in the 100KHz to 30MHz range and precise-tuned bandpass filters with low noise GaAsFETs in VHF and upper frequency bands. Exceptionally high sensitivity, intermod immunity and frequency stability in all ranges.

Multi-Function Five Inch CRT. Displays frequencies, modes, memory contents, operator-entered notes and function menus. Features a subdisplay area for printed modes such as RTTY, SITOR and PACKET (external T.U. required).

Spectrum Scope. Indicates all signal activities within a +/-25, 50 or 100KHz range of your tuned frequency. It's ideal for spotting random signals that pass unnoticed with ordinary monitoring receivers.

1000 Multi-Function Memories. Store frequencies, modes, and tuning steps. Includes an editor for moving contents between memories, plus an on-screen notepad for all memory locations.

Eight Scanning Modes. Includes programmable limits, automatic frequency and time-mark storage of scanned signals, full, restricted or mode-selected memory scanning, priority channel watch, voice-sense scanning and scanning a selectable width around your tuned frequency. Absolutely the last word in full spectrum monitoring.

Professional Quality Throughout. The revolutionary IC-R9000 features IF Shift, IF Notch, a fully adjustable noise blanker, and more. The Direct Digital Synthesizer assures the widest dynamic range, lowest noise and rapid scanning. Designed for dependable long-term performance. Backed by a full one-year warranty at any one of ICOM's four North American Service Centers!

○ ICOM

First in Communications

ICOM America, Inc., 2380-116th Ave. N.E., Bellevue, WA 98004
Customer Service Hotline (206) 454-7619
3150 Premier Drive, Suite 126, Irving, TX 75063 /
1777 Phoenix Parkway, Suite 201, Atlanta, GA 30349
ICOM CANADA, A Division of ICOM America, Inc.,
3071 - #5 Road, Unit 9, Richmond, B.C. V6X 2T4 Canada
All stated specifications are subject to change without notice or obligation. All ICOM radios significantly exceed FCC regulations limiting spurious emissions. 9000489

ALISTAIR COOKE: THE LONGEST LETTER

by Joe Rosenbloom III

The letters pour forth—a torrent from around the world, at least 1,000 a week. No way can Alistair Cooke read, much less answer, all his mail.

"Of course, you get angry letters from people who say, 'I wrote to you six times.' People *are* amazing," says Cooke in the droll, fine-timbred voice known to millions of BBC listeners from Picadilly Circus to New Zealand's fjords.

What's new about his mail, Cooke says, is the U.S. postmark. It tells him the vast audience for his weekly, 15-minute talks on things American includes a growing number of Americans themselves—tuned, of course, to world band radio.

It's early Friday evening in Boston. Cooke sits in his suite at the Ritz Carlton Hotel, smoking filter-tipped Merits. At 82 the ruddy, silver-haired man-cum-institution looks remarkably fit. This day he spent taping *Masterpiece Theatre,* the TV drama series he hosts on the Public Broadcasting Service. *Masterpiece Theatre* has established him as a kind of British icon in America. No matter that he's an American citizen, residing in the United States for 55 years as student, newspaperman and BBC correspondent.

He's reminiscing not about his TV appearances, but about his first love, the vintage *Letter from America* radio show he started in 1947, and which since has become his trademark. His original mandate: talk about "anything that comes to mind."

Much has come to mind. For more than 43 years, Cooke has never missed a week, even recording from a hospital bed. The *Guinness Book of World Records* cites *Letter* as the longest-running talk show on radio.

A secret to the talks' success, Cooke says, is their loose, almost rambling style. They are supposed to resemble conversation—one person to another in a room—rather than an essay or lecture. The paradoxically self-conscious aim is to let his unconscious run free: "That's the fun of it. It's free association. And it took years, really, for me to have the courage to do that."

Not that he actually talks off the cuff. The process starts Thursday morning in his New York apartment overlooking Central Park, when he scratches for a topic. "I never know when I get up in the morning what it's going to be, unless the President has been assassinated, or we've invaded Panama, or there's something that obviously has to be talked about."

Alistair Cooke is better known for his weekly world band radio show, *Letter from America,* than for his TV appearances. *Letter* is cited by the *Guinness Book of World Records* as the longest-running talk show on radio.

An item in the papers or on radio sometimes kindles the spark. A folk song he heard on the radio just before Earth Day 1990 triggered a flashback to the 1930s, days he rummaged through the Deep South recording spirituals for the BBC. So, that week his *Letter from America* salutation was, "What's the word, brother?" Dredged from his memory of an old Christian sect encountered during those vintage Dixie travels, his meandering vignette leads by artful turns to some personal reflections on the U.S. environmental movement.

His audience includes a growing number of Americans tuned to world band radio.

Mind spinning, Cooks bangs at his typewriter until the piece is honed, as a Stateside Southerner would say, to a fare-thee-well. Thursday afternoon he ushers the finished draft to the BBC's New York office and tapes his weekly offering, which is then flown to London for broadcast Friday evening and Sunday morning (and later in the week for points the world across).

The several-day lag between recording and airing adds a wild card. If Cooke comments on breaking news, he risks being overtaken by events.

Once, he taped a talk about Watergate while President Richard M. Nixon's fate hung in the balance. "So I wrote this thing saying, 'If he were to be brought down, it would not be just the liberals, it would not be just *The Washington Post*, it would not be just the Democratic Party, it would be the men and women in his own party,' and so on and so on," Cooke recounts.

"And for the end I invented the line, 'The rest you know.'"

"It was played on the Friday evening he abdicated. I got more letters from people saying, 'What a talk!' And of course the assumption of everyone listening is: 'I know you know what happened.' You can't use that one every week!"

Cooke's urbane wit suggests to Americans an aristocratic lineage. In fact, he's a metalworker's son from England's industrial north. And while Americans may think Cooke's accent the epitome of proper English diction, to the British, he insists, he's an "enlightened American" speaking the New World tongue.

"They're both right," he laughs. "Everyone notices the different way you pronounce something. My inflections and tune tend to be more American than British. That's what the British hear. The Americans notice the British sounds that I've retained." Splitting the difference, one English writer says Cooke speaks with a NATO accent.

In the same sense, Cooke is blessed with a NATO (read: cross-cultural) perspective. Thanks to his wide-open original marching orders, he's been able to make the comparative study of American culture his life's work. By now it's second nature: "I instinctively notice what is American about America."

He was fresh from Cambridge (first honors in English) when at age 23 he crossed the Atlantic for the first time, destination Yale University on a Commonwealth Fellowship. "I was going to be a theater director. That was my whole interest in life." But the fellowship stipulated that he buy a car and travel around the States. All summer. He was smitten, and theater's loss was radio's gain.

"It was a new country," he says, "and nobody covered it. I mean, there were three British correspondents in Washington, five in New York, and maybe six in Hollywood who occasionally jumped to Chicago to interview Al Capone. It was a revelation to me. And I thought, 'My God, here is a whole continent and a way of life that people know nothing about.'"

For 43 years, Cooke has never missed a week, even recording from a hospital bed.

Cooke resolved to fill the void someday. Back in England, he did a three-year stint as a BBC film critic, marrying an American and immigrating to America with the intent to stay. The marriage ended in divorce five years later, and Cooke eventually married a British war widow, Jane White Hawkes. They have two grown children—son John, a novelist in Wyoming, and daughter Susan, who is studying for the ministry in Vermont.

Over the years Cooke's Anglo–American expertise has earned him his crust variously as U.S. correspondent for the BBC,

Times of London, and *Manchester Guardian.* He is still mining material accumulated in decades beating shoe leather as a reporter. He's crisscrossed the nation 16 times by car, as much on back country roads as main highways, and used to keep a notebook for jotting down American slang. The notebook is gone, but slang continues as a passion: he corresponds on the subject with ranking authority William Safire of *The New York Times.*

Cook's urbane wit suggests an aristocratic lineage. In fact, he's a metalworker's son.

Cooke's American English is far from faultless, as he's glad to point out. When he goes wrong, he says, it's apt to be an elementary mistake: "Until about eight years ago, I'd gone to a deli or supermarket and asked for a bottle of soda water. When I think of the number of times people have said, 'Would that be lemon squash or something?' And I suddenly realized I'd never asked for club soda. I started talking about club soda when everyone else started calling it seltzer."

The anecdote ends, not uncharacteristically, with a muffled guffaw. Cooke's replies tend toward the wry anecdote, spun with vaudevillian verve. Small wonder—he's trotted the same anecdotes around the track for years. Often he is amusing, and no less amused himself. His merriment is infectious.

But merriment is not all. Cooke is first and foremost a reporter, and the reporter's life is serious. His voice loses its fizz when the subject turns to America's future, a subject on which he was asked to speak by no less than the U.S. House of Representatives. That was in 1974, for the Congressional bicentennial. Cooke was forthright:

"Americans are activists in the sense that they believe tomorrow is going to be at least as good as today, and certainly better than yesterday," he pronounced. And therein lies the danger.

As he sees it, America's optimistic impulse is as potent today as ever—for better or worse. "I think it explains a good deal," he says now, "of whatever is vital about the country. And it also explains the way we plunge into the most hideous errors in foreign policy, of thinking it's got to be done by Monday morning. You got to change the world by Monday morning, and we're all for democracy, so, by golly, uplift Lithuania and screw Gorbachev."

Cooke sees a dark lining in Americans' perennial silver cloud: "I've always been a sort of short-term optimist, but in the last 20 years a long-term pessimist. I think the Sixties were a ghastly period. American civilization is very much going down."

"I think the Sixties were a ghastly period. American civilization is very much going down."

Up or down, Cooke intends to keep talking about America every week on the BBC World Service. How much longer? "Till I keel over," he says. After all, Cooke has license to knock about the country, eyeball its people, and hobnob with what he calls on the air, "all possible variations of the same types that you know in England," and thereby "to double your enjoyment of life and indulge your curiosity."

No wonder he decided long ago to make talking about America his life's work. The rest you know.

Joe Rosenbloom is Staff Reporter for the Public Broadcasting Service's Frontline.

WHEN TO TUNE IN

Letter From America is heard Saturday at 1015 World Time to Europe on 9410, 12095 and 15070 kHz; and to East Asia and the Pacific on 15360 kHz. Sunday (Saturday evening in North America) it's on to North America at 0545 on 5975 and 9640 kHz; to Europe on 3955, 6195, 9410 and 12095 kHz; and to East Asia on 21715 kHz. Again Sunday there's a repeat at 1645 to North America on 9515 (or 11775) and 15260 kHz; and to Europe on 6195, 7325, 9410, 12095 and 15070 kHz. Finally, there's Sunday at 2315 to North America on 5975, 6175, 7325, 9590 and 9915 kHz; and to East Asia and the Pacific on 11955 kHz.

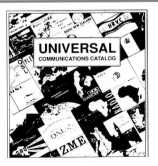

TEN OF THE BEST: TOP SHOWS FOR 1991

N o, not *the* ten best! Who can say? World band radio carries *thousands* of programs, and no one can hear them all.

But we here at *Passport to World Band Radio* listen to a lot of them, and we've chosen what we think conveys world band's cream. Many are easy to hear in most parts of the globe, and usually on more than one frequency. If we've leaned in one direction, it's toward the growing interrelationship between science and politics—especially *vis-à-vis* the environment. All in all, it's a bag full of goodies. Let's open it.

"European Journal" Deutsche Welle

Eastern Europe and the Soviet Union have been in the throes of history since last year's *Passport,* the perfect stage for world band radio to strut its stuff.

Few stations were as well-poised as Deutsche Welle. As the Berlin Wall forcibly crumbled, programs on "consolidation," "democratization" and "reconstruction" filled the German station's schedule. Created in haste, not all were of high quality, something Deutsche Welle followers knew would not last. It was no surprise, then, when in March, 1990, it inaugurated *European Journal,* a regular program on not only East–West German relations, but also about events in Greater Europe stretching,

as Gen. de Gaulle used to point out, from the Atlantic Ocean to the Ural Mountains.

Journal was a precocious creation; it took off right from the start. Essentially news and commentary, with coverage of politics, economics, interstate relations and ecology, its quality rivals that of the BBC World Service's European news—no small feat.

European Journal is broadcast, week-days only, at nine minutes past the hour, and ending about 24 minutes later. North Americans have three chances to hear it: 0109, 0309 and 0509 World Time, Tuesday through Saturday. At 0109, try 6040, 6085, 6145, 9565, 9735, 11865 or 15105 kHz; at 0309, tune to 6085, 6130, 9545, 9605, 11810 or 15205 kHz. For the final repeat at 0509, try 5960, 6120, 9670, 9700 or 11845 kHz.

Listeners in Asia and the Pacific may tune in at 2109, Sunday through Thursday, on 7130, 9670, 9765, 11785, 11810, 13780 or 15435 kHz. Deutsche Welle has no scheduled English-language European transmission, but listeners can try for the West Africa version at 0600 on 11765, 13790, 15185 and 17875 kHz.

"One Norway Street" Christian Science Monitor World Service

"Features drawn mainly from the United States," says a single line in the Christian Science Monitor program guide about *One Norway Street.* It's hardly the sort of

One Norway Street, hosted over the Christian Science Monitor World Service by Kim Shippey.

A delightful native wind instrument, the *roncador*, played on *Música del Ecuador* over HCJB—The Voice of the Andes. HCJB, operated by American missionaries, is the best-heard station from Latin America.

HCJB world radio

description to spur you to leap into your listening chair.

A pity, because *One Norway Street* is one of the most comprehensive programs on world band radio, 20-odd minutes of just about anything. Topics can be thorny: animal rights one moment, perhaps American small-town racism the next. Other recent examples have included an interview with a Paul Robeson biographer, a review of baseball books for children, and an item on the influence of Albert Einstein's first wife. Variety abounds—low key, but agreeable.

One Norway Street finds its way to different parts of the world every two hours on Mondays, Wednesdays and Thursdays at 1706, 1906, and so forth. All editions from 0106 to 1506, inclusive, are heard on Tuesdays, Thursdays and Fridays, and are repeats of the previous day's program. For North America, the schedule is: 0106 (not Monday) on 7400 or 9410 kHz (East); 0306, 0506 and 0706 on 9455 kHz; 1106 and 1306 on 9495 kHz (East); 1506 on 13760 or 17555 kHz (West); 2106 on 15610 kHz (East); and 2306 on 9465 kHz (East).

Europeans can tune in at 0706 and 0906 on 9840 or 11705 kHz; 1506 on 21780 kHz; and at 2106 on 13770 and 15610 kHz. In East Asia, try 0506 on 17780 kHz; 0906, 1106 and 1506 on 9530 kHz; 1906 on 11980 or 17555 kHz; 2106 on 9455 kHz;

and 2306 on 15405 kHz. For Australia and New Zealand the best times are 0906 on 17855 kHz; 1306 on 15285 kHz; 1906 on 9455 or 13720 kHz; and 2106 on 13625 kHz.

"Global Concerns" BBC World Service

Our endangered earth is a hot topic today. Where once such terms as acid rain, the ozone layer and greenhouse effect were only the private argot of scientific specialists, they are now even talked about on street corners. Several world band stations now feature environmental topics, and the Beeb's *Global Concerns* is the best.

From time to time, the program features items which, although scientific in nature, might best be classified as curiosities. A case in point was an elephant fitted with a 20-pound (9 kg.) satellite beacon so his meandering through Eastern Africa could be monitored by the London Zoo. The signals were picked up by satellite, relayed to the French city of Toulouse, then on to London.

In just 15 minutes, *Global Concerns* may cover anything related to the environment, directly or indirectly: toxic waste, ocean dumping, acid rain, "green economics," environmental conferences, tropical rain forests—all in adequate, but not excessive, detail. A program for all ages and every corner of the world, *Global Concerns* is on its way to becoming a listening "must."

In Europe, *Global Concerns* can be heard Thursdays at 2130 on 3955, 6195 and 9410 kHz; with a repeat the next morning at 1115 on 5975, 6045, 7325, 9750, 12095 and 15070 kHz. Canadian and U.S. listeners can tune in Fridays at 0145 (that is, Thursday evening in the Americas) on 5975, 6175, 7325, 9590, 9915 or 12095 kHz. There is a second opportunity a few hours later, at 1115, on 9515 and 11775 kHz.

Surprisingly, this program is not beamed to East Asia, but Australians can try 11750 or 15140 kHz on Thursdays at 2130.

"The Jazz Place" Radio Habana Cuba

What do people associate with Fidel Castro's Cuba? Sugarcane? Cigars? Communism? Political persecution? Not jazz, surely!

"The Best Results throughout the Shortwave Spectrum."

*— Larry Magne, Radio Database International
White Paper*

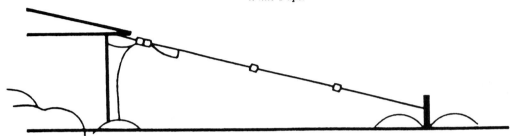

Get world-class, multi-band reception with

ALPHA DELTA DX–SWL
SLOPER ANTENNA

Just $69.95 plus shipping from your Alpha Delta dealer!

- Fully assembled, ready to use and built for long life. So strong, it can even be used to transmit—up to 2 kW! Stainless steel hardware.

- Superior multi-band performance on 13, 16, 19, 21, 25, 31, 41, 49, 60, 90, 120 meters plus the AM broadcast band (.5-1.6 MHz). All in a single compact antenna. Alpha Delta first!

- Efficient multi-band frequency selection by means of special RF choke-resonators—instead of lossy, narrow band traps.

- Overall length just 60 feet. Requires only a single elevated support—easier to install than a dipole.

- 50 ohm feedpoint at apex of antenna for maximum DX reception. A UHF connector is provided on the mounting bracket for easy connection to your coax.

- A top overall rating in Radio Database International's hard-hitting White Paper, "RDI Evaluates the Popular Outdoor Antennas."

At your dealer or add $4.00 for direct U.S. orders (exports quoted)
- *MODEL DX-SWL,* AM bdcst thru 13 mtrs, 60 ft. long $69.95
- *MODEL DX-SWL-S,* as above but 90 thru 13 mtrs, only 40 ft. long $59.95

ALPHA DELTA COMMUNICATIONS, INC.

1232 East Broadway, Suite 210 • Tempe, AZ 85282 • (602) 966-2200

Deutsche Welle's new *European Journal* covers fascinating stories, including from Europe's hidden byways, that tend to be overlooked by media outside Europe.

Yes, jazz. For all the bad Western press it gets, Cuba abounds in artistic talent—albeit talent often blessed with official money and encouragement. There's variety, as well, from two stupendous ballet companies to a corps of outstanding jazz musicians. On Havana radio, the "cats" hang out at *The Jazz Place*, and they aren't all *cubanos*.

Thirty minutes of top-class music, and one of the few places where the aficionado has a chance to hear examples of the excellent *jazz latino*.

North Americans should tune in on Mondays at 0030, 0230, 0430 or 0630 (Sunday evening in the Americas). The first and second airings are on 11820 kHz (plus 9710 kHz at 0230), the third on 5965 or 9750, 11760 and 11820 kHz; and the fourth on 11835 kHz. Europeans face complexity, as the program goes out on Saturday one week, and Sunday the next. The exact time of transmission is hard to pin down, but try between 1900 and 2100 on 11800 kHz.

"Sounds of Soweto" Radio RSA

Sadly, Soweto's name has for years meant strikes and civil disobedience, the latter often violent. Few outside South Africa—or in it, for that matter—realize its wealth of musical talent. This little gem, a mere 10 minutes on Tuesdays and Saturdays, showcases a surprising range, from traditional Miriam Makeba-like vocals to soft soul reminiscent of the late Otis Redding. Thelma Mbhalati is the program's speaking voice, and a delightful one.

> **Few realize Soweto's wealth of musical talent, from Miriam Makeba-like vocals to soft soul.**

Sounds of Soweto is part of the first half of a two-hour Tuesday broadcast beginning at 1400. Although primarily aimed at Europe and Africa, it sometimes reaches parts of North America, usually on 17835 kHz. Repeated Saturdays during the 1800 transmission on 15270 and 17765 kHz.

"Discovery" BBC World Service

Here's the best science program on radio, any radio—AM, FM or world band. Subatomic particles, genetic engineering, earthquake prediction, intergalactic winds—no matter the subject, you find yourself understanding it, even if you knew nothing at the start.

Discovery has been around for years, and rightfully so. Never have so many difficult subjects been made to sound so simple, yet retain the hard facts necessary to satisfy professionally interested listeners. While its sister program, *Science in Action*, deals mainly with applied science, *Discovery's* realm is research. Not only is the program extremely up to date, it is consistently of high quality.

In North America, you can hear it Wednesdays at 0330 (Tuesday nights your local time) at 0330 on 5975, 6175 and 9915 kHz. Europeans can listen Tuesdays at 1001 on 5975, 6045, 9750, 12095 or 15070 kHz, with a repeat at 1830 on 3955, 6195, 7325 and 9410 kHz.

In East Asia and the Pacific, try

(continued on page 101)

GETTING STARTED WITH WORLD BAND RADIO

by Harry L. Helms

You did it—you've got that new world band radio!

Quick, unpack it. Admire the styling and design, then scan the front panel. All those buttons and dials—looks complicated, doesn't it?

Not so. Remember, you thought your VCR was a monster when you brought it home, yet you mastered it quickly enough. A world band radio is no more mysterious than that, or a CD player, or even a microwave oven—plus it's a lot more interesting, and doesn't get you fat. So, settle down with the owner's manual and *Passport to World Band Radio*, and you'll be on top of things in short order.

What is World Band Radio?

The technology for world band radio was developed about the same time as that of television—the late Twenties and early Thirties. TV receivers were ready for mass consumption by the late Forties—color about 15 years later. Yet, world band receivers were generally mediocre, unfriendly performers until the early Eighties, when a variety of technological developments came together to lift them into the mainstream.

Old-technology world band radios still abound, and should be avoided—refer to *Passport's* Buyer's Guide for more on this. But new world band technology continues to expand, and there's more to come. These are exciting, almost pioneering, times for world band radio. The changes happening today in world band radio are as important to audio as will be the changes brought about in video by high-definition TV.

What, then, is this medium that, like Rip Van Winkle, has been asleep for so long? World band is actually just another broadcasting range, like the mediumwave AM and FM bands you're used to. In fact, world band is right between them, in terms of wavelength. If you could tune your AM radio above 1600 kHz, you'd eventually run right into it.

There are two main differences. Regular AM and FM stations cannot be heard worldwide, and they use the same channels year in and year out. World band, of course, covers the globe, and its stations change channels—frequencies—much more often.

Finding Your Way Around

World band radio uses 13 groups—"segments"—of frequencies in the shortwave portion of the radio spectrum. Shortwave goes long distance, taking music, news and entertainment around the world on a regular basis, although with only Spartan

In Beijing, Mark Hopkins of the Voice of America interviews a Chinese student.

audio fidelity. With a world band radio, it's possible—in fact common—to have a simultaneous choice between stations from London, Moscow, Beijing, Paris, Boston, Berlin or Jerusalem.

These are exciting, almost pioneering, times for world band radio.

The frequencies used by world band stations are measured in either *kiloHertz* (kHz) or *MegaHertz* (MHz). A MegaHertz is equal to 1000 kiloHertz, so 9.58 MHz is the same as 9580 kHz.

You'll hear world band stations announce their operating frequencies both ways, but *Passport* uses only kHz, for uniformity. Some advanced radio sets display the frequency to one-tenth or even one-hundredth of a kHz, but that's splitting hairs. Scientists may need it; you won't.

World band stations can't operate just anywhere within the radio spectrum—chaos would result. No, there's a method to this wonderful madness. Flip through the Blue Pages of *Passport,* and you'll notice most stations spaced exactly five kHz apart. For example, look at the 15100 to 15600 kHz listings. Most stations use frequencies ending in zero or five. The pattern holds in other ranges, too: 5950 to 6200, 7100 to 7300, 9500 to 9900, 11650 to 12050 and 13600 to 13800 kHz.

Advanced world band receivers boast digital frequency display, but old-technology models are *analog,* or slide-rule tuned.

(continued on page 103)

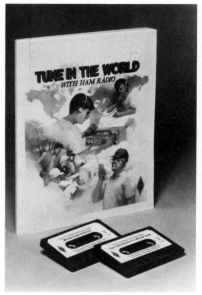

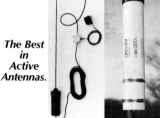

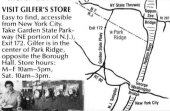

Voice of America's wealth of news programming includes in-depth coverage of lay topics and personalities. Here, China is examined.

NEWS I:
HEAR IT NOW

For the news junkie, world band is the ultimate fix. Peruvian terror, Burmese elections, Fijian insurrection—you're there.

It's a mystery how so juicy a fruit, so ripe for the picking, can be left to rot by domestic radio and television networks, but it is. What little that's picked bears the picker's prejudice, too—an obvious parochial eye.

No, the usual newscasts won't do, not if you want real juice. For that you need world band. Tune around. You'll hear news happening, where it's happening and when—bulletins, features, propaganda and paranoia, editorial and press reviews. World band is whatever there is to report, from wherever it may come.

Fresh perspectives? They're here, the farthest and freshest. A paragraph in your local paper can be a world event elsewhere. The opposite can be true, as well: The biggest story in the United States often makes mere ripples outside its borders.

Different eyes, different ears—a worldwide, world band network finds it all, not just some.

Nearly every world band broadcast opens with seven to 15 minutes of regional, national and international news, of which the BBC World Service has earned and upheld a world standard. The BBC's scope is national and international and—unlike, say, Radio Pyongyang or Radio Baghdad—grinds no ideological axe. BBC bulletins are accurate, diverse in format, comprehensive and up-to-the-minute, with plentiful on-scene reporting from a generous correspondent network.

An American voice fast rivaling the Beeb is the World Service of the Christian Science Monitor. Although religiously affiliated, the station scrupulously segregates religion and opinion, as does its Pulitzer-winning print counterpart. And like its namesake newspaper, the station's analysis emphasizes international news—not American affairs. The Monitor's style differs from that of the BBC in that the BBC feels

Radio France Internationale in studio, with French Communist leader Georges Marchais participating via television monitor.

more like it's "at the front," whereas the Monitor gives the impression of sober reporting coupled with reasoned, knowledgeable analysis.

Another gem is Radio Canada International's *As It Happens*, aired weekdays. Although it covers Canada generously—its primary audience is Canadian—the newscast delves superbly into broad international issues and events. Don't be fooled into thinking that just because this is a Canadian show, it's pretty much the same as a U.S. newscast. *As It Happens* offers a perspective quite distinct from that of its neighbor to the south, and it's as refreshing to Americans as it is good.

Outside Britain and the Americas, a number of relatively objective news voices penetrate the air, including Swiss Radio International, Radio Nederland, Radio Japan, Radio Australia, the Deutsche Welle, and UAE Radio/Dubai.

Dubai? Yes, and what makes it special is that its bulletins often include items which most other stations, including the majors, have missed. It's sometimes among the first with breaking news, as well.

Significantly, in the past year or so Eastern European radio reporting has grown to be of a high caliber. Even Radio Moscow's reporting can be surprisingly candid and professional. During the 1990 Lithuanian crisis, for example, its reporting was excellent by any standard.

Aside from regular news bulletins, most world band broadcasters offer news features in detail, much as *CBS Reports* or *20/20* do on American television. Among the best are the BBC World Service's *Newshour, Newsdesk, Twenty-Four Hours* and *The World Today*, as well as Radio Australia's *International Report*. Other noteworthy offerings include the Voice of America's *Encounter*, which usually features press bureau chiefs or former public officials, and Radio Moscow's *Update*.

A few stations specialize in news from their part of the world. East Asia is well-handled, if dryly, on Radio Japan's *Asia Now*, and Asia as a whole is targeted by Radio Nederland's *Asiascan*. Indeed, Radio Japan is arguably the best source for coverage of day-to-day events in China, just as Radio Beijing is now one of the worst.

In the same vein, Radio Australia concentrates on Pacific events. Also, Radio France Internationale's one-hour broadcast at 1600 World Time and the BBC's special programs for Africa offer needed coverage of African issues from two very different perspectives.

For a regional perspective of Eastern European events, two good choices are Radio Yugoslavia and Radio Austria International. Radio Yugoslavia, in addition to its broad, if somewhat dull, coverage of Eastern European affairs, also reports on a wide variety of Balkan matters. The Austrian station, on the other hand, provides some worthwhile coverage of political, economic and cultural changes in Czechoslovakia, Hungary and Romania. Radio France Internationale—notably in its French-language services, though—also does a superior job in covering developments in volatile Romania.

What's happening in Western Europe? Perhaps the best way to find out is to tune in the Deutsche Welle's *European Journal*. This is the world band edition of the television show of the same name seen in various cities of the world. While the radio version has the edge, both are highly recommended for coverage of European affairs.

Another European-oriented offering is Radio Nederland's *Newsline*. Swiss Radio International's newscasts traditionally provide worthy coverage of European matters, as well. More targeted still are Radio Finland's *Northern Report* and Radio Sweden's *Weekday*, both of which focus their energies on Scandinavia.

"Press review" programs give reliable assessments of a nation's mood, and spotlight stories and editorials from the main newspapers of Britain, France, Finland, Israel and Belgium. Radio France Internationale, for example, reads editorials from major French newspapers—even the political extremes. Other jewels include the BBC's *Review of the British Press* and *From the Weeklies*, plus excellent coverage of Soviet newspapers over Radio Moscow's *Update*.

Does a single issue interest you over others? If so, world band is your dish. Specialty programs on sports, the environment, science and technology, agriculture, business and finance, religious activity, and music and the fine arts all abound. Whatever the kind of news you seek, you'll find it somewhere, sometime, on world band radio. Check *Passport's* hour-by-hour "What's On Tonight" section to see what you can hear.

NEWS II: THE RELUCTANT LISTENER

"It's meant to drive him crazy," chuckled a jubilant Panamanian, one of a crowd of onlookers standing near a U.S. military checkpoint outside the Vatican embassy in the seaside Paitilla district of Panama City.

"Him" was deposed Panamanian strongman General Manuel Antonio Noriega, who had taken refuge in the Papal Nunciature on Christmas Eve, four days after American troops overthrew his government in late December, 1989.

"It" was rock-and-roll music—supplied at ear-splitting volume by Army loudspeakers in the square—broadcast by the Salt Lake City world band station, Superpower KUSW Radio Worldwide.

The popular American world band station played a small, but fascinating, role in the psychological warfare waged for three days by the United States' military against the pop-music-hating ex-dictator holed up in the Vatican mission.

For other, more-willing KUSW listeners, it was another example of world band radio doing what it does best—keeping in touch with what's happening, when it's happening.

"We were excited about broadcasting rock and roll that the boys down there liked," said KUSW air personality Sheryl

Sheafor. Sheafor often gets musical requests from overseas GIs. "We kept playing them whether Manuel Noriega liked it or not!"

The "psywar" scenario started on Tuesday night, December 26, when paratroopers from the U.S. 82nd Airborne Division sealed off the palm-lined avenue, shot out streetlights, and ringed the neighborhood with banks of tripod-mounted loudspeakers.

On Wednesday, those speakers came alive, first relaying newscasts from the U.S. Armed Forces Radio and Television Service's AM station at Fort Clayton, in the old Canal Zone. After the news, a little entertainment was in order.

Amplified by the speakers at full blast, Linda Ronstadt's already powerful voice indicted Noriega with "You're No Good," after which the Army deejays poured it on with another appropriate number, Motown's 1965 "Nowhere to Run." More lovingly-loaded musical bullets peppered the former dictator's second-floor window: "I Fought the Law and the Law Won," "Voodoo Chile," and—naturally—Don Henley's "Smuggler's Blues."

Noriega's reaction? No one knew, although diplomatic contacts reported the high-impact music was keeping Papal Nuncio Msgr. Jose Sebastian Laboa awake at night.

Manuel Noriega's nemesis, Skinny Johnny Mitchell, displays the tools of his trade. KUSW, a private American station, broadcasts rock music, news, weather and live basketball games worldwide from Salt Lake City, Utah.

A spokesman for the Vatican, already edgy as host to an unwelcome house guest, complained about the musical bombardment. Presidential spokesman Marlin Fitzwater claimed there had been some attempt to "disrupt communications" among the American forces, and that the loud music was necessary to guarantee "the security of our conversations."

Later, the military would claim that the blaring rock music was really intended to thwart the press corps, holed up at a Holiday Inn a hundred yards away, from using listening devices to eavesdrop on negotiations between the American commander, Gen. Maxwell Thurman, and the papal nuncio.

During the U.S. invasion of Panama, it was the USS *Emory S. Land*, shown here at dusk, that picked up KUSW's rock music over world band. The ship relayed it ashore to be force fed to Manuel Noriega.

"We kept playing whether Manuel Noriega liked it or not!"

Asked about the play list, Fitzwater added he was "certainly glad to see the American sense of whimsy come forward in this situation."

KUSW received first word of its unwitting role late Thursday morning, when Sheafor got a phone call from an American sailor on an AS39 submarine tender, the USS *Emory S. Land,* at sea off Costa Rica. The sailor, a third class petty officer who identified himself only as "Buck," asked her to play James McCurty's "Painting by Numbers," which contains the words, "You may be down in the Canal Zone, being all you can be . . . ."

Oh, and by the way, Buck said, did you know your music was being force-fed to Manuel Noriega? *Emory Land,* he told the startled station staff, was now picking the signal off the air and beaming it ashore, for doorstep delivery to the well-known deposed despot.

KUSW jocks Sheafor, John Florence and Skinny Johnny Mitchell adroitly ad-libbed, tailoring their musical choices for GI listeners in Panama—songs like Bruce Springsteen's "Born in the USA," Jimi Hendrix's Woodstock guitar solo of the "Star Spangled Banner," and "Panama Red," by the New Riders of the Purple Sage.

One listener said it sounded like a party at the station. Sheafor admitted it was "very exciting."

Friday morning found the speakers blaring away, but repeated Vatican protests were having an effect in Washington. "It's time to cool it," the commander-in-chief, President George Bush, concluded. That afternoon the volume was turned down. On Saturday, the music stopped.

"It's time to cool it," President Bush concluded.

Gen. James J. Lindsay, commander of special operations during the invasion, would admit later that from the military's standpoint blasting the music had been a mistake. "We'll never do that again. We took some real flak over the thing."

Even today, KUSW General Manager Ralph J. Carlson is still a little surprised by it all.

"We didn't set out to get involved. It just happened," he said. "But we do get a lot of requests from servicemen, and we do have a worldwide audience."

For three days, that audience—estimated at four million—increased by one. Under the circumstances, it's pretty safe to assume that that one would have been happier *not* listening to world band radio!

Prepared by Don Jensen.

MUSIC BEYOND THE CURTAIN

Only two nationalities on earth sing as God and the muses intended: the Russians and the Welsh. At least, so once claimed a member of a prominent Welsh male choir.

He wasn't referring to mere technical ability. He meant the singer's total commitment—the giving of his very soul to the music. To him it was best described by the untranslatable Welsh word *hwyl.* Applying it to Russians was his highest praise.

The sound of a Russian tenor singing praise to his native earth, accompanied by a *balalaika,* is not easily forgotten. Neither are the melancholic strains of "Moscow Nights." The Russian is an emotional being, his character clearly heard in the music. Moreover, the ethnic Russian is not alone in the Soviet sphere.

At present, the Soviet Union includes 15 separate republics, encompassing more than 80 ethnolinguistic groups. Small wonder such a melting pot should offer so great a variety. From the Baltic republics to the Pacific shore lies rich musical abundance, from spontaneous to ceremonial.

The western republics, from Estonia in the north to Moldavia in the south, are justifiably famous not only for superb folk choirs, but for fine individual performances, both vocal and instrumental. The accordion, which adds vitality, is important in many of these republics.

Armenia produces some of the most delightful melodies in the U.S.S.R. Nothing exotic, mind you—just nice. Hear some works by Komitas. Your ears will thank you.

Armenia's neighbor—and hardly its best one, as recent events have under-scored—is Azerbaijan. Strife is nothing new in this predominantly Muslim state, as its music amply reflects. It was invaded by Arabs in the seventh century, by Turks in the 11th, and has historical ties to Iran, so its music evinces all these historical influences.

The Soviet Union's three southernmost republics—Turkmenistan, Tajikistan and Kirghizia—are likewise predominantly Muslim, and their inhabitants speak either Turkic or Iranian languages. Not surprisingly, their national music parallels the Middle East's, but with Asian overtones that make it gentler to the Western ear.

> Orchestras feature a variety of instruments, not the least of which are the wonderfully named *Kashgar rubabs.*

Uzbekistan shares a common border with those republics, and a Turkic language and Muslim religion as well. But it has evolved a different music, one Westerners find easy to identify through its combination of indigenous instruments, such as the *chang,* with such classical western ones as the violin and 'cello. They're often found together in "folk orchestras," which vary from the very small to the very large. These orchestras often feature a variety of instruments, not the least of which are the wonderfully named *Kashgar rubabs.*

Throughout the U.S.S.R. there is probably no single style of music as distinctive as that of Kazakhstan. As an instrumental solo or as musical accompaniment for one or more singers, the monotonous—yet strangely attractive—resonant strumming is as individual a style as you'll likely find anywhere on our planet. Totally different, but equally enjoyable, is the music pro-duced by such diverse instruments as the Jew's harp and the Kazakh shepherd's flute, both of which feature prominently in this, the Soviet Union's second-largest republic.

While much of Soviet music is unknown

HOW TO TUNE IN

In the Americas, the best time to hear traditional music programming from Eastern Europe and the Soviet Union is around 0000-0600 World Time; in Europe, try in the evening, several hours earlier.

A good starting point is Kazakh Radio's Second Program, which airs authentic folk music at 0015-0100, and again around 0115 and 0415 (an hour earlier in summer). Frequencies include 5260, 5945, 5970, 7115, 7235, 9690 and 17730 kHz.

For more music from Soviet Central Asia, try Radio Liberty in Kazakh between 0100 and 0300, and in Tatar-Bashkir from 0200 to 0400 (both an hour earlier in summer). Program content varies considerably from day to day, so don't be put off if all you hear is talk the first time around. The Kazakh service was extended at the end of March, 1990, and frequencies change periodically. Try 7255, 9660, 11750 and 11770 kHz in the winter; and in summer, try 6170, 9660, 11815 and 11915 kHz. For Tatar-Bashkir, good winter frequencies are 7245, 9725, 9750 and 11725; and in summer 9750, 11725, 11855 and 15145 kHz.

Although not an easy catch, Tajik Radio is another station that broadcasts delightfully exotic music. Try 4635 and 9785 kHz about 0330, and again at 0435-0500. That later slot includes some of the best indigenous music anywhere in the world band spectrum.

Possibly the two most enjoyable folk music programs ever to hit the airwaves are Radio Moscow's *Folk Box* and Radio Romania International's *The Skylark*. *Folk Box*, carried several times a week on the Radio Moscow World Service, covers virtually the whole of Soviet folk music, offering fare otherwise nearly impossible to find.

Unfortunately, many of Moscow's World Service programs are rescheduled every six months, so forecasting is chancy. At this writing, *Folk Box* can be heard in most parts of the world on Tuesdays at 1132-1159. Since Radio Moscow's signals are so plentiful throughout the world band spectrum, just tune around at those times and you're likely to find it. If it's not strong, look around some more—perhaps a different frequency is stronger in your locale.

Another time to try Radio Moscow for folk music is after the end of *Update*, a program aired several times daily. *Update* finishes at 40 minutes past the hour, and the ensuing 20 minutes are sometimes devoted to music of the Soviet republics. Jazz is also a frequent feature, so don't be surprised.

The Skylark is nominally scheduled to North America on Fridays at about 0225, but can just as easily surface on other days—sometimes as often as three times a week. It's worth seeking out, consisting as it does of some of the most beautiful and emotive music to come out of Europe, East or West. Try 5990, 6155, 9510, 9570, 11830 and 11940 kHz. Europeans should try for the 1930-2030 broadcast on 6105, 7105, 7195, 9690, 11810 or 11940 kHz.

Folk music is aired over other Eastern European stations, although not as much as it once was. The best bet is probably Radio Sofia, Bulgaria, which can be heard in Europe at 1930 and 2230 on 6070, 7155 and 9700 kHz (an hour earlier summer on 11660, 11720 and 15330 kHz). North Americans can find Radio Sofia at 0000-0100 on 9700 and 11660 (or 11680) kHz in the winter; and in summer at 2300-2400 on 11660 (or 11680) and 15330 kHz. A second transmission may also reach North America at 0400-0500 on 7115 and 9700 kHz winters; and in summer at 0300-0300 on 11720, 11735 or 15290 kHz.

to people in the West, the same cannot be said of East European music. Emigration and cultural exchanges—even with the most dictatorial regimes—have given the music wide Western exposure.

Eastern Europe has abundant musical variety, with the bagpipes of Bulgaria arguably the most unusual. Bulgarian folk rhythms are difficult to describe to the uninitiated: lively, with a definite Balkan flavor—haunting, some would say. But of all the music that emanates from this part of Europe, the most invigorating is found primarily in Hungary, Romania and Czechoslovakia. The three have two instruments in common: the violin and the cimbalom—which looks like an overgrown

zither sometimes plucked, as was the zither in the classic *The Third Man* thriller, but more often struck.

> The combination of violin, cimbalom and panpipes has virtually no equal, burrowing into the very soul.

Much Czechoslovak music is devoted to dance, celebration and general diversion—an effective cure for the blues in any language. Wedding songs abound, and so do those on wine. Never a dull moment.

Hungarian music, on the other hand, is often bittersweet, depicting beauty, passion,

KAZAKHSTAN

Aral Sea

UZBEKISTAN

KIRGIZIYA

TAJIKISTAN

GEORGIA

AZER-
BAIJAN

ARMENIA

TURKMENISTAN

Caspian Sea

AFGHANISTAN

sadness—the gamut of human emotions. Not for that is it any less desirable. Hungarian music is often called "Gypsy music," although it bears little resemblance to that of genuine gypsies in other European countries, such as Ireland and Spain.

The attraction of Romanian music lies as much in the instruments themselves—and the versatility with which they are played— as with the compositions. The combination of violin, cimbalom and panpipes has virtually no equal, burrowing into the very soul.

Within Eastern Europe and the greater U.S.S.R., then, lies music for everyone—and much of it may be heard over world band radio. As to where and when, much depends on your location.

Many stations in the Soviet republics now relay through transmitters in the Moscow area, which together with transmitters in the republics themselves afford improved reception abroad. But North Americans may still have trouble. Listeners in the United States and Canada probably have a better chance to hear Munich-based Radio Liberty, which broadcasts in 13 of the Soviet Union's minority languages. Unfortunately, Radio Liberty doesn't carry much in the way of traditional music—the excellent Kazakh and Tatar-Bashkir services excepted.

Prepared by Don Swampo.

Make your station really perform

Need to hear the weak ones? No room for an outside long wire? Looking for a great little speaker? Choose the accessories for the

Use this 54 inch active antenna to receive strong signals from all over-the-world MFJ-1024 ... $129.95

Receive strong clear signals from all-over-the world with this 54 inch active antenna that rivals long wires hundreds of feet long. The authoritative *World Radio TV Handbook* rates the MFJ-1024 as 'a first-rate easy-to-operate active antenna . . . quiet . . . excellent

dynamic range . . . good gain . . . very low noise factor . . . broad frequency coverage . . . excellent choice'.

You'll receive all frequencies 50 KHz to 30 MHz from VLF thru lower VHF - including long wave, medium wave, broadcast and shortwave bands. Mounts anywhere away from electrical noise for maximum signal and minimum noise pickup -- mount on houses, buildings, balconies, mobile homes, apartments, on board ships -- anywhere space is a premium.

High dynamic range eliminates intermodulation so you never hear 'phantom' signals.

A 20 dB attenuator and a gain control prevents overloading your receiver. You can select between 2 receivers and an auxiliary antenna. Has weather-proofed electronics. Use 12 VDC or 110 VAC with MFJ-1312, $9.95.

The MFJ-1024 comes complete with a 50 foot coax cable and connector - ready to use!

WORLD TIME CLOCK

MFJ-109 ... $19.95

The new MFJ-109 World Time Clock gives you a dual LCD display that shows both the local time and the time in any of 24 world cities.

Easy-slide control lets you instantly select the city.

Or you can instantly check GMT by setting it on our convenient GMT pointer.

It also features an alarm with snooze, night light, Daylight Savings Time adjustment, suede-like carrying case, international date change indicators, and a flip stand. AAA batteries are also included along with an attractive gift box.

It has silver casing, a gray background and black lettering with a red MFJ logo. It measures a shirt-pocket sized 2x4½x½ inches.

Multi-mode Data Controller

MFJ-1278 ... $279.95

Use you world band radio, computer and MFJ software to receive AP wire photos, news over Radio teletype, AMTOR ship to shore communications, weather maps, morse code, slow scan tv pictures and more -- all on your computer screen.

It also teaches you Morse code so you can get your ham license in no time -- you can talk to hams all over the world.

Available Software:
MFJ-1289 MultiCom™ for IBM or compatible, $59.95. MFJ also has less powerful programs for Macintosh (MFJ-1287) and Commodore 64/128 (MFJ-1282), $24.95 each. MFJ-1278 also includes AC power supply, dual radio ports and tons more.

AP photo received on 20.738 MHz using MFJ-1278 and MFJ-1289 MultiCom™.

PRESELECTING SW/MW/LW TUNER

MFJ-956 ... .39.95

This MFJ-956 short, medium, long wave preselector/tuner lets you boost your favorite station while rejecting images, intermod and other phantom signals on your shortwave receiver! It greatly improves reception of 150 KHz thru 30 MHz signals. It has convenient tuner bypass and ground receiver positions. 2x3x4 inches

COMPACT SPEAKER

MFJ-280 ... $19.95

A rugged, compact communications speaker with a tilt bracket on a magnetic base. Has 3½ mm phone plug on 30 inch cord. Use with all 8 & 4 ohm impedances. Handles up to 3 watts of audio. Mounting plates, screws included. Its dark gray military color matches your rig. 2x2½x3 inches.

12/24 HOUR LCD CLOCKS

MFJ-108B ... $19.95
MFJ-107B ... $9.95

Know the exact 24 hour UTC time and your local 12 hour time at a single glance so

you'll tune in your favorite stations on time and keep accurate logs for DXing. Huge 5/8 inch LCD digits makes glare-free reading easy. MFJ-108, dual 24/12 hour clock, 4½x1x2 in. MFJ-107, single 24 hour clock, 2¼x1x2 in. Long lasting lithium battery included.

MFJ ... making quality affordable

with MFJ shortwave accessories

Troubled by 'phantom' signals? Need convenient access to UTC? kind of performance you need from the many models MFJ offers

ANTENNA MATCHER

MFJ-959B . . . $89.95

Don't lose signal power! The MFJ-959B Antenna Tuner provides proper impedance matching so you transfer maximum power from your antenna to your receiver from 1.8 to 30 MHz. You'll be surprised by significant increases in signal strength.

20 dB preamp with gain control boosts weak stations and 20 dB attenuator prevents overload. Select from 2 antennas and 2 receivers. 9x2x6 inches. 9-18 VDC or 110 VAC with MFJ-1312.

RTTY ASCII CW Interface
MFJ-1225 . . . $79.95

Use your Commodore or IBM compatible computer to pick up exciting communications on your SW radio. Software: disk (MFJ-1265) or tape (MFJ-1264) for C-64/128 or disk (MFJ-1285B) for IBM or compatible, $19.95 each. Get yours today!Use 12 VDC or110 VAC with MFJ-1312, $12.95.

"The Shortwave Listener's Bible for Completely Indoors Listening"

If you're in an apartment or city and can't pick anything up, Ed Noll's newest book is the key to the indoor SWL. Everything you need to know -- antennas, frequencies, etc. MFJ-36, $9.95. Available soon.

ALL MODE FILTER

MFJ-752C . . . $99.95

Maybe the only filter you'll ever need. Why? Because the all mode dual tunable filters let you zero in AM/SSB/RTTY/CW/AMTOR/Packet signals and notch out interference at the same time.

The primary filter lets you peak, notch, low or high pass filter out interference.

The auxilary filter gives deep notches and sharp peaks.

Both tune 300 to 3000 Hz with variable bandwidth from 40 Hz to virtually flat. Select 2 receivers. Drive speaker. Use 9-18 VDC or 110 VAC with MFJ-1312.   10x2x6 in.

Gray Line DX Advantage
MFJ-1286 . . . $29.95

Here's a computerized DXing tool that predicts DX

propagation. Now even the casual DXer can snag rare DX by knowing exactly when DX conditions are best. You get a high resolution world map that displays the gray line aa a moving area of day and night that changes with time. It also shows you the position of the sun, time in 24 places, more. IBM compatible, any graphics. Run memory resident or alone. Check gray line for any date. 3 maps.

Morse Code Practicer
MFJ-557 . . . $14.95

Learn to send perfect Morse code with this MFJ Deluxe Code Practice Oscillator. Straight key mounted on heavy steel base with oscillator. Volume, tone controls. Earphone jack. Use 9 V battery (not included) or optional AC power supply, $12.95. Sturdy unit small enough to be portable.

Rival outside long wires with this INDOOR active antenna

Now you'll rival or exceed the reception of outside long wires with the new and improved MFJ-1020A Indoor Tuned Active Antenna with higher gain. Here's what the 'World Radio TV Handbook' says about the MFJ-1020: 'Fine value...fair price...best offering to date...**performs very well indeed.**'

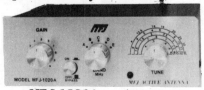

MFJ-1020A . . . $79.95

You get continuous coverage of low, medium and short wave bands from 300 KHz to 30 MHz so you can listen to all your favorite stations. It even functions as a preselector with an external antenna.

Its unique tuned circuitry minimizes intermodulation, improves selectivity and reduces noise so you're less bothered by images, and other out-of-band signals.

The adjustable telescoping antenna that gives you maximum signal and minimum noise. There's a full set of controls for tuning, band selection, gain, ON/OFF/Bypass and an LED power 'ON' indicator. It measures just 5x2x6 inches. Use a 9 volt battery,9-18 VDC or 110 VAC with MFJ-1312.

Call toll-free 800-647-1800 and charge to your VISA or Master Card. Order any product from MFJ and try it -- no obligation! If not satisfied, return it within 30 days for a full no-hassle refund, less shipping. One-year **unconditional** guarantee. Add $5 each for shipping/ handling. Free catalog. For technical info. or outside USA or in Miss. call 601-323-5869; telex 53-4590 MFJ STKV; FAX: 601-323-6551.

800-647-1800

MFJ ENTERPRISES, INC.
P.O. Box 494
Miss. State, MS 39762

MFJ . . . making quality affordable

OFF THE BEATEN PATH

"*Bonjour Afrique! Bonjour Africains!*"
With a greeting reminiscent of Robin Williams' "Gooood morning Vietnaaam," Afrique Numéro Un sends its daily hello across the continent to some 16 million listeners.

For a decade now, the powerful world band station at Libreville, capital of West Africa's Gabon, has been steadily gaining listeners. Afrique Numéro Un, with its fast-paced commercial programming and lively music, has climbed to the top of the hill, leaving many of the duller state-run stations in the African dust.

There's nothing small-time about Afrique Numéro Un, found daytime on 15475 and 17630 kHz. With several huge 500,000-watt shortwave transmitters, it is the third largest user of electricity on Africa's west coast. It has so much broadcasting capacity that it leases air time for program relays by such world band biggies as Radio France Internationale, Radio Japan and Swiss Radio International. Its listener response is impressive—more than 3,000 letters a month.

So why isn't Afrique Numéro Un among the most popular stations with *Passport to World Band Radio* readers? Probably because most English-speaking shortwave listeners shy away from a French-language station.

That's a shame, too, since an adventurous listener who strays from the beaten path to tune in Afrique Numéro Un doesn't need to know the language to love the music. It's easy to get hooked on the rhythms of Africa, with hits by such stars as Alpha Blondy and Papa Wemba—household names from Abidjan to Zaire, but little-known elsewhere in the world.

If you're willing to break your habits, there's a lot of good programming on world band. Some stations, like Afrique Numéro Un, seldom if ever broadcast in English, but still offer musical programs you will enjoy. Others do broadcast in English, but at inconvenient times—very late at night or in the predawn, for instance. Yet other broadcasters run lower transmitting power, making their signals less dominant than the major international stations, and sometimes harder to tune in.

But even among the stronger signals, you may find a few offbeat surprises.

Radio Cairo, for instance, is one you may have heard with its English programs to North America during the evening hours. But there's another side to Radio Cairo which you may have missed: its relay of Home Arabic language programming directed mainly to listeners in North Africa and Southern Europe, where many Egyptians work.

Now Cairo is the Middle East's music city. The Egyptian capital and its recording industry is to Arab pop music what Nashville is to American country and western.

One of the Voice of America's most popular programs to Africa is *Music Time in Africa*, presented by Rita Rochelle and Leo Sarkisian. Although beamed to Africa, it can be heard elsewhere, including North America and Europe.

Folk arts continue to be important in Egypt. Radio Cairo's shows on Egyptian life and culture are nightly fare to most parts of the world.

To non-Arab ears, this style of music may sound dissonant, but if you give it half a chance you may come to appreciate its exotic sound. It is a real ethnic experience, one worth taking. Instead of tuning to your usual Radio Cairo frequency, try listening on 9850 kHz around 2200 World Time.

> It's easy to get hooked on the rhythms of Africa by such stars as Alpha Blondy and Papa Wemba.

Many veteran world band listeners maintain that the broadcasts of Latin America offer the world's most varied musical menu. There are Brazilian rhythms, Dominican merengues, galloping Colombian cumbias, lilting Guatemalan melodies, the brassy mariachi of Mexico, and so much more. But to enjoy the sound buffet you must, with few exceptions, tune into stations that never broadcast in English.

Brazil, French Guiana, Belize, Suriname and Guyana excepted, Spanish rules the South and Central American airwaves, and dozens of stations are audible to world band listeners during the evening hours. Some are found among the major international stations in the 25, 31 and 49 meter segments. But a better place to hunt is within the tropical segments below 5700 kHz. Even if you don't know a word of Spanish, just tune until you hit some music that catches you ear. Colombia and Venezuela are among the easiest to sniff out.

Stay up late or get up early, and discover some of the best. Andean *música folclórica* is a generic label for a number of distinctive musical styles from the countries along South America's mountainous spine. They differ from country to country, but be they *huaynos* (pronounced "why-knows") of Peru or Bolivia, or Ecuadorian *pasacalles*, they reflect an exotic blend of the Spanish and much older Inca cultures.

The world was introduced to the Andean musical sound—dominated by the flute-like instrument Peruvians call the *quena*—by U.S. recording stars Simon and Garfunkel with their version of "El Cóndor Pasa," a huayno.

Tune around the lower world band frequencies an hour or so before dawn in North America—earlier during the hours of darkness in Europe—and unless it's summer you may unearth more than one station playing Andean music. Among them are Radio Andina in Huancayo, Peru, on 4995 kHz, and La Voz de Cutervo, another Peruvian, on 5660 kHz.

> ## Cairo is to Arab pop music what Nashville is to country and western.

Tahiti is no longer quite the remote Pacific paradise it was when French impressionist Paul Gaugin discovered the local color for his vivid paintings of carefree, bare-bosomed maidens. Today, the tourists are more likely than the Tahitians to be carefree and skimpily clothed. They fly in droves to this mid-ocean vacation magnet where, beneath the tropical stars on a palm-fringed shore, they can still marvel at Tahitians dancing to gentle island strains—sounds unlike any other in the world.

It's an experience world band listeners can share via Tahiti's Radio Télévision Française d'Outre-Mer, or simply RFO, France's overseas station in Tahiti. Programming is in French, of course. But with all that strumming, who cares? Of RFO's several frequencies, 11815 kHz and 15170 kHz are best bets, especially after around 0300 or 0400 World Time.

As long as our quest for off-the-beaten-track world band listening has brought us to the Pacific, how about Kiribati? This tiny independent country, a series of dots in the ocean across some 300 square miles, is about as far out and far away as you can get. Until 1979, Kiribati was part of the British colonial territory known as the Gilbert Islands.

Radio Kiribati (the pronunciation may surprise you, KIR-eh-bass) is not the easiest station to hear, mostly due to its low 250-watt power. It is enough to carry the broadcasts to Kiribati's outer islands, but it's not intended for international reception. Still, at times this upper-sideband mode signal can travel a long way, and be heard at a surprisingly decent level in North America and even Europe on its frequency of 14919.7 kHz. If your radio permits, try about 0555 World Time, when it comes on the air.

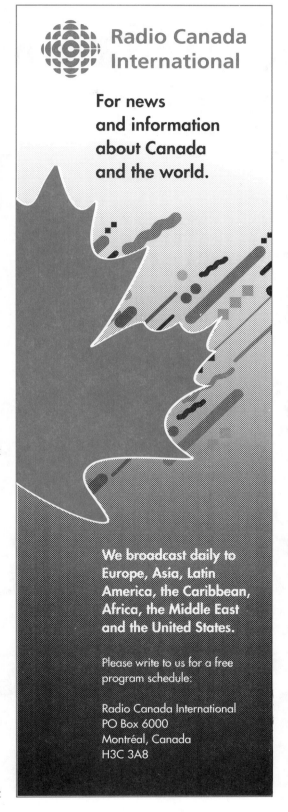

Want to party? Come to Salvador, Brazil, for the annual Carnival. Or do the next best thing—listen to lively Radio Nacional do Brasil, audible throughout North America and Europe.

Even among the familiar there is the unusual. Consider Radio Australia, Radio Canada International or Radio RSA—all widely popular international broadcasters. Less well-known, though, are the world band transmissions by the same broadcasting organizations intended for domestic consumption.

Marvel at Tahitian island strains—sounds unlike any other in the world.

For instance, the domestic commercial network of the South African Broadcasting Corporation, Radio Five, provides FM and mediumwave AM programs for English-speaking South Africans. This also is carried over world band, including on 11885 kHz. It can give the overseas listener a different perspective of South Africa than that heard on RSA's External Service.

You can hear the Home Service news at 0600 World Time, followed by a string of ads for such things as life insurance, cigarettes and jeans, with South African

sponsors whose brand names and claims may be completely unfamiliar to you.

Similarly, the Australian Broadcasting Corporation, which operates Radio Australia, also has a series of world band stations which program to Australians in the remote Outback. They include 4920 and 9660 kHz from Brisbane, and 9610 kHz from Wanneroo, in suburban Perth in Western Australia. Try listening during the predawn to hear what Australians are hearing on their radios at home.

Besides the easily heard Radio Canada International, the Canadian Broadcasting Corporation also reaches internal audiences in the remote north country with the Northern Quebec Service, which operates on 9625 kHz, 18 hours a day. Programs are not only in English and French, but also in Eskimo and the Indian languages Inuktitut, Cree and Attikameque. Word has it that this service may vanish soon from world band, so grab it while you can.

There are other unusual languages to be heard on world band radio. Romansch is one. Along with French, Italian and German—the correct version, not the oft-used local variation, *Schweizerdeutsch*—

Romansch is one of the four official languages of Switzerland.

There are only 50,000 persons who speak Romansch, which linguists say is the closest living language to the ancient Latin vernacular of the days of the Caesars. And the number of Romansch speakers diminishes with every census.

Swiss Radio International is doing its part to keep a living language alive by broadcasting a limited Romansch schedule—two 15-minute segments each week, with regular repeats to different parts of the world. Though you won't understand it, you may want to tune in at 0315 World Time Wednesdays and Saturdays (Tuesday and Friday evenings in North America) on SRI's regular frequencies to North America, just to hear what the language is like.

Tok Pisin, formerly known as Pidgin, is one of the world's oddest languages. Its origins date to the 1600s, when British merchants began trading with the people of Asia and the East Indies. Arrogantly assuming the natives could never learn to use proper English, the white traders devised a simplified language, stringing basic English words together with local syntax, disregarding linguistic niceties like gender and number, and with verbs timeless and invariable. Eventually·the jargon evolved into a real and separate, though curious, language known as Pidgin—the name itself a corruption of the word "business."

On world band, there's more than a smidgin of Tok Pisin, broadcast by the stations of the National Broadcasting Commission of Papua New Guinea. One of the outlets, for example, identifies in Tok Pisin as "Maus Bilong Sunkamup," which can be rendered in English as the Mouth-Belong-Sun-Come-Up, meaning voice of the sunrise, or east.

A different NBC station at Port Moresby may be easier to hear around dawn in North America, on 4890 kHz. Or, try tuning Radio Australia's broadcasts in Tok Pisin at 0930 World Time on 6080, 7240, 9710 or 11930kHz.

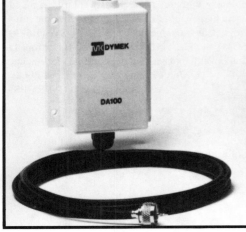

Over 150 countries broadcast over the world band airwaves. But the United Nations, which once had an extensive schedule of programs broadcast over Voice of America facilities, lost most of its world band voice following a dispute over airtime charges by the U.S. for use of the transmitters. Now, it's audible in Europe over the Italian Radio Relay Service's frequency of 9860 kHz. The Organization of American States, however, does use VOA transmitters for its daily Spanish programs from Washington, D.C. to Latin America at 2345 World Time.

> **Over 150 countries broadcast over the world band airwaves.**

Additionally, the International Red Cross has an arrangement with Swiss authorities for the use of its world band facilities. From a transmitter at Beromünster, Switzerland, the Red Cross airs programs in four languages on 7210 kHz—at 1100 and 1700 World Time on the first or last Monday and Thursday of each month.

A better bet for those listening in North America is an English program beamed to the United States and Canada on regular Swiss Radio International world band frequencies in the 25, 31 and 49 meter segments. Look for this brief—only 17 minutes long—program at 0310 World Time on the first or last Tuesday and Friday (Monday and Thursday evenings in North America) of each month. It includes Red Cross news and interviews, information briefs and actuality tapes, and replies to reader letters.

These are but a few of the unusual stations and programs you can hear when you stray from your customary world band rounds. World band offers countless offbeat surprises for the adventurous listener. Try it!

Prepared by Don Jensen.

TOUR OF WORLD BAND AND POINTS BETWEEN

by Harry L. Helms

The shortwave spectrum, which includes world band radio, is just another tuning range, like the AM or FM bands you know. But it offers much more room to roam—30 times AM!

Such wide-open spaces accommodate tens of thousands of stations, but navigating the dial may seem daunting. Fortunately, the shortwave spectrum has segments, or bands—each with its own personality.

Depending on when and where you tune, you can hear major international broadcasters, such as Radio Moscow and the BBC; smaller, local-language stations, such as Venezuela's Ecos del Torbes, from remote areas; airplanes, military and ham operators; and bewildering bleeps and braaps that send photographs to special terminals. A look at the shortwave spectrum, and who does what, where, will help.

Frequencies are measured in kiloHertz (kHz) or MegaHertz (MHz). One MHz equals 1000 kHz; so, the frequency 9580 kHz is the same thing as 9.58 MHz. You might also hear or see things like "31 meters" or "19 meters." That is a holdover from when frequencies were measured in wavelength. Some major world band broadcasters still use that shorthand on the air, as when announcing frequencies. It's all explained in *Passport's* Glossary at the back of this book.

The Big Picture

One of the first things you'll notice is that some frequencies are better at different times of the day than others. As a very general rule of thumb, frequencies below 9 MHz (that is, 9000 kHz) offer better reception during your local night. The 9-to-14 MHz range is transitional; you'll hear some stations there almost around the clock—although either daytime or nighttime might give better reception, depending on the season.

Frequencies above 14 MHz are usually heard during the day. A couple of hours before and after your local sunrise and sunset often give a mixed reception bag. For example, at 7 am your local time, Americans can usually hear stations from Europe on frequencies above 14 MHz, and also find Asian stations on frequencies below 9 MHz. Later, at 7 pm, they tend to hear Europe and Africa below 9 MHz, while Asia and Australia are coming through above 14 MHz. After you've been listening to world band a short while, the patterns in

The American Radio Relay League has top-notch equipment for its visitors to use. Shown are Chuck Bender, left, and Greg Bonaguide.

your own part of the world will become second nature.

World band stations generally operate on channels spaced 5 kHz apart; e.g., 9505, 9510, 9515 and 9520 kHz. And while some stations use the same frequencies year-round, many use different ones at different times of the year to ensure best reception. These seasonal frequencies are indicated in *Passport* by a "J" (June) for summer and a "D" (December) for winter. If the listing doesn't have a letter, that frequency is used all year.

Workhorse Segments

As you flip through the Blue Pages of this *Passport,* you'll note that major broadcasters like the BBC, Radio Moscow and Deutsche Welle tend to be found within a few frequency ranges. These are the *international* broadcasting segments, used mainly by stations transmitting programs for foreign consumption. Here are those ranges, and the segment (wavelength) each is known by. If you're like most *Passport* readers, these are where you'll spend most of your listening time.

World Band—International Broadcasting

Frequency Range		Segment (Wavelength)
3900-4000	kHz	75 meters*
5950-6200	kHz	49 meters
7100-7300	kHz	41 meters*
9500-9900	kHz	31 meters
11650-12050	kHz	25 meters
13600-13800	kHz	22 meters
15100-15600	kHz	19 meters
17550-17900	kHz	16 meters
21450-21850	kHz	13 meters
25670-26100	kHz	11 meters

*Used only outside the Americas.
(Used by hams in the Americas.)

While most international broadcasters stick to these frequency ranges, there's been a growing tendency to operate adjacent to, but outside of, the established segments. For more on the "real world" segments and best listening times, see the Glossary at the rear of this *Passport.*

Not all these segments are equally crowded. 11 meters is very lightly used because it comes to life during the non-prime-time hours of daylight, and also

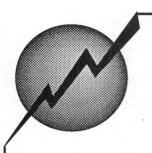

because of its highly erratic nature: It doesn't always work; but when it works, it works well. 22 meters is not as heavily populated as most others because it is the newest and still not entirely "official." Many broadcasters have yet to acquire equipment for it.

Don't let the relative lack of popularity of these two segments turn you away. Because they're relatively lightly used, interference from competing stations is minimal, making reception clearer than in the other segments.

On the other hand, 49 and 31 meters are packed to the gunwales at night. Even 25 meters tends to be crowded evenings.

Listening is usually easy within the international broadcasting segments. Stations use these to schedule their programming during our local evening hours, use English, and select frequencies that allow reasonably clear, reliable reception. With a little familiarity and a current *Passport* in hand, pulling in the news from Tokyo or a soccer match from Britain can be almost as easy as tuning in a weather or traffic report on your car radio.

World Band Radio Goes Native: The Tropical Segments

Ads for world band radio used to say, "Travel the world from your armchair." Within the international segments, that's a fair description. After all, listening to a major international station is rather like staying at a comfortable five-star hotel.

But, as with real touring, it's often interesting to sacrifice comfort for adventure. Enter the backroads signals—the smaller stations secreted within the *tropical* broadcasting segments:

World Band—Tropical Broadcasting

Frequency Range	Segment (Wavelength)
2300-2498 kHz	120 meters
3200-3400 kHz	90 meters
4750-5060 kHz	60 meters

Not all world band stations broadcast to audiences outside their borders. Nations with large, sparsely populated areas find world band radio the only practical way to offer residents any radio at all. Much of this takes place within these special tropical segments that are nominally off limits to the big international broadcasters. Most of these stations are in the tropics; so, needless to say, you won't hear lots of English, unless it happens to be the local lingua franca.

If you can overlook that, you might find string music from the Indian subcontinent, Brazilian soccer matches with screaming announcers, recitations from the Holy Koran, and opportunities to brush up on your foreign language skills with idioms from native speakers.

Listening to tropical stations can be exhausting. Signals are much weaker than in the international broadcasting segments, static and noise are high, and reception tends to be hit-or-miss, with daytime and summertime reception being downright hopeless. Serious receivers and antennas are a necessity.

The rewards, then, are best appreciated by world band connoisseurs, whose experienced palates can relate to such tongues as Indonesian, Swahili, Hindustani and Malay; music played on a cora, a valiha, a mbira or a vivo; or a concert on a Tongan noseflute (yes, that's how it's played).

Clandestine Broadcasters

Passport's Blue Pages list some stations that are considered "clandestine." Clandestine broadcasters are world band's equivalent of the Twilight Zone: hidden, extralegal stations using deceptive practices to promote a political/ideological aim. Typically, a clandestine station will keep its actual location secret—although a false one may be announced—and sometimes will also mask its true sponsor or purpose.

Clandestine broadcasting began 1941 with Radio España Independiente, operated by the Spanish Communist Party. After its defeat and exile by Gen. Francisco Franco, the Party began broadcasting to Spain from the U.S.S.R.

During World War II, many clandestines sprang up, some claiming to transmit from occupied territories. In the postwar era, East and West alike sponsored clandestine broadcasters in such global hot spots as East and Southeast Asia, Iran, Central and Southern Europe, and the Caribbean.

More recently, the focus has been the Middle East and Central America. North

UTILITY ACTION FREQUENCIES

Utility stations are prolific—they use more frequencies than international and tropical broadcasting stations combined. Listing every utility station and its frequency would take a book larger than *Passport,* and would swiftly be out of date. But if you'd like a sample of what's on, here are some of the most commonly used utility frequencies and their main purpose. All are voice channels, with USB normally used:

Frequency (kHz)	Main Use
2182	Ship emergency and calling
2670	U.S. Coast Guard maritime weather bulletins
3485	Aviation weather for North Atlantic routes
4125	International ship-to-ship communications
4449	U.S. Air Force communications
6218.6	Inland (rivers, lakes) ship-to-shore
6221.6	U.S. Coast Guard communications
6683	U.S. Air Force (often used by Air Force One)
8257	International ship calling
8825	Aircraft flying North Atlantic routes
10072	Ground-to-air communications
11182	U.S. Air Force
12429.2	International ship-to-ship communications
15041	U.S. Air Force
16523	International ship calling
22124	International ship-to-ship communications

American listeners who understand Spanish have been able to follow the conflicts between factions in Nicaragua and El Salvador over such stations as *Radio Venceremos* and *Radio Quince de Septiembre.* If English is your only tongue, you may have the dubious experience of hearing the neo-Nazi U.S. station, *Voice of To-morrow,* which for years has broadcast irregularly from a secret site believed to be in Virginia.

Since clandestine broadcasters are political creatures, they appear and vanish as political winds shift. The odds are good that some of the clandestine stations listed in *Passport's B*lue Pages will have already ceased by the time you read this, while others probably will have taken their place.

Amateur ("Ham") Radio

Since the dawn of radio, certain sections of the radio spectrum have been set aside for use by private individuals for direct radio communication with others—just for fun. These are the amateur radio, or "ham," bands.

Hams are licensed by their national governments to transmit within the radio spectrum. Ham radio operators communi-

cate with each other in several modes, including Morse telegraphy and such exotic means as "packet radio," which links computers through the airwaves. Certain portions of each ham radio band are allocated for voice, and in the shortwave spectrum upper and lower sideband (USB and LSB) are the widest choices by far. In most cases, voice communication is confined to the higher part of each band, with Morse, radio teletype (RTTY), digital modes such as ASCII and AMTOR, and even amateur television down lower. The ham bands are:

Amateur Radio

Frequency Range		Segment (Wavelength)	
1800-2000	kHz	160	meters
3500-4000	kHz	80	meters
7000-7300	kHz	40	meters
10100-10150	kHz	30	meters
14000-14350	kHz	20	meters
18068-18168	kHz	17	meters
21000-21450	kHz	15	meters
24890-24990	kHz	12	meters
28000-29700	kHz	10	meters

Listening to hams, you'll discover most of their conversations are inconsequential chitchat. But in major emergencies—such as 1989's Hurricane Hugo and San Francisco earthquake—the chatter disappears, replaced by emergency communications networks staffed and run entirely by those same hams. In fact, the ham bands are often the best place to listen for information during and immediately after a widespread emergency. It often happens that ham radio communications function far better in those situations than those operated by local, state or federal agencies!

Getting the Work Done: "Utility" Stations

Most world band frequencies not used for broadcasting or amateur radio are used by what's loosely referred to as "utility" stations. As the term implies, utility stations facilitate some activity: air or sea travel, law enforcement, shipping, the military, and so forth. Much of what goes on in the utility bands is unintelligible without special receiving equipment to convert those bleeps, buzzes, and zzaapps into photographs, maps or

text. But there's a lot of chitchat to be heard on upper sideband (USB).

Unlike world band broadcasters, utility stations are merely point-to-point; that is, they're not meant to be heard by the public, and there are laws in various countries governing the listening to utility stations. In Europe, for example, much of this sort of listening is prohibited.

In the U.S., however, it's usually okay to eavesdrop on utility stations, including the occasional conversation from Air Force One. But you're not supposed to divulge what you've heard. That same rule of the road also applies to the Government. Although the huge National Security Agency eavesdrops silently on all electronic communications, including telephone calls—indeed, it's against the law for Americans to encrypt communications such that the NSA can't decipher them—they virtually always keep the findings to themselves except where national security is involved.

As utility stations are for point "A" to make contact with point "B," and no more, they generally keep no set schedule, and sometimes even change frequencies minute by minute. Much of what you can hear is cryptic ("Two Alfa Niner, go to Delta Sierra in red mode"), and it's often hard to know what station you're hearing or where it's at.

However, the various international emergency frequencies do offer dramatic listening at times. During emergencies, the jargon stops and the emphasis is on communicating as clearly and quickly as possible. An "emergency" can range from an out-of-gas pleasure boat to an airliner with a burning engine.

Standard Time and Frequency Stations

Several stations continuously transmit the exact time and other useful information. They are the standard time and frequency stations. They're termed "standard" because their operating frequencies and time signals are so accurate they can be used for scientific purposes.

In North America, the most widely heard stations are WWV in Colorado and WWVH in Hawaii, both of which operate on 2500, 5000, 10000 and 15000 kHz. They announce the precise World Time ("Coordinated Universal Time") each minute, and occasionally oceanographic weather, with WWV using a male voice and WWVH a female voice.

Of special interest to world band aficionados is that WWV and WWVH also transmit a brief announcement of world band radio reception conditions at 18 minutes after the hour. The bulletin is straightforward, describing reception conditions as quiet, unsettled or active. They also offer information on solar flux and the "K-index," which are measures of the Earth's geomagnetic field. As a general rule, the higher the solar flux reading and lower the K-index, the better the world band reception.

There are other standard time and frequency stations throughout the world. One heard well across North America is Canada's CHU, on 3330, 7335 and 14670 kHz. CHU doesn't use World Time, instead announcing Eastern Standard Time—but at least they do so in both English and French!

Harry L. Helms is one of the principals of HighText Publishing. His Shortwave Listening Guidebook _will be published by DX/SWL Press in early 1991._

BELOW WORLD BAND RADIO

The standard mediumwave AM band runs from about 540 to 1600 kHz. Frequencies above that, but below 30,000 kHz, are considered to be shortwave, which includes world band. But many radios covering world band also tune frequencies below 540 kHz. These are commonly referred to as longwave, and were among the first frequencies used in radio's infancy.

In Europe, the U.S.S.R., North Africa and the Near East, the 153 to 281 kHz range is used for broadcasting. Longwave reception distances are short during daylight, but reception of stations within a few hundred miles is common at night. For this reason, listeners in many parts of the world continue to seek out radios with longwave coverage, the inclusion or absence of which is given for each radio in _Passport's_ Buyer's Guide.

Passport specializes in coverage of world band broadcasting. If you're interested in utility stations, however, there are a number of excellent references available from radio and book dealers in North America and Europe, as well as from their publishers/distributors:

Shortwave Directory (published by Grove Enterprises, P.O. Box 98, Brasstown, NC 28902 USA); *Confidential Frequency List* (published by Gilfer Shortwave, 52 Park Ave., Park Ridge, NJ 07656 USA); and *Guide to Utility Stations, HF Aeronautical Communications Handbook* and *Maritime Radio Handbook* (distributed by Universal Radio, 1280 Aida Drive, Reynoldsburg OH 43068 USA).

If you're an American and interested in getting your own ham radio license, contact the nonprofit American Radio Relay League (ARRL). The venerable "League," as it's known among hams, is the national association of ham radio operators in the U.S. The ARRL publishes numerous authoritative books on amateur radio, plus the popular magazine *QST,* and has a wealth of materials to help people obtain their own ham license. The ARRL may be reached at at 225 Main St., Newington, CT 06111 USA.

Canadian? Contact the Canadian Radio Relay League at Box 7009, Station E, London ON, N5Y 4J9. In the United Kingdom, write to David Evans, Secretary/CEO, at the Radio Society of Great Britain—an excellent publisher, too—Lambda House, Cranborne Road, Potter's Bar, Herts EN6 3JE.

STATIONS: WHO AND WHERE TO WRITE

H ave a complaint? Want to pat somebody on the back for a job well done?

While some world band stations regard listeners' opinions as being beside the point, a number of others are genuinely interested in hearing from you. After all, while domestic radio and TV networks can afford to take exacting listener surveys within the one country they broadcast to, world band stations rarely find it feasible to do this for the dozens of countries they're heard in.

Free Goodies

In order to stimulate listener correspondence, stations resort to a variety of reward schemes. No, you won't get $1,000 for being the fifth caller to identify Elvis Presley as the guy singing "Milkcow Blues Boogie." But you can get a variety of freebies, such as program schedules, calendars, magazines, brochures, program guides, souvenir "QSL" postcards, pins, pennants, T-shirts, stickers and decals—even, on rare occasion, coins and stamps.

Probably the all-time King of the Giveaways was Radio Peking, as Radio Beijing was known back then, some 20 years ago. During the Cultural Revolution, those writing the station were showered with bundles of communist kitsch: beaming Mao buttons, Little Red Books of Mao's

"thoughts," calendars exalting the People's Liberation Army, station pennants, and various propaganda magazines. Sometimes, they would even throw in free records . . . of Mao's wife's music.

By those standards, today's broadcasters—including Radio Beijing—are downright parsimonious. But worthwhile responses still come from such stations as Deutsche Welle (arguably the best, overall), Voice of the UAE, Radio Tirana, Radio RSA, Radio Habana Cuba, Radio Portugal International, Radio Nacional España, Radio Budapest, Turkish RTV Corporation, Radio Station Peace and Progress and, of course, Radio Beijing. It is real flesh-and-blood human beings that read your letter, so it never hurts to send along a little souvenir of your own—a photo of your family or a local tourist brochure, for example—to help stimulate a friendly response.

Buying via World Band

Most world band stations, being government entities, take the mandarin viewpoint on earning a profit and simply give away token items. However, a growing number—such as the Christian Science Monitor and KUSW—also sell world band and other merchandise by mail. The BBC World Service, which sells a wide variety of goods, goes one step further. If you want to receive its excellent *London Calling* schedule regularly, you have to cough up for it.

Radio Canada International receives up to 50,000 letters each year from appreciative listeners.

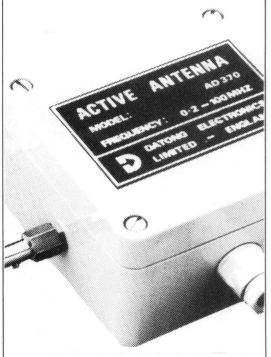

Where someone is responsible for listener
correspondence, his—or her—name is
given. Otherwise, simply address your letter
to the station itself.

AFGHANISTAN
Radio Afghanistan, P.O. Box 544, Kabul,
Afghanistan.

ALBANIA
Radio Tirana, Tirana, Albania.

ALGERIA
RTV Algerienne, 21 Boulevard des Martyrs,
Algiers, Algeria.

ARGENTINA
Radio Argentina al Exterior—RAE, Casilla
de Correo 555, 1000 Buenos Aires, Argentina. Contact: Ms. Silvana Licciardi, English
Department.

AUSTRALIA
Radio Australia, GPO Box 428G, Mel-
bourne VIC 3001, Australia. Contact:
Michael Taft, Correspondence Officer.

AUSTRIA
Radio Austria International, A-1136 Vienna,
Austria. Contact: Paul Lendvai, Director.

BANGLADESH
Radio Bangladesh, External Services, P.O.
Box No. 2204, Dhaka, Bangladesh. Contact:
Masudul Hasan, Deputy Director.

BELGIUM
Belgische Radio TV, Postbus 26, B-1000
Brussels, Belgium.
RT Belge Francaise, B.P. 202, B-1040
Brussels, Belgium.

BRAZIL
Radio Nacional, C.P. 04/0340, 70323
Brasília, Brazil.

BULGARIA
Radio Sofia, 4 Dragan Tsankov Blvd., Sofia,
Bulgaria. Contact: Ms. Nadezhda Gecheva,
Listeners' Letters Department.

CANADA
CFCX-CFCF, 200 McGill College Avenue,
Montréal PQ, H3B 4G7 Canada.
CFRX-CFRB, 2 St. Clair Avenue West,
Toronto ON, M4V 1L6 Canada.
Radio Canada International, P.O. Box
6000, Montréal PQ, H3C 3A8 Canada.
Contact: Ms. Judith Suavé, Listeners' Letters;
Ian McFarland, DX Producer.

CHINA (PR)
Radio Beijing, Beijing 100866, People's Republic of China. Contact: Li Dan, Head, English Department; Chen Xiaoyu, English Department; Wu Xiaoyung, English Department.

CHINA (TAIWAN)
Voice of Free China, P.O. Box 24-38, Taipei, Taiwan, Republic of China. Contact: Daniel Dong, Public Affairs Officer.

COSTA RICA
Adventist World Radio—see "USA."

CUBA
Radio Habana Cuba, P.O. Box 70-26, Havana, Cuba. Contact: Rolando Peláez, Head of Correspondence; Manolo de la Rosa, DX Producer.

CZECHOSLOVAKIA
Radio Prague International, Czechoslovak Radio, 12099 Prague 2, Vinohradska 12, Czechoslovakia. Contact: Karel Stary, Director of International Relations.

ECUADOR
HCJB, Casilla de Correo 691, Quito, Ecuador; **or** Box 553000, Opa Locka FL 33055 USA. Contact: Glen Voltshadt, Director of Broadcasting (Quito).

EGYPT
Radio Cairo, P.O. Box 1186, Cairo, Egypt.

FINLAND
Radio Finland, Oy. Yelisradio Ab., PL 95, SF-00241 Helsinki, Finland; **or** P.O. Box 462, Windsor CT 06095 USA. Contact: U.K. Haarma, Director of Public Relations (Helsinki).

FRANCE
Radio France Internationale, B.P. 9516, F-75016 Paris Cedex 16, France. Contact: Simon Najovits, Chief, English Department.

GERMANY
Deutsche Welle, Postfach 10 04 44, D-5000 Cologne 1, Federal Republic of Germany. Contact: Ernst Peterssen, Head of Audience Research and Listeners' Mail.
Radio Berlin International, DDR Berlin 1160, German Democratic Republic.

GHANA
Radio Ghana, Ghana Broadcasting Corporation, P.O. Box 1633, Accra, Ghana. Contact: Ms. Maud Blankson-Mills, Head, Audience Research.

GREECE
Foni tis Helladas, 5th Program, ERT, P.O. Box 60019, Mesogion 432, Aghia Paraskevi 15310, Athens, Greece. Contact: Kosta Valetas, Director, Programs for Abroad.

GUAM
Adventist World Radio and *Trans World Radio*—see "USA."

GUINEA
RTV Guinéenne, B.P. 391, Conakry, Guinea.

HOLLAND
Radio Nederland Wereldomroep, Postbus 222, NL-1200 JG Hilversum, Holland. Contact: J.C. Veltkamp Helbach, Director of Public Relations.

HUNGARY
Radio Budapest, Budapest, Hungary.

INDIA
All India Radio, External Services Division, P.O. Box No. 500, New Delhi, India.

INDONESIA
Voice of Indonesia, P.O. Box 157, Jakarta, Indonesia.

IRAN
Voice of the Islamic Republic of Iran, P.O. Box 19395/3333, Tehran, Iran; **or** Aria Shahr. 14518, Golnaz Jonubi, St. 29, No. 29, Tehran, Iran. Contact: Hamid Yasamin, Public Affairs.

IRAQ
Radio Baghdad, P.O. Box 8145, Baghdad, Iraq.

ISRAEL
Kol Israel, P.O. Box 1082, 91010 Jerusalem, Israel. Contact: Ms. Sara Manobla, Head of English Department.

ITALY
Adventist World Radio—See "USA."
Italian Radio Relay Service, P.O. Box 10980, I-20110 Milan MI, Italy. Contact: Alfredo E. Cotroneo, General Manager.
RTV Italiana, Viale Mazzini 14, I-00195 Rome, Italy; **or** RAI—Radio Division, 21st floor, 1350 Avenue of the Americas, New York NY 10019 USA.

JAPAN
Radio Japan/NHK, 2-2-1 Jinnan, Shibuyaku, Tokyo, Japan. Contact: Ms. Rika Kobayashi, DX Producer.

JORDAN
Radio Jordan, P.O. Box 909, Amman, Jordan. Contact: Jawad Zada, Director of English Service.

KIRIBATI
Radio Kiribati, Tarawa, Kiribati.

KOREA (DPR)
Radio Pyongyang, Pyongyang, Democratic People's Republic of Korea.

KOREA (REPUBLIC)
Radio Korea, Korean Broadcasting System, Seoul, Republic of Korea.

KUWAIT
Radio Kuwait, P.O. Box 193, Safat, Kuwait.

LUXEMBOURG
Radio Luxembourg, B.P. 1002, Villa Louvigny à Luxembourg, Luxembourg; **or** 38 Hertford Street, London W1Y 8BA, United Kingdom. Contact: M. Vaas, Chief, English Service (Luxembourg).

MALAYSIA
Voice of Malaysia, Box 11272-KL, Kuala Lumpur, Malaysia. Contact: Lin Chew, Director of Engineering.

MALTA
Voice of the Mediterranean, Box 143, Valletta, Malta.

MONACO
Trans World Radio—see "USA."

MONGOLIA
Radio Ulan Bator, English Department, External Services, Ulan Bator, Mongolia.

MOROCCO
RTV Marocaine, 1 rue el-Brihi, Rabat, Morocco. Contact: Tanane Mohammed Jamal Eddine, Public Affairs.

NETHERLANDS ANTILLES
Trans World Radio—see "USA."

NEW ZEALAND
Radio New Zealand, P.O. Box 2092, Wellington, New Zealand. Contact: Rudi Hill, Manager.

NICARAGUA
Radio Nicaragua, Apartado de Correo 3170, Managua, Nicaragua.

NIGERIA
Voice of Nigeria, P.M.B. 12504, Ikoyi, Lagos, Nigeria.

NORTHERN MARIANA ISLANDS

Christian Science Monitor—see "USA."

NORWAY

Radio Norway International, 0340 Oslo 3, Norway. Contact: Sverre Fredheim, Head of External Broadcasting.

PAKISTAN

Radio Pakistan, External Services, National Broadcasting House, Constitution Avenue, Islamabad, Pakistan. Contact: Anwar Inayat Khan, Senior Broadcast Engineer.

PHILIPPINES

Radio Veritas Asia, P.O. Box 939, Manila, Philippines. Contact: Ms. Cleofe R. Labindao.

POLAND

Radio Polonia, 00 950 Warsaw, Poland. Contact: Miroslaw Lubon, Editor of English Section.

PORTUGAL

Radio Portugal International, Rua São Marçal 1, Lisbon, Portugal. Contact: Ms. Carminda Días da Silva.
Adventist World Radio—see "USA."

WILL WRITING GET YOU INTO TROUBLE?

Not long back, writing certain foreign stations could earn an American a slot within the FBI's files of suspicious persons. Even in tolerant Britain, those writing Eastern European stations sometimes used to find themselves being interrogated by the authorities. After all, the reasoning went, your letter could be communicating secrets to the enemy.

Occasionally, the concern was to keep unorthodox ideas at bay. For example, during the early Sixties the U.S. government sometimes intercepted mail it viewed as communist propaganda. If you wished to receive it, you had to sign a form requesting that the Government release it to you. Later, during the Vietnam War, tapes to American listeners from such stations as the Voice of Vietnam were sometimes erased by the authorities, as well. Even certain world band programs, such as those containing comments by Ramsey Clark and Jane Fonda, that had already been aired and heard by thousands, were classified as "secret" by the CIA's Foreign Broadcast Information Service.

Because of this history, Americans of a certain age still tend to be reluctant to communicate with foreign stations that might be considered "anti-American." But although the laws allowing these Government activities are still on the books, in practice since the early Seventies the American government has pretty much quit regarding ordinary communication with communist radio stations as suspicious behavior.

So, will writing foreign stations get you into hot water? In 1991, with the Cold War over and virtually won, almost certainly not. However, if security clearance is important to your career objectives, use common sense. Avoid writing the Four Bad Bears— Albania, Cuba, North Korea and Vietnam. But if you must write, use post cards, rather than sealed envelopes.

A footnote to this is that there are scams in world band, just as in any other field. Fortunately, they are few, and we don't list the addresses of these offending stations in *Passport*. Here are the ones to watch.

For years, some of those writing the smaller Nigerian stations have found themselves being approached by Nigerian "students" or allegedly devout Christians seeking goods, money or sponsorship to emigrate to Western countries. Similarly, the Somalian station Radio Hargeisa recently has become known for its staffers' extended palms.

African stations are not the only offenders. Letters to a handful of the smaller Latin American stations have been known to generate "love letter" replies, sometimes accompanied by appealing photos. Invariably, these evolve into pleas for money, merchandise or emigration sponsorship.

If you wish to reach out and aid suffering people abroad, donate to any of the several worthwhile charities that exist for this purpose—not to world band bunko artists.

ROMANIA
Radio Romania International, Str. Nuferilor 60-62, 79756 Bucharest, Romania.

SAUDI ARABIA
Broadcasting Service of the Kingdom of Saudi Arabia, Riyadh, Saudi Arabia. Contact: Suliman A. Samnan, Director of Frequency Management.

SOCIETY ISLANDS
RFO-Tahiti, B.P. 125, Papeete, Tahiti, French Polynesia.

SOUTH AFRICA
Radio RSA, Piet Meyer Building, Henley Road, Broadcasting Centre, Johannesburg 2000, Republic of South Africa. Contact: B.R. Leeman, Manager, English External Services.
South African Broadcasting Corporation, P.O. Box 91312, Auckland Park 2006, South Africa. Contact: Ms. Helena Boshoff, Public Relations Officer.

SPAIN
Radio Exterior de España, Apartado de Correo 156.202, E-28080 Madrid, Spain.

SRI LANKA
Sri Lanka Broadcasting Corporation, P.O. Box 574, Colombo 7, Sri Lanka.

SURINAME
Radio Suriname International, Postbus 2979, Paramaribo, Suriname. Contact: Saskia de Bruin.

SWEDEN
Radio Sweden, S-105 10 Stockholm, Sweden.

SWITZERLAND
Swiss Radio International, P.O. Box, CH-3000 Berne 15, Switzerland. Contact: Walter Fankhauser, Press and Public Relations Officer; Bob Zanotti, DX Editor.

SYRIA
Radio Damascus, Ommayad Square, Damascus, Syria.

THAILAND
Radio Thailand, External Service, Bangkok 10200, Thailand. Contact: Bupha Laemluang, Director.

TOGO
Radio Lomé, Lomé, Togo.

TURKEY

Turkish Radio TV Corporation, P.K. 333, 06-443 Ankara, Turkey. Contact: Raymen Somer, Director.

UNITED ARAB EMIRATES

UAE Radio & TV, Dubai, P.O. Box 1695, Dubai, United Arab Emirates. Contact: Ahmed A. Shouly, Director.

Voice of the UAE, P.O. Box 63, Abu Dhabi, United Arab Emirates.

UNITED KINGDOM

BBC World Service, P.O. Box 76, Bush House, Strand, London WC2B 4PH, United Kingdom; **or** 630 Fifth Avenue, New York NY 10020 USA.

USA

Adventist World Radio, 12501 Old Columbia Pike, Silver Spring MD 20904 USA. Contact: Tulio R. Haylock, Director.

The Christian Science Monitor, Shortwave World Service, One Norway Street, Boston MA 02115 USA. Contact: Thomas Nickell, Manager.

KGEI—Voice of Friendship, 1400 Radio Road, Redwood City CA 94065 USA.

KNLS, P.O. Box 473, Anchor Point AK 99556 USA. Contact: Ms. Beverly Jones, Promotions Department.

KUSW, P.O. Box 57040, Salt Lake City UT 84157 USA. Contact: Ms. Jana Carlson, Promotions Director.

KVOH, High Adventure Ministries, Box 7466, Van Nuys CA 91409 USA; **or** Box 425, Station "E", Toronto, M6H 4E3 Canada; **or** BM Box 2575, London WC1N 3XX, United Kingdom. Contact: David Lawrence, International Program Director (U.S.).

RFE-RL, Oettingenstrasse 67, D-8000 Munich 22, Federal Republic of Germany; **or** 1201 Connecticut Avenue, N.W., 11th floor, Washington DC 20036 USA; **or** 1775 Broadway, New York NY 10019 USA.

Trans-World Radio, P.O. Box 700, Cary NC 27512 USA. Contact: Ms. Rosemarie Jaszzka, Director of Public Affairs.

Voice of America, 330 Independence Avenue, S.W., Washington DC 20547 USA.

WHRI—World Harvest Radio, P.O. Box 12, South Bend IN 46624 USA. Contact: Brad Butler, staff assistant.

WINB, P.O. Box 88, Red Lion PA 17356 USA. Contact: John W. Norris, Jr., Manager.

WMLK—Assemblies of Yahweh, P.O. Box C, Bethel PA 19507 USA. Contact: Elder Jacob O. Mayer, Manager.

WRNO, 4539 I-10 Service Road North, Metairie LA 70002 USA. Contact: Joseph M. Costello III, General Manager.

WWCR, 3314 West End Avenue, Nashville TN 37203 USA. Contact: Jay Litton, Public Affairs.

WYFR—Family Radio, Family Stations, Inc., 290 Hegenberger Road, Oakland CA 94621 USA. Contact: Thomas A. Schaff, Shortwave Program Manager.

USSR

Radio Kiev, Ul. Kreshchatik 26, Kiev 252001, Ukrainian SSR, USSR.

Radio Moscow, 25 Pyatnitskaya Street, Moscow 113326, USSR. Contact: Pavel Kuznetsov, American Section Chief; Vladimir Srebnitsky, Chief Producer.

Radio Station Peace and Progress, Moscow, USSR.

Radio Tashkent, 49 Khorezm Street, Tashkent 700047, Uzbekistan, USSR. Contact: Ms. Nadira Dabadjanova, Correspondence Section.

Radio Vilnius, Televizija. Radijas, Vilnius 232674, Lithuanian SSR, USSR. Contact: Edvinas Butkus, Deputy Chief Editor.

Radio Yerevan, 5 Mravian Street, Yerevan 375025, Armenian SSR, USSR.

VATICAN STATE

Vatican Radio, Vatican City, Vatican State.

VIETNAM

Voice of Vietnam, 58 rue Quan Su, Hanoi, Vietnam. Contact: Dao Dinh Tuan, Director of External Broadcasting.

YUGOSLAVIA

Radio Yugoslavia, P.O. Box 200, 11000 Belgrade, Yugoslavia. Contact: Aleksandar Georgiev.

There are literally thousands of other world band stations on the air—most of which you'll never hear. Keeping track of the ever-changing addresses of the more obscure stations, especially those in Latin America and Indonesia, is a passion reserved for radio enthusiasts seeking official written verification—a QSL postcard or letter—that the listener actually heard that station. Associations and publications keeping track of this sort of information abound worldwide (DX editors and producers listed above can provide information on these), but probably the most widely read for address information, as opposed to the details of verifications, is *Monitoring Times* (Box 98, Brasstown NC 28902 USA).

MORE WORLD BAND
FREQUENCIES POSSIBLE

The upcoming 1992 World Administrative Radio Conference of the International Telecommunication Union (ITU) will reallocate the radio spectrum. Among its chief missions is to consider expanding the frequencies available for world band radio.

This expansion has been needed for years so stations can be heard in the countries their signals are targeted to. However, as the receding of the Cold War has prompted world band to be more of a news and entertainment medium, rather than a propaganda or Cold War tool, the need to have reception of high quality has assumed greater importance. People in enslaved countries with little else worth hearing tend to endure mediocre signal quality. Listeners with good media alternatives have less incentive to suffer it out.

It's much too early to tell what the outcome of this crucial Conference will be. However, based on proposals made thus far, the new frequencies could be as shown in the table below.

Some of these new frequencies have already been agreed upon, but not allocated (see *Passport/90*). Whatever the final outcome, it will almost surely mean less congestion—which means clearer signals for world band listeners worldwide.

Prepared by Lawrence Magne and the staff of Passport to World Band Radio.

Existing ITU Allocations (kHz)	Possible New ITU Allocations (kHz)	Possible Increase (kHz)
2300- 2498*	2300- 2498*	—
3200- 3400*	3200- 3400*	—
3900- 4000**	3900- 4000	100***
4750- 5060*	4750- 5060*	—
—	5060- 5200	140
5950- 6200	5850- 6200	100
7100- 7300**	7100- 7750	650***
9500- 9775	9350- 9900	275
11700- 11975	11550- 12050	225
—	13600- 13900	300
15100- 15450	15100- 15700	250
17700- 17900	17450- 17900	250
—	18900- 19300	400
21450- 21750	21450- 21850	100
25600- 26100	25670- 26100	(70)

   * For tropical domestic broadcasting only.
  ** Not for use in all parts of the world.
 *** Includes additional allocations for parts of the world not now covered.

Holland

Transmitters in Holland, Madagascar and the Netherlands Antilles ensure a sizeable audience for **Radio Nederland's** news and specialty features, for which it has a justifiable reputation. Lots on Dutch and European affairs weekdays, with Sundays devoted to the cheerful, long-running family show, *The Happy Station.*

Radio Nederland is heard well throughout much of North America at 0030-0125 on 6020, 6165 and 15315 kHz; 0330-0425 on 6165 and 9590 kHz; and 1830-1925 on 17605 and 21685 kHz. The 1830 transmission is beamed to Africa, and sometimes contains different programming from what North America hears.

Radio Nederland beams to Europe at 1130-1225 on 5955 and 9715 kHz, and 1430-1525 on 5955 kHz. Best Asian bets are at 0830 on 17575 and 21485 kHz; 1130 on 17575, 21480 and 21615 kHz; and again at 1430 on 13770, 15150, 17575 and 17605 kHz. In the Pacific, try 0730 on 9630 and 9715 kHz; 1030 on 11890 kHz; plus a briefer transmission, weekdays only, at 0830-0855 on 9770 kHz.

United Kingdom

What's left to say about **The British Broadcasting Corporation**? Even people who wouldn't know a shortwave from a microwave know of "The Beeb." With Britain's Empire but a memory and its economy less robust than those of some other nations, it has been said, with good reason, that the jewel in Britain's crown today is the BBC World Service. Here, Britannia still very much rules the waves—the airwaves.

> Even people who wouldn't know a shortwave from a microwave know of "The Beeb."

Its audience may be unsurpassed. Some estimates say it runs to over *120 million* listeners every day! Only the Voice of America rivals the BBC World Service's network of worldwide transmitter relays, which includes sites in the United Kingdom, Hong Kong, Singapore, Cyprus, the Seychelles, Lesotho, Canada, the United States, and Ascension and Antigua Islands. The BBC World Service, in English and other languages, carries an impact far beyond the British sphere.

Mornings, the BBC World Service is best heard in Eastern North America at 1100-1330 on 5965, 6195, 9515 or 11775 kHz; and again at 1600-1745 on 9515, 11775 or 15260 kHz. In Western North America, try 1030-1515 on 9740 kHz, and 1600-1745 on 15260 kHz.

Early evenings, Eastern North Americans can tune in at 2000-2200 on a wealth of frequencies, including 5975 or 15260 kHz. *Caribbean Report* airs at 2115-2130, Monday through Friday, on 5975 and 17715 kHz—but not on 15260 kHz.

Later in the evening, North Americans can hear London calling at 2200-0815 on many frequencies. Best bets are 5975 (to 0730), 6175 (to 0430), 9640 (0500 to 0815), and 9915 (to 0430).

In Europe, try 6195, 7325, 9410, 12095 or 15070 kHz at various times between 0300 and 2300. In East Asia, among the many popular choices are 0600-1115 on 15360 kHz, and 1030-1515 on 9740 kHz. In Australia and New Zealand, tune to 7150, 9660, 9760, 11750, 11955, 15360 and 17830 kHz at various prime-time hours. See "Worldwide Broadcasts in English" and the Blue Pages in this *Passport* for complete schedule details.

U.S.S.R.

Hard although it is to imagine, the Soviet Union occupies roughly 15 percent of the earth's land mass. The signals from **Radio Moscow** befit such a giant, both in power and in scope.

Moscow's broadcasts to Europe and North America are virtually continuous, and consist of the North American Service, which operates from early to mid-evening, and the World Service, which operates the rest of the time.

Radio Moscow airs a wide array of programs, including news, interviews, political commentary, music and features on life in the Soviet Union. Its folk and jazz programs are particularly worthy.

Where to find them? Nobody broadcasts on as many frequencies, or from as many locations—day or night, summer or winter. Just dial around. You'll find them, over and again, with little difficulty.

MIDDLE EAST
Egypt

Although it reaches both Europe and North America quite easily, **Radio Cairo** is slightly questionable for inclusion in a list of the best-heard stations. Why? Audio quality.

Radio Cairo announcers often sound as though they're speaking with a mouthful of mush. The station is thus easy to pick out, but less easy to enjoy.

Radio Cairo broadcasts to North America at 0200-0300 on 9475 and 9675 kHz, and transmits to Europe at 2115-2245 on 9900 kHz. Staple fare includes Middle East news, together with Egyptian history and enjoyable music.

United Arab Emirates

Combining as it does both technical excellence and interesting programming, **UAE Radio** in Dubai is something of a Middle Eastern rarity. The close relationship between its listeners and the station's technical department ensures it is well heard in both Europe and North America.

> UAE Radio's news can be more complete and up to the minute than those of the BBC and Voice of America.

All English broadcasts either start or finish with a news bulletin, and the rest of the time is dedicated to features on Arab life, culture and history—including fascinating translations from Arab literature. UAE Radio's news gives superior coverage of events worldwide, including items of interest concerning South Asian matters. Perhaps surprisingly, its bulletins can be more complete and up to the minute than those of the major international broadcasters—including the BBC World Service and the Voice of America.

One of the friendliest stations on the air, UAE Radio can be heard in North America at 0330-0400 on 11940, 15400, 15435 and 17890 kHz. English is beamed to Europe at 1030-1100 and 1330-1400 on

15320, 15435, 17775 and 21605 Khz; and at 1600-1645 on 11790, 15320, 15435 and 21605 kHz. Some of these signals can also be heard in North America. East Asian and Pacific listeners can tune in at 0530-0600 on 15435, 17830 and 21700 kHz.

Israel

Like Belgium's BRT, **Kol Israel** broadcasts from a small country and has no overseas relay. But that doesn't mean it can't punch out a supersignal—clear throughout Europe and Eastern North America. And, like South Africa's Radio RSA, Kol Israel spends its share of time explaining official government policy.

Those of you with little ear for politics needn't worry. There's lighter stuff as well. But news dominates this station—and all Kol Israel newscasts are live.

Kol Israel can be heard three times daily with half-hour broadcasts to North America in English at 0000, 0100 and 0200 on 9435, 9930, 11605, 15615 or 15640 kHz. Its transmission to Europe and Eastern North America at 2230, on such frequencies as 9435, 11605, 13750, 15615, 15640, 17575 or 17630 kHz, is usually clear in North America, as well. Europeans can also tune in at 2000 on most of those frequencies.

News from an Israeli domestic-service network is in English to Europe and North America for 15 minutes each day at 1800 on 9930, 11585 or 11655 kHz; and again at 0500 on 11585, 11655, 15640 or 17575 kHz. Yet another domestic-service program segment, combining news and features, is heard in Europe at 1100-1130 on 11585, 15650, 17575, 17590 or 21780 kHz. You won't be alone—many journalists start their day with Kol Israel.

Listeners in Asia and the South Pacific get just one 15-minute slot per day, at 0500, on 17630 kHz.

All transmissions are one hour earlier in the summer.

ASIA
China (People's Republic)

Radio Beijing has relay arrangements with Canada, Mali, France (including French Guiana), Spain and Switzerland—but it's still not the powerhouse you'd expect from so vast a network. Reception is usually better in Western North America than in the East, although most Canadian and U.S. listeners have a decent shot. Varied programming includes ethnic music, travel, Chinese festivals, ecology and history.

Radio Beijing broadcasts English six times a day to North America—or rather, the same transmission six times. Try at 0000 on 9665, 9770, 11715, 15100 or 17705 kHz; 0300 on 9690, 9770, 11715, 15100 or 17855 kHz; 0400 (possibly 0500 from next winter) on 11685 (or 11695) and 11840 kHz; 1200 on 9665 or 17855 kHz; and 1300 and 1400 on 7405 or 11855 kHz.

Europeans can hear Radio Beijing at 2000-2055 and 2100-2155 on 6920, 9920 or 11500 kHz, and via Switzerland at 2200-2230 (2100-2130 summers) on 3985 kHz. In much of Asia, listeners can tune in at 1200-1255 and 1300-1355 on 11600, 11660, 11890 or 15285 kHz. In Australia and New Zealand, one-hour broadcasts can be heard at 0900 and 1000 on 11755, 15440 and 17710 kHz.

China (Taiwan)

Several years ago, the **Voice of Free China** signed a reciprocal agreement with Family Radio, a North American religious broadcaster with transmitters in Okeechobee, Florida. Now the station's signal blankets North America, but it is still iffy in Europe. The 0200 broadcast on one evening repeats the next at 0300; if you miss it one night, you can catch it the next.

> The Voice of Free China's signal blankets North America, but is iffy in Europe.

Taiwan's programming is mellower, but less diverse, than its continental counterpart's. Both the 0200 and 0300 broadcasts are on 5950 kHz. The Voice of Free China also broadcasts to Asia at 0200 on 15345 and 11860 kHz, and to Europe at 2200 on 9852.5 or 17845 kHz.

Japan

Like Radio Beijing and the Voice of Free China, **Radio Japan** takes advantage of overseas relays, including Radio Canada's facilities at Sackville, New Brunswick. Japan's signal is loud and clear throughout much of North America—especially along the populous coasts.

Radio Japan's General Service, via the Canadian relay, to Eastern North America airs at 1100 on 6120 kHz, and again at 0300 (0100 summers) on 5960 kHz. Radio Japan reaches Western North America direct from Tokyo at 0100 on 17755 kHz; and again at 0300 on 11870 (or 15195), 17825 and 21610 kHz. Too, the General Service to Europe via Gabon is heard not only in Europe, but also in Western North America at 1500 on 21700 kHz, and again at 2100 on 11835 kHz.

Listeners in Australasia can hear Radio Japan's Regional Service at 0900 on 15270 and 17890 kHz. The General Service is aired at 0500 and 0700 on 17890 kHz; 1900 on 11850 and 15270 kHz; and 2100 on 15270 and 17890 kHz.

THE PACIFIC
Australia

Radio Australia is on the air around the clock, but only to Asia and the Pacific. Officially, that is. Fortunately for world band buffs, the station's also heard well beyond.

In Eastern North America, try in the morning between 0830 and 1500 on 9580 kHz. On the North American Pacific coast, you can hear Radio Australia on 17795 kHz evenings from 2100 until 0400 or later. For a challenge, Eastern North Americans can try those same evening times and frequencies in spring, summer and fall; plus from 0200 on 15320 and 21740 kHz.

European listeners can try before 0700 on 15240 kHz.

LATIN AMERICA
Brazil

Brazil is a country of superlatives: the largest tropical rain forest and hydroelectric plant in the world, and even the largest foreign debt. From the architecture of its capital, Brasília, to the parade of the *escolas da samba* in Rio de Janeiro's world famous *carnaval*, is a wealth of talent and originality.

> Much of the programming is music, from the samba of Rio to the Mato Grosso's *música sertaneja*.

The English language programs of **Radio Nacional do Brasil,** better known as **Radiobras**—Brazil's only international world band station—reflect that. Much of the programming is structured around the country's diverse music, from the samba of Rio to the Mato Grosso's *música sertaneja*.

Radiobras can be heard in North America at 0200-0250 on 11745 kHz; and listeners in Europe and North Africa can listen in at 1800-1850 on 15265 kHz.

Ecuador

One of the oldest—and friendliest—of all South American broadcasters is the evangelical station, **HCJB,** in Quito, Ecuador. It broadcasts mornings to North America at 1130-1500 on 11740 kHz, and 1200-1600 on 15115 and 17890 kHz. The evening broadcast is at 0030-0430 and 0500-0700 on any two of the following frequencies: 6230, 9745, 11775, 15155 or 17875 kHz. HCJB also beams to Europe, where it is less clear, at 0700-0830 on 9610, 11835 and 15270 kHz; plus 1900-2000 on 15270,

17790 and 21470 kHz and 2130-2200 on 15270 (or 21470) and 17790 kHz. Programs for the South Pacific are broadcast at 0700-1130 on 9745 and 11925 kHz.

Religious commentary is the station's staple. It is, after all, a missionary organ. But there are also many programs tied only loosely to the religious message, including *Música del Ecuador, Saludos Amigos* and *Dateline*. Of all the religious broadcasters found on world band, HCJB is one the best.

Cuba

Although strong in North America, **Radio Habana Cuba** is usually weak in Europe. It broadcasts in English to North America in the evenings at 0000-0200 on 11820 kHz; 0200-0450 on 9710 and 11820 kHz; 0450-0600 on 11820; and 0600-0800 on 11835 kHz. The initial hour-long broadcast at 0000-0100 repeats at 0200 and 0400, and the 0100-0200 broadcast re-airs at 0300 and 0500. Europeans can try their luck at 1900-2100 on 11800 or 15340 kHz.

Radio Habana Cuba's programming and presentation have gained sophistication in recent years, but it is no longer the lively Caribbean station it once was. There is still some music, but the spoken word—Fidel's—predominates.

NORTH AMERICA
Canada

Proximity ensures **Radio Canada International** is clearly heard throughout Eastern and much of Central North America, but RCI has met with less success in Europe and Western North America, despite relays.

Broadcasts for North America are at 1300-1400 weekdays on 9635, 11855 and 17820 kHz; 1400-1700 Sundays on 11955 and 17820; 0000-0130 daily, plus 0130-0200 Sundays and Mondays, on 9755 and 5960 kHz. The 0000-0130/0200 transmission features the likes of the Canadian Broadcasting Corporation's excellent public affairs products, *The World at Six* and *As It Happens*.

Mornings include special interviews, plus such regular programs as *Innovation Canada, Coast to Coast* and *SWL Digest*. The afternoon transmission to Africa, heard fairly well in North America, begins at 1800 on 13670, 15260 and 17820 kHz, and follows a slightly different format: 1800-1830 and 1900-1930 Mondays through Fridays, and 1800-1900 Saturdays and Sundays.

Again, RCI is spotty in Europe, but try 1930-2000 Mondays through Fridays on 5995, 7235, 15325, 17875 and 11945 or 21675 kHz. There is also a daily broadcast at 2200-2300 on 9760 and 11745, or 15325 and 17875 kHz. On weekdays, this transmission relays *The World at Six* and *As It Happens.*

A twice-daily program for Asian listeners airs at 1300-1330 on 11955 and 15210 or 15385 kHz; and 2200-2230 on 11705 kHz.

Most of RCI's English-language broadcasts are an hour earlier during the summer, although not those intended for Asia.

United States

Eastern Africa possibly excepted, there is no place on earth where the **Voice of America** doesn't reach. Powerful transmitters and a massive worldwide relay network see to that.

The two best times to hear it in North America are at 0000-0200 (to 0230 Tuesdays through Saturdays) on 5995, 6130, 9455, and 11580 kHz; and 1000-1200 on 6030 (or 15120), 9590 and 11915 kHz, when VOA aims at the Caribbean and South America. The VOA's African Service is also audible in North America, at 1600-2200 on 15410, 15445, 15580, 15600, 17785, 17800 and 17870 kHz. Listeners in Europe can tune in at 1700-2200 on 6040, 9760, 11760 and 15205 kHz.

Voice of America

Helen Hung-Hui Shen presents the news over the Voice of America. The mighty VOA is well heard worldwide—including within the United States—in over 40 languages, including English.

The relatively new—and highly popular—Pacific Service may be heard at 1900-2000 and 2100-2200 on 9525, 11965 and 15185 kHz. In East Asia, good bets for the regular VOA English Service include 1000-1100 on 11720 kHz; 1100-1330 on 9760, 11720 or 15160 kHz; 1330-1500 on 9760 or 15160; 2200-2400 on 15290, 15305, 17735 or 17820 kHz; and 0000-0100 on 15290, 17735 or 17820 kHz.

Prepared by the staff of Passport to World Band Radio.

FORMER *PASSPORT* COLLEAGUES VICTIMS OF CANCER

Amnon Nadav, who as a young man emigrated from Israel to New York to make his mark in the psychology of hypnosis, died while he was but in his early 40s. He gave generously of aid and encouragement to the *Passport* team during those difficult early days when the book was known as *Radio Database International.* If life's true friends can be defined as those who support and encourage during the lean times, we couldn't have asked for a better friend than Amnon. We all miss him deeply. Survivors include his wife, Esthera, children Ophir and Orly, and both parents.

Ralf Munster, who in 1926 as a young man also emigrated to the United States—from the deteriorating German Weimar Republic—died at 77. Ralf, who earned his Ph.D. from Duke University, was assistant editor in the preparation of Merriam-Webster's *Third New International Dictionary,* the definitive reference for the American language. He taught at Duke, the University of Georgia, and ultimately was professor emeritus at Georgia State University. Ralf, a doer as well as a philosopher, not only contributed freely of his talents to *Radio Database International,* but also aided several world band broadcasters in Europe, Israel and Africa.

NEW COMRADES ON THE BLOC

(continued from page 24)

bars from Dvorak's New World symphony, rather than the former Communist anthem, "Forward Left."

Albania
Radio Tirana

The movement for democracy has not been televised here. In fact, it probably hasn't even been heard very often.

For one thing, world band radios, although legal, are scarce in this poverty-stricken country. Radio Moscow's Albanian service has not so much as received a single letter from an Albanian listener . . . yet, the show has been on the air for over 45 years!

Radio Tirana's broadcasts have always been strange. They seem to hate everyone without fear or favor: American "imperialists," Soviet "revisionists"—even, for a while after Mao's death, the sternly communist Chinese. Although Tirana's programs have been toned down in recent years—they used to speak approvingly of Stalin's firing squads and death camps—they still represent the last vestigial hope to hear The World According to Uncle Joe.

Hungary
Radio Budapest

Radio Budapest has for decades been the great liberal voice amidst a field of strait-jacketed Communist Bloc stations. Some years back, a *Passport* staffer was astonished to see receivers in Budapest's newsroom tuned to the Hungarian services of Radio Free Europe and the BBC. "This is where we get much of our news," he was told matter-of-factly.

This maverick spirit continues. During the Romanian revolution, world band listeners were startled to hear Radio Budapest not backing the besieged comradely government but, instead, supporting the uprising of "our Romanian brothers."

Romania
Radio Romania International

Before December 21, 1989, the usual programs of Radio Bucharest—that's what it was called then—were news, commentary, music, and the usual numbing reports on the bumper harvests of Romanian agriculture.

On December 21, the station referred briefly to "a large rally" in Bucharest, but indicated that it was in support of the beloved leader, Nicolae Ceaucescu. Shortly thereafter, Radio Bucharest's external broadcasts were suspended.

On December 23, the station returned to the air. A taped announcement in several languages was repeated throughout the afternoon: "This is Radio Bucharest, Romania. The Revolution of December 22nd that removed the Ceaucescu leadership is in full

Boston Globe

While those formerly under the Kremlin's yoke move into a new era, Asian communist countries muddle along as before. Here, Chinese students risk arrest and torture by listening to the Voice of America. Although VOA is intensely jammed by Chinese authorities, millions listen daily.

swing in our homeland. Supported by the Army, the Romanian People is defending with might the great conquest. The victory of the People cannot be avoided."

The broadcast continued by airing a communique addressed to the country by the revolutionary Council of the Front of National Salvation. The message included a statement about freedom of the press.

Later that evening the tape was changed to what seemed to be the text of a speech. "Dear Citizens," it went, "we have had a full and dear struggle today, owing to the criminal actions of some gangs of terrorists, especially trained to fight against the popular masses and for the protection of the dictator Ceaucescu."

On Christmas eve, the station broadcast Christmas carols and music by Wagner, all previously banned by Ceaucescu. Then the big shoe was dropped:

"December 24th, 1989 . . . the third day of Romania's freedom, on Christmas Eve, we wish you all a Merry Christmas. Listen to the most important news of the last twenty-four hours. Nicolae Ceaucescu and Elena Ceaucescu have been arrested and will be put on trial by the People."

Then, silence—no radio on Christmas Day. But, the day after, the other shoe fell:

"On Monday the 25th of December 1989, Nicolae Ceaucescu and Elena Ceaucescu were tried by an extraordinary Military Court. The defendants . . . were sentenced to death . . . and the confiscation of their wealth. The sentence was final and was executed. The sentence struck like a hatchet: death by shooting. The free Romanian people decided that he who spits bullets will be fed by bullets."

On the last day of the year, another remarkable broadcast, an apology:

"Until December 22nd, we were not allowed to transmit, and so you could not hear the voice of real Romania. Aware of the wrong we have done to you, we now apologize for the daily flood of lies and misrepresentations we have been broadcasting. The fist of tyranny forced us to say what was convenient to the dictatorship. We set out to real work in the first days of the Revolution, at first under a shower of gunfire, so we made the voice of truth reach your home. We step into 1990 purified in the heat of the Revolution. The freed Voice of the People will forever be the voice of our own conscience, the voice of truth."

These are but a sampling of what . sprang forth from Communist Bloc broadcasters during recent historic events. Of course, there are other stations and other stories. But history continues to be made, and its front line is none other than world band radio.

Daniel Lorenzetti is President of Acumen, a professional problem-solving firm, and Adjunct Instructor of Law at Florida Atlantic University.

BEST BETS FOR 1991

Communism hasn't rolled over and died . . . just yet. For 1991, there could be upheavals in any of a number of present or former communist countries, but some are better bets than others.

In Asia, try Radio Pyongyang in North Korea, as well as Radio Beijing and even the Voice of Vietnam. During the events of June, 1989, Radio Beijing sometimes aired remarkable reports. (See *Passport/90,* page 129.) Burma, although not strictly communist, is another good bet.

In the Americas, of course, there's always the tireless voice of Radio Habana Cuba.

Elsewhere, Europe's Radio Tirana, from the xenophobic People's Socialist Republic of Albania, might be one of the handful of sources for up-to-the-minute communication in the event of a mass uprising or coup. Radio Yugoslavia, a reliable reporter, also bears watching for activities in either Albania or Yugoslavia.

The Ukraine is not only the Soviet Union's breadbasket, it's also the location for a large number of powerful world band transmitters beamed to Europe and the Americas. Should long-smoldering Ukrainian nationalist sentiment result in a clash with Moscow, Radio Kiev could remain on the air without the need for Russian-based facilities.

TEN OF THE BEST
(continued from page 40)

(continued from page 40)

Tuesdays at 1001 on 11750, 15360 or 21715 kHz. Listeners in the South Pacific have a second chance at 1830 on 11750 kHz, while those in East Asia can tune in again on Wednesdays at 0330 on 15280 or 21715 kHz.

"Caribbean Report"
Voice of America

Cricket is hardly an American game. But did you know a U.S. government radio station broadcasts some of the latest important cricket scores? And that these scores sometimes overshadow those for baseball?

Hard to believe? Tune into *Caribbean Report,* part of the Voice of America's service to that part of the world, heard Tuesday through Saturday at 0010 (Monday through Friday, local evenings, in the Americas).

The first quarter-hour is news from correspondents in the various Caribbean countries, with good insight into numerous island problems. Not all is gloom and doom, though; some of the local political squabbles can amuse the outsider, though islanders take them seriously.

Coverage is good, the range of topics varied, and the information up to date. The final five minutes are a financial spot, currency rates and the Dow Jones Index, followed by three minutes of sports news (including those cricket scores) and a Caribbean weather update. If you have an interest in the Caribbean, this program is for you.

Year-round frequencies are 6130, 9455 and 11695 kHz. The signal is virile throughout the eastern Caribbean and much of South America, but reception in the U.S. and Canada is patchy and varies by season. Reception is also possible in East Asia, interference permitting.

"Música del Ecuador"
HCJB—Voice of the Andes

Now and then, the world band listener stumbles onto a program which attracts not so much by its excellence, but because it is different. Such is *Música del Ecuador,* broadcast by the mighty South American evangelical station, HCJB, in Quito, Ecuador.

Unique is a better description, really. When propagation is right, and faint local Ecuadorian stations peek through the static, listeners with elaborate receiving equipment may be able to eavesdrop on the music of the *campesinos,* the peasants. *Música del Ecuador,* on the other hand, airs a more refined Andean musical potpourri—and it's easily heard in North America on almost any world band radio. To be sure, HCJB plays the traditional, but it shares pride of place with such as the Quito Municipal Marching Band or the local symphony orchestra's extracts from an Ecuadorian folk opera.

Listeners seldom set out to hear it, but having found they tend to stay to the end. It is so unlike anything else on world band radio that it is well worth listening to.

> It shares pride of place with the Quito Municipal Marching Band or an Ecuadorian folk opera.

Música del Ecuador is beamed to North America Saturdays (Friday nights your local time) at 0100 on 9745, 11795, 15155 or 17875 kHz; and is repeated at 0300 on 11795, 15155 or 17875 kHz. There is a third opportunity to hear it at 0530 on 6230, 9745, 11795, 15155 or 17875 kHz. Not all these channels are available at any one time, so dial around.

The program can also be heard in Europe Fridays at 0800 on 9585, (or 15270), 9610 and 11835 kHz; and at 1930 on 15270, 17790 and 21470 kHz; and in the South Pacific the same day at 0800 and 1030 on 9745 and 11925 kHz.

"People and Politics"
BBC World Service

What a refreshing change: a program that promises little, but delivers a lot. The BBC's publication *London Calling* describes it as "background to the British political scene," and that's just what it is.

Scope is the success secret of this 30-minute staple. Starting with highlights of the past week in Parliament (when in session, or "sitting," as the British say), the announcer then branches out in any one of several directions, depending on the subject.

Grass roots politics, law and order, and constitutional issues—particularly interesting in that the United Kingdom does not have a written constitution—are but a few of the domestic topics. Foreign policy issues include some prickly ones, such as the Anglo-U.S. dispute over repatriation of Vietnamese boat people, or moves towards a unified Europe. How about differences with the International Court of Justice over human rights violations in Northern Ireland? The program usually concludes with a round table discussion among the host and representatives of opposing factions.

> ## A window on the workings of the world's oldest surviving democracy.

People and Politics not only reports on the week's political events, it is a window on the workings of the world's oldest surviving parliamentary democracy.

Except for a short summer recess, the program can be heard all year around in its regular weekend spot. If you live in North America, tune in Saturdays at 0230 (Friday night your local time) on 5975, 7325, 9915 or 12095 kHz. European listeners have two options: Fridays at 2130 on 3955, 6195, 9410 and 12095 kHz, with a repeat the following morning at 1030 on 5975, 9410, 9750, 12095 and 15070 kHz. In the South Pacific, tune in Fridays at 2130 on 11750 and 15140 kHz, or Saturdays at 1030 on 9740 and 15360 kHz. That last transmission is also available to East Asia on the same frequencies.

"Music Time in Africa"
Voice of America

Some of the best world band programs are not intended for a worldwide audience; they're beamed, instead, to specific parts of the planet.

That's the bad news. The good news is that thanks to world band propagation, broadcasts don't only go just where they are intended. Such is the case of *Music Time in Africa.*

Although aimed at African ears, this excellent two-part program can be heard with varying success throughout the Americas. It can also be heard in parts of the South Pacific, but listeners in Europe and East Asia will find good reception elusive.

Music Time in Africa is exactly what it says, encompassing virtually every African music both traditional and modern. Segments often devote themselves to the music of a particular country or region, such as Angola or Nigeria's Anambra State. The variety of rhythms and sounds is astounding, from the traditional lute-like *ud* of the Sudan to the up-tempo saxophone of South African dance bands.

Program hosts don't stop at just playing records. There are often detailed descriptions of featured instruments or short biographies of better-known artists, some of whom are the sole focus of one 30-minute broadcast. *Music Time's* musicologist, Leo Sarkisian, deserves much credit. While commercial recordings are part of the fare, much is recorded on-location, with occasional performer profiles.

Whatever your taste, be it South Africa's Kati Namanono, Ghana's Amponsah Konimo, or Guinea's *Les Amazones de Guinée,* you won't be disappointed. If it's available, *Music Time in Africa* will eventually get around to it.

> ## The variety of sounds is astounding, from the lute-like *ud* to the up-tempo saxophone.

Both segments of the program—at 1730 and 1930—can be heard Sundays on 15410, 15445, 15580, 15600, 17785, 17800 and 17870 kHz. Listeners in North America should try all those frequencies; however, 17785 kHz is usually best along the West Coast.

Prepared by the staff of Passport to World Band Radio.

GETTING STARTED
(continued from page 44)

The two compare something like digital and conventional clocks. If your radio is analog, finding the station you want takes trial and error. Patience and practice help the analog owner, but digital frequency readout is very nearly a "must" if you value your time. There are, after all, some *1,100* world band channels from which to choose, and finding your way through this thicket is far easier and quicker with digital readout.

Bells and Whistles

Today's world band radios pack an array of knobs and buttons, sliders and switches into a remarkably compact space. The owner's manual should describe your set's controls. However, here's a list of the more common ones. Yours may not have them all, or it may have more.

   –Digital frequency display. If your radio has a digital readout, it shows the exact frequency the radio is tuned to, either in kHz or MHz. Some display to the nearest kHz, as in 9580 kHz, while others display fractional frequencies, as in 9580.5 kHz.

   –Tuning knob. No mystery here! Turn it until the frequency of the station you want to hear shows on the display. Or browse through *Passport's* Blue Pages and go "fishing" (see box).

   Instead of a tuning knob, a few radios have *slewing* controls—elevator-like up/down buttons for tuning. Slewing buttons are fine for your TV or VCR, with reasonably

AN EVENING WITH WORLD BAND RADIO

The day is done—let's check the BBC first. Tonight, there's an auto tour of the Isle of Lewis, where Harris tweed has been hand-woven for generations. I can practically hear the looms clicking, idyllic and peaceful, a haven from the rat race. Settling back, I tune in. Radio Moscow's World Service, straining to sound like the BBC World Service, explains why the Soviet attitude toward the Baltic States is so reasonable. Enough of that. Up the band.

   Vatican Radio plays songs recorded in Vermont by the monks of Weston Priory. Small world—in two hours' drive, I could hear them live. I turn the dial.

   Wait a minute. Deutsche Welle is reporting on a foot race, a kind of vertical marathon on the slopes of Africa's 11,000-foot Mount Cameroon. I grab the atlas, find Cameroon. Hmm. Its equatorial locus bids me to think I can resist the urge to get in shape for next year. I jump to another band and begin tuning around.

   Radio Habana Cuba, helped by a young lady announcer with a distinctly Brooklyn lilt (no Hispanic tones here!), verbally spanks the United States for its nasty, capitalist ways. Presently, she produces an American "economist" to explain why this is so. It certainly changes my perspective to know that I am listening to Cuba. The rhetoric is more subtle than it used to be. In the old days, it was *cha-cha* bolshevism of the airwaves.

   Radio France Internationale plays a kind of bebop *Marseillaise*, followed by a French language lesson. Lesson past, I am convinced that "the bus will be here in ten minutes" sounds romantic.

   On a higher frequency, a Middle Eastern station pumps out steamy ethnic music, the kind I associate with ball-bearing hips. Radio Australia is also broadcasting music—pop, broken by word of a dry heat wave in seaside Perth. Looking at our frosted panes, I envy the Aussies' weather and beaches, and turn the knob.

   A time warp! British music hall tunes, early century, fill my ears. Rod Serling, the Twilight Zone, come to life? No, it's Radio New Zealand International's new 100,000-watt service to the Pacific. The music ends, the news begins, referring to island people and places invisible in American and European news bulletins: Fiji, Johnson Atoll, the Maoris. I check my watch; time to call it a night. Flick the radio, close my *Passport.*

   I smile. The TV's still cold.

—*Jock Elliott*

limited channels. But for the vastness of world band radio, slew tuning is a mediocre substitute for a conventional tuning knob.

–Tuning keypad. This works much like the keypad on a Touch-Tone telephone or calculator. Punch in the frequency you want, tap the *enter* or *execute* key, and the radio instantly finds the frequency. For example, if you want 9580 kHz, you would typically press 9-5-8-0, and execute.

Not all keypads operate the same way. As most world band stations are on frequencies ending in either zero or five, a few keypads allow only frequencies ending in zero or five. If you try to enter a frequency like 9582 kHz, you'll get either an error message on the display, or a truncated frequency such as 9580 kHz. A handful of models confuse things, making you fiddle with an *AM* key or some other control before entering a frequency.

–BFO or SSB control. Single sideband (SSB) is a transmission mode that's used by amateur radio operators and utility stations that operate near world band frequencies. ("Tour of World Band and Points Between" in this *Passport* explains these.) Almost no world band stations use SSB, so leave this control off or, on some models, set to AM.

–Bandwidth (Wide/Narrow) control. For best audio, leave this in the *wide* position. If there's annoying interference from other stations, try *narrow*. A few top-class radios offer more than two bandwidths.

–Sensitivity, or attenuator, control. You can often hear weak stations better, and stronger stations with less hiss, by setting this to *high*—or *normal* or *DX,* depending on the manufacturer's nomenclature. However, under certain conditions the high position may cause strong stations to *overload* the radio, resulting in a babble of false signals that dims listening pleasure. In such cases, which with better radios are not common, the *local* position can help.

For best results, leave this control switched to high. But if you hear a mishmash of stations that sound as though they're piled atop each other on the same channel, feel free to experiment with the local setting.

–RF (or IF) gain control. Leave this one on *high,* or perhaps *DX.* With Grundig Satellit series receivers, leave the setting at *AGC.* In practice, this control doesn't do much, but if set improperly—turned down for instance—it can make you think the receiver's dead. It's one of the first places to look when you can't hear anything.

Tuning in Stations

You've looked around, seen the switches. It's time to put them to work. Let's try tuning in an easily heard station.

If you're in North America and it's daytime, turn to the Blue Pages in the back of this book to the listing for 15000 kHz. You'll see that stations WWV in Colorado and WWVH in Hawaii both operate there. They are run by the U.S. National Bureau of Standards, and transmit the precise official time and a station identification once each minute. Since they're fairly strong throughout North America, they are good stations to try for first.

If you're in Europe, try instead the BBC World Service on 9410 or 12095 kHz. In Asia or the Pacific the BBC on 15360 kHz is a good bet. The Blue Pages tell when they're on.

Before tuning, turn the BFO or SSB control to off; set the sensitivity to high; and choose the wide bandwidth. If there is an RF gain control, adjust it to maximum. Extend the telescopic antenna, if it has one, all the way, or attach a wire to the antenna terminals. If you're in a metal-framed building, a high-rise or mobile home, try placing your radio near a window. Metal tends to block radio waves.

Ready to go?

1. Turn your radio on. (A few travel portables require two controls to be switched on, to avoid its happening accidentally in transit.)

2. Turn the tuning knob, or punch in 1-5-0-0-0 on the keypad, to tune in 15000 kHz. (On some sets a band selector or "AM" button may have to be used first.)

3. Adjust the volume to the desired level. On WWV or WWVH, you will hear a time tick each second. On the BBC, you will hear English-language programming.

That's it! In most cases, operating a world band radio requires only these three steps. Try tuning in some other stations. Take a crack at some of the "easy pickings" stations, or maybe a few of the ten best programs for 1991, both described elsewhere in this *Passport*.

> In most cases, operating a world band radio requires only three steps.

Reception Varies

As you use your radio, you'll soon notice reception on different world band frequencies varies with the time of day. The 5950 to 6200 kHz range is loaded with stations at night, but you'll hear very little there at your local noon. By contrast, you can hear plenty of stations at noon in the 21450 to 21850 kHz range, but few at your local midnight.

Too, signals are often strongest during your local prime-time evening hours. That's because stations try to beam their signals so they are audible when most people are at home to listen.

Nevertheless, there is still a wealth of choices during the day, even though signals tend to be weaker. For the most fruitful

daytime results, a better-than-average radio—one unusually sensitive to reception of weak signals—can be a real plus. Look to *Passport's* Buyer's Guide for what's what here.

There are some notable exceptions to the prime-time dictum, though. For example, in much of North America the best time to hear Radio Australia is not in the evening, when its signals are weak and noisy. Rather, it's in the early hours of the morning—on 9580 kHz.

> Signals are often strongest during your local prime-time evening hours. Nevertheless, there is a wealth of choices during the day.

As a loose rule of thumb, the most choice reception is below 10000 kHz during the evening and at night, best above 15000 kHz during the day and early evening, with the 10000 to 15000 kHz range mixed. There are specific tips under "World Band Spectrum" in the Glossary. With the *Passport*

schedules and a little experience, you'll soon know exactly which frequencies and times are best for the stations you want to hear. If your radio has station memories, you can set them to these frequencies, like the buttons on a car radio, for easy future access.

Most of us have heard the TV expression, "live via satellite." Signals bounced off space satellites have made our world smaller. Because world band radio bounces signals off the earth's own "natural satellite," the *ionosphere*, reception varies. Like the weather, it varies not only daily, but seasonally. At certain times of the year you can listen to smaller, weaker stations that you otherwise might not be able to hear.

For example, frequencies beginning with threes, fours, fives, sixes and sevens are most vigorous during or near darkness in winter. That's why winter is the best time for Europeans and North Americans to try for stations in Latin America and Africa, as most of these are found in the "low ranges" below 8 MHz.

Spring and fall, on the other hand, are especially good for very distant signals crossing the Equator, such as from Papua New Guinea to New York. Summer evenings are appropriate for long-distance reception above 15000 kHz. So you can take your portable outside and entertain the mosquitos—and yourself—by the barbecue grill.

WHAT IS WORLD TIME?

You'd like to catch Alistair Cooke's *Letter from America* on the BBC World Service? Good. What time does it come on? Is that your time—or BBC time? After all, there are 24 time zones around the planet, and world band touches every one. How do we know which to use?

World Time is the answer. You've probably heard of it. It goes by several names: GMT (Greenwich Mean Time), UTC (Coordinated Universal Time), or especially in the military, Zulu Time. For the sake of simplicity, we've called it World Time here in *Passport*, and world band radio schedules follow it. It can be a little confusing at first, but you'll catch on—here's how.

First, get used to the 24-hour format (often called military time, because the services all use it). From midnight to noon, no problem; 24-hour time is the same, for those hours, as 12-hour time. That is, 10:20 am is just that, 1020 hours, or simply 1020 ("ten-twenty"). After noon, though, 24-hour time doesn't start over, it keeps right on going—1 pm is 1300 ("thirteen hundred"), 2 pm 1400, and so on. Thus, 2400 and 0000 ("zero hours") are the same time (well, practically). Practice a little. It'll save time later.

Converting local to World Time is the next step. Find out how many hours your local time differs from World Time, then add or subtract. In Eastern North America, for instance, add five hours—four hours summer. (World Time is four or five hours "later" than yours.) A program on at 1900 World Time winter thus would be on at 1400 your local time—2 pm.

Live elsewhere? Central Time in the United States and Canada is six hours behind World Time, Mountain seven, and Pacific eight (an hour less—five, six and seven, respectively—if you're on daylight-saving time). Let's try somewhere else.

In Continental Western Europe, subtract one hour—two hours summer. In the United Kingdom, World Time is the same as local time except during summer, when you subtract one hour. In Japan, subtract nine hours year-round, and in Western Australia subtract eight.

Well, now, do you have to go take the square root and cube it each time you listen?

Nay. You only have to figure the difference *once* for your location. Your radio may already have a 24-clock; if not, buy one—they're cheap (MFJ, for example, makes one for less than ten bucks) and worth every penny. Set it once, and that's that.

By the way, World Time also applies to the date. If a BBC drama program is scheduled for 0215 World Time Sunday, in Ohio you would listen at 9:15 pm *Saturday*.

Most broadcasters adhere to the same schedule year-round. But a few, including some of the biggest, vary by season, especially summer and winter. *Passport* denotes these seasonal schedules with a "J" ("June") for summer and a "D" ("December") for winter.

> **If your radio has station memories, you can set them, like the buttons on a car radio, for easy future access.**

Another way world band stations differ from local stations is that any number of broadcasters—even a dozen or more—may use a given channel. Because world band signals travel so far, this is more of a problem on world band than on AM or FM. Fortunately, you usually hear only one station at a time. Sometimes, though, an unwanted station makes listening less pleasant, penetrating through to bother the station you're trying to hear.

While listening to specific stations and programs is interesting, don't miss the fun of tuning around with the help of *Passport's* Blue Pages (see box). While most major stations are heard pretty regularly, there are at least as many—some quite worthwhile—that only come in now and then. Too, new stations come on the air, and old ones change frequencies and schedules. This dynamism is part of world band's allure.

Communication doesn't have to be one-way. If you'd like to write some of the stations that broadcast shows you particularly like—or dislike—by all means do so.

(*Passport's* address list tells you who and where to write.) Some will provide you with their latest program schedules, calendars, souvenirs and information on their country. Most especially, nearly all are eager to hear what you have to say about their programs.

Prepared by Harry Helms and the staff of Passport to World Band Radio.

"FISHING" FOR STATIONS

Some of the finest enjoyment can be had by simply tuning around to see what the world has to offer. Because world band reception conditions vary throughout the year, it's sort of like fishing. You're never completely sure of what you're going to catch, but it's always interesting.

The pros call this *bandscanning*, and *Passport's* Blue Pages are your "map" to these airwaves.

1991 BUYER'S GUIDE TO WORLD BAND RADIO

HOW TO CHOOSE A WORLD BAND RADIO

There's no mystery to buying a TV set. You look, listen, check *Consumer Reports*. Even shopping blind, you'll probably get one that performs like the rest. TV sets are pretty much alike.

Not so world band radios. Some use 1960s technology and barely function. Others perform superbly—they're usually state of the art. As usual, money talks, but even that's a fickle barometer in this exceptional field.

Exceptional? We should say jungle, for that's what world band can be without a good radio: hundreds of channels, scrunched cheek by jowl, even worse than ordinary AM, all weakened in their long-haul bout with the heavens. Listening is a long haul, too, with a subpar radio.

The good news? There's no need to settle for second best. The selection is vast, dozens upon dozens of models, and many perform very well, indeed.

Which ones? Since 1977 we've been testing world band radio products. These independent evaluations, not swayed by advertising, include both hands-on use by veteran listeners and highly specialized laboratory tests. These form the basis of this to-the-point Buyer's Guide, as well as our unabridged *Radio Database International White Paper* series.

First: How much do you want to spend? Don't fool yourself—world band radios are sophisticated electronic devices. Unless you want a small radio for the road, recognize that an acceptable world band radio runs in the same range as a video cassette recorder, a VCR.

Yes, a VCR could sell for $99.95— stripped of counter, timer, clock, channel indicator and remote control, and susceptible to interference. But you wouldn't buy something like that, and nobody else would, either. That's why they don't sell cheap. Use the same reasoning for world band, and avoid disappointment.

Second: If you know world band, think your listening needs through. Do you want a few powerful stations? Or hanker for softer voices from more exotic lands? A good $200 portable will do for the former. For the latter, think at least twice as much.

If you don't know world band listening, but think you're going to take it seriously, the best bet is to go for a mid-sized or compact portable in the $200–$300 range—up to $500 if you feel it's worth it. Most of those are snug enough to take on trips, yet big enough to be daily home companions.

If you just want to gain a nodding acquaintance with world band, some sets about or under $100 will give a taste, albeit unpalatable, of what the fuss is about.

Third: Think of your location. Signals tend to be strongest around Europe, and almost as good in Eastern North America. If you live in either place, you might get by with less radio. If you live in Western North America, Australia or New Zealand, you're better off digging deeper. You'll need a

---

Technician Kathleen Nace measures tabletop receivers for the *Passport* Buyer's Guide.

$200, give or take, is lowball for a radio heard day in and day out. Less, performance plummets. Shown: Sangean's popular ATS-803A, also sold as Radio Shack's Realistic DX-440.

sensitive receiver, and maybe an outdoor antenna, too, for good reception. Central North America and the Caribbean are better, but think twice.

A tabletop model? Probably not, if this is to be your first world band radio. A good portable will do all but the dirtiest work. If you decide on a tabletop later, save the portable for trips, even if only to the balcony or backyard.

You're an experienced hand? A longtime listener, frustrated with your present radio? One of the better tabletop models may make good sense. Remember, though, they aren't cheap. A first-rate tabletop matches the very best Super-VHS VCR, dime for dime.

Fourth: What features make sense to you? Break them into two categories: those that affect performance, and those that don't. Don't rely on performance figures alone. A lot more besides features goes into perform-ance. Check *Passport's* Buyer's Guide.

Performance features are important nevertheless, especially on costlier portable models. They includes *multiple conversion*, essential to pleasant world band reception; two *bandwidths* for adjacent-channel rejection; properly functioning *synchronous selectable sideband* for more adjacent-channel rejection and to reduce fading; perhaps a 5 kHz *slot filter* to quell howls and squeals; separate, continuously tuned, bass and treble; and *single-sideband* (SSB) reception capability.

Heavy-hitting tabletop models, de-signed to flush out even the most stubborn signal, can offer more: a tunable *notch filter* for those howls and squeals; *passband tuning*, also known as *IF shift*, for still more adjacent-channel rejection and audio contouring; three or more AM-mode bandwidths, plus two or more SSB band-

widths (and/or continuously variable bandwidth) for the best adjacent-channel rejection; an attenuator, preferably multi-step, to curb overloading; multiple *AGC decay* rates and *AGC off*. A *noise blanker* doesn't hurt, either.

Non-performance features include digital frequency readout, a virtual *must;* a 24-hour World Time clock, especially one that always shows; such tuning aids as a keypad, tuning knob, channel memories and up/down slewing controls; on/off timing, especially if it can control a tape recorder; illuminated display and controls; and a good signal-strength indicator.

Fifth: Unlike TVs and ordinary radios, world band sets rarely test well in stores, except perhaps in specialty houses with the right outdoor antennas. Even so, given the fluctuations in world band reception, long-term satisfaction is hard to gauge from a spot test. The exception is audio quality. Even if a radio can't pick up any world band stations in the store, you can get a thumb-nail idea of fidelity by catching some mediumwave AM stations. Otherwise, whether you buy in the neighborhood or through the mail makes little difference. Use the same horse sense you would for any other expensive appliance.

Repair? Judging from both our experi-ences and reports from *Passport* readers, this tends to correlate with price. At one ex-treme, some off-brand plastic portables from such places as Hong Kong and the People's Republic of China seem essentially unserv-iceable, although most outlets will replace a defective one within warranty. On the other hand, for high-priced tabletop models factory-authorized service is usually avail-able to keep them purring for years to come.

Finally: a good way to judge a store is by bringing your *Passport* book when you shop. Reputable dealers welcome it as a sign that you are serious and knowledge-able. The rest react accordingly.

Performance to the max? Reach deep. Kenwood's top-rated R-5000 runs a kilobuck, yet sells so well it's in short supply.

WORLD BAND'S HALL OF FAME (AND SHAME)

by Lawrence Magne

Funk to junk, over 13 years we've seen it all. Strong memories, yea and nay:

Best Portable: Sony's discontinued ICF-6800W "Orange." One of our team calls it "The Gold Standard," and for sheer listenability it still is.

Worst Portable: Nearly anything "multiband," especially from the People's Republic of China or Hong Kong. It's always the Year of the Dog.

Best Simple-to-Use, High-Tech Portable: Panasonic's RF-B65. Real radio for real people.

Worst Simple-to-Use, High-Tech Portable: Sangean's ATS-801 and ATS-802, both discontinued. Simple, and simply awful.

Best Travel Radio: The ICF-SW1S and ICF-SW1E, both from Sony. Big gems, small settings.

Worst Travel Radio: Homer's discontinued EP-8, hands down. This $30 egg-sized wonder laid one: no speaker, no antenna, no readout, no buyers. Hatched 1980, buried 1980.

Best Starter Radio: Sangean ATS-803A. Too much? Then try the new Sangean ATS-800.

Worst Starter Radio: Sony CRF-V21. Howard Hughes couldn't afford it, Hulk Hogan couldn't carry it, Harry Houdini couldn't work it.

Best All-Around Tabletop: Kenwood R-5000. Brings in the weak and the great with aplomb. Keep an eye on Drake's upcoming R-8, as well.

Best Tabletop for Program Listening: Lowe HF-225. Beneath plain exterior and lowball price throb the heart of a lion and the voice of a Pavarotti.

Worst Tabletop for Program Listening: The Sharper Image's Tunemaster Classic Radio. An eyestopper that should have come with an earstopper.

Best DX Tabletop: Drake's discontinued R-7A. If price is no object, Icom's IC-R9000 does even better. Cooks eggs, too.

Worst DX Tabletop: Tunemaster, again—nothing else even comes close. Reproduction of a French art-deco radio? *Quel chien!*

Lawrence Magne with some of the tools of his trade.

COMPARATIVE RATINGS OF WORLD BAND PORTABLES

The good news for 1991 goes beyond new models. There are some, of course, but more exciting is the apparent end of ever-higher prices—at least in the thriving United States market. Sony, Panasonic and Sangean have all announced price cuts on some world band portables, and the street prices of some other makes have been falling, too. World band popularity has mushroomed in North America, making demand outrun supply now and then—but delays of more than several weeks have been rare, especially among dealers with substantial inventory.

The results of our hands-on and laboratory testing follow—evaluations of virtually every widely distributed world band portable that meets minimum standards. Models are listed by size; and, within size, in order of world band listening suitability. Unless otherwise indicated:

- each radio covers the usual 88.7-107.9 MHz FM band;
- mediumwave AM band coverage in models with *digital* frequency display includes the forthcoming 1600-1705 kHz segment for the Americas; and
- mediumwave AM band coverage in models with *analog* frequency display stops short of 1705 kHz.

Longwave is used for domestic broadcasts in Europe, North Africa and the U.S.S.R. If you listen from these parts of the world, longwave coverage is a plus. Otherwise, forget it.

We excluded those models, such as the Icom IC-R1 and Kenwood RZ-1, which lack bandwidths narrow enough to qualify for acceptable world band reception.

For the United States and Canada, we quote suggested retail ("list") prices. Discounts, of course, are common. As "list" prices are largely a North American phenomenon, observed *selling* price parameters are given in pounds for the United Kingdom and, to have a common benchmark, U.S. dollars for continental Europe. Prices elsewhere vary widely, with Japan among the highest, and Dubai, Hong Kong, Singapore and parts of Latin America among the lowest.

Duty-free shopping? In Europe, it may save you 10 to 20 percent, *provided* you don't have to declare the radio at your destination. Be sure to check on warranty coverage, though. In the United States, where prices are already among the world's lowest, you're better off buying from regular stores. Canada, too.

Naturally, all prices are as we go to press and may fluctuate. Some will probably have changed before the ink dries.

What *Passport's* Ratings Mean

Star ratings: ★★★★★ is best. We award stars solely for overall performance and meaningful features, both here and in our tabletop model reviews elsewhere in this *Passport*. The same star-rating standard applies regardless of price, size or what have you. So you can cross-compare any radio—little or big, portable or tabletop—with any other radio evaluated in *Passport*. A star is a star.

A portable rating of three-and-a-half stars should please most day-to-day listeners. However, for occasional use on trips a small portable with as little as two stars may suffice. Four stars is the best we've given any portable, although a few five-star tabletops shine. (So, by the way, do their price tags.)

Editor's Choice models are our test team's personal picks of the litter—what we would buy ourselves.

¢ denotes a price-for-performance bargain. It may or may not be a great set, but gives uncommon value for the money.

113

MINI-PORTABLES

Mini-portables weigh under a pound, or half-kilogram, and are about the size of a hand-held calculator or a bit larger than an audio cassette case. They operate off two to four ordinary little "AA" (penlite) batteries. These tiny models do one job well: provide news and entertainment when you're traveling, especially abroad by air. A few will do for day-to-day listening, but only through good headphones—not an attractive prospect, given that none has the full array of Walkman-type features, such as a hidden antenna.

Best bet? Sony's ICF-SW1S or ICF-SW1E, if you can stand the sticker shock. No other minis come close.

★ ★ ★ $\frac{1}{2}$ *Editor's Choice*

Sony ICF-SW1S
Portable Receiving System

Price: $349.95 in the United States, CAN$599.95 in Canada, under £250 in the United Kingdom, $370-480 elsewhere in Europe.

Advantages: Superior overall world band performance for size class. Very high-quality, low-distortion audio when earpieces (supplied) are used. Various helpful tuning features. Unusually straightforward to operate for a high-tech model. World Time clock. Alarm/sleep settings. Travel power lock, which also disables alarm and display illumination. FM stereo through earpieces. Receives longwave and Japanese FM. Amplified outboard antenna (supplied), in addition to the usual built-in antenna, enhances weak-signal reception below about 15 MHz. Supplied self-regulating AC power supply adjusts automatically to local current, protecting against excess voltage. American and most other versions supplied with American-style flat-prong plug, as well as European-style round-prong. Rugged travel case for radio and accessories.

Disadvantages: Tiny speaker has mediocre audio. No tuning knob. Tunes only in coarse 5 kHz increments, providing substandard reception of the relatively

Globetrotting? Best bet is Sony's ICF-SW1S receiving system, complete with carrying case and useful accessories.

few "off-channel" broadcasts. World Time clock readable only when radio is switched off. Volume control at rear, vulnerable to accidental change. For price class, substandard rejection of some spurious signals ("images"). No meaningful signal-strength indicator. Earpieces less comfortable than foam-padded headphones. Amplified antenna does not switch on and off with radio.

Bottom Line: Although pricey, the new Sony ICF-SW1S—the closest thing to a world band Walkman—is the hands-down best mini-portable on the market.

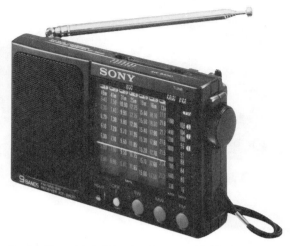

Sony ICF-SW1E
"Sony ICF-SW1"

Price: *ICF-SW1E:* under £170 (about $290) in the United Kingdom, $260-340 elsewhere in Europe; *"ICF-SW1":* CAN$449.95 in Canada.

Comment: Identical to Sony ICF-SW1S, less carrying case and most accessories. Not available in the United States. "ICF-SW1" is the informal designation given to the equivalent of the 'SW1E at one Canadian retail outlet, Atlantic Ham Radio. Otherwise, this radio is available in Canada only in the ICF-SW1S version.

Even with outdated technology and limited world band coverage, the Sony ICF-SW20 is still the best of the low-cost mini-portables.

The Sony ICF-SW1E is the same radio as the ICF-SW1S, but less expensive and without accessories or carrying case.

★ ★ ½   ¢

Sony ICF-SW20

Price: $99.95 in the United States, CAN$169.95 in Canada, under £75 in the United Kingdom, $110-150 elsewhere in Europe.

Advantages: Superior adjacent-channel rejection, comparable to the pricier ICF-SW1S and ICF-SW1E siblings, for size and class. Travel power lock.

Disadvantages: No digital frequency display. Limited world band spectrum coverage, omits important 13 MHz segment. Tiny speaker offers mediocre audio. No longwave reception. No meaningful signal-strength indicator. No AC power supply.

Bottom Line: Although its circuitry is getting long in the tooth, the ICF-SW20 remains the best low-cost teeny travel radio. It's a shame Sony didn't provide 13 MHz coverage.

FIVE-MINUTE, FIVE-DOLLAR ANTENNA

Portables work fine with built-in antennas. But if yours needs extra oomph, simply buy around 30 feet (10 meters) of doorbell wire, an alligator clip, and two insulators at an electronics store.

    Wrap one end of the wire onto an insulator and attach it to a nearby tree—height isn't important. Connect the other end, through an insulator, to the alligator clip, which snaps onto your radio's telescopic antenna. Don't run the wire near or across any utility wires, and disconnect the alligator clip when there are storms nearby.

Customs and security officials, even in totalitarian countries, almost never concern themselves with ordinary little world band radios. However, larger, more exotic-looking radios—world band or otherwise—can invite unwelcomed attention . . . and theft.

Best bet: When globetrotting, stick to mini or compact portables without built-in tape recorders.

★ ★

Sangean MS-103
Sangean MS-103L

Price: *MS-103:* $99.00 in the United States; *MS-103L:* $75-150 in Europe.

Advantages: Better world band coverage than otherwise-identical MS-101. Travel power lock. FM stereo through headphones.

Disadvantages: No digital frequency display, and display not lighted. Slightly limited world band coverage. Mediocre adjacent-channel and image rejection. Inferior audio. No meaningful signal-strength indicator. No AC power supply.

Bottom Line: Preferable to the cheaper MS-101, but interesting only to the weight- and price-conscious traveler. Also sold under a wide and ever-changing variety of brand names, including Goodmans and Siemens.

Comment: The MS-103 includes tropical world band coverage from 2.3 to 5.2 MHz, but has no longwave coverage. The MS-103L excludes 2.3-5.2 MHz, but receives longwave broadcasts.

The Sangean MS-101 is similar to the costlier MS-103, but covers fewer frequencies.

★ ★

Sangean MS-101

Price: $84.00 in the United States, CAN$99.95 in Canada, $65-125 in Europe.

Advantages: Inexpensive. FM stereo through headphones. Travel power lock.

Disadvantages: No digital frequency display. Limited world band coverage. Mediocre adjacent-channel and image rejection. Inferior audio. Display not lighted. No meaningful signal-strength indicator. No AC power supply.

Bottom Line: A low-priced, plain-vanilla portable of interest almost exclusively to the weight- and price-conscious traveler. Also sold under a wide and ever-changing variety of brand names, including Goodmans and Siemens.

None of the various Sangean minis inspires, but they are attractively priced. The MS-103 is the pick of that litter.

★ ★

Sangean SG-789
Sangean SG-789L

Price: *SG-789:* $69.00 in the United States, CAN$149.95 in Canada; *SG-789L:* $60-95 in Europe.

Advantages: Inexpensive. FM stereo through headphones.

Disadvantages: No digital frequency display. Somewhat limited coverage, omits important 13 MHz band. Mediocre adjacent-channel and image rejection. Inferior audio. No meaningful signal-strength indicator. No AC power supply.

Bottom Line: Similar to the Sangean MS-101, but with less complete coverage. If this isn't cheap enough for you, try the Sangean ATS-796, which lists in the United States for $59.95—same play, fewer acts.

Comments: SG-789 covers world band from 2.3 to 5.2 MHz, but has no long-wave coverage. SG-789L has no 2.3-5.2 MHz coverage, but receives longwave broadcasts.

That Canadian list price? Don't believe it. The actual selling price is around half that, sometimes less.

Panasonic makes some fine world band radios, but the RF-B10 isn't one of them.

★ $\frac{1}{2}$

Panasonic RF-B10
National B10

Price: *Panasonic:* $79.95 in the United States, CAN$139.95 in Canada, $95-135 in Europe.

Advantages: Relatively inexpensive. Travel lock switch. Two-year warranty.

Disadvantages: No digital frequency display. Limited coverage omits important 13 MHz segment. Substandard overall performance includes mediocre adjacent-channel and image rejection. Mediocre audio. No display illumination. No meaningful signal-strength indicator. No AC power supply.

Bottom Line: Why bother?

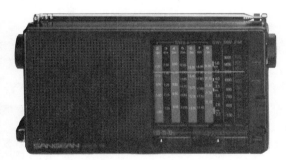

Cheapest of the acceptable minis is Sangean's SG-789.

MARKET TICKER: MULTIBAND OFF, WORLD BAND UP

So-called "multiband portables," usually made in Hong Kong or the People's Republic of China, use outdated technology that can't cope with the uncommon rigors of world band. These sets, such as the Alconic 2959, are hard to endure once the novelty of hearing distant stations wears off.

Consumers appear to be catching on. Sales of low-technology multiband portables reportedly are beginning to taper off. On the other hand, manufacturers and retailers report that last year's sales of true world band radios rose between 20 and 30 percent.

COMPACT PORTABLES

Compacts weigh between 1.0-1.5 pounds, or 0.5-0.7 kg, and are typically sized 8 × 5 × 1.5 in, or 20 × 13 × 4 cm. Like minis, they feed off "AA" batteries—but more of them. They travel almost as well as minis, but sound better and usually receive better, too. For some travelers, they also suffice as home sets—something minis can't really do. However, if you don't travel much by air, you will probably find better value in a mid-sized portable.

Two models stand out: Panasonic's RF-B65, and Sony's new ICF-SW7600. The Sangean ATS-808, also new for 1991, also is appropriate—especially in certain parts of the world, such as Western North America.

★ ★ ★ ½　　　　*Editor's Choice*

Panasonic RF-B65
Panasonic RF-B65D
National B65

Price: *RF-B65:* $269.95 in the United States, CAN$499.95 in Canada; *RF-B65D:* under £200 in the United Kingdom, $290-450 elsewhere in Europe. RP-65 120V AC power supply $13.95 in the United States.

Advantages: Superior overall world band performance for size class. Very easy to operate for an advanced-technology radio. Pleasant audio. Various helpful tuning features. Signal-strength indicator. World Time clock, plus second time-zone clock. Alarm/sleep settings. One of the

Panasonic's RF-B65: An advanced-technology radio for people who don't like advanced technology.

few lightweight portables capable of demodulating single-sideband signals, used by hams and utility stations (see "Tour of World Band and Points Between"). Receives longwave. In the United States, attractively priced for a superior performer within its size class. Travel power lock. Two-year warranty. AC power supply supplied (outside North America).

Disadvantages: Cumbersome tuning knob inhibits speed. With built-in antenna, weak-signal sensitivity very slightly below top-rated portables. Selectivity, although adequate, not quite equal to some competing models. Clocks not displayed separately from frequency. No display illumination. AC power supply extra (North America).

Bottom Line: A very nice, easy-to-use portable. If you live in Europe or Eastern North America, where world band signals tend to be fairly strong, and want to hear major international broadcasters, the RF-B65 makes an excellent choice.

New for 1991
★ ★ ★ ½　　　　*Editor's Choice*

Sony ICF-SW7600

Price: $249.95 in the United States, CAN$449.95 in Canada, under £170 in the United Kingdom, $250-400 elsewhere in Europe.

Advantages: Superior overall for size class. When supplied earpieces are used, very high-quality, low-distortion audio. Easy to operate for level of technology. Helpful tuning features, including properly configured keypad. World Time clock. Alarm/sleep settings. One of the few lightweight portables that demodulates single sideband, used by hams and utility stations (see "Tour of World Band and Points Between"). Lighted display. Travel power lock, also disables display light. Comes with reel-in portable wire antenna, besides built-in telescopic one. Stereo FM through earpieces, also covers Japanese FM band. Receives longwave. Comes with AC power supply.

Disadvantages: No tuning knob. With built-in antenna and on battery power, weak-signal sensitivity slightly below that of top-rated portables. No meaningful signal-

Sony's new ICF-SW7600 gives superior performance and features, all at an attractive price. No tuning knob, though.

strength indicator. Supplied earpieces less comfortable than foam-padded headphones.

Bottom Line: Similar to the Sony ICF-SW1E, but a little bigger, the Sony ICF-SW7600 is an excellent value for air travel, especially in North America where the 'SW1E is not available and the ICF-SW1S costs $100 more.

Evaluation of New Model: Rising production costs and unfavorable foreign exchange movement have pressured Taiwan and Japan to stretch the useful life of each model. Sometimes, as with Sony's ICF-2010/ICF-2001D, a model stays on the market for many years "as is." At other times, when a model's sales become anemic, a basic design gets reworked to produce a forward evolutionary step. Sony's new ICF-SW7600 is just such an offering.

The 'SW7600 succeeds the ICF-2003 and ICF-7600DS which, in turn succeeded the original ICF-2002 and ICF-7600D. This time around, though, the cabinet was thoroughly redesigned.

Of greater interest, of course, are the operative improvements, beginning with ergonomics. Among various refinements to make controls fall easily to hand: putting the zero key where it belongs, under the "8" in the three-by-three-over-one design in the familiar pattern of telephones. This is an improvement over past Sony practice of the zero key under the "7". Including a handy display light is another ergonomic improvement. The light extinguishes itself after 15 seconds.

The 'SW7600 comes with FM stereo and stereo earpieces, improving not only FM listening, but world band sound quality, too. Compact speakers, after all, can do only so much. The only aural demerit? No meaningful tone controls.

Unfortunately, in one respect the receiver is less useful than its predecessor. The 24-hour World Time clock, once displayed separately, is now visible only when the set is turned off. Too, the supplied earpieces are less comfortable than are the ubiquitous Walkman-type foam headphones.

Otherwise, the 'SW7600 continues the tradition. Weak signal sensitivity is good on battery power and with the built-in telescopic antenna, but not quite the equal of the best bigger portables and even some earlier '2003 samples. However, a reel-in outboard wire antenna helps suck in the weak ones, and it's supplied with the radio. Selectivity—the ability to reject interference from stations on adjacent channels—is as good as you can expect from a portable with only a single bandwidth.

Although the 'SW7600's digital synthesizer tunes world band in relatively coarse 5 kHz—one-channel—increments (mediumwave AM tunes in 9 or 10 kHz increments, longwave in 3 kHz increments), there is an analog control on the side of the set for interpolation. This feature can be used to reduce adjacent-channel interference, and is necessary for single sideband to receive hams and utility signals.

This control demands a safecracker's touch, does not adjust frequency readout, and its tuning range is far wider than it should be. Furthermore, it doesn't reset to zero automatically, so it's easily left on. If it is, you may find stations on "wrong" frequencies, off by 5 or 10 kHz.

Like its forebears, the 'SW7600 tunes with a keypad, 10 programmable memories, a meter-segment selector, a rudimentary scanner, and a set of two-speed up/down slewing controls—the kind found on many TV/VCR remote controls.

However, unlike Panasonic's RF-B65, the 'SW7600 has neither tuning knob nor meaningful indication of signal strength—just a lone LED "glow light."

The biggest cause for celebrating may be price: $50 *less* than its predecessor, making it, after discounts, one of the better buys on the world band market.

Sangean's new ATS-808 includes two bandwidths for superior performance.

New for 1991
★ ★ ★ ½

Editor's Choice

Sangean ATS-808

Price: $259.00 in the United States, CAN$399.95 in Canada. ADP-808 120V AC power supply $7.99 in the United States.

Advantages: Easy to operate for a high-tech radio. Already-pleasant speaker audio improves with earpieces. Various helpful features, including dual-speed tuning knob. Weak-signal sensitivity above average for size class. Dual bandwidths, exceptional in this size, offer flexibility in the struggle against adjacent-channel interference. Keypad has exceptional feel and tactile response—the best we've seen. Receives longwave. World Time clock, displayed separately from frequency, and local 24-hour clock. Alarm/sleep settings. Signal strength indicator. Travel power lock. Stereo FM via earpieces (supplied).

Disadvantages: Spurious-signal rejection only adequate. Fast tuning tends to mute receiver. Tunes only in coarse 5 kHz increments. No carrying strap or handle. Supplied earpieces inferior to comparable foam-padded headphones. AC power supply extra.

Bottom Line: A superior model, especially for Central and Western North America, where its weak-signal sensitivity arguably makes it the best choice in its size class. *Editor's Choice* for Western North America, Latin America, sub-Saharan Africa and Oceania only.

Evaluation of New Model: Sangean's popular ATS-803A qualifies as the best world band radio in or below its price class. However, for travel by air it's a tad beefy. To get around that, Sangean recently introduced a smaller advanced-technology entry, the ATS-808.

The '808's tuning is unusually versatile, especially for such a small radio. Besides a pair of up/down slew buttons, which second as controls for a rudimentary scanner, there's a two-speed tuning knob. There's also a three-function keypad. The default function level controls memories, the second is direct-frequency access, while the third selects meter segments. The keypad is an ergonomic breakthrough, the best we've ever tested, but it still takes getting used to—the keypad numbers are arranged three-by-three-over-one; however, the zero is under the "7," not the "8" as on telephones.

Of 45 programmable memories, only 18 work on world band—the rest are for FM and mediumwave AM.

World band tuning is only in 5 kHz increments, unrelieved by any fine-tuning control. That would normally dictate that a few signals would be received quite poorly. However, the '808's second, wider bandwidth can snare these off-channel stations "on the side." It's not the best arrangement, but it works.

Longwave and mediumwave AM tuning is channel by channel—a sensible arrangement, which includes a switch to choose between 9 kHz and 10 kHz mediumwave AM channel spacing. (In the Americas, spacing is 10 kHz; elsewhere, it's usually 9 kHz.) FM tunes in relatively precise 50 kHz increments, which allows it to function properly anywhere in the world.

Frequency coverage in the North American and most other versions is all the way from 150 kHz at the low end of the longwave band, to 30 MHz at the upper end of the shortwave spectrum (world band segments are found between 2.3-26.1 MHz).

FM performance is quite good, with stereo FM, to boot. Although the set comes with only one speaker, it also comes with earpieces and a headband for true stereo.

Yes, there are two bandwidths, unlike nearly every other compact, which has one. But there is no provision for single sideband. On the larger Sangean 803A, demodulation of single-sideband signals is not only possible, but actually quite good by portable standards. While of little moment to world band listeners, single sideband makes the '808 inappropriate for ham or utility signals.

For travel, the '808 comes with a power lock switch and a soft case. Surprisingly, however, the '808 has no strap or handle.

Travelers often use radios both to wake them at precise times and to lull themselves to sleep. A radio, after all, can often override those traffic and adjacent-room noises that keep light sleepers awake. For that reason, the '808 has a sleep-shutoff control, as well as an alarm switch to trigger either the receiver or a buzzer. However, once the timer triggers the radio, it must be shut off by hand like a true alarm clock, rather than automatically as with the true timers found on some other world band radios and virtually all VCRs.

The display, although unlit, has superior contrast and reasonably large numbers. It also has two 24-hour clocks, for World and local time, although neither displays seconds numerically. American civilians, unused to 24-hour local clocks, will probably stick to wristwatches for local time.

A handy plus is that the time is displayed whether the radio is on or off. On many other models, the time shows only when the radio—or at least the frequency readout—is off. The display also shows meter segment, battery strength and signal strength—albeit in an unorthodox one-to-seven scale.

As of press time, no AC power was supplied—an oddity, considering one comes standard with the less-costly ATS-803A. However, there is a socket for a supply of suitable polarity. In North America, Sangean offers one, the ADP-808, which lists for $7.99.

Overall performance is quite decent. Those two bandwidths, for example, help make the '808 a serious contender in its size class.

Sensitivity to weak signals is superior, too. Indeed, in this regard the '808 outperforms some compacts, and even larger portables. That makes the '808 particularly appropriate for those parts of the world, such as Western North America and Oceania, where signal strengths tend to be relatively modest. It also makes the '808 an obvious choice for portable faint-signal reception.

Spurious-signal rejection, however, disappoints. False "repeats" of world band stations occur on various frequencies—between 6.2 and 6.3 MHz, in particular—sometimes at perfectly listenable levels. This tends to be more of a problem in such places as Europe, where signals are usually strong. However, in Western North America and Oceania these "ghosts" tend to appear less often, and at lower strength.

Because tuning is in synthesized 1 kHz increments, there is always the potential for "thoop-thoop" chuffing sounds, as on a steam locomotive, proportionate to the speed at which the radio is tuned. Other receivers have been faulted for this, so Sangean's design mutes the receiver when the tuning knob is turned. It eliminates the chuffing all right. Unfortunately, it also mutes the receiver so much it's hard to tell when a station's tuned in without slowing down a lot. That characteristic will annoy.

Speaker audio is reasonably pleasant for such a small set, although it would have been better with worthwhile tone controls. Audio quality is at least comparable through the supplied earpieces, but foam-padded Walkman-type headphones are better still—especially on FM.

Those listening in Europe—and certain other parts of the world outside the Americas—will appreciate the '808's ability to receive longwave broadcasts. However, inadequate front-end selectivity mars reception, allowing mediumwave AM ghosts to disrupt longwave.

Overall? The Sangean ATS-808 has for the most part been carefully thought out. The bigger ATS-803A is still better and cheaper and has more features, but for a compact travel portable the new '808 is a welcomed entry—especially for Western and Central North America.

Want a scanner that receives world band? The Sony ICF-PRO80 may be the answer—if you can accept its dreadful ergonomics.

★ ★ ★ ½

Sony ICF-PRO80
Sony ICF-PRO70

Price: $449.95 in the United States, CAN$689.95 in Canada, under £330 in the United Kingdom, $550-700 elsewhere in Europe.

Advantages: Superior overall performance for size class. Above average at bringing in weak world band stations. Helpful tuning features, including scanning, and comes with versatile VHF scanner (reduced coverage in 'PRO70 version). One of the few lightweight portables suitable for utility signals (see "Tour of World Band and Points Beyond"). Receives Japanese FM band, longwave, VHF-TV audio. Illuminated display.

Disadvantages: Awkward to operate, especially outboard scanner module, which requires removal and replacement of antenna and battery pack. Mediocre audio. No tuning knob, few travel features. No signal-strength indicator. No AC power supply.

Bottom Line: Great for puzzle lovers: Otherwise, of value mainly to weak-signal chasers who need a small world band portable with a VHF scanner.

★ ★ ★

Panasonic RF-B40
Panasonic RF-B40DL
National B40

Price: *RF-B40:* $189.95 in the United States, CAN$329.95 in Canada; *RF-B40DL:* $220-320 in Europe. RP-65 120V AC power supply $13.95 in the United States.

Advantages: Very easy to use. Some helpful tuning features. Receives longwave broadcasts. Two-year warranty.

Disadvantages: Tunes only in coarse 5 kHz increments. Inferior adjacent-channel rejection. No tuning knob. AC power supply extra.

Bottom Line: Although lacking strong pluses and with mediocre selectivity, the 'B40 is a reasonably pleasant and very easy-to-use portable for noncritical listening.

$40 cheaper than last year, the RF-B40 now occupies Panasonic's middle price range.

Sony's ICF-7700, also sold as the ICF-7600DA, is advanced tech cleverly disguised as low tech. Sounds it, too.

★ ★ ★

Sony ICF-7700
Sony ICF-7600DA

Price: *ICF-7700:* $199.95 in the United States, CAN$339.95 in Canada; *ICF-7600DA:* under £150 in the United Kingdom, $230-300 elsewhere in Europe.

Advantages: Very easy to use. World Time clock. Alarm/sleep settings. Only new receiver offering digital frequency display complemented by unusual digitalized "analog" tuning scale. Helpful tuning aids include 15 memories—five for world band—and a tuning knob. Travel power lock. Covers longwave and Japanese FM bands.

Disadvantages: Slightly limited world band coverage. Mediocre adjacent- and unwanted-signal rejection. Coarse 5 kHz

tuning increments. No display illumination. No meaningful signal-strength indicator. No AC power supply.

Bottom Line: Nice try, no cigar. In this size and price class, a much better bet for the technically timid is either the Panasonic RF-B65, Sony's new ICF-SW7600 or even the Sangean ATS-808.

New for 1991
★ ★ ½

Editor's Choice

Magnavox AE 3805
Philips AE 3805

Price: *Magnavox:* $149.95 in the United States.

Bottom Line: Essentially similar, except for layout and stereo, to Sangean ATS 800, below.

Advanced technology doesn't come simpler than the Philips AE 3805, also sold as the Magnavox AE 3805. Targeted to newcomers, it's fun to fiddle with.

TRAVELING TO GERMANY?

German radio regulations require that world band receivers be unable to tune above about 26.1 MHz—the upper limit of the world band spectrum. However, many digitally tuned world band radios cover up to 30 MHz—the upper limit of the short-wave spectrum.

Fortunately, in practice German customs officials almost never hassle travelers bringing in small radios that cover the forbidden 26.1-30 MHz range. If you are still concerned, bring along a compact or mini model with needle-and-dial (analog) tuning. None of the current analog models tested for this year's *Passport* Buyer's Guide tunes above 26.1 MHz.

Sangean's new ATS 800, also sold as Radio Shack's Realistic DX-370, brings a measure of advanced technology to the $100 price range. It's simple and fun—the MG of world band radios.

New for 1991

★ ★ ½

Editor's Choice

Sangean ATS 800
Realistic DX-370

Price: *Sangean:* $139.00 in the United States. ADP-808 120V AC power supply $7.99 in the United States. *Realistic:* $119.95 in the United States.

Advantages: Relatively inexpensive for model with digital frequency display and memories. Already-pleasant speaker audio improves with headphones. Five memory buttons provide up to 10 world band and 10 AM/FM preset stations. Relatively selective for price class. Simple to operate for radio at this technology level. World Time clock. Timer/sleep/alarm settings. Travel power lock. Low-battery indicator, unusual in price category. Stereo FM via earpieces (supplied in Sangean version).

Disadvantages: Does not tune 2.3-2.5, 7.3-7.6, 9.3-9.5, 21.75-21.85 and 25.6-26.1 MHz world band segments. Tunes world band only in coarse 5 kHz steps. FM and mediumwave AM tuning steps do not conform to channel spacing in much of the world outside North America. Mediocre spurious-signal rejection. No tuning knob. Does not receive longwave broadcasts or 1635-1705 kHz portion of forthcoming expanded AM band in Americas. On/off LCD signal-strength indicator nigh useless. No display illumination. Clock not displayed separately from frequency. No carrying strap

or handle. Supplied earpieces (Sangean version) inferior to comparable foam-padded earphones. AC power supply extra.

Bottom Line: Sangean's new ATS 800 *et al.*, although no Lamborghini, is easily the best low-cost model with digital frequency display. Excellent value for money.

Evaluation of New Model: Is the new DAK MR-101 a cheap imitation? Yes, and here's the set they've flattered so by trying to copy. The Sangean original—also sold under Radio Shack's *Realistic* label, as well as by Philips and its Magnavox U.S. subsidiary—is clearly better performing and constructed than the imitation. Of course, it's also more costly.

The ATS 800—alone among those in the Sangean line, it has no hyphen—is compact enough for trips, yet is just about large enough for daily use around the home. It covers FM in 200 kHz steps, mediumwave AM from 530 to 1630 kHz in 10 kHz steps, and the world band spectrum from 3.2 to 7.3 and 9.5-21.75 MHz in 5 kHz steps.

Missed altogether are the 120 and 11 meter segments; as well as the 7.3-7.6, 9.3-9.5, and 21.75-21.85 MHz portions of the 41, 31 and 13 meter segments. Complete world band coverage is a rarity in the '800's price category, but listeners will very much miss the rich offerings between 7.3-7.6 and 9.3-9.5 MHz. Whatever theoretician specced out the frequency coverage for the '800 and its DAK lookalike—same chip?—must have divined these parameters from a dusty textbook. A pity, but it may not be crucial to your listening requirements. Look over *Passport's* Blue Pages to see whether you find the missing 7305-9495 kHz slice to be essential.

The 200 kHz and 10 kHz tuning steps for FM and mediumwave AM, respectively, are fine for the Americas—but not for most other parts of the world, where narrower channel spacing is the norm. So while the '800 tends to be a worthy travel set, it's hardly adequate for listening to FM or mediumwave AM outside the Americas. Even in the Americas, the forthcoming expanded AM band will be covered to only 1630 kHz—not the planned upper limit of 1705 kHz.

Tuning features are minimal. Not only is there no tuning knob whatsoever, there's also no keypad. Instead, you're left with a single pair of up/down multi-speed slewing buttons and 10 easily programmed memories for world band, plus five more each for AM and FM.

Fortunately, the slew buttons are so flexible—when pressed, they chirp, too—you can chug the radio up or down at one channel per tap, bandscan at a comfortable rate, or soar up and down the spectrum at lightning speed. Tuning from 9.5 to 21.7 MHz, for example, takes a mere 10 seconds—and sharp reflexes, to glide successfully to a halt near the desired channel.

However, tuning is complicated slightly by an old-fashioned "SW1 SW2" control. SW1 tunes from 3.2 to 7.3 MHz, SW2 from 9.5 to 21.75 MHz. It's an outdated concept and a nuisance, but hardly a major drawback in a low-cost radio. Indeed, except for that the '800 is relatively simple to operate for a receiver with digitally synthesized tuning.

There is only a binary-type on/off signal-strength indicator, which serves no worthwhile purpose. However, there is a useful 24-hour-format World Time clock. This displays when the set is off, but to see it when the set is on requires that a button be pushed to have time replace frequency on the digital display.

That display, although unlit, has superior contrast and reasonably large numbers. On the other hand, instead of using the straightforward XXXXX kHz frequency layout, it is displayed as XX.XXx MHz. For frequencies ending in "5" that's okay. But the last digit is dropped when it's a zero. So, say, 6175 kHz displays as 6.175 MHz, but 6170 kHz comes out as 6.17 MHz. You get used to it, but it's yet another indication, like the 7.3-9.5 MHz tuning gap, that whoever designed this set has had zilch practical experience in the field.

For traveling, there's also a lock switch to keep the power from coming on accidentally during transit. Also for travel, the '800 comes with a soft case and power lock switch. This lock switch prevents the radio from turning on accidentally inside a suitcase.

Perhaps surprisingly, the '800 has no strap or handle. For some, this is a

drawback. For others, wrist straps are just a nuisance best left off, anyway.

Travelers often use radios to soothe them to sleep and to be awakened. A radio, after all, can mask traffic and room noises that keep the sandman at bay. For that reason, the '800 has a sleep-shutoff control, plus an alarm switch to trigger either the receiver or a buzzer. However, once the timer turns on the radio, it has to be turned off manually, like an alarm clock rather than the complete on/off timing found on some other world band radios and VCRs.

Performance? About what you would expect from one of the better models in this price range that lacks digital frequency display. Sensitivity to weak signals is quite good below 7.3 MHz; less impressive, but still adequate, from 9.5 to 21.75 MHz. Adjacent-channel rejection—selectivity—is a bit broad, but nonetheless is a touch above average for this price group.

The one drawback of the '800's performance is in its spurious-signal rejection. Repeats ("images") of stations tend to appear 900 kHz away. It's the one area in which some comparably priced models with analog readout—Sony's ICF-7601, for example—fare better.

Speaker audio is reasonably pleasant for such a small set, provided it's not played too loudly. Less pleasant is the stiff operation of the volume slider control. Audio quality is at least comparable through the supplied earpieces, but foam-padded Walkman-type headphones are better still—especially on FM.

FM? Yes, its performance is also quite good, with stereo, to boot. Although the set is equipped with only one speaker, those earpieces and headband it comes with provide true stereo.

As of press time, no AC power was supplied—an oddity, considering one comes standard with the slightly less-costly ATS-803A. However, there is a socket for a supply of suitable polarity. In North America, Sangean offers one, the ADP-808, which lists for $7.99.

Presumably, any version of the '800 destined for European markets would be hard-wired for channel spacing within the FM and mediumwave AM bands in accordance with European norms.

Overall, the Sangean ATS 800, in its

several incarnations, fills an important niche in the world band market. It's not the cheapest set, nor is it the best. But it is the first under-$150 model to combine reasonably good performance with digital frequency display. This virtually guarantees its popularity, and rightly so.

★ ★ ½   ₵

Sony ICF-7601

Price: $129.95 in the United States, CAN$209.95 in Canada, $125-170 in Europe.

Advantages: Weak-signal sensitivity above average for size class. Travel power lock. Covers Japanese FM band.

Disadvantages: No digital display. Display not illuminated. Slightly limited world band coverage. Adjacent-channel rejection, although reasonable, not equal to other Sony models. Some crosstalk among adjacent world band segments. No longwave coverage. No meaningful signal-strength indicator. No AC power supply.

Bottom Line: This latest entrant in a popular series—well over a million sold—provides reasonable performance at a very attractive price. The ICF-7601 is a proven performer within its class, especially for Central and Western North America, where world band signals tend to be weaker. A favorite among foreign correspondents.

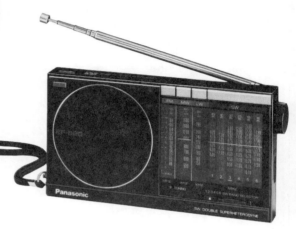

Panasonic's RF-B20, no longer sold in the United States, has little to offer.

★ ★

Panasonic RF-B20L
Panasonic RF-B20
National B20

Price: CAN$189.95 in Canada, $120-195 elsewhere outside the United States.

Advantages: Unusually good audio, including continuous tone control, for such a small radio. Weak-signal sensitivity slightly above average for class, so radio is suitable for such low-signal regions as Australia and New Zealand. Receives longwave. Two-year warranty.

Disadvantages: No digital display. Limited world band coverage, omits important 13 and 21 MHz segments. Mediocre adjacent-channel rejection. No meaningful signal-strength indicator. No AC power supply. No longer in Panasonic's U.S. line, but RF-B20 version may still be available for under $150 in some stores.

Bottom Line: A reasonable performer that would be much better could it sort stations out more successfully.

The Sony ICF-7601 is the latest in a series that has been unusually successful—almost two million sold. An excellent value for traveling.

★ ★

Grundig Yacht Boy 230
Grundig Travel Kit 230

Price: *Yacht Boy 230:* $149.00 in the United
States, CAN$249.95 in Canada, $120-
175 in Europe. *Travel Kit 230:* $249.00 in
the United States, CAN$349.95 in
Canada.

Advantages: Includes World Time and
worldwide multicountry clock/alarm/
sleep timer with electronic map. Illuminated display. Receives longwave. Stereo
FM through earphones. Extra-cost Travel
Kit version, apparently available only in
North America, comes with zippered
carrying case, pocket knife, alarm clock,
pen/pencil set and flashlight.

Disadvantages: No digital display. Slightly
limited world band coverage. Mediocre
image and adjacent-channel rejection.
Tricky on/off switch. Pushbutton volume
control increases or decreases sound in
sizable bites, compromising adjustability.
Annoying tuner backlash at lower end of
each band. No meaningful signal-
strength indicator. No AC power supply.

Bottom Line: A decent but undistinguished
radio made attractive only by its novel
world clock, pocket knife and other non-
radio extras. Are cheese slicers next?

$249 for *this* model? Yes, but much of what
you're paying for are the several geegaws
Grundig throws in along with the radio.

The Magnavox D1875, also sold as the Philips
D1875, is a decent little radio at a decent little
price—under $100.

★ ★   ¢

Magnavox D1875
Philips D1875

Price: *Magnavox:* $99.95 in the United
States; *Philips:* under £50 in the United
Kingdom, $85-125 elsewhere in Europe.

Advantages: Receives longwave. More
likely than most models to be heavily
discounted in the United States, making
the D1875 an attractive value for trips.

Disadvantages: No digital display. Limited
world band coverage. Mediocre adjacent-channel and image rejection. No
meaningful signal-strength indicator. No
display illumination. No AC power
supply. Not distributed in Canada.

Bottom Line: A so-so performer; after
discounting the D1875 is nonetheless
one of the better low-cost portables if the
Sony ICF-7601 is outside your budget.

Comment: According to unconfirmed
industry reports, this model is shortly to
be replaced by the AE 3205.

★ ★

Price: *Yacht Boy 220:* $119.00 in the United States, CAN$149.95 in Canada, $95-150 in Europe; *Travel Kit 220:* $229.00 in the United States, CAN$329.95 in Canada.

Advantages: Receives longwave. Travel Kit version, apparently available only in North America, supplied with alarm clock, pocket knife, flashlight, pen/pencil set and calculator.

Disadvantages: No digital display. Display not lit. Limited world band coverage. Mediocre spurious and adjacent-channel rejection. Pushbutton volume control takes sizable bites, hard to adjust. No meaningful signal-strength indicator. No AC power supply.

Bottom Line: An adequate, if uninspiring, travel radio. Note, however, that the '220 has less dial backlash than its more costly Yacht Boy 230 sibling, and that the '220's on/off switch is easier to use.

$229 gets you a Yacht Boy 220 radio, calculator, alarm clock, shiv, pen, pencil and, by golly, a little flashlight, too.

DAK's MR-101 provides lots of features for precious little money, but has major deficiencies.

New for 1991

★ $\frac{1}{2}$

DAK MR-101

Price: $49.90 by mail order in the United States, but reportedly seen selling for as low as $29.50 at DAK's California warehouse. Not yet available elsewhere.

Advantages: Least-costly portable tested with digital frequency display. Least-costly portable tested with memories. Five memory buttons for up to 10 world band and 10 AM/FM preset stations. More selective than usual for price category. Relatively simple to operate for radio in this technology class. Clock/alarm/sleep timer. Illuminated display. Available on 30-day money-back basis.

Disadvantages: Grossly deficient in weak-signal sensitivity. Flimsy antenna swivel. Does not tune 2.3-2.5, 7.3-7.6, 9.3-9.5,

FREE BATTERIES!

If you live in the United States, you can power your world band portable without spending a dime.

Radio Shack offers one free battery per person per month to each of its "battery club members." To join this "club," simply walk into any participating Radio Shack store—there are thousands nationwide—and ask for one of their membership cards, usually at the counter for the taking. Each card is good for one year, or 12 batteries, and when it runs out they'll give you a new card. All this is completely gratis—no purchase necessary.

These are garden-variety batteries, not alkalines, NiCds or platinum-plated cells. But they work fine, and it's hard to argue with the price.

21.75-21.85 and 25.6-26.1 MHz world band segments. Tunes world band only in coarse 5 kHz steps. FM and mediumwave AM tuning steps do not conform to channel spacing in much of the world outside North America. Mediocre spurious-signal rejection. No tuning knob. Does not receive longwave broadcasts or 1635-1705 kHz portion of forthcoming expanded AM band in the Americas. No signal-strength indicator. No power lock switch. No AC power supply. Reportedly prone to breaking down. Currently known to be sold by only one firm.

Bottom Line: *Beaucoup* radio for very little money, but still no bargain.

Evaluation of New Model: When the MR-101 first showed up in DAK's 1990 catalogs, it aroused more interest than we'd seen in 14 years of evaluating world band products. Here was the promise of truly advanced world band reception—lighted digital display, programmable memories, a clock/timer, and more—all for less than $50! Indeed, samples reportedly have been seen inside DAK's California warehouse priced as low as $29.50. (Presumably, these are units that have been returned or otherwise different from regular samples.)

What is it? Remember when "Taiwanese" and "knockoff" were practically one word in computer circles? Now, in world band, the Taiwanese are making the originals and the Chinese are doing the knocking off.

The MR-101, made in the People's Republic of China, is a compact world band portable small enough to ride along on trips. It covers FM in 200 kHz steps, mediumwave AM from 530 to 1630 kHz in 10 kHz steps, and the world band spectrum from 3.2 to 7.3 and 9.5-21.75 MHz in 5 kHz steps. The tuned frequency is displayed digitally—an enormous plus in this price category—but somewhat oddly. 5970 kHz, for example, shows as 5.97 MHz.

The fertile 7.3-7.6 and 9.3-9.5 MHz world band ranges are completely missed, as are the 120 meter segment, the 11 meter segment, and the 21.75-21.85 MHz portion of the 13 meter segment. Too, the 200 kHz and 10 kHz tuning steps for FM and mediumwave AM, respectively, are fine for the Americas—but not for elsewhere, where

narrower channel spacing is the norm. So while the MR-101 is in many ways a worthy travel set, it's hardly adequate for FM or mediumwave AM outside the Americas. Even in the Americas, the forthcoming expanded AM band is covered to only 1630 kHz—not the planned upper limit of 1705 kHz.

Tuning features are minimal, an apparent cost-cutting gesture. Not only is there no tuning knob whatsoever, there's also no keypad. Instead, you're left with a single pair of up/down multispeed slewing buttons and 20 easily programmed memories (only 10 are for world band).

Fortunately, the slew controls are so flexible you can chug the radio up or down at one channel per tap, bandscan at a comfortable rate, or soar up and down the spectrum at lightning speed. Tuning from 9.5 to 21.7 MHz, for example, takes a mere 10 seconds—and sharp reflexes, to screech successfully to a halt near the desired channel.

However, tuning is complicated slightly by an old-fashioned "SW1 SW2" control. SW1 tunes from 3.2 to 7.3 MHz, SW2 from 9.5 to 21.75 MHz. It's an outdated concept and a nuisance, but hardly a major drawback in such a low-cost radio. Indeed, except for that the MR-101 is relatively simple to operate for a receiver with digitally synthesized tuning.

Having a clock with timing capability on a world band radio is also a plus. You can use the clock to keep track of time, and as a timer it allows for at least some hands-off taping, as on a VCR.

Trouble is, the MR-101's clock uses 12-hour format, not 24-hour as World Time demands. And the timer is a simple on-only alarm—fine for waking up, but of little use for taping. There's also a sleep-off control to help summon the sandman.

In principle, a lock switch is handy for travel. Normally, locks prevent radios from turning on accidentally inside a suitcase.

The MR-101 has a lock switch, all right, but this one is improperly designed, turning off only the tuning circuitry—*not* the main power or the easily activated display light. If either trips en route, you'll likely arrive with dead batteries.

Performance is a mixed bag. On one hand, selectivity is pretty good—better than some sets costing over twice as much. Audio quality, while a bit tinny and lacking in any kind of tone control, isn't too shabby, either.

All this is very nice, but turn it on and you'll find why it's $50: It has the sensitivity of a stevedore.

Trying to tune a weak signal? Or even a moderate one? Forget it! Ergo, this radio is useless for chasing tough signals. But even more importantly, because most world band signals tire out as they wing inland from North America's East Coast, the MR-101 makes a poor choice for North America's Central, Mountain or Pacific time zones.

An external antenna is no help, either. The set's extremely limited dynamic range can't handle such high signal input without overloading—an awful-sounding mishmash, stations sounding jumbled atop each other. Indeed, even with its built-in telescopic antenna, overloading is troublesome in such strong signal bastions as Europe. (If this happens, collapse the antenna slowly until the situation clears up.)

> By and large, this set is a novelty.

A lesser shortcoming is the MR-101's single-conversion IF (intermediate frequency) circuitry. Hardly surprising for a receiver in this price class, but it means you can hear "repeats" of signals from almost a Megahertz away. Ironically, the model's woeful sensitivity somewhat offsets that.

Finally, the MR-101's overall construction quality seems cheesy. For one thing, the telescopic antenna's non-rotating swivel mount bends easily and can break. Too, the front slider controls feel loose and sloppy. Indeed, we have come across a report suggesting that the MR-101 is unusually prone to breaking down after relatively brief periods of use.

The upshot is that DAK's MR-101 is much more receiver than you would expect to find at its price. In some respects—such as selectivity and digital frequency display—it resembles radios costing at least twice as much. California-based DAK calls it a "breakthrough," and to that extent it is.

Still, if a radio can't pick up a signal in the first place, signal processing and digital display are both academic. The MR-101 sorely needs a sensitivity boost, more adequate dynamic range, and fuller coverage of the 7.3-9.5 MHz zone.

By and large, this set is a novelty and hardly in the same league as the Sangean ATS-800 it tried to copy. Still, for casual listening in Eastern North America—say, as a starter set to get a basic world band feel—the MR-101 can give you a taste of world band on the cheap. It's also suitable for European world band listening—*provided* you aren't interested in mediumwave AM or FM, and *provided* you're willing to run the risk of world band overloading.

DAK, the only firm we've come across so far selling this model, gives a no-questions-asked, money-back refund for the first 30 days. That's a real plus—more firms should do this—allowing you as it does a chance to check out the radio for the requirements where you live. DAK also tells us that parts and service will continue to be provided by them once the 30-day trial and 90-day warranties have expired.

As a footnote: The radio itself isn't the only thing that's copied from Sangean. The frequency guide for this Chinese-made set is, except for the front cover, virtually a copy of Sangean's. Being Taiwanese, Sangean doesn't recognize the People's Republic of China. So that guide lists the Voice of Free China in Taiwan . . . but breathes nary a word about the People's Republic—not even Radio Beijing! *A él que mal hace, mal viene.*

We may not yet have heard the last of this radio. If precedent holds, the Chinese manufacturer will almost surely offer this model to other than DAK. Presumably, any version destined to be sold in Europe would be hard-wired for channel spacing within the FM and mediumwave AM bands in accordance with European norms.

Five cents won't buy a good cigar, and $50 won't get you a decent world band radio. The Cougar H-88 is no exception.

The poorly rated Opal OP-35, also sold as the Siemens RK 702, features the "World Time Handy Humane Wake System."

★

Cougar H-88

Price: $49.95 in the United States, $40-70 in Europe.
Advantages: Inexpensive. Receives long-wave.
Disadvantages: No digital display. Limited world band coverage. Mediocre adjacent-channel and spurious-signal rejection. Modest sensitivity to weak signals. Tuning knob somewhat stiff. Power switch easily activated by accident, as when radio packed on trips. No display illumination. No meaningful signal-strength indicator. No AC power supply.
Bottom Line: Tinker's toy.

★

Opal OP-35 Siemens RK 702

Price: *OP-35:* $99.95 in the United States; *RK 702:* $75-160 in Europe.
Advantages: Includes novel World Time and worldwide multicountry clock/timer, the "World Time Handy Humane Wake System." Tends to be heavily discounted. Available duty-free on Lufthansa flights.
Disadvantages: No digital display. World band coverage limited to 6, 7, 9, 11 and 15 MHz segments. Inferior adjacent-channel rejection makes for unpleasant listening. Poor spurious-signal rejection in both in world band and mediumwave AM band. Modest weak-signal sensitivity. Drifts off frequency when held. No signal-strength indicator. Does not receive longwave. Not widely available. No AC power supply.
Bottom Line: Clock in drag.

RADIOS FROM EASTERN EUROPE AND THE U.S.S.R.

A number of radios with at least some world band coverage are made in what was, at least until recently, the "Soviet Bloc." Most are designed to receive domestic stations below 12 MHz, although a couple of Soviet models and at least one Polish set cover up through the 21 MHz world band segment. Once upon a time, restriction of coverage above 12 MHz served to discourage listening to then-jammed foreign broadcasts.

Virtually all these radios are miserable world band performers, with woefully outdated technology. A few, such as the Vega Selena, are available on the cheap in parts of Western Europe and the United Kingdom. That Selena, the most widely distributed, is about as mediocre a world band receiver as any we have seen. However, it is quite pleasant for FM and mediumwave AM reception—and it comes in an attractive wooden cabinet.

What the future holds for radio producers in these nations is anybody's guess. Stay tuned!

MID-SIZED PORTABLES

If you're looking for a home set, but also one that can be taken out in the backyard and on the occasional trip, you'll probably gravitate to a mid-sized portable. They're large enough to perform well and sound pretty good; yet compact enough to tote in your suitcase now and then. Most take 3-4 "D" cells, plus a couple of "AA" cells for their fancy computer circuits.

How large? Typically just under a foot wide—that's 30 cm—and weighing in around 3-4 pounds, or 1.3-1.8 kg. For air travel, that's okay if you're a dedicated listener, but a bit much otherwise. Too, larger sets with snazzy controls sometimes attract unwanted attention from customs and security personnel.

Two stand out: the ultra-high-tech Sony ICF-2010, also sold as the ICF-2001D; and the much cheaper Sangean ATS-803A, sold under many names. The '2010 is the finest true portable around, while the '803A is the best buy if you feel the '2010 is too pricey.

★ ★ ★ ★   *Editor's Choice*

Sony ICF-2010
Sony ICF-2001D

Price: *ICF-2010:* $429.95 in the United States, CAN$689.95 in Canada; *ICF-2001D:* under £330 in the United Kingdom, $500-950 elsewhere in Europe.

Serious about world band radio? Sony's ICF-2010, also sold as the ICF-2001D, is the portable to grab. It outperforms radios costing up to twice as much.

Advantages: Superior overall world band performance. High-tech synchronous detector circuit with selectable sideband rejects adjacent-channel interference and counters fading distortion on world band, longwave and mediumwave AM signals. Two bandwidths offer superior trade-off between audio fidelity and adjacent-channel rejection. Tunes in precise 0.1 kHz increments. Numerous helpful tuning features, including 36 memories with handy individual push-buttons. Separately displayed World Time clock. Alarm/sleep/timer settings. Some reception of air band signals (most versions). Illuminated display. Best travel-weight portable for single sideband. Travel power lock. Signal-strength indicator. Covers longwave and Japanese FM bands. AC power supply. In Europe, available for under $600 in a special version supplied with Sony AN-1 amplified antenna. Elsewhere, the AN-1 may be purchased separately for around $90.

> ## The Big Enchilada, and fairly priced for all it does so well.

Disadvantages: Controls and high-tech features may intimidate or confuse. Memories and clock/timer settings sometimes erase when set is jostled. Wide bandwidth somewhat broad for world band reception (remediable by at least one specialty firm, Radio West). Audio only average, with mediocre tone control. Synthesizer chuffs a bit. First RF transistor reportedly prone to damage by static electricity, as from nearby lightning strikes, with outdoor wire antenna deployed; no such antenna should be connected during snow, sand, dry-wind or thunder storms. Telescopic antenna swivel gets slack with use, requiring periodic screw adjustment.

Bottom Line: The Big Enchilada, and fairly priced for all it does so well. Except for audio and operating ease, Sony's very-high-tech offering remains the best performing travel-weight portable—regardless of where you are.

 An *RDI WHITE PAPER* is available for this model.

Improved for 1991 is Grundig's Satellit 500. Unlike most Grundig world band radios, this model is made in Portugal, not Asia.

Changed for 1991

★ ★ ★ ★   *Editor's Choice*

Grundig Satellit 500

Price: $599.00 in the United States, but actual selling price has been as high as $699.00; CAN$799.95 in Canada; $400-550 in Europe.

Advantages: Superior overall world band performance. Two excellent bandwidths give superior trade-off between audio fidelity and adjacent-channel rejection. Bandwidth circuitry has best ultimate rejection of any portable tested. Relatively easy to operate, with superior ergonomics. Tunes in precise 0.1 kHz increments. Numerous helpful, well-thought-out tuning features, including 42 memories. Superior tuning knob. Large-character display shows station name in memory mode. Some world band channels factory-programmed (Central European version only). Above-average audio for size class, with separate continuous bass and treble tone controls. World Time clock and another 24-hour clock, one of which is displayed separately from frequency. Alarm/sleep/timer, including two-event timer that also controls certain tape recorders. Illuminated keypad and display. One of the best travel-weight portables for single sideband. Signal-strength indicator. Travel power lock disables all functions. Stereo FM through headphones and speaker (neither supplied). Generally superior FM and mediumwave AM performance. Receives longwave. Worldwide AC power supply (supplied). Built-in NiCd battery charger. Mounting screw holes for securing radio in mobile

WORLDBAND CASSETTE RECORDERS

It's hardly a new idea—set a timer to record programs so you can enjoy them at your convenience. We do this every day with VCRs.

Alas, most world band radios with built-in cassette recorders (WCRs) are dreadful performers—so bad, in fact, that they don't even meet the minimum criteria for being tested by *Passport*. There are some exceptions, though.

Take Sony's WA-8000MKII. Although it's not a sterling performer, if you simply must have a WCR, it's far and away the best. It comes with an auto-reverse stereo cassette recorder and mic, FM stereo, and stereo speakers. There's also a World Time clock with alarm, sleep and timer facilities.

Performance? It earns two-and-a-half stars, with superior sensitivity to weak signals and spurious-signal rejection. However, selectivity is only average, and there's no digital frequency display or programmable channel memories. Without such memories, the ability to record different stations automatically at different times—multi-event recording—is unrealized.

Something cheaper? Most other available choices are dreadful. An uninspiring, but passable, alternative is the '8000MKII's sibling, the Sony WA-6000. Its coverage of the world band spectrum is limited, as is its performance. For world band, it barely musters two stars.

The rub for Americans: Neither model is available in the United States or Canada. Yanks and Canadians have to ferret it out at electronic and airport shops abroad. The Sony WA-8000MKII is about £200 in the United Kingdom, ¥50,000 in Japan—about $340 either way—the WA-6000 just under half as much. Prices within Continental Europe are, as usual, higher.

For now, the Sony WA-8000MKII is the best the market has to offer. Until high-technology performers with programmable channel memories come along, WCRs will continue to offer more sizzle than steak.

environments. Telescopic antenna, with spring-loaded detents, unusually rugged.

Disadvantages: Synchronous detector circuit gives neither selectable sideband nor reduced fading distortion, but sometimes causes slight whistle ("heterodyne"). High overall distortion in single-sideband mode at certain audio frequencies. Dynamic range poor at 5 kHz channel spacing. Built-in battery charger reportedly overheats certain NiCd cells. Pushbuttons push hard. Synthesizer chuffs some. AGC control may deaden reception if switched on accidentally. Keypad default is AM mode, which complicates single-sideband tuning. Factory-programmed channels (Central European version) can't be changed (and schedules do). AC power supply poorly labeled, possibly leading some to adjust it to wrong voltage; could cause serious receiver damage if power supply adjusted to 110-127V, when actual power is 220-240V (not a concern in North America). Batteries on our sample sometimes lost contact when set turned on its side, wiping out clock-related data. Telescopic antenna tends to flop over from its own weight when adjusted to certain angles. Radio relatively costly in North America.

Bottom Line: Improved since its introduction in 1989, the '500 is noteworthy for its features, appearance and ergonomic niceties. Overall performance is, in some ways, the best available in a portable. But the set still suffers from a flawed synchronous detector which, instead of improving reception as it does on the Sony ICF-2010 and ICF-2001D, actually makes matters a bit worse.

Changes for 1991: Since about the beginning of 1990, Grundig has modified the '500. The original suffered from a serious lack of sensitivity to weak signals in the lower world band reaches. It's now quite adequate.

Front-end selectivity is also much better—excellent, in fact—which is important to those near local medium-wave AM stations. Assembly looks like it got some needed attention, too.

Ironically, though, the original version measured better in some respects. Our laboratory measurements of dynamic range, image rejection, IF rejection, blocking and phase noise in our latest

unit are decent, but not, alas, like before. Was it our sample, or the engineering redesign? Time will tell.

The upshot is that the Grundig Satellit 500 is now a noticeably better receiver than it was at its inception. Shakeout largely behind, it now merits four stars. Steep price and flawed detector notwithstanding, its virtues make it an *Editor's Choice*.

By the way, practically every '500 now on the market is an improved one. In North America, check the AC supply's prongs. If they're flat, it's new. The original's were round, with a round-to-flat converter.

An *RDI WHITE PAPER* is available for this model.

★ ★ ★ ½   *Editor's Choice*

> Sangean ATS-803A
> Realistic DX-440
> Clairtone PR-291
> TMR 7602 Hitech Tatung
> Matsui MR-4099
> Eska RX 33
> Siemens RK 651
> Quelle Universum

Price: *Sangean:* $249.00 in the United States, CAN$449.95 in Canada, $150-330 in Europe; *Realistic:* $199.95 plus AC power supply in the United States, CAN$299.00 in Canada, $230-260 plus AC power supply in Europe; *Clairtone:* CAN$229.95 in Canada; *Tatung:* under £110 in the United Kingdom; *Matsui:* $160-220 in Europe; *Eska:* Dkr. 1995 (about $315) in Denmark; *Siemens:* $180-250 in Europe; *Quelle Universum:* $180-250 in Europe. *#273-1454 Radio Shack 120V AC power supply for DX-440:* $7.95 in the United States.

The best world band radio that lists for under $400 continues to be Sangean's ATS-803A, also sold as Radio Shack's Realistic DX-440.

Advantages: Superior overall world band performance. Numerous tuning features. Two bandwidths, for good fidelity/interference trade-off. Superior image rejection and good weak-signal sensitivity—a plus for Central or Western North America. Superior reception of utility signals for price class. Illuminated display. Signal-strength indicator. World Time clock. Alarm/sleep/timer. Travel power lock. FM stereo through headphones (usually supplied). Separate bass and treble controls. Receives longwave. Sangean ATS-803A and most other designations supplied with AC adaptor.

Disadvantages: Synthesizer chuffs a little. Audio no prize—only slightly above average. Clock not displayed separately from frequency. On Realistic DX-440, sold by Radio Shack in the United States and Tandy elsewhere, AC power supply is extra.

Bottom Line: A dollar cigar for 75 cents. True, it's not quite equal to Sony's ICF-2010/ICF-2001D, but it costs little more than half as much. A nigh-perfect model for getting started.

Footnotes for 1991: The dual-voltage worldwide AC power supply formerly provided with the Sangean ATS-803A in North America has, alas, been replaced by a single-voltage version. According to the manufacturer, the switch was prompted by consumer complaints about "dead" radios when their power supplies were set incorrectly to 220V.

According to an unconfirmed industry report, the bargain-priced TMR 7602 Hitech Tatung has been discontinued, although at press time units were still being sold in the United Kingdom.

★ ½

Philips D2615

Price: Under $100 in Europe.
Advantages: Pleasant audio.
Disadvantages: No meaningful frequency display, so finding stations is a struggle. Mediocre overall performance. Not available in North America.
Bottom Line: To find out why nobody used to listen to foreign broadcasts, try this 1960s-technology number. Just don't buy it.

FULL-SIZED PORTABLES

Let's call big portables tabletop models that run off batteries—usually several "D" cells, plus some "AA" cells for their computer circuitry. Tabletop models, however, have the advantage of laying flat, and thus are better-suited for everyday home use. Tabletop models also provide more performance for the money.

Some of these weigh as much as a stuffed suitcase, and are almost as large. Take one on a worldwide air excursion and you should have your head examined. The first customs or security inspector that sees your radio will probably do it for you.

None of the present full-sized portable crop really excites. However, the Sony CRF-V21 is full of techy goodies, and the Grundig Satellit 650 has superior audio.

★ ★ ★ ★

Sony CRF-V21

Price: $6,500.00 in the United States, under £3,000 in the United Kingdom, $4,500-6,500 elsewhere in Europe.
Advantages: Superior overall world band performance. High-tech synchronous detector circuit with selectable sideband cuts adjacent-channel interference and fading distortion on world band, longwave and mediumwave AM. Two bandwidths mean superior trade-off between audio fidelity and adjacent-channel rejection. Helpful tuning features, including 350 memories. Unusually straightforward keypad. Processes off-

Sony's CRF-V21 is, by a small margin but big price, the best world band portable around. Some video capability, too.

the-air narrow-band FM, RTTY (radio teletype) and fax. Covers longwave down to 9 kHz, as well as four satellite fax frequencies. Liquid-crystal video display (LCD) for various functions, including frequency, station name (in memory mode), separately displayed World Time/Date, and RTTY. Display doubles as spectrum monitor. Built-in thermal printer allows print-screen and fax hard-copy with very high resolution. World Time/Date clock displays seconds numerically. Alarm/sleep/timer/scanner/activity-search can also do hands-off spectrum surveys. Tunes and displays in precise 10 Hz increments. World's best tuning knob, a pure delight. Best portable (in a squeaker) for ham and utility signals. Superior weak-signal sensitivity, plus blocking, AGC threshold, dynamic range, ultimate rejection, skirt selectivity, phase noise, image rejection, IF rejection and stability. Very low audio distortion in the AM and synchronous-detection modes. Illuminated display. Precise signal-strength indicator. Amplified antenna. Receives Japanese FM broadcasts. Worldwide AC power supply and rechargeable NiCd battery pack. Except for U.S. version, comes with RS-232C port for computer interface.

Disadvantages: Expensive. Complex and generally not user-friendly. Mediocre ergonomics. Video display lacks contrast, very hard to read. Size, weight and no fixed telescopic antenna mar portable operation. Wide bandwidth setting a bit broad for world band. Audio only average. Tuning knob rates are either too slow or too fast. Flip-over night light ineffective—and easily mistaken for carrying handle, and thus broken. Slow-sweep spectrum-occupancy display not real-time. Two of three spectrum-occupancy slices too wide for shortwave use, and the other so narrow it's barely of any use at all. AGC decay much too fast for single sideband. For premium device, only so-so unwanted-sideband suppression. Mediocre front-end selectivity. RS-232C port not supplied with U.S. version, as it does not meet U.S. FCC Part 15 spurious-emission requirements.

Bottom Line: A fax-oriented receiver with more goodies than Dolly Parton. On world band, however, the CRF-V21 doesn't equal some tabletops costing a fifth as much, and only modestly exceeds the performance of some portables that are cheaper, yet.

 An *RDI WHITE PAPER* is available for this model.

SUN OF WORLD BAND?

Surveys say *Passport* readers are a pretty affluent lot, and nearly all live in economically advanced countries.

It's easy for us to lose sight of the fact that most world band listeners live in impoverished "Third World" countries. There, not only affordable radios and repairs are scarce, but electricity itself can be an unthinkable luxury compared to food. Although most low-cost radios run on batteries, even the cells themselves strain meager budgets.

Graham Mytton, head of audience research for the BBC World Service, proposed a common-sense solution at a recent conference in Canada: solar-powered radios. Pure solar radios, of course, would restrict listening to cloud-free daylight. But solar-charged NiCd cells could lick that shortcoming. Although NiCds cost more up front, and eventually must be replaced, the cost per listening hour would drop.

We discussed this proposal with two of the largest world band manufacturers that serve poorer countries. "Intriguing," they mused, but it's doubtful such a radio would find a receptive market. If people can't afford fresh batteries, the reasoning goes, how could they possibly afford the necessarily higher up-front price of solar circuitry and rechargeable cells?

Mytton nonetheless suggests that international broadcasters open dialogue with major electronics manufacturers on this subject. Who knows? Maybe the heavens will power the radios, as well as bring in the signal.

The Grundig Satellit 650 may not equal similarly priced tabletop models, but it has unsurpassed audio quality.

★ ★ ★ ★   *Editor's Choice*

Grundig Satellit 650

Price: $999.00 in the United States, CAN$1,299.95 in Canada, $700-900 in Europe.

Advantages: Superior world band performance. Excellent audio. Two full bandwidths and a third pseudo-bandwidth give good trade-off between audio fidelity and adjacent-channel rejection. Superior spurious-signal rejection. High weak-signal sensitivity. Helpful tuning features. World Time clock, displayed separately. Alarm/timer. Precise signal-strength indicator. Superior FM reception. Receives longwave. Built-in worldwide AC power supply.

Disadvantages: Size and weight. Less likely to be steeply discounted. Motorized preselector tuning requires some manual tweaking for best performance and means mechanical complexity. Construction quality below norm for price class.

Bottom Line: Biceps builder's boombox. Superior speakers and generous, high-quality audio make the '650 a favorite for pleasant hour-after-hour listening—but enthusiasts chasing faint signals should shop among tabletop models, instead.

 An *RDI WHITE PAPER* is available for this model.

★ $\frac{1}{2}$

Marc II NR-108F1 Pan Crusader

Price: $300-550 worldwide.

Advantages: Unusually broad coverage, from 150 kHz longwave to 520 MHz UHF, plus 850-910 MHz UHF (North American/Japanese version). Many helpful tuning features. World Time clock, displayed separately from frequency. Sleep/timer. Signal-strength indicator. Illuminated display.

Disadvantages: Marginal overall performance within certain portions of world band, including hissing, buzzing and serious overloading. Poor adjacent-channel rejection. Poor spurious-signal rejection. Poorly performing preselector tuning complicates operation. Excessive battery drain. Mediocre construction quality, including casual alignment. Not widely available.

Bottom Line: Made in Japan, but performance smacks of Albania. Poorest showing when used in Europe, Near East, North Africa and Eastern North America. Performance improves in some respects within Western North America and Australia/New Zealand.

Who says more money buys a better radio? The Marc II, also sold as the Pan Crusader, is outperformed by models costing a fourth as much.

The Alconic Series 2959, also called the Venturer and Rhapsody, does many things—none well.

★

Alconic Series 2959
Venturer Multiband
Rhapsody Multiband
MBR7 Mark II

Price: *Basic model:* $79.95-99.95; *With cassette player:* $129.95; *With cassette player, stereo audio and digital clock:* $159.00.

Advantages: Inexpensive. Covers VHF-TV channels and air/weather bands. Audio at least average. Built-in cassette player (two versions only). Stereo audio (one version only). Digital clock (one version only), displayed separately from frequency. Signal-strength indicator. Rotating ferrite-bar direction finder (mediumwave AM). Built-in AC power supply.

Disadvantages: No remotely accurate frequency display, so finding a station is a struggle. World band coverage omits the 2, 3, 13, 15, 17, 21 and 26 MHz segments. Performance mediocre in nearly every respect. Does not receive longwave.

Bottom Line: Pink flamingo. Sold widely throughout North America and Europe under various names—or even no advertised name—but with identical appearance, by a wide variety of American mail order stores, as well as by some credit-card companies. One (Haverhills) to its credit does not promote the Venturer for world band reception. Assembled in Hong Kong from China-made components.

New for 1991
★

Electro Brand 2971

Price: $169.50, including cassette player, stereo audio and digital clock.

Bottom Line: Essentially identical to Alconic Series 2959, above, except Electro Brand is made *and assembled* in the People's Republic of China.

China's Electro Brand 2971, new for 1991, is long on features, short on performance.

OLDIES, SOME GOODIES

The following models reportedly have been discontinued, yet may still be available new at some retail outlets. Cited are typical sale prices in the United States and United Kingdom as *Passport/91* went to press. Prices elsewhere may be higher.

★ ★ ★ ★

Panasonic RF-9000
National RF-9000

Excellent overall performance but too big and heavy for portable use. £1,800.00 (about $3,100) in the United Kingdom.

★ ★ ★ $\frac{1}{2}$　　　*Editor's Choice*

Magnavox D2999
Philips D2999

A fine-sounding receiver that works equally well as a large portable and tabletop. Grab it while you can! Under $300, but not available in Canada.

★ ★ ★ $\frac{1}{2}$

Grundig Satellit 400

Pleasant overall mid-sized model, but poor single sideband. Under $400.

★ ★ ★ $\frac{1}{2}$　　　*Editor's Choice*

Magnavox D2935
Philips D2935

One of the great affordable portables of all time—a classic. Similar to the Magnavox/Philips D2999 (above), but mid-sized, with traditional portable layout and fewer features. Around $200, and worth more. Nigh impossible to find in the United States—Sears is the best bet—but the odd unit still available in the United Kingdom for around £125 (about $215) as of press time. Not available in Canada.

★ ★ ★ $\frac{1}{2}$

Sony ICF-2003
Sony ICF-7600DS
Sony ICF-2002
Sony ICF-7600D

Precursors to the current compact Sony ICF-SW7600 (see), they all perform similarly. Under $260.

★ ★ $\frac{1}{2}$

Sony ICF-7600A
Sony ICF-7600AW

Similar to the current compact Sony ICF-7601 (see), but 13 MHz coverage omitted. No digital display. Under $100 in the United States, under £110 in the United Kingdom.

★ ★ $\frac{1}{2}$　　　　　　　　　　¢

Sony ICF-4920
Sony ICF-4900II
Sony ICF-5100

Identical in all but styling to the current mini Sony ICF-SW20 (see). No digital display. Under $100.

★ ★

Grundig Yacht Boy 215

A modest compact performer notable only for its World Time clock/timer. No digital display, no 13 MHz coverage. Under $140.

★ ★

Grundig Yacht Boy 210

Identical to Grundig Yacht Boy 215, preceding, except clock/timer omitted. Under $120.

★ ★　　　　　　　　　　　　　¢

Magnavox D1835
Philips D1835

Identical performance with current compact Magnavox D1875 and Philips D1875 (see). No digital display. Under $70, but not available in Canada.

★

Realistic DX-360

The Yugo of world band radios. No trace of meaningful frequency display. Under $80.

★

Sangean ATS-802

Radio for the deaf. Dreadful performance, tortoise-slow tuning. Under $100.

The Passport *equipment review team: Lawrence Magne, along with Jock Elliott and Tony Jones, with laboratory measurements by Robert Sherwood.*

New from Radio Shack . . .

As we go to press, Radio Shack is about to introduce the Realistic DX-350, a small—apparently mini—$69.95 portable that replaces the DX-360. Spectrum coverage includes 87.5-108 MHz FM; 150-270 kHz longwave; 520-1700 kHz mediumwave AM; plus world band 5.85-6.2, 7.05-7.5, under 9.45-9.9, under 11.6-over 12.0, 13.55-13.85, under 15.1-15.6, 17.45-18.0, 21.45-21.95, and 25.65-26.15 MHz. For a model in this price class, that's reasonable world band coverage, even if the key BBC World Service channels of 9410 and 12095 seem to be missing. One plus is that the forthcoming 1600-1705 kHz AM band segment for the Americas is included.

We haven't tested it, as it's not yet available. However, it is virtually certain to be a single-conversion, needle-and-dial model with bandspreading. This genre typically provides pedestrian, but acceptable, performance—two stars or so. In any event, because of its bandspreading and lower price, it is likely to be a better value than the discontinued '360—even if its smaller speaker is unlikely to provide world class audio quality.

Radio Shack appears to be diving into the world band market with new-found gusto. Their 1991 line is expected to expand even more under both the traditional Realistic, as well as the new Optima, brand names.

. . . and from Philips/Magnavox . . .

In recent years, Philips and its U.S. subsidiary, Magnavox, have been turning out a number of world band portables that offer performance clearly superior for the money.

Alas, sharply rising costs of production have caused these models—D2999, D2935, D1835 and possibly the D1875, as well—to be discontinued. The new top-end model, the AE 3805, is reviewed in this edition. The new low-end model, the AE 3205, is due out shortly.

The '3205 is to list in the United States at the bargain-basement price of $49.95. Like the Realistic DX-350, above, it appears to be a single-conversion, needle-and-dial mini-portable with bandspreading. Coverage reportedly is FM 88-108 MHz; longwave; mediumwave AM 530-1600 kHz; and world band 5.95-6.2, 7.0-7.3, 9.55-9.9, 11.6-12.0, 15.0-15.5 and 17.6-18.2 MHz. This omits, among others, the 7.3-7.6, 9.3-9.55, 11.5-11.6, 12.0-12.1, 13.6-13.8, 15.5-15.7, 21.45-21.85 and 25.6-26.1 MHz world band segments, as well as the 1600-1705 kHz expanded AM band due to be inaugurated in the Americas. This is disappointing coverage as compared to the D1875, but the new set costs only half as much.

The AE 3205 hasn't been tested, of course. However, this sort of model typically earns between one-and-a-half and, at best, two stars.

. . . and from Sangean

In the pipeline for 1991 is the $49.95 700SGL analog (needle-and-dial) tuned mini-portable covering 12 world band segments. Too, there may be yet another advanced-technology portable coming up from Sangean—this one to be priced just below the popular ATS-803A.

Pretuned Radio from Sony

In mid-1989, when *Passport* was presenting a paper to the IEEE's International Conference on Consumer Electronics in Chicago, Sony engineering representatives unveiled the prototype of the ICF-SW700, a simple, low-cost AM/world band radio with replaceable magnetic station schedule data. By changing a gumstick-type magnetic card, a limited amount of new schedule data—three cards' worth—could be inputted into the radio, simplifying tuning.

The target market was to be Japan, where it would be used in the outlying islands to receive world band relays of domestic Japanese radio networks. However, later that year there were reports of a version—the ICF-SW800—covering FM, as well, being shown abroad. Would this version be introduced outside Japan? In 1989, Sony said no.

As of now, the ICF-SW700 is sold only in Japan. If Sony ever decides to introduce the ICF-SW800 into the North American or European markets, it is the sort of radio that would probably sell for around $125-175 Stateside.

Sized at 7 × 4 × 1.5 in (18 × 10 × 4 cm), the 'SW800 has 60 preset channels, a keypad, and up/down slewing buttons. However, it has no tuning knob. Coverage is only 3700-17900 kHz, so some world band segments aren't included.

This is a set designed for extreme simplicity of use, and even its gumstick feature has only limited utility. Still, it incorporates innovative engineering that should appeal to what one all-thumbs wag calls, "we, the technologically disabled."

An American World Band Portable?

Hold on to your hat: An American firm is considering production of a U.S.-made advanced-technology world band portable, possibly in the $400 price range. It's all very iffy, but should it pan out look for introduction around 1993 or late 1992.

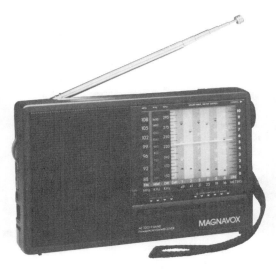

The Magnavox AE 3205, also sold as the Philips AE 3205, promises little besides low cost and small size.

Radio Shack's Realistic DX-350 costs less than its predecessor, the DX-360. Should be better, too.

COMPARATIVE RATINGS OF TABLETOP RECEIVERS

For most, a good portable is more than adequate to enjoy the offerings found on world band radio. Others, though, seek something more.

That "more" is a tabletop receiver. These often excel at flushing out the really tough game—faint stations, or those swamped by interference from competing signals. Tabletops also do unusually well with non-broadcasting signals, such as ham and utility stations, many of which use single sideband. Tabletop models can also be useful if you live in a part of the world, such as Central and Western North America, where signals tend to be weak and made choppy by "flutter" fading—a common problem when world band signals have to follow high-latitude paths. To get an idea how much this phenomenon might affect your listening, place a string on a globe, between where you live and where the signals come from. If it passes near the arctic, beware.

Tabletops also excel for daytime listening, when most signals are relatively modest. A good tabletop won't guarantee getting a favorite weak daytime station, but it will certainly help.

What tabletop receivers don't necessarily do is to deliver better audio. As our findings show, tabletop models—like portables—run the audio gamut from shrill to mellow.

For the most part, tabletop receivers are pricier than portables. Too, most tabletop models also require, and should have, an outboard antenna—indeed, tabletop performance is largely determined by antenna quality and placement. A good outdoor wire antenna, such as the various Antenna Supermarket models or the Alpha Delta Sloper, usually runs from $60 to $80— these are best. A short amplified antenna, suitable for indoors and sometimes outdoors when space is at a premium, sells for more.

Models new for 1991 are covered at length in this year's Buyer's Guide. Every model, regardless of its introduction year, has taken the various testing hurdles we established and have honed since 1977, when IBS first started evaluating world band equipment.

Each model is thoroughly tested in the laboratory, using criteria developed specially for the strenuous requirements of world band reception. The receiver then undergoes hands-on evaluation, usually for weeks, before we begin preparing our detailed internal report. That report, in turn, forms the basis for our findings, summarized in this *Passport* Buyer's Guide.

Our unabridged laboratory and hands-on test results are far too exhaustive to reproduce here, as they run many pages per model. However, they are now being made available as *Passport's Radio Database International White Papers*—details may be found elsewhere in this edition.

Receivers are listed in order of suitability for listening to difficult-to-hear world band radio broadcasts. Models that are unusually appropriate for hour-after-hour listening to favorite programs are so indicated under "Advantages."

Unless otherwise stated, all tabletop models have:

- digital frequency synthesis and illuminated digital display;
- a wide variety of helpful tuning features;
- meaningful signal-strength indication;
- the ability to properly demodulate single-sideband and CW (Morse code) signals; and
- full coverage of at least the 155-26099 kHz longwave, mediumwave AM and world band spectra.

Unless otherwise stated, all tabletop models do *not*:

- tune the FM broadcast range between 87.5-107.9 MHz; and
- come equipped with synchronous selectable sideband.

In this regard, keep in mind that if you listen mainly to weaker stations—or to speech, such as newscasts—audio quality is less important than for music programs over strong, clear stations. Too, when shopping, remember that most tabletop models, unlike portables, are available only from electronics and world band specialty outlets.

For the United States and Canada, suggested retail ("list") prices are quoted. As the gap between dealer cost and list price tends to be relatively modest with world band tabletops, discounts are common, but rarely substantial.

As "list" prices are largely a North American phenomenon, observed *selling* price parameters are given in pounds for the United Kingdom and, to have a common benchmark, U.S. dollars for continental Europe. Prices elsewhere vary widely. World band tabletop models are virtually unavailable at duty-free shops.

> ## Tabletops excell at flushing out really tough stations.

Of course, all prices are as of when we go to press and subject to fluctuation. Prices for tabletop models, unlike portables, continue to crawl upward.

What *Passport's* Ratings Mean

Star ratings: ★★★★★ is best. We award stars solely for overall performance and meaningful features. To facilitate comparison, the same rating system is used for portable models, reviewed elsewhere in this *Passport*. Whether a radio is a portable or a tabletop model, a given rating—three stars, say—means essentially the same thing.

Editor's Choice models are our test team's personal picks of the litter—what we would buy ourselves.

¢ denotes a price-for-performance bargain. It may or may not be a great set, but gives uncommon value for the money.

PROFESSIONAL MONITOR RECEIVERS

If your backyard has become another Spindletop, or your name is—was?—Donald Trump, look here for your next receiver. Otherwise, look over the best of the regular tabletop models, which offer essentially the same performance for far less money.

★ ★ ★ ★ ★   *Editor's Choice*

Icom IC-R9000

Price: $5,459.00 in the United States, CAN$7,999 in Canada, under £4,000 in the United Kingdom.

Advantages: Unusually appropriate for hour-after-hour world band listening. Exceptional tough-signal performance. Flexible, above-average audio for a tabletop model, when used with suitable outboard speaker. Three AM-mode bandwidths. Tunes and displays frequency in precise 10 Hz increments. Video display of radio spectrum occupancy. Sophisticated scanner/timer. Extraordinarily broad coverage of radio spectrum. Exceptional assortment of flexible operating controls and sockets. Very good ergonomics. Superb reception of utility and ham signals. Two 24-hour clocks.

Disadvantages: Very expensive. Power supply runs hot. Both AM-mode bandwidths too broad for most world band applications. Both single-sideband bandwidths almost identical. Dynamic range merely adequate. Reliability, especially when roughly handled, thus far appears wanting. Front-panel controls of only average construction quality.

Best by a skootch is Icom's IC-R9000—one of the costliest models tested.

Bottom Line: The Icom IC-R9000, with at least one changed AM-mode bandwidth filter—available from world band specialty firms—is, by a wee margin, the best-performing model we have ever tested.

 An *RDI WHITE PAPER* is available for this model.

★ ★ ★ ★ ★   *Editor's Choice*

Japan Radio NRD-93

Price: $6,850.00 in the United States, $6,000 to $10,000 elsewhere.

Advantages: Unusually appropriate for hour-after-hour world band listening. Superb all-around performance. Professional-quality construction with legendary durability to survive around-the-clock use in punishing environments. Unusually easy to repair on-the-spot. Excellent ergonomics and unsurpassed control feel. Above-average audio for a tabletop model. Sophisticated optional scanner allows some degree of automated listening. Superb reception of utility and ham signals.

No other radio tested by *Passport* approaches the ruggedness and quality of construction of the Japan Radio NRD-93.

Disadvantages: Very expensive. Lacks some advanced-technology tuning aids. Distribution limited to Japan Radio offices and a few specialty organizations, such as shipyards.

Bottom Line: Crafted like a Swiss watch, but tough as an Israeli tank, the Japan Radio NRD-93 is a breed apart. It is a pleasure to operate for bandscanning hour after hour, but its overall performance is not appreciably different from that of some cheaper tabletop models, and it lacks certain handy features.

 An *RDI WHITE PAPER* is available for this model.

TWO PROFESSIONAL RECEIVERS TO BE INTRODUCED

Japan Radio's NRD-240 Features Self-Diagnosis

Japan Radio is shortly to commence production of its new GMDSS (Global Maritime Distress and Safety System) receiver, the NRD-240. We haven't laid hands on one yet, and thus can't begin to say how well—or poorly—it will perform. However, it appears to be a straightforward, relatively uncomplicated piece of hardware with excellent specifications and, if precedent is any guide, tank-tough construction.

Features include plug-in type circuit boards, 100 memories, scanning, nominal 3 kHz (narrow) and 6 kHz (wide) voice bandwidths and frequency resolution to the nearest Hz. Among other things, this virtually eliminates the possibility of chuffing, or "bagpiping," during tuning. Synchronous selectable sideband? Who knows, but there may be—or may not be, depending on how you read JRC's prerelease specifications—DSB (AM-mode) synchronous detection, similar to that of the Lowe HF-225. On the other hand, there is no sign of a tunable notch filter or passband tuning.

A key feature is to be built-in test equipment (BITE) to allow, in principle, circuits to be checked within the modular circuitry on a board-by-board basis. There's also to be complete remote control via an RS-423A port, plus a noise blanker to protect against atmospheric static, as well as the usual pulse noise.

The price has not yet been announced, but reach deep—it will almost certainly will be well into the *thousands* of dollars.

HF-235 Receiver Due Out from Lowe

The Lowe HF-225 reviewed in this *Passport* Buyer's Guide is, in terms of ruggedness and reliability, very much a professional-caliber receiver—but at a consumer-caliber price. Almost as *Passport/91* will be coming off press, Lowe will be adding a professional model, the HF-235, to its lineup.

The British-made '235 is to be rack mounted, with a forward-facing speaker and a conventional built-in keypad in lieu of the '225's ergonomically excellent mouse-type keypad. Additionally, there is to be a version, the HF-235/R, with an RS-232 port to allow for what the manufacturer calls "powerful" scan/search and other control via personal computer, as well for use of a computer video display for receiver data. Otherwise, controls and features are to be similar to those of the '225, except that the '235 is to have an IF Gain in lieu of the '225's tone control—a plus for some commercial users, but a drawback for world band listeners.

Inside, however, there are a number of planned changes to make the '235 a superior tough-signal device. Among these are higher-quality bandwidth filters, greater stability (in the extra-cost HF-235H version) and improved dynamic range. On the other hand, the HF-235/F fax version—which costs nothing extra—has no lower sideband capability (most commercial applications use only upper sideband).

Price? £950 (about $1,625), plus VAT, for the basic HF-235 receiver; £1,286 (about $2,200), plus VAT, with all options in the HF-235/H/R or HF-235/H/R/F versions—low by professional standards.

Japan Radio's NRD-240 is to stress construction quality, ruggedness and performance—while keeping controls to a minimum.

The Lowe HF-235 is to be of professional caliber, but will lack the tone control and handy mouse-type keypad found on the cheaper HF-225.

American Manufacturer To Produce Advanced-Tech Model

Several years back, the R.L. Drake Company of Miamisburg, Ohio, was renowned for its tabletop receivers. The last, the R7 and related models, are still considered by many *cognoscenti* to be the finest tough-signal receivers ever made—regardless of price.

Now, Drake has reversed gears and will be reentering the world band market with a premium tabletop receiver, the R8. If history is any precedent, it could be an exceptional piece of equipment. Of course, we won't know for sure until we have tested it.

Lifting up the tent flap, what we see is a tabletop receiver that nominally has superior tough-signal-handling specifications, plus a variety of features to endear it to the knowledgeable world band enthusiast: at least three bandwidths for voice and music, passband offset tuning, a tunable notch filter, slow/fast/off AGC, a preamplifier, two antenna inputs, a computer interface . . . plus an exceptionally complete array of helpful tuning aids. The first three of these features, if properly implemented, should put the R8 ahead of other tabletop models in reducing interference without unnecessarily degrading audio fidelity.

The R8 is scheduled to come, just as did the R7, with 0.5 and 1.8 kHz bandwidths, as well as 6, 4 and 2.3 kHz for voice and music. As of when we go to press, 3 kHz is to be neither standard nor optional.

The ergonomics look pretty good, too. Although the keypad would have made much more sense in the upper right corner—or outboard, as with a computer mouse—the layout is otherwise uncluttered and handy, with sensibly sized, well-spaced controls. There's also a genuine analog signal-strength meter, not a skittish digital indicator.

Particularly interesting is that Drake's receiver, unlike most other tabletop models, appears to have been designed specifically for world band listeners and DXers, rather than hams or commercial users. In this vein, the R8 and the new Japan Radio NRD-535 will be the *only* tabletop models available with synchronous selectable sideband—a fidelity enhancing, high-tech advance that reduces interference and distortion. Drake claims theirs will be even easier to use than that of the Sony ICF-2010/ICF-2001D, and work better too. We'll see.

For a set to look promising, then to fulfill that promise, are two sometimes very different things. This we know from years of testing and disappointment. Still, given Drake's track record—much of the engineering of the R8 was done by those involved in the creation of the earlier R7—there is cause for optimism.

Price? Drake won't say, yet, but they do expect it to be under $1,000, fully equipped. (World band dealers should know the exact price before the R8 is released.) When it comes out, our test panel and laboratory will give it a rigorous workout, then issue an *RDI White Paper* with our findings. We'll know at that time whether it's as good as it promises to be . . . or falls short of its potential of being the best world band radio on the market.

When? Hopefully, by spring or summer of 1991. Stay tuned!

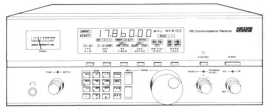

Drake's R8 receiver, due out in 1991, is the latest in a distinguished series from this American manufacturer.

Japan Radio's NRD-535, intended to improve upon earlier JRC models' substandard audio quality.

New JRC Model to Feature Synchronous Selectable Sideband

About the time Drake left the world band market, Japan Radio entered it with a series of superb performers: the NRD-505, NRD-515 and NRD-525. Each of these has been characterized by superior quality of construction and excellent tough-signal performance; but, with the '515 and '525, pedestrian audio quality.

For 1991, Japan Radio is to introduce yet another model—the NRD-535. While full details are not available as we go to press—and, of course, we haven't had a chance to test the unit—it appears to be quite similar to the forthcoming Drake R8 discussed above. Most important, it, like the R8, is to feature synchronous selectable sideband ("ECSS") and, JRC claims, much-improved audio quality. Too, the '535 appears to be ergonomically well thought out.

However, there are at least some apparent differences between the '535 and the R8.

First, the '535 is to tune in *1 Hz* increments, although the display is to be only to the nearest 10 Hz. The R8 is to tune and display in 10 Hz increments. The practical difference between 10 Hz and 1 Hz tuning is all but imperceptible, but it means that the '535 should tune virtually as smoothly as an analog circuit.

Second, the '535 makes use of single-function knobs, whereas the R8 uses the concentric variety. This means that the '535 sprouts more knobs, but arguably is more ergonomically sound.

Third, the '535's keypad, with long, thin buttons, appears to be similar to that used on the '525. The square-ish buttons on the R8's keypad are more likely than those of the '535 to be comfortable to use.

On the other hand, the '535's keypad is located in the upper-right corner—a distinct ergonomic advantage over the unhandy location on the R8.

Fourth, the '535 has twice as many memories—200—as does the R8.

Fifth, the '535 has a digital signal-strength indicator. The R8 uses a genuine analog meter, which is preferable except for computer applications. (Both models are to have computer interface provisions, according to the manufacturers.)

Finally, the bandwidth configurations of the two models differ. The R8 has five bandwidths, at least three of which—nominally 6, 4 and 2.3 kHz—are for world band. The '535 has only four positions, of which only two—nominally 6 and 2.0 kHz (there's a better 2.4 kHz crystal-lattice replacement to be made available as an option)—are suitable for world band broadcasts.

However, the '535 has a control that allows each bandwidth to be "choked" continuously by as much as 0.8 kHz. The 2.0 and 2.4 kHz bandwidths are probably already too narrow to make meaningful use of this feature, but choking the 6 kHz bandwidth down to around 5.2 kHz may well prove to be useful. Still, this leaves a substantial gap between the '535's two bandwidths. On the R8, a third filter—4 kHz—prevents this problem.

How much for all this? Under $1,500 in the United States, more in Canada and Europe. As to the NRD-525, it is expected to remain in Japan Radio's line for some time to come, possibly at a reduced price.

Prices aside, the sum of the surface differences between the Japan Radio NRD-535 and Drake R8 don't add up to much. The real meat will show up during testing. Both models have the potential—right now, it's only that—of outperforming the current crop of tabletop models. Once we have thoroughly tested the NRD-535, we will issue a special *RDI White Paper* with our full laboratory and hands-on findings.

A New Tabletop for 1992?

One manufacturer of communications equipment has expressed an interest in producing a high-quality tabletop receiver selling for under $1,500. The existing design does not call for synchronous selectable sideband, but this could change.

TABLETOP RECEIVERS

If you want a top performer, here is where your money stretches most. Any model with four or five stars should satisfy all but the fussiest world band enthusiast.

The best tabletop models are the Ferraris and Porsches of the radio world. Like their automotive counterparts, however, like-ranked receivers may come out of the curve at the same speed, though how they do it can differ greatly from model to model. So, if you're thinking of choosing from the top end, study each contender in detail.

★ ★ ★ ★ ★ *Editor's Choice*

Kenwood R-5000

Price: $1,049.95 in the United States, CAN$1,349.95 in Canada, under £900 in the United Kingdom, $1,000-1,500 elsewhere in Europe.

Advantages: Unusually appropriate for hour-after-hour world band listening. Superb all-around performance. Unusually good audio for a tabletop, provided a suitable outboard speaker is used.

A best seller, Kenwood's R-5000 excels at bringing in tough signals. And it sounds good, too.

Exceptionally flexible operating controls. Tunes and displays frequency in precise 10 Hz increments. Excellent reception of utility and ham signals.

Disadvantages: Ergonomics only fair, especially keypad. Mediocre wide bandwidth filter supplied with set; replacement with high-quality YK-88A-1 substitute adds $88.95 to cost. Audio significantly distorted at tape-recording output.

Bottom Line: The Kenwood R-5000's combination of superior tough-signal performance and above-average audio quality makes it the optimum receiver in its price class for those who need a receiver for both quality program listening and weak-signal DXing.

Comment: At press time, demand for this model has placed it in short supply, with waits of up to several weeks common.

 An *RDI WHITE PAPER* is available for this model.

GROVE RECEIVER POSTPONED INDEFINITELY

The Grove SR1000 professional communications receiver, intended to be sold in the $3,000 price class, has been put off for the foreseeable future. Serious engineering problems arose during the long and costly development process, causing Grove management to suspend the project.

Grove advises us that the considerable knowledge gained during this activity may yet be put to good use. At present, the firm is considering a variety of options to bring out a less-costly, yet high-caliber, tabletop world band receiver.

The Japan Radio NRD-525 is a gem flawed by woolly audio.

★ ★ ★ ★ ★   *Editor's Choice*

Japan Radio NRD-525

Price: $1,349.00 in the United States, CAN$2,099.95 in Canada, under £1,100 in the United Kingdom, $1,300-2,000 elsewhere in Europe.

Advantages: Superb all-around performance. Highly flexible operating controls. Very good ergonomics. Construction quality slightly above average. Computer-type modular plug-in circuit boards ease repair. Sophisticated scanner allows some automated listening. Superior reception of utility and ham signals. Tunes and displays frequency in precise 10 Hz increments. Two 24-hour clocks.

Disadvantages: Woolly audio, a major drawback for program listening. Dynamic range below par for genre. Keypad lacks proper feel. Jittery signal-strength indicator readout. Surface-mounted devices make discrete component replacement difficult. Relatively limited dealer network.

Bottom Line: A superb performer that's well put together—although hardly like its sibling the NRD-93—but lacks audio fidelity. The prominent choice in its price class for listening in diverse modes.

Comment: When tested with Sherwood SE-3 synchronous selectable sideband device fitted to a Realistic Minimus 7 speaker, audio quality improved to excellent.

 An *RDI WHITE PAPER* is available for this model.

★ ★ ★ ★ $\frac{1}{2}$

Icom IC-R71A
Icom IC-R71E
Icom IC-R71D

Price: *IC-R71A:* $999.00 in the United States, CAN$1,559.00 in Canada; *IC-R71E:* under £900 in the United Kingdom; *IC-R71E and IC-R71D:* $1,000-1,600 in continental Europe.

Advantages: Superb reception of weak, hard-to-hear signals. Reception of faint signals alongside powerful competing ones aided by superb ultimate selectivity, as well as excellent dynamic range. Flexible operating controls. Excellent reception of utility and ham signals. Tunes in precise 10 Hz increments (reads in 100 Hz increments).

Disadvantages: Mediocre audio. Diminutive controls, and otherwise generally substandard ergonomics. Should backup battery die, operating system software erases, requiring reprogramming by Icom service center (expected battery life is in excess of 10 years). Units on sale since March, 1989, lack certain helpful operating features found on original version.

Bottom Line: The Icom IC-R71, especially in its original incarnation, has long been a favorite among those seeking faint, hard-to-hear signals. However, the 'R71 is not equal to some other tabletops for hour-on-hour program listening.

 An *RDI WHITE PAPER* is available for this model.

A traditional favorite among serious DXers, the Icom IC-R71 now has fewer features than it once did.

Swimming refreshingly against the cultural mainstream, Lowe provides a superior product in a plain-vanilla package. Shown, the excellent HF-225.

tive to weak signals. Frequency reads in relatively coarse 1 kHz increments. Currently not distributed outside Europe.

Note: Heretofore, units shipped to customers in North America arrived with no plug on the AC power supply, as the customary British plug does not work outside the U.K. However, the manufacturer informs us that AC power supplies with American-type flat prongs are now being provided to American customers.

Bottom Line: A hardy, easy-to-operate set with superior audio quality. *Grand cru* at a *petit cru* price.

 An *RDI WHITE PAPER* is available for this model.

New for 1991
★ ★ ★ ★

Icom IC-R72

Price: £599 (about $1,024) in United Kingdom; more in continental Europe.

Advantages: Pleasant audio with outboard speaker or headphones. Generally superior ergonomics. Tunes and displays frequency in precise 10 Hz increments. World clock/timer. Operates for about one hour off built-in rechargeable battery—useful during power failure. Novel center-tuning LED for world band and certain other signals. Superb image and IF rejection. Small footprint. Smoothly operating tuning knob. 10 dB switchable preamplifier.

Disadvantages: Receiver, parts and factory-authorized service currently not available in United States or Canada. Wide bandwidth too broad. Dreadful audio from built-in speaker. Noisy synthesizer. Relatively few features,

★ ★ ★ ★   *Editor's Choice*

Lowe HF-225

Price: £395, plus power supply and accessories, in the United Kingdom; around $695—including keypad, power supply, shipping and tariff—if sent to the United States.

Advantages: Among the very best for listening to world band programs hour after hour. Superior audio with outboard speaker. Straightforward to operate. Generally excellent ergonomics, especially with keypad. Best bandwidth flexibility of any model tested. Tunes in precise, if unusual, 8 Hz increments. Rugged, with frequency-of-repair record that appears to be exceptional. Optional synchronous detector reduces distortion. Optional field-portable configuration. Small footprint. Attractively priced.

Disadvantages: Limited operational flexibility, including AGC. Two of four bandwidths too wide for most world band applications. Front-end selectivity only fair. In tabletop use, less sensitive to weak signals than top-rated models. Optional portable configuration relatively insensi-

Icom's new IC-R72 is a lower-cost alternative to the IC-R71. It's available in Europe, Asia and the Pacific, but not in North America.

compared to better models. In our test unit, poor low-frequency audio reproduction in upper sideband.

Bottom Line: Nice, but nothing special. A number of other models offer better value.

Evaluation of New Model: Icom's new IC-R72 is designed as a lower-cost alternative, by about £250 (about $425) in the United Kingdom, to Icom's venerable IC-R71.

This set presents a problem for North Americans, and it's a whopper: not only is it not available in the United States or Canada, it's probably not going to be until later in 1991, if ever. Ditto Icom's new IC-R1 and IC-R100 receivers. And Icom America won't service them, either.

The 'R72 is a cleanly designed, attractive model, measuring 9.5 in wide by 3.7 in high by 9 in deep (24 × 9.5 × 23 cm), so it occupies relatively little desktop real estate. The bright orange-on-black display is highly legible, too, and so is the analog signal-strength meter. The tuning knob, replete with (non-rotating) speed dimple, spins with silky smoothness.

Features include worldwide multivoltage AC operation; 99 tunable memories plus two separate programmable scan-edge memories; a 10 dB preamplifier to help flush out faint signals; a keypad for direct frequency and memory selection; two kinds of antenna connectors; a variety of scanning options; computer control capability; a World Time clock and timer; and provision for operation from a built-in lead storage battery. That last feature, which gives around an hour of operation per charge, won't meet portable requirements, but it's useful when the electricity fails, as during earthquakes or electrical storms. There's also a center-tune LED that glows when the receiver is tuned to a broadcaster's frequency.

The noise blanker, although nowhere as complex as the one on the sibling 'R71, has two positions: normal, for ordinary pulse-type noises, plus high for weak pulse noises.

When we ran the 'R72 through our laboratory paces, measurement confirmed it as a worthy piece of gear. Except for sensitivity in the mediumwave AM band, nearly all measurements are at least "good." Some—image rejection, IF rejection, and world band sensitivity with the preselector on—are superb.

In the past, we've often faulted Icom for its inattention to ergonomics: the art of orienting controls to people, rather than the other way around. The 'R72 represents a major improvement, partly because it has fewer and less-complex features.

The 'R72's frequency synthesizer tunes in 10 Hz increments, and the readout also displays to that exacting degree of resolution. This is a plus over the 'R71, which tunes in 10 Hz increments, but displays only to the nearest 100 Hz.

Tuning is flexible, too. You can select tuning steps as fine as 10 Hz, or as massive as 1 MHz. In fact, you can program the receiver to tune in whole kHz increments anywhere from 1 to 10. If you want the receiver to tune, say, in 1 kHz increments, it's easily done.

Clutter on the 'R72 has been controlled by making some buttons serve two related functions. For example, instead of separate buttons for lower sideband (LSB) and upper sideband (USB), there's a single control marked "SSB." Push once, there's USB; twice, LSB.

Same thing for the AM/N button. Push it once, AM-wide; twice, AM-narrow. A "beep" confirms each push, and the 'R72 remembers the last setting of each mode. Single-function controls may be best for foolproof operation, but the 'R72's dual-function buttons—once you've gotten the hang of them—are handy and useful.

Less agreeable is the relatively small volume (AF gain) control, located close to the headphone receptacle on the left side of the receiver.

Presumably to keep costs down, a number of goodies that world band enthusiasts value are missing: no tunable notch filter, no passband tuning, no IF shift, no RF gain control. And the 'R72's tiny, tinny speaker is awful. This radio definitely requires headphones or a good external speaker. With either of these, however, audio becomes quite pleasant.

The bandwidths are bad-widths. At nearly 8 kHz, the wider setting is too broad to be of much use for world band listening.

Real world, what does this mean? On the 'R72, you can easily hear powerful stations 5 kHz away. In fact, we heard stations in the wide position, only to have them "vanish" in the narrow. In other words, in wide you can hear a station that is actually a whole channel—5 kHz—away. Loud and clear.

As our experience implies, the other (narrow) bandwidth gets rid of the problem. But it's truly narrow, 2.4 kHz, and sounds muffled unless the receiver is detuned 1 kHz or so, which helps. So we found ourselves listening to most world band broadcasts not in the usual AM mode, but in the single-sideband mode, which also makes use of that narrow filter. That's okay for flushing out flyspeck stations, but for ordinary world band listening it's an impractical alternative. Tuning world band signals in the SSB mode does have benefits, but it's fussy and time-consuming.

Because of its disappointing wide bandwidth, the Icom IC-R72 all but begs for the sort of replacement filtering offered by shortwave specialty firms. Of course, that would raise the price, tending to defeat its positioning as a lower-cost alternative to the 'R71A.

Lesser downers include various slight internally generated noises. In narrow AM and lower sideband there's minor hum, whereas in upper sideband there is an occasional bit of buzz on faint, DX-caliber signals. Lab tests unearthed the source that USB buzz: the frequency synthesizer, arguably the heart of any serious modern receiver. It's one of the least-clean synthesizers we've encountered in recent times, and stands out all the more because of Icom's heretofore long-standing practice of turning out models with superior synthesizers.

Another non-critical disappointment is that on our unit, at any rate, the USB mode was adjusted so high that virtually no low audio frequencies made it through to the speaker.

Overall, the 'R72 is a nice little set that's in serious need of a slimmer—say, 5 or 5.5 kHz—"wide" bandwidth. That, and an outboard speaker, would make it suitable for serious listening to world band broadcasts. The 'R72's superior sensitivity makes it useful for snaring faint signals, but to some extent the noisy synthesizer keeps the receiver from fully reaching this potential.

★ ★ ★ ★

Yaesu FRG-8800

Price: $784.00 in the United States, CAN$1,229.00 in Canada, under £650 in the United Kingdom, $800-1,100 elsewhere in Europe.

Advantages: Flexible controls. Slightly above-average audio for tabletop model. Superior sensitivity and related blocking measurements help weak-signal reception. Fairly good ergonomics. Two 24-hour clocks. Established circuit design, going back several years, is by now thoroughly proven.

Disadvantages: "Wide" bandwidth too broad for most world band receiving applications. "Narrow" bandwidth somewhat wide for a "narrow," yet rather narrow for a "wide." Spurious-signal ("image") rejection only fair. Front-end selectivity only fair. Utility and ham signal reception, though acceptable, is below average for tabletop model. Some control settings difficult to see, and a couple of controls are unhandy to reach.

Bottom Line: The only world band receiver sold by Yaesu, the FRG-8800 is a proven, well-balanced performer in need of tighter selectivity, which can be provided by some world band specialty firms.

 An *RDI WHITE PAPER* is available for this model.

Yaesu's FRG-8800 is a balanced performer that's well established in the marketplace.

Kenwood's R-2000, which features good audio quality, succeeds with clearer world band signals. It is less successful with tough catches.

★ ★ ★ $\frac{1}{2}$

Kenwood R-2000

Price: $799.95 in the United States, CAN$1,049.95 in Canada, under £600 in the United Kingdom, $750-1,250 elsewhere in Europe.

Advantages: Straightforward to operate, with generally good ergonomics. Audio slightly above average for tabletop model. Utility and ham reception, though not outstanding, are at least average within its price class. Superior sensitivity makes model relevant to needs of listeners in places like Western North America and Oceania, where world band signals tend to be weaker. Two 24-hour clocks.

Disadvantages: Mediocre dynamic range materially compromises performance by allowing overloading to take place in many parts of the world, such as Europe and even Eastern North America—especially with high-gain antennas. Wide bandwidth too broad for most world band applications. Keypad uses nonstandard, unhandy layout.

Bottom Line: This model can be quite pleasurable for listening to the major world band stations—especially if you live in Western North America. But for other, more demanding applications, it is in need of tighter selectivity and better dynamic range.

★ ★ $\frac{1}{2}$

Heathkit/Zenith SW-7800

Price: $299.95 in the United States.

Advantages: One of the lowest-priced tabletop models tested. Fairly straightforward to operate. Relatively visible availability in North America through Heath's vast catalog mailings. Kit construction made nigh foolproof by the well-written assembly manual, plus helpful assistance that's available from factory advisors.

Disadvantages: Mediocre performance for a tabletop. Only one true IF bandwidth available; second bandwidth is merely an audio filter. Considerable frequency drift. Barely functional for utility and ham reception. Proliferation of whistles and other spurious signals cause unnecessary interference. Available only in kit form, requiring dozens of hours to construct.

Bottom Line: At this price, the SW-7800 may be attractive, but only *vis-à-vis* increasingly higher-priced Japanese tabletop alternatives . . . or if you insist on buying the only world band radio more or less made in the United States. However, unless kits are your special passion, you should consider instead one of the better portables, such as the Sangean ATS-803A, which provides much better performance for a lot less money.

Heathkit's SW-7800 is a mediocre performer, but is relatively inexpensive. It's only available in kit form.

Sharper Image's Tunemaster Classic Radio—an eyestopper that should come with an earstopper.

★

Tunemaster Classic Radio

Price: $129.00 plus $7.50 shipping in the United States.

Advantages: Eye-catching appearance; styled after a French art-deco radio originally built in the 1940s. Also covers VHF from 110 to 137 and 144-164 MHz. Audio quality at least average. Very inexpensive for a tabletop model, and now $70 less than it was last year.

Disadvantages: No digital frequency display or synthesized tuning circuitry. Coarse analog readout provides virtually no indication of what channel is being tuned. Portions of analog readout misaligned or mislabeled. Lacks any tuning facilities except spongy knob and a fine-tuning knob on the back of the set. Mediocre adjacent-channel selectivity. Poor image rejection. Mediocre dynamic range results in significant overloading when connected to outdoor antenna (comes with no built-in antenna or attenuator). Relatively unstable, making for marginal single-sideband reception. Does not receive longwave.

Bottom Line: What a dog! According to industry reports, once The Sharper Image disposes of its existing Tunemaster inventory, the model will be replaced by a more conventional, digitally tuned world band portable.

The Passport review team: Lawrence Magne, along with Jock Elliott and Tony Jones, with laboratory measurements by Robert Sherwood.

ICOM RECEIVER THAT'S NOT ICOM'S RECEIVER

Nowhere in Icom's line of receivers is there an "ICR7000HF" receiver to be found. But it can be found at the English firm of ARE Communications.

We haven't tested it, but a reliable industry source tells us that it is the Icom IC-R7000 scanner, which normally doesn't cover world band frequencies, coupled to a shortwave converter produced by ARE. Converters are, by dint of their role, limited in the ability to provide first-rate performance.

This source, who has installed an ARE converter in an 'R7000, reports that—aside from the considerable complexities of installation—the result has been disappointing performance within the world band spectrum. The "ICR7000HF" apparently comes with the converter already installed, which eliminates one of the two reported short-comings. (A third may be invalidation of the factory warranty.)

The cost? £989 (around $1,700), plus shipping, for the receiver and converter together as one unit.

WORLD BAND IN YOUR CAR

Wouldn't it be nice if there were a *real* world band car radio? Not a radio designed for "DXing," mind you—after all, chasing faint stations usually requires large antennas, reasonable quiet and considerable concentration. But how about a radio that, after you're done listening to the usual mix of AM and FM stations or your favorite cassettes, would allow you to punch a button or two and wile away the time with the BBC World Service, Deutsche Welle or Radio Japan?

Well, here it is: The $500 Philips DC777. It's a full-blown car stereo designed for in-dash installation, replete with AM, FM, longwave, auto-reverse cassette, power to drive four speakers . . . and world band frequencies from 3200 to 21850 kHz.

Press a single button marked "SW" and you can step through the various world band segments, which are legibly identified in the display as 90m, 60m, and so forth. Then press either the up or down search button, and the DC777 will mute itself, search the band in 5 kHz steps until it locks onto a strong world band station, then turn the sound back on so you can hear it. You can fine tune in 1 kHz increments with a pair of slewing buttons, but that's usually not necessary in the autosearch mode.

Curiously, the DC777 has no tuning knob, but there is direct frequency entry. Press a button on the face of the radio, and a small drawer flops out, presenting a 12-button keypad at a handy 45-degree angle. The clunky ergonomics of the six-over-six keypad don't lend themselves to handy operation while your car is in motion, but the software is designed for a minimum of button-pushing so that a frequency can be entered quickly while you are stopped at a light. If you want the BBC World Service on 6175 kHz, for example, press 6, 1, 7, 5, Enter—*voilà*, there it is.

More conveniently, you can store up to 20 favorite stations in four preselect-button memories. Each stores up to five frequencies, and another button allows you to carousel, one by one, through the four memories. In all, the tuning arrangements of the DC777 acquit themselves well for the driver with urgent business elsewhere and a need to hear world band.

Audio is where the DC777 really shines. When connected to a pair of high-quality speakers, the DC777 produces world band audio that is among the best we have encountered. There were times during our tests when strong world band stations sounded very nearly as good as local AM broadcasters. That the radio excels with strong signals is just as well, as the DC777 has no provision for selecting a narrower filter or sideband mode—options that are virtually necessary for tough-signal reception. The DC777 is a mobile receiver designed to make strong world band stations as accessible as the push buttons on your car radio. As such, it succeeds very well in its mission.

At last, a world band car radio that really works—the Philips DC777.

On the Other Hand . . .

A million years from now, a world band paleontologist digging through the fossils of our civilizations might examine the Icom IC-R100 and conclude that it had taken a different evolutionary path than that of the DC777. While the DC777 is derived from the genus *car radio*, the 'R100 appears to be a close relative of the family *mobile scanner*, but with added world band capabilities.

Designed for in-dash or alongside-the-console installation, the tiny—6 × 2 × 7 in, or 15 × 5 × 18 cm—'R100 covers from 500 kHz to 1.8 GHz in the AM, wide-FM, and narrow-FM modes. Vast as is this tuning range, it does not embrace the longwave broadcasting band found on the Philips DC777. The 'R100 offers a variety of scanning and search functions, as well as 100 memory channels—far more than are on the Philips unit. There's also a tiny and surprisingly good speaker in the bottom of the 'R100, and a plug on the back for connection to an external speaker. However, the 'R100, unlike the Philips unit, does not offer stereo audio or other fidelity-oriented features.

Unlike the Philips unit, which accepts a standard automotive antenna connector, the 'R100 uses a PL-259 connector for a world band antenna and another connector for a VHF/UHF antenna. As with the Philips unit, the 'R100 offers no narrow-band AM or sideband facilities, but the single 6 kHz AM filter does a reasonable job of rejecting adjacent-channel interference. The sensitivity of the 'R100 is good enough for mobile use, but inadequate for a tabletop radio.

On the face of the 'R100 are three knobs—volume, squelch and tuning (adjustable from 1–25 kHz steps)—and a keypad, and herein lies the rub. The 12-button keypad measures just 1.5 × 1.25 in, or about 4 × 3 cm. Each button is obviously quite small and, as fully half the buttons offer up to three different functions, there is writing—tiny writing—both on and above each button. Too, the keypad is in the same plane as the 'R100's face plate so that, if viewed from any angle other than head-on, keypad legibility becomes even worse.

Thus, even though the keypad numerals are in the handy three-by-three-over-one configuration found on most telephones, we found ourselves picking up the receiver so we could read the keypad and press those tiny buttons. As we did so, we found ourselves imagining drivers trying to stick their heads under the dash or in front of the console to squint at the 'R100's buttons as they whiz through rush-hour traffic.

To make matters worse, frequency entry requires more button-pushing than is necessary. To enter the BBC World Service on 6175 kHz, for example, you must press ENT, 6, . (decimal), 1, 7, 5, and ENT again. It takes a steady hand and a high degree of concentration to push those Lilliputian buttons in the right order.

In short, the electrical performance of the 'R100 is adequate for mobile world band reception. The ergonomics, however, are a driver's nightmare.

If you live in the United States or Canada, whether or not to buy this new offering from Icom is moot . . . as it isn't offered there. However, in Europe, Asia and other parts of the world the street price runs from about the equivalent of $700 to around $1,000.

A Final Caveat

If you are considering buying a radio for world band listening in your car, keep in mind that automotive ignition noise is the key factor limiting reception opportunities. Because of this, don't expect to hear more than the major outlets clearly.

Unless, of course, you drive a diesel—in which case you will have only the electrical spark noise from the wiper motors to interfere with your listening.

Icom's new IC-R100 is a driver's nightmare. It's available throughout Europe, but not North America.

WORLDSCAN

WHAT'S ON TONIGHT?

Passport's Hour-by-Hour Guide to World Band Shows

World band radio is like a patchwork quilt—some bits may be a little ragged, but the final product remains a joy. It's all there, news to nostalgia, exotic to exquisite. News, as it breaks and from the source, analysis and actuality. But that's only part. There's also comedy, plays, language lessons (including Arabic and Russian), science, travel, history and music. And what music! From London's Royal Albert Hall to the steppes of Central Asia and virtually all points in between.

Variety abounds. There's always something to be heard, day or night. In fact, there's often so much, the problem is when and where to tune. That is why the *Passport* team prepared this listener's guide.

All shows are listed in World Time, also known as Greenwich Mean Time (GMT), Coordinated Universal Time (UTC), and Zulu Time—all of which is explained elsewhere in this *Passport*. Many world band stations announce it at the beginning of a broadcast, on the hour, or both.

Key channels are given for North America, Western Europe, East Asia and the Pacific, including Australia and New Zealand. Information on secondary and seasonal channels, as well as channels for other parts of the world, may be found in the "Worldwide Broadcasts in English" and Blue Pages sections of this volume.

Unless otherwise noted, "summer" and "winter" refer to seasons in the Northern Hemisphere; readers south of the equator should transpose those items as they occur.

Whatever your taste, with *Passport* as your guide, you'll find plenty to suit you.

EVENING PRIME TIME—NORTH AMERICA
0000

BBC World Service. First, there's the half-hour *Newsdesk,* which includes both international and British news. This is followed by any one of a wide variety of programs, including *The Ken Bruce Show* (Sunday), *Recording of the Week* (Saturday) and *Comedy Show* (Thursday). On other days you can hear such offerings as *In Praise of God* (Monday), *Omnibus* (Wednesday), or *From the Weeklies* (Saturday). Continuous to North America on 5975, 6175, 9590, 9915 and 15260 kHz; to East

---

World band station RTV Italiana, like Venice, may be slowly on the mend. It's widely heard throughout much of Eastern North America and Europe.

Kurt Kroszner

Asia until 0030 on 11945 and 11955 kHz; and to the Pacific until 0030 on 11955 kHz.

Christian Science Monitor World Service, USA. *News* and *News Focus*—news analysis and news-related features with emphasis on international developments. This is followed by *Kaleidoscope*—a program of general human interest. On Saturday (Friday evening in North America), *Home Forum* replaces *Kaleidoscope*. The first part of a two-hour cyclical broadcast repeated throughout the day to various parts of the globe. To North America and Europe Tuesday through Saturday (Monday through Friday, local American date) on 9410 and 9850 kHz.

Kol Israel. *News,* followed by a variety of feature programs—some of which are aired now, others of which can be heard an hour later or, in summer, an hour earlier. Depending on the time of year, features include *Israel Sound* (latest Israeli pop songs), *Studio Three* (arts in Israel), *Shabbat Shalom* (greetings and music requests), *Calling All Listeners* (replies to questions), *DX Corner* (for radio enthusiasts), *Spotlight* (current events), *Spectrum* (science and technology), *With Me in the Studio* (guest interviews), *This Land* (a travel magazine), *Thank Goodness It's Friday* (Sabbath eve program), *Faith to Faith* (religious affairs), *Israel Mosaic* (a weekly magazine), *Letter from Jerusalem, Jewish News Review,* and *Living Here.* Half hour to Eastern North America and Europe on 9435, 9930, 11605 or 15640 kHz.

Spanish Foreign Radio. *News,* followed most days by *Panorama,* which features commentary, a review of the Spanish press, weather, and foreign press comment on matters affecting Spain. Extracts are not restricted to the major international newspapers; there are even quotes from specialized publications like *The Wine Spectator.* The remainder of the program is given over to a mixed bag of literature, science, music and general programming. On weekends the format is varied somewhat, including *Who's Visiting Spain?* and *Radio Club.* Sixty minutes to Eastern North America on 9630 and 11880 kHz.

Radio Canada International. On weekdays during winter, relays the excellent CBC domestic service *news* programs *World at Six* and *As It Happens,* which feature international stories, Canadian news

and general human interest features. On Sunday (Saturday evening in North America), there is *News,* sports and weather, followed by *Innovation Canada* and *SWL Digest.* Mondays are given over to relays of comedy programs from the CBC domestic network—*Royal Canadian Air Farce* and *Double Exposure.* For summer programs, see 0100. To North America on 5960 and 9755 kHz.

Radio Moscow—North American Service. The second hour of a two-hour cyclical broadcast. *News,* followed by *Outlook,* a series of editorial features and commentary. There are then various *ad hoc* features, as well as regulars like *Newmarket, Home in the USSR, People,* and *Science and Engineering.* Just dial around to find a clear frequency. An hour earlier in the summer.

Radio Yugoslavia. Summers only at this time. *News,* followed by features (see 2100). Forty-five minutes to Eastern North America on 7215, 9620, 11735 and 15105 kHz.

Radio Prague International, Czechoslovakia. *News,* followed by information on Czechoslovak political and cultural happenings. Fifteen minutes to North America on 7345, 11680 and 11990 kHz.

Radio Sofia, Bulgaria. Winters only at this time. *News,* followed by commentary in *Events and Developments* or *Balkan Panorama.* This, in turn, is followed by such features as *Cultural Scene, Mailbag, DX Corner,* and *Across the Map of Bulgaria,* plus a fair helping of lively Bulgarian music. One hour to Eastern North America on 9700, 11660, 11680 or 11720 kHz.

Radio Finland. Winters only at this time. Repeat of the 0730 transmission. To North America on 9645 and 11755 kHz.

Radio Pyongyang, North Korea. See 1100 for program details. Fifty minutes to the Americas on 15115 and 15160 kHz.

Radio Korea, South Korea. The hourlong broadcast opens with *news,* followed on most days by commentary, *Seoul Calling* (magazine format), *Let's Learn Korean!,* and features like *Korean Cultural Variety* (Wednesday) and *Pulse of Korea* (Thursday). On other days, the news is followed by features such as *Sites and Sounds* (Sunday) and *Echoes of Korean Music* (Monday). To North America on 15575 kHz.

Voice of America. First hour of VOA's two-hour broadcasts to the Caribbean and

Latin America. *News,* followed by split programming Tuesday through Sunday. Listeners in the Caribbean can tune in to *Caribbean Report* followed by *Music, U.S.A.,* except for Sunday (Saturday evening in the Americas), when *Press Conference, U.S.A.* is aired. For Latin America there is *Newsline* and Special English news and features. On Monday the programs are the same for both services—*Encounter* and *Studio One.* An excellent way to keep in touch with events in the western hemisphere. The service to the Caribbean is on 6130, 9455 and 11695 kHz; the service to the Americas is on 5995, 9775, 9815, 11580, and 15205 kHz. The final hour of a separate service to East Asia (see 2200) can be heard on 9770, 11760, 11775, 15185, 15290 and 17735 kHz.

Radio Beijing, China. *News,* followed by *News About China,* then *Current Affairs.* There are then various feature programs, such as *Culture in China* (Friday), *Listeners' Letterbox* (Monday/Wednesday), *Travel Talk* (Sunday), *Cooking Show* (Sunday) or *In the Third World* (Saturday). The highly recommended *Music from China* is aired Sunday (local Saturday evening in the Americas). One hour to Eastern North America winters on 9665, 9770 and 11715 kHz; summers on 15100, 17705 and 17855 kHz.

Radio Habana Cuba. The start of a two-hour cyclical broadcast to North America. *News,* followed by such feature programs as *Newsbreak* (daily except Monday), *Spotlight on Latin America* (Tuesday through Saturday), *DXers Unlimited* (Sunday), *Dateline Havana* (Monday), or *The Jazz Place* (Monday). Some good Cuban and Caribbean music. To Eastern North America on 11820 kHz.

WRNO, New Orleans, USA. This station broadcasts mostly rock music, plus a little jazz. Offerings to date have included *Crusin' America, Rock Over London, Profiles of Rock Stars,* and NBC's *The Jazz Show.* To North America throughout much of the evening on 7355 kHz.

Radio Luxembourg, Luxembourg. Rock music and some religious programs for three hours each evening. Audible in the United Kingdom, Continental Europe—and sometimes Eastern North America, as well—on 6090 kHz.

Radio Kiev, Ukrainian SSR. Winters only at this time; see 2000 for program

details, although all programs air one day later. One hour directed to Eastern North America on various frequencies, including 7400, 9765, 15180 and 17665 kHz.

0030

Radio Nederland. *News,* followed by *Newsline,* a current affairs program. There is then a different feature each night, including *Research File* (Tuesday; science), *Rembrandt Express* (a Saturday magazine program), *Images* (Wednesday; arts in Holland), or *Over to You* (Sunday)—a listener response program. Monday (Sunday evening local time in North America) are devoted to *The Happy Station,* an ever-popular program of chat, letters and light music. This has the distinction of being the longest-running program on radio, having begun in the 1920s. Fifty-five minutes to Eastern North America on 6020, 6165 and 15315 kHz.

Belgische Radio en Televisie, Belgium. Winters only at this time; see 1730 for program details, although are one day later. To Eastern North America for 25 minutes on 9925 or 13675 kHz.

Radio Budapest, Hungary. This time Tuesday through Sunday winters; daily in summer. *Newsroom,* followed by interviews, features and music. Unlike most stations, Radio Budapest's regularly scheduled feature programs are aired several times a month, rather than on a weekly basis. The exceptions are *Sportarama* (Tuesday), *The Weeklies* (Thursday), and *168 Hours*—a look at events of the week just past—on Saturday. All this from the country which some experts have called "the most Westernized of the Eastern Bloc nations." To Eastern North America on 6110, 9520, 9585, 9835, 11910 and 15160 kHz.

HCJB, Ecuador. *Studio 9,* featuring five minutes of Latin American *news,* followed Tuesday through Saturday (Monday through Friday, local American date) by 15 minutes of in-depth *news,* current affairs, interviews and features. On Sunday (Saturday evening in the Americas) the Latin American news is followed by a science program, *Focus 2000,* which in turn is replaced Monday by *Get Set*—a program of interviews and features from the world of sports. The final portion of *Studio 9* is given over to one of a variety of 30-minute features—including *Saludos Amigos* (Monday),

Dateline (Tuesday), *Happiness Is* (Wednesday), *Música del Ecuador* (Saturday) and programs for radio enthusiasts—plus a five-minute bulletin of world *news*. To North America on 9745, 11795, 15155 or 17875 kHz.

0050

Vatican Radio. Each weekday at this time, the station looks at issues in the news and how they affect Catholics around the world. It also analyzes the role of the Church in coping with events, as well as the involvement of the Church, priests and the laity in these matters. Different programs are aired on weekends. Twenty-five minutes to Eastern North America on 9605, 11780 and 15180 kHz.

0100

BBC World Service. *News Summary*, followed on Tuesday through Saturday (weekday evening in North America) by *Outlook*, a program of news and human-interest stories, and *Financial News*. These are succeeded by one or more of a variety of feature programs, including *Society Today* (Thursday), *Waveguide* (Thursday), *Short Story* (Thursday), *Europe's World* (Tuesday) and *Global Concerns* (Friday). On Sunday and Monday (weekends in North America), look for longer drama, music and book reviews. Continuous to North America on 5975, 6175, 9590, 9915 and 12095 or 15260 kHz.

Christian Science Monitor World Service, USA. Continuation of 0100 broadcast to North America and Europe. *News*, then *One Norway Street*—a wide variety of features drawn mainly from the United States—replaced Wednesday (Tuesday evening in the Americas) by *Curtain Call*, a music program, and on Friday by *Encore*, reruns of earlier features. The final half hour includes *Letterbox*—a listener response program. Tuesday through Friday on 9410 and 9850 kHz.

Kol Israel. *News* at the top of the hour, then various feature programs (see 0000). A half hour to Eastern North America and Europe on 9435, 9930, 11605 or 15640 kHz.

Radio Canada International. Winters only. Weekday programming (Tuesday through Saturday World Time) consists of the final 30 minutes of *As It Happens* (see 0000). The broadcasts are extended to one hour at the weekend, and include *Coast to Coast* (Saturday), *Spotlight on Science* (Friday), *L'Attitude* (Thursday) and *Listeners' Corner* (Monday). One hour earlier in summer. To North America on 5960 and 9755 kHz.

Radio Japan. One hour to Eastern North America summers only on 5960 kHz via the powerful relay facilities of Radio Canada International in Sackville, New Brunswick, Canada. See 0300 for program details—all programs are one day later.

Spanish Foreign Radio. Repeat of the 0000 transmission. To Eastern North America on 9630 and 11880 kHz.

Radio Moscow—North American Service. *News*, followed by feature programs, including *Top Priority*, *Moscow Mailbag*, *Home in the USSR*, *Science and Engineering*, *Actuality*, and *Sidelights on Soviet Life*. This basic programming is supplemented by interviews, reports and music. Just dial around—you'll find it! An hour earlier in the summer.

Radio Habana Cuba. See 0000 for program details. Continues to North America on 11820 kHz.

Radio Yugoslavia. Winters only at this time. *News*, with concentration on events in Eastern Europe. This is followed by commentary and one of several feature programs, including *Sidewalk Rock* (Saturday; popular music in the Third World), *Science and Ecology Report* (Friday), and *Spotlight on Culture* (Thursday). Unbiased reporting, but presentation somewhat dry. Usually good reception in North America. Forty-five minutes to Eastern North America on 5980, 7215, 9620 and 11735 kHz.

Voice of America. *News*, then *Report to the Americas*, a series of news features about the United States and other countries in the Americas. This is replaced Sunday by *Weekend Magazine*, and Monday by *New Horizons* and *Issues in the News*. To the Americas on 5995, 6130, 9455, 9775, 9815, 11580 and 15205 kHz.

Deutsche Welle, West Germany. *News*, followed weekdays by the relatively recent—but excellent—*European Journal*, which includes commentary, interviews, background reports and analysis. The broadcast ends with *Transatlantic Diary*, a look at cultural, scientific, economic and bilateral developments. Sunday (Saturday night in North America) is given over to *Commentary, Mailbag* (or *Phone in*) and *German by Radio* ; while the Monday broadcast features *Living in Germany* and Larry Wayne's ever-popular *Random Selection.* Very good reception in North America on 6040, 6085, 6145, 9565, 9735 and 11865 or 15105 kHz.

KUSW, Salt Lake City, USA. Mostly popular music and regional weather reports, plus *news* five minutes before the hour. Well-heard throughout the evening Thursday–Sunday (Wednesday–Saturday in North America); on 11695 or 15590 kHz.

0130

Radio Austria International. *Report from Austria,* which includes a brief bulletin of *news* followed by a series of current events and human interest stories. Domestic topics are amply covered, and there is also substantial information about events in Eastern Europe. Twenty-five minutes to North America on 9870, 9875 and 13730 kHz.

HCJB, Ecuador. Sixty minutes of mainly religious programming. *Musical Mailbag*—a listener response program—is featured Sunday (Saturday evening in the Americas) at 0130. To North America on 9745, 11795, 15155 or 17875 kHz.

Voice of Greece. Preceded, and to a lesser extent followed, by lots of delightful Greek music, plus news and features in Greek. There's a ten-minute English *newscast,* more or less at 0130, heard daily except Sunday (Saturday evening local North American date). To Eastern North America on 7430 or 11645 kHz, plus 9395 and 9420 kHz.

Radio Budapest, Hungary. Winters only. See 0030 for program details. To Eastern North America on 6110, 9520, 9835, 11910 and 15160 kHz.

0145

BBC World Service for Asia. Thirty minutes of special programming to Asia. In addition to regular programs like *Newsreel* and *The World Today,* check out *South Asia Survey* (Saturday). Audible in North America and the Pacific as well, on 7135, 9580, 11955 and 15380 kHz.

0200

BBC World Service. *News,* followed by *British Press Review.* These are succeeded, on different days of the week, by a variety of features, including *Network UK* (Tuesday, Thursday and Saturday), *Health Matters* (Wednesday), *Andy Kershaw's World of*

Music (Monday), *People and Politics* (Saturday), *Album Time,* a dramatized novel, *Science in Action* (Monday), *Sports International* (Tuesday), and *Assignment* (Thursday). Continuous to North America on 5975, 6175, 9590 (to 0230), 9915 and 15260 kHz.

BBC World Service for Asia. Continuation of the 0145 broadcast. On 7135, 9580, 11955 and 15380 kHz.

Christian Science Monitor World Service, USA. See 0000 for program details. To North America and Europe Tuesday through Friday on 9455 kHz, and Monday through Friday on 9850 kHz.

Radio Nacional do Brasil (Radiobras), Brazil. Brazilian *news,* followed by abundant examples of the wide variety of musical styles for which the country is rightly famous. From the bossa nova to the blues, you are unlikely to hear as rich a collection of sounds anywhere on world band radio. The music is interspersed with short features on Brazilian folklore, cultural events, contemporary Brazil, tourist attractions, and the like. The talk and music often complement each other very nicely. A pleasant 50 minutes to North America on 11745 kHz.

Radio Cairo. A potpourri of exotic Arab music and features reflecting Egyptian life and culture, with *news* and commentary about events in Egypt and the Arab world, including the Palestinian question. On a lighter level, there are quizzes and answers to listeners' questions. Ninety minutes of fair reception in North America on 9475 and 9675 kHz.

Voice of America. *News,* then *Focus—* an examination of the major issues of the day. Thirty minutes to the Americas, Tuesday through Saturday, on 5995, 9775, 9815, 11580 and 15205 kHz.

Radio Argentina al Exterior—R.A.E. Similar to the 1900 transmission. To North America Tuesday through Saturday (Monday through Friday local American days) on 11710 kHz.

Voice of Free China, Taiwan. *News* and commentary focusing on events in China, then three different features. The last is *Let's Learn Chinese,* which has a series of segments for beginners, intermediate and advanced learners. Other features include the *Republic of China Today* (Tuesday), *Jade Bells and Bamboo Pipes* (Thursday) and *Journey into Chinese Culture* (Saturday). One hour to North and Central

America on 5950, 9680 and 11740 kHz; and to the Pacific on 9765 kHz.

Kol Israel. Winters only at this time. *News,* followed by various features (see 0000). A half hour to North America on 9435, 9930, and 11605 kHz.

Radio Moscow—North American Service. Continuation of the evening transmission to North America, and repeat of 0000 broadcast. On numerous frequencies—simply dial about. An hour earlier in summer.

Radio Habana Cuba. Repeat of the 0000 transmission. To North America on 9710 and 11820 kHz.

Swiss Radio International. *News* and *Dateline* (except Monday)—a thoroughly workmanlike compilation of news and analysis of world and Swiss events. On Sunday, the last 15 minutes air *Swiss Shortwave Merry-go-Round,* which answers technical questions sent in by listeners; Monday are devoted alternately to *Supplement, Roundabout Switzerland* and *The Grapevine,* a listeners' contact program where humor plays a major role. A half hour to North America on 6095, 6135, 9650 or 9725, 9885, 12035 and 17730 kHz.

KUSW, Salt Lake City, USA. Continuous with popular music, *news* and weather Thursday–Sunday (Wednesday–Saturday evenings in North America) to North America on 11695 or 15590 kHz.

Radio Romania International. *News,* then commentary. This is followed by several feature programs, including *Youth Club, Friendship and Cooperation,* and *The Skylark*—a charming selection of Romanian folk songs. To North America on 5990, 9510, 9570, 11830 and 11940 kHz.

"Radio Free America," WWCR, Nashville, Tennessee. This time summers only, see 0300 for details.

0230

Radio Tirana, Albania. *News,* followed by commentary and different feature programs for each day of the week. These include such self-explanatory titles as *Marxism–Leninism—An Ever Young and Scientific Doctrine* (Monday), *Leafing Through the Marxist–Leninist Press* (Tuesday), and *Leafing Through the Albanian Calendar* (Tuesday). If you are interested, tune in before autumn! To North America on 9500, 9760 or 11825 kHz.

Radio Portugal. *News*—which usually takes up at least half the broadcast—followed by feature programs, including Thursday's *The Challenge of '92,* a look at the problems facing Portugal as it prepares for a unified European market. There are no broadcasts on Sunday or Monday (Saturday and Sunday evening local North American dates). Only fair reception in Eastern North America—worse to the west—on 9600, 9680, 9705 and 11840 kHz.

Radio Sweden. Repeat of the 1530 transmission. Thirty minutes to North America on 9695 (or 15295) and 11705 kHz.

HCJB, Ecuador. Repeat of the 0030 transmission of *Studio 9.* Good reception throughout North America on 11775, 11795, 15155 or 17875.

0250

Radio Yerevan, Armenian SSR. Summers only at this time. English consists solely of up to four minutes of *news* of interest mainly to Armenians abroad. To North America on 11675, 11790, 13645, 15180 and 15485 kHz.

0300

BBC World Service. *News,* then *News About Britain,* followed daily except Monday at 0315 by news analysis on *The World Today* or *From Our Own Correspondent.* Apart from Wednesday, when *Discovery* is aired, the next half hour is taken up by music, quiz shows or religion. Continuous to North America on 5975, 6175 and 9915 kHz; to early risers in parts of Western Europe on 6195, 9410 and sometimes 12095 kHz; and to East Asia on 15280 and 21715 kHz.

Christian Science Monitor World Service, USA. See 0100 for program details. Continuation of transmission to North America and Europe Tuesday through Friday on 9455 kHz, and Monday through Friday on 9850 kHz.

Voice of Free China, Taiwan. Similar to the 0200 transmission, but with the same programs broadcast on different days of the week. To North and Central America on 5950 and 9680 kHz; to East Asia on 15345 kHz; and to the Pacific on 9765 kHz.

Radio Beijing, China. Repeat of the 0000 transmission. To North America on 9690, 9770, 11715, 15100, or 17855 kHz.

Deutsche Welle, West Germany. Repeat of the 0100 transmission. To North America on 6085, 6130, 9545, 9605, 11810 or 15205 kHz.

Radio Moscow—North American Service. Continuous to North America throughout the evening on numerous frequencies. Repeat of 0100 broadcast. An hour earlier in summer.

Radio Habana Cuba. Repeat of the 0100 transmission; see 0000 for program details. To North America on 9710 and 11820 kHz.

KUSW, Salt Lake City, USA. Continuous with popular music, *news* and weather Thursday–Sunday (Wednesday–Saturday evenings in North America) to North America on 9815 kHz.

Radio Japan. On most days *news,* followed by *Radio Japan Magazine Hour,* an umbrella for features like *Out and Around* (Tuesday–Thursday), *Asia Contact* (Wednesday) and *Music Mix* (Friday). Saturday, it's an hour of *This Week,* with *DX Corner* on Sunday. News and commentary round out the broadcast. One hour winters to Eastern North America on 5960 kHz. There is also a separate year-round broadcast to the Americas, consisting of *News,* followed by *Let's Learn Japanese* or a feature program. Thirty minutes on 15325, 17825 and 21610 kHz.

Voice of Turkey. Summers only at this time. *News* and press review, followed by such arcane offerings as *Turkish Art in Anatolia* (Monday) and *Kemal Ataturk and Contemporary Turkey* (Wednesday). Probably more to the liking of the average listener is the feature *Turkey's World of Culture,* aired Saturday (Friday evening in the Americas). Fifty minutes to North America on 9445 kHz, and to the Pacific (also heard in Western North America) on 17760 or 17880 kHz.

Radio Prague International, Czechoslovakia. *News,* followed by information on Czechoslovakia's democracy, as well as environmental and cultural happenings in the country. Thirty minutes to North America on 5930, 7345 and 11680 kHz.

"Radio Free America," WWCR, Nashville, Tennessee. Nearly 20 years ago, the fiery conservative preacher, Rev. Carl McIntire, took to the airwaves for one day from an unlicensed offshore station, "Radio Free America." Now, a talk show not affiliated with McIntire, but decidedly to the populist right—"the international banking conspiracy" is among the topics—is aired under that same name via the facilities of WWCR. Hosted by Tom Valentine, it's heard in North America Tuesday through Saturday (Monday through Friday evenings, local American date) for two hours from 0300 winters, 0200 summers, on 7520 kHz.

0315

Radio France Internationale. *News*, then a review of the French press, followed by such feature programs as *Land of France* (Wednesday), *Drum Beat* (Monday), *Science Notes* (Friday), *Development Magazine* (Tuesday) and *Press Comment on Africa* (Thursday). Thirty minutes on 9800 or 11670 kHz.

0330

Radio Tirana, Albania. *News* and commentary, then features in the same mould as the 0230 broadcast, although not necessarily the same ones. To North America on 9500, 9760 or 11825 kHz.

HCJB, Ecuador. See 0130 for program details. One hour of religion to North America on 11775, 11795, 15155 or 17875 kHz.

United Arab Emirates Radio, Dubai. Similar to the transmission at 1330, but on 11940 and 15435 kHz. Heard best in North America during the warm-weather months. See 1330 transmission for program details.

Why do Greeks converse so excitedly over *ouzo*? Thanks to the Voice of Greece, you can find out during English segments sandwiched between oodles of music and yet more of that Greek chitchat.

Radio Nederland. Repeat of the 0030 transmission. Fifty-five minutes to North America on 6165 and 9590 kHz.

United Arab Emirates Radio, Dubai. News, followed by a feature on Arab life, history or culture. Thirty minutes to North America on 11940, 15400, 15435 and 17890 kHz.

BBC World Service for Africa. The BBC World Service for Africa airs excellent special programs for and about that continent, which otherwise tends to be poorly covered by the international media. Although this special BBC service is beamed only to Africa, it can sometimes be heard in other parts of the world, as well. Try 3255, 6005, 6190, 9600, 11740 or 15420 kHz.

Voice of Greece. Repeat of the 0130 transmission. Ten minutes of English, surrounded by long periods of Greek music and programming, to North America, except Sunday (Saturday evening local American date), on 9395, 9420 and 11645 kHz.

0350

Radio Yerevan, Armenian SSR. Winters only at this time. English consists solely of up to four minutes of *news* of interest mainly to Armenians abroad. To North America on 7400, 9765, 15180 and 17665 kHz.

0400

BBC World Service. Starting off the hour is *Newsdesk*, which airs both international and British news. This is usually followed by a first-rate musical or drama-reading feature program, such as Saturday's *Here's Humph* jazz show and *Andy Kershaw's World of Music* on Thursday. Continuous to North America and the Pacific on 5975 kHz; to Western Europe on 3955, 6195, 9410 and 12095 kHz; and to East Asia on 15280 and 21715 kHz.

Christian Science Monitor World Service, USA. See 0000 for program details. Tuesday through Friday to North America on 9455 kHz; Monday through Friday to Europe on 9840 kHz, and to East Asia on 17780 kHz.

Radio Habana Cuba. Repeat of the 0000 broadcast. To North America on 5965, 9710, 11760 and 11820 kHz.

Swiss Radio International. Repeat of

the 0200 transmission. To North America on 6135, 9725, 9885 and 12035 kHz.

Voice of America. Directed to Europe and North Africa 0400-0700, but widely heard elsewhere. *News*, followed Monday through Friday by *Morning Newsline* and *VOA Morning*—a conglomeration of popular music, interviews, human interest stories, science digest, sports news, and so on, with news summaries at the half hour. On weekends, the *news* is followed by either *Saturday Morning* or *Sunday Morning*. Not the most original of titles, but at least you'll know on which day of the week you're listening. On 5995, 6040, 7170, 7200 and 9740 kHz.

Radio Beijing, China. Repeat of the 0000 transmission; to North America on 11685 or 11695 kHz plus, summers only, 11840 kHz.

Radio Romania International. An abbreviation of the 0200 transmission, beginning with national and international *news* and commentary, then the feature program from the first half hour of the 0200 broadcast. To North America on 5990, 9510, 9570, 11830 and 11940 kHz.

Kol Israel. Summers only at this time. News for 15 minutes from Israel Radio's domestic network. To Europe and North America on 9435, 11605, 11655, 12077 and 15640 kHz, and to Asia and the Pacific on 17630 kHz.

KUSW, Salt Lake City, USA. Winters only at this time. Continuous, usually with popular music, *news* and weather, Thursday–Sunday (Wednesday–Saturday evenings in North America) to North America on 9815 kHz.

Voice of Turkey. Winters only at this time. See 0300 for program details. To North America for fifty minutes on 9445 kHz, and to the Pacific on 17760 or 17880 kHz.

Radio Moscow—North American Service. *News*, then a continuation of Moscow's evening transmissions to North America. Good reception on a broad variety of frequencies.

"Radio Free America," WWCR, Nashville, Tennessee. This time winters only. See 0300 for details.

0430

BBC World Service for Africa. See 0330. Try 3255, 6005, 6190, 9600, 15400 or 15420 kHz.

0500

BBC World Service. *News,* then *Twenty-Four Hours,* which is one of many of the BBC's in-depth news analysis programs. This is followed by *Financial News, Words of Faith,* and another news-analysis program—*The World Today.* The latter is replaced Sunday by Alistair Cooke's ubiquitous *Letter from America* and Monday by *Recording of the Week.* Continuous to North America and the Pacific on 5975 kHz; to Western Europe on 3955, 6195, 7120, 9410 and 12095 kHz; and to East Asia on 15280 and 21715 kHz.

Christian Science Monitor World Service, USA. See 0100 for program details. Tuesday through Friday to North America on 9455 kHz; Monday through Friday to Europe on 9840 kHz, and to East Asia on 17780 kHz.

Deutsche Welle, West Germany. Repeat of the 0100 transmission to North America, but on 5960, 6120, 9670 and 11705 kHz.

HCJB, Ecuador. Repeat of 0030 transmission. To North America on any two of the following: 6230, 9745, 11775, 11795, 15155 and 17875 kHz.

Spanish Foreign Radio. Repeat of the 0000 and 0100 transmissions to North America, but on 9630 kHz only.

Voice of America. Continues with the morning broadcast to Europe and North Africa on the same frequencies as at 0400, plus 11925 and 15205 kHz.

Voice of Nigeria. Usually clearer in winter than in summer, but never brilliant. Opens with *Jamboree* (African popular music and mailbag), followed by *news,* editorials, commentary and more music until 0700, when the station begins its broadcast in other languages. Two hours on 7255 kHz.

Kol Israel. Winters only at this time. *News* for 15 minutes from Kol Israel's domestic network. To Europe and North America on 7460, 9435, 11588, 11655 and 15485 kHz, and to Asia and the Pacific on 17630 kHz.

Radio Beijing, China. This time winters only. Repeat of the 0000 transmission; to North America on 11840 kHz.

Radio Moscow—North American Service. Continuation of the transmission beamed to the west coast of North America. Tune around to find the best of the numerous Moscow frequencies.

Radio Habana Cuba. Repeat of the

0100 transmission; see 0000 for program details. Well-heard throughout North and Central America on 5965, 11760 or 11820 kHz.

KUSW, Salt Lake City, USA. Weekends only at this time. Similar programming—popular music, *news* and weather—as on weekdays. To North America Sundays (Saturday evenings in North America) only on 9870 kHz.

WHRI, Indiana, USA. WHRI, although a religious broadcaster, carries some secular programs. Weekdays at 0500 it's *The Mediator,* a look at Hollywood. This is followed, after religious programming, at 0530 by *Passport International,* information on various countries. To North America (sometimes heard in Europe) on 7315 and 9495 kHz.

0515

Radio Canada International. Summers only at this time. See 0615 for program details. To Western Europe and Africa on 6050, 6150, 7295, 9750, 11775 and 17840 kHz.

0530

Radio Austria International. *Report from Austria;* see 0130 for more details. To North America on 6015 kHz.

United Arab Emirates Radio, Dubai. See 0330 for program details. To East Asia and the Pacific on 15435, 17830 and 21700 kHz.

EVENING PRIME TIME—EAST ASIA AND THE PACIFIC
0600

BBC World Service. *Newsdesk,* followed by such diverse features as *Meridian* (Wednesday, Friday and Saturday; an arts show), *Jazz for the Asking* (Sunday), *Counterpoint* and dramatized novels. Continuous to North America on 5975 and 9640 kHz; to Western Europe on 3955, 6195, 7120, 9410 and 12095 kHz; to East Asia on 15280, 15360 and 21715 kHz; and to the Pacific on 5975, 7150, 9640, 11955 and either 17710 or 17830 kHz.

Christian Science Monitor World Service, USA. See 0000 for program details. Monday through Friday to North America on 9455 and 11980 kHz; to Europe on 9840 kHz; and to East Asia on 17780 kHz.

Radio New Zealand International. The first half of a two-hour package beamed to the Pacific, but often heard in North America as well. *News* airs on the hour, followed much of the year (otherwise one hour earlier) by features like *Drum Beat* (Monday), *The Kiwi Countdown* (Wednesday), and the *Totally Kiwi Music Show* (Sunday). Listen for sports on Saturday. On 17675 (or 17680) kHz.

Radio Habana Cuba. Repeat of the 0000 transmission. To Western North America on 11835 kHz.

Voice of America. Final hour of the transmission to Europe and North Africa. See 0400 for program details. On 6040, 6060, 6095, 7170, 7200, 7325 and 15205 kHz.

Radio Moscow—North American Service. Another hour of programming to the west coast of North America. Available on a variety of frequencies—just turn the dial.

KUSW, Salt Lake City, USA. Part of the evening-long broadcast to North America, but featuring at this time *Music and the Spoken Word,* which reportedly is the longest-running continuous program in the U.S. Too, the Mormon Tabernacle choir sings classic songs, as well as religious favorites. Heard Sunday only on 9870 kHz.

HCJB, Ecuador. See 0130. Additionally, *Music in the Night* can be heard Monday, Wednesday and Friday at 0600. To North America on any two of the following: 6230, 9745, 11775, 11795, 15155 or 17875 kHz.

0615

Radio Canada International. Winters only. Forty-five minutes of programming produced by the domestic Canadian Broadcasting System. First, there's *news,* sports, weather and stock market report. At around 0630 there's *The Inside Track* (Monday; sports), *The Food Show* (Tuesday), *Open House* (Wednesday), *Media File* (Thursday), or *The Arts Tonight* (Friday). To Western Europe and Africa, Monday through Friday, on 6050, 6150, 7155, 9760, 9740 and 11840 kHz.

0630

BBC World Service for Africa. See 0330. Try 6190, 9600, 11940 or 15400 kHz.

Radio Finland. Summers only at this time. See 0730 winter transmission for program details. Twenty-five minutes to Europe on 6120, 9560 and 11755 kHz.

Swiss Radio International. Summers only at this time. See 0830 for program details. To Europe on 3985, 6165 and 9535 kHz.

Radio Sofia, Bulgaria. Summers only at this time. An abbreviated version of the 2300 broadcast to North America, concentrating on *news* and commentary. To Europe on 11720, 15160 and 17825 kHz.

Belgische Radio en Televisie, Belgium. Summers only at this time. Weekdays, there's *news,* followed by *Belgium Today*—a magazine program—and features like *Tourism in Flanders* (Monday) and *Around the Arts* (Wednesday). On weekends, features include *Record of the Week* (Saturday) and *The Fourth Community* (Sunday; on English speakers in Belgium). To Europe on 6035 and 13675 kHz; to the Pacific on 11695 kHz.

0645

Ghana Broadcasting Corporation. Designed for listeners in neighboring countries, so reception is marginal—especially during the summer months. The broadcast begins with West African music, followed by *news,* then a further serving of lively African rhythms. On 6130 kHz.

0700

BBC World Service. *News,* followed by the in-depth news program *Twenty-Four Hours.* Shows that are usually oriented to current events follow at 0730, except Thursday, when Keith Hindell's *Mediawatch* rotates with the listener-correspondence show *Write On . . .,* hosted by Britain's popular sportscaster Paddy Feeny. Continuous to North America on 9640 kHz; to Europe on 7325, 9410, 12095 and 15070 kHz; to East Asia on 15360 and 21715 kHz; and to the Pacific on 7150, 9640, 11955 and 17710 or 17830 kHz.

Radio New Zealand International. Continuation of the 0600 broadcast, on 17675 (or 17680) kHz.

Christian Science Monitor World Service, USA. See 0100 for program details. Monday through Friday to North America on 9455 and 11980 kHz; to Europe

on 9840 kHz; and to East Asia on 17780 kHz.

Radio Australia. Part of a 24-hour service to Asia and the Pacific, but which can also be heard at this time in parts of Western Europe and North America. World and Australian *news* is followed—most days—by *Music of RA,* then any one of a number of features, including *Monitor* (Tuesday; science), *One World* (Saturday; the environment), *Science File* (Thursday), *Innovations* (Friday) and *World of Country Music* (Sunday). To East Asia on 17715 kHz. Best bet for North America is 21740 kHz (to 0730), and in Europe try 15240 kHz.

Radio Habana Cuba. Repeat of the 0100 transmission; see 0000 for program details. To Western North America on 11835 kHz.

Radio Moscow—North American Service. Winters only. The final 60-minute broadcast to the west coast of North America. On a variety of frequencies—just tune around.

Voice of Free China, Taiwan. Repeat of the 0200 transmission. To North America on 5950 kHz.

HCJB, Ecuador. Thirty minutes of religious programming—except for Saturday, when *Musical Mailbag* is on the air—followed by the hour-long *Studio 9.* See 0030 for program details, except that weekend variations are on Saturday and Sunday (rather than Sunday and Monday). To Europe on 9610, 11835 or 15270 kHz; and to the Pacific (from 0730) on 9745 and 11925 kHz.

0730

Radio Finland. Winters only at this time. Finnish and Nordic *news,* followed by a press review. Tuesday through Saturday there's *Northern Report.* Feature programs include *Names in the News* (Friday), *Out and About* (Saturday), *Sports Fare* (Wednesday) and *Learning Finnish* (Thursday). Twenty-five minutes to Europe on 6120, 9560 and 11755 kHz.

Radio Prague International, Czechoslovakia. *News,* followed by information on Czechoslovakia's democracy, as well as environmental and cultural happenings in the country. Thirty minutes to Asia and the Pacific on 17840 and 21705 kHz.

Radio Nederland. *News,* followed by *Newsline* and a variety of features (see

0030; all features are one day earlier). Fifty-five minutes to Australasia on 9630 and 9715 or 15560 kHz.

Swiss Radio International. Winters only at this time. See 0830 for program details. To Europe on 3985, 6165 and 9535 kHz.

Radio Sofia, Bulgaria. Winters only at this time. An abbreviated version of the 0000 broadcast to North America. Less music, and more accent on *news* and commentary. To Europe on 11720, 15160 and 17825 kHz.

BBC World Service for Africa. See 0330. To 0800 on 9600, 11860 and 15105 kHz.

Belgische Radio en Televisie, Belgium. Winters at this time. See 0630 for program details. To Europe on 6035 and 13675 kHz; to the Pacific on 11695 kHz.

0800

BBC World Service. *News,* then the religious *Words of Faith,* followed by a wide variety of programming depending on the day of the week. Choice programs include *Music for a While with Richard Baker* (Sunday), *Anything Goes* (Monday), *Health Matters* (Tuesday), and *Music Review* (Friday). Starting time may be either 0815 or 0830. Continuous to Western Europe on 7325, 9410, 12095 and 15070 kHz; to East Asia on 15360 and 21715 kHz; and to the Pacific on 11955 and 17710 or 17830 kHz.

Christian Science Monitor World Service, USA. See 0000 for program details. Monday through Friday to North America on 9455 kHz; to Europe on 9840 or 11705 kHz; to East Asia on 9530 and 17780 kHz; and to the Pacific on 13760 kHz.

KNLS, Alaska, USA. Although a religious station, KNLS has some interesting secular fare on offer—such as *American Magazine,* part of the broadcast on Wednesday and Friday. Best of all, though, is the weekday program *The Swinging Years*—world band radio's most reliable source of Big Band music. To East Asia, but also well-heard in parts of North America, winters on 7355 or 7365 kHz, and summers on 9840 or 11715 kHz.

Radio Australia. Begins with *International Report,* followed Monday through Friday by *Stock Exchange Report,* then the daily Sports Report. The hour is rounded off (except for Sunday and Thursday, when

there are lottery results) with a 10-minute music program. Good reception in East Asia on 17715 kHz. Listeners in North America can tune in on 9580 kHz, while those in Europe can try 15240 kHz.

Radio Finland. Summers only at this time; see 0730 for program details. To East Asia and the Pacific on 17795 (or 17800) and 21550 kHz.

Radio Korea, South Korea. See 0000 for program details, although all programs air one day earlier. To Europe on 7550 and 13670 kHz.

0830

Radio Finland. Summers only at this time; see 0730 for program details. To East Asia on 17800 and 21550 kHz.

HCJB, Ecuador. Continues with religious programming to the Pacific on 9745 and 11925 kHz.

Swiss Radio International. *News,* then *Dateline* (except Sunday). On Saturday, the last 15 minutes are given over to the technically oriented *Swiss Shortwave Merry-go-Round;* Sunday is devoted to *Supplement, Roundabout Switzerland* or *The Grapevine*—a listener participation program. Thirty minutes to East Asia and the Pacific on 9560, 13685, 17670 and 21695 kHz.

Radio Nederland. A 25-five minute weekday program of news and current events, beamed to Australia and the Pacific on 9770 kHz.

0900

BBC World Service. *News, British Press Review* and news analysis, including *The World Today,* plus financial and sports news most days to 0945. The final 15 minutes is rather a mixed bag, with most listeners opting for Sunday's *Short Story,* Monday's *Andy Kershaw's World of Music,* or Saturday's *World Brief.* Continuous to Western Europe on 6045, 7325, 9750, 9760, 12095, 15070 and 17640 kHz; to East Asia on 15360 and 21715 kHz, and to the Pacific on 11750 and 11955 kHz, the latter switching from 15360 kHz at 0915.

Christian Science Monitor World Service, USA. See 0100 for program details. Monday through Friday to North America on 9455 kHz; to Europe on 9840 or 11705 kHz; to East Asia on 9530 and 17780 kHz; and to the Pacific on 13760 kHz.

Deutsche Welle, West Germany. *News,* followed Monday through Friday by *Newsline Cologne* and *Asia-Pacific Report.* These are replaced Saturday by *International Talking Point, Development Forum* and *Religion and Society;* and Sunday by *Arts on the Air* and *German By Radio.* To Asia and the Pacific on 6160, 17820, 21650 and 21680 kHz.

HCJB, Ecuador. Another 60 minutes of predominantly religious fare; to the Pacific on 9745 and 11925 kHz.

Radio Australia. World and Australian *news,* followed most days by music (replaced Monday by *Back Page*—a sporting feature). Then comes any one of a wide variety of features, including *Education Focus* (Monday), *AgriNews* (Tuesday), *Women of Asia* (Wednesday) and *Points of Law* (Saturday). To North America on 9580 kHz; to East Asia on 9760 and 17715 kHz.

Radio Finland. Winters only at this time; see 0730 for program details. To East Asia and the Pacific on 17800 and 21550 kHz.

WHRI, Indiana, USA. WHRI, although a religious broadcaster, carries some secular programs. Weekdays at 0915 summers it's *The Mediator,* a look at Hollywood. To North America (sometimes heard in Europe) year-round on 7355 kHz, plus 7315 kHz winters.

0930

Radio Finland. Winters only at this time; see 0730 for program details. To East Asia on 15245 and 17800 kHz.

1000

BBC World Service. *News Summary,* followed by some of the best that the BBC has to offer (some of which starts at 1015 or 1030). The list includes *Here's Humph* (Saturday), *Letter from America* (Saturday), *People and Politics* (Saturday), *The Vintage Chart Show* (Monday), *Science in Action* (Sunday), *Sports International* (Tuesday), *Jazz for the Asking* (Wednesday), *Assignment* (Thursday) and *Omnibus* (Wednesday). Tune in any day of the week for some high-quality programming. Continuous to Western Europe on 6045, 7325, 9750, 9760, 12095, 15070 and 17640 kHz; and to East Asia and the Pacific on 15360 kHz.

Christian Science Monitor World Service, USA. See 0000 for program

details. Monday through Friday to North America on 9455 and 9495; and to East Asia on 9530 kHz.

Radio Australia. *International Report,* followed Monday through Friday by *Stock Exchange Report,* then one of several feature programs, including *Arts Roundabout* (Sunday), *Innovations* (Tuesday), *Points of Law* (Wednesday), *Monitor* (Saturday) and *Interaction* (Thursday). Heard well in North America on 9580 kHz.

Voice of Vietnam. Better heard in Europe than in North America. Begins with *news,* then political commentary, interviews, short features, and Vietnamese music. Omnidirectional on 9840 and 12019 or 15010 kHz. Repeats of this transmission can be heard on the same frequencies at 1230, 1330, 1600, 1800, 1900, 2030 and 2330 World Time.

Swiss Radio International. Repeat of 0830 transmission. To East Asia and the Pacific on 9560, 13685, 17670 and 21695 kHz.

Voice of America. The start of VOA's daily broadcasts to the Caribbean. *News, Newsline* and *VOA Morning*—a compendium of sports, science, business and features—on 9590, 11915 and 6030 or 15120 kHz. For a separate service to the Pacific, see the next item.

Voice of America. *News,* followed weekdays by *Newsline* and *Magazine Show.* On weekends, there are features such as *Weekend Magazine* (Saturday) and *Critic's Choice* (Sunday). To the Pacific on 5985, 11720 and 15425 kHz.

All India Radio. *News,* then a composite program of commentary, press review and features—accompanied by sizable portions of highly enjoyable subcontinental music. To the Pacific on 15335 kHz; and to East Asia on 15050, 17387, 17865 and 21735 kHz.

HCJB, Ecuador. *Studio 9.* As 0030, but one day earlier. To the Pacific on 9745 and 11925 kHz.

Kol Israel. Summers only at this time. *News* from Israel Radio's domestic network, followed by various features: *Mainstream* (consumer and community affairs), *With Me in the Studio* (guest interviews), *Israel Mosaic* (variety of topics), *Studio Three* (arts in Israel), *This Land* (a travel magazine), and *Thank Goodness It's Friday.* A half hour to Europe—occasionally audible in Eastern North America—on 11585, 17575, 17590,

21745 and 21780 kHz. To Asia and the Pacific on 15485 and 15650 kHz.

1030

Radio Korea, South Korea. Summers only at this time. Monday–Saturday, *news,* followed by *Seoul Calling* Monday and Tuesday, music Wednesday–Friday, and *From Us to You* Saturday. *Shortwave Feedback* follows *Weekly News in Review* on Sunday. On 11715 kHz via Canadian relay, so this morning slot is the best chance for North Americans to tune in this station.

Radio Nederland. Repeat of the 0730 transmission. To the Caribbean on 6020 kHz; to the Pacific on 11890 kHz.

United Arab Emirates Radio, Dubai. *News,* then a feature dealing with aspects of Arab life and culture. Weekends, there are replies to listeners' letters. To Europe on 15320, 15435, 17775 and 21605 kHz.

Radio Austria International. See 1130 for program details. Twenty-five minutes to the Pacific on 15450 and 21490 kHz.

1100

BBC World Service. *News,* followed by *News About Britain,* then such feature programs as *Health Matters* (Monday), *Composer of the Month* (Monday), *Waveguide* (Tuesday), *Country Style* (Wednesday), *Global Concerns* (Friday), *Meridian* (Wednesday, Friday, Saturday) and *The Ken Bruce Show* (Sunday). Continuous to North America on 5965, 6195, 9515, 9740 or 11775 kHz; to Western Europe on 6045, 7325, 9750, 9760, 12095, 15070 and 17640 kHz; and to East Asia and the Pacific on 9740 kHz (except 1115-1130, see below).

Christian Science Monitor World Service, USA. See 0100 for program details. Monday through Friday to North America on 9455 and 9595 kHz; and to East Asia on 9530 kHz.

Radio Australia. World and Australian *news,* then music, followed at 1130 by a 30-minute feature, such as *One World* (Sunday), *Land and Culture* (Monday), *Business Horizons* (Tuesday), *AgriNews* (Thursday) or *Science File* (Wednesday). Heard clearly in North America on 9580 kHz, and in East Asia on 6080, 9710 or 11800 kHz.

Voice of Vietnam. Repeat of the 1000 transmission. To Asia on 7420 and 9730 kHz.

HCJB, Ecuador. Thirty minutes of religious programming to the Pacific on 9745 and 11925 kHz.

Voice of America. The second—and final—hour of the morning broadcast to the Caribbean. *News,* followed weekdays by *Focus* and *VOA Morning.* On Saturday there is *Closeup* and *Music U.S.A.,* while Sunday features *Critic's Choice* and *Studio One.* On 6030 (or 15120), 9590 and 11915 kHz. For a separate service to Asia and the Pacific, see the next item.

Voice of America. *News,* followed Saturday by *Focus* and *Press Conference, U.S.A.,* Sunday by *New Horizons* and *Issues in the News,* and weekdays by special features and *Music U.S.A..* To East Asia on 9760 and 15155 kHz; to the Pacific on 5985 kHz; and to both areas on 11720 and 15425 kHz.

Radio RSA, South Africa. *News* and comment, followed weekdays by *Africa South, Sport RSA* (Monday), *Economic Desk* (Wednesday), *Talking Point* (Friday and Sunday), *Around and About* (Saturday), *Profile* (Saturday) and *Conversation Corner* (Sunday). Fifty-five minutes aimed at African listeners, but occasionally heard in Europe and beyond on 9555, 11805, 11900 and 17835 kHz.

Swiss Radio International. Repeat of the 0830 transmission. A half hour to Asia and the Pacific on 13635, 15570, 17830 and 21550 or 21770 kHz.

Radio Japan. On weekdays, opens with *Radio Japan News-Round,* with news oriented to Japanese and Asian affairs. *Radio Japan Magazine Hour* follows, with more feature content, including *CrossCurrents* (Monday), *Asia Contact* (Wednesday) and *A Glimpse of Japan* (Friday). *Commentary* and *news* finish the hour. On Saturday, hear *This Week;* Sunday features *news, Hello from Tokyo,* and *Viewpoint.* One hour to North America on 6120 kHz, and to East Asia on 11815 and 11840 kHz.

Radio Beijing, China. See 0000 for program details. To North America winters on 9665 kHz; summers on 17855 kHz.

Radio Pyongyang, North Korea. *News,* much of it devoted to the "great leader, Kim Il-Sung." This is followed by Korean patriotic music and such features as *Immortal Ideas* (Friday). A plethora of political commentary throughout. Fifty minutes to North America and Asia on 9600 (or 9645), 9977 and 11735 kHz.

Kol Israel. Winters only at this time. *News* from Israel Radio's domestic network, followed by various features (see 1000). A half hour to Europe—sometimes heard in Eastern North America—on 11585, 15485, 17575, 17590 or 21780 kHz. To Asia and the Pacific on 15650 kHz.

Voice of Asia, Taiwan. Broadcasts open with features like *Asian Culture* (Monday) and *Touring Asia* (Tuesday), followed by *news, Festival Asia,* and *Let's Learn Chinese.* Heard in East Asia and the Pacific—and occasionally in North America—on 5980 and 7445 kHz.

Radio Jordan. *News summary,* followed by various programs from Radio Jordan's domestic service in English. Nominally, this is beamed to North America. However, because of the early hour and low frequency—both woefully inappropriate for signals from that part of the world—it is virtually inaudible there. Nevertheless, it's well-heard in Europe on 13655 kHz.

1115

BBC World Service for Asia. On Friday the BBC World Service airs *Dateline East Asia.* Although beamed only to Asia, this service can sometimes be heard in other parts of the world—notably the Pacific and North America—as well. Until 1130, try 6195, 9740, 11750 and 15360 kHz.

1130

Radio Korea, South Korea. Winters only at this time. See 1030 for program details. On 9700 kHz via Canadian relay, so this morning slot is the best chance for North Americans to tune in the station.

Radio Austria International. Monday through Friday features *Report from Austria* (see 0130 for further details). On Saturday, there's *Austrian Coffeetable,* which consists of light chat and different kinds of music, including classical, popular, jazz, or German and Austrian popular songs from the Twenties and Thirties. On Sunday, it's *Shortwave Panorama* for radio enthusiasts. Thirty minutes to North America on 21475 or 21495 kHz; to Europe on 6155 and 13730 kHz; and to East Asia on 15430 kHz.

Radio Nederland. See 0730 for program details. To Europe on 5955 and 9715 kHz; and to Asia on 17575, 21480 and 21520 or 21615 kHz.

HCJB, Ecuador. First 30 minutes of a four-and-a-half-hour block of religious programming to North America. On 11740 kHz.

Radio Sweden. This time summers only; see 1530 for program details. To Asia and the Pacific on 17740, 21570 and 21610 kHz.

1145

BBC World Service for Asia. See 1115. In Asia and North America, try 7180 or 15280 kHz.

EVENING PRIME TIME—ASIA AND WESTERN AUSTRALIA
1200

BBC World Service. Except for Sunday, the hour starts with *Newsreel,* followed by *Multitrack* (Tuesday, Thursday, Saturday), *The Farming World* (Wednesday), a quiz, or a special feature, with *Sports Roundup* at 45 minutes past the hour. Sunday features *Play of the Week*—the very best in radio theater, after a *news* summary. Continuous to North America on 5965, 6195, 9515, 9740 and 11775 kHz; to Western Europe on 6045, 7325, 9750, 9760, 12095, 15070 and 17640 kHz; and to East Asia and the Pacific on 9740 kHz.

Christian Science Monitor World Service, USA. See 0000 for program details. Monday through Friday to North America on 9495 and 11930 kHz; and to the Pacific on 15285 kHz.

Radio Canada International. Summers only at this time; see 1300 for program details. Monday through Friday to North and Central America on 9635, 11855 and 17820 kHz.

Radio Tashkent, Uzbek SSR. *News* and commentary, followed by such features as *Life in the Village, Youth Program,* and *On the Asian Continent.* Heard better in Asia, the Pacific and Europe than in North America. Thirty minutes winters on 5945, 9540, 9600, 11785 and 15470 kHz; and summers on 7325, 9715, 11785, 15460 and 11740 kHz.

Radio Australia. *International Report,* followed 30 minutes later, Sunday through Thursday, by *Soundabout*—a program of contemporary popular music. On Friday there is a documentary program, *This Australia,* and Saturday features *Ring the Bells,* a look at Australian politics. To East Asia on 6080, 9710 or 11800 kHz; and to North America on 9580 kHz.

HCJB, Ecuador. Continuous to North America on 11740, 15115 and 17890 kHz.

Voice of America. *News,* then—weekdays—*Newsline* and *Magazine Show.* Weekend programming consists of features like *Encounter* (Sunday), *Studio One* (Sunday) and *Weekend Magazine* (Saturday). To East Asia on 9760, 15155 and 15425 kHz.

Radio Beijing, China. *News* and various features—see 0000 for specifics. To North America winters on 9665 kHz, and summers on 11855 kHz; to East Asia on 11600 (or 15285) and 11660 kHz; and to the Pacific on 11600 and 15285 kHz.

Vatican Radio. Twenty-five minutes Monday through Saturday to Asia and the Pacific on 17865 and 21515 kHz.

Swiss Radio International. Summers only at this time; see 0830 for program details. To Europe on 6165, 9535 and 12030 kHz.

Radio Yugoslavia. Summers only at this time. *News,* followed by various features (see 2100). Thirty minutes to Asia, the Pacific and Eastern North America on 17740, 21555 and 25795 kHz.

Radio RSA, South Africa. *News,* followed by *Yours and Mine, Meditation* (Thursday and Friday), *S.A. Review* (Saturday), *P.O. Box 91313* (Saturday), and *The Message.* Fifty-five minutes to Africa on 9555, 11805, 11900 and 17835 kHz, but sometimes audible in Europe and beyond.

Radio Moscow World Service. The hour starts with *news,* followed by *Newmarket* (Sunday and Monday; new products), or *Focus on Asia and the Pacific* (Tuesday-Saturday). At half-past, a *news* brief, generally followed by *music.* Saturday is an exception, when it's *Roundtable Discussion.* An hour to North America, Asia and the Pacific on 11840, 15110, 15550, 17815, 21690 and 21785 kHz.

WHRI, Indiana, USA. Whatever happened to Pat Boone, whose non-rock versions of rock songs have vanished even from the oldies airwaves? If you really want to find out, tune in your pink-and-black world band radio to the *Pat Boone Show,* Saturday at this time to North America on 9465 and 11790 kHz.

1215

Radio Cairo. Seventy-five minutes of *News,* comment, culture and authentic Egyptian music; to East Asia on 17595 kHz.

1230

Radio France Internationale. *News,* which gives in-depth coverage of French politics and international events. This is then usually followed by a short feature such as *Land of France* (Tuesday) or *Arts in France* (Thursday). A half hour to North America on 17650, 21635 and 21645 kHz; and to Europe on 9805, 11670, 15155 and 15195 kHz.

Radio Sweden. This time winters only; see 1530 for program details. To Asia and the Pacific on 17740, 21570 and 21610 (or 15190) kHz.

Belgische Radio en Televisie, Belgium. Summers only at this time, Monday through Saturday. On Sunday the broadcast airs at 11:30. See 1330 for program details. Twenty-five minutes to North America and East Asia on 17555 and 21810 kHz.

1300

BBC World Service. *News* and analysis on *Twenty-Four Hours.* This is followed by a variety of features, including *Jazz Scene UK* or *Folk in Britain* (Thursday), *Development* (Wednesday), music, or sports. On Sunday, catch the integrated package *News* and *Twenty-Four Hours on Sunday,* a 45-minute news extravaganza. To North America until 1330 (1345 weekends) on 6195, 9515, 9740 or 11775 kHz. Continuous to Western Europe on 5975, 7325, 9410, 9750, 9760, 12095, 15070 and 17640 kHz; to East Asia from 1300 to 1330 World Time on 5995, 7180 and 9740 kHz; and to the Pacific on 9740 kHz.

Christian Science Monitor World Service, USA. See 0100 for program details. Monday through Friday to North America on 9495 and 11930 kHz; and to the Pacific on 15285 kHz.

Radio Canada International. Winter weekdays only at this time. Relay of CBC domestic network's *World Report,* followed by *North Country*—a program of *news,* interviews, human interest stories and current events. Regular features like *SWL Digest* (Tuesday) and *Spotlight on Science*

(Thursday) fit into *North Country* at about 1230. One hour Monday through Friday to North and Central America on 9635, 11855 and 17820 kHz. For an additional service, see next item.

Radio Canada International. Summers only at this time; see 1400 for program details. Sunday only to North and Central America on 11955 and 17820 kHz.

Radio Pyongyang, North Korea. Repeat of the 1100 transmission. To Europe on 9325 and 9345 kHz; and to North America and East Asia on 9645, 13650, and 15230.

Swiss Radio International. Winters only at this time. See 0830 for program details. To Europe on 6165, 9535 and 12030 kHz.

Radio Yugoslavia. Winters only at this time. *News,* followed by various features (see 2100). Thirty minutes to Asia, the Pacific and Eastern North America on 11735, 15325 and 15380 kHz.

Radio Australia. World and Australian *news,* followed by *Sports Report* and a half hour of music. To North America on 9580 kHz; and to East Asia on 6080, 11930, or 21525 kHz.

HCJB, Ecuador. Sixty minutes of predominantly religious broadcasting. Continuous to North America on 11740, 15115 and 17890 kHz.

Voice of America. *News,* followed by *Focus* (weekdays), *American Viewpoints* (Saturday) or *Critic's Choice* (Sunday). The last half hour includes special features. To East Asia on 9760, 15155 and 15425 kHz.

1330

United Arab Emirates Radio, Dubai. *News,* then a documentary feature which runs in a series from beginning to end. Recent selections have included *Arab and Islamic Encyclopedia, History of Islam,* and *Islamic Traditions Through the Ages.* A half hour to Europe on 15320, 15435, 17775 and 21605 kHz.

Radio Austria International. *Report from Austria;* see 0130 for more details. Twenty-five minutes to East Asia on 15430 kHz.

Belgische Radio en Televisie, Belgium. Winters only at this time, Monday through Saturday. On Sunday, the broadcast airs at 1230. See 0630 for program details. *News,* press review, and such

features as *Belgium Today, Living in Belgium* and *Musical Roundabout.* To North America and East Asia on 17555, 21810, 21815 or 21820 kHz.

Radio Tashkent, Uzbek SSR. Repeat of the 1200 transmission. Heard in Asia, the Pacific, Europe and parts of North America winters on 5945, 9540, 9600, 11785 and 15470 kHz; and summers on 7325, 9715, 11785, 15460 and 17740 kHz.

Swiss Radio International. Repeat of the 0830 transmission. A half hour to Asia and the Pacific on 9620, 11695, 13635, 15570, 17830 and 21695 kHz.

1400

BBC World Service. On weekdays, catch the *news,* followed by *Outlook.* On the half hour the programs are mainly of a cultural nature, such as *Off the Shelf* (Monday, Friday) and *Business Matters* (Wednesday). On weekends, after the news summary, you can hear *Sportsworld* (Saturday) or feature programming. Continuous to Western North America, East Asia and the Pacific on 9740 kHz; to Western Europe on 5975, 7325, 9410, 9750, 9760, 12095, 15070 and 17640 kHz; and to East Asia on 5995 and 7180 kHz.

Christian Science Monitor World Service, USA. See 0000 for program details. Monday through Friday to North America on 17555 kHz; to Europe on 21780 kHz; and to East Asia on 9530 kHz.

Radio Korea, South Korea. Repeat of the 0800 transmission, but to East Asia on 9570 kHz.

Radio France Internationale. *News,* press review and a variety of short features, including *Letterbox* (Sunday) and *Made in France* (Saturday). Thirty minutes to Southeast Asia and the Pacific on 7125, 11925 and 21770 kHz.

Radio Australia. *International Report,* followed Monday through Friday by *Stock Exchange Report* and, on the half hour, special feature programs like *Science File* (Friday) and *Women of Asia* (Saturday). To North America on 9580 kHz. To East Asia on 6080, 7240 or 11930 kHz.

Radio RSA. First hour of a two-hour broadcast. *News,* followed by *Historical Almanac* and *Africa South* (weekdays); the excellent *Our Wild Heritage* (Sunday, Monday); *Conversation Corner* (Sunday, Monday, Friday); the enjoyable entertain-

Jolly England? No, it's Ottawa, Canada's capitol. Most foreign television networks scarcely mention Canada. So Radio Canada International, plus CFRX–CFRB/Toronto and sometimes CFCX–CFCF/Montréal, fill in the gap with some of the best programming around.

ment shows *Black Choirs* (Monday), *Sounds of Soweto* (Tuesday), and *Artist of the Week* (Friday); *Talking About Towns* (Monday); *Women in Africa* (Tuesday, Thursday); *Changing the Face of Africa* (Wednesday); *Medical File* (Wednesday); *Economic Desk* (Wednesday); *Profile* (Thursday); *Not in the Headlines* (Friday); *A Contribution by Colin Jackson* (Saturday); *Kaleidoscope* (Saturday); *Science and Technology* (Sunday); and *Sunday Magazine.* Two hours targeted to Africa, but sometimes also heard outside Africa on 9555, 11925 and 17835 kHz.

Radio Moscow World Service. *News,* followed by *Mailbag* or *News and Views.* At half-past, *News in Brief* and then features like *Roundtable Discussion* (Sunday), *Folk Box* (Monday), and *Vasily's Weekend* (Saturday; music). On scads of frequencies to East Asia, the Pacific, and North America; examples include 9755, 11840, 12050, 15375, 17815 and 21690 kHz.

Radio Finland. *Northern Report* is featured Tuesday through Saturday, with *Compass North* (Sunday; news review) and *Business Monday* completing the week. Other features include such titles as *Airmail*

(Tuesday), *Faiths in Finland* (Wednesday), *Learning Finnish* (Thursday), and *Names in the News* (Friday). Twenty-five minutes (extended to one hour at weekends) to North America on 15400 and 21550 kHz. One hour earlier in summers.

HCJB, Ecuador. Another hour of mainly religious fare. To North America on 11740, 15115 and 17890 kHz.

Voice of America. *News.* This is followed weekdays by *Asia Report.* On Saturday there is jazz, and Sunday is given over to classical music. At 1455, there's a daily editorial. To East Asia on 9760, 15160 and 15425 kHz.

Radio Canada International. *News,* followed by *Sunday Morning*—a program from the CBC domestic network. Sunday only to North and Central America on 11955 and 17820 kHz.

KUSW, Salt Lake City, USA. Winters, there's *M.D. Radio,* a public-service medical program, at 1500. Popular music, *news,* weather and sports continuous to North America Saturday and Sunday on 15590 kHz.

CFRX-CFRB, Toronto, Canada. Audible throughout much of the northeastern United States and southeastern Canada during the hours of daylight with a modest, but clear, signal on 6070 kHz. With programs for an Ontario audience, this pleasant, friendly station carries news, sports, weather, traffic reports—and, at times, music. Arguably most interesting are talk-show discussions concerning such topics as the status of neighboring Quebec. Call in if you'd like at 514/790-0600—comments from outside Ontario are welcomed.

CFCX-CFCF, Montréal, Canada. Locally oriented programming. Its weak signal is sometimes audible on good radios in parts of the northeastern United States and southeastern Canada during the hours of midday and early afternoon on 6005 kHz.

1430

Radio Nederland. *News* and a variety of features, for the most part in the 0730 broadcast. One exception airs on Friday: *Asiascan,* a live magazine show featuring 45 minutes of programming specially designed for Asian listeners. To Europe on 5955 kHz; and to Asia on 13770, 15150, 17575 and 17605 kHz.

Radio Austria International. Repeat of 1130 transmission. To Europe on 6155, 13730 and 21490 kHz; to Asia on 11780 kHz.

WHRI, Indiana, USA. WHRI, although a religious broadcaster, carries some secular programs. Weekdays at 1445 summers it's *Passport International,* information on various countries. To North America (sometimes heard in Europe) on 9465 and 15105 kHz.

1500

BBC World Service. *Newsreel,* followed by sports, music or the arts. A treat for classical music aficionados: *Music Review,* on Friday. Continuous to Western North America on 9740 kHz; to North America weekends on 9515 or 11775 and 15260 kHz; daily to Western Europe on 6195, 7325, 9410, 9750, 9760, 12095, 15070 and 17640 kHz; and to East Asia on 5995, 7180 and 9740 kHz. Also, until 1515, to the Pacific on 7180 and 9740 kHz.

Christian Science Monitor World Service, USA. See 0100 for program details. Monday through Friday to North America on 17555 kHz; to Europe on 21780 kHz; and to East Asia on 9530 kHz.

KNLS, Alaska, USA. Tuesday through Sunday only at this time; see 0800 for

program details. To East Asia and the Pacific winters on 7355 kHz, and summers on 9750 or 11715 kHz.

BBC World Service for Africa. See 0330. Try 11860, 15420 or 21490 kHz.

Radio Canada International. Continuation of CBC domestic program *Sunday Morning.* Sunday only to North and Central America on 11955 and 17820 kHz.

Radio Japan. *News* and various features. See 0300 for details. One hour to North America on 11865 kHz; to Europe on 21700 kHz; and to East Asia on 11815 kHz.

Radio RSA. Second hour of a two-hour broadcast to the African continent. *News* and features about South Africa, also heard in Europe and Eastern North America on 17835 kHz.

HCJB, Ecuador. Continues with religious programming to North America on 15115 and 17890 kHz.

KUSW, Salt Lake City, USA. Popular music, *news,* weather and sports. Continuous until 0300 Saturday and Sunday to North America on 15590 kHz.

CFRX-CFRB, Toronto, Canada. See 1400.

1530

Belgische Radio en Televisie, Belgium. Summers only at this time, Monday through Saturday. Repeat of the 0630 transmission, but on 17580 and 21810 kHz. Although beamed to Africa, these frequencies are often audible in Europe and Eastern North America.

Radio Sweden. Each broadcast is called *Weekday, Saturday* or *Sunday,* and begins with world and Nordic *news,* followed by human interest features and interviews. On Monday, the accent is on sport; Wednesday features *Business Scan;* and Friday's broadcast contains Scandinavian jazz and popular music. On Saturday, there's a look back at the week's events in Scandinavia in *Nordic Newsweek.* Thirty minutes to North America on 17880 and 21500 kHz; and to Europe on 21665 kHz.

1600

BBC World Service. *News,* followed by *News About Britain.* Feature programs that follow include sports, drama, science or music. Particularly worthwhile are *Assignment* (Thursday) and *Science in Action*

(Friday). At 1645, on Sunday there's Alistair Cooke's popular *Letter from America* (see the interview with Cooke in this edition of *Passport*), and on weekdays at the same time you can hear a news analysis program, *The World Today*. Continuous to North America on 9515 or 11775 and 15260 kHz; and to Western Europe on 6195, 7325, 9410, 12095 and 15070 kHz. Also, to East Asia until 1615 on 5995 and 7180 kHz.

Christian Science Monitor World Service, USA. *News* and *News Focus*—30 minutes of news analysis and news-related features, with emphasis on international developments—followed by *Kaleidoscope*, an interesting collection of human-interest features, replaced Friday by *The Home Forum*. Monday through Friday to East Asia on 13745 kHz and to parts of North America and Europe on 21640 kHz.

Radio France Internationale. This program, formerly called *Paris Calling Africa,* is heard quite well in North America and Europe. Begins with world and African *news,* followed by feature programs, including the *Land of France* (Tuesday), *Arts in France* (Thursday), *Mailbag* (Sunday), *Drumbeat* (Wednesday; African arts), *Spotlight on Africa* and, perhaps surprisingly, *Latin American Notes* (Sunday, Wednesday). One hour, audible in Europe and North America, on 6175, 11705, 12015, 15360, 17620, 17795 and 17850 kHz.

United Arab Emirates Radio, Dubai. Starts with a feature on Arab history or culture, followed by music at 1615 and a bulletin of *news* at 1630. Answers listeners' letters at weekends. To Europe on 11790, 15320, 15435 and 21605 kHz.

Radio Korea, South Korea. See 0800 for program details. To Asia and beyond on 5975 and 9870 kHz.

Deutsche Welle, West Germany. Repeat of the 0900 transmission. To Asia on 6170, 7225, 15105, 15595, 17825 and 21680 kHz.

Radio Canada International. Winters only. Final hour of CBC's *Sunday Morning;* Sunday only to North and Central America on 11955 and 17820 kHz.

Voice of America. *News,* followed by *Nightline Africa*—special news and features on African affairs. Heard beyond Africa—including North America—on many frequencies, including 15410, 15580, 17785, 17800 and 17870 kHz.

KUSW, Salt Lake City, USA. Weekends only, mostly popular music and regional weather reports, plus *news* five minutes before the hour. Summer Sundays, the Mormon Tabernacle Choir is aired until 1630. Interestingly, Mormon missionaries scattered throughout the Western Hemisphere can't listen to this, or any other program from KUSW—they're not allowed to have radios! To North America on 15590 kHz.

Radio Moscow World Service. *News,* generally followed by *Focus on Asia and the Pacific* (a notable exception is Monday's *International Listeners' Club*). After a *news* brief at half-past, features like *History Club* (Friday) and *Mailbox* (Saturday). Beamed to virtually everywhere, on virtually every band. Try 9655, 11840, 11900, 11995, 12010, 12050 and 15375 kHz.

CFRX-CFRB, Toronto, Canada. See 1400.

1615

BBC World Service for Africa. See 0330. Until 1645, on 6190, 9630, 15400, 15420 and 17880 kHz.

1630

Belgische Radio en Televisie, Belgium. Winters only at this time, Monday through Saturday. Repeat of the 0630 transmission, but on 17580 and 21810 kHz. Beamed to Africa, but often audible in Europe and Eastern North America.

1700

BBC World Service. *News,* followed by *Commentary* (Monday–Friday) or *Book Choice* (Saturday and Sunday), and then a quiz show, drama, music or sports. There is a daily summary of world sporting news at 1745, in *Sports Roundup*. Until 1745 to North America on 9515 or 11775 and 15260 kHz. Continuous to Western Europe on 6195, 7325, 9410, 12095 and 15070 kHz.

BBC World Service for Africa. See 0330. Until 1745, on 6005, 9630, 11940, 15400, 15420 and 17880 kHz.

Christian Science Monitor World Service, USA. *News,* followed Monday, Wednesday and Thursday by *One Norway Street*—a highly varied selection of features

Gong with the Wind, traditional Japanese style. Less traditional, but even more appreciated, is the livelier style of programming now heard over Radio Japan. Stronger signal, too.

dealing mostly with items from the United States. On Tuesday there is *Curtain Call,* and on Friday an edition of *Encore*—featuring items from earlier broadcasts that listeners have asked to hear again. Monday through Friday only, to East Asia on 13745 kHz and to parts of North America and Europe on 21640 kHz.

Radio Prague International, Czechoslovakia. *News,* followed by information on Czechoslovakia's democracy, as well as environmental and cultural happenings in the country. Thirty minutes to Europe on 5930, 6055, 7345 and 11990 kHz.

Voice of America. Produced for Africa. *News,* then *African Panorama,* interviews, current affairs, music and human-interest features. Weekend programming is somewhat different, and includes the excellent *Music Time in Africa* at 1730 Sunday. Audible in many parts of the world on 15410, 15445, 15580, 15600, 17785, 17800 and 17870 kHz.

Kol Israel. Summers only at this time. *News* from Israel Radio's domestic network.

To Europe—sometimes audible in Eastern North America—for 15 minutes on 11585 and 11655 kHz.

KUSW, Salt Lake City, USA. Wednesday–Sunday summers, but only Saturday winters, there's popular music and regional weather reports, plus *news* five minutes before the hour. Winter Sundays, the Mormon Tabernacle Choir airs until 1730. To North America on 15590 kHz.

CFRX-CFRB, Toronto, Canada. See 1400.

1730

Belgische Radio en Televisie, Belgium. Summers only at this time. On weekdays, there's *news, Press Review,* and *Belgium Today,* followed by features like *Musical Roundabout* (Wednesday) and *Around the Arts* (Friday). Weekends include features like *Radio World* (Saturday) and *Music Through the Ages* (Sunday). Twenty-five minutes to Europe on 5910, 5915, 11695 or 13675 kHz.

Swiss Radio International. Summers only at this time; see 0830 for program details. To Europe on 3985. 6165 and 9535 kHz.

EVENING PRIME TIME—EUROPE
1800

BBC World Service. *Newsdesk* for a half hour, followed most days by pop, jazz or classical music. An exception is the quality science program *Discovery,* broadcast Tuesday at 1830. Continuous to Western Europe on 6195, 7325, 9410, 12095 and 15070 kHz; and to the Pacific on 11750 kHz.

Christian Science Monitor World Service, USA. See 1600 for program details. Monday through Friday to North America and Europe on 21640 and 21780 kHz; to East Asia on 11980 or 17555 kHz; and to the Pacific on 9455 or 13720 kHz.

Radio Canada International. Targeted to Africa, but heard quite well in North America. *News,* sports, weather and current affairs. Expands to an hour on weekends, and includes *Coast to Coast* (Saturday), *Spotlight on Science* (Saturday), *L'Attitude* (Sunday) and *SWL Digest*—a program for world band listeners. Half hour weekdays, one hour weekends on 13670, 15260 and 17820 kHz.

Radio Nacional do Brasil (Radio-bras), Brazil. For program details, see the 0200 broadcast, which is a repeat of this transmission. Fifty minutes to Europe on 15265 kHz.

Radio Kuwait. Popular and rock music, plus occasional features on Islam and Kuwaiti history. Heard in Europe and Eastern North America for three hours on 13610 kHz.

Radio RSA. *News* and features about South Africa. Fifty-five minutes targeted to the African continent, but also audible in Europe and beyond on 7230, 15270 and 17765 kHz.

Radio Moscow World Service. Besides *news* on the hour and half hour, features. In the first slot: *Mailbag* (Sunday/ Monday), *Focus on Perestroika* (Wednesday), and *Newmarket* (Friday). At 1832, catch *Your Top Tune* (Sunday), *Music Humor* and *Imagination* (Monday), and *Gypsy Melodies* (Wednesday). To Europe and North America on 11840, 12010, 12050, 13605, 15375 and 15425, among others.

Voice of America. *News,* followed weekdays by *Focus; Encounter* is aired Sunday, and *American Viewpoints* on Saturday. The second half hour is devoted to news and features in "special English"— that is, simplified talk in the American language for those whose mother tongue is other than English. To Europe on 6040, 9760, 11760 and 15205 kHz; to Africa, but often heard elsewhere, on 15410, 15580, 17785 and 17800 kHz.

Radio Sweden. *News* and features, with a predominantly Nordic slant; see 1530 for program details. To Europe on 6065 and 7265 or 9615 kHz.

Kol Israel. Winters only at this time. *News* from Israel Radio's domestic network. To Europe—sometimes audible in Eastern North America—for 15 minutes on 11585 and 11655 kHz.

Radio Korea, South Korea. *News,* followed by features; see 0800 for program details. One hour to Europe—sometimes also heard in North America—on 15575 kHz.

KUSW, Salt Lake City, USA. Popular music, news, weather and sports from Salt Lake City to North America until around 0300 on 15590 kHz Wednesday–Sunday.

CFRX-CFRB, Toronto, Canada. See 1400.

1830

Radio Yugoslavia. Summers only at this time. *News,* followed by various features (see 2100). Thirty minutes for Europe on 7215, 9660 and 11735 kHz.

Belgische Radio en Televisie, Belgium. Winters only at this time; see 1730 for program details. Twenty-five minutes to Europe on 5910, 5915, 11695 or 13675 kHz.

Radio Budapest, Hungary. Summers only. See 1930 for program details. To Europe on 6110, 7220, 9585, 9835, 11910 and 15160 kHz.

Swiss Radio International. Winters only at this time; see 0830 for program details. Thirty minutes to Europe on 3985, 6165 and 9535 kHz.

Radio Canada International. Summers only at this time. See 1900 for program details. Monday through Friday to Western Europe on 5995, 7235, 15325, 17875 and 21675 kHz.

BBC World Service for Africa. See 0330. Thirty minutes on 3255, 6005, 6190, 9630, 15400 and 17880 kHz.

1900

BBC World Service. Begins on weekdays with *News Summary,* followed by the magazine program *Outlook, Financial News,* and such feature programs as *Short Story* (Monday) and *Development* (Tuesday). The excellent *Play of the Week* can be heard Sunday at this time. Continuous to Western Europe on 6195, 7325, 9410, 12095 and 15070 kHz; and to the Pacific on 11750 kHz, plus 15140 kHz Sunday.

Christian Science Monitor World Service, USA. See 1700 for program details. Monday through Friday to North America and Europe on 21640 and 21780 kHz; to East Asia on 11980 or 17555 kHz; and to the Pacific on 9455 or 13720 kHz.

Radio Algiers, Algeria. *News,* then rock and popular music. Also some occasional brief features, such as *Algiers in a Week,* which covers the main events in Algeria during the past week. One hour of so-so reception on one or more of the following channels: 9535, 9640, 9685, 15215 and 17745 kHz.

Kol Israel. Summers only at this time. *News,* followed by various features (see 0000). A half hour to Europe—often audible in Eastern North America—on 11605, 12077, 15640 and 17590 kHz.

HCJB, Ecuador. The first evening transmission for Europe. Repeat of the 1000 broadcast to the Pacific, *Studio 9.* On 15270, 17790 and 21470 kHz.

Deutsche Welle, West Germany. This African-oriented transmission includes *Newsline Cologne* and *African News,* along with such features as *Economic Notebook* (Friday), *Living in Germany* (Wednesday) and *Africa in the German Press* (Sunday). To West Africa, but heard elsewhere, on 11785, 11810, 13790, 15390 and 17810 kHz.

Radio Canada International. *News,* sports, weather and current affairs. Monday through Friday to Africa—but heard well in parts of North America—on 13670, 15260 and 17820 kHz.

Radio Portugal. Summers only at this time, Monday through Friday. See 0230 for program details; programs in this time slot are one day earlier. Thirty minutes to Europe on 11740 kHz.

Spanish Foreign Radio. *News,* followed by features and Spanish music; see 0000 for program details. To Europe and Africa on 11790, 12035, 15375 and 15395 kHz.

Radio Kuwait. Mainly music, but with short features like *Understanding the Koran* and *Kuwait in a Week.* The second part of a three-hour broadcast to Europe and Eastern North America on 13610 kHz.

Voice of America. *News.* For Europe and the Pacific there then follows *Newsline* and a variety of features; and for Africa— weekdays—there is *African Panorama* and *Sound of Soul.* Weekend offerings on this service include the second part of the highly entertaining *Music Time in Africa* Sunday at 1930. The European transmission is on 6040, 9760, 11760 and 15205 kHz; the broadcast to the Pacific on 9525, 11870 and 15180 kHz; and the African service (also heard in North America) on 15410, 15445, 15580, 17785, 17800 and 17870 kHz.

Radio Argentina al Exterior - R.A.E. Monday through Friday only. Lots of mini-features covering all aspects of life in Argentina, interlaced with enjoyable samples of the country's various musical styles. Fifty-five minutes to Europe on 15345 kHz. May be broadcast an hour earlier during summer in Argentina (winter in the northern hemisphere).

KUSW, Salt Lake City, USA. Popular Music and news to North America until around 0300 Wednesday–Sunday on 15590 kHz.

CFRX-CFRB, Toronto, Canada. See 1400.

1920

Voice of Greece. Comparable to the 0130 English transmission, but to Europe on 7430, 9395 or 11645 kHz.

1930

Radio Austria International. *Report from Austria.* See 0130 for complete details. A half hour to Europe on 5945, 6155 and 13730 kHz.

Voice of the Islamic Republic of Iran. Sixty minutes of *news,* commentary and religion—all from the Iranian point of view. To Europe on 9022, plus 6030, 6080 or 11895 kHz.

Radio Budapest, Hungary. Winters only. See 0030 for complete program details, although programs in this broadcast are actually one day earlier. To Europe on 6110, 7220, 9585, 9835, 11910 and 15160 kHz.

Radio Canada International. Winters only. See 1900 for program details. Monday through Friday to Western Europe on 5995, 7235, 11945, 15325 and 17875 kHz.

Radio Yugoslavia. Winters only at this time. *News,* followed by various features (see 2100). Thirty minutes to Europe on 5980, 9620 and 9660 kHz.

WHRI, Indiana, USA. WHRI, although a religious broadcaster, carries some secular programs. Weekdays at 1930 summers it's *The Mediator,* a look at Hollywood. To North America (sometimes heard in Europe) on 13760 and 17830 kHz.

2000

BBC World Service. *News,* then news analysis weekdays on *The World Today.* Saturday, there's *From Our Own Correspondent,* and Sunday you can hear *Personal View.* These are followed by *Words of Faith,* then a quiz or feature program. Gems at this time include *Meridian* (Tuesday, Thursday, Saturday), *The Vintage Chart Show* (Monday), *Science in Action* (Friday) or *Assignment* (Wednesday). Continuous to most of Eastern North

America on 5975 and 15260 kHz; to Western Europe on 3955, 6195, 7325, 9410, 12095 and 15070 kHz; to East Asia on 7180 and 11715 kHz; and to the Pacific on 11750 and 15140 kHz.

Christian Science Monitor World Service, USA. See 1600 for program details. Monday through Friday to North America and Europe on 13770, 15610 and 17555 kHz; to East Asia on 9455 kHz; and to the Pacific on 13625 and 13720 kHz.

Radio Damascus, Syria. Actually starts at 2005. *News,* followed by lots of Syrian music and a daily press review, then a different feature for each day of the week. These include *Portrait from Our Country, Around the World in a Week* and *Reflections on Arab Literature.* Most of the transmission, however, airs Syrian and some Western popular music. One hour to Europe, often also audible in Eastern North America, on 11625, 12085 or 15095 kHz.

Radio Baghdad, Iraq. Summers only at this time. See 2100 for program details. To Europe, often also audible in Eastern North America, on 13660 kHz.

Radio Moscow World Service. *News* on the hour and half hour. *News and Views* airs at 2011, except on Sunday, when *Newmarket* (new products) runs instead. At 2030, various music programs. To Europe

(although heard elsewhere) on such frequencies as 11840, 12050, 13605 and 17695 kHz.

Radio Kiev, Ukrainian SSR. Summers only at this time. *News,* followed by commentary and *The Ukraine Today,* a show covering all aspects of Ukrainian life. The broadcast ends with a different feature each day, including *Society* (Monday), *Dialogue* (Saturday) and *Sunday with Radio Kiev.* One hour to Europe on 9865 kHz. One hour later in winter.

Radio Budapest, Hungary. Summers only. See 1930 for program details. To Europe on 6110, 7220, 9585, 9835, 11910 and 15160 kHz.

Radio Beijing, China. *News,* then various feature programs; see 0000 for details, although all programs are one day earlier. To Europe winters on 6920 and 9920 kHz, summers on 9820 and 11500 kHz.

Voice of Turkey, Summers only at this time. Check 0300 for program details—all programs are one day earlier. To Western Europe on 9795 kHz.

Radio Pyongyang, North Korea. Repeat of the 1100 transmission. To Europe and beyond on 6576, 9345, 9640 and 9977 kHz.

Radio Portugal. Winters only at this time. *News,* followed by a feature about

Strollers in New Delhi. India is more than the doom and gloom seen on evening newscasts. All India Radio conveys the rich tapestry of Indian life to several parts of the world, including Europe.

Portugal; see 1900 for program details. A half hour to Europe Monday through Friday on 11740 kHz.

Kol Israel. Winters only at this time. *News,* followed by various features (see 0000). A half hour to Europe—often also audible in Eastern North America—on 7462, 9435, 11605, 13750 or 15640 kHz.

Voice of America. *News.* Listeners in Europe and North Africa can then hear the VOA's long-running and highly popular jazz program (replaced Sunday by *The Concert Hall*) on 6040, 9760, 11760 and 15205 kHz. For the rest of Africa there is the daily *Nightline Africa*—with news, interviews and background reports—on 15410, 15445, 15580, 17785, 17800 and 17870 kHz. Both transmissions are also audible elsewhere, including parts of North America.

Radio Kuwait. Mainly pop and rock music; final hour of transmission to Europe and Eastern North America on 13610 kHz.

KUSW, Salt Lake City, USA. Popular music, news, weather and sports until around 0300 to North America on 15590 kHz Wednesday–Sunday.

Radio Prague International, Czechoslovakia. *News,* followed by features on Czechoslovakia's politics, as well as environmental and cultural happenings in the country. Thirty minutes to Europe on 5930, 6055, 7345 and 11990 kHz.

CFRX-CFRB, Toronto, Canada. See 1400.

2030

Radio Korea, South Korea. See 0800 for program details. One hour to Europe and beyond on 6480, 7550 and 15575 kHz.

2045

All India Radio. Press review, Indian music, regional and international *news,* commentary and a variety of talks and features of general interest. Continuous till 2230; to Europe on 7412, 9910 and 11620; and to the Pacific on 7265 and 9550 kHz.

2100

BBC World Service. *News Summary,* then *Sports Roundup.* These are followed by a variety of features, including *Europe's World* (Monday), *Sports International* (Monday), *Business Matters* (Tuesday), *Megamix*

(Tuesday), *Recording of the Week* (Wednesday), *Global Concerns* (Thursday) and *People and Politics* (Friday). Continuous to most of Eastern North America on 5975 and 15260 kHz, (except 2115-2130 weekdays on 5975 kHz, see below); to Western Europe on 3955, 6195, 7325, 9410 and 12095 kHz; and to the Pacific on 11750 and 15140 kHz.

Christian Science Monitor World Service, USA. See 1700 for program details. Monday through Friday to North America and Europe on 13770, 15610 and 17555 kHz; to East Asia on 9455 kHz; and to the Pacific on 13625 or 13720 kHz.

Radio Yugoslavia. Summers only at this time. *News,* followed by well-prepared accounts of events in Eastern Europe, and features on East–West relations—interspersed by a variety of Yugoslav music. Although there are now other stations from Eastern Europe which provide objective information, Radio Yugoslavia is still a valuable source of news about the region. It can be heard for 45 minutes in Europe and Eastern North America on 7215, 9660, 11735 and 15105 kHz.

Spanish Foreign Radio. Repeat of 1900 transmission. To Europe on 11790 and 15280 kHz.

Radio Baghdad, Iraq. *News,* then a generous helping of Iraqi music, and a press review just prior to the second hour of transmission. A few brief features, including *Guests in Baghdad* and *The Song of Today,* with some *ad hoc* interviews and current events. Two hours to Europe—sometimes also heard in Eastern North America— winters on 7295, 9770 or 11720 kHz; summers on 13660 kHz.

Radio Sweden. Repeat of the 1800 transmission, directed to Europe and West Africa on 9655 and 11705 kHz.

Belgische Radio en Televisie, Belgium. Summers only at this time. Repeat of the 1730 transmission; 25 minutes daily to Europe on 5910 and 9925 or 13675 kHz.

Radio Beijing, China. Repeat of the 2000 transmission; see 0000 for program details. To Europe winters on 6920 and 9920 kHz, summers on 9920 and 11500 kHz.

Deutsche Welle, West Germany. *News,* followed Sunday through Thursday by the highly recommended *European Journal* and such features as *Man and Environment* (Monday), *Science and*

Bavaria has its own world band station, Bayerischer Rundfunk, located in suburban Munich. It's a tough catch outside of Central Europe on the crowded channel of 6085 kHz.

Technology (Sunday), *Insight* (Tuesday), *Living in Germany* (Wednesday) and *Spotlight on Sport* (Thursday). Friday and Saturday programs include *Panorama* (Friday), *Economic Notebook* (Friday), *Asia in the German Press* (Saturday) and *Mailbag Asia* (Saturday). To Asia and the Pacific on 9670, 9765 and 13780 kHz, plus other, seasonal frequencies.

Radio Japan. Repeat of the 0300 transmission. An hour to Europe, East Asia and the Pacific on 15270, 17765, 17810 and 21610 kHz.

Radio Canada International. Summers only at this time. See 2200 for program details. To Western Europe on 15325 and 17875 kHz.

Radio Romania International. *News,* followed by various features—including *Newsreel, Home News* and *Science Magazine*—plus some thoroughly enjoyable folk music. A half hour to Europe on 7195, 9690, 9750 or 11940 kHz.

Voice of Turkey. Winters only at this time. See 2000 for program details. To Western Europe on 9795 kHz.

Radio Finland. Summers only; see 0730 for program details, except that programs are a day earlier for this transmission. Twenty-five minutes to Europe on 6120 kHz, and to the Pacific on 11775 kHz.

Radio Budapest, Hungary. Winters only. See 1930 for program details. To Europe on 6110, 7220, 9585, 9835, 11910 and 15160 kHz.

Voice of America. *News,* followed on weekdays by *World Report* and on weekends by a variety of features. These depend on the area being served, and include *New Horizons* (Africa, Europe; Sunday), *Press Conference, U.S.A.* (Pacific; Saturday) and *Issues in the News* (Africa; Sunday). To Europe on 6040, 9760, 11760 and 15205 kHz; to Africa, but often heard elsewhere, on 15410, 15445, 15580, 17785 and 17800 kHz; and to the Pacific on 11870, 15185 and 17735 kHz.

Radio Damascus, Syria. Actually starts at 2110. See 2000 for program details. Sixty minutes to North America and the Pacific on 12085 and 15095 kHz.

All India Radio. Continues to Europe on 7412, 9910 and 11620 kHz; and to the Pacific on 7265 and 9550 kHz.

KUSW, Salt Lake City, USA. Popular music, news, weather and sports to North America until around 0300 on 15580 or 15590 kHz Wednesday–Sunday.

WRNO, USA. Rock music and the like, to North America until around 2400 on 13720 or 15420 kHz.

CFRX-CFRB, Toronto, Canada. See 1400.

2115

BBC World Service for the Caribbean. *Caribbean Report,* although intended for listeners in the area, can also be clearly heard throughout much of Eastern North America. This brief, 15-minute program provides experienced coverage of Caribbean economic and political affairs, especially of those which tend to receive little coverage elsewhere in the international media. Too, there's the all-important news of sports, including cricket, for which Barbadian and other island players are justifiably renowned. Monday through Friday only on 5975 kHz.

Radio Cairo. A wide variety of features dealing with Egypt and the Middle East, interlaced with exotic Arab music. These include *Egypt–Europe Weekly Report* (Monday), *Spotlight on the Middle East* (Tuesday), and *Cairo This Week* on Saturday. There are also features on Egyptian history, architecture and tourism. Ninety minutes to Europe on 9900 kHz.

2130

BBC World Service for the Falkland Islands. *Calling the Falklands* might seem esoteric, but it's about as chatty as the BBC gets. Good curiosity value. Tuesday and Friday on 9915 kHz—easily heard in North America.

Kol Israel. Summers only at this time. *News,* followed by various features (see 0000). A half hour beamed to Europe and Eastern North America on 11605, 12077, 15640 and 17575 kHz.

Swiss Radio International. Summers only; see 0830 for program details. To Europe on 6190 kHz.

HCJB, Ecuador. The self-explanatory

Musical Mailbag is aired on Saturday, while the rest of the week is devoted to religious offerings. Thirty minutes to Europe on 17790 and 21470 kHz.

2200

BBC World Service. *Newshour,* arguably the finest newscast to be found anywhere on the airwaves, and aired only once each day, is a must for those interested in comprehensive and up-to-the-minute news coverage. Sixty minutes of sheer professionalism, it is broadcast to Eastern North America on 5975, 6175, 9590, 9915 and 15260 kHz; to Western Europe on 3955, 6195, 7325, 9410 and 12095 kHz; to East Asia on 11955 kHz; and to the Pacific on 9570, 11955 and 15140 kHz.

Christian Science Monitor World Service, USA. See 1600 for program details. Monday through Friday to North America on 9465 and 17555 kHz; to East Asia on 15405 kHz; and to the Pacific on 15300 kHz.

Radio Yugoslavia. Winters only at this time. *News,* followed by features (see 2100).

Forty-five minutes heard in Europe and Eastern North America on 5980, 7130, 9620 and 9660 kHz.

Radio Finland. Winters only at this time; see 0730 for program details, except that programs are a day earlier for this transmission. Twenty-five minutes to Europe on 6120 kHz, and to the Pacific on 11755 kHz.

Voice of America. The beginning of a three-hour block of *News*, sports, science, business, music and features. To East Asia on 9770, 11760, 11775, 15185, 15290, 15305 and 17735 kHz.

Radio Moscow—North American Service. Summers only (See 2300). Beamed to Eastern North America on a variety of frequencies—dial around, and find the one that suits you best.

Voice of Free China, Taiwan. See 0200. For Western Europe on any two of the following: 9852.5, 11805, 15440, 17845, 21500 or 21720 kHz.

Voice of Turkey. Summers only at this time. See 2300 for program details. Fifty minutes to North America on 9445 kHz; to Europe on 9685 kHz; and to East Asia and the Pacific on 17760 or 17880 kHz.

Radio Vilnius, Lithuanian SSR. Summers only at this time. See 2300 for program details. To Europe and Eastern North America on 6100, 11790, 13645, 15180, 15455 and 15485 kHz.

Belgische Radio en Televisie, Belgium. Winters only at this time. See 1730 for program details. Daily for 25 minutes to Europe on 5910 and to Eastern North America on 9925 kHz.

Radio Canada International. Winters only at this time. Monday through Friday, relays CBC's domestic news programs *World at Six* and *As It Happens.* Saturday features *Innovation Canada* and *Listeners' Corner;* and Sunday's programming includes *L'Attitude* and *SWL Digest.* To Western Europe on 9760 and 11945 kHz. For a separate summer service to North America, see next item.

Radio Canada International. Summers only. Monday through Friday feature relays of CBC's *World at Six.* On Saturday there is *News*, sports and weather, followed by *Innovation Canada,* while the Sunday broadcast consists of *News* and comedy— the *Royal Canadian Air Farce.* To North America on 5960, 9755 and 11905 kHz.

Radio for Peace International, Costa Rica. This World Peace University-sponsored station carries mostly UN programming in this time slot. On Sunday, the broadcast includes *Music from Everywhere,* a program produced by Radio Earth, a Chicago-based broadcasting concern. Weak, but often audible in North America on 13660 and 21565 kHz.

Voice of United Arab Emirates, Abu Dhabi. Begins with *Readings from the Holy Koran,* in which verses are chanted in Arabic, then translated into English. Then there is a documentary series, such as *Palestine Under the Muslims.* The last half hour is a relay of Capital Radio in Abu

HOW *PASSPORT* PREPARES WORLD BAND SCHEDULES

How to obtain television schedules? Easy—ask stations for them. That's how *TV Guide* and hundreds of other television publications acquire grist for their mills.

Not so world band. Some stations provide accurate, up-to-date and complete schedule information upon demand. Most don't. You have to dig it out on your own.

That's why *Passport* came into existence. We set up a worldwide network of data-gathering sites to determine what's actually being aired. These—combined with what accurate information is available from stations, official administrative bodies and the like—constitute the basis of our schedules.

There are some *17,000* separate schedule items processed each year at *Passport.* New ones are added, old ones carefully checked and adjusted as necessary. Rounding things off, predictive data is included when feasible.

This major effort continues even after much of the book has already gone to press. How? By printing the Worldscan section at the very last minute. When *Passport* comes off press, the schedule data is as fresh, accurate and complete as possible.

From what's shown on television and the movies, you'd never guess nearly all Australians live in thriving cities, such as Sydney, above. Unless, of course, you tune in the friendly shows on Radio Australia to get the straight poop.

Jennifer Wilde

Dhabi, complete with rock music and local contests. To Eastern North America and Europe on 9600, 11985 and 13605 kHz.

All India Radio. Final half hour of transmission to Europe on 7412, 9910 and 11620 kHz; and to the Pacific on 7265 and 9550 kHz. Also sometimes audible in Eastern North America on 11620 kHz.

KUSW, Salt Lake City, USA. To North America until 0100 or later with continuous popular music, *news,* weather and sports, all on 15590 kHz Wednesday–Sunday.

Radio Baghdad, Iraq. Winters only at this time; see 2100 for program details. To Europe, and sometimes also audible in Eastern North America, on 7295, 9770 or 11720 kHz.

WHRI, Indiana, USA. There's isn't much in the way of country music over world band—not much gospel music, either. *Country Gospel* helps remedy this by giving you both at once Saturday on 13760 and 17830 kHz.

CFRX-CFRB, Toronto, Canada. Live in the northeastern United States or southeastern Canada? Try this pleasant little local station, usually audible for hundreds of miles/kilometers during the hours of day-

light. Among the treats: Big Band and Gaelic music Saturday around 2200-2300 summers on 6070 kHz.

2230

Kol Israel. Winters only at this time. *News,* followed by various features (see 0000). A half hour beamed to Europe and Eastern North America on 9435, 9930, 11605 and 13750 kHz.

Swiss Radio International. Winters only; see 0830 for program details. To Europe on 6190 kHz.

2300

BBC World Service. *News,* then *Commentary* (Monday–Friday) or *Words of Faith* (Saturday/Sunday), followed weekdays by *Financial News* and weekends by *Book Choice.* The remaining 45 minutes are mainly taken up by music programs like *Multitrack, International Recital* or *A Jolly Good Show,* but there are some interesting talks to be found in between. The best of these is Alistair Cooke's *Letter from America,* heard Sunday at 2315. Continuous to North

America on 5975, 6175, 9590, 9915 and 15260 kHz; to East Asia on 11945, 11955 and 17830 or 17875 kHz; and to the Pacific on 9570 and 11955 kHz.

Christian Science Monitor World Service, USA. See 1700 for program

details. Monday through Friday to North America on 9465 and 17555 kHz; to East Asia on 15405 kHz; and to the Pacific on 15300 kHz.

Voice of Turkey. Winters only. See 2000 for program details. To Eastern North

WEIGHING IN

Jesus on the Volga

In Japan, when private firms come up with sensible ideas, their government encourages them. It's a notion they may have lifted from the United States, whose government over the years has helped nurture such industries as canals, railroads, airplanes and computers.

Pioneering American entrepreneurs and religious groups have recently launched world band radio stations to take advantage of a growing audience in the United States and Canada. Some, such as the Christian Science Monitor World Service, are journalistic gems. None is yet financially successful, but the future could be promising. After all, unlike AM or FM, one transmitter covers not just a city, but a whole continent and even beyond. Sound economics, and a major environmental plus.

The Government's reaction?

For starters, the Federal Communications Commission (FCC), which regulates broadcasting in the United States, has decreed that American world band broadcasters may not beam their signals to the United States. No matter that private world band broadcasters in Canada, Mexico, and most countries of Central and South America routinely target their broadcasts to a home audience. In the United States, as in Cuba, *es ist verboten*.

Unfortunately for Washington functionaries, the laws of ionospheric physics march to a more sensible drummer. This means American world band signals are heard in the United States, anyway—no matter where they are beamed. Broadcasters simply aim their signals at some convenient foreign shore to meet the letter of the law. Problem is, this wastes electricity—much of the power winds up in the ocean—and so adds to the stations' operating costs.

As if this were not enough, the FCC recently instituted a tax ("user fee" in political Newspeak) of up to $40,000 a year for each private world band station—including those, such as Family Radio, that are strictly religious and non-commercial. A new tax to soak the rich? Hardly. American world band stations are currently running in the red. This is, remember, a pioneering medium, just as FM was until 30 years ago.

The result has been predictable. Stations are cutting back on operations—the tax is levied on a per-frequency-hour basis—and some may shut down altogether.

Why is the American government hacking away at an American growth industry?

The answer may lie within the plenipotentiary cloisters of the State Department. Insiders relate that State and its friends want American broadcasting to speak to the world . . . provided it comes only from secular Government stations: the Voice of America, RFE-RL and Radio Marti. Never mind that people the world over watch CNN, CBS and other private American television networks daily. With radio, only the sovereign is sovereign.

Never mind, too, that in the motherland of bolshevism Radio Moscow has arranged for private American broadcasters to utilize its facilities. If Washington has its way, private American world band radio may eventually wind up being heard only via such foreign transmitters.

Unless that gets outlawed, too.

—Lawrence Magne

America on 9445 kHz; to Europe on 9685 kHz; and to South East Asia and the Pacific on 17760 or 17880 kHz.

Radio Vilnius, Lithuanian SSR. Winters only at this time. *News* about events in Lithuania, features about the republic's history and culture, and some highly pleasant Lithuanian music. A half hour to Europe and Eastern North America on 6100, 7400, 9765, 15180 and 17665 kHz.

Radio Japan. Similar to 0300 broadcast, but with *Hello from Tokyo* on Sunday instead of *DX Corner.* One hour to Europe on 11835 kHz; and to East Asia on 15195, plus 11815 or 17765 kHz.

Radio Pyongyang, North Korea. See 1100 for program details. Fifty minutes to the Americas on 11735 and 13650 kHz.

Radio Moscow—North American Service. In winter, the broadcast begins with world and national *news,* followed by any number of features, including *Actuality, Top Priority, Science and Engineering, Sidelights on Soviet Life, Home in the USSR* and *Moscow Mailbag,* all aired two or three times a week. In summer, it's hour two of the eight-hour program. On numerous frequencies—dial about for the clearest channel.

Radio Sofia, Bulgaria. Summers only at this time; see 0000 for program details. One hour on 9700, 11660, 11680 or 15330 kHz.

Radio Finland. Summers only at this time. Repeat of the 0630 transmission. To North America on 11775 and 15185 kHz.

Voice of the United Arab Emirates, Abu Dhabi. The first half hour is a review of articles and editorials from the Arab press, which is then followed by a feature with an Islamic slant. Heard in Eastern North America and Europe on 9600, 11985, and 13605 kHz.

Kol Israel. Summers only at this time.

News, followed by various features (see 0000). A half hour beamed to Eastern North America and Europe on 9435, 11605 and 15640 kHz.

Voice of America. The second hour of programming to East Asia (see 2200) on 9770, 11760, 11775, 15185, 15290, 15305 and 17735 kHz.

KUSW, Salt Lake City, USA. To North America until 2330 (summers) or 0030 (winters) with popular music, *news,* weather, sports and religious programming—all on 15590 kHz Wednesday–Sunday.

Radio Kiev, Ukrainian SSR. Summers only at this time; see 2000 for program details. One hour to North America on 11790, 13645, 15180, 15455, 15485 and 15525 kHz.

CFRX-CFRB, Toronto, Canada. See 2200.

2305

Radio Polonia, Poland. *News* and commentary, followed by a variety of feature programs, including *Focus* (culture; Thursday), *Panorama* (Wednesday), and *Postbag* (Monday). Fifty minutes to Europe (and sometimes audible in Eastern North America) on 5995, 6135, 7125 and 7270 kHz.

2330

Belgische Radio en Televisie, Belgium. Summers only at this time. See 1730 for program details. To Eastern North America for 25 minutes on 9925 or 13675 kHz.

Radio Canada International. Summers only at this time. A relay of CBC's excellent weekday *news* program *As It Happens,* with weekends being given over to *News,* followed by *SWL Digest* (Saturday) and *Double Exposure* (Sunday). To Eastern North America on 5960 and 9755 kHz.

Radio Tirana, Albania. See 0230 for the sort of programming you can expect, albeit one day earlier. Occasionally enlivened by very pleasant Albanian music. To North America on 6120, 9760 and 11825kHz.

Radio Budapest, Hungary. This time Monday through Saturday, summers only. See 0030 for program details, with all broadcasts one day earlier. To Eastern North America on 6110, 9520, 9585, 9835, 11910 and 15160 kHz.

WHRI, Indiana, USA. WHRI, although a religious broadcaster, carries some secular programs. Weekdays during the summer it's *Passport International,* information on various countries. To North America (sometimes heard in Europe) on 13760 and 17830 kHz.

Prepared by Don Swampo; assisted by Kannon Shanmugam, who also edits for Monitoring Times *and the* Harvard Independent; *Lawrence Magne; and others on the staff of* Passport to World Band Radio.

MONITORING THE EXPLOSIVE MIDDLE EAST

Nearly all world band stations from Arab countries orient their programs to Arabic-speaking audiences. Indeed, during recent crises what English-language programming that does exist has sometimes been preempted by special shows in Arabic. For those who understand them, these offerings can be rich—even exciting.

In time, this emphasis could shift as Arab countries find, as Israel has, that political and religious information targeted to Western audiences can serve useful national purposes. So during crises in that part of the world, also try tuning around the Middle Eastern channels listed in "Voices from Home" and the Blue Pages for unscheduled transmissions in English.

WORLDWIDE BROADCASTS IN ENGLISH

Country-by-Country Guide to Best-Heard Stations

Dozens of countries, large and small, reach out to us in English over world band radio. Here are the frequencies and times you're most likely to hear them.

A few helpful tips . . .

- Best frequencies are usually 3900-12100 kHz evenings, higher during the day. See *World Band Spectrum* in the glossary at the back of the book for more specific information.
- Best frequencies are usually those in bold—say, **6175**—as they are from transmitters that may be located near you.
- Best time to listen, in general, is during the evening. This is when most programs are targeted to your location.
- Best times for listeners in North America and Europe are in bold (for example, **2200-0430**).
- Time *and days of the week* are given in World Time, explained on page 106. Some programs are heard an hour earlier in summer.

Broadcasts in other than English? Turn to the next two sections—"Voices from Home" and the "Blue Pages."

AFGHANISTAN
RADIO AFGHANISTAN -- **(Europe)**
  6020 **1830-1930**
  9635 **1830-1930**

ALBANIA
RADIO TIRANA
  6121 **2330-2400 (E North Am)**
  7155 **1830-1900 (W Europe)**
  7235 **2230-2300 (W Europe)**
  7300 **0630-0700 (Europe)**
  9480 1030-1100 (Australia), **1730-1800, 1830-1900, 2130-2200 & 2230-2300 (Europe)**
  9500 **0230-0300 (N America), 0530-0600 & 0630-0700 (Europe)**, 0800-0830 & 1400-1430 (Australia)
  9760 **0230-0300 & 0330-0400 (N America)**, **2330-2400 (E North Am** & C America)
  11825 **0230-0300, 0330-0400 & 2330-2400 (E North Am)**
  11835 0800-0830 (Australia)
  11855 1030-1100 (Australia)

ALGERIA
RTV ALGERIENNE -- **(Europe)**
  9509 **1900-2000**
  9685 **1900-2000**

ARGENTINA
RADIO ARGENTINA-RAE
  11710 Tu-Sa **0200-0300 (Americas)**
  15345 M-F **1900-2000 (Europe)**

AUSTRALIA
ABC/BRISBANE -- (Australia)
  9660 24h

ABC/PERTH -- (Australia)
  6140 0900-0100
  9610 24h
  15425 2245-0915
RADIO AUSTRALIA
  5995 0900-2030 (Pacific)
  6060 1400-1630 (Pacific)
  6080 0800-0930 & 1100-2030 (Pacific)
  7215 1330-2130 (Pacific)
  9580 **0830-2100 (Pacific & N America)**
  9655 0930-1130 (Pacific)
  9710 1100-1230 (E Asia & Pacific)
  9760 0900-1000 (E Asia)
  11720 1200-1330 (Pacific)
  11855 1700-2100 (Pacific)
  13705 0600-0830 (Pacific)
  13745 1930-2130 (Pacific)
  15160 0030-0600 & 0800-0830 (Pacific)
  15240 2200-0130 (Pacific)
  15320 0200-0600 (Pacific)
  15395 **2100-0100 (Pacific & N America)**
  15465 2100-0730 (Pacific)
  15560 0230-0600 (Pacific)
  17630 0000-0330, Sa/Su 0330-0430, 0430-1000 & 2300-2400 (E Asia)
  17750 0000-0330, Sa/Su 0330-0430 & 0430-0600 (E Asia)
  17795 **0800-0830 & 2100-0600 (Pacific & N America)**
  21525 0100-0900 (E Asia)
  21825 0900-1000 & 1100-1230 (E Asia)

AUSTRIA
RADIO AUSTRIA INTERNATIONAL
  5945 **1730-1800 & 1930-2000 (Europe)**
  6015 **0530-0600 (N America)**

6155	**0530-0600, 0730-0800, 0830-0900, 1130-1200, 1430-1500, 1630-1700, 1730-1800 & 1930-2000 (Europe)**
9875	**0130-0200 (N America** & C America)
13730	**0130-0200 (N America), 0530-0600, 0730-0800, 0830-0900, 1130-1200, 1430-1500 & 1630-1700 (Europe)**
15430	1130-1200 & 1330-1400 (E Asia)
15450	0830-0900 & 1030-1100 (Australia)
21490	0830-0900 & 1030-1100 (Australia), **1130-1200 (E North Am)**

BANGLADESH

RADIO BANGLADESH -- (Europe)

11705	**0800-0830, 1230-1300**
11862	**1815-1900**
15195	**0800-0830, 1230-1300**
15255	**1815-1900**
15510	**1230-1300**
17850	**0800-0830, 1230-1300**

BELGIUM

BELGISCHE RADIO & TV

5910	**1830-1855 & 2200-2225 (Europe)**
6035	**0730-0755 & M-F 1000-1025 (Europe)**
9925	**0030-0055 & 2200-2225 (Americas)**
11695	0630-0655 & 0730-0755 (Australia), M-F **1000-1025 (Europe)**
13675	**0630-0655**, M-F **0900-0925, 1730-1755 & 1830-1855 (Europe)**
17555	Su **1130-1155** & M-Sa **1230-1255 (E North Am** & C America)
21810	Su **1230-1255** & M-Sa **1330-1355 (E North Am)**

BRAZIL

RADIO NACIONAL (RADIOBRAS)

11745	**0200-0250 (Americas)**
15265	**1800-1850 (Europe)**

BULGARIA

RADIO SOFIA

6070	**1930-2000 & 2130-2200 (Europe)**
7115	**0400-0500 (E North Am & Europe)**
7155	**1930-2000 & 2130-2200 (Europe)**
9700	**0000-0100 (E North Am** & C America), 0400-0500 (C America), **1930-2000, 2130-2200 & 2230-2330 (Europe)**
11660	**1830-1900, 2030-2100 & 2130-2230 (Europe), 2300-2400 (E North Am** & C America)
11680	**0000-0100 & 2230-2330 (E North Am** & C America)
11720	0300-0400 (C America), **0730-0800 (Europe)**
11765	**1830-1900 & 2030-2100 (Europe)**
11785	**1830-1900 & 2030-2100 (Europe)**
15160	**0730-0800 (Europe)**
15290	**0300-0400 (E North Am** & C America)
15330	**1830-1900, 2030-2100 & 2130-2230 (Europe), 2300-2400 (E North Am)**
17825	**0730-0800 (Europe)**

CANADA

CANADIAN BC CORP -- (E North Am)

9625	Su **0000-0300**, Tu-Sa **0200-0300**, M **0300-0310**, M **0330-0610**, Tu-Sa **0500-0610**, Su **0400-0610**, Su **1200-1700**, Sa **1200-1505**, M-F **1200-1255**, Sa **1700-1805**, Su **1800-2400**, M-F **2200-2225**, M-F **2240-2330**

CFCX-CFCF, Montreal

6005	**24h (N America)**

CFRX-CFRB, Toronto

6070	**24h (N America)**

RADIO CANADA INTERNATIONAL

5960	Su/M **0030-0100**, Su/M **0130-0200**, **2200-2230 & 2330-0130 (E North Am &** C America)
5995	**1715-1730**, M-F **1830-1900** & M-F **1930-2000 (Europe)**
6050	M-F **0515-0600** & M-F **0615-0700 (Europe)**
6150	M-F **0515-0600** & M-F **0615-0700 (Europe)**
7155	M-F **0615-0700 (Europe)**
7235	**1715-1730**, M-F **1830-1900** & M-F **1930-2000 (Europe)**
7295	M-F **0515-0600 (Europe)**
9555	**1515-1530 (Europe)**
9750	M-F **0515-0600 (Europe)**
9755	**0000-0130**, Su/M **0100-0200**, Tu-Sa **0200-0300**, Su/M **0030-0100**, Su/M **0130-0200, 2200-2230 & 2300-2400 (E North Am &** C America)
9760	M-F **0615-0700 & 2200-2300 (Europe)**
11730	2300-2330 (C America)
11845	Su/M 0100-0200 & Tu-Sa 0200-0300 (C America)
11855	M-F **1200-1400 (E North Am)**
11905	**2200-2230 (E North Am &** C America)
11915	**1515-1530 (E Europe)**
11935	**1415-1430, 1515-1530 & 1615-1630 (Europe)**
11945	M-F **1930-2000 & 2200-2300 (Europe)**
11955	Su **1300-1700 (E North Am)**
13650	M-Sa **1515-1530 & 1715-1730 (Europe)**
15305	M-Sa **1415-1430 & 1615-1630 (E Europe)**
15315	**1515-1530**
15315	**1415-1430 (E Europe)**
15325	**1715-1730**, M-F **1830-1900**, M-F **1930-2000, 2100-2200**
15325	**1415-1430, 1515-1530 & 1615-1630 (Europe)**
17795	M-Sa **1415-1430 (Europe)**
17820	M-F 1200-1400, Su 1300-1600 & Su 1400-1700 (C America), M-Sa **1515-1530, 1615-1630 & 1715-1730 (Europe)**
17820	**1415-1430 (E Europe)**
17875	M-F **1830-1900**, M-F **1930-2000 & 2100-2200 (Europe)**
21545	M-Sa **1415-1430**, M-Sa **1515-1530, 1615-1630 & 1715-1730 (Europe)**
21675	M-F **1830-1900 (Europe)**

CHINA (PEOPLE'S REPUBLIC)
RADIO BEIJING
3985	**2200-2230 (Europe)**
6920	**2000-2200 (Europe)**
9665	**0000-0100 & 1100-1300 (E North Am & C America)**
9690	**0300-0400 (N America** & C America)
9710	**2000-2200 (Europe)**
9820	**2000-2200 (Europe)**
9920	**2000-2200 (Europe)**
11500	**2000-2200 (Europe)**
11600	1200-1400 (Pacific)
11685	**0400-0500 (W North Am)**
11695	**0400-0500 (W North Am)**
11715	**0000-0100 & 0300-0400 (N America)**
11755	0900-1100 (Australia)
11840	**0400-0600 (N America)**
11855	**1300-1500 (W North Am)**
11980	**0400-0500 (W North Am)**
15100	**0000-0100 & 0300-0400 (E North Am & C America)**
15285	1200-1400 (Australia)
15440	0900-1100 (Australia)
15455	**0300-0400 (W North Am)**
17705	**0000-0100 (E North Am** & C America)
17710	0900-1100 (Australia)
17855	**1200-1300 (E North Am** & C America)

CHINA (TAIWAN)
VOICE OF FREE CHINA
5950	**0200-0300 (E North Am)**, 0300-0400 **(E North Am** & C America), 0700-0800 (C America)
9680	**0200-0400 (W North Am)**
9765	0200-0400 (Australia)
9852	**2200-2300 (Europe)**
11740	0200-0300 (C America)
11805	**2200-2300 (Europe)**
15345	0200-0400 (E Asia)
15370	2200-2300 (Australia)
21500	**2200-2300 (Europe)**
21720	**2200-2300 (Europe)**

CUBA
RADIO HABANA
5965	0400-0600 (C America)
7215	**2200-2300 (W Europe)**
9710	**0200-0450 (N America)**
11760	0400-0600 (C America)
11800	**1900-2100 (Europe)**
11820	**0000-0600 (E North Am)**
11835	**0600-0800 (W North Am)**
11930	**2200-2300 (Europe)**

CZECHOSLOVAKIA
RADIO PRAGUE INTERNATIONAL
5930	**0100-0130, 0300-0330 & 0400-0415 (Americas), 1700-1730, 2000-2030 & 2100-2115 (Europe)**
6055	**0640-0700, 0740-0800, 0840-0900, 0940-1000, 1040-1100, 1140-1200, 1700-1730, 1830-1845, 2000-2030 & 2100-2115 (Europe)**

7345	**0000-0015, 0100-0130, 0300-0330 & 0400-0415 (Americas), 0640-0700, 0740-0800, 0840-0900, 0940-1000, 1040-1100, 1140-1200, 1700-1730, 1830-1845, 2000-2030 & 2100-2115 (Europe)**
9505	**0640-0700, 0740-0800, 0840-0900, 0940-1000, 1040-1100 & 1140-1200 (Europe)**
11680	**0000-0015, 0100-0130, 0300-0330 & 0400-0415 (Americas)**
11990	**0000-0015 (Americas), 1700-1730, 2000-2030 & 2100-2115 (Europe)**
17840	0730-0800 (Australia)
21705	0730-0800 (Australia)

ECUADOR
HCJB-VOICE OF THE ANDES
6130	0700-1030 (Pacific)
6230	**0500-0700 (N America** & C America)
9610	M-F **0645-0700 & 0700-0830 (Europe)**
9745	**0030-0300 & 0500-0700 (C America & N America)**, 0700-1130 (Australia)
11740	**1130-1500** (C America & **E North Am)**
11775	**0030-0430 & 0500-0700 (C America & N America)**
11925	0700-1130 (Australia & Pacific)
15115	**1200-1600 (Americas)**
15155	**0030-0430 & 0500-0700 (N America &** C America)
15270	M-F **0645-0700, 0700-0830, 1900-2000 & 2130-2200 (Europe)**
17790	**1900-2000 & 2130-2200 (Europe)**
17890	**1200-1600 (N America** & C America)
21470	**1900-2000 & 2130-2200 (Europe)**

EGYPT
RADIO CAIRO
9475	**0200-0330 (N America &** C America)
9675	**0200-0330 (N America)**
9900	**2115-2245 (Europe)**

FINLAND
RADIO FINLAND
6120	**0730-0755, 1930-1945 & 2200-2225 (Europe)**
9530	**1930-1945 (Europe)**
9550	**1830-1845 (Europe)**
9560	**0730-0755 (Europe)**
9635	**0330-0400 (N America)**
9640	**1505-1530 (E Europe)**
9670	2200-2225 (E Asia)
11755	**0330-0400 (Americas), 0730-0755, 1930-1945 & 2200-2225 (Europe)**
11855	0930-0955 (E Asia)
11925	**1405-1430 (E Europe)**
11945	M-F **1200-1225,** M-F **1300-1325, 1400-1425 &** Sa/Su **1425-1500 (E North Am & C America)**, 2100-2125 (E Asia)
15185	**0230-0300 (Americas), 1830-1845 (Europe)**
15245	0930-0955 (E Asia)

15400	M-F **1200-1225**, M-F **1300-1325**, **1400-1425** & Sa/Su **1425-1500** (**E North Am** & C America)
17795	0800-0825 (Australia), 0830-0855 (E Asia), 0900-0925 (Australia)
21550	0800-0825 (Australia), M-F **1100-1125**, M-F **1200-1225**, **1300-1325** & Sa/Su **1325-1400** (**N America** & C America)

FRANCE
RADIO FRANCE INTERNATIONALE
5990	**0315-0345 (E Europe)**
6045	**0315-0345 (E Europe)**
6175	**1600-1700 (Europe)**
7280	**0315-0345 (E Europe)**
9550	**0315-0345 (E Europe)**
9745	**0315-0345 (E Europe)**
9800	0315-0345 (C America)
9805	**1230-1300 (E Europe)**
11670	**1230-1300 (E Europe)**
11790	**0315-0345 (E Europe)**
15155	**1230-1300 (E Europe)**
15195	**1230-1300 (E Europe)**
15360	1600-1700 (Mideast)
17620	1600-1700 (Africa)
17650	**1230-1300 (E North Am** & C America)
17795	1600-1700 (Africa)
17845	1600-1700 (Africa)
17850	1600-1700 (Africa)
21635	**1230-1300 (E North Am)**
21645	1230-1300 (C America)

GERMANY (DR)
RADIO BERLIN INTERNATIONAL
(merges with Deutsche Welle in 1991)
6080	**0045-0130, 0245-0330** & **0400-0445** (**E North Am**)
7185	**0645-0730** & Sa/Su **0845-0930** (**Europe**)
7260	**1645-1730 (Europe)**
7295	**1645-1730** & **2245-2330 (W Europe)**
9665	**1845-1930** & **2045-2130 (Europe)**
9730	**0045-0130** & **0400-0445 (E North Am** & C America), Sa/Su **0845-0930** (**Europe**)
11785	**0845-0930** & **1000-1045 (E North Am** & C America)
11890	**0045-0130, 0245-0330, 0445-0530** & **1000-1045 (E North Am)**
13610	0045-0130 & 0245-0330 (C America)
13770	**0245-0330, 0445-0530** & **2245-2330 (N America)**
15240	0045-0130 & 0245-0330 (C America)
21465	Sa/Su 0845-0930 & Sa/Su 1000-1045 (E Asia)
21540	0845-0930 & 1000-1045 (E Asia & Australia)

GERMANY (FR)
DEUTSCHE WELLE
5960	**0500-0550 (N America** & C America)
6040	**0100-0150 (N America)**

6085	**0100-0150 (N America)**
6085	**0300-0350 (N America** & C America)
6120	**0500-0550 (N America)**
6130	**0300-0350 (N America)**
6145	**0100-0150 (N America)**
6160	0900-0950 (C America & Australia)
9545	**0300-0350 (N America** & C America)
9565	**0100-0150 (E North Am** & C America)
9605	**0300-0350 (N America)**
9670	**0500-0550 (N America)**, 2100-2150 (Australia)
9700	**0500-0550 (W North Am)**
9735	**0100-0150 (N America** & C America)
9765	2100-2150 (Australia)
11705	**0500-0550 (W North Am)**
11740	0900-0950 (Australia)
11785	2100-2150 (Australia)
11810	**0300-0350 (E North Am** & C America)
11810	2100-2150 (Australia)
11845	**0500-0550 (N America)**
11865	**0100-0150 (N America** & C America)
11945	0900-0950 (Australia)
13780	2100-2150 (E Asia)
15105	**0100-0150 (E North Am** & C America)
15205	**0300-0350 (E North Am** & C America)
15435	2100-2150 (Australia)
17765	0900-0950 (Australia)
17780	0900-0950 (Australia)
17820	0900-0950 (Australia)
21650	0900-0950 (Australia)
21680	0900-0950 (Australia)

GREECE
FONI TIS HELLADAS ("Voice of Greece")
7430	**0135-0145** & **0335-0345 (N America)**, 1920-1930 (Europe)
9395	**0135-0145** & **0335-0345 (N America)**, 1920-1930 (Europe)
9420	**0135-0145** & **0335-0345 (N America)**
9425	1920-1930 (Europe)
11645	**0135-0145** & **0335-0345 (N America)**, 1035-1045 (E Asia), **1235-1245 (N America)**, 1535-1545 (**N America** & Europe), 1920-1930 (Europe)
15625	0835-0845 (Australia), 1035-1050 (E Asia), **1235-1245** & **1530-1540 (N America & Europe)**
15630	1035-1050 (E Asia), **1235-1245** & **1530-1540 (N America & Europe)**
15650	**1235-1245 (N America & Europe)**
17535	0835-0845 (Australia), 1035-1045 (E Asia), **1235-1245** & **1530-1540 (N America & Europe)**
17550	0835-0845 (Australia), **1235-1245 (N America & Europe)**

HOLLAND
RADIO NEDERLAND
5955	**1130-1225** & **1430-1525 (Europe)**
6020	**0030-0125 (E North Am)**
6020	1030-1125 (C America)
6165	**0030-0125 (E North Am)**, 0330-0425 (**W North Am**)

9590	0330-0425 (W North Am)
9630	0730-0825 (Australia)
9715	1130-1225 (Europe)
9715	0730-0825 (Australia)
9770	M-Sa 0830-0855 (Australia)
11890	1030-1125 (Australia)
15315	0030-0125 (E North Am)
15560	0730-0825 (Australia)
17575	1130-1225 (E Asia)

HUNGARY
RADIO BUDAPEST

6110 Tu-Su **0030-0100, 0130-0200**, W/Sa
0200-0230 & Tu/W/F/Sa **0230-0245**
(**E North Am**), **1930-2000, 2100-2130** &
Tu/F **2230-2300** (**Europe**)

7220 Su **1045-1100**, Sa **1130-1145**, M/Th
1615-1630, 1930-2000 & **2100-2130**
(**Europe**)

9520 Tu-Su **0030-0100, 0130-0200**, W/Sa
0200-0230 & Tu/W/F/Sa **0230-0245**
(**E North Am**)

9585 Tu-Su **0030-0100, 0130-0200**, W/Sa
0200-0230 & Tu/W/F/Sa **0230-0245**
(**E North Am**), Su **1045-1100**, Sa
1130-1145, M/Th **1615-1630, 1930-2000**
& **2100-2130** (**Europe**)

9835 Tu-Su **0030-0100, 0130-0200**, W/Sa
0200-0230 & Tu/W/F/Sa **0230-0245**
(**E North Am**), Su **1045-1100**, Sa
1130-1145, M/Th **1615-1630, 1930-2000**
& **2100-2130** (**Europe**)

11910 Tu-Su **0030-0100, 0130-0200**, W/Sa
0200-0230 & Tu/W/F/Sa **0230-0245**
(**E North Am**), Su **1045-1100**, Sa
1130-1145, M-Th **1615-1630, 1930-2000**
& **2100-2130** (**Europe**)

15160 Tu-Su **0030-0100, 0130-0200**, W/Sa
0200-0230 & Tu/W/F/Sa **0230-0245**
(**E North Am**), Su **1045-1100**, Sa
1130-1145, M/Th **1615-1630, 1930-2000**
& **2100-2130** (**Europe**)

15220 Su **1045-1100**, Sa **1130-1145** & M-Th
1615-1630 (**Europe**)

INDIA
ALL INDIA RADIO

7265	2045-2230 (Australia)
7412	**1845-1945 & 2045-2230 (Europe)**
9550	2045-2230 (Australia)
9665	**1845-1945 & 2045-2230 (Europe)**
9910	**2045-2230 (Europe)**, 2245-0115 (E Asia)
11620	**1845-1945 & 2045-2230 (Europe)**
11715	2245-0115 (E Asia)
11810	**1845-2230 (Europe)**
11860	1000-1100 (Australia)
15050	1000-1100 (E Asia)
15265	2045-2230 (Australia)
15335	1000-1100 (Australia)
15345	2245-0115 (Australia)
17387	1000-1100 (E Asia)
17865	1000-1100 (E Asia)
21735	1000-1100 (E Asia)

INDONESIA
VOICE OF INDONESIA
11744   0100-0200 & 0800-0900 (Pacific),
        2000-2100 (Europe)
11788   **2000-2100 (Europe)**

IRAN
VOICE OF THE ISLAMIC REPUBLIC
6030   **1930-2030 (Europe)**
9022   **1930-2030 (Europe & C America)**

IRAQ
RADIO BAGHDAD
7290   **2100-2255 (Europe)**
9515   **0230-0425 (E North Am & C America)**
11755   **0130-0325 (Americas)**
13660   **2000-2155 (Europe)**

ISRAEL
KOL ISRAEL
7462   **0500-0515 & 2000-2030 (W Europe &
        E North Am)**
9435   **0000-0030, 0100-0125, 0200-0225 &
        0400-0415 (W Europe & E North Am),
        1745-1800 (E Europe), 2000-2030 &
        2230-2330 (W Europe & E North Am)**
9930   **0000-0030, 0100-0125, 0200-0230 &
        2230-2300 (E North Am)**
11585   **0500-0515 (Europe & E North Am),
        1000-1030 (Europe), 1100-1130
        (Europe & E North Am), 1700-1715
        (Europe)**
11605   **0000-0030, 0100-0125, 0200-0225 &
        0400-0415 (Europe, E North Am &
        C America), 0500-0515 (Europe &
        C America), 1900-1930, 2000-2030,
        2130-2200 & 2230-2330 (Europe,
        E North Am & C America)**
11655   **0400-0415, 0500-0515 & 1700-1715
        (E Europe)**
15640   **0000-0025, 0100-0125, 0400-0415,
        1645-1700, 1900-1930, 2130-2155 &
        2300-2330 (E North Am & C America)**
15650   **1000-1030 & 1100-1130 (Australia)**
17575   **1000-1030, 1100-1130 & 2130-2200
        (W Europe & E North Am)**
17590   **1900-1930 (W Europe & E North Am)**
17630   **0400-0415 & 0500-0515 (Australia)**
21745   **1000-1030 & 1645-1700 (W Europe &
        E North Am)**
21780   **1100-1130 (W Europe & E North Am)**

ITALY
ADVENTIST WORLD RADIO
9670   **Su 0900-1000 (W Europe)**
RTV ITALIANA
5990   **0425-0440 (Europe)**, 2200-2225
        (E Asia)
7235   **2025-2045 (E Europe)**
7275   **0425-0440 & 1935-1955 (Europe)**
9575   **0100-0120 (E North Am), 0425-0440
        (Europe)**

9710   **1935-1955 (Europe)**, 2200-2225
        (E Asia)
11800   **0100-0120 (E North Am & C America),
        1935-1955 (Europe)**, 2200-2225
        (E Asia)
15330   2200-2225 (E Asia)

JAPAN
RADIO JAPAN/NHK
5960   **0100-0200 & 0300-0400 (E North Am &
        C America)**
6120   **1100-1200 (N America)**
7140   1700-1800 (E Asia)
9505   **1400-1600, 1700-1800 & 1900-1930
        (Pacific & W North Am)**
9695   1700-1800 (E Asia)
11815   2100-2200 & 2300-2400 (E Asia)
11835 **2300-2400 (Europe)**
11840   0900-1000 & 1100-1300 (E Asia)
11850   1900-1930 (Australia)
11865 **1400-1600, 1700-1800 & 1900-1930
        (Pacific & N America)**
11870   **0300-0330 & 0500-0600 (W North Am)**
15195   0300-0400 (E Asia), **0500-0600
        (Pacific & N America)**, 2300-2400
        (E Asia)
15270   0900-1000, 1900-1930 & 2100-2130
        (Australia)
15325   **0700-0800 (Europe)**
15325 0300-0330 (C America)
17765   0000-0200, 0500-0600, 0700-0800,
        2100-2200 & 2300-2400 (E Asia)
17825   **0300-0330 & 0400-0600 (W North Am &
        C America)**
17835   0100-0200 (E Asia)
17890   0500-0600, 0700-0800, 0900-1000 &
        2100-2130 (Australia)
21500   **0700-0800 (Europe)**
21610   0300-0330 (Pacific)
21690 **0700-0800 (Europe)**
21700 **1500-1600 (Europe)**

JORDAN
RADIO JORDAN -- (Europe)
9560   **1420-1730**
13655   **1200-1415**

KOREA (DPR)
RADIO PYONGYANG
6576   **2000-2050 (Europe)**
9325   **1300-1350, 1500-1550 & 1700-1750
        (Europe)**
9345   **1300-1350 & 2000-2050 (Europe)**
9600   **1100-1150 (C America)**
9640   **1500-1550, 1700-1750 & 2000-2050
        (Europe)**
9977   1100-1150 (C America)
11735   1100-1150 & 2300-2350 (C America)
11760   **1500-1550 & 1700-1750 (Europe)**
13650   2300-2350 (C America)
15115   0000-0050 (C America)
15160   0000-0050 (C America)

KOREA (REPUBLIC)
RADIO KOREA
6165 0245-0300 (E Asia)
6480 **2030-2130 (Europe)**
7275 0045-0100, 1115-1130, 1330-1345 &
      1545-1600 (E Asia)
7550 **0800-0900 (Europe)**
9570 **0600-0800 (W North Am** & C America)
9700 **1130-1200 (N America)**
11715 **1030-1100 (N America)**
11740 1115-1130 & 1330-1345 (E Asia)
13670 **0800-0900 & 0915-0930 (Europe)**
15575 **0000-0100 & 0245-0300 (E North Am)**,
      1800-1900 & 2030-2130 (Europe)

KUWAIT
RADIO KUWAIT (when operating)
13610 **1800-2100 (Europe & E North Am)**

LUXEMBOURG
RADIO LUXEMBOURG
6090 **0000-0300 (Europe)**

MALTA
VO MEDITERRANEAN -- **(Europe)**
9765 **0600-0700**
11925 **1400-1500**

MONGOLIA
RADIO ULAN BATOR (weak)
11850 W/Th/Sa-M 0910-0940 (E Asia &
      Australia), W/Th/Sa-M 1200-1230
      (E Asia), W/Th/Sa-M **1940-2010**
      (Europe)
12015 W/Th/Sa-M 0910-0940 & W/Th/Sa-M
      1200-1230 (E Asia)
13780 W/Th/Sa-M 1445-1515 (E Asia)

MOROCCO
RTV MAROCAINE -- **(Europe)**
11920 Su **1900-2000**
17595 M-F **1530-1700**
17815 Sa **1700-1800**

NETHERLANDS ANTILLES
TRANS WORLD RADIO
11815 **1100-1255, Sa/Su 1255-1335 & Sa**
      1330-1400 (E North Am)
11930 **0300-0430 (N America)**

NEW ZEALAND
R NEW ZEALAND INTL -- (Pacific)
9855 Sa 0645-0715, M-Sa 0715-0830, Sa
      0830-1100
15485 M-F 1750-1815, Su-F 1845-2205
17675 M-Sa 0000-0150, 0150-0645, Su-F
      0645-0715, Su 0715-0800, Su/F 2305-
      2400

NORWAY
RADIO NORWAY INTERNATIONAL
5980 Sa/Su **0600-0630 (Europe)**
9590 Sa/Su **1300-1330 (Europe)**

9605 Sa/Su **2300-2330 (E North Am)**
15165 Sa/Su **0600-0630 & Sa/Su 0800-0830**
      (W North Am & Pacific), Sa/Su **1200-**
      1230 (N America), Sa/Su **1900-1930**
      (Europe), Sa/Su **2300-2330**
      (E North Am & C America)
15220 Sa/Su **1900-1930 (Europe)**
15305 Sa/Su **1700-1730 (W North Am)**
17740 Sa/Su 0900-0930 (Australia)
17765 Sa/Su **1600-1630 (N America)**, Sa/Su
      1700-1730 (W North Am)
17840 Sa/Su 0900-0930 (E Asia), Sa/Su
      1600-1630 (E North Am & C America)
21705 Sa/Su **1600-1630 (E North Am &**
      C America)
25730 Sa/Su **0800-0830** (E Asia & Australia)

PAKISTAN
RADIO PAKISTAN
17660 **1100-1120 (Europe)**

POLAND
RADIO POLONIA
6095 **1200-1225 (Europe)**
6135 **0630-0700, 1430-1455, 1600-1630,**
      1830-1855 & 2230-2355 (Europe)
7125 **2230-2355 (Europe)**
7270 **0630-0700 & 2230-2355 (Europe)**
7285 **1200-1225, 1430-1455 & 1830-1855**
      (Europe)
9525 **1230-1300, 1630-1700, 1830-1855 &**
      2000-2030 (Europe)
9540 **1430-1455 & 1600-1630 (Europe)**
9675 **0630-0700 (Europe)**
11815 **1200-1230 (Europe)**, 1430-1455
      (W Europe)
11840 **1230-1300, 1630-1700, 1830-1855 &**
      2000-2030 (W Europe)
15120 **1230-1300 & 1630-1700 (Europe)**

PORTUGAL
RADIO PORTUGAL INTERNATIONAL
9615 Sa/Su **0845-0900 (Europe)**
9680 Tu-Sa **0230-0300 (E North Am)**
9705 Tu-Sa **0230-0300 (N America)**
11740 M-F **2000-2030 (Europe)**

ROMANIA
RADIO ROMANIA INTERNATIONAL
5990 **0200-0300 & 0400-0430 (Americas)**,
      2100-2130 (Europe)
6105 **1930-2030 & 2100-2130 (Europe)**
6155 **0200-0300 & 0400-0430 (Americas)**
7105 **1930-2030 & 2100-2130 (Europe)**
7195 **1930-2030 & 2100-2130 (Europe)**
9510 **0200-0300 & 0400-0430 (Americas)**
9570 **0200-0300 & 0400-0430 (Americas)**
9690 **1930-2030 & 2100-2130 (Europe)**
9750 **1930-2030 & 2100-2130 (Europe)**
11810 **1930-2030 (Europe)**
11830 **0200-0300 & 0400-0430 (Americas)**
11940 **0200-0300 & 0400-0430 (Americas)**,
      0645-0715 (Australia), **1300-1330,**
      1930-2030 & 2100-2130 (Europe)

15250 0645-0715 (Australia)
15335 0645-0715 (Australia)
15365 **1300-1400 (Europe)**
15380 **0200-0300 & 0400-0430 (Americas)**
17720 0645-0715 (Australia)
17805 0645-0715 (Australia)
17850 **1300-1400 (W Europe)**
21550 0645-0715 (Australia), **1300-1400 (W Europe)**

SAUDI ARABIA
BS OF THE KINGDOM
9705 **1600-2100 (Europe)**

SOUTH AFRICA
RADIO RSA
17765 1800-1855 (C Africa)
17835 1100-1155 (W Africa), 1200-1255 (E Africa), 1400-1555 (W Africa)

SPAIN
RADIO NACIONAL DE ESPANA
9630 **0000-0200 (E North Am & C** America), **0500-0600 (N America & C** America)
9765 **1900-2000 & 2100-2200 (Europe)**
11790 **1900-2000 & 2100-2200 (Europe)**
11880 **0000-0200 (E North Am & C** America)
15110 **0000-0200 & 0500-0600 (E North Am &** C America)
15280 **1900-2000 & 2100-2200 (Europe)**

SRI LANKA
SRI LANKA BROADCASTING CORPORATION
11800 **1845-1915 (Europe)**
11835 1030-1135 (Australia)
15120 1030-1135 (E Asia)

SURINAME
RADIO SURINAME INTERNATIONAL
17755 M-F 1730-1740 (Europe)

SWEDEN
IBRA RADIO
7110 Sa/Su 1930-2000 (Europe)
RADIO SWEDEN
6065 **1700-1730 & 1800-1830 (Europe)**
7265 **1800-1830 (Europe)**
9615 **1700-1730 (Europe)**
9655 **2100-2130 (Europe)**
9695 **0230-0300 (N America)**
11705 **0230-0300 (N America), 2100-2130 (W Europe)**
11905 1400-1430 (Australia)
15190 1230-1300 (E Asia)
15295 **0230-0300 (E North Am** & C America)
15405 0100-0130 (Australia)
17860 0100-0130 (Australia), **1530-1600 (E North Am)**
17880 **1530-1600 (N America)**
21570 1130-1200 & 1230-1300 (Australia)
21610 1130-1200 & 1400-1430 (E Asia & Australia), **1530-1600 (E North Am)**
21655 **1530-1600 (Europe)**

SWITZERLAND
RED CROSS (airs one week per month)
6135 Tu/F **0310-0330 (N America & C America)**
7210 Su **1100-1130** & M **1700-1730 (Europe)**
9560 M/Th 0740-0800 (Australia)
9620 M/Th 1310-1330 (E Asia)
9725 Tu/F **0310-0330 (N America & C America)**
9885 Tu/F **0310-0330 (N America)**
12035 Tu/F **0310-0330 (N America)**
13635 M/Th 1040-1100 (Australia), M/Th 1310-1330 (E Asia)
13685 M/Th 0740-0800 (Australia)
15570 M/Th 1040-1100 (E Asia & Australia)
17670 M/Th 0740-0800 (Australia)
17830 M/Th 1040-1100 (Australia)
21695 M/Th 0740-0800 (Australia)
25680 M/Th 1310-1330 (E Asia)
SWISS RADIO INTERNATIONAL
3985 **0730-0800 & 1830-1900 (Europe)**
6095 0200-0230 (C America)
6135 **0200-0230 & 0400-0430 (N America & C America)**
6165 **0730-0800, 1300-1330 & 1830-1900 (Europe)**
6190 **2230-2300 (W Europe)**
9535 **0730-0800, 1300-1330 & 1830-1900 (Europe)**
9560 0830-0900 & 1000-1030 (Australia)
9620 1330-1400 (E Asia)
9725 0200-0230 (C America), **0400-0430 (N America & C America)**
9885 **0200-0230 (E North Am & C America), 0400-0430 (N America)**
12030 **1300-1330 (Europe)**
12035 **0200-0230 (E North Am** & C America), **0400-0430 (N America)**
13635 1100-1130 (Australia), 1330-1400 (E Asia)
13685 0830-0900 & 1000-1030 (Australia)
15570 1100-1130 (E Asia & Australia)
17670 0830-0900 & 1000-1030 (Australia)
17730 **0200-0230 (C America & W North Am)**
17830 1100-1130 (Australia)
21695 0830-0900 & 1000-1030 (Australia)
25680 1330-1400 (E Asia)

SYRIA
SYRIAN BROADCASTING SERVICE
11625 **2005-2105 (Europe)**
12085 **2005-2105 (Europe)**, 2110-2210 (Australia)
15095 **2005-2105 (Europe)**, 2110-2210 **(N America)**

TURKEY
VOICE OF TURKEY
9445 **0400-0450 & 2300-2350 (E North Am)**
9685 **2200-2250 (Europe)**
9795 **2000-2050 (Europe)**
9875 **2100-2150 & 2300-2350 (Europe)**
17880 0400-0450 & 2300-2350 (Australia)

UNITED ARAB EMIRATES
UAE RADIO, Dubai
11940	**0330-0400 (E North Am & C America)**
13675	**0330-0400 (E North Am & C America)**
15400	**0330-0400 (E North Am)**
15435	**0330-0400 (E North Am)**, 0530-0600 (Australia), **1030-1100, 1330-1400 & 1600-1645 (Europe)**
17775	**1030-1100 & 1330-1400 (Europe)**
17830	0530-0600 (E Asia)
17865	**1030-1100 & 1330-1400 (Europe)**
17890	**0330-0400 (E North Am** & C America)
21605	**1030-1100, 1330-1400 & 1600-1645 (Europe)**
21675	**0330-0400 (E North Am)**
21700	0530-0600 (Australia)

VOICE OF THE UAE, Abu Dhabi
9600	**2200-2400 (E North Am)**
11985	**2200-2400 (E North Am)**
13605	**2200-2400 (N America)**

UNITED KINGDOM
BBC WORLD SERVICE
3955	**1830-2300 (Europe)**
5965	**1100-1130 & M-Sa 1130-1200 (N America)**
5975	**0730-1515 (W Europe), 0900-1515 (Europe)**
5975	2000-0730, except M-F 2115-2130 (C America)
5995	0900-1000, 1245-1430 & 1500-1615 (E Asia)
6045	**0900-1515 (Europe)**
6175	**2200-0430 (N America)**
6180	**0300-0730 (Europe)**, Sa/Su **0730-0900 (E Europe), 0900-1515 & 1700-2300 (Europe)**
6195	**0400-0915 & 1700-2300 (Europe)**
6195	0900-1615 (E Asia), 1100-1330 & Su 1330-1400 (C America), 2100-0045 (E Asia)
7120	**0400-0730 (Europe), 0500-0730 (W Europe)**
7150	0600-0815 (Australia)
7180	0900-1000, 1145-1200, 1300-1615 & 2000-2130 (E Asia)
7230	**0500-0730 (Europe)**
7325	**0700-2300 (Europe)**, 2200-0330 (C America)
9410	**0300-2300 (Europe)**
9515	**1100-1330 & Su 1330-1400 (N America)**
9580	**0400-0730 (Europe)**
9590	0030-0230 (C America), **2200-0030 (N America)**
9640	0500-0815 (C America)
9660	Sa/Su **0730-0900 & 0900-1515 (Europe)**
9740	1030-1515 (Australia)
9750	**0900-1615 (Europe)**
9760	**0900-1615 (Europe)**

9915	**0330-0430 (N America** & C America), **2200-0530 (W North Am), 1600-1630 (Europe)**, Tu/F 2130-2200 (Atlantic), **2200-0330 (Americas)**
11715	2000-2115 (E Asia)
11750	0900-1030 & 1800-2200 (Australia)
11775	1100-1330 & Su 1330-1400 (C America), Sa/Su **1500-1600 & 1600-1745 (N America)**
11945	2200-0045 (E Asia)
11955	0600-0915 (Australia), 0930-1000 (E Asia), 2200-0030 (E Asia & Australia)
12095	**0400-2300 (Europe), 2200-0330 (E North Am)**
15070	**0500-1745 (Europe)**
15140	Su 1900-2000 & 2000-2300 (Australia)
15260	Sa/Su **1500-1600 & 1600-1745 (N America)**
15280	0100-1000 (E Asia)
15360	0600-0915 (E Asia), 0915-1130 (E Asia & Australia)
17830	0600-0915 (Australia), 2215-0045 (E Asia)
21715	0100-1030 (E Asia)

BBC WORLD SERVICE (CARIBBEAN)
5975	M-F 2115-2130
17715	M-F 2115-2130

USA -- (All stations audible to some extent within North America, regardless of where they are targeted.)
AFRTS-US MILITARY -- (Atlantic)
(LSB or USB, aired very irregularly on any one or two of the following frequencies:)
9239	24h
9242	24h
9244	24h
9334	24h
13651	24h
16041	24h
16454	24h

CHRISTIAN SCIENCE MONITOR
9410	M-Sa **0000-0100, 0100-0120 & Tu-Su 0120-0155 (E North Am & C America)**
9455	**0200-0300, M-F 0300-0315 & Tu-F 0315-0355 (W North Am & C America), 0400-0500, M-F 0500-0515, Tu-F 0515-0555, 0600-0700 & M-F 0700-0755 (W North Am)**
9455	Su-F 1800-1855 & 1855-1955 (Australia), 2000-2155 (E Asia)
9465	**2200-2300, Su-F 2300-2315 & M-F 2315-2355 (E North Am)**
9495	**1000-1100, M-F 1100-1155, 1200-1300 & M-F 1305-1355 (E North Am)**
9530	0800-1155 & 1400-1555 (E Asia)
9840	M-F **0600-0700, 0700-0755**, M-F **0800-0900 & 0900-0955 (Europe)**
9895	M-F 1200-1255 & 1255-1355 (Australia)
11705	M-F **0800-0900 & 0900-0955 (Europe)**

11930   M-F 1200-1300 & 1300-1355
       (C America)
11980   M-F 0600-0700 & 0700-0755
       (C America)
11980   Su-F 1800-1855, 1855-1920 & M-Sa
       1920-1955 (E Asia)
13625   Su-F 2000-2055 & 2055-2155
       (Australia)
13720   Su-F 1800-1855 & 1855-1955
       (Australia)
13760   M-F 0400-0500, 0500-0515 & Tu-Su
       0515-0555 (C America), 0800-0900 &
       M-F 0900-0955 (C America &
       Australia), M-F **1400-1500 & 1500-1555**
       (W North Am)
13770   Su-F **2000-2120 (E North Am), 2000-**
       2100 & Su-F 2100-2155 (Europe), M-F
       2120-2155 (E North Am)
15405   2200-2355 (E Asia)
15610   Su-F **2000-2120 (E North Am &**
       Europe), 2000-2100 & Su-F 2100-2155
       (Europe), M-F 2120-2155 (E North Am
       & Europe)
15610   M-F 0800-0855 & 0855-1000
       (Australia)
17555   M-F 1400-1500 & 1500-1555
       (C America)
17555   Su-F 1800-1855, 1855-1920 & M-Sa
       1920-1955 (E Asia)
17780   0400-0755 (E Asia)
21780   **1400-1500 & M-F 1500-1555 (Europe),**
       Su-F **1800-1900, 1900-1920 & M-Sa**
       1920-1955 (E North Am)

KNLS, Alaska -- (E Asia)
7355   0800-0900, Tu-Su 1500-1600
11715   0800-0900
11800   Tu-Su 1500-1600

KUSW, Utah -- (E North Am)
9815   Th-Su **0300-0400**, Su **0400-0500**
9870   Su **0500-1315**, Sa/Su **1315-1400**
15590   Th-M **0000-0030**, Th-Su **0030-0300**,
       Sa/Su **1400-1800**, W-Su **1800-2400**

KVOH, California
17775   **2000-2200 (W North Am** & C America)

VOICE OF AMERICA
5985   1000-1200 (Pacific & Australia)
5995   0000-0200 & Tu-Sa 0200-0230
       (C America)
5995   **0400-0500 (Europe), 0400-0700**
       (E Europe)
6030   1000-1200 (C America)
6040   **0400-0600 & 1700-2200 (Europe)**
6060   **0500-0700 (E Europe)**
6130   0000-0200 (C America)
6140   **0400-0700 (E Europe)**
7200   **0400-0700 (Europe)**
7325   **0600-0700 (Europe)**
9455   0000-0200 (C America)
9590   1000-1200 (C America)
9640   M-F 2200-2215 (C America)
9760   **1630-2200 (Europe)**
9775   0000-0200 & Tu-Sa 0200-0230
       (C America)

9815   0000-0200 & Tu-Sa 0200-0230
       (C America)
11580   0000-0200 & Tu-Sa 0200-0230
       (C America)
11695   0000-0100 (C America)
11760   **1700-2200 (Europe)**
11870   1900-2000 & 2100-2200 (E Asia &
       Australia)
11880   M-F 2200-2215 (C America)
11915   1000-1200 (C America)
15120   1000-1200 (C America)
15160   **1400-1500 (E Asia)**
15205   0000-0200 & Tu-Sa 0200-0230
       (C America)
15205   **1500-1700 (Europe)**
15225   M-F 2200-2215 (C America)
15290   **2200-0100 (E Asia)**
17735   **2100-0100 (E Asia & Australia)**

WINB, Pennsylvania -- (Europe)
15145   **2250-2345**
15185   **2005-2245**
15295   **1600-2000**

WMLK, Pennsylvania -- (Europe)
9465   M-Sa **0400-0700**, Su-F **1700-2000**

WHRI, Indiana
7315   **0000-0100 & 0300-1100 (E North Am)**
7355   **0800-1100 (E North Am & C America)**
9465   **1100-1500 (E North Am)**
9495   0300-0800 (C America)
9620   **0600-0800 (E North Am & W Europe)**
11790   1100-1400 (C America)
13760   **1700-2400 (E North Am & W Europe)**
15105   1400-1500, Su 1600-1700 & 1700-1800
       (C America)
17830   1800-2400 (C America)
21840   **1500-1600 (E North Am & W Europe)**

WRNO, Louisiana -- (E North Am)
6185   **0300-0600**, Su **0600-1200**
7355   **0000-0400, 2300-2400**
9715   Su **1200-1400**
13720   **2100-2400**
15420   **1400-2400**

WWCR, Tennessee -- (E North Am & Europe)
7520   **0100-0600**
15690   M-F **1330-1400, 1400-0100**

FAMILY RADIO
5950   **1000-1545 (E North Am)**
5985   **0500-0700 (W North Am), 2300-0245**
       (E North Am)
6015   **1200-1445 (W North Am)**
6065   **0300-0445 (E North Am), 0600-0800**
       (W North Am)
7355   **0600-0745 (Europe), 1100-1245**
       (W North Am)
9455   **2000-2145 (Europe)**
9505   **2300-0445 (W North Am)**
9680   **0100-0200 (W North Am), 0600-0745**
       (Europe)
9705   **1300-1445 (W North Am)**
11580   **0500-0600 (Europe), 1100-1645 &**
       2200-2345 (W North Am)
11720   **0100-0245 (C America)**
11830   **1200-2245 (W North Am)**

13695	**0000-0045 (W North Am), 1300-2245 (E North Am)**
13760	**0600-0745 (Europe)**
15215	**1500-2245 (W North Am)**
15440	**1700-2145 (W North Am)**, 2300-0245 (C America)
15566	**1600-1700 & 1900-2200 (Europe)**
17612	**0100-0145 (W North Am)**
17640	1200-1645 (C America)
17750	1200-1645 (C America), **1700-1900 (Europe)**
17895	1700-2245 (C America)
21615	**1600-1700 & 1900-2145 (Europe)**

USSR -- (Soviet schedules currently changing often and without notice.)
RADIO KIEV, Ukraine

7400	**0000-0100 (E North Am)**
9800	**0000-0100 (E North Am & C America)**
9865	**2000-2100 (Europe)**
11790	**2300-2400 (E North Am)**
13645	**2300-2400 (W North Am)**
15180	**0000-0100 (W North Am)**
15455	**2300-2400 (W North Am)**
15485	**2300-2400 (W North Am)**
15525	**2300-2400 (E North Am & C America)**

RADIO MOSCOW

5960	1300-1400 (E Asia)
6000	**0000-0500 & 1000-1300 (N America)**
6045	**2200-0400 (N America)**
7115	**2200-0400 (E North Am)**
7150	**1800-2200 (Europe), 2200-0600 (E North Am)**
7195	**1800-2400 (Europe & E North Am)**
7310	**0030-0900 (E North Am & C America)**
7315	1300-1400 (E Asia)
7330	**2000-2200 (Europe** & Atlantic)
7370	1300-1500 (E Asia)
9450	**0500-1000 & 1100-1700 (Europe)**, 2130-2300 (Atlantic)
9795	**0400-0900 (Europe)**
11690	**2200-0300 (E North Am)**
11710	**2200-0400 (N America)**
11830	**0630-1500 (Europe)**
11840	**1330-2200 (N America)**
11850	**0000-0600 (N America)**
12010	**0200-0500 (W North Am)**
12050	**1500-0700 (Pacific & W North Am)**
12060	**1900-2200 (W Europe & C America)**
13680	**0700-1600 (W Europe & Atlantic)**
15150	**1000-1530 (Europe & Atlantic)**, **1630-2100 (Europe, E North Am & C America)**
15180	**0400-0800 (W North Am)**
15245	**0400-0700 (W North Am)**
15290	**2200-0300 (E North Am** & C America)
15420	0000-1000 (Australia), **0900-1100, 0800-0900 & 1130-1500 (Europe)**
15425	**1930-0700 (W North Am)**
15455	**0300-0600 (W North Am)**
17685	2300-1200 (E Asia)

17850	0130-0800 & 2230-2400 (Australia)
17860	2330-0700 (Australia)

RADIO VILNIUS, Lithuania

7400	**2300-2330 (E North Am)**
11790	**2200-2230 (E North Am)**
13645	**2200-2230 (W North Am)**
15180	**2300-2330 (W North Am)**
15455	**2200-2230 (W North Am)**

RADIO YEREVAN, Armenia

11790	**0252-0256 (E North Am)**
13645	**0252-0256 (W North Am)**
15180	**0352-0356 (W North Am)**
15455	**0352-0356 (W North Am)**

VATICAN RADIO

6185	**0600-0620 (Europe)**
6190	M-Sa **2000-2010 (Europe), 2050-2110 (W Europe)**
7250	**1445-1500**, M-Sa **1600-1630**, M-Sa **2000-2010 & 2050-2110 (Europe)**
9605	**0050-0115 (E North Am)**
9615	2205-2230 (E Asia)
9645	**0600-0620**, M-Sa **0700-0800**, M-Sa **1130-1200, 1445-1500**, M-Sa **1600-1630**, M-Sa **2000-2010 & 2050-2110 (Europe)**
11725	**0310-0330 (E North Am & C America)**
11740	M-Sa **0700-0800**, M-Sa **1130-1200, 1445-1500 & M-Sa 1600-1630 (Europe)**
11780	**0050-0115 (E North Am)**
11830	2205-2230 (Australia)
15105	2205-2230 (E Asia)
15180	**0050-0115 (E North Am)**
17865	M-Sa 1200-1230 (E Asia)
21515	M-Sa 1200-1230 (E Asia)

YUGOSLAVIA
RADIO LJUBLJANA

5980	M **2100-2130 (Europe)**
9620	M **2100-2130 (W Europe)**

RADIO YUGOSLAVIA

5980	**0100-0145 (W Europe & E North Am), 1930-2000 & 2200-2245 (W Europe)**
7130	2200-2245 (E Asia & Australia)
7215	**0000-0045, 1830-1900 & 2100-2145 (Europe)**
9620	**0100-0145 (E North Am), 1730-1800 & 1930-2000 (Europe)**, 2200-2245 (E Asia & Australia)
9660	**0100-0145 (E North Am), 1830-1900 & 1930-2000 (Europe), 2200-2245 (Europe & E North Am)**
11735	**0000-0045 (E North Am), 1830-1900 (Europe)**
15105	**0000-0045 & 2100-2145 (W Europe & E North Am)**
15325	**1300-1330 (E North Am)**
15380	1300-1330 (E Asia & Australia)
17740	**1200-1230 (E North Am)**
21555	1200-1230 (E Asia & Australia)

For some, the offerings in English on world band radio are just icing on the cake. Their real interest is in listening to programs aimed at national compatriots. Voices from home.

"Home" may be a place of birth, or perhaps it's a favorite country you once visited or lived in. Vacationers and business travelers also turn to world band radio to keep in touch with the events that mean so much: politics, stocks, weather . . . how the local ball team is faring. For yet others, it is the perfect way to keep limber in a second tongue.

Following are frequencies for the most popular such stations. Those in bold usually come in best, as they are from relay transmitters close to the listening audience. For full details on times and target zones, please refer the the Blue Pages.

ALGERIA
"VOICE OF PALESTINE"
Arabic 11715 kHz (weak)
RTV ALGERIENNE
Arabic 6145, 7145, 11715, 17745 kHz
French 9509, 9535, 9685, 15160, 15205, 15215, 17745 kHz

ARGENTINA -- Spanish
RADIO ARGENTINA-RAE
11710, 15345 kHz
RADIO NACIONAL
6060, 11710, 15345 kHz

AUSTRIA -- German
RADIO AUSTRIA INTERNATIONAL
5945, **6015**, 6155, 9870, 9875, 11780, 12010, 13730, 15410, 15430, 15450, 21490 kHz

BELGIUM -- French
RADIO-TV BELGE FRANCAISE
5965, 9925, 11660, 13745, 15540, 17675, 21460, 25645 kHz

BRAZIL -- Portuguese
RADIO NACIONAL (RADIOBRAS)
9760, 15230 kHz
RADIO NACIONAL DA AMAZONIA
6180, 11780 kHz
RADIO CULTURA
17815 kHz (weak)

CANADA -- French
CANADIAN BROADCASTING CORPORATION
9625 kHz
RADIO CANADA INTERNATIONAL
5960, **5995**, **6050**, 6120, 6150, **7155**, **7230**, **7235**, **7295**, 9535, **9555**, 9635, 9650, **9670**, **9740**, 9750, 9755, 9760, **11705**, 11730, **11775**, **11840**, 11855, 11880, **11915**, **11925**, **11935**, 11940, 11945, 13650, 13670, 13720, 15140, 15150, 15260, 15305, 15315, 15320, 15325, 15425, 17795, 17820, **17840**, 17875, 21545, 21675 kHz

CHILE -- Spanish
RADIO NACIONAL
15140 kHz

CHINA (PR) -- Standard Chinese
CENTRAL PEOPLES BS (weak)
7504, 7516, 7525, 7620, 7770, 8007, 9020, 9080, 9390, 9455, 9775, 10010, 11000, 11040, 11100, 11330, 11505, 11610, 12120, 15030, 15390, 15500, 17700 kHz
RADIO BEIJING
6995, 7315, 7335, 7350, 7420, 7590, 7660, 7780, 7800, 8450, 9455, 9480, **9690**, **9745**, **9770**, 9945, 11445, 11650, 11685, 11695, **11715**, **11790**, 11945, 11975, 12015, 12055, 15100, **15110**, **15130**, 15150, 15165, 15195, 15260, 15320, 15330, 15435, 15455, 17533, 17705, **17715** kHz

CHINA (TAIWAN) -- Chinese
VOICE OF FREE CHINA
5950, 6200, 7130, 7445, 9510, 9575, **9680**, 9765, 11745, 11825, 11860, 11915, **15130**, **15215**, 15270, 15345, 15370, **15440**, 17720, **17805**, **17845**, **21500**, **21720** kHz

CLANDESTINE (CENTRAL AMERICA)
-- Spanish
"15 DE SETIEMBRE"
6214 kHz (weak)
"LA VOZ DEL CID"
6305, 7340, 9942, 11635 kHz
"RADIO CAIMAN"
9965 kHz

CLANDESTINE (MIDDLE EAST) -- Persian
"IRAN FLAG OF FREEDOM RADIO"
9045, 11615, 15100 kHz
"RADIO IRAN"
6970, 9400, 15650 kHz

COLOMBIA -- Spanish
CARACOL BOGOTA
5075 kHz
LA VOZ DEL LLANO
6116 kHz (weak)

CUBA -- Spanish
RADIO HABANA
5985, 9550, 9590, 9640, 9655, 11705, **11755**, 11760, 11820, 11910, **11920**, 11950, 11970, 15230, 15285, 15300, 15340, **15350**, 15425, **17710**, 17800, **21670** kHz

RADIO REBELDE
3365, 5025 kHz

ECUADOR -- Spanish
HCJB-VOICE OF THE ANDES
9765, 11910, 11960, 15160, 17890 kHz

EGYPT -- Arabic
RADIO CAIRO
6195, 9455, 9620, 9670, 9700, 9755, 9770,
9805, 9850, 9900, 9940, 11665, 11785, 11905,
11980, 12050, 15115, 15175, 15220, 15285,
17670, 17745, 17770, 17800 kHz

FRANCE -- French
RADIO FRANCE INTERNATIONALE
3965, **4890**, 5945, 5990, 5995, 6040, 6045,
6175, 7120, **7125**, 7135, 7160, 7280, 9550,
9605, 9715, 9745, 9790, 9800, 9805, 9830,
11660, 11670, 11695, 11700, 11705, **11735**,
11790, 11800, 11845, **11890**, **11910**, 11930,
11965, 11995, **12025**, 15135, 15155, 15180,
15190, 15195, **15215**, **15275**, **15285**, 15300,
15315, 15360, **15365**, 15425, 15435, 15460,
15530, 17620, 17650, 17695, **17705**, **17710**,
17720, 17775, 17785, 17795, 17800, 17845,
17850, **17860**, **21520**, 21580, 21620, 21635,
21645, 21685, 21730, **21765**, 21770, **21810**,
25820 kHz

GABON -- French
AFRIQUE NUMERO UN
9580, 15475, 17630 kHz

GERMANY (DR) -- German
DEUTSCHLANDSENDER-KULTUR
6115 kHz (weak)
RADIO BERLIN INTERNATIONAL
(merges with Deutsche Welle in 1991)
5965, 6040, 6080, 6115, 7185, 7260, 7295,
9635, 9665, 9730, 9760, 11705, 11785, 11890,
11970, 13610, 13690, 13700, 13770, 15145,
15240, 15350, 15440, 15445, 17780, 21465,
21540 kHz

GERMANY (FR) -- German
BAYERISCHER RUNDFUNK
6085 kHz (weak)
DEUTSCHE WELLE (may carry ARD
network starting in 1991)
3995, 6075, **6085**, 6100, 6145, 7130, 9545,
9605, 9650, **9690**, 9700, 9715, 9735, 9760,
11765, 11795, **11810**, 11950, **11965**, 13780,
15105, **15245**, **15250**, 15270, 15275, **15410**,
15510, **17715**, **17795**, **17810**, 17830, 17845,
17860, 17875, 21560, 21600, **21640**, 21680,
25740 kHz
SENDER FREIES BERLIN
6190 kHz (weak)
RADIO IN THE AMERICAN SECTOR
6005 kHz (weak)
RADIO BREMEN
6190 kHz (weak)

SUDDEUTSCHER RUNDFUNK
6030 kHz (weak)
SUDWESTFUNK
7265 kHz (weak)

GREECE -- Greek
FONI TIS HELLADAS
7430, 9395, 9420, 9425, 9935, 11645, 12105,
15625, 15630, 15650, 17535, 17550 kHz

IRAN
VOICE OF THE ISLAMIC REPUBLIC
Persian 3778, 9022, 9720, 15084 kHz
Arabic 5975, 6080, 6140, 6150, 7215, 7230,
9022, 9525, 9680, 9685, 11780, 15084 kHz

IRAQ -- Arabic
"VOICE OF PALESTINE"
9705 kHz
RADIO BAGHDAD
6130, 7240, 9605, 9760, 11755, 12025, 13650,
13680, 13800, 15150, 15170, 15310, 15400,
15415, 17720, 17880 kHz

ISRAEL -- Hebrew
KOL ISRAEL (Reshet He)
9435, 9930, 11585, 11605, 11655, 12077, 15485,
15640, 17575, 21745, 21760 kHz
RASHUTH HASHIDUR (Reshet Bet)
7410, 9385, 11585, 11655, 15615, 15640, 17545,
17590 kHz

ITALY -- Italian
RTV ITALIANA -- Domestic
6060, 7175, 9515 kHz (weak)
RTV ITALIANA -- External
5990, 7235, 7275, 7290, 9575, 9710, 11800,
11905, 15245, 15330, 15385, 17780, 17795,
17800, 21515, 21560, 21690 kHz

JAPAN -- Japanese
RADIO JAPAN/NHK
5960, 5990, 6025, 6080, **6120**, **7125**, 7140,
7210, 9505, 9535, 9580, **9645**, **9675**, **9685**,
9695, 11815, **11835**, 11840, 11850, 11865,
11870, 15140, 15195, **15210**, 15270, 15325,
15350, 15390, 17765, 17810, 17825, 17835,
17845, 17890, 21500, 21610, **21635**, **21640**,
21690, **21700** kHz

JORDAN -- Arabic
RADIO JORDAN
9560, 11810, 11940, 11955, 13655, 15435 kHz

KOREA (DPR) -- Korean
KOREAN CENTRAL BROADCASTING
11680 kHz
RADIO PYONGYANG
6125, 6540, 6576, 7200, 7230, 9220, 9325,
9345, 9540, 9600, 9640, 9977, 11735, 11760,
11845, 12000, 13650, 15115, 15160, 15230,
15340, 17765, 17795 kHz

KOREA (REPUBLIC) -- Korean
RADIO KOREA
  5975, 6060, 6135, **6145**, 6165, 6480, 7275,
  7550, 9570, 9640, **9650**, 9750, 9870, 11740,
  13670, 15375, 15575 kHz

KUWAIT -- Arabic
RADIO KUWAIT (when operating)
  6055, 11990, 13610, 13620, 15345, 15495,
  15505, 17850, 17885, 17895, 21675 kHz

LIBYA -- Arabic
RADIO JAMAHIRIYA
  15235, 15415, 15450 kHz

MOROCCO
RADIO MEDI UN
  French 9575 kHz (weak in Americas)
RTV MAROCAINE
  Arabic 15105, 15330, 15335, 15360, 17815 kHz
  French 11920, 17595, 17815 kHz

NICARAGUA -- Spanish
RADIO NICARAGUA
  6002 kHz (weak)

PARAGUAY -- Spanish
RADIO NACIONAL
  9735 kHz

SAUDI ARABIA -- Arabic
BS OF THE KINGDOM
  7150, 7210, 7220, 7275, 9870, 9885, 11730,
  11780, 11935, 21505, 21665 kHz

SOCIETY ISLANDS -- French
RFO-TAHITI
  11825, 15170 kHz (weak)

SPAIN -- Spanish
RADIO NACIONAL DE ESPANA
  6020, 7450, 9360, **9620**, 9630, 9650, 9745,
  9765, 9875, 11730, 11775, 11790, 11815, 11880,
  11915, 11920, 11945, 12035, 15110, 15125,
  15395, 17715, 17730, 17815, 17845, 17890,
  21460, 21495, 21555, 21570, 21595 kHz

SWEDEN -- Swedish
RADIO SWEDEN
  6065, 7225, 7265, 9615, 9630, 9655, 9695,
  11705, 11760, 15190, 15240, 15290, 15295,
  15390, 15405, 17740, 17860, 17880, 21570,
  21610, 21655, 21690 kHz

SWITZERLAND
SWISS RADIO INTERNATIONAL
  French 3985, 6135, 6165, 9535, 9560, **9620**,

  9725, 9810, 9885, **11695**, 11955, 12030, 12035,
  13635, 13685, 15420, 15430, 15525, 15570,
  17570, 17670, **17730**, 17830, 21630, 21695,
  21770, 25680 kHz
  German 3985, 6095, 6135, 6165, 9535, 9560,
  9620, 9725, 9810, 9885, **11695**, 11955, 12030,
  12035, 13635, 13685, 15420, 15430, 15525,
  15570, 17570, 17670, **17730**, 17830, 21630,
  21695, 21770, 25680 kHz

SYRIA -- Arabic
SYRIAN BROADCASTING SERVICE
  11625, 12085, 15095 kHz

TUNISIA -- Arabic
RTV TUNISIENNE
  7475, 9675, 11550, 12005, 15450, 17610 kHz

TURKEY
VOICE OF TURKEY
  Turkish 5980, 6140, 9445, 9460, 9515, 9685,
  11775, 11925, 11955, 15160, 15267, 15405,
  17880 kHz
  Arabic 11955, 15160 kHz

UNITED ARAB EMIRATES -- Arabic
UAE RADIO
  11790, 11940, 13675, 15320, 15400, 15435,
  17775, 17830, 17865, 17890, 21605, 21675,
  21700 kHz
VOICE OF THE UAE
  7280, 9600, 9695, 9780, 11815, 11965, 11985,
  13605, 15315, 15480, 17645, 17705, 17820,
  17855, 21515, 21725, 21735, 25890 kHz

USSR -- Russian
RADIO MOSCOW
  9790, 9800, 9810, 9820, 9830, 9865, 9890,
  11670, 11675, 11680, 11690, 11695, 12000,
  12005, 12015, 12020, 12025, 12030, 12035,
  12040, 12045, 12050, 12055, 12060, 12065,
  12070, 12100, 13615, 13625, 13630, 13645,
  13690, 13700, 13735, 13745, 15455, 15470,
  15485, 15490, 15495, 15510, 15525, 15530,
  15535, 15550, 15570, 15585, 15590, 15595,
  17560, 17590, 17595, 17600, 17605, 17610,
  17615, 17645, 17675, 17680, 17690, 17695,
  21490, 21615, 21750, 21795, 21820 kHz

VENEZUELA -- Spanish
ECOS DEL TORBES
  4980, 9640 kHz
RADIO RUMBOS
  4970, 9660 kHz (weak)
RADIO TACHIRA
  4830 kHz (weak)

WORLDSCAN: THE BLUE PAGES

Quick-Access Guide to World Band Frequencies

There are hundreds of channels of news and entertainment available on world band radio, with some channels being shared by many stations. With such an abundance from which to choose, it can take some doing to figure out what is actually on the air.

Ordinary listings of what's on world band radio are unwieldy because there is such a vast quantity of data. That's why *Passport to World Band Radio* includes these quick-access "Blue Pages." Now, everything—stations, times, languages, targets and more—can be found at a glance. If something is not clear, the glossary at the back of the book explains it. There is also a handy key to languages and symbols at the bottom of each set of Blue Pages.

For example, if you're in North America listening to the channel of 6175 kHz at 2300 World Time, you'll see that the BBC World Service is broadcast in English to this area at that time. The transmitter is located in Canada and operates at a power of 250 kW.

World Time Simplifies Listening

World Time (UTC)—a handy concept also known as GMT—is used to eliminate the potential complication of so many time zones throughout the world. It treats the entire planet as a single zone and is announced regularly on the hour by many world band stations.

For example, if you're in New York and it's 6:00 AM EST, you will hear the time announced as "11 hours UTC." A glance at your clock shows that this is five hours ahead of your local time. You can either keep this "add five hours" figure in your head or use a separate clock for World Time. A growing number of world band radios come with World Time clocks built in, and 24-hour UTC clocks are also widely available as accessories.

World Band Stations Heard Outside Intended Target

With several hundred stations on the air at the same time, many piled atop each other like so much cordwood, you can't begin to hear all—or even most—of them. Nevertheless, even stations not targeted to your part of the world may be audible. Tune around, using the Blue Pages as your "radio map," and you'll discover a wealth of stations that can be enjoyed even though they're beamed to completely different parts of our planet.

GUIDE TO BLUE PAGES FORMAT

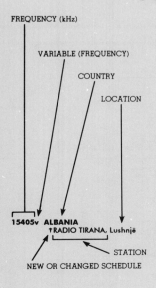

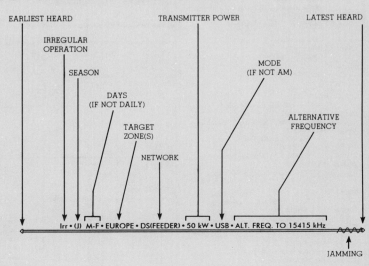

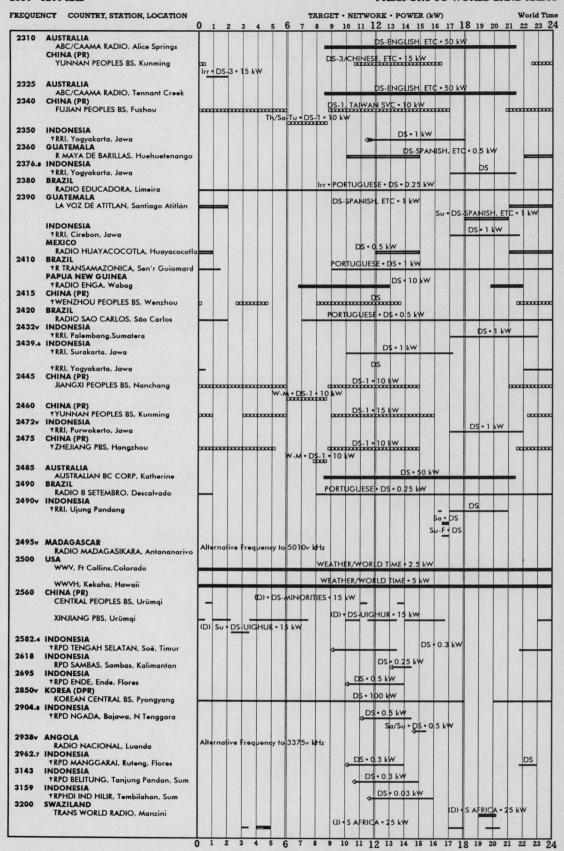

FREQUENCY   COUNTRY, STATION, LOCATION

TARGET • NETWORK • POWER (kW)

World Time

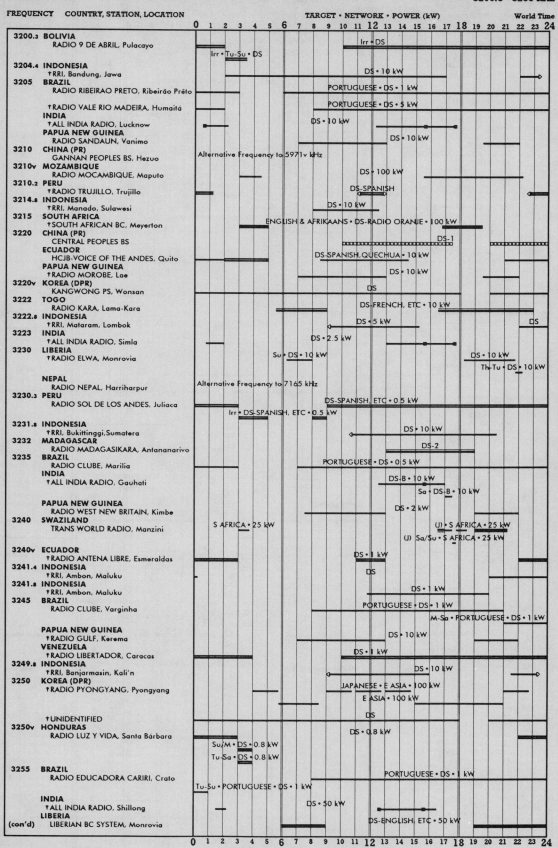

Frequency	Country, Station, Location	Notes
3200.3	**BOLIVIA** RADIO 9 DE ABRIL, Pulacayo	Irr • DS; Irr • Tu-Su • DS
3204.4	**INDONESIA** †RRI, Bandung, Jawa	DS • 10 kW
3205	**BRAZIL** RADIO RIBEIRAO PRETO, Ribeirão Prêto	PORTUGUESE • DS • 1 kW
	†RADIO VALE RIO MADEIRA, Humaitá	PORTUGUESE • DS • 5 kW
	INDIA †ALL INDIA RADIO, Lucknow	DS • 10 kW
	PAPUA NEW GUINEA RADIO SANDAUN, Vanimo	DS • 10 kW
3210	**CHINA (PR)** GANNAN PEOPLES BS, Hezuo	Alternative Frequency to 5971v kHz
3210v	**MOZAMBIQUE** RADIO MOCAMBIQUE, Maputo	DS • 100 kW
3210.2	**PERU** †RADIO TRUJILLO, Trujillo	DS-SPANISH
3214.8	**INDONESIA** †RRI, Manado, Sulawesi	DS • 10 kW
3215	**SOUTH AFRICA** †SOUTH AFRICAN BC, Meyerton	ENGLISH & AFRIKAANS • DS-RADIO ORANJE • 100 kW
3220	**CHINA (PR)** CENTRAL PEOPLES BS	DS-1
	ECUADOR HCJB-VOICE OF THE ANDES, Quito	DS-SPANISH, QUECHUA • 10 kW
	PAPUA NEW GUINEA †RADIO MOROBE, Lae	DS • 10 kW
3220v	**KOREA (DPR)** KANGWONG PS, Wonsan	DS
3222	**TOGO** RADIO KARA, Lama-Kara	DS-FRENCH, ETC • 10 kW
3222.8	**INDONESIA** †RRI, Mataram, Lombok	DS • 5 kW; DS
3223	**INDIA** †ALL INDIA RADIO, Simla	DS • 2.5 kW
3230	**LIBERIA** †RADIO ELWA, Monrovia	Su • DS • 10 kW; DS • 10 kW; Th-Tu • DS • 10 kW
	NEPAL RADIO NEPAL, Harriharpur	Alternative Frequency to 7165 kHz
3230.3	**PERU** RADIO SOL DE LOS ANDES, Juliaca	DS-SPANISH, ETC • 0.5 kW; Irr • DS-SPANISH, ETC • 0.5 kW
3231.8	**INDONESIA** †RRI, Bukittinggi, Sumatera	DS • 10 kW
3232	**MADAGASCAR** RADIO MADAGASIKARA, Antananarivo	DS-2
3235	**BRAZIL** RADIO CLUBE, Marilia	PORTUGUESE • DS • 0.5 kW
	INDIA †ALL INDIA RADIO, Gauhati	DS-B • 10 kW; Sa • DS-B • 10 kW
	PAPUA NEW GUINEA RADIO WEST NEW BRITAIN, Kimbe	DS • 2 kW
3240	**SWAZILAND** TRANS WORLD RADIO, Manzini	S AFRICA • 25 kW; (J) • S AFRICA • 25 kW; (J) Sa/Su • S AFRICA • 25 kW
3240v	**ECUADOR** †RADIO ANTENA LIBRE, Esmeraldas	DS • 1 kW
3241.4	**INDONESIA** †RRI, Ambon, Maluku	DS
3241.8	**INDONESIA** †RRI, Ambon, Maluku	DS • 1 kW
3245	**BRAZIL** RADIO CLUBE, Varginha	PORTUGUESE • DS • 1 kW; M-Sa • PORTUGUESE • DS • 1 kW
	PAPUA NEW GUINEA †RADIO GULF, Kerema	DS • 10 kW
	VENEZUELA †RADIO LIBERTADOR, Caracas	DS • 1 kW
3249.8	**INDONESIA** †RRI, Banjarmasin, Kali'n	DS • 10 kW
3250	**KOREA (DPR)** †RADIO PYONGYANG, Pyongyang	JAPANESE • E ASIA • 100 kW; E ASIA • 100 kW
	†UNIDENTIFIED	DS
3250v	**HONDURAS** RADIO LUZ Y VIDA, Santa Bárbara	DS • 0.8 kW; Su/M • DS • 0.8 kW; Tu-Sa • DS • 0.8 kW
3255	**BRAZIL** RADIO EDUCADORA CARIRI, Crato	PORTUGUESE • DS • 1 kW; Tu-Su • PORTUGUESE • DS • 1 kW
	INDIA †ALL INDIA RADIO, Shillong	DS • 50 kW
(con'd)	**LIBERIA** LIBERIAN BC SYSTEM, Monrovia	DS-ENGLISH, ETC • 50 kW

ENGLISH ▬   ARABIC ⣿   CHINESE ∞∞∞   FRENCH ═══   GERMAN ▬▬   RUSSIAN ══   SPANISH ▬▬   OTHER ▬

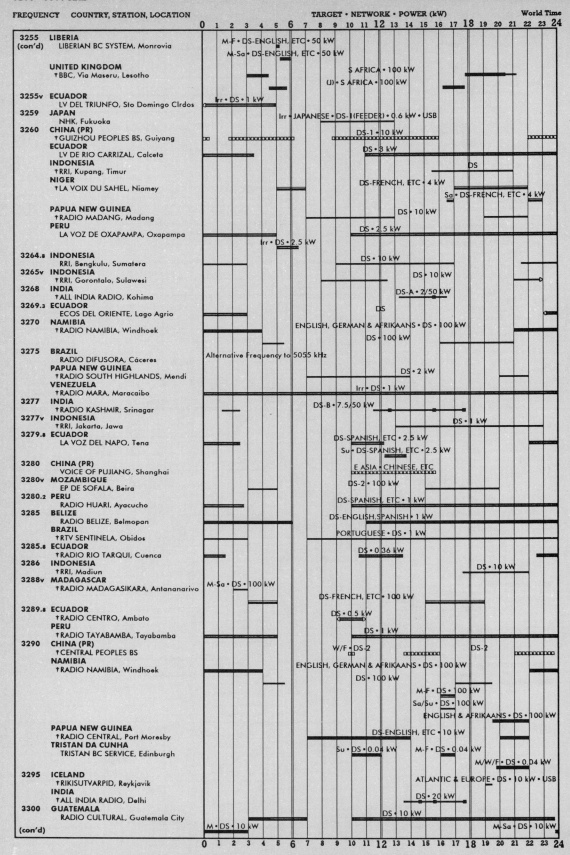

FREQUENCY   COUNTRY, STATION, LOCATION

TARGET • NETWORK • POWER (kW)   World Time

3255   LIBERIA
(con'd)   LIBERIAN BC SYSTEM, Monrovia   M-F • DS-ENGLISH, ETC • 50 kW
                                                             M-Sa • DS-ENGLISH, ETC • 50 kW

          UNITED KINGDOM
             †BBC, Via Maseru, Lesotho   S AFRICA • 100 kW
                                                                            (J) • S AFRICA • 100 kW

3255v   ECUADOR
             LV DEL TRIUNFO, Sto Domingo Clrdos   Irr • DS • 1 kW
3259   JAPAN
             NHK, Fukuoka   Irr • JAPANESE • DS-1 (FEEDER) • 0.6 kW • USB
3260   CHINA (PR)
             †GUIZHOU PEOPLES BS, Guiyang   DS-1 • 10 kW
          ECUADOR
             LV DE RIO CARRIZAL, Calceta   DS • 3 kW
          INDONESIA
             †RRI, Kupang, Timur   DS
          NIGER
             †LA VOIX DU SAHEL, Niamey   DS-FRENCH, ETC • 4 kW
                                                                     Sa • DS-FRENCH, ETC • 4 kW

          PAPUA NEW GUINEA
             †RADIO MADANG, Madang   DS • 10 kW
          PERU
             LA VOZ DE OXAPAMPA, Oxapampa   DS • 2.5 kW
                                                             Irr • DS • 2.5 kW

3264.8   INDONESIA
             RRI, Bengkulu, Sumatera   DS • 10 kW
3265v   INDONESIA
             †RRI, Gorontalo, Sulawesi   DS • 10 kW
3268   INDIA
             †ALL INDIA RADIO, Kohima   DS-A • 2/50 kW
3269.3   ECUADOR
             ECOS DEL ORIENTE, Lago Agrio   DS
3270   NAMIBIA
             †RADIO NAMIBIA, Windhoek   ENGLISH, GERMAN & AFRIKAANS • DS • 100 kW
                                                                      DS • 100 kW

3275   BRAZIL
             RADIO DIFUSORA, Cáceres   Alternative Frequency to 5055 kHz
          PAPUA NEW GUINEA
             †RADIO SOUTH HIGHLANDS, Mendi   DS • 2 kW
          VENEZUELA
             †RADIO MARA, Maracaibo   Irr • DS • 1 kW
3277   INDIA
             †RADIO KASHMIR, Srinagar   DS-B • 7.5/50 kW
3277v   INDONESIA
             †RRI, Jakarta, Jawa   DS • 1 kW
3279.8   ECUADOR
             LA VOZ DEL NAPO, Tena   DS-SPANISH, ETC • 2.5 kW
                                                             Su • DS-SPANISH, ETC • 2.5 kW

3280   CHINA (PR)
             VOICE OF PUJIANG, Shanghai   E ASIA • CHINESE, ETC
3280v   MOZAMBIQUE
             EP DE SOFALA, Beira   DS-2 • 100 kW
3280.2   PERU
             RADIO HUARI, Ayacucho   DS-SPANISH, ETC • 1 kW
3285   BELIZE
             RADIO BELIZE, Belmopan   DS-ENGLISH, SPANISH • 1 kW
          BRAZIL
             †RTV SENTINELA, Obidos   PORTUGUESE • DS • 1 kW
3285.8   ECUADOR
             †RADIO RIO TARQUI, Cuenca   DS • 0.36 kW
3286   INDONESIA
             †RRI, Madiun   DS • 10 kW
3288v   MADAGASCAR
             †RADIO MADAGASIKARA, Antananarivo   M-Sa • DS • 100 kW
                                                             DS-FRENCH, ETC • 100 kW

3289.8   ECUADOR
             †RADIO CENTRO, Ambato   DS • 0.5 kW
          PERU
             †RADIO TAYABAMBA, Tayabamba   DS • 1 kW
3290   CHINA (PR)
             †CENTRAL PEOPLES BS   W/F • DS-2   DS-2
          NAMIBIA
             †RADIO NAMIBIA, Windhoek   ENGLISH, GERMAN & AFRIKAANS • DS • 100 kW
                                                                      DS • 100 kW
                                                                      M-F • DS • 100 kW
                                                                      Sa/Su • DS • 100 kW
                                                                      ENGLISH & AFRIKAANS • DS • 100 kW

          PAPUA NEW GUINEA
             †RADIO CENTRAL, Port Moresby   DS-ENGLISH, ETC • 10 kW
          TRISTAN DA CUNHA
             TRISTAN BC SERVICE, Edinburgh   Su • DS • 0.04 kW   M-F • DS • 0.04 kW
                                                                      M/W/F • DS • 0.04 kW

3295   ICELAND
             †RIKISUTVARPID, Reykjavik   ATLANTIC & EUROPE • DS • 10 kW • USB
          INDIA
             †ALL INDIA RADIO, Delhi   DS • 20 kW
3300   GUATEMALA
             RADIO CULTURAL, Guatemala City   DS • 10 kW
(con'd)   M • DS • 10 kW   M-Sa • DS • 10 kW

FREQUENCY   COUNTRY, STATION, LOCATION

TARGET • NETWORK • POWER (kW)

World Time

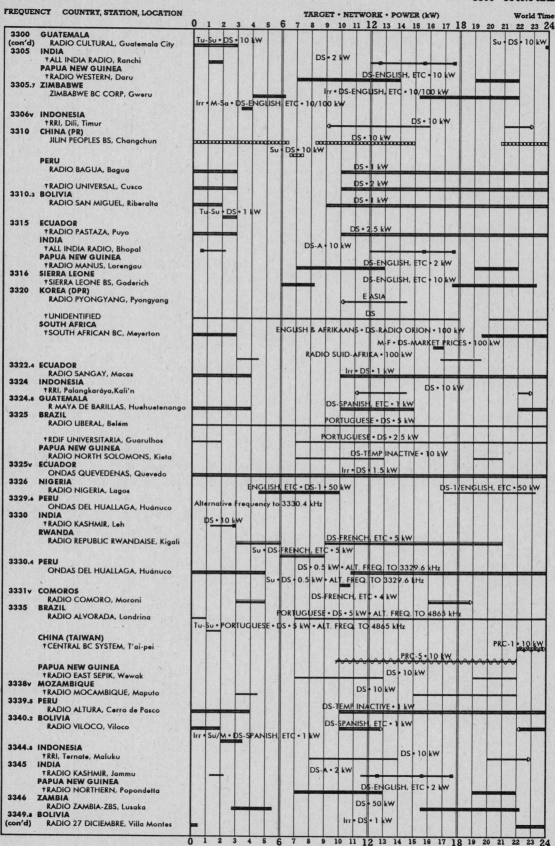

Frequency	Country, Station, Location	Notes
3300 (con'd)	**GUATEMALA** RADIO CULTURAL, Guatemala City	Tu-Su • DS • 10 kW Su • DS • 10 kW
3305	**INDIA** †ALL INDIA RADIO, Ranchi	DS • 2 kW
	PAPUA NEW GUINEA †RADIO WESTERN, Daru	DS-ENGLISH, ETC • 10 kW
3305.7	**ZIMBABWE** ZIMBABWE BC CORP, Gweru	Irr • DS-ENGLISH, ETC • 10/100 kW Irr • M-Sa • DS-ENGLISH, ETC • 10/100 kW
3306v	**INDONESIA** †RRI, Dili, Timur	DS • 10 kW
3310	**CHINA (PR)** JILIN PEOPLES BS, Changchun	DS • 10 kW Su • DS • 10 kW
	PERU RADIO BAGUA, Bagua	DS • 1 kW
	†RADIO UNIVERSAL, Cusco	DS • 2 kW
3310.3	**BOLIVIA** RADIO SAN MIGUEL, Riberalta	DS • 1 kW Tu-Su • DS • 1 kW
3315	**ECUADOR** †RADIO PASTAZA, Puyo	DS • 2.5 kW
	INDIA †ALL INDIA RADIO, Bhopal	DS-A • 10 kW
	PAPUA NEW GUINEA †RADIO MANUS, Lorengau	DS-ENGLISH, ETC • 2 kW
3316	**SIERRA LEONE** †SIERRA LEONE BS, Goderich	DS-ENGLISH, ETC • 10 kW
3320	**KOREA (DPR)** RADIO PYONGYANG, Pyongyang	E ASIA
	†UNIDENTIFIED	DS
	SOUTH AFRICA †SOUTH AFRICAN BC, Meyerton	ENGLISH & AFRIKAANS • DS-RADIO ORION • 100 kW M-F • DS-MARKET PRICES • 100 kW RADIO SUID-AFRIKA • 100 kW
3322.4	**ECUADOR** RADIO SANGAY, Macas	Irr • DS • 1 kW
3324	**INDONESIA** †RRI, Palangkaráya, Kali'n	DS • 10 kW
3324.8	**GUATEMALA** R MAYA DE BARILLAS, Huehuetenango	DS-SPANISH, ETC • 1 kW
3325	**BRAZIL** RADIO LIBERAL, Belém	PORTUGUESE • DS • 5 kW
	†RDIF UNIVERSITARIA, Guarulhos	PORTUGUESE • DS • 2.5 kW
	PAPUA NEW GUINEA RADIO NORTH SOLOMONS, Kieta	DS-TEMP INACTIVE • 10 kW
3325v	**ECUADOR** ONDAS QUEVEDENAS, Quevedo	Irr • DS • 1.5 kW
3326	**NIGERIA** RADIO NIGERIA, Lagos	ENGLISH, ETC • DS-1 • 50 kW DS-1 ENGLISH, ETC • 50 kW
3329.6	**PERU** ONDAS DEL HUALLAGA, Huánuco	Alternative Frequency to 3330.4 kHz
3330	**INDIA** †RADIO KASHMIR, Leh	DS • 10 kW
	RWANDA RADIO REPUBLIC RWANDAISE, Kigali	DS-FRENCH, ETC • 5 kW Su • DS-FRENCH, ETC • 5 kW
3330.4	**PERU** ONDAS DEL HUALLAGA, Huánuco	DS • 0.5 kW • ALT. FREQ. TO 3329.6 kHz Su • DS • 0.5 kW • ALT. FREQ. TO 3329.6 kHz
3331v	**COMOROS** RADIO COMORO, Moroni	DS-FRENCH, ETC • 4 kW
3335	**BRAZIL** RADIO ALVORADA, Londrina	PORTUGUESE • DS • 5 kW • ALT. FREQ. TO 4865 kHz Tu-Su • PORTUGUESE • DS • 5 kW • ALT. FREQ. TO 4865 kHz
	CHINA (TAIWAN) †CENTRAL BC SYSTEM, T'ai-pei	PRC-1 • 10 kW PRC-5 • 10 kW
	PAPUA NEW GUINEA †RADIO EAST SEPIK, Wewak	DS • 10 kW
3338v	**MOZAMBIQUE** †RADIO MOCAMBIQUE, Maputo	DS • 10 kW
3339.5	**PERU** RADIO ALTURA, Cerro de Pasco	DS-TEMP INACTIVE • 1 kW
3340.2	**BOLIVIA** RADIO VILOCO, Viloco	DS-SPANISH, ETC • 1 kW Irr • Su/M • DS-SPANISH, ETC • 1 kW
3344.8	**INDONESIA** †RRI, Ternate, Maluku	DS • 10 kW
3345	**INDIA** †RADIO KASHMIR, Jammu	DS-A • 2 kW
	PAPUA NEW GUINEA †RADIO NORTHERN, Popondetta	DS-ENGLISH, ETC • 2 kW
3346	**ZAMBIA** RADIO ZAMBIA-ZBS, Lusaka	DS • 50 kW
3349.8 (con'd)	**BOLIVIA** RADIO 27 DICIEMBRE, Villa Montes	Irr • DS • 1 kW

ENGLISH ▬   ARABIC ⁵⁵⁵   CHINESE ▫▫▫   FRENCH ═   GERMAN ▭   RUSSIAN ═   SPANISH ▬   OTHER ▬

| FREQUENCY | COUNTRY, STATION, LOCATION | TARGET • NETWORK • POWER (kW) / World Time |

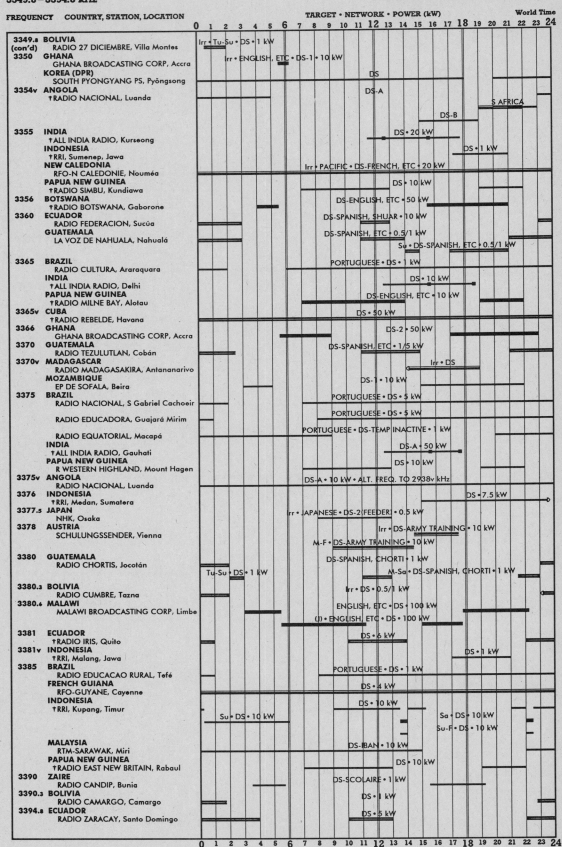

- **3349.8 BOLIVIA** (con'd) — RADIO 27 DICIEMBRE, Villa Montes — Irr • Tu-Su • DS • 1 kW
- **3350 GHANA** — GHANA BROADCASTING CORP, Accra — Irr • ENGLISH, ETC • DS-1 • 10 kW
- **KOREA (DPR)** — SOUTH PYONGYANG PS, Pyŏngsong — DS
- **3354v ANGOLA** — †RADIO NACIONAL, Luanda — DS-A / S AFRICA / DS-B
- **3355 INDIA** — †ALL INDIA RADIO, Kurseong — DS • 20 kW
- **INDONESIA** — †RRI, Sumenep, Jawa — DS • 1 kW
- **NEW CALEDONIA** — RFO-N CALEDONIE, Nouméa — Irr • PACIFIC • DS-FRENCH, ETC • 20 kW
- **PAPUA NEW GUINEA** — †RADIO SIMBU, Kundiawa — DS • 10 kW
- **3356 BOTSWANA** — †RADIO BOTSWANA, Gaborone — DS-ENGLISH, ETC • 50 kW
- **3360 ECUADOR** — RADIO FEDERACION, Sucúa — DS-SPANISH, SHUAR • 10 kW
- **GUATEMALA** — LA VOZ DE NAHUALA, Nahualá — DS-SPANISH, ETC • 0.5/1 kW / Su • DS-SPANISH, ETC • 0.5/1 kW
- **3365 BRAZIL** — RADIO CULTURA, Araraquara — PORTUGUESE • DS • 1 kW
- **INDIA** — †ALL INDIA RADIO, Delhi — DS • 10 kW
- **PAPUA NEW GUINEA** — †RADIO MILNE BAY, Alotau — DS-ENGLISH, ETC • 10 kW
- **3365v CUBA** — †RADIO REBELDE, Havana — DS • 50 kW
- **3366 GHANA** — GHANA BROADCASTING CORP, Accra — DS-2 • 50 kW
- **3370 GUATEMALA** — RADIO TEZULUTLAN, Cobán — DS-SPANISH, ETC • 1/5 kW
- **3370v MADAGASCAR** — RADIO MADAGASAKIRA, Antananarivo — Irr • DS
- **MOZAMBIQUE** — EP DE SOFALA, Beira — DS-1 • 10 kW
- **3375 BRAZIL** — RADIO NACIONAL, S Gabriel Cachoeir — PORTUGUESE • DS • 5 kW
- RADIO EDUCADORA, Guajará Mirim — PORTUGUESE • DS • 5 kW
- RADIO EQUATORIAL, Macapá — PORTUGUESE • DS-TEMP INACTIVE • 1 kW
- **INDIA** — †ALL INDIA RADIO, Gauhati — DS-A • 50 kW
- **PAPUA NEW GUINEA** — R WESTERN HIGHLAND, Mount Hagen — DS • 10 kW
- **3375v ANGOLA** — RADIO NACIONAL, Luanda — DS-A • 10 kW • ALT. FREQ. TO 2938v kHz
- **3376 INDONESIA** — †RRI, Medan, Sumatera — DS • 7.5 kW
- **3377.5 JAPAN** — NHK, Osaka — Irr • JAPANESE • DS-2 (FEEDER) • 0.5 kW
- **3378 AUSTRIA** — SCHULUNGSSENDER, Vienna — Irr • DS-ARMY TRAINING • 10 kW / M-F • DS-ARMY TRAINING • 10 kW
- **3380 GUATEMALA** — RADIO CHORTIS, Jocotán — DS-SPANISH, CHORTI • 1 kW / Tu-Su • DS • 1 kW / M-Sa • DS-SPANISH, CHORTI • 1 kW
- **3380.3 BOLIVIA** — RADIO CUMBRE, Tazna — Irr • DS • 0.5/1 kW
- **3380.6 MALAWI** — MALAWI BROADCASTING CORP, Limbe — ENGLISH, ETC • DS • 100 kW / (J) • ENGLISH, ETC • DS • 100 kW
- **3381 ECUADOR** — †RADIO IRIS, Quito — DS • 6 kW
- **3381v INDONESIA** — †RRI, Malang, Jawa — DS • 1 kW
- **3385 BRAZIL** — RADIO EDUCACAO RURAL, Tefé — PORTUGUESE • DS • 1 kW
- **FRENCH GUIANA** — RFO-GUYANE, Cayenne — DS • 4 kW
- **INDONESIA** — †RRI, Kupang, Timur — DS • 10 kW / Su • DS • 10 kW / Sa • DS • 10 kW / Su-F • DS • 10 kW
- **MALAYSIA** — RTM-SARAWAK, Miri — DS-IBAN • 10 kW
- **PAPUA NEW GUINEA** — †RADIO EAST NEW BRITAIN, Rabaul — DS • 10 kW
- **3390 ZAIRE** — RADIO CANDIP, Bunia — DS-SCOLAIRE • 1 kW
- **3390.3 BOLIVIA** — RADIO CAMARGO, Camargo — DS • 1 kW
- **3394.8 ECUADOR** — RADIO ZARACAY, Santo Domingo — DS • 5 kW

SUMMER ONLY (J)   WINTER ONLY (D)   JAMMING / OR ∧   EARLIEST HEARD ◁   LATEST HEARD ▷   NEW OR CHANGED FOR 1991 †

FREQUENCY   COUNTRY, STATION, LOCATION

TARGET • NETWORK • POWER (kW)

World Time

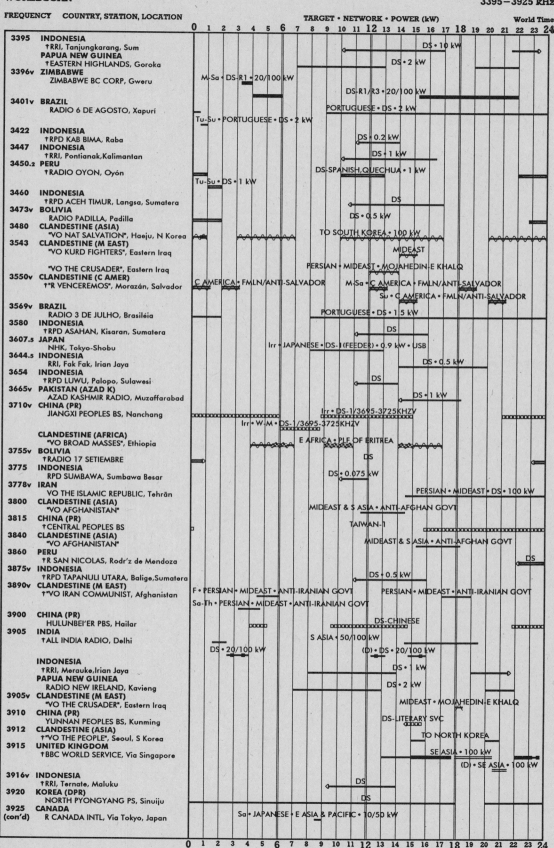

Frequency	Country, Station, Location	Target • Network • Power
3395	INDONESIA †RRI, Tanjungkarang, Sum	DS • 10 kW
	PAPUA NEW GUINEA †EASTERN HIGHLANDS, Goroka	DS • 2 kW
3396v	ZIMBABWE ZIMBABWE BC CORP, Gweru	M-Sa • DS-R1 • 20/100 kW; DS-R1/R3 • 20/100 kW
3401v	BRAZIL RADIO 6 DE AGOSTO, Xapurí	PORTUGUESE • DS • 2 kW; Tu-Su • PORTUGUESE • DS • 2 kW
3422	INDONESIA †RPD KAB BIMA, Raba	DS • 0.2 kW
3447	INDONESIA †RRI, Pontianak, Kalimantan	DS • 1 kW
3450.2	PERU †RADIO OYON, Oyón	DS-SPANISH, QUECHUA • 1 kW; Tu-Su • DS • 1 kW
3460	INDONESIA †RPD ACEH TIMUR, Langsa, Sumatera	DS
3473v	BOLIVIA RADIO PADILLA, Padilla	DS • 0.5 kW
3480	CLANDESTINE (ASIA) "VO NAT SALVATION", Haeju, N Korea	TO SOUTH KOREA • 100 kW
3543	CLANDESTINE (M EAST) "VO KURD FIGHTERS", Eastern Iraq	MIDEAST
	"VO THE CRUSADER", Eastern Iraq	PERSIAN • MIDEAST • MOJAHEDIN-E KHALQ
3550v	CLANDESTINE (C AMER) †"R VENCEREMOS", Morazán, Salvador	C AMERICA • FMLN/ANTI-SALVADOR; M-Sa • C AMERICA • FMLN/ANTI-SALVADOR; Su • C AMERICA • FMLN/ANTI-SALVADOR
3569v	BRAZIL RADIO 3 DE JULHO, Brasiléia	PORTUGUESE • DS • 1.5 kW
3580	INDONESIA †RPD ASAHAN, Kisaran, Sumatera	DS
3607.5	JAPAN NHK, Tokyo-Shobu	Irr • JAPANESE • DS-1 (FEEDER) • 0.9 kW • USB
3644.5	INDONESIA RRI, Fak Fak, Irian Jaya	DS • 0.5 kW
3654	INDONESIA †RPD LUWU, Palopo, Sulawesi	DS
3665v	PAKISTAN (AZAD K) AZAD KASHMIR RADIO, Muzaffarabad	DS • 1 kW
3710v	CHINA (PR) JIANGXI PEOPLES BS, Nanchang	Irr • DS-1/3695-3725KHZV; Irr • W-M • DS-1/3695-3725KHZV
	CLANDESTINE (AFRICA) "VO BROAD MASSES", Ethiopia	E AFRICA • PLF OF ERITREA
3755v	BOLIVIA †RADIO 17 SETIEMBRE	DS
3775	INDONESIA RPD SUMBAWA, Sumbawa Besar	DS • 0.075 kW
3778v	IRAN VO THE ISLAMIC REPUBLIC, Tehrān	PERSIAN • MIDEAST • DS • 100 kW
3800	CLANDESTINE (ASIA) "VO AFGHANISTAN"	MIDEAST & S ASIA • ANTI-AFGHAN GOVT
3815	CHINA (PR) †CENTRAL PEOPLES BS	TAIWAN-1
3840	CLANDESTINE (ASIA) "VO AFGHANISTAN"	MIDEAST & S ASIA • ANTI-AFGHAN GOVT
3860	PERU †R SAN NICOLAS, Rodr'z de Mendoza	DS
3875v	INDONESIA †RPD TAPANULI UTARA, Balige, Sumatera	DS • 0.5 kW
3890v	CLANDESTINE (M EAST) †"VO IRAN COMMUNIST", Afghanistan	F • PERSIAN • MIDEAST • ANTI-IRANIAN GOVT; Sa-Th • PERSIAN • MIDEAST • ANTI-IRANIAN GOVT; PERSIAN • MIDEAST • ANTI-IRANIAN GOVT
3900	CHINA (PR) HULUNBEI'ER PBS, Hailar	DS-CHINESE
3905	INDIA †ALL INDIA RADIO, Delhi	S ASIA • 50/100 kW; DS • 20/100 kW; (D) • DS • 20/100 kW
	INDONESIA †RRI, Merauke, Irian Jaya	DS • 1 kW
	PAPUA NEW GUINEA RADIO NEW IRELAND, Kavieng	DS • 2 kW
3905v	CLANDESTINE (M EAST) †"VO THE CRUSADER", Eastern Iraq	MIDEAST • MOJAHEDIN-E KHALQ
3910	CHINA (PR) YUNNAN PEOPLES BS, Kunming	DS-LITERARY SVC
3912	CLANDESTINE (ASIA) †"VO THE PEOPLE", Seoul, S Korea	TO NORTH KOREA
3915	UNITED KINGDOM †BBC WORLD SERVICE, Via Singapore	SE ASIA • 100 kW; (D) • SE ASIA • 100 kW
3916v	INDONESIA †RRI, Ternate, Maluku	DS
3920	KOREA (DPR) NORTH PYONGYANG PS, Sinuiju	DS
3925 (con'd)	CANADA R CANADA INTL, Via Tokyo, Japan	Sa • JAPANESE • E ASIA & PACIFIC • 10/50 kW

FREQUENCY   COUNTRY, STATION, LOCATION

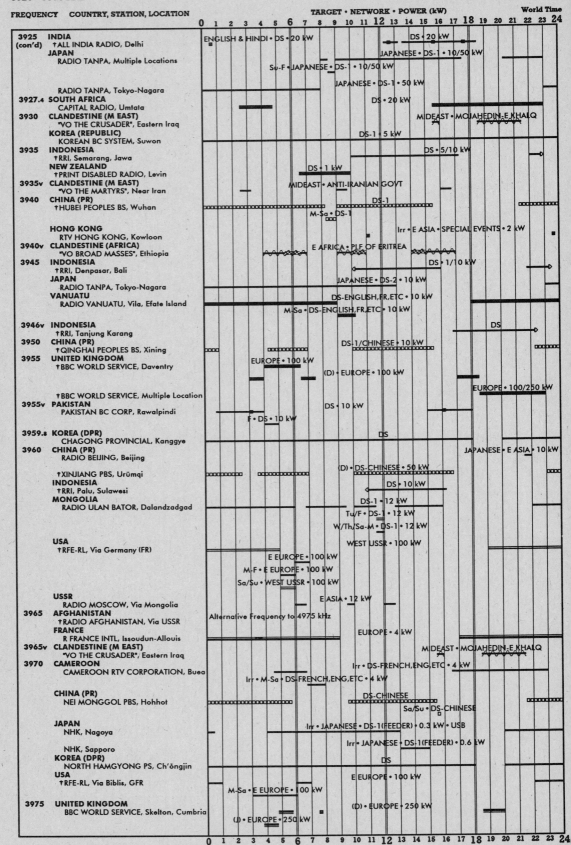

3925 (con'd)	INDIA †ALL INDIA RADIO, Delhi	ENGLISH & HINDI • DS • 20 kW / DS • 20 kW
	JAPAN RADIO TANPA, Multiple Locations	JAPANESE • DS-1 • 10/50 kW / Su-F • JAPANESE • DS-1 • 10/50 kW
	RADIO TANPA, Tokyo-Nagara	JAPANESE • DS-1 • 50 kW
3927.4	SOUTH AFRICA CAPITAL RADIO, Umtata	DS • 20 kW
3930	CLANDESTINE (M EAST) "VO THE CRUSADER", Eastern Iraq	MIDEAST • MOJAHEDIN-E KHALQ
	KOREA (REPUBLIC) KOREAN BC SYSTEM, Suwon	DS-1 • 5 kW
3935	INDONESIA †RRI, Semarang, Jawa	DS • 5/10 kW
	NEW ZEALAND †PRINT DISABLED RADIO, Levin	DS • 1 kW
3935v	CLANDESTINE (M EAST) "VO THE MARTYRS", Near Iran	MIDEAST • ANTI-IRANIAN GOVT
3940	CHINA (PR) †HUBEI PEOPLES BS, Wuhan	DS-1 / M-Sa • DS-1
	HONG KONG RTV HONG KONG, Kowloon	Irr • E ASIA • SPECIAL EVENTS • 2 kW
3940v	CLANDESTINE (AFRICA) "VO BROAD MASSES", Ethiopia	E AFRICA • PLF OF ERITREA
3945	INDONESIA †RRI, Denpasar, Bali	DS • 1/10 kW
	JAPAN RADIO TANPA, Tokyo-Nagara	JAPANESE • DS-2 • 10 kW
	VANUATU RADIO VANUATU, Vila, Efate Island	DS-ENGLISH,FR,ETC • 10 kW / M-Sa • DS-ENGLISH,FR,ETC • 10 kW
3946v	INDONESIA †RRI, Tanjung Karang	DS
3950	CHINA (PR) †QINGHAI PEOPLES BS, Xining	DS-1/CHINESE • 10 kW
3955	UNITED KINGDOM †BBC WORLD SERVICE, Daventry	EUROPE • 100 kW / (D) • EUROPE • 100 kW
	†BBC WORLD SERVICE, Multiple Location	EUROPE • 100/250 kW
3955v	PAKISTAN PAKISTAN BC CORP, Rawalpindi	DS • 10 kW / F • DS • 10 kW
3959.8	KOREA (DPR) CHAGONG PROVINCIAL, Kanggye	DS
3960	CHINA (PR) RADIO BEIJING, Beijing	JAPANESE • E ASIA • 10 kW
	†XINJIANG PBS, Urümqi	(D) • DS-CHINESE • 50 kW
	INDONESIA †RRI, Palu, Sulawesi	DS • 10 kW
	MONGOLIA RADIO ULAN BATOR, Dalandzadgad	DS-1 • 12 kW / Tu/F • DS-1 • 12 kW / W/Th/Sa-M • DS-1 • 12 kW
	USA †RFE-RL, Via Germany (FR)	WEST USSR • 100 kW / E EUROPE • 100 kW / M-F • E EUROPE • 100 kW / Sa/Su • WEST USSR • 100 kW
	USSR RADIO MOSCOW, Via Mongolia	E ASIA • 12 kW
3965	AFGHANISTAN †RADIO AFGHANISTAN, Via USSR	Alternative Frequency to 4975 kHz
	FRANCE R FRANCE INTL, Issoudun-Allouis	EUROPE • 4 kW
3965v	CLANDESTINE (M EAST) "VO THE CRUSADER", Eastern Iraq	MIDEAST • MOJAHEDIN-E KHALQ
3970	CAMEROON CAMEROON RTV CORPORATION, Buea	Irr • DS-FRENCH,ENG,ETC • 4 kW / Irr • M-Sa • DS-FRENCH,ENG,ETC • 4 kW
	CHINA (PR) NEI MONGGOL PBS, Hohhot	DS-CHINESE / Sa/Su • DS-CHINESE
	JAPAN NHK, Nagoya	Irr • JAPANESE • DS-1 (FEEDER) • 0.3 kW • USB
	NHK, Sapporo	Irr • JAPANESE • DS-1 (FEEDER) • 0.6 kW
	KOREA (DPR) NORTH HAMGYONG PS, Ch'ŏngjin	DS
	USA †RFE-RL, Via Biblis, GFR	E EUROPE • 100 kW / M-Sa • E EUROPE • 100 kW
3975	UNITED KINGDOM BBC WORLD SERVICE, Skelton, Cumbria	(D) • EUROPE • 250 kW / (J) • EUROPE • 250 kW

FREQUENCY   COUNTRY, STATION, LOCATION

TARGET • NETWORK • POWER (kW)

World Time

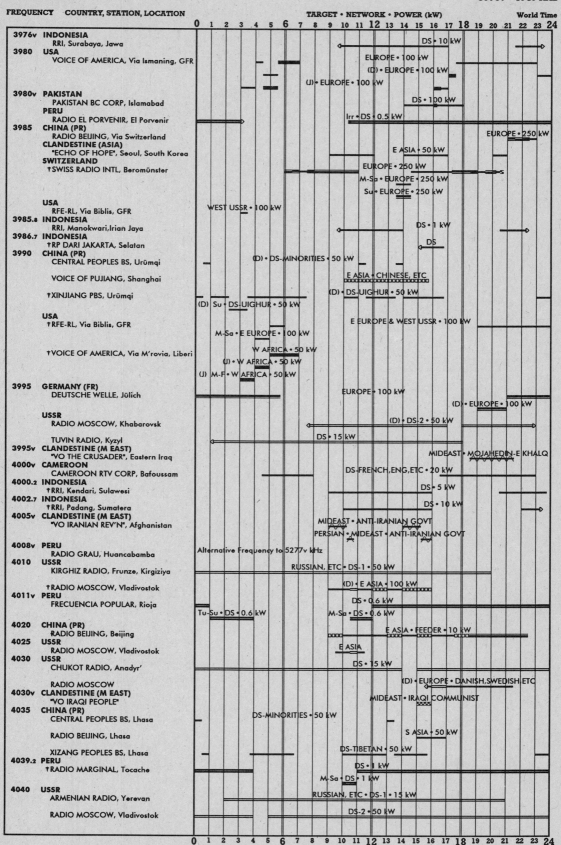

FREQUENCY	COUNTRY, STATION, LOCATION	TARGET • NETWORK • POWER (kW)
3976v	INDONESIA	
	RRI, Surabaya, Jawa	DS • 10 kW
3980	USA	
	VOICE OF AMERICA, Via Ismaning, GFR	EUROPE • 100 kW
		(D) • EUROPE • 100 kW
		(J) • EUROPE • 100 kW
3980v	PAKISTAN	
	PAKISTAN BC CORP, Islamabad	DS • 100 kW
	PERU	
	RADIO EL PORVENIR, El Porvenir	Irr • DS • 0.5 kW
3985	CHINA (PR)	
	RADIO BEIJING, Via Switzerland	EUROPE • 250 kW
	CLANDESTINE (ASIA)	
	"ECHO OF HOPE", Seoul, South Korea	E ASIA • 50 kW
	SWITZERLAND	
	†SWISS RADIO INTL, Beromünster	EUROPE • 250 kW
		M-Sa • EUROPE • 250 kW
		Su • EUROPE • 250 kW
	USA	
	RFE-RL, Via Biblis, GFR	WEST USSR • 100 kW
3985.8	INDONESIA	
	RRI, Manokwari, Irian Jaya	DS • 1 kW
3986.7	INDONESIA	
	†RP DARI JAKARTA, Selatan	DS
3990	CHINA (PR)	
	CENTRAL PEOPLES BS, Urümqi	(D) • DS-MINORITIES • 50 kW
	VOICE OF PUJIANG, Shanghai	E ASIA • CHINESE, ETC
	†XINJIANG PBS, Urümqi	(D) • DS-UIGHUR • 50 kW
		(D) Su • DS-UIGHUR • 50 kW
	USA	
	†RFE-RL, Via Biblis, GFR	E EUROPE & WEST USSR • 100 kW
		M-Sa • E EUROPE • 100 kW
	†VOICE OF AMERICA, Via M'rovia, Liberi	W AFRICA • 50 kW
		(J) • W AFRICA • 50 kW
		(J) M-F • W AFRICA • 50 kW
3995	GERMANY (FR)	
	DEUTSCHE WELLE, Jülich	EUROPE • 100 kW
		(D) • EUROPE • 100 kW
	USSR	
	RADIO MOSCOW, Khabarovsk	(D) • DS-2 • 50 kW
	TUVIN RADIO, Kyzyl	DS • 15 kW
3995v	CLANDESTINE (M EAST)	
	"VO THE CRUSADER", Eastern Iraq	MIDEAST • MOJAHEDIN-E KHALQ
4000v	CAMEROON	
	CAMEROON RTV CORP, Bafoussam	DS-FRENCH, ENG, ETC • 20 kW
4000.2	INDONESIA	
	†RRI, Kendari, Sulawesi	DS • 5 kW
4002.7	INDONESIA	
	†RRI, Padang, Sumatera	DS • 10 kW
4005v	CLANDESTINE (M EAST)	
	"VO IRANIAN REV'N", Afghanistan	MIDEAST • ANTI-IRANIAN GOVT
		PERSIAN • MIDEAST • ANTI-IRANIAN GOVT
4008v	PERU	
	RADIO GRAU, Huancabamba	Alternative Frequency to 5277v kHz
4010	USSR	
	KIRGHIZ RADIO, Frunze, Kirgiziya	RUSSIAN, ETC • DS-1 • 50 kW
	†RADIO MOSCOW, Vladivostok	(D) • E ASIA • 100 kW
4011v	PERU	
	FRECUENCIA POPULAR, Rioja	DS • 0.6 kW
		Tu-Su • DS • 0.6 kW M-Sa • DS • 0.6 kW
4020	CHINA (PR)	
	RADIO BEIJING, Beijing	E ASIA • FEEDER • 10 kW
4025	USSR	
	RADIO MOSCOW, Vladivostok	E ASIA
4030	USSR	
	CHUKOT RADIO, Anadyr'	DS • 15 kW
	RADIO MOSCOW	(D) • EUROPE • DANISH, SWEDISH, ETC
4030v	CLANDESTINE (M EAST)	
	"VO IRAQI PEOPLE"	MIDEAST • IRAQI COMMUNIST
4035	CHINA (PR)	
	CENTRAL PEOPLES BS, Lhasa	DS-MINORITIES • 50 kW
	RADIO BEIJING, Lhasa	S ASIA • 50 kW
	XIZANG PEOPLES BS, Lhasa	DS-TIBETAN • 50 kW
4039.2	PERU	
	†RADIO MARGINAL, Tocache	DS • 1 kW
		M-Sa • DS • 1 kW
4040	USSR	
	ARMENIAN RADIO, Yerevan	RUSSIAN, ETC • DS-1 • 15 kW
	RADIO MOSCOW, Vladivostok	DS-2 • 50 kW

ENGLISH ▬ ARABIC ﹏ CHINESE ┉ FRENCH ═ GERMAN ▬ RUSSIAN ▭ SPANISH ▬ OTHER ▬

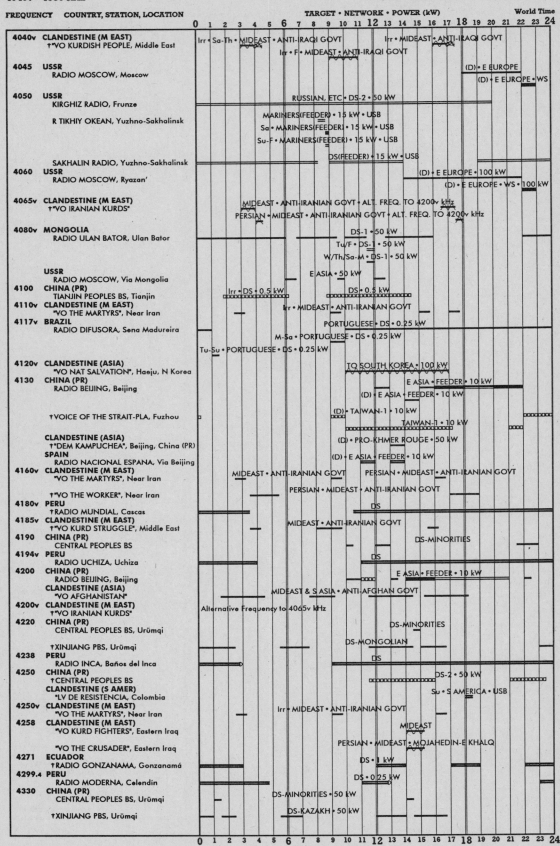

FREQUENCY　　COUNTRY, STATION, LOCATION　　　　TARGET • NETWORK • POWER (kW)　　　World Time

FREQUENCY	COUNTRY, STATION, LOCATION	TARGET • NETWORK • POWER (kW)
4040v	CLANDESTINE (M EAST) †"VO KURDISH PEOPLE, Middle East	Irr • Sa-Th • MIDEAST • ANTI-IRAQI GOVT / Irr • MIDEAST • ANTI-IRAQI GOVT / Irr • F • MIDEAST • ANTI-IRAQI GOVT
4045	USSR RADIO MOSCOW, Moscow	(D) • E EUROPE / (D) • E EUROPE • WS
4050	USSR KIRGHIZ RADIO, Frunze	RUSSIAN, ETC • DS-2 • 50 kW
	R TIKHIY OKEAN, Yuzhno-Sakhalinsk	MARINERS(FEEDER) • 15 kW • USB / Sa • MARINERS(FEEDER) • 15 kW • USB / Su-F • MARINERS(FEEDER) • 15 kW • USB
	SAKHALIN RADIO, Yuzhno-Sakhalinsk	DS(FEEDER) • 15 kW • USB
4060	USSR RADIO MOSCOW, Ryazan'	(D) • E EUROPE • 100 kW / (D) • E EUROPE • WS • 100 kW
4065v	CLANDESTINE (M EAST) †"VO IRANIAN KURDS"	MIDEAST • ANTI-IRANIAN GOVT • ALT. FREQ. TO 4200v kHz / PERSIAN • MIDEAST • ANTI-IRANIAN GOVT • ALT. FREQ. TO 4200v kHz
4080v	MONGOLIA RADIO ULAN BATOR, Ulan Bator	DS-1 • 50 kW / Tu/F • DS-1 • 50 kW / W/Th/Sa-M • DS-1 • 50 kW
	USSR RADIO MOSCOW, Via Mongolia	E ASIA • 50 kW
4100	CHINA (PR) TIANJIN PEOPLES BS, Tianjin	Irr • DS • 0.5 kW / DS • 0.5 kW
4110v	CLANDESTINE (M EAST) "VO THE MARTYRS", Near Iran	Irr • MIDEAST • ANTI-IRANIAN GOVT
4117v	BRAZIL RADIO DIFUSORA, Sena Madureira	PORTUGUESE • DS • 0.25 kW / M-Sa • PORTUGUESE • DS • 0.25 kW / Tu-Su • PORTUGUESE • DS • 0.25 kW
4120v	CLANDESTINE (ASIA) "VO NAT SALVATION", Haeju, N Korea	TO SOUTH KOREA • 100 kW
4130	CHINA (PR) RADIO BEIJING, Beijing	E ASIA • FEEDER • 10 kW / (D) • E ASIA • FEEDER • 10 kW
	†VOICE OF THE STRAIT-PLA, Fuzhou	(D) • TAIWAN-1 • 10 kW / TAIWAN-1 • 10 kW
	CLANDESTINE (ASIA) †"DEM KAMPUCHEA", Beijing, China (PR)	(D) • PRO-KHMER ROUGE • 50 kW
	SPAIN RADIO NACIONAL ESPANA, Via Beijing	(D) • E ASIA • FEEDER • 10 kW
4160v	CLANDESTINE (M EAST) "VO THE MARTYRS", Near Iran	MIDEAST • ANTI-IRANIAN GOVT / PERSIAN • MIDEAST • ANTI-IRANIAN GOVT
	†"VO THE WORKER", Near Iran	PERSIAN • MIDEAST • ANTI-IRANIAN GOVT
4180v	PERU †RADIO MUNDIAL, Cascas	DS
4185v	CLANDESTINE (M EAST) †"VO KURD STRUGGLE", Middle East	MIDEAST • ANTI-IRANIAN GOVT
4190	CHINA (PR) CENTRAL PEOPLES BS	DS-MINORITIES
4194v	PERU RADIO UCHIZA, Uchiza	DS
4200	CHINA (PR) RADIO BEIJING, Beijing	E ASIA • FEEDER • 10 kW
	CLANDESTINE (ASIA) "VO AFGHANISTAN"	MIDEAST & S ASIA • ANTI-AFGHAN GOVT
4200v	CLANDESTINE (M EAST) †"VO IRANIAN KURDS"	Alternative Frequency to 4065v kHz
4220	CHINA (PR) CENTRAL PEOPLES BS, Urümqi	DS-MINORITIES
	†XINJIANG PBS, Urümqi	DS-MONGOLIAN
4238	PERU RADIO INCA, Baños del Inca	DS
4250	CHINA (PR) †CENTRAL PEOPLES BS	DS-2 • 50 kW
	CLANDESTINE (S AMER) "LV DE RESISTENCIA, Colombia	Su • S AMERICA • USB
4250v	CLANDESTINE (M EAST) "VO THE MARTYRS", Near Iran	Irr • MIDEAST • ANTI-IRANIAN GOVT
4258	CLANDESTINE (M EAST) "VO KURD FIGHTERS", Eastern Iraq	MIDEAST
	"VO THE CRUSADER", Eastern Iraq	PERSIAN • MIDEAST • MOJAHEDIN-E KHALQ
4271	ECUADOR †RADIO GONZANAMA, Gonzanamá	DS • 1 kW
4299.4	PERU RADIO MODERNA, Celendin	DS • 0.25 kW
4330	CHINA (PR) CENTRAL PEOPLES BS, Urümqi	DS-MINORITIES • 50 kW
	†XINJIANG PBS, Urümqi	DS-KAZAKH • 50 kW

World Time scale: 0 1 2 3 4 5 6 7 8 9 10 11 12 13 14 15 16 17 18 19 20 21 22 23 24

SUMMER ONLY (J)　　　WINTER ONLY (D)　　　JAMMING / OR ∧　　　EARLIEST HEARD ◁　　　LATEST HEARD ▷　　　NEW OR CHANGED FOR 1991 †

FREQUENCY   COUNTRY, STATION, LOCATION

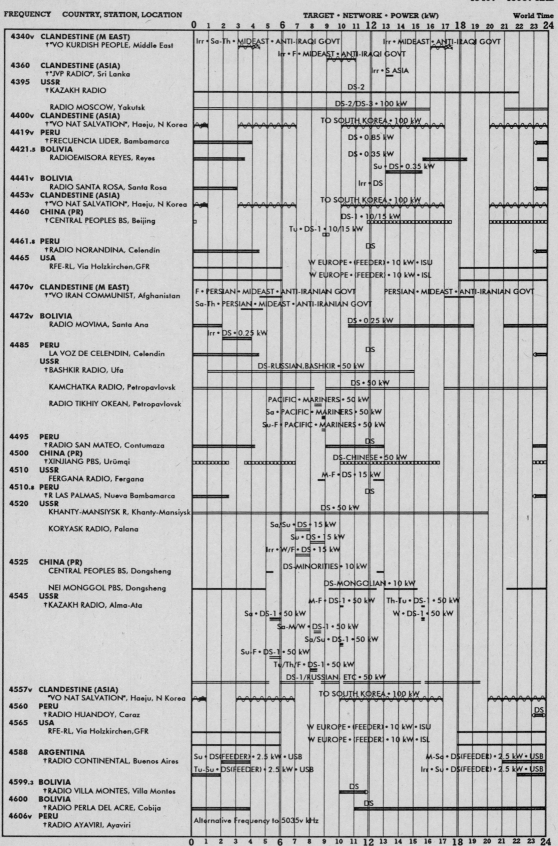

TARGET • NETWORK • POWER (kW)   World Time

Freq	Country, Station, Location	Schedule/Network
4340v	CLANDESTINE (M EAST) †"VO KURDISH PEOPLE, Middle East	Irr • Sa-Th • MIDEAST • ANTI-IRAQI GOVT / Irr • MIDEAST • ANTI-IRAQI GOVT / Irr • F • MIDEAST • ANTI-IRAQI GOVT
4360	CLANDESTINE (ASIA) †"JVP RADIO", Sri Lanka	Irr • S ASIA
4395	USSR †KAZAKH RADIO	DS-2
	RADIO MOSCOW, Yakutsk	DS-2/DS-3 • 100 kW
4400v	CLANDESTINE (ASIA) †"VO NAT SALVATION", Haeju, N Korea	TO SOUTH KOREA • 100 kW
4419v	PERU †FRECUENCIA LIDER, Bambamarca	DS • 0.85 kW
4421.5	BOLIVIA RADIOEMISORA REYES, Reyes	DS • 0.35 kW / Su • DS • 0.35 kW
4441v	BOLIVIA RADIO SANTA ROSA, Santa Rosa	Irr • DS
4453v	CLANDESTINE (ASIA) †"VO NAT SALVATION", Haeju, N Korea	TO SOUTH KOREA • 100 kW
4460	CHINA (PR) †CENTRAL PEOPLES BS, Beijing	DS-1 • 10/15 kW / Tu • DS-1 • 10/15 kW
4461.8	PERU †RADIO NORANDINA, Celendín	DS
4465	USA RFE-RL, Via Holzkirchen,GFR	W EUROPE • (FEEDER) • 10 kW • ISU / W EUROPE • (FEEDER) • 10 kW • ISL
4470v	CLANDESTINE (M EAST) †"VO IRAN COMMUNIST, Afghanistan	F • PERSIAN • MIDEAST • ANTI-IRANIAN GOVT / PERSIAN • MIDEAST • ANTI-IRANIAN GOVT / Sa-Th • PERSIAN • MIDEAST • ANTI-IRANIAN GOVT
4472v	BOLIVIA RADIO MOVIMA, Santa Ana	DS • 0.25 kW / Irr • DS • 0.25 kW
4485	PERU LA VOZ DE CELENDIN, Celendin	DS
	USSR †BASHKIR RADIO, Ufa	DS-RUSSIAN, BASHKIR • 50 kW
	KAMCHATKA RADIO, Petropavlovsk	DS • 50 kW
	RADIO TIKHIY OKEAN, Petropavlovsk	PACIFIC • MARINERS • 50 kW / Sa • PACIFIC • MARINERS • 50 kW / Su-F • PACIFIC • MARINERS • 50 kW
4495	PERU †RADIO SAN MATEO, Contumaza	DS
4500	CHINA (PR) †XINJIANG PBS, Urümqi	DS-CHINESE • 50 kW
4510	USSR FERGANA RADIO, Fergana	M-F • DS • 15 kW
4510.8	PERU †R LAS PALMAS, Nueva Bambamarca	DS
4520	USSR KHANTY-MANSIYSK R, Khanty-Mansiysk	DS • 50 kW
	KORYASK RADIO, Palana	Sa/Su • DS • 15 kW / Su • DS • 15 kW / Irr • W/F • DS • 15 kW
4525	CHINA (PR) CENTRAL PEOPLES BS, Dongsheng	DS-MINORITIES • 10 kW
	NEI MONGGOL PBS, Dongsheng	DS-MONGOLIAN • 10 kW
4545	USSR †KAZAKH RADIO, Alma-Ata	M-F • DS-1 • 50 kW / Th-Tu • DS-1 • 50 kW / Sa • DS-1 • 50 kW / W • DS-1 • 50 kW / Sa-M/W • DS-1 • 50 kW / Sa/Su • DS-1 • 50 kW / Su-F • DS-1 • 50 kW / Tu/Th/F • DS-1 • 50 kW / DS-1/RUSSIAN, ETC • 50 kW
4557v	CLANDESTINE (ASIA) "VO NAT SALVATION", Haeju, N Korea	TO SOUTH KOREA • 100 kW
4560	PERU †RADIO HUANDOY, Caraz	DS
4565	USA RFE-RL, Via Holzkirchen,GFR	W EUROPE • (FEEDER) • 10 kW • ISU / W EUROPE • (FEEDER) • 10 kW • ISL
4588	ARGENTINA †RADIO CONTINENTAL, Buenos Aires	Su • DS(FEEDER) • 2.5 kW • USB / M-Sa • DS(FEEDER) • 2.5 kW • USB / Tu-Su • DS(FEEDER) • 2.5 kW • USB / Irr • Su • DS(FEEDER) • 2.5 kW • USB
4599.3	BOLIVIA †RADIO VILLA MONTES, Villa Montes	DS
4600	BOLIVIA †RADIO PERLA DEL ACRE, Cobija	DS
4606v	PERU †RADIO AYAVIRI, Ayaviri	Alternative Frequency to 5035v kHz

0 1 2 3 4 5 6 7 8 9 10 11 12 13 14 15 16 17 18 19 20 21 22 23 24

ENGLISH ▬   ARABIC ⋙   CHINESE ▭▭▭   FRENCH ══   GERMAN ▬▬   RUSSIAN ══   SPANISH ▬▬   OTHER ──

FREQUENCY   COUNTRY, STATION, LOCATION

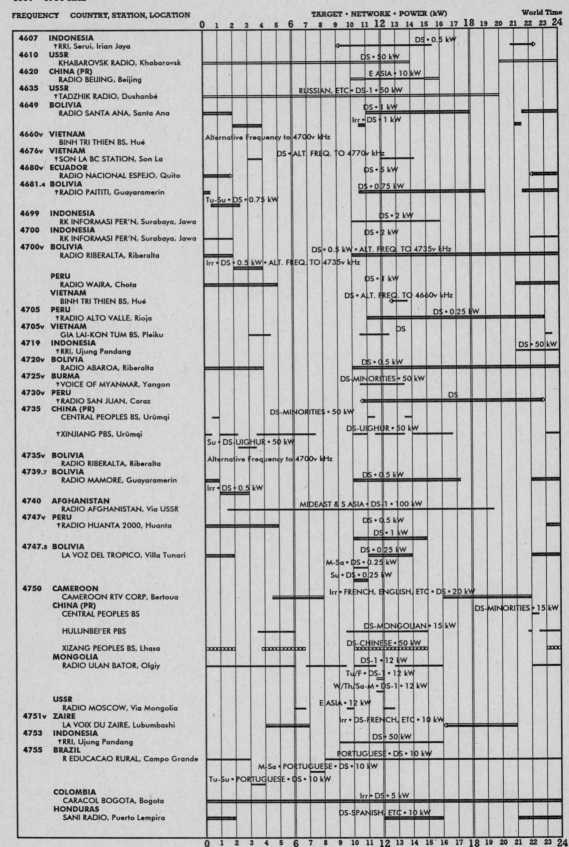

Frequency	Country, Station, Location	Notes
4607	INDONESIA — †RRI, Serui, Irian Jaya	DS • 0.5 kW
4610	USSR — KHABAROVSK RADIO, Khabarovsk	DS • 50 kW
4620	CHINA (PR) — RADIO BEIJING, Beijing	E ASIA • 10 kW
4635	USSR — †TADZHIK RADIO, Dushanbé	RUSSIAN, ETC • DS-1 • 50 kW
4649	BOLIVIA — RADIO SANTA ANA, Santa Ana	DS • 1 kW / Irr • DS • 1 kW
4660v	VIETNAM — BINH TRI THIEN BS, Hué	Alternative Frequency to 4700v kHz
4676v	VIETNAM — †SON LA BC STATION, Son La	DS • ALT. FREQ. TO 4770v kHz
4680v	ECUADOR — RADIO NACIONAL ESPEJO, Quito	DS • 5 kW
4681.4	BOLIVIA — †RADIO PAITITI, Guayaramerín	DS • 0.75 kW / Tu-Su • DS • 0.75 kW
4699	INDONESIA — RK INFORMASI PER'N, Surabaya, Jawa	DS • 2 kW
4700	INDONESIA — RK INFORMASI PER'N, Surabaya, Jawa	DS • 2 kW
4700v	BOLIVIA — RADIO RIBERALTA, Riberalta	DS • 0.5 kW • ALT. FREQ. TO 4735v kHz / Irr • DS • 0.5 kW • ALT. FREQ. TO 4735v kHz
	PERU — RADIO WAIRA, Chota	DS • 1 kW
	VIETNAM — BINH TRI THIEN BS, Hué	DS • ALT. FREQ. TO 4660v kHz
4705	PERU — †RADIO ALTO VALLE, Rioja	DS • 0.25 kW
4705v	VIETNAM — GIA LAI-KON TUM BS, Pleiku	DS
4719	INDONESIA — †RRI, Ujung Pandang	DS • 50 kW
4720v	BOLIVIA — RADIO ABAROA, Riberalta	DS • 0.5 kW
4725v	BURMA — †VOICE OF MYANMAR, Yangon	DS-MINORITIES • 50 kW
4730v	PERU — †RADIO SAN JUAN, Caraz	DS
4735	CHINA (PR) — CENTRAL PEOPLES BS, Urümqi	DS-MINORITIES • 50 kW
	†XINJIANG PBS, Urümqi	DS-UIGHUR • 50 kW / Su • DS-UIGHUR • 50 kW
4735v	BOLIVIA — RADIO RIBERALTA, Riberalta	Alternative Frequency to 4700v kHz
4739.7	BOLIVIA — RADIO MAMORE, Guayaramerín	DS • 0.5 kW / Irr • DS 0.5 kW
4740	AFGHANISTAN — RADIO AFGHANISTAN, Via USSR	MIDEAST & S ASIA • DS-1 • 100 kW
4747v	PERU — †RADIO HUANTA 2000, Huanta	DS • 0.5 kW / DS • 1 kW
4747.5	BOLIVIA — LA VOZ DEL TROPICO, Villa Tunari	DS • 0.25 kW / M-Sa • DS • 0.25 kW / Su • DS • 0.25 kW
4750	CAMEROON — CAMEROON RTV CORP, Bertoua	Irr • FRENCH, ENGLISH, ETC • DS • 20 kW
	CHINA (PR) — CENTRAL PEOPLES BS	DS-MINORITIES • 15 kW
	HULUNBEI'ER PBS	DS-MONGOLIAN • 15 kW
	XIZANG PEOPLES BS, Lhasa	DS-CHINESE • 50 kW
	MONGOLIA — RADIO ULAN BATOR, Olgiy	DS-1 • 12 kW / Tu/F • DS-1 • 12 kW / W/Th/Sa-M • DS-1 • 12 kW
	USSR — RADIO MOSCOW, Via Mongolia	E ASIA • 12 kW
4751v	ZAIRE — LA VOIX DU ZAIRE, Lubumbashi	Irr • DS-FRENCH, ETC • 10 kW
4753	INDONESIA — †RRI, Ujung Pandang	DS • 50 kW
4755	BRAZIL — R EDUCACAO RURAL, Campo Grande	PORTUGUESE • DS • 10 kW / M-Sa • PORTUGUESE • DS • 10 kW / Tu-Su • PORTUGUESE • DS • 10 kW
	COLOMBIA — CARACOL BOGOTA, Bogota	Irr • DS • 5 kW
	HONDURAS — SANI RADIO, Puerto Lempira	DS-SPANISH, ETC • 10 kW

SUMMER ONLY (J)   WINTER ONLY (D)   JAMMING / OR ∧   EARLIEST HEARD ◁   LATEST HEARD ▷   NEW OR CHANGED FOR 1991 †

FREQUENCY   COUNTRY, STATION, LOCATION

TARGET • NETWORK • POWER (kW)

World Time

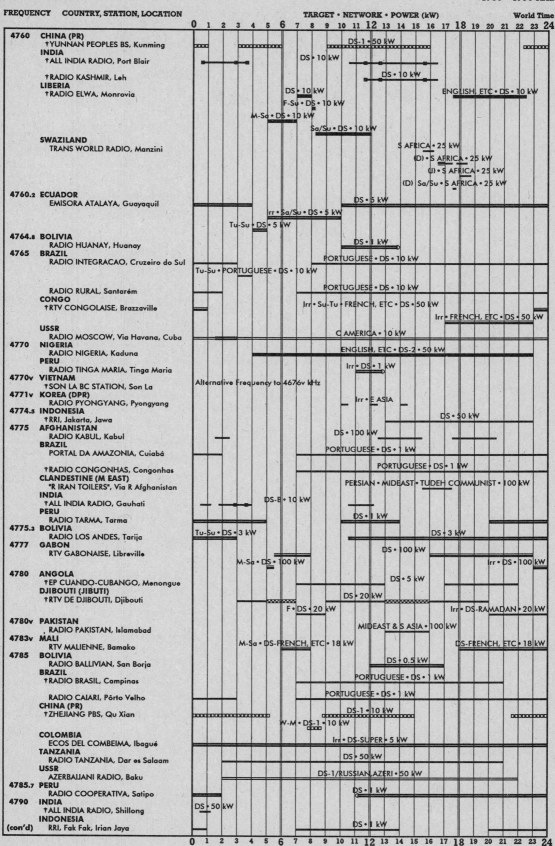

FREQUENCY	COUNTRY, STATION, LOCATION	TARGET • NETWORK • POWER (kW)
4760	**CHINA (PR)**	
	†YUNNAN PEOPLES BS, Kunming	DS-1 • 50 kW
	INDIA	
	†ALL INDIA RADIO, Port Blair	DS • 10 kW
	†RADIO KASHMIR, Leh	DS • 10 kW
	LIBERIA	
	†RADIO ELWA, Monrovia	DS • 10 kW / ENGLISH, ETC • DS • 10 kW
		F-Su • DS • 10 kW
		M-Sa • DS • 10 kW
		Sa/Su • DS • 10 kW
	SWAZILAND	
	TRANS WORLD RADIO, Manzini	S AFRICA • 25 kW
		(D) • S AFRICA • 25 kW
		(J) • S AFRICA • 25 kW
		(D) Sa/Su • S AFRICA • 25 kW
4760.2	**ECUADOR**	
	EMISORA ATALAYA, Guayaquil	DS • 5 kW
		Irr • Sa/Su • DS • 5 kW
		Tu-Su • DS • 5 kW
4764.8	**BOLIVIA**	
	RADIO HUANAY, Huanay	DS • 1 kW
4765	**BRAZIL**	
	RADIO INTEGRACAO, Cruzeiro do Sul	PORTUGUESE • DS • 10 kW
		Tu-Su • PORTUGUESE • DS • 10 kW
	RADIO RURAL, Santarém	PORTUGUESE • DS • 10 kW
	CONGO	
	†RTV CONGOLAISE, Brazzaville	Irr • Su-Tu • FRENCH, ETC • DS • 50 kW
		Irr • FRENCH, ETC • DS • 50 kW
	USSR	
	RADIO MOSCOW, Via Havana, Cuba	C AMERICA • 10 kW
4770	**NIGERIA**	
	RADIO NIGERIA, Kaduna	ENGLISH, ETC • DS-2 • 50 kW
	PERU	
	RADIO TINGA MARIA, Tinga Maria	Irr • DS • 1 kW
4770v	**VIETNAM**	
	†SON LA BC STATION, Son La	Alternative Frequency to 4676v kHz
4771v	**KOREA (DPR)**	
	RADIO PYONGYANG, Pyongyang	Irr • E ASIA
4774.5	**INDONESIA**	
	†RRI, Jakarta, Jawa	DS • 50 kW
4775	**AFGHANISTAN**	
	RADIO KABUL, Kabul	DS • 100 kW
	BRAZIL	
	PORTAL DA AMAZONIA, Cuiabá	PORTUGUESE • DS • 1 kW
	†RADIO CONGONHAS, Congonhas	PORTUGUESE • DS • 1 kW
	CLANDESTINE (M EAST)	
	"R IRAN TOILERS", Via R Afghanistan	PERSIAN • MIDEAST • TUDEH COMMUNIST • 100 kW
	INDIA	
	†ALL INDIA RADIO, Gauhati	DS-B • 10 kW
	PERU	
	RADIO TARMA, Tarma	DS • 1 kW
4775.3	**BOLIVIA**	
	RADIO LOS ANDES, Tarija	Tu-Su • DS • 3 kW / DS • 3 kW
4777	**GABON**	
	RTV GABONAISE, Libreville	DS • 100 kW
		M-Sa • DS • 100 kW
		Irr • DS • 100 kW
4780	**ANGOLA**	
	†EP CUANDO-CUBANGO, Menongue	DS • 5 kW
	DJIBOUTI (JIBUTI)	
	†RTV DE DJIBOUTI, Djibouti	DS • 20 kW
		F • DS • 20 kW
		Irr • DS-RAMADAN • 20 kW
4780v	**PAKISTAN**	
	RADIO PAKISTAN, Islamabad	MIDEAST & S ASIA • 100 kW
4783v	**MALI**	
	RTV MALIENNE, Bamako	M-Sa • DS-FRENCH, ETC • 18 kW / DS-FRENCH, ETC • 18 kW
4785	**BOLIVIA**	
	RADIO BALLIVIAN, San Borja	DS • 0.5 kW
	BRAZIL	
	†RADIO BRASIL, Campinas	PORTUGUESE • DS • 1 kW
	RADIO CAIARI, Pôrto Velho	PORTUGUESE • DS • 1 kW
	CHINA (PR)	
	†ZHEJIANG PBS, Qu Xian	DS-1 • 10 kW
		W-M • DS-1 • 10 kW
	COLOMBIA	
	ECOS DEL COMBEIMA, Ibagué	Irr • DS-SUPER • 5 kW
	TANZANIA	
	RADIO TANZANIA, Dar es Salaam	DS • 50 kW
	USSR	
	AZERBAIJANI RADIO, Baku	DS-1/RUSSIAN, AZERI • 50 kW
4785.7	**PERU**	
	RADIO COOPERATIVA, Satipo	DS • 1 kW
4790	**INDIA**	
	†ALL INDIA RADIO, Shillong	DS • 50 kW
	INDONESIA	
(con'd)	RRI, Fak Fak, Irian Jaya	DS • 1 kW

FREQUENCY   COUNTRY, STATION, LOCATION

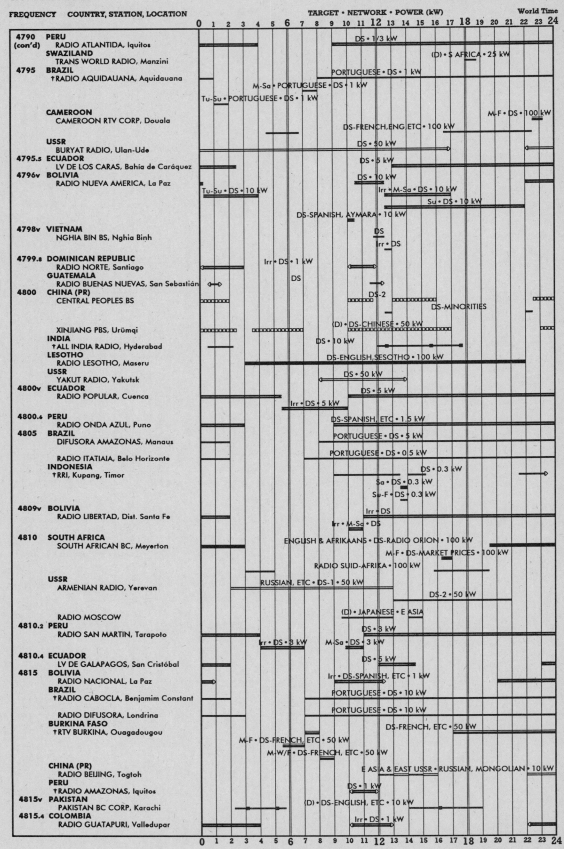

4790	PERU	
(con'd)	RADIO ATLANTIDA, Iquitos	DS • 1/3 kW
	SWAZILAND	
	TRANS WORLD RADIO, Manzini	(D) • S AFRICA • 25 kW
4795	BRAZIL	
	†RADIO AQUIDAUANA, Aquidauana	PORTUGUESE • DS • 1 kW
		M-Sa • PORTUGUESE • DS • 1 kW
		Tu-Su • PORTUGUESE • DS • 1 kW
	CAMEROON	M-F • DS • 100 kW
	CAMEROON RTV CORP, Douala	DS-FRENCH, ENG, ETC • 100 kW
	USSR	
	BURYAT RADIO, Ulan-Ude	DS • 50 kW
4795.5	ECUADOR	
	LV DE LOS CARAS, Bahía de Caráquez	DS • 5 kW
4796v	BOLIVIA	
	RADIO NUEVA AMERICA, La Paz	DS • 10 kW
		Tu-Su • DS • 10 kW
		Irr • M-Sa • DS • 10 kW
		Su • DS • 10 kW
		DS-SPANISH, AYMARA • 10 kW
4798v	VIETNAM	
	NGHIA BIN BS, Nghia Binh	DS
		Irr • DS
4799.8	DOMINICAN REPUBLIC	
	RADIO NORTE, Santiago	Irr • DS • 1 kW
	GUATEMALA	
	RADIO BUENAS NUEVAS, San Sebastián	DS
4800	CHINA (PR)	
	CENTRAL PEOPLES BS	DS-2
		DS-MINORITIES
	XINJIANG PBS, Urümqi	(D) • DS-CHINESE • 50 kW
	INDIA	
	†ALL INDIA RADIO, Hyderabad	DS • 10 kW
	LESOTHO	
	RADIO LESOTHO, Maseru	DS-ENGLISH, SESOTHO • 100 kW
	USSR	
	YAKUT RADIO, Yakutsk	DS • 50 kW
4800v	ECUADOR	
	RADIO POPULAR, Cuenca	DS • 5 kW
		Irr • DS • 5 kW
4800.6	PERU	
	RADIO ONDA AZUL, Puno	DS-SPANISH, ETC • 1.5 kW
4805	BRAZIL	
	DIFUSORA AMAZONAS, Manaus	PORTUGUESE • DS • 5 kW
	RADIO ITATIAIA, Belo Horizonte	PORTUGUESE • DS • 0.5 kW
	INDONESIA	
	†RRI, Kupang, Timor	DS • 0.3 kW
		Sa • DS • 0.3 kW
		Su-F • DS • 0.3 kW
4809v	BOLIVIA	
	RADIO LIBERTAD, Dist. Santa Fe	Irr • DS
		Irr • M-Sa • DS
4810	SOUTH AFRICA	
	SOUTH AFRICAN BC, Meyerton	ENGLISH & AFRIKAANS • DS-RADIO ORION • 100 kW
		M-F • DS-MARKET PRICES • 100 kW
		RADIO SUID-AFRIKA • 100 kW
	USSR	
	ARMENIAN RADIO, Yerevan	RUSSIAN, ETC • DS-1 • 50 kW
		DS-2 • 50 kW
	RADIO MOSCOW	(D) • JAPANESE • E ASIA
4810.2	PERU	
	RADIO SAN MARTIN, Tarapoto	DS • 3 kW
		Irr • DS • 3 kW
		M-Sa • DS • 3 kW
4810.4	ECUADOR	
	LV DE GALAPAGOS, San Cristóbal	DS • 5 kW
4815	BOLIVIA	
	RADIO NACIONAL, La Paz	Irr • DS-SPANISH, ETC • 1 kW
	BRAZIL	
	†RADIO CABOCLA, Benjamim Constant	PORTUGUESE • DS • 10 kW
	RADIO DIFUSORA, Londrina	PORTUGUESE • DS • 10 kW
	BURKINA FASO	
	†RTV BURKINA, Ouagadougou	DS-FRENCH, ETC • 50 kW
		M-F • DS-FRENCH, ETC • 50 kW
		M-W/F • DS-FRENCH, ETC • 50 kW
	CHINA (PR)	
	RADIO BEIJING, Togtoh	E ASIA & EAST USSR • RUSSIAN, MONGOLIAN • 10 kW
	PERU	
	†RADIO AMAZONAS, Iquitos	DS • 1 kW
4815v	PAKISTAN	
	PAKISTAN BC CORP, Karachi	(D) • DS-ENGLISH, ETC • 10 kW
4815.4	COLOMBIA	
	RADIO GUATAPURI, Valledupar	Irr • DS • 1 kW

FREQUENCY	COUNTRY, STATION, LOCATION	TARGET • NETWORK • POWER (kW)

World Time

0 1 2 3 4 5 6 7 8 9 10 11 12 13 14 15 16 17 18 19 20 21 22 23 24

4819.7	ECUADOR	
	RADIO PAZ Y BIEN, Ambato	DS-SPANISH, ETC • 1.5 kW
		Tu-Su • DS-SPANISH, ETC • 1.5 kW
4820	HONDURAS	
	LA VOZ EVANGELICA, Tegucigalpa	DS • 5 kW
		M • DS • 5 kW
		Tu-Su • DS • 5 kW
	INDIA	
	ALL INDIA RADIO, Calcutta	DS-A • 10 kW
	USSR	
	KHANTY-MANSIYSK R, Khanty-Mansiysk	DS • 50 kW
4820v	VIETNAM	
	†HA TUYEN BS, Ha Tuyen	DS
4820.2	ANGOLA	
	ER DA HUILA, Lubango	DS • 10 kW
4820.8	PERU	
	RADIO ATAHUALPA, Cajamarca	DS • 1 kW
4825	BRAZIL	
	R CANCAO NOVA, Cachoeira Paulista	PORTUGUESE • DS • 10 kW
	RADIO EDUCADORA, Bragança	PORTUGUESE • DS • 10 kW
	GUATEMALA	
	RADIO MAM, Cabricán	DS/SPANISH, ETC • 1 kW
	USSR	
	TURKMEN RADIO, Ashkhabad	DS-1/RUSSIAN, ETC • 50 kW
4825v	PERU	
	LV DE LA SELVA, Iquitos	DS • 10 kW
4826.3	PERU	
	RADIO SICUANI, Sicuani	DS-SPANISH, ETC • 0.35 kW
4830	BOLIVIA	
	RADIO GRIGOTA, Santa Cruz	Tu-Su • DS • 1 kW
		Irr • Tu-Su • DS • 1 kW DS • 1 kW
	BOTSWANA	
	RADIO BOTSWANA, Gaborone	DS-ENGLISH, ETC • 50 kW
	THAILAND	
	†RADIO THAILAND, Pathum Thani	DS-1 • 10 kW
	VENEZUELA	
	RADIO TACHIRA, San Cristóbal	DS • 10 kW
4831	PERU	
	RADIO HUANTA, Huanta	Alternative Frequency to 4890v kHz
4831v	MONGOLIA	
	RADIO ULAN BATOR, Altai	DS • 12 kW
		Tu/F • DS • 12 kW
		W/Th/Sa-M • DS • 12 kW
	USSR	
	RADIO MOSCOW, Via Mongolia	E ASIA • 12 kW
4832	COSTA RICA	
	RADIO RELOJ, San José	Irr • DS • 3 kW
4835	AUSTRALIA	
	ABC/CAAMA RADIO, Alice Springs	DS-ENGLISH, ETC • 50 kW
	GUATEMALA	
	RADIO TEZULUTLAN, Cobán	DS-SPANISH, ETC • 2.5/3 kW
	MALAYSIA	
	†RTM-SARAWAK, Kuching-Stapok	DS-MALAY, MELANEU • 10 kW
	PERU	
	RADIO MARANON, Jaén	DS • 1 kW
4835v	MALI	
	RTV MALIENNE, Bamako	Irr • M-Sa • DS-FRENCH, ETC • 18 kW Irr • DS-FRENCH, ETC • 18 kW
	PAKISTAN	
	PAKISTAN BC CORP, Islamabad	(D) • DS • 100 kW
4839v	ZAIRE	
	RADIO BUKAVU, Bukavu	Alternative Frequency to 4862v kHz
4840	CHINA (PR)	
	HEILONGJIANG PBS, Harbin	DS-CHINESE, KOREAN • 50 kW
	†VOICE OF THE STRAIT-PLA, Fuzhou	TAIWAN-1 • 10 kW
		(D) • TAIWAN-1 • 10 kW
	ECUADOR	
	RADIO INTEROCEANICA, Santa Rosa	DS • 1 kW
	INDIA	
	†ALL INDIA RADIO, Bombay	DS-B • 10 kW
	PERU	
	RADIO ANDAHUAYLAS, Andahuaylas	DS-SPANISH, QUECHUA • 2 kW
	VENEZUELA	
	RADIO VALERA, Valera	DS • 1 kW
		Tu-Su • DS • 1 kW
4844.4	GUATEMALA	
	RADIO K'EKCHI, San Cristóbal V	DS-SPANISH, ETC • 1/5 kW
		M-Sa • DS-SPANISH, ETC • 1/5 kW Su • DS-SPANISH, ETC • 1/5 kW
		Tu-Su • DS-SPANISH, ETC • 1/5 kW
4845	BRAZIL	
	†RADIO METEOROLOGIA, Ibitinga	PORTUGUESE • DS • 1 kW
	†RADIO CABOCLA, Manaus	PORTUGUESE • DS • 250 kW
	MALAYSIA	
	RADIO MALAYSIA, Kajang	DS-TAMIL • 50 kW
		Sa-Th • DS-TAMIL • 50 kW
		Sa/Su • DS-TAMIL • 50 kW
		Su • DS-TAMIL • 50 kW

(con'd)

0 1 2 3 4 5 6 7 8 9 10 11 12 13 14 15 16 17 18 19 20 21 22 23 24

ENGLISH ▪▪▪   ARABIC ≈≈≈   CHINESE □□□   FRENCH ▬▬▬   GERMAN ▬▬▬   RUSSIAN ══   SPANISH ▪▪▪   OTHER ▬▬

| FREQUENCY | COUNTRY, STATION, LOCATION | TARGET • NETWORK • POWER (kW) | World Time |

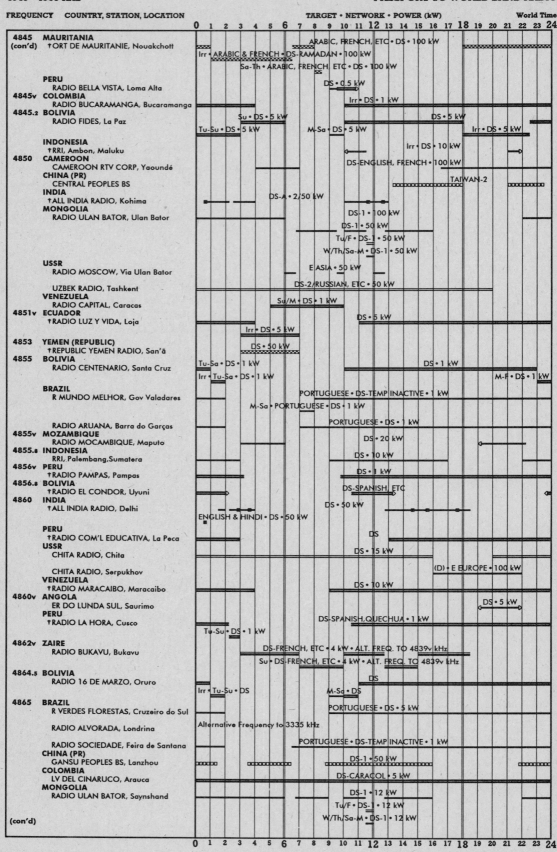

FREQUENCY — COUNTRY, STATION, LOCATION — TARGET • NETWORK • POWER (kW) — World Time

0 1 2 3 4 5 6 7 8 9 10 11 12 13 14 15 16 17 18 19 20 21 22 23 24

4845 MAURITANIA
(con'd) †ORT DE MAURITANIE, Nouakchott
- ARABIC, FRENCH, ETC • DS • 100 kW
- Irr • ARABIC & FRENCH • DS-RAMADAN • 100 kW
- Sa-Th • ARABIC, FRENCH, ETC • DS • 100 kW

PERU
RADIO BELLA VISTA, Loma Alta — DS • 0.5 kW
4845v COLOMBIA
RADIO BUCARAMANGA, Bucaramanga — Irr • DS • 1 kW
4845.2 BOLIVIA
RADIO FIDES, La Paz
- Su • DS • 5 kW
- DS • 5 kW
- Tu-Su • DS • 5 kW
- M-Sa • DS • 5 kW
- Irr • DS • 5 kW

INDONESIA
†RRI, Ambon, Maluku — Irr • DS • 10 kW
4850 CAMEROON
CAMEROON RTV CORP, Yaoundé — DS-ENGLISH, FRENCH • 100 kW
CHINA (PR)
CENTRAL PEOPLES BS — TAIWAN-2
INDIA
†ALL INDIA RADIO, Kohima — DS-A • 2/50 kW
MONGOLIA
RADIO ULAN BATOR, Ulan Bator
- DS-1 • 100 kW
- DS-1 • 50 kW
- Tu/F • DS-1 • 50 kW
- W/Th/Sa-M • DS-1 • 50 kW

USSR
RADIO MOSCOW, Via Ulan Bator — E ASIA • 50 kW
UZBEK RADIO, Tashkent — DS-2/RUSSIAN, ETC • 50 kW
VENEZUELA
RADIO CAPITAL, Caracas — Su/M • DS • 1 kW
4851v ECUADOR
†RADIO LUZ Y VIDA, Loja — DS • 5 kW
- Irr • DS • 5 kW

4853 YEMEN (REPUBLIC)
†REPUBLIC YEMEN RADIO, San'ā — DS • 50 kW
4855 BOLIVIA
RADIO CENTENARIO, Santa Cruz
- Tu-Sa • DS • 1 kW
- DS • 1 kW
- Irr • Tu-Sa • DS • 1 kW
- M-F • DS • 1 kW

BRAZIL
R MUNDO MELHOR, Gov Valadares
- PORTUGUESE • DS-TEMP INACTIVE • 1 kW
- M-Sa • PORTUGUESE • DS • 1 kW
RADIO ARUANA, Barra do Garças — PORTUGUESE • DS • 1 kW
4855v MOZAMBIQUE
RADIO MOCAMBIQUE, Maputo — DS • 20 kW
4855.8 INDONESIA
RRI, Palembang, Sumatera — DS • 10 kW
4856v PERU
†RADIO PAMPAS, Pampas — DS • 1 kW
4856.8 BOLIVIA
†RADIO EL CONDOR, Uyuni — DS-SPANISH, ETC
4860 INDIA
†ALL INDIA RADIO, Delhi
- DS • 50 kW
- ENGLISH & HINDI • DS • 50 kW

PERU
†RADIO COM'L EDUCATIVA, La Peca — DS
USSR
CHITA RADIO, Chita — DS • 15 kW
CHITA RADIO, Serpukhov — (D) • E EUROPE • 100 kW
VENEZUELA
†RADIO MARACAIBO, Maracaibo — DS • 10 kW
4860v ANGOLA
ER DO LUNDA SUL, Saurimo — DS • 5 kW
PERU
†RADIO LA HORA, Cusco
- DS-SPANISH, QUECHUA • 1 kW
- Tu-Su • DS • 1 kW
4862v ZAIRE
RADIO BUKAVU, Bukavu
- DS-FRENCH, ETC • 4 kW • ALT. FREQ. TO 4839v kHz
- Su • DS-FRENCH, ETC • 4 kW • ALT. FREQ. TO 4839v kHz
4864.5 BOLIVIA
RADIO 16 DE MARZO, Oruro
- DS
- Irr • Tu-Su • DS
- M-Sa • DS
4865 BRAZIL
R VERDES FLORESTAS, Cruzeiro do Sul — PORTUGUESE • DS • 5 kW
RADIO ALVORADA, Londrina — Alternative Frequency to 3335 kHz
RADIO SOCIEDADE, Feira de Santana — PORTUGUESE • DS-TEMP INACTIVE • 1 kW
CHINA (PR)
GANSU PEOPLES BS, Lanzhou — DS-1 • 50 kW
COLOMBIA
LV DEL CINARUCO, Arauca — DS-CARACOL • 5 kW
MONGOLIA
RADIO ULAN BATOR, Saynshand
- DS-1 • 12 kW
- Tu/F • DS-1 • 12 kW
- W/Th/Sa-M • DS-1 • 12 kW

(con'd)

0 1 2 3 4 5 6 7 8 9 10 11 12 13 14 15 16 17 18 19 20 21 22 23 24

SUMMER ONLY (J)   WINTER ONLY (D)   JAMMING / OR ∧   EARLIEST HEARD ◁   LATEST HEARD ▷   NEW OR CHANGED FOR 1991 †

FREQUENCY   COUNTRY, STATION, LOCATION   TARGET • NETWORK • POWER (kW)   World Time

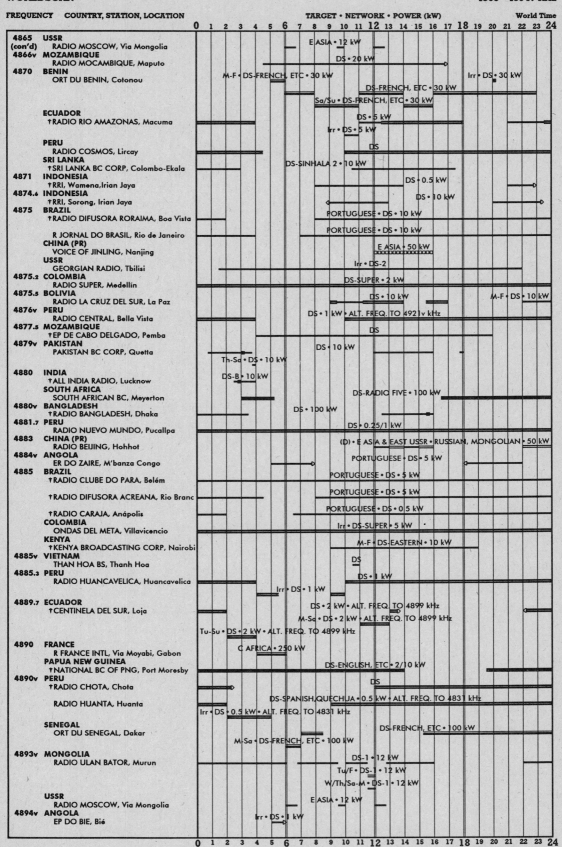

FREQUENCY	COUNTRY, STATION, LOCATION	TARGET • NETWORK • POWER (kW)
4865 (con'd)	USSR — RADIO MOSCOW, Via Mongolia	E ASIA • 12 kW
4866v	MOZAMBIQUE — RADIO MOCAMBIQUE, Maputo	DS • 20 kW
4870	BENIN — ORT DU BENIN, Cotonou	M-F • DS-FRENCH, ETC • 30 kW / Irr • DS • 30 kW / DS-FRENCH, ETC • 30 kW / Sa/Su • DS-FRENCH, ETC • 30 kW
	ECUADOR — †RADIO RIO AMAZONAS, Macuma	DS • 5 kW / Irr • DS • 5 kW
	PERU — RADIO COSMOS, Lircay	DS
	SRI LANKA — †SRI LANKA BC CORP, Colombo-Ekala	DS-SINHALA 2 • 10 kW
4871	INDONESIA — †RRI, Wamena, Irian Jaya	DS • 0.5 kW
4874.6	INDONESIA — †RRI, Sorong, Irian Jaya	DS • 10 kW
4875	BRAZIL — †RADIO DIFUSORA RORAIMA, Boa Vista	PORTUGUESE • DS • 10 kW
	R JORNAL DO BRASIL, Rio de Janeiro	PORTUGUESE • DS • 10 kW
	CHINA (PR) — VOICE OF JINLING, Nanjing	E ASIA • 50 kW
	USSR — GEORGIAN RADIO, Tbilisi	Irr • DS-2
4875.2	COLOMBIA — RADIO SUPER, Medellín	DS-SUPER • 2 kW
4875.5	BOLIVIA — RADIO LA CRUZ DEL SUR, La Paz	DS • 10 kW / M-F • DS • 10 kW
4876v	PERU — RADIO CENTRAL, Bella Vista	DS • 1 kW • ALT. FREQ. TO 4921v kHz
4877.5	MOZAMBIQUE — †EP DE CABO DELGADO, Pemba	DS
4879v	PAKISTAN — PAKISTAN BC CORP, Quetta	DS • 10 kW / Th-Sa • DS • 10 kW
4880	INDIA — †ALL INDIA RADIO, Lucknow	DS-B • 10 kW
	SOUTH AFRICA — SOUTH AFRICAN BC, Meyerton	DS-RADIO FIVE • 100 kW
4880v	BANGLADESH — †RADIO BANGLADESH, Dhaka	DS • 100 kW
4881.7	PERU — RADIO NUEVO MUNDO, Pucallpa	DS • 0.25/1 kW
4883	CHINA (PR) — RADIO BEIJING, Hohhot	(D) • E ASIA & EAST USSR • RUSSIAN, MONGOLIAN • 50 kW
4884v	ANGOLA — ER DO ZAIRE, M'banza Congo	PORTUGUESE • DS • 5 kW
4885	BRAZIL — †RADIO CLUBE DO PARA, Belém	PORTUGUESE • DS • 5 kW
	†RADIO DIFUSORA ACREANA, Rio Branc	PORTUGUESE • DS • 5 kW
	†RADIO CARAJA, Anápolis	PORTUGUESE • DS • 0.5 kW
	COLOMBIA — ONDAS DEL META, Villavicencio	Irr • DS-SUPER • 5 kW
	KENYA — †KENYA BROADCASTING CORP, Nairobi	M-F • DS-EASTERN • 10 kW
4885v	VIETNAM — THAN HOA BS, Thanh Hoa	DS
4885.3	PERU — RADIO HUANCAVELICA, Huancavelica	DS • 1 kW / Irr • DS • 1 kW
4889.7	ECUADOR — †CENTINELA DEL SUR, Loja	DS • 2 kW • ALT. FREQ. TO 4899 kHz / M-Sa • DS • 2 kW • ALT. FREQ. TO 4899 kHz / Tu-Su • DS • 2 kW • ALT. FREQ. TO 4899 kHz
4890	FRANCE — R FRANCE INTL, Via Moyabi, Gabon	C AFRICA • 250 kW
	PAPUA NEW GUINEA — †NATIONAL BC OF PNG, Port Moresby	DS-ENGLISH, ETC • 2/10 kW
4890v	PERU — †RADIO CHOTA, Chota	DS
	RADIO HUANTA, Huanta	DS-SPANISH, QUECHUA • 0.5 kW • ALT. FREQ. TO 4831 kHz / Irr • DS • 0.5 kW • ALT. FREQ. TO 4831 kHz
	SENEGAL — ORT DU SENEGAL, Dakar	DS-FRENCH, ETC • 100 kW / M-Sa • DS-FRENCH, ETC • 100 kW
4893v	MONGOLIA — RADIO ULAN BATOR, Murun	DS-1 • 12 kW / Tu/F • DS-1 • 12 kW / W/Th/Sa-M • DS-1 • 12 kW
	USSR — RADIO MOSCOW, Via Mongolia	E ASIA • 12 kW
4894v	ANGOLA — EP DO BIE, Bié	Irr • DS • 1 kW

ENGLISH ▬   ARABIC ░░░   CHINESE ▭▭▭   FRENCH ▬▬   GERMAN ▬▬   RUSSIAN ═══   SPANISH ▬▬   OTHER ▬

FREQUENCY   COUNTRY, STATION, LOCATION

TARGET • NETWORK • POWER (kW)   World Time

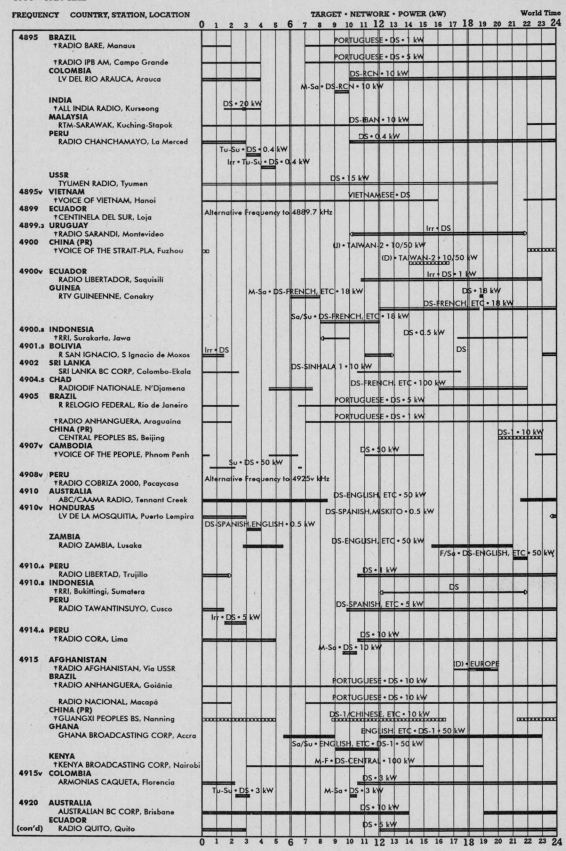

4895	BRAZIL	
	†RADIO BARE, Manaus	PORTUGUESE • DS • 1 kW
	†RADIO IPB AM, Campo Grande	PORTUGUESE • DS • 5 kW
	COLOMBIA	
	LV DEL RIO ARAUCA, Arauca	DS-RCN • 10 kW
		M-Sa • DS-RCN • 10 kW
	INDIA	
	†ALL INDIA RADIO, Kurseong	DS • 20 kW
	MALAYSIA	
	RTM-SARAWAK, Kuching-Stapok	DS-IBAN • 10 kW
	PERU	
	RADIO CHANCHAMAYO, La Merced	DS • 0.4 kW
		Tu-Su • DS • 0.4 kW
		Irr • Tu-Su • DS • 0.4 kW
	USSR	
	TYUMEN RADIO, Tyumen	DS • 15 kW
4895v	VIETNAM	
	†VOICE OF VIETNAM, Hanoi	VIETNAMESE • DS
4899	ECUADOR	
	†CENTINELA DEL SUR, Loja	Alternative Frequency to 4889.7 kHz
4899.3	URUGUAY	
	†RADIO SARANDI, Montevideo	Irr • DS
4900	CHINA (PR)	
	†VOICE OF THE STRAIT-PLA, Fuzhou	(J) • TAIWAN-2 • 10/50 kW
		(D) • TAIWAN-2 • 10/50 kW
4900v	ECUADOR	
	RADIO LIBERTADOR, Saquisilí	Irr • DS • 1 kW
	GUINEA	
	RTV GUINEENNE, Conakry	M-Sa • DS-FRENCH, ETC • 18 kW DS • 18 kW
		DS-FRENCH, ETC • 18 kW
		Sa/Su • DS-FRENCH, ETC • 18 kW
4900.8	INDONESIA	
	†RRI, Surakarta, Jawa	DS • 0.5 kW
4901.5	BOLIVIA	
	R SAN IGNACIO, S Ignacio de Moxos	Irr • DS DS
4902	SRI LANKA	
	SRI LANKA BC CORP, Colombo-Ekala	DS-SINHALA 1 • 10 kW
4904.5	CHAD	
	RADIODIF NATIONALE, N'Djamena	DS-FRENCH, ETC • 100 kW
4905	BRAZIL	
	R RELOGIO FEDERAL, Rio de Janeiro	PORTUGUESE • DS • 5 kW
	†RADIO ANHANGUERA, Araguaína	PORTUGUESE • DS • 1 kW
	CHINA (PR)	
	CENTRAL PEOPLES BS, Beijing	DS-1 • 10 kW
4907v	CAMBODIA	
	†VOICE OF THE PEOPLE, Phnom Penh	DS • 50 kW
		Su • DS • 50 kW
4908v	PERU	
	†RADIO COBRIZA 2000, Pacaycasa	Alternative Frequency to 4925v kHz
4910	AUSTRALIA	
	ABC/CAAMA RADIO, Tennant Creek	DS-ENGLISH, ETC • 50 kW
4910v	HONDURAS	
	LV DE LA MOSQUITIA, Puerto Lempira	DS-SPANISH, MISKITO • 0.5 kW
		DS-SPANISH, ENGLISH • 0.5 kW
	ZAMBIA	
	RADIO ZAMBIA, Lusaka	DS-ENGLISH, ETC • 50 kW
		F/Sa • DS-ENGLISH, ETC • 50 kW
4910.6	PERU	
	RADIO LIBERTAD, Trujillo	DS • 1 kW
4910.8	INDONESIA	
	†RRI, Bukittingi, Sumatera	DS
	PERU	
	RADIO TAWANTINSUYO, Cusco	DS-SPANISH, ETC • 5 kW
		Irr • DS • 5 kW
4914.6	PERU	
	†RADIO CORA, Lima	DS • 10 kW
		M-Sa • DS • 10 kW
4915	AFGHANISTAN	
	†RADIO AFGHANISTAN, Via USSR	(D) • EUROPE
	BRAZIL	
	†RADIO ANHANGUERA, Goiânia	PORTUGUESE • DS • 10 kW
	RADIO NACIONAL, Macapá	PORTUGUESE • DS • 10 kW
	CHINA (PR)	
	†GUANGXI PEOPLES BS, Nanning	DS-1 /CHINESE, ETC • 10 kW
	GHANA	
	GHANA BROADCASTING CORP, Accra	ENGLISH, ETC • DS-1 • 50 kW
		Sa/Su • ENGLISH, ETC • DS-1 • 50 kW
	KENYA	
	†KENYA BROADCASTING CORP, Nairobi	M-F • DS-CENTRAL • 100 kW
4915v	COLOMBIA	
	ARMONIAS CAQUETA, Florencia	DS • 3 kW
		Tu-Su • DS • 3 kW M-Sa • DS • 3 kW
4920	AUSTRALIA	
	AUSTRALIAN BC CORP, Brisbane	DS • 10 kW
	ECUADOR	
(con'd)	RADIO QUITO, Quito	DS • 5 kW

SUMMER ONLY (J)   WINTER ONLY (D)   JAMMING / OR ⋀   EARLIEST HEARD ◁   LATEST HEARD ▷   NEW OR CHANGED FOR 1991 †

FREQUENCY   COUNTRY, STATION, LOCATION   TARGET • NETWORK • POWER (kW)   World Time

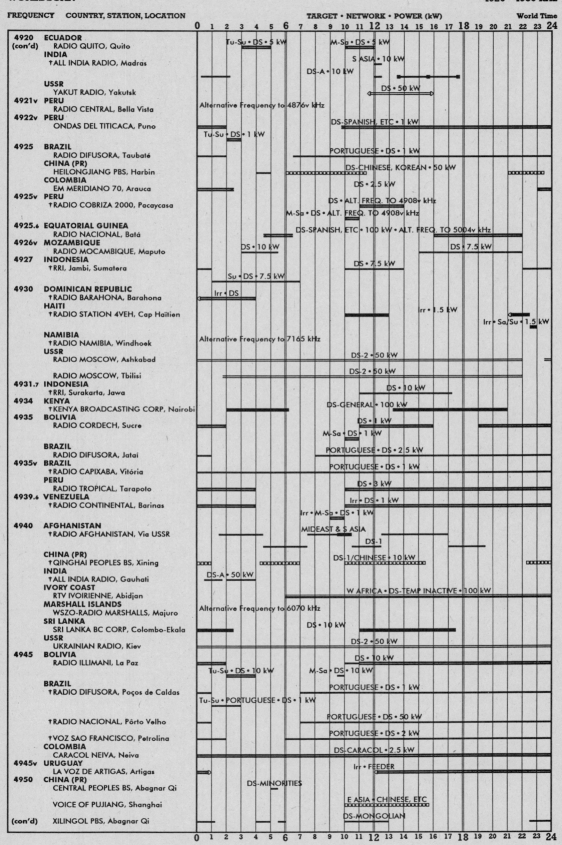

FREQUENCY	COUNTRY, STATION, LOCATION	TARGET • NETWORK • POWER (kW)
4920 (con'd)	**ECUADOR** RADIO QUITO, Quito	Tu-Su • DS • 5 kW / M-Sa • DS • 5 kW
	INDIA †ALL INDIA RADIO, Madras	S ASIA • 10 kW / DS-A • 10 kW
	USSR YAKUT RADIO, Yakutsk	DS • 50 kW
4921v	**PERU** RADIO CENTRAL, Bella Vista	Alternative Frequency to 4876v kHz
4922v	**PERU** ONDAS DEL TITICACA, Puno	DS-SPANISH, ETC • 1 kW Tu-Su • DS • 1 kW
4925	**BRAZIL** RADIO DIFUSORA, Taubaté	PORTUGUESE • DS • 1 kW
	CHINA (PR) HEILONGJIANG PBS, Harbin	DS-CHINESE, KOREAN • 50 kW
	COLOMBIA EM MERIDIANO 70, Arauca	DS • 2.5 kW
4925v	**PERU** †RADIO COBRIZA 2000, Pacaycasa	DS • ALT. FREQ. TO 4908v kHz / M-Sa • DS • ALT. FREQ. TO 4908v kHz
4925.6	**EQUATORIAL GUINEA** RADIO NACIONAL, Bata	DS-SPANISH, ETC • 100 kW • ALT. FREQ. TO 5004v kHz
4926v	**MOZAMBIQUE** RADIO MOCAMBIQUE, Maputo	DS • 10 kW / DS • 7.5 kW
4927	**INDONESIA** †RRI, Jambi, Sumatera	DS • 7.5 kW / Su • DS • 7.5 kW
4930	**DOMINICAN REPUBLIC** †RADIO BARAHONA, Barahona	Irr • DS
	HAITI †RADIO STATION 4VEH, Cap Haïtien	Irr • 1.5 kW / Irr • Sa/Su • 1.5 kW
	NAMIBIA †RADIO NAMIBIA, Windhoek	Alternative Frequency to 7165 kHz
	USSR RADIO MOSCOW, Ashkabad	DS-2 • 50 kW
	RADIO MOSCOW, Tbilisi	DS-2 • 50 kW
4931.7	**INDONESIA** †RRI, Surakarta, Jawa	DS • 10 kW
4934	**KENYA** †KENYA BROADCASTING CORP, Nairobi	DS-GENERAL • 100 kW
4935	**BOLIVIA** RADIO CORDECH, Sucre	DS • 1 kW / M-Sa • DS • 1 kW
	BRAZIL RADIO DIFUSORA, Jataí	PORTUGUESE • DS • 2.5 kW
4935v	**BRAZIL** †RADIO CAPIXABA, Vitória	PORTUGUESE • DS • 1 kW
	PERU RADIO TROPICAL, Tarapoto	DS • 3 kW
4939.6	**VENEZUELA** †RADIO CONTINENTAL, Barinas	Irr • DS • 1 kW / Irr • M-Sa • DS • 1 kW
4940	**AFGHANISTAN** †RADIO AFGHANISTAN, Via USSR	MIDEAST & S ASIA / DS-1
	CHINA (PR) †QINGHAI PEOPLES BS, Xining	DS-1/CHINESE • 10 kW
	INDIA †ALL INDIA RADIO, Gauhati	DS-A • 50 kW
	IVORY COAST RTV IVOIRIENNE, Abidjan	W AFRICA • DS-TEMP INACTIVE • 100 kW
	MARSHALL ISLANDS WSZO-RADIO MARSHALLS, Majuro	Alternative Frequency to 6070 kHz
	SRI LANKA SRI LANKA BC CORP, Colombo-Ekala	DS • 10 kW
	USSR UKRAINIAN RADIO, Kiev	DS-2 • 50 kW
4945	**BOLIVIA** RADIO ILLIMANI, La Paz	DS • 10 kW / Tu-Su • DS • 10 kW / M-Sa • DS • 10 kW
	BRAZIL †RADIO DIFUSORA, Poços de Caldas	PORTUGUESE • DS • 1 kW / Tu-Su • PORTUGUESE • DS • 1 kW
	†RADIO NACIONAL, Pôrto Velho	PORTUGUESE • DS • 50 kW
	†VOZ SAO FRANCISCO, Petrolina	PORTUGUESE • DS • 2 kW
	COLOMBIA CARACOL NEIVA, Neiva	DS-CARACOL • 2.5 kW
4945v	**URUGUAY** LA VOZ DE ARTIGAS, Artigas	Irr • FEEDER
4950	**CHINA (PR)** CENTRAL PEOPLES BS, Abagnar Qi	DS-MINORITIES
	VOICE OF PUJIANG, Shanghai	E ASIA • CHINESE, ETC
(con'd)	XILINGOL PBS, Abagnar Qi	DS-MONGOLIAN

ENGLISH ▬▬   ARABIC ▧▧▧   CHINESE ▢▢▢   FRENCH ▬▬   GERMAN ▬▬   RUSSIAN ═══   SPANISH ▬▬   OTHER ▬

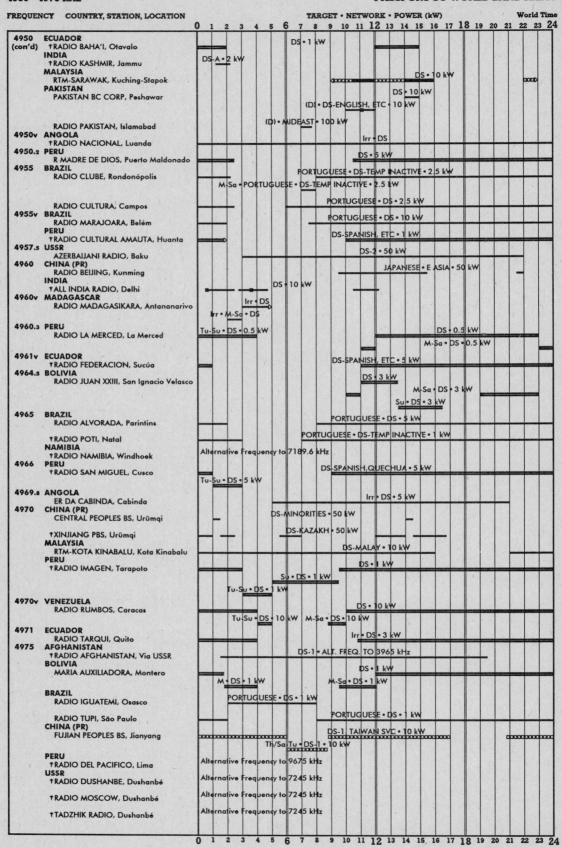

FREQUENCY	COUNTRY, STATION, LOCATION	TARGET • NETWORK • POWER (kW)	World Time

4950 (con'd) **ECUADOR** †RADIO BAHA'I, Otavalo — DS • 1 kW

INDIA †RADIO KASHMIR, Jammu — DS-A • 2 kW

MALAYSIA RTM-SARAWAK, Kuching-Stapok — DS • 10 kW

PAKISTAN PAKISTAN BC CORP, Peshawar — DS • 10 kW — (D) • DS-ENGLISH, ETC • 10 kW

RADIO PAKISTAN, Islamabad — (D) • MIDEAST • 100 kW

4950v ANGOLA †RADIO NACIONAL, Luanda — Irr • DS

4950.2 PERU R MADRE DE DIOS, Puerto Maldonado — DS • 5 kW

4955 BRAZIL RADIO CLUBE, Rondonópolis — PORTUGUESE • DS-TEMP INACTIVE • 2.5 kW / M-Sa • PORTUGUESE • DS-TEMP INACTIVE • 2.5 kW

RADIO CULTURA, Campos — PORTUGUESE • DS • 2.5 kW

4955v BRAZIL RADIO MARAJOARA, Belém — PORTUGUESE • DS • 10 kW

PERU †RADIO CULTURAL AMAUTA, Huanta — DS-SPANISH, ETC • 1 kW

4957.5 USSR AZERBAIJANI RADIO, Baku — DS-2 • 50 kW

4960 CHINA (PR) RADIO BEIJING, Kunming — JAPANESE • E ASIA • 50 kW

INDIA †ALL INDIA RADIO, Delhi — DS • 10 kW

4960v MADAGASCAR RADIO MADAGASIKARA, Antananarivo — Irr • DS / Irr • M-Sa • DS

4960.3 PERU RADIO LA MERCED, La Merced — Tu-Su • DS • 0.5 kW / DS • 0.5 kW / M-Sa • DS • 0.5 kW

4961v ECUADOR †RADIO FEDERACION, Sucúa — DS-SPANISH, ETC • 5 kW

4964.5 BOLIVIA RADIO JUAN XXIII, San Ignacio Velasco — DS • 3 kW / M-Sa • DS • 3 kW / Su • DS • 3 kW

4965 BRAZIL RADIO ALVORADA, Parintins — PORTUGUESE • DS • 5 kW

†RADIO POTI, Natal — PORTUGUESE • DS-TEMP INACTIVE • 1 kW

NAMIBIA †RADIO NAMIBIA, Windhoek — Alternative Frequency to 7189.6 kHz

4966 PERU †RADIO SAN MIGUEL, Cusco — DS-SPANISH, QUECHUA • 5 kW / Tu-Su • DS • 5 kW

4969.8 ANGOLA ER DA CABINDA, Cabinda — Irr • DS • 5 kW

4970 CHINA (PR) CENTRAL PEOPLES BS, Urümqi — DS-MINORITIES • 50 kW

†XINJIANG PBS, Urümqi — DS-KAZAKH • 50 kW

MALAYSIA RTM-KOTA KINABALU, Kota Kinabalu — DS-MALAY • 10 kW

PERU †RADIO IMAGEN, Tarapoto — DS • 1 kW / Su • DS • 1 kW / Tu-Su • DS • 1 kW

4970v VENEZUELA RADIO RUMBOS, Caracas — DS • 10 kW / Tu-Su • DS • 10 kW / M-Sa • DS • 10 kW

4971 ECUADOR RADIO TARQUI, Quito — Irr • DS • 3 kW

4975 AFGHANISTAN †RADIO AFGHANISTAN, Via USSR — DS-1 • ALT. FREQ. TO 3965 kHz

BOLIVIA MARIA AUXILIADORA, Montero — DS • 1 kW / M • DS • 1 kW / M-Sa • DS • 1 kW

BRAZIL RADIO IGUATEMI, Osasco — PORTUGUESE • DS • 1 kW

RADIO TUPI, São Paulo — PORTUGUESE • DS • 1 kW

CHINA (PR) FUJIAN PEOPLES BS, Jianyang — DS-1 TAIWAN SVC • 10 kW / Th/Sa-Tu • DS-1 • 10 kW

PERU †RADIO DEL PACIFICO, Lima — Alternative Frequency to 9675 kHz

USSR †RADIO DUSHANBE, Dushanbé — Alternative Frequency to 7245 kHz

†RADIO MOSCOW, Dushanbé — Alternative Frequency to 7245 kHz

†TADZHIK RADIO, Dushanbé — Alternative Frequency to 7245 kHz

FREQUENCY   COUNTRY, STATION, LOCATION

TARGET • NETWORK • POWER (kW)

World Time

0 1 2 3 4 5 6 7 8 9 10 11 12 13 14 15 16 17 18 19 20 21 22 23 24

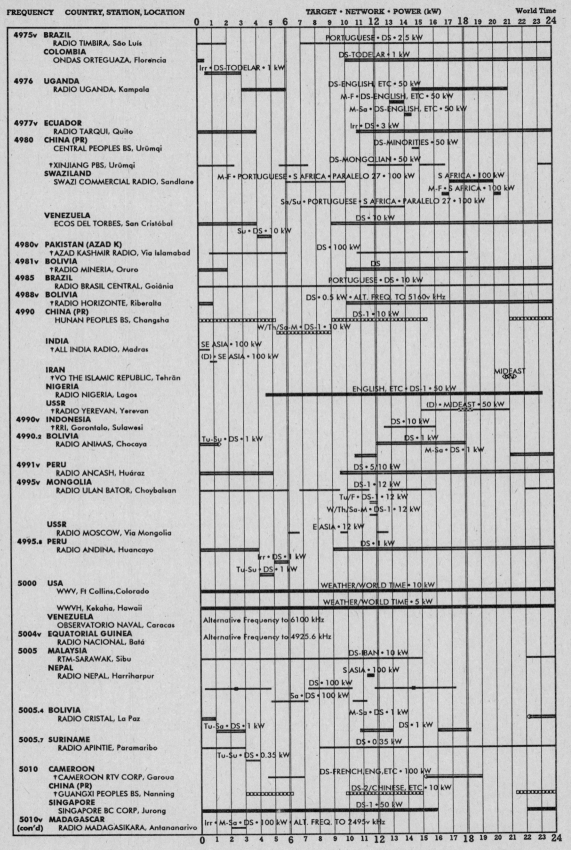

Frequency	Country, Station, Location	Notes
4975v	**BRAZIL** RADIO TIMBIRA, São Luís	PORTUGUESE • DS • 2.5 kW
	COLOMBIA ONDAS ORTEGUAZA, Florencia	DS-TODELAR • 1 kW / Irr • DS-TODELAR • 1 kW
4976	**UGANDA** RADIO UGANDA, Kampala	DS-ENGLISH, ETC • 50 kW / M-F • DS-ENGLISH, ETC • 50 kW / M-Sa • DS-ENGLISH, ETC • 50 kW
4977v	**ECUADOR** RADIO TARQUI, Quito	Irr • DS • 3 kW
4980	**CHINA (PR)** CENTRAL PEOPLES BS, Urümqi	DS-MINORITIES • 50 kW / DS-MONGOLIAN • 50 kW
	†XINJIANG PBS, Urümqi **SWAZILAND** SWAZI COMMERCIAL RADIO, Sandlane	M-F • PORTUGUESE • S AFRICA • PARALELO 27 • 100 kW / S AFRICA • 100 kW / M-F • S AFRICA • 100 kW / Sa/Su • PORTUGUESE • S AFRICA • PARALELO 27 • 100 kW
	VENEZUELA ECOS DEL TORBES, San Cristóbal	DS • 10 kW / Su • DS • 10 kW
4980v	**PAKISTAN (AZAD K)** †AZAD KASHMIR RADIO, Via Islamabad	DS • 100 kW
4981v	**BOLIVIA** †RADIO MINERIA, Oruro	DS
4985	**BRAZIL** RADIO BRASIL CENTRAL, Goiânia	PORTUGUESE • DS • 10 kW
4988v	**BOLIVIA** †RADIO HORIZONTE, Riberalta	DS • 0.5 kW • ALT. FREQ. TO 5160v kHz
4990	**CHINA (PR)** HUNAN PEOPLES BS, Changsha	DS-1 • 10 kW / W/Th/Sa-M • DS-1 • 10 kW
	INDIA †ALL INDIA RADIO, Madras	SE ASIA • 100 kW / (D) • SE ASIA • 100 kW
	IRAN †VO THE ISLAMIC REPUBLIC, Tehrän	MIDEAST
	NIGERIA RADIO NIGERIA, Lagos	ENGLISH, ETC • DS-1 • 50 kW
	USSR †RADIO YEREVAN, Yerevan	(D) • MIDEAST • 50 kW
4990v	**INDONESIA** †RRI, Gorontalo, Sulawesi	DS • 10 kW
4990.2	**BOLIVIA** RADIO ANIMAS, Chocaya	Tu-Su • DS • 1 kW / DS • 1 kW / M-Sa • DS • 1 kW
4991v	**PERU** RADIO ANCASH, Huáraz	DS • 5/10 kW
4995v	**MONGOLIA** RADIO ULAN BATOR, Choybalsan	DS-1 • 12 kW / Tu/F • DS-1 • 12 kW / W/Th/Sa-M • DS-1 • 12 kW
	USSR RADIO MOSCOW, Via Mongolia	E ASIA • 12 kW
4995.8	**PERU** RADIO ANDINA, Huancayo	DS • 1 kW / Irr • DS • 1 kW / Tu-Su • DS • 1 kW
5000	**USA** WWV, Ft Collins, Colorado	WEATHER/WORLD TIME • 10 kW
	WWVH, Kekaha, Hawaii	WEATHER/WORLD TIME • 5 kW
	VENEZUELA OBSERVATORIO NAVAL, Caracas	Alternative Frequency to 6100 kHz
5004v	**EQUATORIAL GUINEA** RADIO NACIONAL, Batá	Alternative Frequency to 4925.6 kHz
5005	**MALAYSIA** RTM-SARAWAK, Sibu	DS-IBAN • 10 kW
	NEPAL RADIO NEPAL, Harriharpur	S ASIA • 100 kW / DS • 100 kW / Sa • DS • 100 kW
5005.4	**BOLIVIA** RADIO CRISTAL, La Paz	M-Sa • DS • 1 kW / Tu-Sa • DS • 1 kW / DS • 1 kW
5005.7	**SURINAME** RADIO APINTIE, Paramaribo	DS • 0.35 kW / Tu-Su • DS • 0.35 kW
5010	**CAMEROON** †CAMEROON RTV CORP, Garoua	DS-FRENCH, ENG, ETC • 100 kW
	CHINA (PR) †GUANGXI PEOPLES BS, Nanning	DS-2/CHINESE, ETC • 10 kW
	SINGAPORE SINGAPORE BC CORP, Jurong	DS-1 • 50 kW
5010v (con'd)	**MADAGASCAR** RADIO MADAGASIKARA, Antananarivo	Irr • M-Sa • DS • 100 kW • ALT. FREQ. TO 2495v kHz

0 1 2 3 4 5 6 7 8 9 10 11 12 13 14 15 16 17 18 19 20 21 22 23 24

ENGLISH ■■ ARABIC ⬚⬚⬚ CHINESE ⬚⬚⬚ FRENCH ══ GERMAN ▬▬ RUSSIAN ══ SPANISH ▬▬ OTHER ▬

| FREQUENCY | COUNTRY, STATION, LOCATION | TARGET • NETWORK • POWER (kW) | World Time |

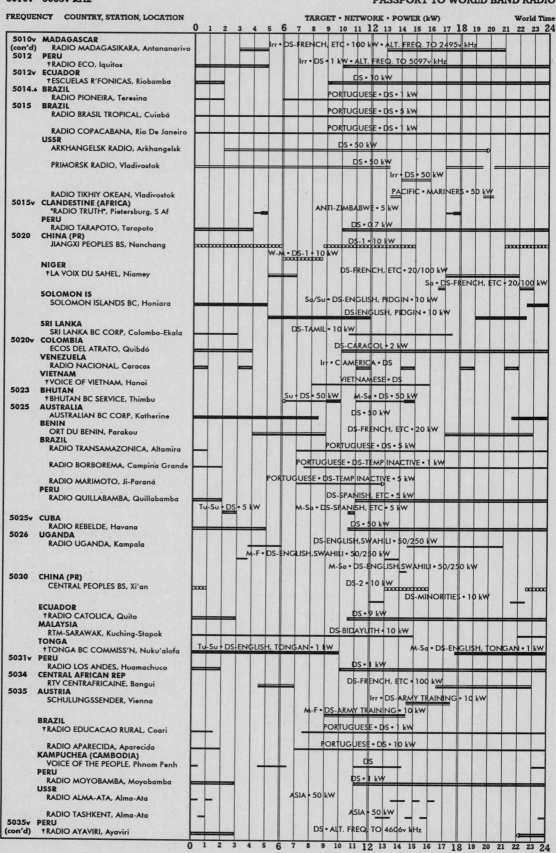

5010v MADAGASCAR
(con'd)   RADIO MADAGASIKARA, Antananarivo — Irr • DS-FRENCH, ETC • 100 kW • ALT. FREQ. TO 2495v kHz
5012 PERU
        †RADIO ECO, Iquitos — Irr • DS • 1 kW • ALT. FREQ. TO 5097v kHz
5012v ECUADOR
        †ESCUELAS R'FONICAS, Riobamba — DS • 10 kW
5014.6 BRAZIL
        RADIO PIONEIRA, Teresina — PORTUGUESE • DS • 1 kW
5015 BRAZIL
        RADIO BRASIL TROPICAL, Cuiabá — PORTUGUESE • DS • 5 kW
        RADIO COPACABANA, Rio De Janeiro — PORTUGUESE • DS • 1 kW
        USSR
        ARKHANGELSK RADIO, Arkhangelsk — DS • 50 kW
        PRIMORSK RADIO, Vladivostok — DS • 50 kW / Irr • DS • 50 kW
        RADIO TIKHIY OKEAN, Vladivostok — PACIFIC • MARINERS • 50 kW
5015v CLANDESTINE (AFRICA)
        "RADIO TRUTH", Pietersburg, S Af — ANTI-ZIMBABWE • 5 kW
        PERU
        RADIO TARAPOTO, Tarapoto — DS • 0.7 kW
5020 CHINA (PR)
        JIANGXI PEOPLES BS, Nanchang — DS-1 • 10 kW / W-M • DS-1 • 10 kW
        NIGER
        †LA VOIX DU SAHEL, Niamey — DS-FRENCH, ETC • 20/100 kW / Sa • DS-FRENCH, ETC • 20/100 kW
        SOLOMON IS
        SOLOMON ISLANDS BC, Honiara — Sa/Su • DS-ENGLISH, PIDGIN • 10 kW / DS-ENGLISH, PIDGIN • 10 kW
        SRI LANKA
        SRI LANKA BC CORP, Colombo-Ekala — DS-TAMIL • 10 kW
5020v COLOMBIA
        ECOS DEL ATRATO, Quibdó — DS-CARACOL • 2 kW
        VENEZUELA
        RADIO NACIONAL, Caracas — Irr • C AMERICA • DS
        VIETNAM
        †VOICE OF VIETNAM, Hanoi — VIETNAMESE • DS
5023 BHUTAN
        †BHUTAN BC SERVICE, Thimbu — Su • DS • 50 kW / M-Sa • DS • 50 kW
5025 AUSTRALIA
        AUSTRALIAN BC CORP, Katherine — DS • 50 kW
        BENIN
        ORT DU BENIN, Parakou — DS-FRENCH, ETC • 20 kW
        BRAZIL
        RADIO TRANSAMAZONICA, Altamira — PORTUGUESE • DS • 5 kW
        RADIO BORBOREMA, Campina Grande — PORTUGUESE • DS-TEMP INACTIVE • 1 kW
        RADIO MARIMOTO, Ji-Paraná — PORTUGUESE • DS-TEMP INACTIVE • 5 kW
        PERU
        RADIO QUILLABAMBA, Quillabamba — DS-SPANISH, ETC • 5 kW / Tu-Su • DS • 5 kW / M-Sa • DS-SPANISH, ETC • 5 kW
5025v CUBA
        RADIO REBELDE, Havana — DS • 50 kW
5026 UGANDA
        RADIO UGANDA, Kampala — DS-ENGLISH, SWAHILI • 50/250 kW / M-F • DS-ENGLISH, SWAHILI • 50/250 kW / M-Sa • DS-ENGLISH, SWAHILI • 50/250 kW
5030 CHINA (PR)
        CENTRAL PEOPLES BS, Xi'an — DS-2 • 10 kW / DS-MINORITIES • 10 kW
        ECUADOR
        †RADIO CATOLICA, Quito — DS • 9 kW
        MALAYSIA
        RTM-SARAWAK, Kuching-Stapok — DS-BIDAYUTH • 10 kW
        TONGA
        †TONGA BC COMMISS'N, Nuku'alofa — Tu-Su • DS-ENGLISH, TONGAN • 1 kW / M-Sa • DS-ENGLISH, TONGAN • 1 kW
5031v PERU
        RADIO LOS ANDES, Huamachuco — DS • 1 kW
5034 CENTRAL AFRICAN REP
        RTV CENTRAFRICAINE, Bangui — DS-FRENCH, ETC • 100 kW
5035 AUSTRIA
        SCHULUNGSSENDER, Vienna — Irr • DS-ARMY TRAINING • 10 kW / M-F • DS-ARMY TRAINING • 10 kW
        BRAZIL
        †RADIO EDUCACAO RURAL, Coari — PORTUGUESE • DS • 1 kW
        RADIO APARECIDA, Aparecida — PORTUGUESE • DS • 10 kW
        KAMPUCHEA (CAMBODIA)
        VOICE OF THE PEOPLE, Phnom Penh — DS
        PERU
        RADIO MOYOBAMBA, Moyobamba — DS • 1 kW
        USSR
        RADIO ALMA-ATA, Alma-Ata — ASIA • 50 kW
        RADIO TASHKENT, Alma-Ata — ASIA • 50 kW
5035v PERU
(con'd)   †RADIO AYAVIRI, Ayaviri — DS • ALT. FREQ. TO 4606v kHz

SUMMER ONLY (J)   WINTER ONLY (D)   JAMMING / OR ∧   EARLIEST HEARD ◁   LATEST HEARD ▷   NEW OR CHANGED FOR 1991 †

FREQUENCY   COUNTRY, STATION, LOCATION   TARGET • NETWORK • POWER (kW)   World Time

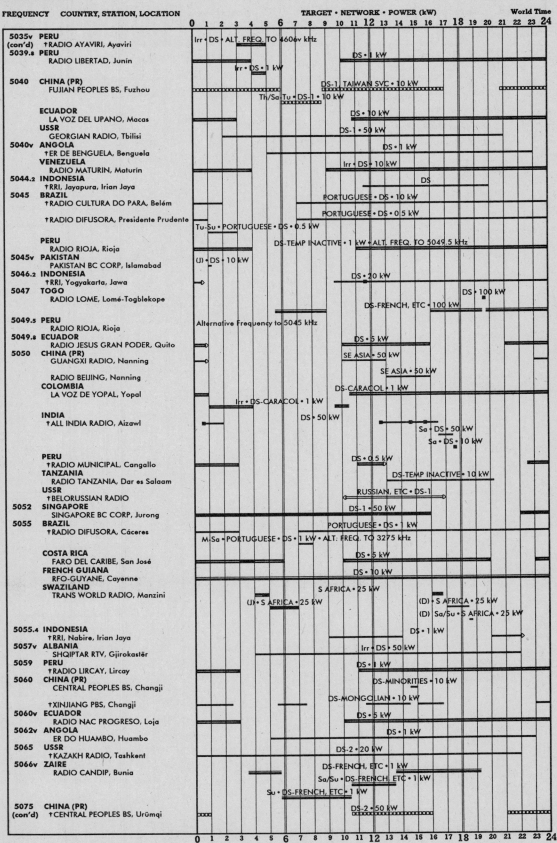

Frequency	Country, Station, Location	Target • Network • Power
5035v (con'd)	PERU †RADIO AYAVIRI, Ayaviri	Irr • DS • ALT. FREQ. TO 4606v kHz
5039.8	PERU RADIO LIBERTAD, Junín	DS • 1 kW / Irr • DS • 1 kW
5040	CHINA (PR) FUJIAN PEOPLES BS, Fuzhou	DS-1 TAIWAN SVC • 10 kW / Th/Sa-Tu • DS-1 • 10 kW
	ECUADOR LA VOZ DEL UPANO, Macas	DS • 10 kW
	USSR GEORGIAN RADIO, Tbilisi	DS-1 • 50 kW
5040v	ANGOLA †ER DE BENGUELA, Benguela	DS • 1 kW
	VENEZUELA RADIO MATURIN, Maturín	Irr • DS • 10 kW
5044.2	INDONESIA †RRI, Jayapura, Irian Jaya	DS
5045	BRAZIL †RADIO CULTURA DO PARA, Belém	PORTUGUESE • DS • 10 kW
	†RADIO DIFUSORA, Presidente Prudente	PORTUGUESE • DS • 0.5 kW / Tu-Su • PORTUGUESE • DS • 0.5 kW
	PERU RADIO RIOJA, Rioja	DS-TEMP INACTIVE • 1 kW • ALT. FREQ. TO 5049.5 kHz
5045v	PAKISTAN PAKISTAN BC CORP, Islamabad	(J) • DS • 10 kW
5046.2	INDONESIA †RRI, Yogyakarta, Jawa	DS • 20 kW
5047	TOGO RADIO LOME, Lomé-Togblekope	DS • 100 kW / DS-FRENCH, ETC • 100 kW
5049.5	PERU RADIO RIOJA, Rioja	Alternative Frequency to 5045 kHz
5049.8	ECUADOR RADIO JESUS GRAN PODER, Quito	DS • 5 kW
5050	CHINA (PR) GUANGXI RADIO, Nanning	SE ASIA • 50 kW
	RADIO BEIJING, Nanning	SE ASIA • 50 kW
	COLOMBIA LA VOZ DE YOPAL, Yopal	DS-CARACOL • 1 kW / Irr • DS-CARACOL • 1 kW
	INDIA †ALL INDIA RADIO, Aizawl	DS • 50 kW / Sa • DS • 50 kW / Sa • DS • 10 kW
	PERU †RADIO MUNICIPAL, Cangallo	DS • 0.5 kW
	TANZANIA RADIO TANZANIA, Dar es Salaam	DS-TEMP INACTIVE • 10 kW
	USSR †BELORUSSIAN RADIO	RUSSIAN, ETC • DS-1
5052	SINGAPORE SINGAPORE BC CORP, Jurong	DS-1 • 50 kW
5055	BRAZIL †RADIO DIFUSORA, Cáceres	PORTUGUESE • DS • 1 kW / M-Sa • PORTUGUESE • DS • 1 kW • ALT: FREQ. TO 3275 kHz
	COSTA RICA FARO DEL CARIBE, San José	DS • 5 kW
	FRENCH GUIANA RFO-GUYANE, Cayenne	DS • 10 kW
	SWAZILAND TRANS WORLD RADIO, Manzini	S AFRICA • 25 kW / (J) • S AFRICA • 25 kW / (D) • S AFRICA • 25 kW / (D) • Sa/Su • S AFRICA • 25 kW
5055.4	INDONESIA †RRI, Nabire, Irian Jaya	DS • 1 kW
5057v	ALBANIA SHQIPTAR RTV, Gjirokastër	Irr • DS • 50 kW
5059	PERU †RADIO LIRCAY, Lircay	DS • 1 kW
5060	CHINA (PR) CENTRAL PEOPLES BS, Changji	DS-MINORITIES • 10 kW
	†XINJIANG PBS, Changji	DS-MONGOLIAN • 10 kW
5060v	ECUADOR RADIO NAC PROGRESO, Loja	DS • 5 kW
5062v	ANGOLA ER DO HUAMBO, Huambo	DS • 1 kW
5065	USSR †KAZAKH RADIO, Tashkent	DS-2 • 20 kW
5066v	ZAIRE RADIO CANDIP, Bunia	DS-FRENCH, ETC • 1 kW / Sa/Su • DS-FRENCH, ETC • 1 kW / Su • DS-FRENCH, ETC • 1 kW
5075 (con'd)	CHINA (PR) †CENTRAL PEOPLES BS, Urümqi	DS-2 • 50 kW

ENGLISH ▬ ARABIC ▒ CHINESE ▫▫▫ FRENCH ▭ GERMAN ▬ RUSSIAN ═ SPANISH ▬ OTHER ▬

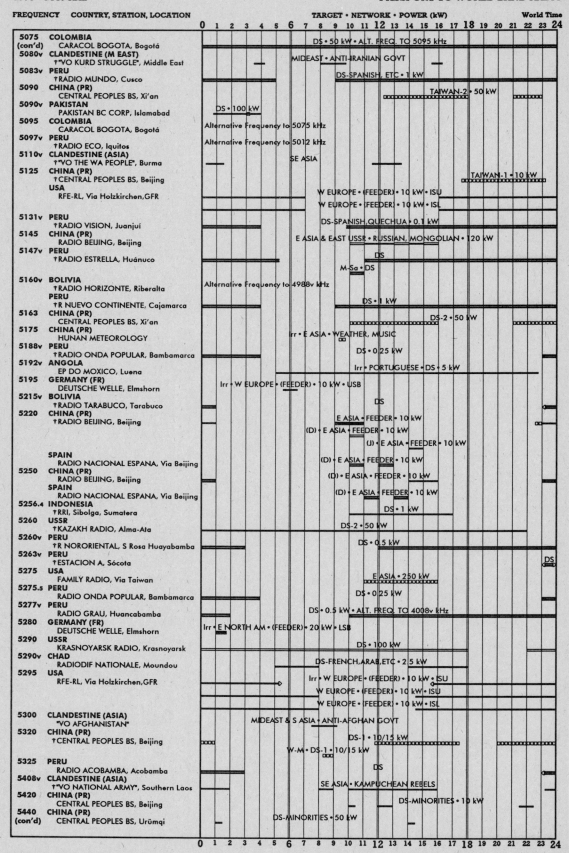

FREQUENCY   COUNTRY, STATION, LOCATION

TARGET • NETWORK • POWER (kW)

World Time

FREQUENCY	COUNTRY, STATION, LOCATION	TARGET • NETWORK • POWER (kW)
5075 (con'd)	COLOMBIA — CARACOL BOGOTA, Bogotá	DS • 50 kW • ALT. FREQ. TO 5095 kHz
5080v	CLANDESTINE (M EAST) — †"VO KURD STRUGGLE", Middle East	MIDEAST • ANTI-IRANIAN GOVT
5083v	PERU — †RADIO MUNDO, Cusco	DS-SPANISH, ETC • 1 kW
5090	CHINA (PR) — CENTRAL PEOPLES BS, Xi'an	TAIWAN-2 • 50 kW
5090v	PAKISTAN — PAKISTAN BC CORP, Islamabad	DS • 100 kW
5095	COLOMBIA — CARACOL BOGOTA, Bogotá	Alternative Frequency to 5075 kHz
5097v	PERU — †RADIO ECO, Iquitos	Alternative Frequency to 5012 kHz
5110v	CLANDESTINE (ASIA) — †"VO THE WA PEOPLE", Burma	SE ASIA
5125	CHINA (PR) — †CENTRAL PEOPLES BS, Beijing	TAIWAN-1 • 10 kW
	USA — RFE-RL, Via Holzkirchen,GFR	W EUROPE • (FEEDER) • 10 kW • ISU / W EUROPE • (FEEDER) • 10 kW • ISL
5131v	PERU — †RADIO VISION, Juanjuí	DS-SPANISH,QUECHUA • 0.1 kW
5145	CHINA (PR) — RADIO BEIJING, Beijing	E ASIA & EAST USSR • RUSSIAN, MONGOLIAN • 120 kW
5147v	PERU — †RADIO ESTRELLA, Huánuco	DS / M-Sa • DS
5160v	BOLIVIA — †RADIO HORIZONTE, Riberalta	Alternative Frequency to 4988v kHz
	PERU — †R NUEVO CONTINENTE, Cajamarca	DS • 1 kW
5163	CHINA (PR) — CENTRAL PEOPLES BS, Xi'an	DS-2 • 50 kW
5175	CHINA (PR) — HUNAN METEOROLOGY	Irr • E ASIA • WEATHER, MUSIC
5188v	PERU — †RADIO ONDA POPULAR, Bambamarca	DS • 0.25 kW
5192v	ANGOLA — EP DO MEXICO, Luena	Irr • PORTUGUESE • DS • 5 kW
5195	GERMANY (FR) — DEUTSCHE WELLE, Elmshorn	Irr • W EUROPE • (FEEDER) • 10 kW • USB
5215v	BOLIVIA — †RADIO TARABUCO, Tarabuco	DS
5220	CHINA (PR) — †RADIO BEIJING, Beijing	E ASIA • FEEDER • 10 kW / (D) • E ASIA • FEEDER • 10 kW / (J) • E ASIA • FEEDER • 10 kW
	SPAIN — RADIO NACIONAL ESPANA, Via Beijing	(D) • E ASIA • FEEDER • 10 kW
5250	CHINA (PR) — RADIO BEIJING, Beijing	(D) • E ASIA • FEEDER • 10 kW
	SPAIN — RADIO NACIONAL ESPANA, Via Beijing	(D) • E ASIA • FEEDER • 10 kW
5256.4	INDONESIA — †RRI, Sibolga, Sumatera	DS • 1 kW
5260	USSR — †KAZAKH RADIO, Alma-Ata	DS-2 • 50 kW
5260v	PERU — †R NORORIENTAL, S Rosa Huayabamba	DS • 0.5 kW
5263v	PERU — †ESTACION A, Sócota	DS
5275	USA — FAMILY RADIO, Via Taiwan	E ASIA • 250 kW
5275.5	PERU — RADIO ONDA POPULAR, Bambamarca	DS • 0.25 kW
5277v	PERU — RADIO GRAU, Huancabamba	DS • 0.5 kW • ALT. FREQ. TO 4008v kHz
5280	GERMANY (FR) — DEUTSCHE WELLE, Elmshorn	Irr • E NORTH AM • (FEEDER) • 20 kW • LSB
5290	USSR — KRASNOYARSK RADIO, Krasnoyarsk	DS • 100 kW
5290v	CHAD — RADIODIF NATIONALE, Moundou	DS-FRENCH, ARAB, ETC • 2.5 kW
5295	USA — RFE-RL, Via Holzkirchen,GFR	Irr • W EUROPE • (FEEDER) • 10 kW • ISU / W EUROPE • (FEEDER) • 10 kW • ISU / W EUROPE • (FEEDER) • 10 kW • ISL
5300	CLANDESTINE (ASIA) — "VO AFGHANISTAN"	MIDEAST & S ASIA • ANTI-AFGHAN GOVT
5320	CHINA (PR) — †CENTRAL PEOPLES BS, Beijing	DS-1 • 10/15 kW / W-M • DS-1 • 10/15 kW
5325	PERU — RADIO ACOBAMBA, Acobamba	DS
5408v	CLANDESTINE (ASIA) — †"VO NATIONAL ARMY", Southern Laos	SE ASIA • KAMPUCHEAN REBELS
5420	CHINA (PR) — CENTRAL PEOPLES BS, Beijing	DS-MINORITIES • 10 kW
5440 (con'd)	CHINA (PR) — CENTRAL PEOPLES BS, Urümqi	DS-MINORITIES • 50 kW

0 1 2 3 4 5 6 7 8 9 10 11 12 13 14 15 16 17 18 19 20 21 22 23 24

SUMMER ONLY (J)   WINTER ONLY (D)   JAMMING / OR ∧   EARLIEST HEARD ◁   LATEST HEARD ▷   NEW OR CHANGED FOR 1991 †

FREQUENCY   COUNTRY, STATION, LOCATION   TARGET • NETWORK • POWER (kW)   World Time

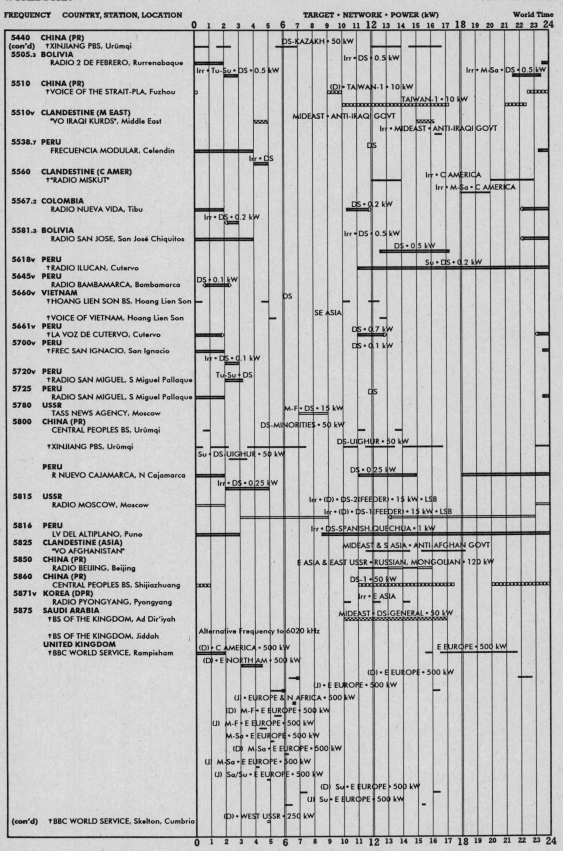

5440	CHINA (PR)
(con'd)	†XINJIANG PBS, Urümqi — DS-KAZAKH • 50 kW
5505.3	BOLIVIA — RADIO 2 DE FEBRERO, Rurrenabaque — Irr • DS • 0.5 kW — Irr • Tu-Su • DS • 0.5 kW — Irr • M-Sa • DS • 0.5 kW
5510	CHINA (PR) — †VOICE OF THE STRAIT-PLA, Fuzhou — (D) • TAIWAN-1 • 10 kW — TAIWAN-1 • 10 kW
5510v	CLANDESTINE (M EAST) — "VO IRAQI KURDS", Middle East — MIDEAST • ANTI-IRAQI GOVT — Irr • MIDEAST • ANTI-IRAQI GOVT
5538.7	PERU — FRECUENCIA MODULAR, Celendín — DS
5560	CLANDESTINE (C AMER) — †"RADIO MISKUT" — Irr • C AMERICA — Irr • M-Sa • C AMERICA
5567.2	COLOMBIA — RADIO NUEVA VIDA, Tibu — DS • 0.2 kW — Irr • DS • 0.2 kW
5581.3	BOLIVIA — RADIO SAN JOSE, San José Chiquitos — Irr • DS • 0.5 kW — DS • 0.5 kW
5618v	PERU — †RADIO ILUCAN, Cutervo — Su • DS • 0.2 kW
5645v	PERU — RADIO BAMBAMARCA, Bambamarca — DS • 0.1 kW
5660v	VIETNAM — †HOANG LIEN SON BS, Hoang Lien Son — DS — †VOICE OF VIETNAM, Hoang Lien Son — SE ASIA
5661v	PERU — †LA VOZ DE CUTERVO, Cutervo — DS • 0.7 kW
5700v	PERU — †FREC SAN IGNACIO, San Ignacio — DS • 0.1 kW — Irr • DS • 0.1 kW
5720v	PERU — †RADIO SAN MIGUEL, S Miguel Pallaque — Tu-Su • DS
5725	PERU — RADIO SAN MIGUEL, S Miguel Pallaque — DS
5780	USSR — TASS NEWS AGENCY, Moscow — M-F • DS • 15 kW
5800	CHINA (PR) — CENTRAL PEOPLES BS, Urümqi — DS-MINORITIES • 50 kW — †XINJIANG PBS, Urümqi — DS-UIGHUR • 50 kW — Su • DS-UIGHUR • 50 kW — PERU — R NUEVO CAJAMARCA, N Cajamarca — DS • 0.25 kW — Irr • DS • 0.25 kW
5815	USSR — RADIO MOSCOW, Moscow — Irr • (D) • DS-2(FEEDER) • 15 kW • LSB — Irr • (D) • DS-1(FEEDER) • 15 kW • LSB
5816	PERU — LV DEL ALTIPLANO, Puno — Irr • DS-SPANISH,QUECHUA • 1 kW
5825	CLANDESTINE (ASIA) — "VO AFGHANISTAN" — MIDEAST & S ASIA • ANTI-AFGHAN GOVT
5850	CHINA (PR) — RADIO BEIJING, Beijing — E ASIA & EAST USSR • RUSSIAN, MONGOLIAN • 120 kW
5860	CHINA (PR) — CENTRAL PEOPLES BS, Shijiazhuang — DS-1 • 50 kW
5871v	KOREA (DPR) — RADIO PYONGYANG, Pyongyang — Irr • E ASIA
5875	SAUDI ARABIA — †BS OF THE KINGDOM, Ad Dir'iyah — MIDEAST • DS-GENERAL • 50 kW — †BS OF THE KINGDOM, Jiddah — Alternative Frequency to 6020 kHz
	UNITED KINGDOM — †BBC WORLD SERVICE, Rampisham — (D) • C AMERICA • 500 kW — E EUROPE • 500 kW — (D) • E NORTH AM • 500 kW — (D) • E EUROPE • 500 kW — (J) • E EUROPE • 500 kW — (J) • EUROPE & N AFRICA • 500 kW — (D) M-F • E EUROPE • 500 kW — (J) M-F • E EUROPE • 500 kW — M-Sa • E EUROPE • 500 kW — (D) • M-Sa • E EUROPE • 500 kW — (J) M-Sa • E EUROPE • 500 kW — (J) Sa/Su • E EUROPE • 500 kW — (D) Su • E EUROPE • 500 kW — (J) Su • E EUROPE • 500 kW
(con'd)	†BBC WORLD SERVICE, Skelton, Cumbria — (D) • WEST USSR • 250 kW

ENGLISH ▬ ARABIC ≈ CHINESE ▭▭▭ FRENCH ▬ GERMAN ▬ RUSSIAN ═ SPANISH ▬ OTHER —

FREQUENCY   COUNTRY, STATION, LOCATION   TARGET • NETWORK • POWER (kW)   World Time

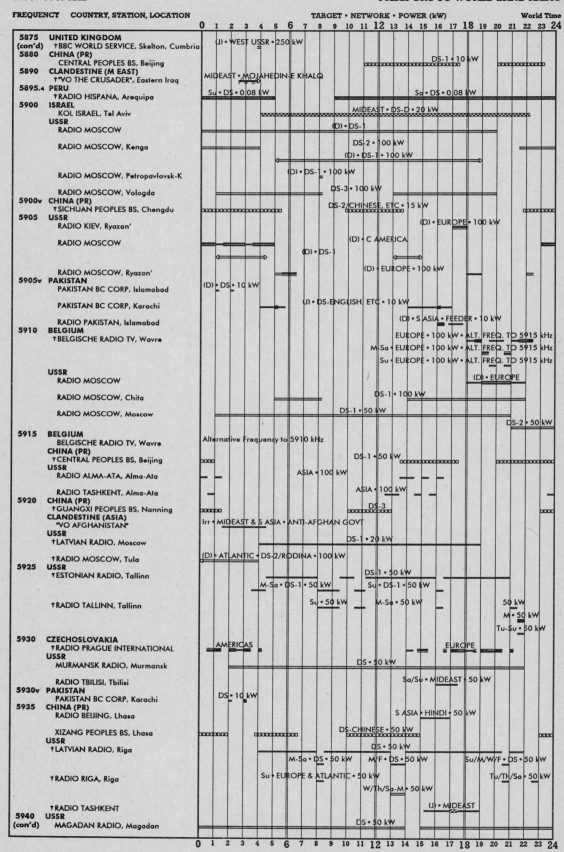

Frequency	Country, Station, Location	Target • Network • Power
5875 (con'd)	**UNITED KINGDOM** †BBC WORLD SERVICE, Skelton, Cumbria	(J) • WEST USSR • 250 kW
5880	**CHINA (PR)** CENTRAL PEOPLES BS, Beijing	DS-1 • 10 kW
5890	**CLANDESTINE (M EAST)** †"VO THE CRUSADER", Eastern Iraq	MIDEAST • MOJAHEDIN-E KHALQ
5895.4	**PERU** †RADIO HISPANA, Arequipa	Su • DS • 0.08 kW Sa • DS • 0.08 kW
5900	**ISRAEL** KOL ISRAEL, Tel Aviv	MIDEAST • DS-D • 20 kW
	USSR RADIO MOSCOW	(D) • DS-1
	RADIO MOSCOW, Kenga	DS-2 • 100 kW
		(D) • DS-1 • 100 kW
	RADIO MOSCOW, Petropavlovsk-K	(D) • DS-1 • 100 kW
	RADIO MOSCOW, Vologda	DS-3 • 100 kW
5900v	**CHINA (PR)** †SICHUAN PEOPLES BS, Chengdu	DS-2/CHINESE, ETC • 15 kW
5905	**USSR** RADIO KIEV, Ryazan'	(D) • EUROPE • 100 kW
	RADIO MOSCOW	(D) • C AMERICA
		(D) • DS-1
	RADIO MOSCOW, Ryazan'	(D) • EUROPE • 100 kW
5905v	**PAKISTAN** PAKISTAN BC CORP, Islamabad	(D) • DS • 10 kW
	PAKISTAN BC CORP, Karachi	(J) • DS-ENGLISH, ETC • 10 kW
	RADIO PAKISTAN, Islamabad	(D) • S ASIA • FEEDER • 10 kW
5910	**BELGIUM** †BELGISCHE RADIO TV, Wavre	EUROPE • 100 kW • ALT. FREQ. TO 5915 kHz
		M-Sa • EUROPE • 100 kW • ALT. FREQ. TO 5915 kHz
		Su • EUROPE • 100 kW • ALT. FREQ. TO 5915 kHz
	USSR RADIO MOSCOW	(D) • EUROPE
	RADIO MOSCOW, Chita	DS-1 • 100 kW
	RADIO MOSCOW, Moscow	DS-1 • 50 kW
		DS-2 • 50 kW
5915	**BELGIUM** BELGISCHE RADIO TV, Wavre	Alternative Frequency to 5910 kHz
	CHINA (PR) †CENTRAL PEOPLES BS, Beijing	DS-1 • 50 kW
	USSR RADIO ALMA-ATA, Alma-Ata	ASIA • 100 kW
	RADIO TASHKENT, Alma-Ata	ASIA • 100 kW
5920	**CHINA (PR)** †GUANGXI PEOPLES BS, Nanning	DS-3
	CLANDESTINE (ASIA) "VO AFGHANISTAN"	Irr • MIDEAST & S ASIA • ANTI-AFGHAN GOVT
	USSR †LATVIAN RADIO, Moscow	DS-1 • 20 kW
	†RADIO MOSCOW, Tula	(D) • ATLANTIC • DS-2/RODINA • 100 kW
5925	**USSR** †ESTONIAN RADIO, Tallinn	DS-1 • 50 kW
		M-Sa • DS-1 • 50 kW Su • DS-1 • 50 kW
	†RADIO TALLINN, Tallinn	Su • 50 kW M-Sa • 50 kW 50 kW
		M • 50 kW
		Tu-Su • 50 kW
5930	**CZECHOSLOVAKIA** †RADIO PRAGUE INTERNATIONAL	AMERICAS EUROPE
	USSR MURMANSK RADIO, Murmansk	DS • 50 kW
	RADIO TBILISI, Tbilisi	Sa/Su • MIDEAST • 50 kW
5930v	**PAKISTAN** PAKISTAN BC CORP, Karachi	DS • 10 kW
5935	**CHINA (PR)** RADIO BEIJING, Lhasa	S ASIA • HINDI • 50 kW
	XIZANG PEOPLES BS, Lhasa	DS-CHINESE • 50 kW
	USSR †LATVIAN RADIO, Riga	DS • 50 kW
		M-Sa • DS • 50 kW M/F • DS • 50 kW Su/M/W/F • DS • 50 kW
	†RADIO RIGA, Riga	Su • EUROPE & ATLANTIC • 50 kW Tu/Th/Sa • 50 kW
		W/Th/Sa-M • 50 kW
	†RADIO TASHKENT	(J) • MIDEAST
5940 (con'd)	**USSR** MAGADAN RADIO, Magadan	DS • 50 kW

SUMMER ONLY (J)   WINTER ONLY (D)   JAMMING / OR ∧   EARLIEST HEARD ◁   LATEST HEARD ▷   NEW OR CHANGED FOR 1991 †

FREQUENCY   COUNTRY, STATION, LOCATION

TARGET • NETWORK • POWER (kW)

World Time

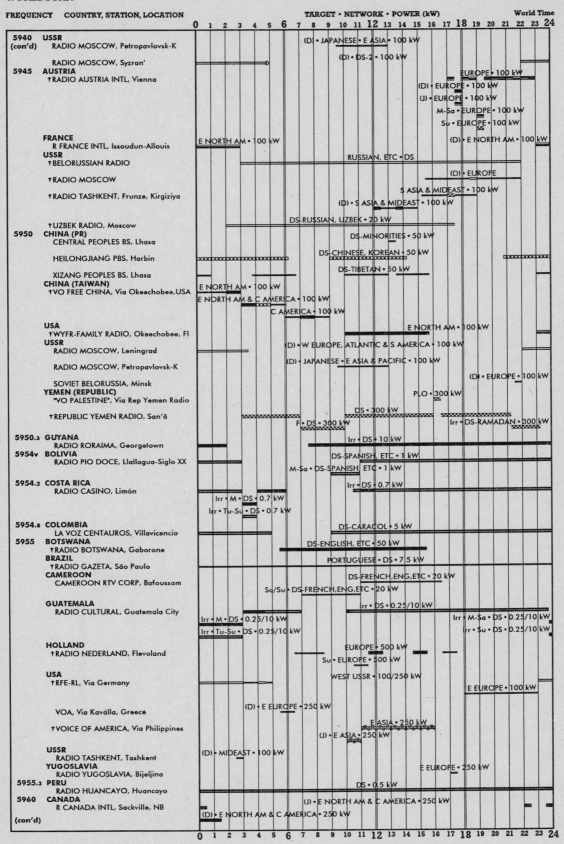

5940 (con'd)	**USSR**
	RADIO MOSCOW, Petropavlovsk-K — (D) • JAPANESE • E ASIA • 100 kW
	RADIO MOSCOW, Syzran' — (D) • DS-2 • 100 kW
5945	**AUSTRIA**
	†RADIO AUSTRIA INTL, Vienna — EUROPE • 100 kW / (D) • EUROPE • 100 kW / (J) • EUROPE • 100 kW / M-Sa • EUROPE • 100 kW / Su • EUROPE • 100 kW
	FRANCE
	R FRANCE INTL, Issoudun-Allouis — E NORTH AM • 100 kW / (D) • E NORTH AM • 100 kW
	USSR
	†BELORUSSIAN RADIO — RUSSIAN, ETC • DS
	†RADIO MOSCOW — (D) • EUROPE
	†RADIO TASHKENT, Frunze, Kirgiziya — S ASIA & MIDEAST • 100 kW / (D) • S ASIA & MIDEAST • 100 kW
	†UZBEK RADIO, Moscow — DS-RUSSIAN, UZBEK • 20 kW
5950	**CHINA (PR)**
	CENTRAL PEOPLES BS, Lhasa — DS-MINORITIES • 50 kW
	HEILONGJIANG PBS, Harbin — DS-CHINESE, KOREAN • 50 kW
	XIZANG PEOPLES BS, Lhasa — DS-TIBETAN • 50 kW
	CHINA (TAIWAN)
	†VO FREE CHINA, Via Okeechobee, USA — E NORTH AM • 100 kW / E NORTH AM & C AMERICA • 100 kW / C AMERICA • 100 kW
	USA
	†WYFR-FAMILY RADIO, Okeechobee, Fl — E NORTH AM • 100 kW
	USSR
	RADIO MOSCOW, Leningrad — (D) • W EUROPE, ATLANTIC & S AMERICA • 100 kW
	RADIO MOSCOW, Petropavlovsk-K — (D) • JAPANESE • E ASIA & PACIFIC • 100 kW
	SOVIET BELORUSSIA, Minsk — (D) • EUROPE • 100 kW
	YEMEN (REPUBLIC)
	"VO PALESTINE", Via Rep Yemen Radio — PLO • 300 kW
	†REPUBLIC YEMEN RADIO, San'ā — DS • 300 kW / F • DS • 300 kW / Irr • DS-RAMADAN • 300 kW
5950.3	**GUYANA**
	RADIO RORAIMA, Georgetown — Irr • DS • 10 kW
5954v	**BOLIVIA**
	RADIO PIO DOCE, Llallagua-Siglo XX — DS-SPANISH, ETC • 1 kW / M-Sa • DS-SPANISH ETC • 1 kW
5954.2	**COSTA RICA**
	RADIO CASINO, Limón — Irr • DS • 0.7 kW / Irr • M • DS • 0.7 kW / Irr • Tu-Su • DS • 0.7 kW
5954.8	**COLOMBIA**
	LA VOZ CENTAUROS, Villavicencio — DS-CARACOL • 5 kW
5955	**BOTSWANA**
	†RADIO BOTSWANA, Gaborone — DS-ENGLISH, ETC • 50 kW
	BRAZIL
	†RADIO GAZETA, São Paulo — PORTUGUESE • DS • 7.5 kW
	CAMEROON
	CAMEROON RTV CORP, Bafoussam — DS-FRENCH, ENG, ETC • 20 kW / Sa/Su • DS-FRENCH, ENG, ETC • 20 kW
	GUATEMALA
	RADIO CULTURAL, Guatemala City — Irr • DS • 0.25/10 kW / Irr • M • DS • 0.25/10 kW / Irr • Tu-Su • DS • 0.25/10 kW / Irr • M-Sa • DS • 0.25/10 kW / Irr • Su • DS • 0.25/10 kW
	HOLLAND
	†RADIO NEDERLAND, Flevoland — EUROPE • 500 kW / Su • EUROPE • 500 kW
	USA
	†RFE-RL, Via Germany — WEST USSR • 100/250 kW / E EUROPE • 100 kW
	VOA, Via Kaválla, Greece — (D) • E EUROPE • 250 kW
	†VOICE OF AMERICA, Via Philippines — E ASIA • 250 kW / (J) • E ASIA • 250 kW
	USSR
	RADIO TASHKENT, Tashkent — (D) • MIDEAST • 100 kW
	YUGOSLAVIA
	RADIO YUGOSLAVIA, Bijeljina — E EUROPE • 250 kW
5955.3	**PERU**
	RADIO HUANCAYO, Huancayo — DS • 0.5 kW
5960	**CANADA**
	R CANADA INTL, Sackville, NB — (J) • E NORTH AM & C AMERICA • 250 kW / (D) • E NORTH AM & C AMERICA • 250 kW
(con'd)	

ENGLISH ▬ ARABIC ξξξ CHINESE □□□ FRENCH ▬ GERMAN ▬ RUSSIAN ══ SPANISH ▬ OTHER ▬

FREQUENCY   COUNTRY, STATION, LOCATION

TARGET • NETWORK • POWER (kW)

World Time

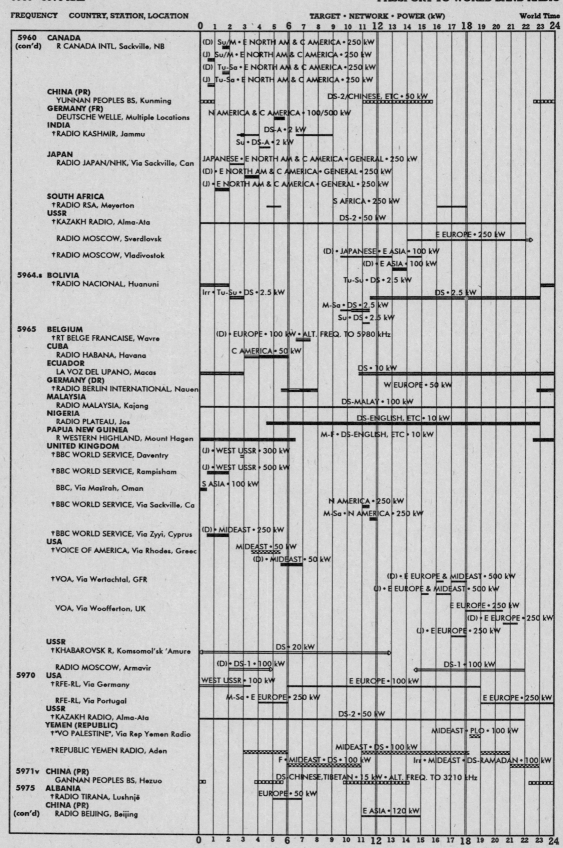

FREQUENCY	COUNTRY, STATION, LOCATION	TARGET • NETWORK • POWER (kW)
5960 (con'd)	**CANADA** R CANADA INTL, Sackville, NB	(D) Su/M • E NORTH AM & C AMERICA • 250 kW
		(J) Su/M • E NORTH AM & C AMERICA • 250 kW
		(D) Tu-Sa • E NORTH AM & C AMERICA • 250 kW
		(J) Tu-Sa • E NORTH AM & C AMERICA • 250 kW
	CHINA (PR) YUNNAN PEOPLES BS, Kunming	DS-2/CHINESE, ETC • 50 kW
	GERMANY (FR) DEUTSCHE WELLE, Multiple Locations	N AMERICA & C AMERICA • 100/500 kW
	INDIA †RADIO KASHMIR, Jammu	DS-A • 2 kW
		Su • DS-A • 2 kW
	JAPAN RADIO JAPAN/NHK, Via Sackville, Can	JAPANESE • E NORTH AM & C AMERICA • GENERAL • 250 kW
		(D) • E NORTH AM & C AMERICA • GENERAL • 250 kW
		(J) • E NORTH AM & C AMERICA • GENERAL • 250 kW
	SOUTH AFRICA †RADIO RSA, Meyerton	S AFRICA • 250 kW
	USSR †KAZAKH RADIO, Alma-Ata	DS-2 • 50 kW
	RADIO MOSCOW, Sverdlovsk	E EUROPE • 250 kW
	†RADIO MOSCOW, Vladivostok	(D) • JAPANESE • E ASIA • 100 kW
		(D) • E ASIA • 100 kW
5964.s	**BOLIVIA** †RADIO NACIONAL, Huanuni	Tu-Su • DS • 2.5 kW
		Irr • Tu-Su • DS • 2.5 kW
		DS • 2.5 kW
		M-Sa • DS • 2.5 kW
		Su • DS • 2.5 kW
5965	**BELGIUM** †RT BELGE FRANCAISE, Wavre	(D) • EUROPE • 100 kW • ALT. FREQ. TO 5980 kHz
	CUBA RADIO HABANA, Havana	C AMERICA • 50 kW
	ECUADOR LA VOZ DEL UPANO, Macas	DS • 10 kW
	GERMANY (DR) †RADIO BERLIN INTERNATIONAL, Nauen	W EUROPE • 50 kW
	MALAYSIA RADIO MALAYSIA, Kajang	DS-MALAY • 100 kW
	NIGERIA RADIO PLATEAU, Jos	DS-ENGLISH, ETC • 10 kW
	PAPUA NEW GUINEA R WESTERN HIGHLAND, Mount Hagen	M-F • DS-ENGLISH, ETC • 10 kW
	UNITED KINGDOM †BBC WORLD SERVICE, Daventry	(J) • WEST USSR • 300 kW
	†BBC WORLD SERVICE, Rampisham	(J) • WEST USSR • 500 kW
	BBC, Via Maṣīrah, Oman	S ASIA • 100 kW
	†BBC WORLD SERVICE, Via Sackville, Ca	N AMERICA • 250 kW
		M-Sa • N AMERICA • 250 kW
	†BBC WORLD SERVICE, Via Zyyi, Cyprus	(D) • MIDEAST • 250 kW
	USA †VOICE OF AMERICA, Via Rhodes, Greec	MIDEAST • 50 kW
		(D) • MIDEAST • 50 kW
	†VOA, Via Wertachtal, GFR	(D) • E EUROPE & MIDEAST • 500 kW
		(J) • E EUROPE & MIDEAST • 500 kW
	VOA, Via Woofferton, UK	E EUROPE • 250 kW
		(D) • E EUROPE • 250 kW
		(J) • E EUROPE • 250 kW
	USSR †KHABAROVSK R, Komsomol'sk 'Amure	DS • 20 kW
	RADIO MOSCOW, Armavir	(D) • DS-1 • 100 kW
		DS-1 • 100 kW
5970	**USA** †RFE-RL, Via Germany	WEST USSR • 100 kW E EUROPE • 100 kW
	RFE-RL, Via Portugal	M-Sa • E EUROPE • 250 kW E EUROPE • 250 kW
	USSR †KAZAKH RADIO, Alma-Ata	DS-2 • 50 kW
	YEMEN (REPUBLIC) †"VO PALESTINE", Via Rep Yemen Radio	MIDEAST • PLO • 100 kW
	†REPUBLIC YEMEN RADIO, Aden	MIDEAST • DS • 100 kW
		F • MIDEAST • DS • 100 kW Irr • MIDEAST • DS-RAMADAN • 100 kW
5971v	**CHINA (PR)** GANNAN PEOPLES BS, Hezuo	DS-CHINESE, TIBETAN • 15 kW • ALT. FREQ. TO 3210 kHz
5975	**ALBANIA** †RADIO TIRANA, Lushnjë	EUROPE • 50 kW
	CHINA (PR)	
(con'd)	RADIO BEIJING, Beijing	E ASIA • 120 kW

FREQUENCY   COUNTRY, STATION, LOCATION   TARGET • NETWORK • POWER (kW)   World Time

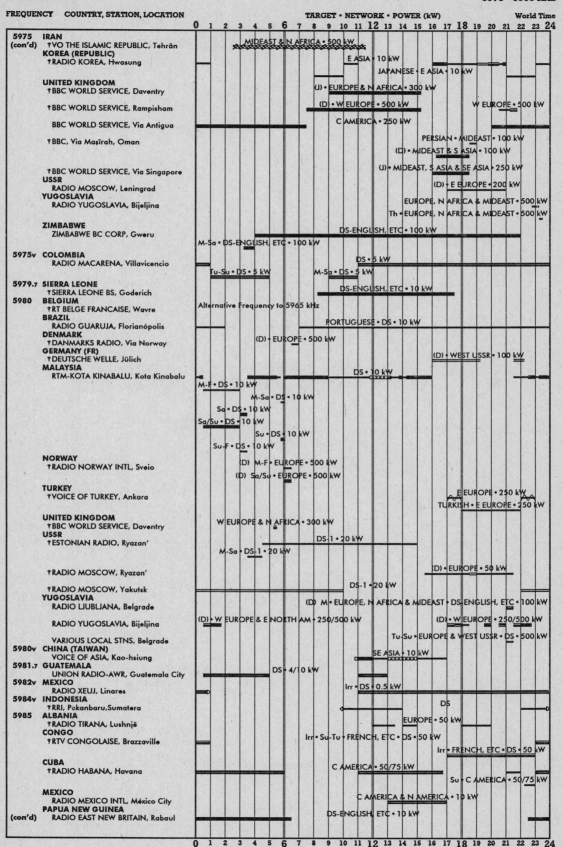

FREQUENCY   COUNTRY, STATION, LOCATION   TARGET • NETWORK • POWER (kW)   World Time

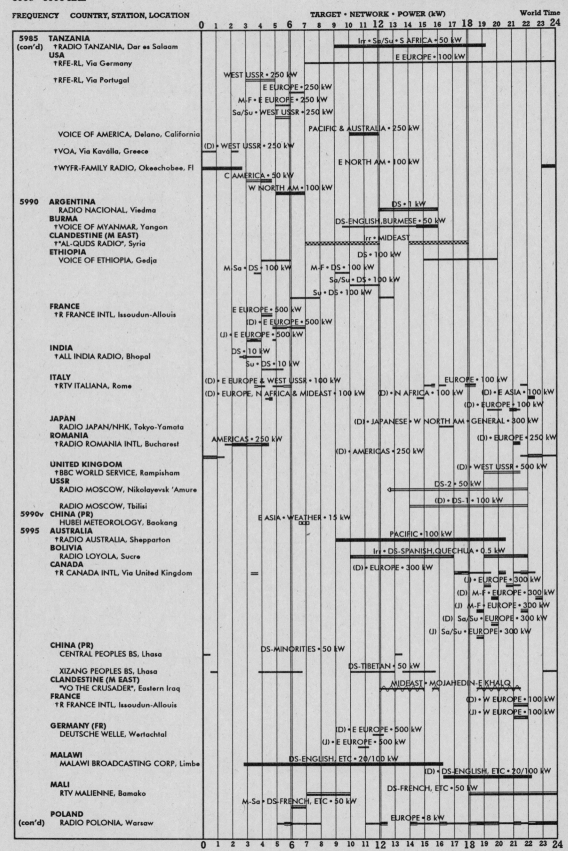

5985	**TANZANIA**
(con'd)	†RADIO TANZANIA, Dar es Salaam
	USA
	†RFE-RL, Via Germany
	†RFE-RL, Via Portugal
	VOICE OF AMERICA, Delano, California
	†VOA, Via Kaválla, Greece
	†WYFR-FAMILY RADIO, Okeechobee, Fl
5990	**ARGENTINA**
	RADIO NACIONAL, Viedma
	BURMA
	†VOICE OF MYANMAR, Yangon
	CLANDESTINE (M EAST)
	†"AL-QUDS RADIO", Syria
	ETHIOPIA
	VOICE OF ETHIOPIA, Gedja
	FRANCE
	†R FRANCE INTL, Issoudun-Allouis
	INDIA
	†ALL INDIA RADIO, Bhopal
	ITALY
	†RTV ITALIANA, Rome
	JAPAN
	RADIO JAPAN/NHK, Tokyo-Yamata
	ROMANIA
	†RADIO ROMANIA INTL, Bucharest
	UNITED KINGDOM
	†BBC WORLD SERVICE, Rampisham
	USSR
	RADIO MOSCOW, Nikolayevsk 'Amure
	RADIO MOSCOW, Tbilisi
5990v	**CHINA (PR)**
	HUBEI METEOROLOGY, Baokang
5995	**AUSTRALIA**
	†RADIO AUSTRALIA, Shepparton
	BOLIVIA
	RADIO LOYOLA, Sucre
	CANADA
	†R CANADA INTL, Via United Kingdom
	CHINA (PR)
	CENTRAL PEOPLES BS, Lhasa
	XIZANG PEOPLES BS, Lhasa
	CLANDESTINE (M EAST)
	"VO THE CRUSADER", Eastern Iraq
	FRANCE
	†R FRANCE INTL, Issoudun-Allouis
	GERMANY (FR)
	DEUTSCHE WELLE, Wertachtal
	MALAWI
	MALAWI BROADCASTING CORP, Limbe
	MALI
	RTV MALIENNE, Bamako
	POLAND
(con'd)	RADIO POLONIA, Warsaw

Programme details (target • network • power):

- Irr • Sa/Su • S AFRICA • 50 kW
- E EUROPE • 100 kW
- WEST USSR • 250 kW
- E EUROPE • 250 kW
- M-F • E EUROPE • 250 kW
- Sa/Su • WEST USSR • 250 kW
- PACIFIC & AUSTRALIA • 250 kW
- (D) • WEST USSR • 250 kW
- E NORTH AM • 100 kW
- C AMERICA • 50 kW
- W NORTH AM • 100 kW
- DS • 1 kW
- DS-ENGLISH, BURMESE • 50 kW
- Irr • MIDEAST
- DS • 100 kW
- M-Sa • DS • 100 kW   M-F • DS • 100 kW
- Sa/Su • DS • 100 kW
- Su • DS • 100 kW
- E EUROPE • 500 kW
- (D) • E EUROPE • 500 kW
- (J) • E EUROPE • 500 kW
- DS • 10 kW
- Su • DS • 10 kW
- (D) • E EUROPE & WEST USSR • 100 kW   EUROPE • 100 kW
- (D) • EUROPE, N AFRICA & MIDEAST • 100 kW   (D) • N AFRICA • 100 kW   (D) • E ASIA • 100 kW
- (D) • EUROPE • 100 kW
- (D) • JAPANESE • W NORTH AM • GENERAL • 300 kW
- AMERICAS • 250 kW
- (D) • AMERICAS • 250 kW   (D) • EUROPE • 250 kW
- (D) • WEST USSR • 500 kW
- DS-2 • 50 kW
- (D) • DS-1 • 100 kW
- E ASIA • WEATHER • 15 kW
- PACIFIC • 100 kW
- Irr • DS-SPANISH, QUECHUA • 0.5 kW
- (D) • EUROPE • 300 kW
- (J) • EUROPE • 300 kW
- (D) M-F • EUROPE • 300 kW
- (J) M-F • EUROPE • 300 kW
- (D) Sa/Su • EUROPE • 300 kW
- (J) Sa/Su • EUROPE • 300 kW
- DS-MINORITIES • 50 kW
- DS-TIBETAN • 50 kW
- MIDEAST • MOJAHEDIN-E KHALQ
- (D) • W EUROPE • 100 kW
- (J) • W EUROPE • 100 kW
- (D) • E EUROPE • 500 kW
- (J) • E EUROPE • 500 kW
- DS-ENGLISH, ETC • 20/100 kW
- (D) • DS-ENGLISH, ETC • 20/100 kW
- DS-FRENCH, ETC • 50 kW
- M-Sa • DS-FRENCH, ETC • 50 kW
- EUROPE • 8 kW

FREQUENCY   COUNTRY, STATION, LOCATION

TARGET • NETWORK • POWER (kW)

World Time

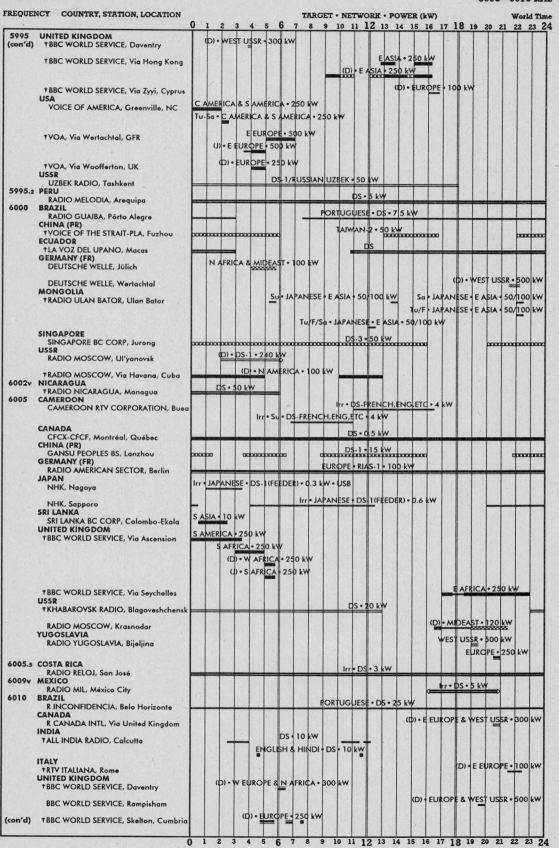

ENGLISH ▬▬ ARABIC ▩ CHINESE ▭▭▭ FRENCH ▬▬ GERMAN ▬▬ RUSSIAN ══ SPANISH ▬▬ OTHER ▬▬

FREQUENCY   COUNTRY, STATION, LOCATION

TARGET • NETWORK • POWER (kW)   World Time

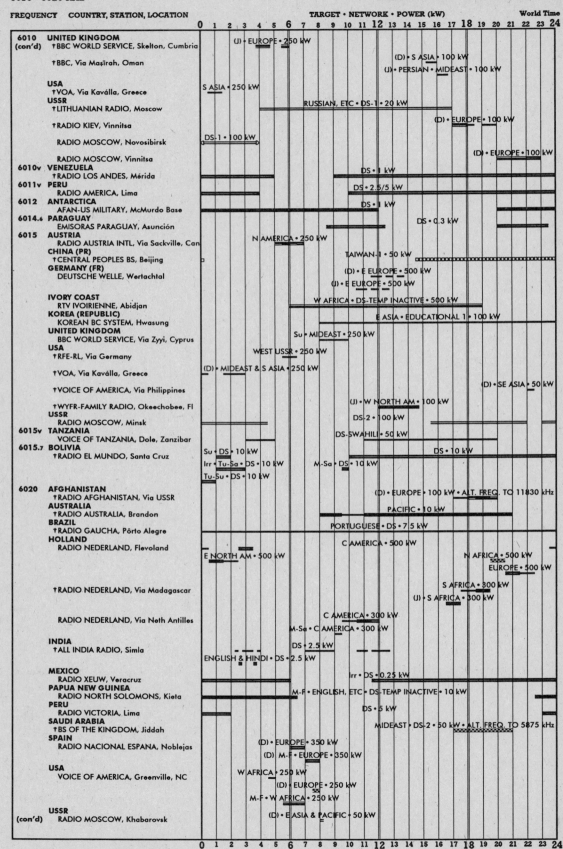

Frequency	Country, Station, Location	Target • Network • Power
6010 (con'd)	**UNITED KINGDOM**	
	†BBC WORLD SERVICE, Skelton, Cumbria	(J) • EUROPE • 250 kW
	†BBC, Via Maṣīrah, Oman	(D) • S ASIA • 100 kW / (J) • PERSIAN • MIDEAST • 100 kW
	USA	
	†VOA, Via Kaválla, Greece	S ASIA • 250 kW
	USSR	
	†LITHUANIAN RADIO, Moscow	RUSSIAN, ETC • DS-1 • 20 kW
	†RADIO KIEV, Vinnitsa	(D) • EUROPE • 100 kW
	RADIO MOSCOW, Novosibirsk	DS-1 • 100 kW
	RADIO MOSCOW, Vinnitsa	(D) • EUROPE • 100 kW
6010v	**VENEZUELA**	
	†RADIO LOS ANDES, Mérida	DS • 1 kW
6011v	**PERU**	
	RADIO AMERICA, Lima	DS • 2.5/5 kW
6012	**ANTARCTICA**	
	AFAN-US MILITARY, McMurdo Base	DS • 1 kW
6014.6	**PARAGUAY**	
	EMISORAS PARAGUAY, Asunción	DS • 0.3 kW
6015	**AUSTRIA**	
	RADIO AUSTRIA INTL, Via Sackville, Can	N AMERICA • 250 kW
	CHINA (PR)	
	†CENTRAL PEOPLES BS, Beijing	TAIWAN-1 • 50 kW
	GERMANY (FR)	
	DEUTSCHE WELLE, Wertachtal	(D) • E EUROPE • 500 kW / (J) • E EUROPE • 500 kW
	IVORY COAST	
	RTV IVOIRIENNE, Abidjan	W AFRICA • DS-TEMP INACTIVE • 500 kW
	KOREA (REPUBLIC)	
	KOREAN BC SYSTEM, Hwasung	E ASIA • EDUCATIONAL 1 • 100 kW
	UNITED KINGDOM	
	BBC WORLD SERVICE, Via Zyyi, Cyprus	Su • MIDEAST • 250 kW
	USA	
	†RFE-RL, Via Germany	WEST USSR • 250 kW
	†VOA, Via Kaválla, Greece	(D) • MIDEAST & S ASIA • 250 kW
	†VOICE OF AMERICA, Via Philippines	(D) • SE ASIA • 50 kW
	†WYFR-FAMILY RADIO, Okeechobee, Fl	(J) • W NORTH AM • 100 kW
	USSR	
	RADIO MOSCOW, Minsk	DS-2 • 100 kW
6015v	**TANZANIA**	
	VOICE OF TANZANIA, Dole, Zanzibar	DS-SWAHILI • 50 kW
6015.7	**BOLIVIA**	
	†RADIO EL MUNDO, Santa Cruz	Su • DS • 10 kW / DS • 10 kW / Irr • Tu-Sa • DS • 10 kW / M-Sa • DS • 10 kW / Tu-Su • DS • 10 kW
6020	**AFGHANISTAN**	
	†RADIO AFGHANISTAN, Via USSR	(D) • EUROPE • 100 kW • ALT. FREQ. TO 11830 kHz
	AUSTRALIA	
	†RADIO AUSTRALIA, Brandon	PACIFIC • 10 kW
	BRAZIL	
	†RADIO GAUCHA, Pôrto Alegre	PORTUGUESE • DS • 7.5 kW
	HOLLAND	
	RADIO NEDERLAND, Flevoland	C AMERICA • 500 kW / E NORTH AM • 500 kW / N AFRICA • 500 kW / EUROPE • 500 kW
	†RADIO NEDERLAND, Via Madagascar	S AFRICA • 300 kW / (J) • S AFRICA • 300 kW
	RADIO NEDERLAND, Via Neth Antilles	C AMERICA • 300 kW / M-Sa • C AMERICA • 300 kW
	INDIA	
	†ALL INDIA RADIO, Simla	DS • 2.5 kW / ENGLISH & HINDI • DS • 2.5 kW
	MEXICO	
	RADIO XEUW, Veracruz	Irr • DS • 0.25 kW
	PAPUA NEW GUINEA	
	RADIO NORTH SOLOMONS, Kieta	M-F • ENGLISH, ETC • DS-TEMP INACTIVE • 10 kW
	PERU	
	RADIO VICTORIA, Lima	DS • 5 kW
	SAUDI ARABIA	
	†BS OF THE KINGDOM, Jiddah	MIDEAST • DS-2 • 50 kW • ALT. FREQ. TO 5875 kHz
	SPAIN	
	RADIO NACIONAL ESPANA, Noblejas	(D) • EUROPE • 350 kW / (D) • M-F • EUROPE • 350 kW
	USA	
	VOICE OF AMERICA, Greenville, NC	W AFRICA • 250 kW / (D) • EUROPE • 250 kW / M-F • W AFRICA • 250 kW
(con'd)	**USSR** RADIO MOSCOW, Khabarovsk	(D) • E ASIA & PACIFIC • 50 kW

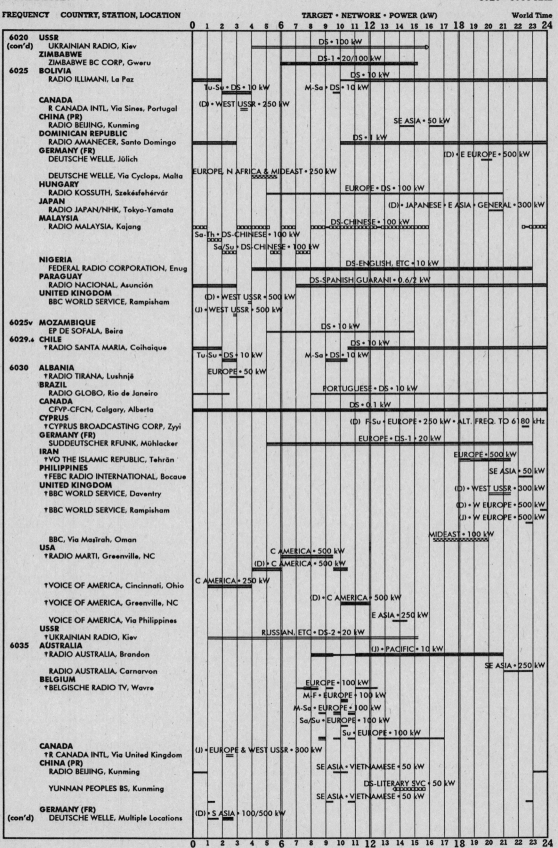

FREQUENCY   COUNTRY, STATION, LOCATION

6020 **USSR**
(con'd)   UKRAINIAN RADIO, Kiev — DS • 100 kW
  ZIMBABWE
    ZIMBABWE BC CORP, Gweru — DS-1 • 20/100 kW
6025 **BOLIVIA**
    RADIO ILLIMANI, La Paz — DS • 10 kW
    Tu-Su • DS • 10 kW   M-Sa • DS • 10 kW
  CANADA
    R CANADA INTL, Via Sines, Portugal — (D) • WEST USSR • 250 kW
  CHINA (PR)
    RADIO BEIJING, Kunming — SE ASIA • 50 kW
  DOMINICAN REPUBLIC
    RADIO AMANECER, Santo Domingo — DS • 1 kW
  GERMANY (FR)
    DEUTSCHE WELLE, Jülich — (D) • E EUROPE • 500 kW
    DEUTSCHE WELLE, Via Cyclops, Malta — EUROPE, N AFRICA & MIDEAST • 250 kW
  HUNGARY
    RADIO KOSSUTH, Székésfehérvár — EUROPE • DS • 100 kW
  JAPAN
    RADIO JAPAN/NHK, Tokyo-Yamata — (D) • JAPANESE • E ASIA • GENERAL • 300 kW
  MALAYSIA
    RADIO MALAYSIA, Kajang — DS-CHINESE • 100 kW
    Sa-Th • DS-CHINESE • 100 kW
    Sa/Su • DS-CHINESE • 100 kW
  NIGERIA
    FEDERAL RADIO CORPORATION, Enug — DS-ENGLISH, ETC • 10 kW
  PARAGUAY
    RADIO NACIONAL, Asunción — DS-SPANISH GUARANI • 0.6/2 kW
  UNITED KINGDOM
    BBC WORLD SERVICE, Rampisham — (D) • WEST USSR • 500 kW
    (J) • WEST USSR • 500 kW

6025v **MOZAMBIQUE**
    EP DE SOFALA, Beira — DS • 10 kW
6029.6 **CHILE**
  †RADIO SANTA MARIA, Coihaique — DS • 10 kW
    Tu-Su • DS • 10 kW   M-Sa • DS • 10 kW

6030 **ALBANIA**
  †RADIO TIRANA, Lushnjë — EUROPE • 50 kW
  BRAZIL
    RADIO GLOBO, Rio de Janeiro — PORTUGUESE • DS • 10 kW
  CANADA
    CFVP-CFCN, Calgary, Alberta — DS • 0.1 kW
  CYPRUS
  †CYPRUS BROADCASTING CORP, Zyyi — (D) F-Su • EUROPE • 250 kW • ALT. FREQ. TO 6180 kHz
  GERMANY (FR)
    SUDDEUTSCHER RFUNK, Mühlacker — EUROPE • DS-1 • 20 kW
  IRAN
  †VO THE ISLAMIC REPUBLIC, Tehrān — EUROPE • 500 kW
  PHILIPPINES
  †FEBC RADIO INTERNATIONAL, Bocaue — SE ASIA • 50 kW
  UNITED KINGDOM
  †BBC WORLD SERVICE, Daventry — (D) • WEST USSR • 300 kW
  †BBC WORLD SERVICE, Rampisham — (D) • W EUROPE • 500 kW
    (J) • W EUROPE • 500 kW
    BBC, Via Maṣīrah, Oman — MIDEAST • 100 kW
  USA
  †RADIO MARTI, Greenville, NC — C AMERICA • 500 kW
    (D) • C AMERICA • 500 kW
  †VOICE OF AMERICA, Cincinnati, Ohio — C AMERICA • 250 kW
  †VOICE OF AMERICA, Greenville, NC — (D) • C AMERICA • 500 kW
    VOICE OF AMERICA, Via Philippines — E ASIA • 250 kW
  USSR
  †UKRAINIAN RADIO, Kiev — RUSSIAN, ETC • DS-2 • 20 kW
6035 **AUSTRALIA**
  †RADIO AUSTRALIA, Brandon — (J) • PACIFIC • 10 kW
    RADIO AUSTRALIA, Carnarvon — SE ASIA • 250 kW
  BELGIUM
  †BELGISCHE RADIO TV, Wavre — EUROPE • 100 kW
    M-F • EUROPE • 100 kW
    M-Sa • EUROPE • 100 kW
    Sa/Su • EUROPE • 100 kW
    Su • EUROPE • 100 kW
  CANADA
  †R CANADA INTL, Via United Kingdom — (J) • EUROPE & WEST USSR • 300 kW
  CHINA (PR)
    RADIO BEIJING, Kunming — SE ASIA • VIETNAMESE • 50 kW
    YUNNAN PEOPLES BS, Kunming — DS-LITERARY SVC • 50 kW
    SE ASIA • VIETNAMESE • 50 kW
  GERMANY (FR)
(con'd)   DEUTSCHE WELLE, Multiple Locations — (D) • S ASIA • 100/500 kW

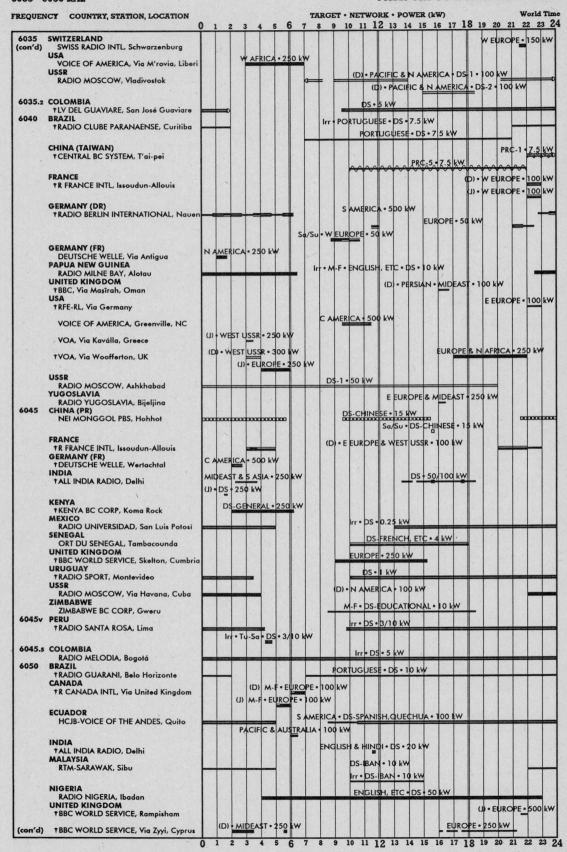

FREQUENCY   COUNTRY, STATION, LOCATION   TARGET • NETWORK • POWER (kW)   World Time

6035   SWITZERLAND
(con'd)   SWISS RADIO INTL, Schwarzenburg   W EUROPE • 150 kW
        USA
            VOICE OF AMERICA, Via M'rovia, Liberi   W AFRICA • 250 kW
        USSR
            RADIO MOSCOW, Vladivostok   (D) • PACIFIC & N AMERICA • DS-1 • 100 kW
                                                         (D) • PACIFIC & N AMERICA • DS-2 • 100 kW

6035.2 COLOMBIA
        †LV DEL GUAVIARE, San José Guaviare   DS • 5 kW
6040   BRAZIL
        †RADIO CLUBE PARANAENSE, Curitiba   Irr • PORTUGUESE • DS • 7.5 kW
                                                         PORTUGUESE • DS • 7.5 kW

        CHINA (TAIWAN)   PRC-1 • 7.5 kW
        †CENTRAL BC SYSTEM, T'ai-pei   PRC-5 • 7.5 kW

        FRANCE   (D) • W EUROPE • 100 kW
        †R FRANCE INTL, Issoudun-Allouis   (J) • W EUROPE • 100 kW

        GERMANY (DR)
        †RADIO BERLIN INTERNATIONAL, Nauen   S AMERICA • 500 kW
                                                                  EUROPE • 50 kW
                                                         Sa/Su • W EUROPE • 50 kW

        GERMANY (FR)
            DEUTSCHE WELLE, Via Antigua   N AMERICA • 250 kW
        PAPUA NEW GUINEA
            RADIO MILNE BAY, Alotau   Irr • M-F • ENGLISH, ETC • DS • 10 kW
        UNITED KINGDOM
        †BBC, Via Maşīrah, Oman   (D) • PERSIAN • MIDEAST • 100 kW
        USA
        †RFE-RL, Via Germany   E EUROPE • 100 kW

            VOICE OF AMERICA, Greenville, NC   C AMERICA • 500 kW

            VOA, Via Kaválla, Greece   (J) • WEST USSR • 250 kW

        †VOA, Via Woofferton, UK   (D) • WEST USSR • 300 kW   EUROPE & N AFRICA • 250 kW
                                                         (J) • EUROPE • 250 kW

        USSR
            RADIO MOSCOW, Ashkhabad   DS-1 • 50 kW
        YUGOSLAVIA
            RADIO YUGOSLAVIA, Bijeljina   E EUROPE & MIDEAST • 250 kW
6045   CHINA (PR)
            NEI MONGGOL PBS, Hohhot   DS-CHINESE • 15 kW
                                                         Sa/Su • DS-CHINESE • 15 kW

        FRANCE
        †R FRANCE INTL, Issoudun-Allouis   (D) • E EUROPE & WEST USSR • 100 kW
        GERMANY (FR)
        †DEUTSCHE WELLE, Wertachtal   C AMERICA • 500 kW
        INDIA
        †ALL INDIA RADIO, Delhi   MIDEAST & S ASIA • 250 kW   DS • 50/100 kW
                                                         (J) • DS • 250 kW

        KENYA
        †KENYA BC CORP, Koma Rock   DS-GENERAL • 250 kW
        MEXICO
            RADIO UNIVERSIDAD, San Luis Potosí   Irr • DS • 0.25 kW
        SENEGAL
            ORT DU SENEGAL, Tambacounda   DS-FRENCH, ETC • 4 kW
        UNITED KINGDOM
        †BBC WORLD SERVICE, Skelton, Cumbria   EUROPE • 250 kW
        URUGUAY
        †RADIO SPORT, Montevideo   DS • 1 kW
        USSR
            RADIO MOSCOW, Via Havana, Cuba   (D) • N AMERICA • 100 kW
        ZIMBABWE
            ZIMBABWE BC CORP, Gweru   M-F • DS-EDUCATIONAL • 10 kW
6045v   PERU
        †RADIO SANTA ROSA, Lima   Irr • DS • 3/10 kW
                                                         Irr • Tu-Sa • DS • 3/10 kW

6045.5 COLOMBIA
            RADIO MELODIA, Bogotá   Irr • DS • 5 kW
6050   BRAZIL
        †RADIO GUARANI, Belo Horizonte   PORTUGUESE • DS • 10 kW
        CANADA
        †R CANADA INTL, Via United Kingdom   (D) M-F • EUROPE • 100 kW
                                                         (J) M-F • EUROPE • 100 kW

        ECUADOR
            HCJB-VOICE OF THE ANDES, Quito   S AMERICA • DS-SPANISH, QUECHUA • 100 kW
                                                         PACIFIC & AUSTRALIA • 100 kW

        INDIA
        †ALL INDIA RADIO, Delhi   ENGLISH & HINDI • DS • 20 kW
        MALAYSIA
            RTM-SARAWAK, Sibu   DS-IBAN • 10 kW
                                                         Irr • DS-IBAN • 10 kW

        NIGERIA
            RADIO NIGERIA, Ibadan   ENGLISH, ETC • DS • 50 kW
        UNITED KINGDOM
        †BBC WORLD SERVICE, Rampisham   (J) • EUROPE • 500 kW

(con'd) †BBC WORLD SERVICE, Via Zyyi, Cyprus   (D) • MIDEAST • 250 kW   EUROPE • 250 kW

FREQUENCY	COUNTRY, STATION, LOCATION	TARGET • NETWORK • POWER (kW)	World Time

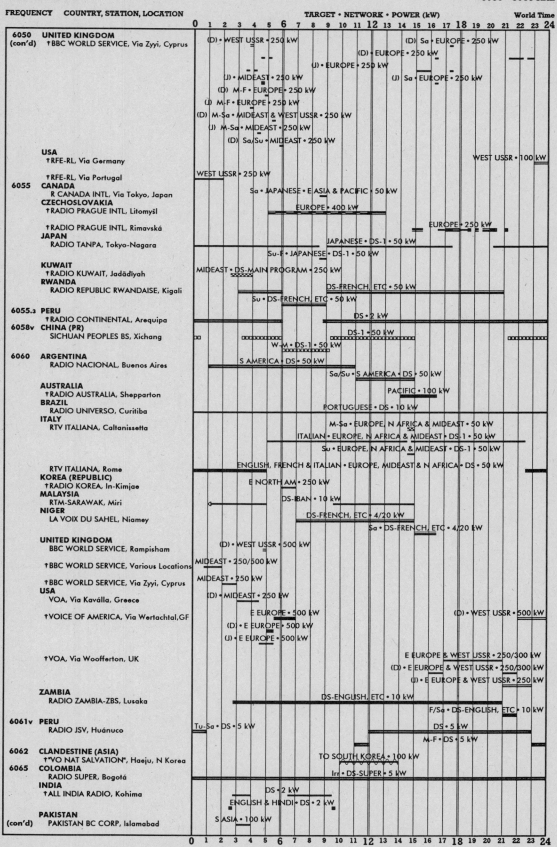

6050 UNITED KINGDOM
(con'd) †BBC WORLD SERVICE, Via Zyyi, Cyprus
- (D) • WEST USSR • 250 kW
- (D) Sa • EUROPE • 250 kW
- (D) • EUROPE • 250 kW
- (J) • EUROPE • 250 kW
- (J) • MIDEAST • 250 kW
- (J) Sa • EUROPE • 250 kW
- (D) M-F • EUROPE • 250 kW
- (J) M-F • EUROPE • 250 kW
- (D) M-Sa • MIDEAST & WEST USSR • 250 kW
- (J) M-Sa • MIDEAST • 250 kW
- (D) Sa/Su • MIDEAST • 250 kW

USA
†RFE-RL, Via Germany
- WEST USSR • 100 kW

†RFE-RL, Via Portugal
- WEST USSR • 250 kW

6055 CANADA
R CANADA INTL, Via Tokyo, Japan
- Sa • JAPANESE • E ASIA & PACIFIC • 50 kW

CZECHOSLOVAKIA
†RADIO PRAGUE INTL, Litomyšl
- EUROPE • 400 kW

†RADIO PRAGUE INTL, Rimavská
- EUROPE • 250 kW

JAPAN
RADIO TANPA, Tokyo-Nagara
- JAPANESE • DS-1 • 50 kW
- Su-F • JAPANESE • DS-1 • 50 kW

KUWAIT
†RADIO KUWAIT, Jadādīyah
- MIDEAST • DS-MAIN PROGRAM • 250 kW

RWANDA
RADIO REPUBLIC RWANDAISE, Kigali
- DS-FRENCH, ETC • 50 kW
- Su • DS-FRENCH, ETC • 50 kW

6055.3 PERU
†RADIO CONTINENTAL, Arequipa
- DS • 2 kW

6058v CHINA (PR)
SICHUAN PEOPLES BS, Xichang
- DS-1 • 50 kW
- W-M • DS-1 • 50 kW

6060 ARGENTINA
RADIO NACIONAL, Buenos Aires
- S AMERICA • DS • 50 kW
- Sa/Su • S AMERICA • DS • 50 kW

AUSTRALIA
†RADIO AUSTRALIA, Shepparton
- PACIFIC • 100 kW

BRAZIL
RADIO UNIVERSO, Curitiba
- PORTUGUESE • DS • 10 kW

ITALY
RTV ITALIANA, Caltanissetta
- M-Sa • EUROPE, N AFRICA & MIDEAST • 50 kW
- ITALIAN • EUROPE, N AFRICA & MIDEAST • DS-1 • 50 kW
- Su • EUROPE, N AFRICA & MIDEAST • DS-1 • 50 kW

RTV ITALIANA, Rome
- ENGLISH, FRENCH & ITALIAN • EUROPE, MIDEAST & N AFRICA • DS • 50 kW

KOREA (REPUBLIC)
†RADIO KOREA, In-Kimjae
- E NORTH AM • 250 kW

MALAYSIA
RTM-SARAWAK, Miri
- DS-IBAN • 10 kW

NIGER
LA VOIX DU SAHEL, Niamey
- DS-FRENCH, ETC • 4/20 kW
- Sa • DS-FRENCH, ETC • 4/20 kW

UNITED KINGDOM
BBC WORLD SERVICE, Rampisham
- (D) • WEST USSR • 500 kW

†BBC WORLD SERVICE, Various Locations
- MIDEAST • 250/500 kW

†BBC WORLD SERVICE, Via Zyyi, Cyprus
- MIDEAST • 250 kW

USA
VOA, Via Kaválla, Greece
- (D) • MIDEAST • 250 kW

†VOICE OF AMERICA, Via Wertachtal, GF
- E EUROPE • 500 kW
- (D) • WEST USSR • 500 kW
- (D) • E EUROPE • 500 kW
- (J) • E EUROPE • 500 kW

†VOA, Via Woofferton, UK
- E EUROPE & WEST USSR • 250/300 kW
- (D) • E EUROPE & WEST USSR • 250/300 kW
- (J) • E EUROPE & WEST USSR • 250 kW

ZAMBIA
RADIO ZAMBIA-ZBS, Lusaka
- DS-ENGLISH, ETC • 10 kW
- F/Sa • DS-ENGLISH, ETC • 10 kW

6061v PERU
RADIO JSV, Huánuco
- Tu-Sa • DS • 5 kW
- DS • 5 kW
- M-F • DS • 5 kW

6062 CLANDESTINE (ASIA)
†"VO NAT SALVATION", Haeju, N Korea
- TO SOUTH KOREA • 100 kW

6065 COLOMBIA
RADIO SUPER, Bogotá
- Irr • DS-SUPER • 5 kW

INDIA
†ALL INDIA RADIO, Kohima
- DS • 2 kW
- ENGLISH & HINDI • DS • 2 kW

PAKISTAN
(con'd) PAKISTAN BC CORP, Islamabad
- S ASIA • 100 kW

ENGLISH ▬ ARABIC ▨ CHINESE ▫▫▫ FRENCH ═ GERMAN ▬ RUSSIAN ═ SPANISH ▬ OTHER —

FREQUENCY   COUNTRY, STATION, LOCATION   TARGET • NETWORK • POWER (kW)   World Time

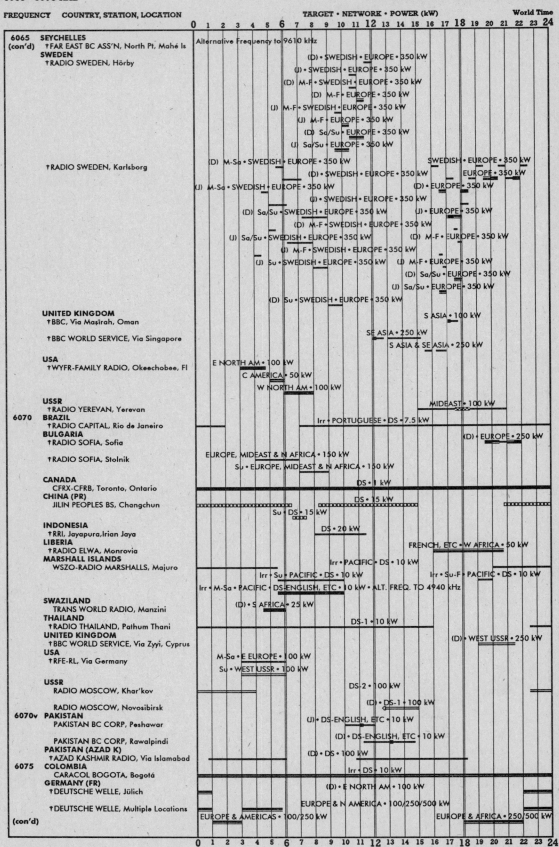

FREQUENCY	COUNTRY, STATION, LOCATION	TARGET • NETWORK • POWER (kW) / World Time
6065 (con'd)	**SEYCHELLES** †FAR EAST BC ASS'N, North Pt, Mahé Is	Alternative Frequency to 9610 kHz
	SWEDEN †RADIO SWEDEN, Hörby	(D) • SWEDISH • EUROPE • 350 kW
		(J) • SWEDISH • EUROPE • 350 kW
		(D) M-F • SWEDISH • EUROPE • 350 kW
		(D) M-F • EUROPE • 350 kW
		(J) M-F • SWEDISH • EUROPE • 350 kW
		(J) M-F • EUROPE • 350 kW
		(D) Sa/Su • EUROPE • 350 kW
		(J) Sa/Su • EUROPE • 350 kW
	†RADIO SWEDEN, Karlsborg	(D) M-Sa • SWEDISH • EUROPE • 350 kW / SWEDISH • EUROPE • 350 kW
		(D) • SWEDISH • EUROPE • 350 kW / EUROPE • 350 kW
		(J) M-Sa • SWEDISH • EUROPE • 350 kW / (D) • EUROPE • 350 kW
		(J) • SWEDISH • EUROPE • 350 kW
		(D) Sa/Su • SWEDISH • EUROPE • 350 kW / (J) • EUROPE • 350 kW
		(D) M-F • SWEDISH • EUROPE • 350 kW
		(J) Sa/Su • SWEDISH • EUROPE • 350 kW / (D) M-F • EUROPE • 350 kW
		(J) M-F • SWEDISH • EUROPE • 350 kW
		(J) Su • SWEDISH • EUROPE • 350 kW / (J) M-F • EUROPE • 350 kW
		(D) Sa/Su • EUROPE • 350 kW
		(J) Sa/Su • EUROPE • 350 kW
		(D) Su • SWEDISH • EUROPE • 350 kW
	UNITED KINGDOM †BBC, Via Maşīrah, Oman	S ASIA • 100 kW
	†BBC WORLD SERVICE, Via Singapore	SE ASIA • 250 kW
		S ASIA & SE ASIA • 250 kW
	USA †WYFR-FAMILY RADIO, Okeechobee, Fl	E NORTH AM • 100 kW
		C AMERICA • 50 kW
		W NORTH AM • 100 kW
	USSR †RADIO YEREVAN, Yerevan	MIDEAST • 100 kW
6070	**BRAZIL** †RADIO CAPITAL, Rio de Janeiro	Irr • PORTUGUESE • DS • 7.5 kW
	BULGARIA †RADIO SOFIA, Sofia	(D) • EUROPE • 250 kW
	†RADIO SOFIA, Stolnik	EUROPE, MIDEAST & N AFRICA • 150 kW
		Su • EUROPE, MIDEAST & N AFRICA • 150 kW
	CANADA CFRX-CFRB, Toronto, Ontario	DS • 1 kW
	CHINA (PR) JILIN PEOPLES BS, Changchun	DS • 15 kW
		Su • DS • 15 kW
	INDONESIA †RRI, Jayapura, Irian Jaya	DS • 20 kW
	LIBERIA †RADIO ELWA, Monrovia	FRENCH, ETC • W AFRICA • 50 kW
	MARSHALL ISLANDS WSZO-RADIO MARSHALLS, Majuro	Irr • PACIFIC • DS • 10 kW
		Irr • Su • PACIFIC • DS • 10 kW / Irr • Su-F • PACIFIC • DS • 10 kW
		Irr • M-Sa • PACIFIC • DS-ENGLISH, ETC • 10 kW • ALT. FREQ. TO 4940 kHz
	SWAZILAND TRANS WORLD RADIO, Manzini	(D) • S AFRICA • 25 kW
	THAILAND †RADIO THAILAND, Pathum Thani	DS-1 • 10 kW
	UNITED KINGDOM †BBC WORLD SERVICE, Via Zyyi, Cyprus	(D) • WEST USSR • 250 kW
	USA †RFE-RL, Via Germany	M-Sa • E EUROPE • 100 kW
		Su • WEST USSR • 100 kW
	USSR RADIO MOSCOW, Khar'kov	DS-2 • 100 kW
	RADIO MOSCOW, Novosibirsk	(D) • DS-1 • 100 kW
6070v	**PAKISTAN** PAKISTAN BC CORP, Peshawar	(J) • DS-ENGLISH, ETC • 10 kW
	PAKISTAN BC CORP, Rawalpindi	(D) • DS-ENGLISH, ETC • 10 kW
	PAKISTAN (AZAD K) †AZAD KASHMIR RADIO, Via Islamabad	(D) • DS • 100 kW
6075	**COLOMBIA** CARACOL BOGOTA, Bogotá	Irr • DS • 10 kW
	GERMANY (FR) †DEUTSCHE WELLE, Jülich	(D) • E NORTH AM • 100 kW
	†DEUTSCHE WELLE, Multiple Locations	EUROPE & N AMERICA • 100/250/500 kW
(con'd)		EUROPE & AMERICAS • 100/250 kW / EUROPE & AFRICA • 250/500 kW

SUMMER ONLY (J)   WINTER ONLY (D)   JAMMING / OR ∧   EARLIEST HEARD ◁   LATEST HEARD ▷   NEW OR CHANGED FOR 1991 †

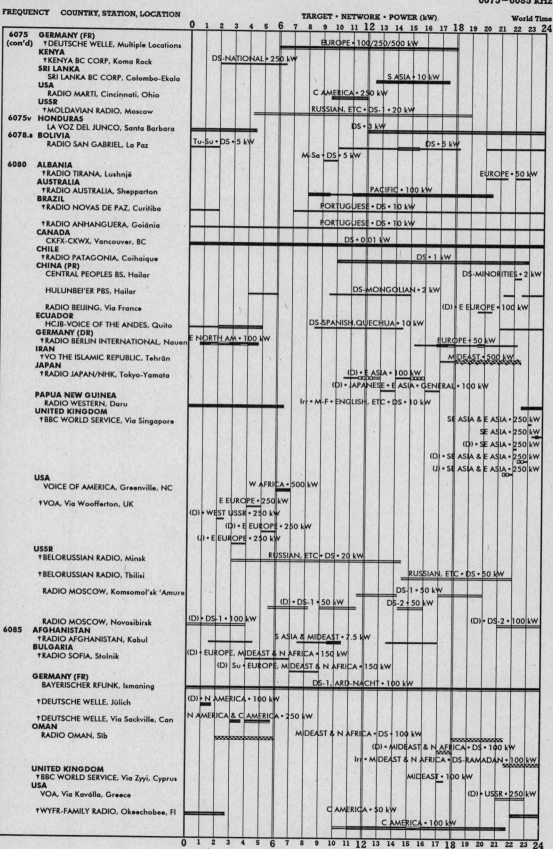

FREQUENCY   COUNTRY, STATION, LOCATION

TARGET • NETWORK • POWER (kW)

World Time

6075	GERMANY (FR)	
(con'd)	†DEUTSCHE WELLE, Multiple Locations	EUROPE • 100/250/500 kW
	KENYA	
	†KENYA BC CORP, Koma Rock	DS-NATIONAL • 250 kW
	SRI LANKA	
	SRI LANKA BC CORP, Colombo-Ekala	S ASIA • 10 kW
	USA	
	RADIO MARTI, Cincinnati, Ohio	C AMERICA • 250 kW
	USSR	
	†MOLDAVIAN RADIO, Moscow	RUSSIAN, ETC • DS-1 • 20 kW
6075v	HONDURAS	
	LA VOZ DEL JUNCO, Santa Barbara	DS • 3 kW
6078.s	BOLIVIA	
	RADIO SAN GABRIEL, La Paz	Tu-Su • DS • 5 kW DS • 5 kW M-Sa • DS • 5 kW
6080	ALBANIA	
	†RADIO TIRANA, Lushnjë	EUROPE • 50 kW
	AUSTRALIA	
	†RADIO AUSTRALIA, Shepparton	PACIFIC • 100 kW
	BRAZIL	
	†RADIO NOVAS DE PAZ, Curitiba	PORTUGUESE • DS • 10 kW
	†RADIO ANHANGUERA, Goiânia	PORTUGUESE • DS • 10 kW
	CANADA	
	CKFX-CKWX, Vancouver, BC	DS • 0.01 kW
	CHILE	
	†RADIO PATAGONIA, Coihaique	DS • 1 kW
	CHINA (PR)	
	CENTRAL PEOPLES BS, Hailar	DS-MINORITIES • 2 kW
	HULUNBEI'ER PBS, Hailar	DS-MONGOLIAN • 2 kW
	RADIO BEIJING, Via France	(D) • E EUROPE • 100 kW
	ECUADOR	
	HCJB-VOICE OF THE ANDES, Quito	DS-SPANISH, QUECHUA • 10 kW
	GERMANY (DR)	
	†RADIO BERLIN INTERNATIONAL, Nauen	E NORTH AM • 100 kW EUROPE • 50 kW
	IRAN	
	†VO THE ISLAMIC REPUBLIC, Tehrān	MIDEAST • 500 kW
	JAPAN	
	†RADIO JAPAN/NHK, Tokyo-Yamata	(D) • E ASIA • 100 kW (D) • JAPANESE • E ASIA • GENERAL • 100 kW
	PAPUA NEW GUINEA	
	RADIO WESTERN, Daru	Irr • M-F • ENGLISH, ETC • DS • 10 kW
	UNITED KINGDOM	
	†BBC WORLD SERVICE, Via Singapore	SE ASIA & E ASIA • 250 kW
		SE ASIA • 250 kW
		(D) • SE ASIA • 250 kW
		(D) • SE ASIA & E ASIA • 250 kW
		(J) • SE ASIA & E ASIA • 250 kW
	USA	
	VOICE OF AMERICA, Greenville, NC	W AFRICA • 500 kW
	†VOA, Via Woofferton, UK	E EUROPE • 250 kW
		(D) • WEST USSR • 250 kW
		(D) • E EUROPE • 250 kW
		(J) • E EUROPE • 250 kW
	USSR	
	†BELORUSSIAN RADIO, Minsk	RUSSIAN, ETC • DS • 20 kW
	†BELORUSSIAN RADIO, Tbilisi	RUSSIAN, ETC • DS • 50 kW
	RADIO MOSCOW, Komsomol'sk 'Amure	DS-1 • 50 kW
		(D) • DS-1 • 50 kW DS-2 • 50 kW
	RADIO MOSCOW, Novosibirsk	(D) • DS-1 • 100 kW (D) • DS-2 • 100 kW
6085	AFGHANISTAN	
	†RADIO AFGHANISTAN, Kabul	S ASIA & MIDEAST • 7.5 kW
	BULGARIA	
	†RADIO SOFIA, Stolnik	(D) • EUROPE, MIDEAST & N AFRICA • 150 kW
		(D) • Su • EUROPE, MIDEAST & N AFRICA • 150 kW
	GERMANY (FR)	
	BAYERISCHER RFUNK, Ismaning	DS-1, ARD-NACHT • 100 kW
	†DEUTSCHE WELLE, Jülich	(D) • N AMERICA • 100 kW
	†DEUTSCHE WELLE, Via Sackville, Can	N AMERICA & C AMERICA • 250 kW
	OMAN	
	RADIO OMAN, Sīb	MIDEAST & N AFRICA • DS • 100 kW
		(D) • MIDEAST & N AFRICA • DS • 100 kW
		Irr • MIDEAST & N AFRICA • DS-RAMADAN • 100 kW
	UNITED KINGDOM	
	†BBC WORLD SERVICE, Via Zyyi, Cyprus	MIDEAST • 100 kW
	USA	
	VOA, Via Kaválla, Greece	(D) • USSR • 250 kW
	†WYFR-FAMILY RADIO, Okeechobee, Fl	C AMERICA • 50 kW C AMERICA • 100 kW

ENGLISH ▬   ARABIC ▓   CHINESE ⊡⊡⊡   FRENCH ▬   GERMAN ▬   RUSSIAN ═   SPANISH ▬   OTHER ▬

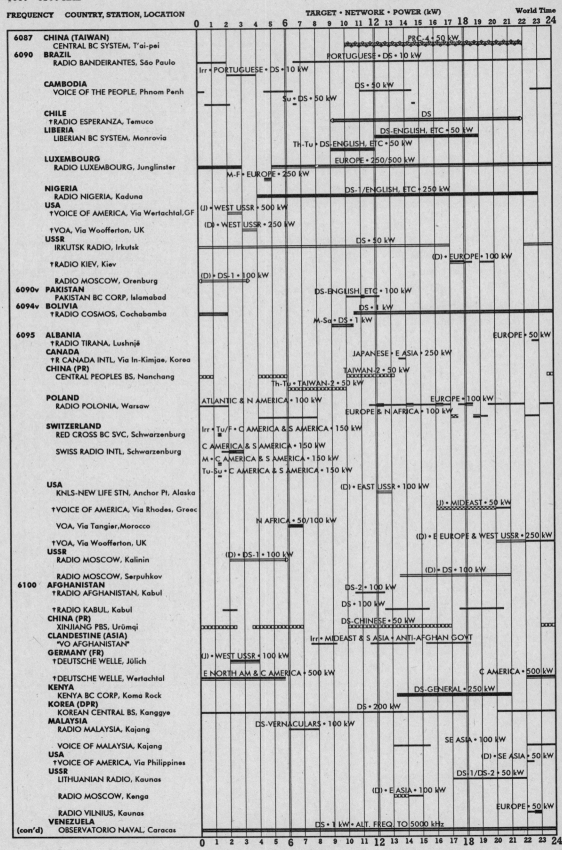

FREQUENCY   COUNTRY, STATION, LOCATION

TARGET • NETWORK • POWER (kW)   World Time

6087   **CHINA (TAIWAN)**
      CENTRAL BC SYSTEM, T'ai-pei
                                     PRC-4 • 50 kW

6090   **BRAZIL**
      RADIO BANDEIRANTES, São Paulo   PORTUGUESE • DS • 10 kW
          Irr • PORTUGUESE • DS • 10 kW

      CAMBODIA
      VOICE OF THE PEOPLE, Phnom Penh   DS • 50 kW
                              Su • DS • 50 kW

      CHILE
      †RADIO ESPERANZA, Temuco   DS
      LIBERIA
      LIBERIAN BC SYSTEM, Monrovia   DS-ENGLISH, ETC • 50 kW
                    Th-Tu • DS-ENGLISH, ETC • 50 kW

      LUXEMBOURG
      RADIO LUXEMBOURG, Junglinster   EUROPE • 250/500 kW
            M-F • EUROPE • 250 kW

      NIGERIA
      RADIO NIGERIA, Kaduna   DS-1/ENGLISH, ETC • 250 kW
      USA
      †VOICE OF AMERICA, Via Wertachtal, GF   (J) • WEST USSR • 500 kW

      †VOA, Via Woofferton, UK   (D) • WEST USSR • 250 kW
      USSR
      IRKUTSK RADIO, Irkutsk   DS • 50 kW

      †RADIO KIEV, Kiev   (D) • EUROPE • 100 kW

      RADIO MOSCOW, Orenburg   (D) • DS-1 • 100 kW
6090v **PAKISTAN**
      PAKISTAN BC CORP, Islamabad   DS-ENGLISH, ETC • 100 kW
6094v **BOLIVIA**
      †RADIO COSMOS, Cochabamba   DS • 1 kW
                        M-Sa • DS • 1 kW

6095 **ALBANIA**
      †RADIO TIRANA, Lushnjë   EUROPE • 50 kW
      CANADA
      †R CANADA INTL, Via In-Kimjae, Korea   JAPANESE • E ASIA • 250 kW
      CHINA (PR)
      CENTRAL PEOPLES BS, Nanchang   TAIWAN-2 • 50 kW
                     Th-Tu • TAIWAN-2 • 50 kW

      POLAND
      RADIO POLONIA, Warsaw   ATLANTIC & N AMERICA • 100 kW   EUROPE • 100 kW
                           EUROPE & N AFRICA • 100 kW

      SWITZERLAND
      RED CROSS BC SVC, Schwarzenburg   Irr • Tu/F • C AMERICA & S AMERICA • 150 kW

      SWISS RADIO INTL, Schwarzenburg   C AMERICA & S AMERICA • 150 kW
                        M • C AMERICA & S AMERICA • 150 kW
                        Tu-Su • C AMERICA & S AMERICA • 150 kW

      USA
      KNLS-NEW LIFE STN, Anchor Pt, Alaska   (D) • EAST USSR • 100 kW

      †VOICE OF AMERICA, Via Rhodes, Greec   (J) • MIDEAST • 50 kW

      VOA, Via Tangier, Morocco   N AFRICA • 50/100 kW

      †VOA, Via Woofferton, UK   (D) • E EUROPE & WEST USSR • 250 kW
      USSR
      RADIO MOSCOW, Kalinin   (D) • DS-1 • 100 kW

      RADIO MOSCOW, Serpuhkov   (D) • DS • 100 kW
6100 **AFGHANISTAN**
      †RADIO AFGHANISTAN, Kabul   DS-2 • 100 kW

      †RADIO KABUL, Kabul   DS • 100 kW
      CHINA (PR)
      XINJIANG PBS, Urümqi   DS-CHINESE • 50 kW
      CLANDESTINE (ASIA)
      "VO AFGHANISTAN"   Irr • MIDEAST & S ASIA • ANTI-AFGHAN GOVT
      GERMANY (FR)
      †DEUTSCHE WELLE, Jülich   (J) • WEST USSR • 100 kW

      †DEUTSCHE WELLE, Wertachtal   E NORTH AM & C AMERICA • 500 kW   C AMERICA • 500 kW
      KENYA
      KENYA BC CORP, Koma Rock   DS-GENERAL • 250 kW
      KOREA (DPR)
      KOREAN CENTRAL BS, Kanggye   DS • 200 kW
      MALAYSIA
      RADIO MALAYSIA, Kajang   DS-VERNACULARS • 100 kW

      VOICE OF MALAYSIA, Kajang   SE ASIA • 100 kW
      USA
      †VOICE OF AMERICA, Via Philippines   (D) • SE ASIA • 50 kW
      USSR
      LITHUANIAN RADIO, Kaunas   DS-1/DS-2 • 50 kW

      RADIO MOSCOW, Kenga   (D) • E ASIA • 100 kW

      RADIO VILNIUS, Kaunas   EUROPE • 50 kW
      VENEZUELA
(con'd)   OBSERVATORIO NAVAL, Caracas   DS • 1 kW • ALT. FREQ. TO 5000 kHz

FREQUENCY   COUNTRY, STATION, LOCATION

TARGET • NETWORK • POWER (kW)

World Time

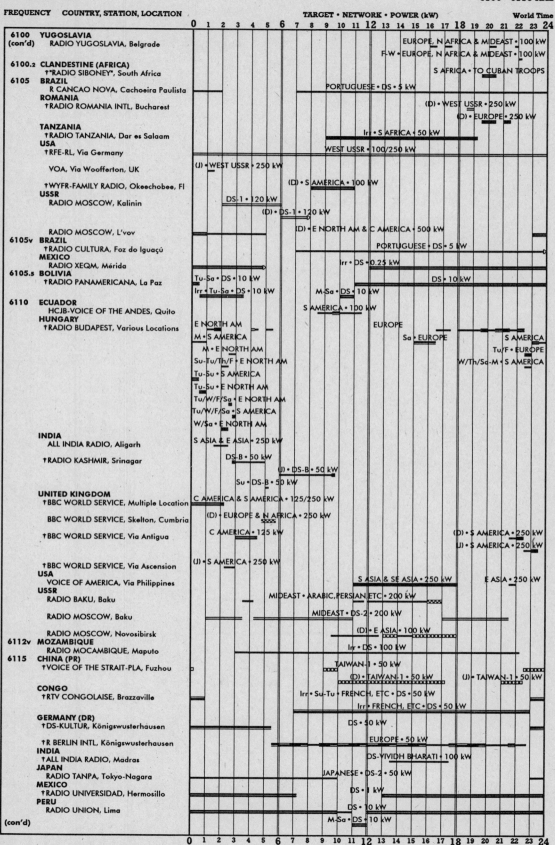

Frequency	Country, Station, Location	Target • Network • Power
6100 (con'd)	YUGOSLAVIA RADIO YUGOSLAVIA, Belgrade	EUROPE, N AFRICA & MIDEAST • 100 kW F-W • EUROPE, N AFRICA & MIDEAST • 100 kW
6100.2	CLANDESTINE (AFRICA) †"RADIO SIBONEY", South Africa	S AFRICA • TO CUBAN TROOPS
6105	BRAZIL R CANCAO NOVA, Cachoeira Paulista	PORTUGUESE • DS • 5 kW
	ROMANIA †RADIO ROMANIA INTL, Bucharest	(D) • WEST USSR • 250 kW (D) • EUROPE • 250 kW
	TANZANIA †RADIO TANZANIA, Dar es Salaam	Irr • S AFRICA • 50 kW
	USA †RFE-RL, Via Germany	WEST USSR • 100/250 kW
	VOA, Via Woofferton, UK	(J) • WEST USSR • 250 kW
	†WYFR-FAMILY RADIO, Okeechobee, Fl	(D) • S AMERICA • 100 kW
	USSR RADIO MOSCOW, Kalinin	DS-1 • 120 kW (D) • DS-1 • 120 kW
	RADIO MOSCOW, L'vov	(D) • E NORTH AM & C AMERICA • 500 kW
6105v	BRAZIL †RADIO CULTURA, Foz do Iguaçú	PORTUGUESE • DS • 5 kW
	MEXICO RADIO XEQM, Mérida	Irr • DS • 0.25 kW
6105.5	BOLIVIA †RADIO PANAMERICANA, La Paz	Tu-Sa • DS • 10 kW DS • 10 kW Irr • Tu-Sa • DS • 10 kW M-Sa • DS • 10 kW
6110	ECUADOR HCJB-VOICE OF THE ANDES, Quito	S AMERICA • 100 kW
	HUNGARY †RADIO BUDAPEST, Various Locations	E NORTH AM M • S AMERICA M • E NORTH AM Su-Tu/Th/F • E NORTH AM Tu-Su • S AMERICA Tu-Su • E NORTH AM Tu/W/F/Sa • E NORTH AM Tu/W/F/Sa • S AMERICA W/Sa • E NORTH AM EUROPE Sa • EUROPE Tu/F • EUROPE W/Th/Sa-M • S AMERICA S AMERICA
	INDIA ALL INDIA RADIO, Aligarh	S ASIA & E ASIA • 250 kW
	†RADIO KASHMIR, Srinagar	DS-B • 50 kW (J) • DS-B • 50 kW Su • DS-B • 50 kW
	UNITED KINGDOM †BBC WORLD SERVICE, Multiple Location	C AMERICA & S AMERICA • 125/250 kW
	BBC WORLD SERVICE, Skelton, Cumbria	(D) • EUROPE & N AFRICA • 250 kW
	†BBC WORLD SERVICE, Via Antigua	C AMERICA • 125 kW (D) • S AMERICA • 250 kW (J) • S AMERICA • 250 kW
	†BBC WORLD SERVICE, Via Ascension	(J) • S AMERICA • 250 kW
	USA VOICE OF AMERICA, Via Philippines	S ASIA & SE ASIA • 250 kW E ASIA • 250 kW
	USSR RADIO BAKU, Baku	MIDEAST • ARABIC, PERSIAN, ETC • 200 kW
	RADIO MOSCOW, Baku	MIDEAST • DS-2 • 200 kW
	RADIO MOSCOW, Novosibirsk	(D) • E ASIA • 100 kW
6112v	MOZAMBIQUE RADIO MOCAMBIQUE, Maputo	Irr • DS • 100 kW
6115	CHINA (PR) †VOICE OF THE STRAIT-PLA, Fuzhou	TAIWAN-1 • 50 kW (D) • TAIWAN-1 • 50 kW (J) • TAIWAN-1 • 50 kW
	CONGO †RTV CONGOLAISE, Brazzaville	Irr • Su-Tu • FRENCH, ETC • DS • 50 kW Irr • FRENCH, ETC • DS • 50 kW
	GERMANY (DR) †DS-KULTUR, Königswusterhausen	DS • 50 kW
	†R BERLIN INTL, Königswusterhausen	EUROPE • 50 kW
	INDIA †ALL INDIA RADIO, Madras	DS-VIVIDH BHARATI • 100 kW
	JAPAN RADIO TANPA, Tokyo-Nagara	JAPANESE • DS-2 • 50 kW
	MEXICO †RADIO UNIVERSIDAD, Hermosillo	DS • 1 kW
	PERU RADIO UNION, Lima	DS • 10 kW M-Sa • DS • 10 kW
(con'd)		

ENGLISH ▬   ARABIC ▨   CHINESE ▤   FRENCH ▬   GERMAN ▬   RUSSIAN ═   SPANISH ▬   OTHER ▬

FREQUENCY   COUNTRY, STATION, LOCATION

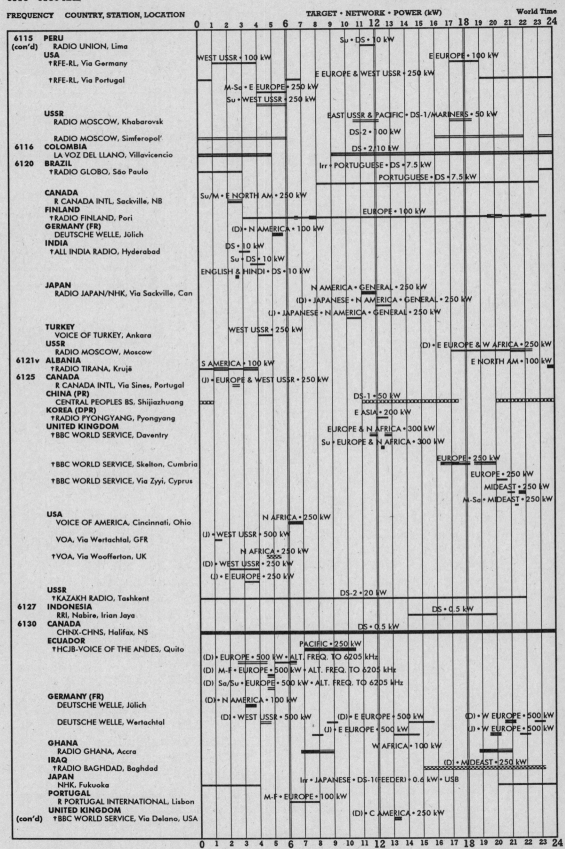

TARGET • NETWORK • POWER (kW)   World Time

6115   PERU
(con'd)   RADIO UNION, Lima   Su • DS • 10 kW
          USA
             †RFE-RL, Via Germany   WEST USSR • 100 kW   E EUROPE • 100 kW

             †RFE-RL, Via Portugal   E EUROPE & WEST USSR • 250 kW

                                             M-Sa • E EUROPE • 250 kW
                                             Su • WEST USSR • 250 kW
          USSR
             RADIO MOSCOW, Khabarovsk   EAST USSR & PACIFIC • DS-1/MARINERS • 50 kW

             RADIO MOSCOW, Simferopol'   DS-2 • 100 kW
6116   COLOMBIA
             LA VOZ DEL LLANO, Villavicencio   DS 2/10 kW
6120   BRAZIL
             †RADIO GLOBO, São Paulo   Irr • PORTUGUESE • DS • 7.5 kW
                                                             PORTUGUESE • DS • 7.5 kW

          CANADA
             R CANADA INTL, Sackville, NB   Su/M • E NORTH AM • 250 kW
          FINLAND
             †RADIO FINLAND, Pori   EUROPE • 100 kW
          GERMANY (FR)
             DEUTSCHE WELLE, Jülich   (D) • N AMERICA • 100 kW
          INDIA
             †ALL INDIA RADIO, Hyderabad   DS • 10 kW
                                                Su • DS • 10 kW
                                             ENGLISH & HINDI • DS • 10 kW

          JAPAN
             RADIO JAPAN/NHK, Via Sackville, Can   N AMERICA • GENERAL • 250 kW
                                                  (D) • JAPANESE • N AMERICA • GENERAL • 250 kW
                                                  (J) • JAPANESE • N AMERICA • GENERAL • 250 kW

          TURKEY
             VOICE OF TURKEY, Ankara   WEST USSR • 250 kW
          USSR
             RADIO MOSCOW, Moscow   (D) • E EUROPE & W AFRICA • 250 kW
6121v   ALBANIA
             †RADIO TIRANA, Krujë   S AMERICA • 100 kW   E NORTH AM • 100 kW
6125   CANADA
             R CANADA INTL, Via Sines, Portugal (J) • EUROPE & WEST USSR • 250 kW
          CHINA (PR)
             CENTRAL PEOPLES BS, Shijiazhuang   DS-1 • 50 kW
          KOREA (DPR)
             †RADIO PYONGYANG, Pyongyang   E ASIA • 200 kW
          UNITED KINGDOM
             †BBC WORLD SERVICE, Daventry   EUROPE & N AFRICA • 300 kW
                                                  Su • EUROPE & N AFRICA • 300 kW

             †BBC WORLD SERVICE, Skelton, Cumbria   EUROPE • 250 kW

             †BBC WORLD SERVICE, Via Zyyi, Cyprus   EUROPE • 250 kW
                                                                 MIDEAST • 250 kW
                                                             M-Sa • MIDEAST • 250 kW

          USA
             VOICE OF AMERICA, Cincinnati, Ohio   N AFRICA • 250 kW

             VOA, Via Wertachtal, GFR   (J) • WEST USSR • 500 kW

             †VOA, Via Woofferton, UK   N AFRICA • 250 kW
                                             (D) • WEST USSR • 250 kW
                                             (J) • E EUROPE • 250 kW

          USSR
             †KAZAKH RADIO, Tashkent   DS-2 • 20 kW
6127   INDONESIA
             RRI, Nabire, Irian Jaya   DS • 0.5 kW
6130   CANADA
             CHNX-CHNS, Halifax, NS   DS • 0.5 kW
          ECUADOR
             †HCJB-VOICE OF THE ANDES, Quito   PACIFIC • 250 kW
                                             (D) • EUROPE • 500 kW • ALT. FREQ. TO 6205 kHz
                                             (D) • M-F • EUROPE • 500 kW • ALT. FREQ. TO 6205 kHz
                                             (D) • Sa/Su • EUROPE • 500 kW • ALT. FREQ. TO 6205 kHz

          GERMANY (FR)
             DEUTSCHE WELLE, Jülich   (D) • N AMERICA • 100 kW

             DEUTSCHE WELLE, Wertachtal   (D) • WEST USSR • 500 kW   (D) • E EUROPE • 500 kW   (D) • W EUROPE • 500 kW
                                                                        (J) • E EUROPE • 500 kW   (J) • W EUROPE • 500 kW

          GHANA
             RADIO GHANA, Accra   W AFRICA • 100 kW
          IRAQ
             †RADIO BAGHDAD, Baghdad   (D) • MIDEAST • 250 kW
          JAPAN
             NHK, Fukuoka   Irr • JAPANESE • DS-1 (FEEDER) • 0.6 kW • USB
          PORTUGAL
             R PORTUGAL INTERNATIONAL, Lisbon   M-F • EUROPE • 100 kW
          UNITED KINGDOM
(con'd)   †BBC WORLD SERVICE, Via Delano, USA   (D) • C AMERICA • 250 kW

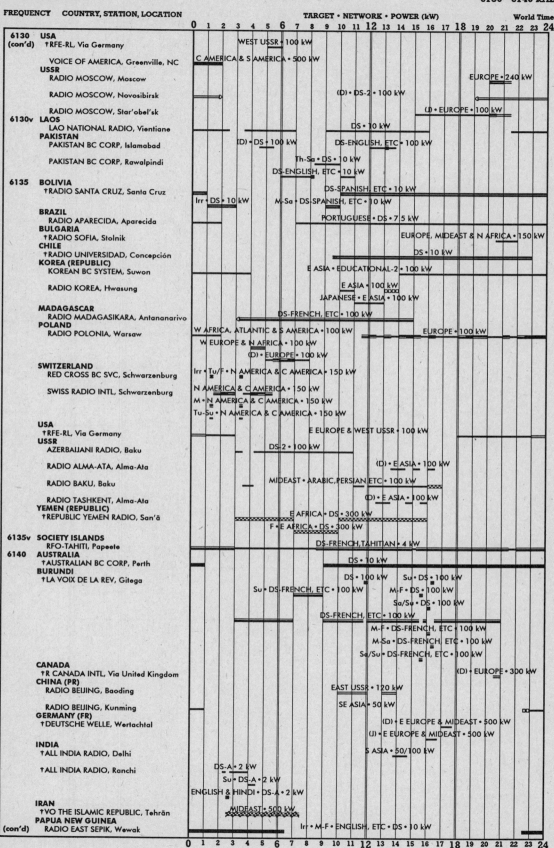

FREQUENCY	COUNTRY, STATION, LOCATION	TARGET • NETWORK • POWER (kW)

6130 (con'd)	USA	
	†RFE-RL, Via Germany	WEST USSR • 100 kW
	VOICE OF AMERICA, Greenville, NC	C AMERICA & S AMERICA • 500 kW
	USSR	
	RADIO MOSCOW, Moscow	EUROPE • 240 kW
	RADIO MOSCOW, Novosibirsk	(D) • DS-2 • 100 kW
	RADIO MOSCOW, Star'obel'sk	(J) • EUROPE • 100 kW
6130v	LAOS	
	LAO NATIONAL RADIO, Vientiane	DS • 10 kW
	PAKISTAN	
	PAKISTAN BC CORP, Islamabad	(D) • DS • 100 kW DS-ENGLISH, ETC • 100 kW
	PAKISTAN BC CORP, Rawalpindi	Th-Sa • DS • 10 kW
		DS-ENGLISH, ETC • 10 kW
6135	BOLIVIA	
	†RADIO SANTA CRUZ, Santa Cruz	DS-SPANISH, ETC • 10 kW
		Irr • DS • 10 kW M-Sa • DS-SPANISH, ETC • 10 kW
	BRAZIL	
	RADIO APARECIDA, Aparecida	PORTUGUESE • DS • 7.5 kW
	BULGARIA	
	†RADIO SOFIA, Stolnik	EUROPE, MIDEAST & N AFRICA • 150 kW
	CHILE	
	†RADIO UNIVERSIDAD, Concepción	DS • 10 kW
	KOREA (REPUBLIC)	
	KOREAN BC SYSTEM, Suwon	E ASIA • EDUCATIONAL-2 • 100 kW
	RADIO KOREA, Hwasung	E ASIA • 100 kW
		JAPANESE • E ASIA • 100 kW
	MADAGASCAR	
	RADIO MADAGASIKARA, Antananarivo	DS-FRENCH, ETC • 100 kW
	POLAND	
	RADIO POLONIA, Warsaw	W AFRICA, ATLANTIC & S AMERICA • 100 kW EUROPE • 100 kW
		W EUROPE & N AFRICA • 100 kW
		(D) • EUROPE • 100 kW
	SWITZERLAND	
	RED CROSS BC SVC, Schwarzenburg	Irr • Tu/F • N AMERICA & C AMERICA • 150 kW
	SWISS RADIO INTL, Schwarzenburg	N AMERICA & C AMERICA • 150 kW
		M • N AMERICA & C AMERICA • 150 kW
		Tu-Su • N AMERICA & C AMERICA • 150 kW
	USA	
	†RFE-RL, Via Germany	E EUROPE & WEST USSR • 100 kW
	USSR	
	AZERBAIJANI RADIO, Baku	DS-2 • 100 kW
	RADIO ALMA-ATA, Alma-Ata	(D) • E ASIA • 100 kW
	RADIO BAKU, Baku	MIDEAST • ARABIC, PERSIAN, ETC • 100 kW
	RADIO TASHKENT, Alma-Ata	(D) • E ASIA • 100 kW
	YEMEN (REPUBLIC)	
	†REPUBLIC YEMEN RADIO, San'ā	E AFRICA • DS • 300 kW
		F • E AFRICA • DS • 300 kW
6135v	SOCIETY ISLANDS	
	RFO-TAHITI, Papeete	DS-FRENCH, TAHITIAN • 4 kW
6140	AUSTRALIA	
	†AUSTRALIAN BC CORP, Perth	DS • 10 kW
	BURUNDI	
	†LA VOIX DE LA REV, Gitega	DS • 100 kW Su • DS • 100 kW
		Su • DS-FRENCH, ETC • 100 kW M-F • DS • 100 kW
		Sa/Su • DS • 100 kW
		DS-FRENCH, ETC • 100 kW
		M-F • DS-FRENCH, ETC • 100 kW
		M-Sa • DS-FRENCH, ETC • 100 kW
		Sa/Su • DS-FRENCH, ETC • 100 kW
	CANADA	
	†R CANADA INTL, Via United Kingdom	(D) • EUROPE • 300 kW
	CHINA (PR)	
	RADIO BEIJING, Baoding	EAST USSR • 120 kW
	RADIO BEIJING, Kunming	SE ASIA • 50 kW
	GERMANY (FR)	
	†DEUTSCHE WELLE, Wertachtal	(D) • E EUROPE & MIDEAST • 500 kW
		(J) • E EUROPE & MIDEAST • 500 kW
	INDIA	
	†ALL INDIA RADIO, Delhi	S ASIA • 50/100 kW
	†ALL INDIA RADIO, Ranchi	DS-A • 2 kW
		Su • DS-A • 2 kW
		ENGLISH & HINDI • DS-A • 2 kW
	IRAN	
	†VO THE ISLAMIC REPUBLIC, Tehrān	MIDEAST • 500 kW
	PAPUA NEW GUINEA	
(con'd)	RADIO EAST SEPIK, Wewak	Irr • M-F • ENGLISH, ETC • DS • 10 kW

ENGLISH ▬   ARABIC ▨▨   CHINESE ▫▫▫   FRENCH ▭▭   GERMAN ▬▬   RUSSIAN ══   SPANISH ▬▬   OTHER ▭

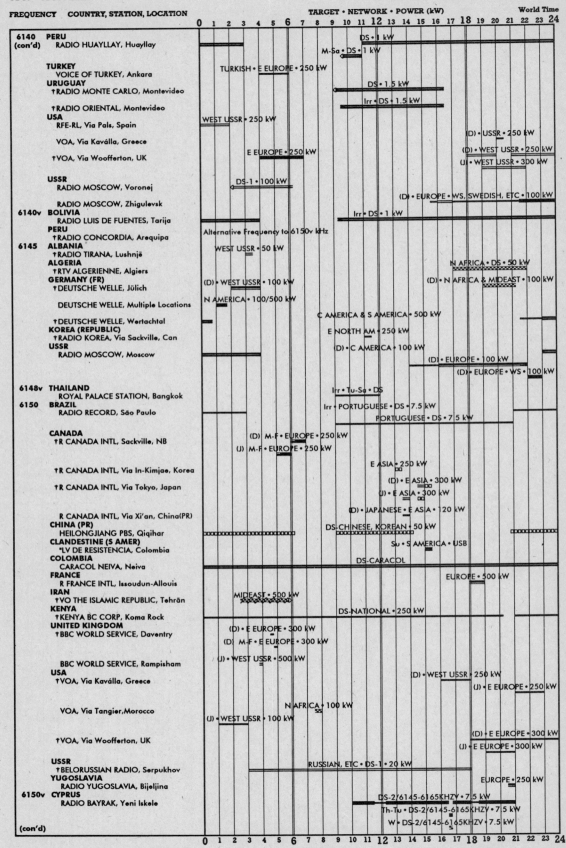

FREQUENCY   COUNTRY, STATION, LOCATION

TARGET • NETWORK • POWER (kW)   World Time

Frequency	Country, Station, Location	Details
6140 (con'd)	**PERU** — RADIO HUAYLLAY, Huayllay	DS • 1 kW / M-Sa • DS • 1 kW
	TURKEY — VOICE OF TURKEY, Ankara	TURKISH • E EUROPE • 250 kW
	URUGUAY — †RADIO MONTE CARLO, Montevideo	DS • 1.5 kW
	†RADIO ORIENTAL, Montevideo	Irr • DS • 1.5 kW
	USA — RFE-RL, Via Pals, Spain	WEST USSR • 250 kW / (D) • USSR • 250 kW
	VOA, Via Kaválla, Greece	E EUROPE • 250 kW / (D) • WEST USSR • 250 kW
	†VOA, Via Woofferton, UK	(J) • WEST USSR • 300 kW
	USSR — RADIO MOSCOW, Voronej	DS-1 • 100 kW
	RADIO MOSCOW, Zhigulevsk	(D) • EUROPE • WS, SWEDISH, ETC • 100 kW
6140v	**BOLIVIA** — RADIO LUIS DE FUENTES, Tarija	Irr • DS • 1 kW
	PERU — †RADIO CONCORDIA, Arequipa	Alternative Frequency to 6150v kHz
6145	**ALBANIA** — †RADIO TIRANA, Lushnjë	WEST USSR • 50 kW
	ALGERIA — †RTV ALGERIENNE, Algiers	N AFRICA • DS • 50 kW
	GERMANY (FR) — †DEUTSCHE WELLE, Jülich	(D) • WEST USSR • 100 kW / (D) • N AFRICA & MIDEAST • 100 kW
	DEUTSCHE WELLE, Multiple Locations	N AMERICA • 100/500 kW
	†DEUTSCHE WELLE, Wertachtal	C AMERICA & S AMERICA • 500 kW
	KOREA (REPUBLIC) — †RADIO KOREA, Via Sackville, Can	E NORTH AM • 250 kW
	USSR — RADIO MOSCOW, Moscow	(D) • C AMERICA • 100 kW / (D) • EUROPE • 100 kW / (D) • EUROPE • WS • 100 kW
6148v	**THAILAND** — ROYAL PALACE STATION, Bangkok	Irr • Tu-Sa • DS
6150	**BRAZIL** — RADIO RECORD, São Paulo	Irr • PORTUGUESE • DS • 7.5 kW / PORTUGUESE • DS • 7.5 kW
	CANADA — †R CANADA INTL, Sackville, NB	(D) M-F • EUROPE • 250 kW / (J) M-F • EUROPE • 250 kW
	†R CANADA INTL, Via In-Kimjae, Korea	E ASIA • 250 kW
	†R CANADA INTL, Via Tokyo, Japan	(D) • E ASIA • 300 kW / (J) • E ASIA • 300 kW
	R CANADA INTL, Via Xi'an, China(PR)	(D) • JAPANESE • E ASIA • 120 kW
	CHINA (PR) — HEILONGJIANG PBS, Qiqihar	DS-CHINESE, KOREAN • 50 kW
	CLANDESTINE (S AMER) — *LV DE RESISTENCIA, Colombia	Su • S AMERICA • USB
	COLOMBIA — CARACOL NEIVA, Neiva	DS-CARACOL
	FRANCE — R FRANCE INTL, Issoudun-Allouis	EUROPE • 500 kW
	IRAN — †VO THE ISLAMIC REPUBLIC, Tehrān	MIDEAST • 500 kW
	KENYA — †KENYA BC CORP, Koma Rock	DS-NATIONAL • 250 kW
	UNITED KINGDOM — †BBC WORLD SERVICE, Daventry	(D) • E EUROPE • 300 kW / (D) M-F • E EUROPE • 300 kW
	BBC WORLD SERVICE, Rampisham	(J) • WEST USSR • 500 kW
	USA — †VOA, Via Kaválla, Greece	(D) • WEST USSR • 250 kW / (J) • E EUROPE • 250 kW
	VOA, Via Tangier, Morocco	N AFRICA • 100 kW / (J) • WEST USSR • 100 kW
	†VOA, Via Woofferton, UK	(D) • E EUROPE • 300 kW / (J) • E EUROPE • 300 kW
	USSR — †BELORUSSIAN RADIO, Serpukhov	RUSSIAN, ETC • DS-1 • 20 kW
	YUGOSLAVIA — RADIO YUGOSLAVIA, Bijeljina	EUROPE • 250 kW
6150v	**CYPRUS** — RADIO BAYRAK, Yeni Iskele	DS-2/6145-6165KHZV • 7.5 kW / Th-Tu • DS-2/6145-6165KHZV • 7.5 kW / W • DS-2/6145-6165KHZV • 7.5 kW

(con'd)

SUMMER ONLY (J)   WINTER ONLY (D)   JAMMING / OR ∧   EARLIEST HEARD ◁   LATEST HEARD ▷   NEW OR CHANGED FOR 1991 †

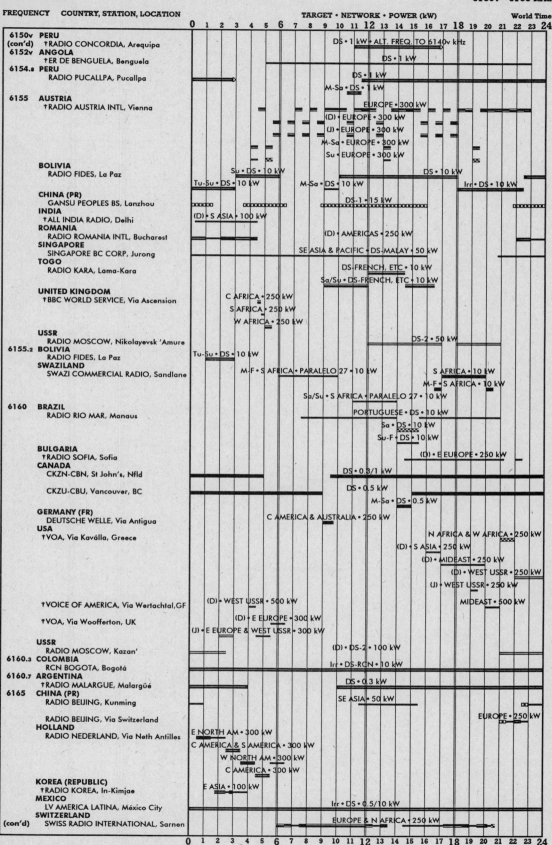

FREQUENCY   COUNTRY, STATION, LOCATION   TARGET • NETWORK • POWER (kW)   World Time

0 1 2 3 4 5 6 7 8 9 10 11 12 13 14 15 16 17 18 19 20 21 22 23 24

6150v   PERU
(con'd)   †RADIO CONCORDIA, Arequipa — DS • 1 kW • ALT. FREQ. TO 6140v kHz
6152v   ANGOLA
           †ER DE BENGUELA, Benguela — DS • 1 kW
6154.8 PERU
           RADIO PUCALLPA, Pucallpa — DS • 1 kW
           M-Sa • DS • 1 kW
6155   AUSTRIA
           †RADIO AUSTRIA INTL, Vienna — EUROPE • 300 kW
           (D) EUROPE • 300 kW
           (J) EUROPE • 300 kW
           M-Sa • EUROPE • 300 kW
           Su • EUROPE • 300 kW

           BOLIVIA
           RADIO FIDES, La Paz — Su • DS • 10 kW / DS • 10 kW
           Tu-Su • DS • 10 kW   M-Sa • DS • 10 kW   Irr • DS • 10 kW

           CHINA (PR)
           GANSU PEOPLES BS, Lanzhou — DS-1 • 15 kW
           INDIA
           †ALL INDIA RADIO, Delhi — (D) • S ASIA • 100 kW
           ROMANIA
           RADIO ROMANIA INTL, Bucharest — (D) • AMERICAS • 250 kW
           SINGAPORE
           SINGAPORE BC CORP, Jurong — SE ASIA & PACIFIC • DS-MALAY • 50 kW
           TOGO
           RADIO KARA, Lama-Kara — DS-FRENCH, ETC • 10 kW
           Sa/Su • DS-FRENCH, ETC • 10 kW

           UNITED KINGDOM
           †BBC WORLD SERVICE, Via Ascension — C AFRICA • 250 kW
           S AFRICA • 250 kW
           W AFRICA • 250 kW

           USSR
           RADIO MOSCOW, Nikolayevsk 'Amure — DS-2 • 50 kW
6155.2 BOLIVIA
           RADIO FIDES, La Paz — Tu-Su • DS • 10 kW
           SWAZILAND
           SWAZI COMMERCIAL RADIO, Sandlane — M-F • S AFRICA • PARALELO 27 • 10 kW   S AFRICA • 10 kW
           M-F • S AFRICA • 10 kW
           Sa/Su • S AFRICA • PARALELO 27 • 10 kW
6160   BRAZIL
           RADIO RIO MAR, Manaus — PORTUGUESE • DS • 10 kW
           Sa • DS • 10 kW
           Su-F • DS • 10 kW

           BULGARIA
           †RADIO SOFIA, Sofia — (D) • E EUROPE • 250 kW
           CANADA
           CKZN-CBN, St John's, Nfld — DS • 0.3/1 kW

           CKZU-CBU, Vancouver, BC — DS • 0.5 kW
           M-Sa • DS • 0.5 kW

           GERMANY (FR)
           DEUTSCHE WELLE, Via Antigua — C AMERICA & AUSTRALIA • 250 kW
           USA
           †VOA, Via Kaválla, Greece — N AFRICA & W AFRICA • 250 kW
           (D) • S ASIA • 250 kW
           (D) • MIDEAST • 250 kW
           (D) • WEST USSR • 250 kW
           (J) • WEST USSR • 250 kW

           †VOICE OF AMERICA, Via Wertachtal, GF — (D) • WEST USSR • 500 kW   MIDEAST • 500 kW

           †VOA, Via Woofferton, UK — (D) • E EUROPE • 300 kW
           (J) • E EUROPE & WEST USSR • 300 kW

           USSR
           RADIO MOSCOW, Kazan' — (D) • DS-2 • 100 kW
6160.3 COLOMBIA
           RCN BOGOTA, Bogotá — Irr • DS-RCN • 10 kW
6160.7 ARGENTINA
           †RADIO MALARGUE, Malargüe — DS • 0.3 kW
6165   CHINA (PR)
           RADIO BEIJING, Kunming — SE ASIA • 50 kW

           RADIO BEIJING, Via Switzerland — EUROPE • 250 kW
           HOLLAND
           RADIO NEDERLAND, Via Neth Antilles — E NORTH AM • 300 kW
           C AMERICA & S AMERICA • 300 kW
           W NORTH AM • 300 kW
           C AMERICA • 300 kW

           KOREA (REPUBLIC)
           †RADIO KOREA, In-Kimjae — E ASIA • 100 kW
           MEXICO
           LV AMERICA LATINA, México City — Irr • DS • 0.5/10 kW
           SWITZERLAND
(con'd)   SWISS RADIO INTERNATIONAL, Sarnen — EUROPE & N AFRICA • 250 kW

0 1 2 3 4 5 6 7 8 9 10 11 12 13 14 15 16 17 18 19 20 21 22 23 24

ENGLISH ▬   ARABIC ≋   CHINESE ▭▭▭   FRENCH ═   GERMAN ▬▬   RUSSIAN ══   SPANISH ▬▬▬   OTHER ──

| FREQUENCY | COUNTRY, STATION, LOCATION | TARGET • NETWORK • POWER (kW) | World Time |

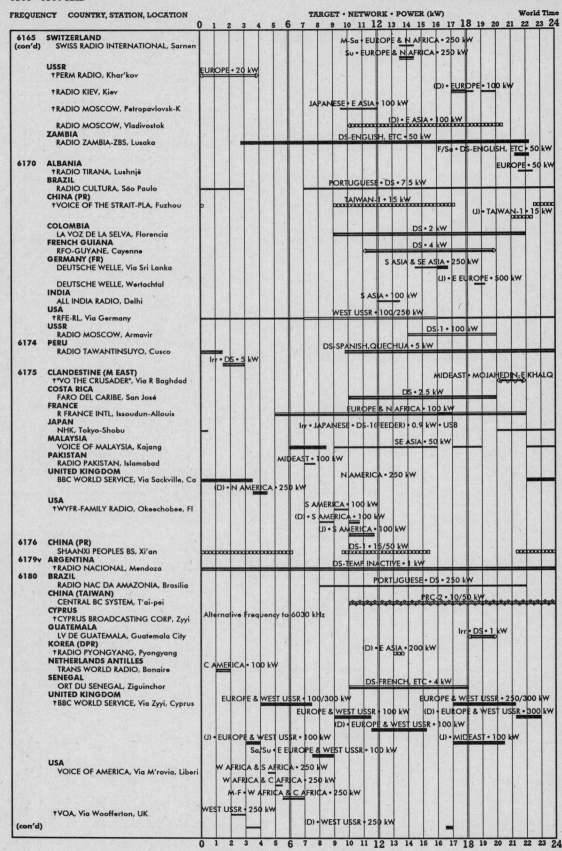

6165 (con'd) SWITZERLAND — SWISS RADIO INTERNATIONAL, Sarnen — M-Sa • EUROPE & N AFRICA • 250 kW / Su • EUROPE & N AFRICA • 250 kW

USSR — †PERM RADIO, Khar'kov — EUROPE • 20 kW

†RADIO KIEV, Kiev — (D) • EUROPE • 100 kW

†RADIO MOSCOW, Petropavlovsk-K — JAPANESE • E ASIA • 100 kW

RADIO MOSCOW, Vladivostok — (D) • E ASIA • 100 kW

ZAMBIA — RADIO ZAMBIA-ZBS, Lusaka — DS-ENGLISH, ETC • 50 kW / F/Sa • DS-ENGLISH, ETC • 50 kW

6170 ALBANIA — †RADIO TIRANA, Lushnjë — EUROPE • 50 kW

BRAZIL — RADIO CULTURA, São Paulo — PORTUGUESE • DS • 7.5 kW

CHINA (PR) — †VOICE OF THE STRAIT-PLA, Fuzhou — TAIWAN-1 • 15 kW / (J) • TAIWAN-1 • 15 kW

COLOMBIA — LA VOZ DE LA SELVA, Florencia — DS • 2 kW

FRENCH GUIANA — RFO-GUYANE, Cayenne — DS • 4 kW

GERMANY (FR) — DEUTSCHE WELLE, Via Sri Lanka — S ASIA & SE ASIA • 250 kW

DEUTSCHE WELLE, Wertachtal — (J) • E EUROPE • 500 kW

INDIA — ALL INDIA RADIO, Delhi — S ASIA • 100 kW

USA — †RFE-RL, Via Germany — WEST USSR • 100/250 kW

USSR — RADIO MOSCOW, Armavir — DS-1 • 100 kW

6174 PERU — RADIO TAWANTINSUYO, Cusco — DS-SPANISH, QUECHUA • 5 kW / Irr • DS • 5 kW

6175 CLANDESTINE (M EAST) — †"VO THE CRUSADER", Via R Baghdad — MIDEAST • MOJAHEDIN-E KHALQ

COSTA RICA — FARO DEL CARIBE, San José — DS • 2.5 kW

FRANCE — R FRANCE INTL, Issoudun-Allouis — EUROPE & N AFRICA • 100 kW

JAPAN — NHK, Tokyo-Shobu — Irr • JAPANESE • DS-1 (FEEDER) • 0.9 kW • USB

MALAYSIA — VOICE OF MALAYSIA, Kajang — SE ASIA • 50 kW

PAKISTAN — RADIO PAKISTAN, Islamabad — MIDEAST • 100 kW

UNITED KINGDOM — BBC WORLD SERVICE, Via Sackville, Ca — N AMERICA • 250 kW / (D) • N AMERICA • 250 kW

USA — †WYFR-FAMILY RADIO, Okeechobee, Fl — S AMERICA • 100 kW / (D) • S AMERICA • 100 kW / (J) • S AMERICA • 100 kW

6176 CHINA (PR) — SHAANXI PEOPLES BS, Xi'an — DS-1 • 15/50 kW

6179v ARGENTINA — †RADIO NACIONAL, Mendoza — DS-TEMP INACTIVE • 1 kW

6180 BRAZIL — RADIO NAC DA AMAZONIA, Brasilia — PORTUGUESE • DS • 250 kW

CHINA (TAIWAN) — CENTRAL BC SYSTEM, T'ai-pei — PRC-2 • 10/50 kW

CYPRUS — †CYPRUS BROADCASTING CORP, Zyyi — Alternative Frequency to 6030 kHz

GUATEMALA — LV DE GUATEMALA, Guatemala City — Irr • DS • 1 kW

KOREA (DPR) — †RADIO PYONGYANG, Pyongyang — (D) • E ASIA • 200 kW

NETHERLANDS ANTILLES — TRANS WORLD RADIO, Bonaire — C AMERICA • 100 kW

SENEGAL — ORT DU SENEGAL, Ziguinchor — DS-FRENCH, ETC • 4 kW

UNITED KINGDOM — †BBC WORLD SERVICE, Via Zyyi, Cyprus — EUROPE & WEST USSR • 100/300 kW / EUROPE & WEST USSR • 250/300 kW / EUROPE & WEST USSR • 100 kW / (D) • EUROPE & WEST USSR • 300 kW / (D) • EUROPE & WEST USSR • 100 kW / (J) • EUROPE & WEST USSR • 100 kW / (J) • MIDEAST • 100 kW / Sa/Su • E EUROPE & WEST USSR • 100 kW

USA — VOICE OF AMERICA, Via M'rovia, Liberi — W AFRICA & S AFRICA • 250 kW / W AFRICA & C AFRICA • 250 kW / M-F • W AFRICA & C AFRICA • 250 kW

†VOA, Via Woofferton, UK — WEST USSR • 250 kW / (D) • WEST USSR • 250 kW

(con'd)

FREQUENCY COUNTRY, STATION, LOCATION — TARGET • NETWORK • POWER (kW) — World Time

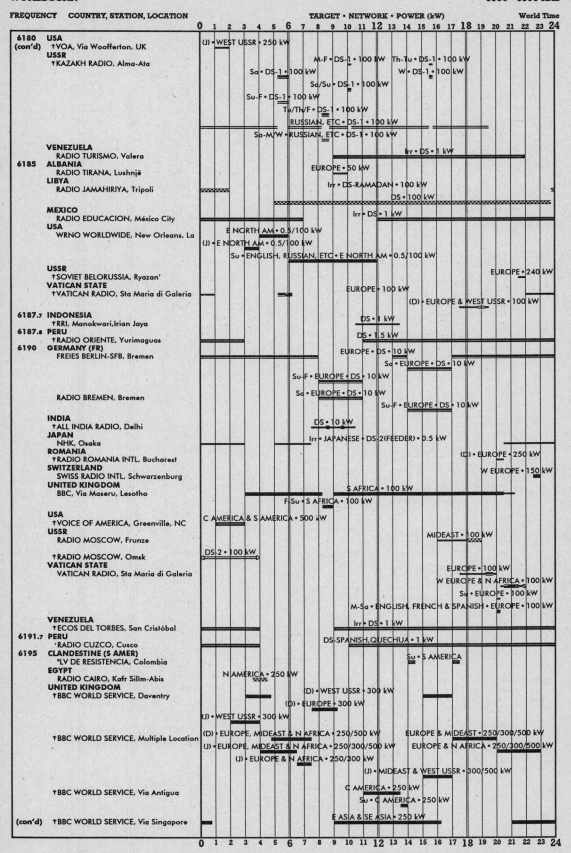

Frequency	Country, Station, Location
6180 (con'd)	**USA** — †VOA, Via Woofferton, UK
	USSR — †KAZAKH RADIO, Alma-Ata
	VENEZUELA — RADIO TURISMO, Valera
6185	**ALBANIA** — RADIO TIRANA, Lushnjë
	LIBYA — RADIO JAMAHIRIYA, Tripoli
	MEXICO — RADIO EDUCACION, México City
	USA — WRNO WORLDWIDE, New Orleans, La
	USSR — †SOVIET BELORUSSIA, Ryazan'
	VATICAN STATE — †VATICAN RADIO, Sta Maria di Galeria
6187.7	**INDONESIA** — †RRI, Manokwari, Irian Jaya
6187.8	**PERU** — †RADIO ORIENTE, Yurimaguas
6190	**GERMANY (FR)** — FREIES BERLIN-SFB, Bremen
	RADIO BREMEN, Bremen
	INDIA — †ALL INDIA RADIO, Delhi
	JAPAN — NHK, Osaka
	ROMANIA — †RADIO ROMANIA INTL, Bucharest
	SWITZERLAND — SWISS RADIO INTL, Schwarzenburg
	UNITED KINGDOM — BBC, Via Maseru, Lesotho
	USA — †VOICE OF AMERICA, Greenville, NC
	USSR — RADIO MOSCOW, Frunze
	†RADIO MOSCOW, Omsk
	VATICAN STATE — VATICAN RADIO, Sta Maria di Galeria
	VENEZUELA — †ECOS DEL TORBES, San Cristóbal
6191.7	**PERU** — ·RADIO CUZCO, Cusco
6195	**CLANDESTINE (S AMER)** — "LV DE RESISTENCIA, Colombia
	EGYPT — RADIO CAIRO, Kafr Silim-Abis
	UNITED KINGDOM — †BBC WORLD SERVICE, Daventry
	†BBC WORLD SERVICE, Multiple Location
	†BBC WORLD SERVICE, Via Antigua
(con'd)	†BBC WORLD SERVICE, Via Singapore

Bar chart entries (TARGET • NETWORK • POWER):

- (J) • WEST USSR • 250 kW
- M-F • DS-1 • 100 kW / Th-Tu • DS-1 • 100 kW
- Sa • DS-1 • 100 kW / W • DS-1 • 100 kW
- Sa/Su • DS-1 • 100 kW
- Su-F • DS-1 • 100 kW
- Tu/Th/F • DS-1 • 100 kW
- RUSSIAN, ETC • DS-1 • 100 kW
- Sa-M/W • RUSSIAN, ETC • DS-1 • 100 kW
- Irr • DS • 1 kW
- EUROPE • 50 kW
- Irr • DS-RAMADAN • 100 kW
- DS • 100 kW
- Irr • DS • 1 kW
- E NORTH AM • 0.5/100 kW
- (J) • E NORTH AM • 0.5/100 kW
- Su • ENGLISH, RUSSIAN, ETC • E NORTH AM • 0.5/100 kW
- EUROPE • 240 kW
- EUROPE • 100 kW
- (D) • EUROPE & WEST USSR • 100 kW
- DS • 1 kW
- DS • 1.5 kW
- EUROPE • DS • 10 kW
- Sa • EUROPE • DS • 10 kW
- Su-F • EUROPE • DS • 10 kW
- Sa • EUROPE • DS • 10 kW
- Su-F • EUROPE • DS • 10 kW
- DS • 10 kW
- Irr • JAPANESE • DS-2 (FEEDER) • 0.5 kW
- (D) • EUROPE • 250 kW
- W EUROPE • 150 kW
- S AFRICA • 100 kW
- F-Su • S AFRICA • 100 kW
- C AMERICA & S AMERICA • 500 kW
- MIDEAST • 100 kW
- DS-2 • 100 kW
- EUROPE • 100 kW
- W EUROPE & N AFRICA • 100 kW
- Su • EUROPE • 100 kW
- M-Sa • ENGLISH, FRENCH & SPANISH • EUROPE • 100 kW
- Irr • DS • 1 kW
- DS-SPANISH, QUECHUA • 1 kW
- Su • S AMERICA
- N AMERICA • 250 kW
- (D) • WEST USSR • 300 kW
- (D) • EUROPE • 300 kW
- (J) • WEST USSR • 300 kW
- (D) • EUROPE, MIDEAST & N AFRICA • 250/500 kW / EUROPE & MIDEAST • 250/300/500 kW
- (J) • EUROPE, MIDEAST & N AFRICA • 250/300/500 kW / EUROPE & N AFRICA • 250/300/500 kW
- (J) • EUROPE & N AFRICA • 250/300 kW
- (J) • MIDEAST & WEST USSR • 300/500 kW
- C AMERICA • 250 kW
- Su • C AMERICA • 250 kW
- E ASIA & SE ASIA • 250 kW

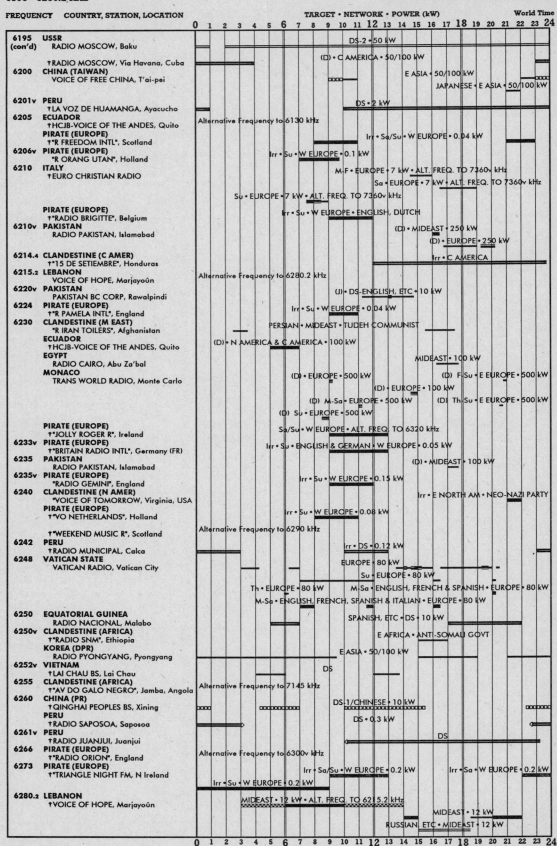

FREQUENCY	COUNTRY, STATION, LOCATION	TARGET • NETWORK • POWER (kW)
6195 (con'd)	USSR RADIO MOSCOW, Baku	DS-2 • 50 kW
	†RADIO MOSCOW, Via Havana, Cuba	(D) • C AMERICA • 50/100 kW
6200	CHINA (TAIWAN) VOICE OF FREE CHINA, T'ai-pei	E ASIA • 50/100 kW JAPANESE • E ASIA • 50/100 kW
6201v	PERU †LA VOZ DE HUAMANGA, Ayacucho	DS • 2 kW
6205	ECUADOR †HCJB-VOICE OF THE ANDES, Quito	Alternative Frequency to 6130 kHz
	PIRATE (EUROPE) †"R FREEDOM INTL", Scotland	Irr • Sa/Su • W EUROPE • 0.04 kW
6206v	PIRATE (EUROPE) "R ORANG UTAN", Holland	Irr • Su • W EUROPE • 0.1 kW
6210	ITALY †EURO CHRISTIAN RADIO	M-F • EUROPE • 7 kW • ALT. FREQ. TO 7360v kHz Sa • EUROPE • 7 kW • ALT. FREQ. TO 7360v kHz Su • EUROPE • 7 kW • ALT. FREQ. TO 7360v kHz
	PIRATE (EUROPE) †"RADIO BRIGITTE", Belgium	Irr • Su • W EUROPE • ENGLISH, DUTCH
6210v	PAKISTAN RADIO PAKISTAN, Islamabad	(D) • MIDEAST • 250 kW (D) • EUROPE • 250 kW
6214.4	CLANDESTINE (C AMER) †"15 DE SETIEMBRE", Honduras	Irr • C AMERICA
6215.2	LEBANON VOICE OF HOPE, Marjayoûn	Alternative Frequency to 6280.2 kHz
6220v	PAKISTAN PAKISTAN BC CORP, Rawalpindi	(J) • DS-ENGLISH, ETC • 10 kW
6224	PIRATE (EUROPE) †"R PAMELA INTL", England	Irr • Su • W EUROPE • 0.04 kW
6230	CLANDESTINE (M EAST) "R IRAN TOILERS", Afghanistan	PERSIAN • MIDEAST • TUDEH COMMUNIST
	ECUADOR †HCJB-VOICE OF THE ANDES, Quito	(D) • N AMERICA & C AMERICA • 100 kW
	EGYPT RADIO CAIRO, Abu Za'bal	MIDEAST • 100 kW
	MONACO TRANS WORLD RADIO, Monte Carlo	(D) • EUROPE • 500 kW (D) • F-Su • E EUROPE • 500 kW (D) • EUROPE • 100 kW (D) M-Sa • EUROPE • 500 kW (D) Th-Su • E EUROPE • 500 kW (D) Su • EUROPE • 500 kW
	PIRATE (EUROPE) †"JOLLY ROGER R", Ireland	Sa/Su • W EUROPE • ALT. FREQ. TO 6320 kHz
6233v	PIRATE (EUROPE) †"BRITAIN RADIO INTL", Germany (FR)	Irr • Su • ENGLISH & GERMAN • W EUROPE • 0.05 kW
6235	PAKISTAN RADIO PAKISTAN, Islamabad	(D) • MIDEAST • 100 kW
6235v	PIRATE (EUROPE) "RADIO GEMINI", England	Irr • Su • W EUROPE • 0.15 kW
6240	CLANDESTINE (N AMER) "VOICE OF TOMORROW", Virginia, USA	Irr • E NORTH AM • NEO-NAZI PARTY
	PIRATE (EUROPE) †"VO NETHERLANDS", Holland	Irr • Su • W EUROPE • 0.08 kW
	†"WEEKEND MUSIC R", Scotland	Alternative Frequency to 6290 kHz
6242	PERU †RADIO MUNICIPAL, Calca	Irr • DS • 0.12 kW
6248	VATICAN STATE VATICAN RADIO, Vatican City	EUROPE • 80 kW Su • EUROPE • 80 kW Th • EUROPE • 80 kW M-Sa • ENGLISH, FRENCH & SPANISH • EUROPE • 80 kW M-Sa • ENGLISH, FRENCH, SPANISH & ITALIAN • EUROPE • 80 kW
6250	EQUATORIAL GUINEA RADIO NACIONAL, Malabo	SPANISH, ETC • DS • 10 kW
6250v	CLANDESTINE (AFRICA) †"RADIO SNM", Ethiopia	E AFRICA • ANTI-SOMALI GOVT
	KOREA (DPR) RADIO PYONGYANG, Pyongyang	E ASIA • 50/100 kW
6252v	VIETNAM †LAI CHAU BS, Lai Chau	DS
6255	CLANDESTINE (AFRICA) †"AV DO GALO NEGRO", Jamba, Angola	Alternative Frequency to 7145 kHz
6260	CHINA (PR) †QINGHAI PEOPLES BS, Xining	DS-1/CHINESE • 10 kW
	PERU †RADIO SAPOSOA, Saposoa	DS • 0.3 kW
6261v	PERU †RADIO JUANJUI, Juanjui	DS
6266	PIRATE (EUROPE) †"RADIO ORION", England	Alternative Frequency to 6300v kHz
6273	PIRATE (EUROPE) †"TRIANGLE NIGHT FM", N Ireland	Irr • Sa/Su • W EUROPE • 0.2 kW Irr • Sa • W EUROPE • 0.2 kW Irr • Su • W EUROPE • 0.2 kW
6280.2	LEBANON †VOICE OF HOPE, Marjayoûn	MIDEAST • 12 kW • ALT. FREQ. TO 6215.2 kHz MIDEAST • 12 kW RUSSIAN, ETC • MIDEAST • 12 kW

FREQUENCY	COUNTRY, STATION, LOCATION	TARGET • NETWORK • POWER (kW)	World Time

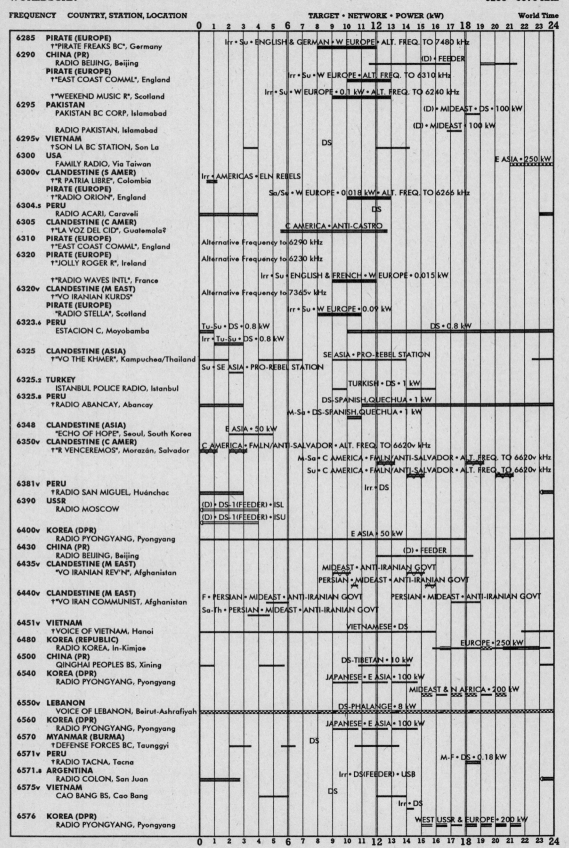

FREQUENCY	COUNTRY, STATION, LOCATION	TARGET • NETWORK • POWER (kW)
6285	PIRATE (EUROPE)	
	†"PIRATE FREAKS BC", Germany	Irr • Su • ENGLISH & GERMAN • W EUROPE • ALT. FREQ. TO 7480 kHz
6290	CHINA (PR)	
	RADIO BEIJING, Beijing	(D) • FEEDER
	PIRATE (EUROPE)	
	†"EAST COAST COMML", England	Irr • Su • W EUROPE • ALT. FREQ. TO 6310 kHz
	†"WEEKEND MUSIC R", Scotland	Irr • Su • W EUROPE • 0.1 kW • ALT. FREQ. TO 6240 kHz
6295	PAKISTAN	
	PAKISTAN BC CORP, Islamabad	(D) • MIDEAST • DS • 100 kW
	RADIO PAKISTAN, Islamabad	(D) • MIDEAST • 100 kW
6295v	VIETNAM	
	†SON LA BC STATION, Son La	DS
6300	USA	
	FAMILY RADIO, Via Taiwan	E ASIA • 250 kW
6300v	CLANDESTINE (S AMER)	
	†"R PATRIA LIBRE", Colombia	Irr • AMERICAS • ELN REBELS
	PIRATE (EUROPE)	
	†"RADIO ORION", England	Sa/Su • W EUROPE • 0.018 kW • ALT. FREQ. TO 6266 kHz
6304.5	PERU	
	RADIO ACARI, Caraveli	DS
6305	CLANDESTINE (C AMER)	
	†"LA VOZ DEL CID", Guatemala?	C AMERICA • ANTI-CASTRO
6310	PIRATE (EUROPE)	
	†"EAST COAST COMML", England	Alternative Frequency to 6290 kHz
6320	PIRATE (EUROPE)	
	†"JOLLY ROGER R", Ireland	Alternative Frequency to 6230 kHz
	†"RADIO WAVES INTL", France	Irr • Su • ENGLISH & FRENCH • W EUROPE • 0.015 kW
6320v	CLANDESTINE (M EAST)	
	†"VO IRANIAN KURDS"	Alternative Frequency to 7365v kHz
	PIRATE (EUROPE)	
	"RADIO STELLA", Scotland	Irr • Su • W EUROPE • 0.09 kW
6323.6	PERU	
	ESTACION C, Moyobamba	Tu-Su • DS • 0.8 kW DS • 0.8 kW / Irr • Tu-Su • DS • 0.8 kW
6325	CLANDESTINE (ASIA)	
	†"VO THE KHMER", Kampuchea/Thailand	SE ASIA • PRO-REBEL STATION / Su • SE ASIA • PRO-REBEL STATION
6325.2	TURKEY	
	ISTANBUL POLICE RADIO, Istanbul	TURKISH • DS • 1 kW
6325.8	PERU	
	†RADIO ABANCAY, Abancay	DS-SPANISH, QUECHUA • 1 kW / M-Sa • DS-SPANISH, QUECHUA • 1 kW
6348	CLANDESTINE (ASIA)	
	"ECHO OF HOPE", Seoul, South Korea	E ASIA • 50 kW
6350v	CLANDESTINE (C AMER)	
	†"R VENCEREMOS", Morazán, Salvador	C AMERICA • FMLN/ANTI-SALVADOR • ALT. FREQ. TO 6620v kHz
		M-Sa • C AMERICA • FMLN/ANTI-SALVADOR • ALT. FREQ. TO 6620v kHz
		Su • C AMERICA • FMLN/ANTI-SALVADOR • ALT. FREQ. TO 6620v kHz
6381v	PERU	
	†RADIO SAN MIGUEL, Huánchac	Irr • DS
6390	USSR	
	RADIO MOSCOW	(D) • DS-1(FEEDER) • ISL / (D) • DS-1(FEEDER) • ISU
6400v	KOREA (DPR)	
	RADIO PYONGYANG, Pyongyang	E ASIA • 50 kW
6430	CHINA (PR)	
	RADIO BEIJING, Beijing	(D) • FEEDER
6435v	CLANDESTINE (M EAST)	
	"VO IRANIAN REV'N", Afghanistan	MIDEAST • ANTI-IRANIAN GOVT / PERSIAN • MIDEAST • ANTI-IRANIAN GOVT
6440v	CLANDESTINE (M EAST)	
	†VO IRAN COMMUNIST, Afghanistan	F • PERSIAN • MIDEAST • ANTI-IRANIAN GOVT PERSIAN • MIDEAST • ANTI-IRANIAN GOVT
		Sa-Th • PERSIAN • MIDEAST • ANTI-IRANIAN GOVT
6451v	VIETNAM	
	†VOICE OF VIETNAM, Hanoi	VIETNAMESE • DS
6480	KOREA (REPUBLIC)	
	RADIO KOREA, In-Kimjae	EUROPE • 250 kW
6500	CHINA (PR)	
	QINGHAI PEOPLES BS, Xining	DS-TIBETAN • 10 kW
6540	KOREA (DPR)	
	RADIO PYONGYANG, Pyongyang	JAPANESE • E ASIA • 100 kW
		MIDEAST & N AFRICA • 200 kW
6550v	LEBANON	
	VOICE OF LEBANON, Beirut-Ashrafiyah	DS-PHALANGE • 8 kW
6560	KOREA (DPR)	
	RADIO PYONGYANG, Pyongyang	JAPANESE • E ASIA • 100 kW
6570	MYANMAR (BURMA)	
	†DEFENSE FORCES BC, Taunggyi	DS
6571v	PERU	
	†RADIO TACNA, Tacna	M-F • DS • 0.18 kW
6571.8	ARGENTINA	
	RADIO COLON, San Juan	Irr • DS(FEEDER) • USB
6575v	VIETNAM	
	CAO BANG BS, Cao Bang	DS / Irr • DS
6576	KOREA (DPR)	
	RADIO PYONGYANG, Pyongyang	WEST USSR & EUROPE • 200 kW

ENGLISH ▬▬   ARABIC ▩▩▩   CHINESE ▭▭▭   FRENCH ▬▬   GERMAN ▬▬   RUSSIAN ▭▭   SPANISH ▬▬   OTHER ▬

FREQUENCY   COUNTRY, STATION, LOCATION   TARGET • NETWORK • POWER (kW)   World Time

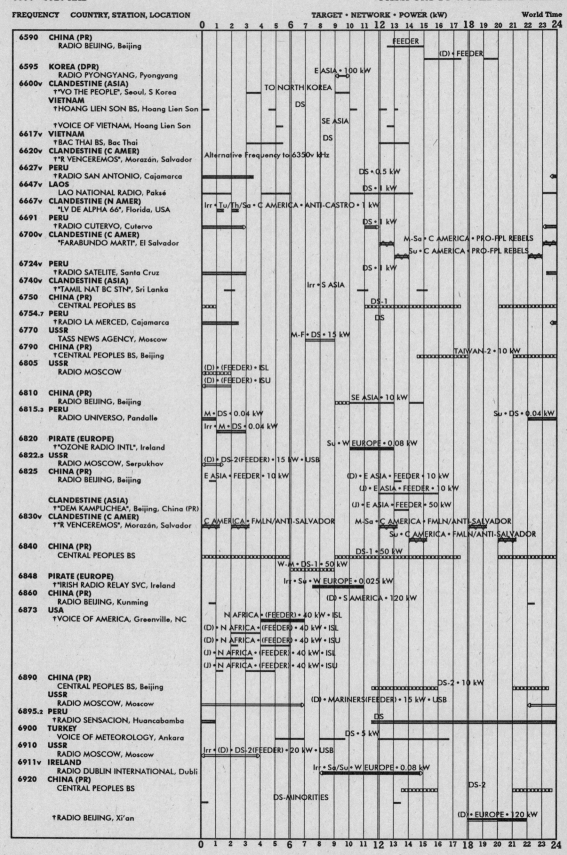

6590	**CHINA (PR)** RADIO BEIJING, Beijing	FEEDER / (D) • FEEDER
6595	**KOREA (DPR)** RADIO PYONGYANG, Pyongyang	E ASIA • 100 kW
6600v	**CLANDESTINE (ASIA)** †"VO THE PEOPLE", Seoul, S Korea	TO NORTH KOREA
	VIETNAM †HOANG LIEN SON BS, Hoang Lien Son	DS
	†VOICE OF VIETNAM, Hoang Lien Son	SE ASIA
6617v	**VIETNAM** †BAC THAI BS, Bac Thai	DS
6620v	**CLANDESTINE (C AMER)** †"R VENCEREMOS", Morazán, Salvador	Alternative Frequency to 6350v kHz
6627v	**PERU** †RADIO SAN ANTONIO, Cajamarca	DS • 0.5 kW
6647v	**LAOS** LAO NATIONAL RADIO, Paksé	DS • 1 kW
6667v	**CLANDESTINE (N AMER)** "LV DE ALPHA 66", Florida, USA	Irr • Tu/Th/Sa • C AMERICA • ANTI-CASTRO • 1 kW
6691	**PERU** †RADIO CUTERVO, Cutervo	DS • 1 kW
6700v	**CLANDESTINE (C AMER)** "FARABUNDO MARTI", El Salvador	M-Sa • C AMERICA • PRO-FPL REBELS / Su • C AMERICA • PRO-FPL REBELS
6724v	**PERU** †RADIO SATELITE, Santa Cruz	DS • 1 kW
6740v	**CLANDESTINE (ASIA)** †"TAMIL NAT BC STN", Sri Lanka	Irr • S ASIA
6750	**CHINA (PR)** CENTRAL PEOPLES BS	DS-1
6754.7	**PERU** †RADIO LA MERCED, Cajamarca	DS
6770	**USSR** TASS NEWS AGENCY, Moscow	M-F • DS • 15 kW
6790	**CHINA (PR)** †CENTRAL PEOPLES BS, Beijing	TAIWAN-2 • 10 kW
6805	**USSR** RADIO MOSCOW	(D) • (FEEDER) • ISL / (D) • (FEEDER) • ISU
6810	**CHINA (PR)** RADIO BEIJING, Beijing	SE ASIA • 10 kW
6815.3	**PERU** RADIO UNIVERSO, Pandallo	M • DS • 0.04 kW / Irr • M • DS • 0.04 kW / Su • DS • 0.04 kW
6820	**PIRATE (EUROPE)** †"OZONE RADIO INTL", Ireland	Su • W EUROPE • 0.08 kW
6822.5	**USSR** RADIO MOSCOW, Serpukhov	(D) • DS-2(FEEDER) • 15 kW • USB
6825	**CHINA (PR)** RADIO BEIJING, Beijing	E ASIA • FEEDER • 10 kW / (D) • E ASIA • FEEDER • 10 kW / (J) • E ASIA • FEEDER • 10 kW
	CLANDESTINE (ASIA) †"DEM KAMPUCHEA", Beijing, China (PR)	(J) • E ASIA • FEEDER • 50 kW
6830v	**CLANDESTINE (C AMER)** †"R VENCEREMOS", Morazán, Salvador	C AMERICA • FMLN/ANTI-SALVADOR / M-Sa • C AMERICA • FMLN/ANTI-SALVADOR / Su • C AMERICA • FMLN/ANTI-SALVADOR
6840	**CHINA (PR)** CENTRAL PEOPLES BS	DS-1 • 50 kW
6848	**PIRATE (EUROPE)** †"IRISH RADIO RELAY SVC, Ireland	W-M • DS-1 • 50 kW / Irr • Su • W EUROPE • 0.025 kW
6860	**CHINA (PR)** RADIO BEIJING, Kunming	(D) • S AMERICA • 120 kW
6873	**USA** †VOICE OF AMERICA, Greenville, NC	N AFRICA • (FEEDER) • 40 kW • ISL / (D) • N AFRICA • (FEEDER) • 40 kW • ISL / (D) • N AFRICA • (FEEDER) • 40 kW • ISU / (J) • N AFRICA • (FEEDER) • 40 kW • ISL / (J) • N AFRICA • (FEEDER) • 40 kW • ISU
6890	**CHINA (PR)** CENTRAL PEOPLES BS, Beijing	DS-2 • 10 kW
	USSR RADIO MOSCOW, Moscow	(D) • MARINERS(FEEDER) • 15 kW • USB
6895.2	**PERU** †RADIO SENSACION, Huancabamba	DS
6900	**TURKEY** VOICE OF METEOROLOGY, Ankara	DS • 5 kW
6910	**USSR** RADIO MOSCOW, Moscow	Irr • (D) • DS-2(FEEDER) • 20 kW • USB
6911v	**IRELAND** RADIO DUBLIN INTERNATIONAL, Dubli	Irr • Sa/Su • W EUROPE • 0.08 kW
6920	**CHINA (PR)** CENTRAL PEOPLES BS	DS-2
	†RADIO BEIJING, Xi'an	DS-MINORITIES / (D) • EUROPE • 120 kW

SUMMER ONLY (J)   WINTER ONLY (D)   JAMMING / OR ∧   EARLIEST HEARD ◁   LATEST HEARD ▷   NEW OR CHANGED FOR 1991 †

FREQUENCY	COUNTRY, STATION, LOCATION	TARGET • NETWORK • POWER (kW)	World Time

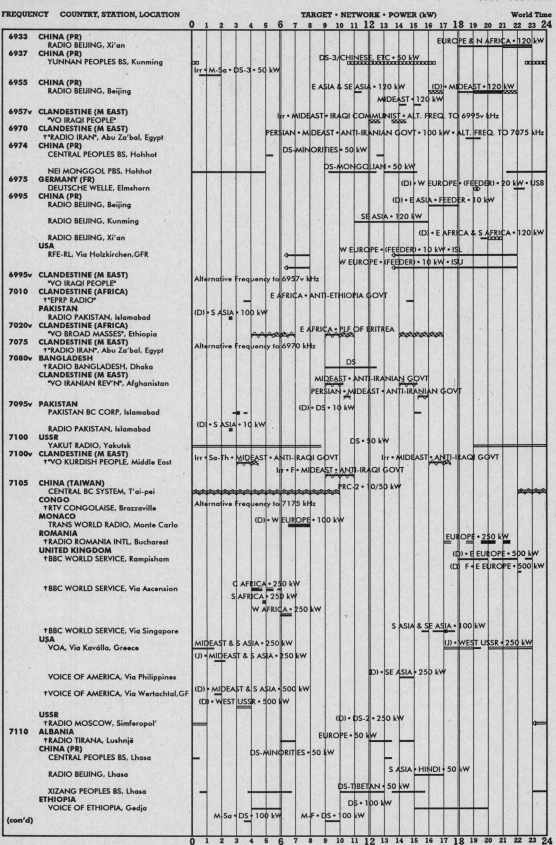

6933	CHINA (PR) RADIO BEIJING, Xi'an	EUROPE & N AFRICA • 120 kW
6937	CHINA (PR) YUNNAN PEOPLES BS, Kunming	DS-3/CHINESE, ETC • 50 kW / Irr • M-Sa • DS-3 • 50 kW
6955	CHINA (PR) RADIO BEIJING, Beijing	E ASIA & SE ASIA • 120 kW / (D) • MIDEAST • 120 kW / MIDEAST • 120 kW
6957v	CLANDESTINE (M EAST) "VO IRAQI PEOPLE"	Irr • MIDEAST • IRAQI COMMUNIST • ALT. FREQ. TO 6995v kHz
6970	CLANDESTINE (M EAST) †"RADIO IRAN", Abu Za'bal, Egypt	PERSIAN • MIDEAST • ANTI-IRANIAN GOVT • 100 kW • ALT. FREQ. TO 7075 kHz
6974	CHINA (PR) CENTRAL PEOPLES BS, Hohhot	DS-MINORITIES • 50 kW
	NEI MONGGOL PBS, Hohhot	DS-MONGOLIAN • 50 kW
6975	GERMANY (FR) DEUTSCHE WELLE, Elmshorn	(D) • W EUROPE • (FEEDER) • 20 kW • USB
6995	CHINA (PR) RADIO BEIJING, Beijing	(D) • E ASIA • FEEDER • 10 kW
	RADIO BEIJING, Kunming	SE ASIA • 120 kW
	RADIO BEIJING, Xi'an	(D) • E AFRICA & S AFRICA • 120 kW
	USA RFE-RL, Via Holzkirchen,GFR	W EUROPE • (FEEDER) • 10 kW • ISL / W EUROPE • (FEEDER) • 10 kW • ISU
6995v	CLANDESTINE (M EAST) "VO IRAQI PEOPLE"	Alternative Frequency to 6957v kHz
7010	CLANDESTINE (AFRICA) †"EPRP RADIO"	E AFRICA • ANTI-ETHIOPIA GOVT
	PAKISTAN RADIO PAKISTAN, Islamabad	(D) • S ASIA • 100 kW
7020v	CLANDESTINE (AFRICA) "VO BROAD MASSES", Ethiopia	E AFRICA • PLF OF ERITREA
7075	CLANDESTINE (M EAST) †"RADIO IRAN", Abu Za'bal, Egypt	Alternative Frequency to 6970 kHz
7080v	BANGLADESH †RADIO BANGLADESH, Dhaka	DS
	CLANDESTINE (M EAST) "VO IRANIAN REV'N", Afghanistan	MIDEAST • ANTI-IRANIAN GOVT / PERSIAN • MIDEAST • ANTI-IRANIAN GOVT
7095v	PAKISTAN PAKISTAN BC CORP, Islamabad	(D) • DS • 10 kW
	RADIO PAKISTAN, Islamabad	(D) • S ASIA • 10 kW
7100	USSR YAKUT RADIO, Yakutsk	DS • 50 kW
7100v	CLANDESTINE (M EAST) †"VO KURDISH PEOPLE, Middle East	Irr • Sa-Th • MIDEAST • ANTI-IRAQI GOVT / Irr • MIDEAST • ANTI-IRAQI GOVT / Irr • F • MIDEAST • ANTI-IRAQI GOVT
7105	CHINA (TAIWAN) CENTRAL BC SYSTEM, T'ai-pei	PRC-2 • 10/50 kW
	CONGO †RTV CONGOLAISE, Brazzaville	Alternative Frequency to 7175 kHz
	MONACO TRANS WORLD RADIO, Monte Carlo	(D) • W EUROPE • 100 kW
	ROMANIA †RADIO ROMANIA INTL, Bucharest	EUROPE • 250 kW
	UNITED KINGDOM †BBC WORLD SERVICE, Rampisham	(D) • E EUROPE • 500 kW / (D) F • E EUROPE • 500 kW
	†BBC WORLD SERVICE, Via Ascension	C AFRICA • 250 kW / S AFRICA • 250 kW / W AFRICA • 250 kW
	†BBC WORLD SERVICE, Via Singapore	S ASIA & SE ASIA • 100 kW
	USA VOA, Via Kaválla, Greece	MIDEAST & S ASIA • 250 kW / (J) • WEST USSR • 250 kW / (J) • MIDEAST & S ASIA • 250 kW
	VOICE OF AMERICA, Via Philippines	(D) • SE ASIA • 250 kW
	†VOICE OF AMERICA, Via Wertachtal,GF	(D) • MIDEAST & S ASIA • 500 kW / (D) • WEST USSR • 500 kW
	USSR †RADIO MOSCOW, Simferopol'	(D) • DS-2 • 250 kW
7110	ALBANIA †RADIO TIRANA, Lushnjë	EUROPE • 50 kW
	CHINA (PR) CENTRAL PEOPLES BS, Lhasa	DS-MINORITIES • 50 kW
	RADIO BEIJING, Lhasa	S ASIA • HINDI • 50 kW
	XIZANG PEOPLES BS, Lhasa	DS-TIBETAN • 50 kW
	ETHIOPIA VOICE OF ETHIOPIA, Gedja	DS • 100 kW / M-Sa • DS • 100 kW / M-F • DS • 100 kW
(con'd)		

ENGLISH ▬ ARABIC ≋ CHINESE ▭▭▭ FRENCH ▬ GERMAN ▬ RUSSIAN ══ SPANISH ▬ OTHER ▬

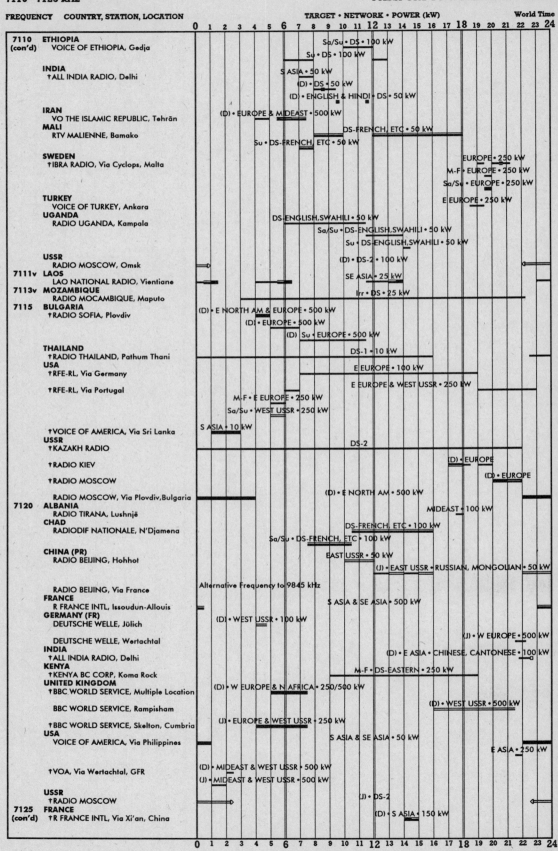

FREQUENCY　COUNTRY, STATION, LOCATION　　　　TARGET • NETWORK • POWER (kW)　　　World Time

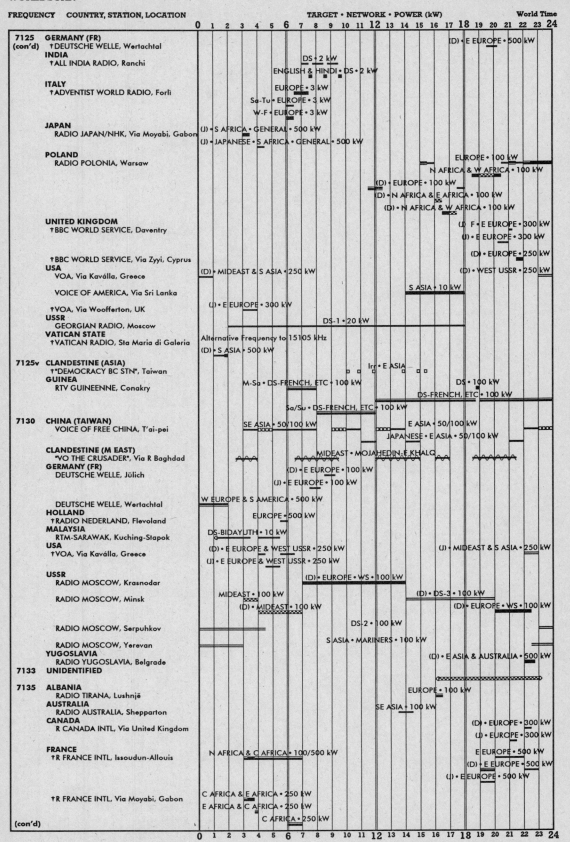

Frequency	Country, Station, Location	Schedule
7125 (con'd)	GERMANY (FR) †DEUTSCHE WELLE, Wertachtal	(D) • E EUROPE • 500 kW
	INDIA †ALL INDIA RADIO, Ranchi	DS • 2 kW / ENGLISH & HINDI • DS • 2 kW
	ITALY †ADVENTIST WORLD RADIO, Forlì	EUROPE • 3 kW / Sa-Tu • EUROPE • 3 kW / W-F • EUROPE • 3 kW
	JAPAN RADIO JAPAN/NHK, Via Moyabi, Gabon	(J) • S AFRICA • GENERAL • 500 kW / (J) • JAPANESE • S AFRICA • GENERAL • 500 kW
	POLAND RADIO POLONIA, Warsaw	EUROPE • 100 kW / N AFRICA & W AFRICA • 100 kW / (D) • EUROPE • 100 kW / (D) • N AFRICA & E AFRICA • 100 kW / (D) • N AFRICA & W AFRICA • 100 kW
	UNITED KINGDOM †BBC WORLD SERVICE, Daventry	(J) F • E EUROPE • 300 kW / (J) • E EUROPE • 300 kW
	†BBC WORLD SERVICE, Via Zyyi, Cyprus	(D) • EUROPE • 250 kW
	USA VOA, Via Kaválla, Greece	(D) • MIDEAST & S ASIA • 250 kW / (D) • WEST USSR • 250 kW
	VOICE OF AMERICA, Via Sri Lanka	S ASIA • 10 kW
	†VOA, Via Woofferton, UK	(J) • E EUROPE • 300 kW
	USSR GEORGIAN RADIO, Moscow	DS-1 • 20 kW
	VATICAN STATE †VATICAN RADIO, Sta Maria di Galeria	Alternative Frequency to 15105 kHz / (D) • S ASIA • 500 kW
7125v	CLANDESTINE (ASIA) †"DEMOCRACY BC STN", Taiwan	Irr • E ASIA
	GUINEA RTV GUINEENNE, Conakry	M-Sa • DS-FRENCH, ETC • 100 kW / DS • 100 kW / DS-FRENCH, ETC • 100 kW / Sa/Su • DS-FRENCH, ETC • 100 kW
7130	CHINA (TAIWAN) VOICE OF FREE CHINA, T'ai-pei	SE ASIA • 50/100 kW / E ASIA • 50/100 kW / JAPANESE • E ASIA • 50/100 kW
	CLANDESTINE (M EAST) "VO THE CRUSADER", Via R Baghdad	MIDEAST • MOJAHEDIN-E KHALQ
	GERMANY (FR) DEUTSCHE WELLE, Jülich	(D) • E EUROPE • 100 kW / (J) • E EUROPE • 100 kW
	DEUTSCHE WELLE, Wertachtal	W EUROPE & S AMERICA • 500 kW
	HOLLAND †RADIO NEDERLAND, Flevoland	EUROPE • 500 kW
	MALAYSIA RTM-SARAWAK, Kuching-Stapok	DS-BIDAYUTH • 10 kW
	USA †VOA, Via Kaválla, Greece	(D) • E EUROPE & WEST USSR • 250 kW / (J) • E EUROPE & WEST USSR • 250 kW / (J) • MIDEAST & S ASIA • 250 kW
	USSR RADIO MOSCOW, Krasnodar	(D) • EUROPE • WS • 100 kW
	RADIO MOSCOW, Minsk	MIDEAST • 100 kW / (D) • DS-3 • 100 kW / (D) • MIDEAST • 100 kW / (D) • EUROPE • WS • 100 kW
	RADIO MOSCOW, Serpuhkov	DS-2 • 100 kW
	RADIO MOSCOW, Yerevan	S ASIA • MARINERS • 100 kW
	YUGOSLAVIA RADIO YUGOSLAVIA, Belgrade	(D) • E ASIA & AUSTRALIA • 500 kW
7133	UNIDENTIFIED	
7135	ALBANIA RADIO TIRANA, Lushnjë	EUROPE • 100 kW
	AUSTRALIA RADIO AUSTRALIA, Shepparton	SE ASIA • 100 kW
	CANADA R CANADA INTL, Via United Kingdom	(D) • EUROPE • 300 kW / (J) • EUROPE • 300 kW
	FRANCE †R FRANCE INTL, Issoudun-Allouis	N AFRICA & C AFRICA • 100/500 kW / E EUROPE • 500 kW / (D) • E EUROPE • 500 kW / (J) • E EUROPE • 500 kW
	†R FRANCE INTL, Via Moyabi, Gabon	C AFRICA & E AFRICA • 250 kW / E AFRICA & C AFRICA • 250 kW / C AFRICA • 250 kW
(con'd)		

ENGLISH ▬　ARABIC ▨　CHINESE ▭▭　FRENCH ═══　GERMAN ▬▬　RUSSIAN ═══　SPANISH ▪▪　OTHER ───

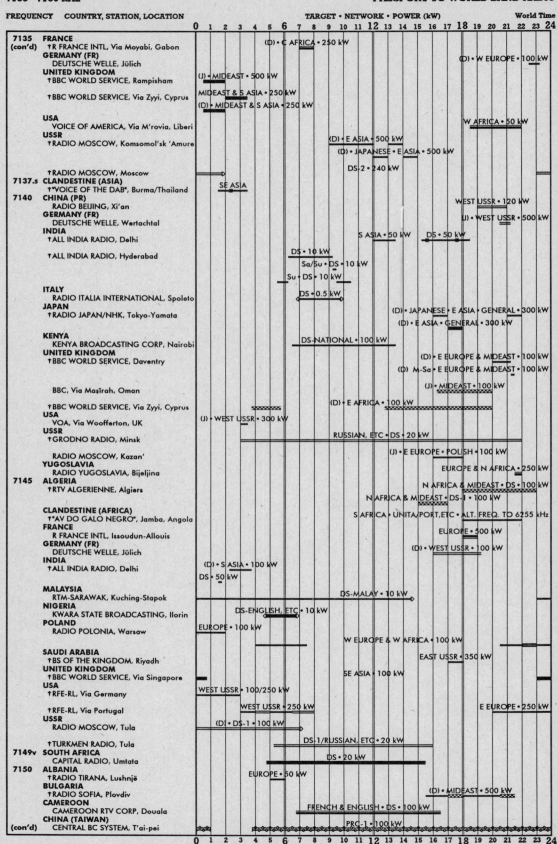

FREQUENCY   COUNTRY, STATION, LOCATION   TARGET • NETWORK • POWER (kW)   World Time

7135 (con'd)	FRANCE	†R FRANCE INTL, Via Moyabi, Gabon	(D) • C AFRICA • 250 kW
	GERMANY (FR)	DEUTSCHE WELLE, Jülich	(D) • W EUROPE • 100 kW
	UNITED KINGDOM	†BBC WORLD SERVICE, Rampisham	(J) • MIDEAST • 500 kW
		†BBC WORLD SERVICE, Via Zyyi, Cyprus	MIDEAST & S ASIA • 250 kW / (D) • MIDEAST & S ASIA • 250 kW
	USA	VOICE OF AMERICA, Via M'rovia, Liberi	W AFRICA • 50 kW
	USSR	†RADIO MOSCOW, Komsomol'sk 'Amure	(D) • E ASIA • 500 kW / (D) • JAPANESE • E ASIA • 500 kW
		†RADIO MOSCOW, Moscow	DS-2 • 240 kW
7137.5	CLANDESTINE (ASIA)	†"VOICE OF THE DAB", Burma/Thailand	SE ASIA
7140	CHINA (PR)	RADIO BEIJING, Xi'an	WEST USSR • 120 kW
	GERMANY (FR)	DEUTSCHE WELLE, Wertachtal	(J) • WEST USSR • 500 kW
	INDIA	†ALL INDIA RADIO, Delhi	S ASIA • 50 kW / DS • 50 kW
		†ALL INDIA RADIO, Hyderabad	DS • 10 kW / Sa/Su • DS • 10 kW / Su • DS • 10 kW
	ITALY	RADIO ITALIA INTERNATIONAL, Spoleto	DS • 0.5 kW
	JAPAN	†RADIO JAPAN/NHK, Tokyo-Yamata	(D) • JAPANESE • E ASIA • GENERAL • 300 kW / (D) • E ASIA • GENERAL • 300 kW
	KENYA	KENYA BROADCASTING CORP, Nairobi	DS-NATIONAL • 100 kW
	UNITED KINGDOM	†BBC WORLD SERVICE, Daventry	(D) • E EUROPE & MIDEAST • 100 kW / (D) • M-Sa • E EUROPE & MIDEAST • 100 kW
		BBC, Via Masīrah, Oman	(J) • MIDEAST • 100 kW
		†BBC WORLD SERVICE, Via Zyyi, Cyprus	(D) • E AFRICA • 100 kW
	USA	VOA, Via Woofferton, UK	(J) • WEST USSR • 300 kW
	USSR	†GRODNO RADIO, Minsk	RUSSIAN, ETC • DS • 20 kW
		RADIO MOSCOW, Kazan'	(J) • E EUROPE • POLISH • 100 kW
	YUGOSLAVIA	RADIO YUGOSLAVIA, Bijeljina	EUROPE & N AFRICA • 250 kW
7145	ALGERIA	†RTV ALGERIENNE, Algiers	N AFRICA & MIDEAST • DS • 100 kW / N AFRICA & MIDEAST • DS-1 • 100 kW
	CLANDESTINE (AFRICA)	†"AV DO GALO NEGRO", Jamba, Angola	S AFRICA • UNITA/PORT, ETC • ALT. FREQ. TO 6255 kHz
	FRANCE	R FRANCE INTL, Issoudun-Allouis	EUROPE • 500 kW
	GERMANY (FR)	DEUTSCHE WELLE, Jülich	(D) • WEST USSR • 100 kW
	INDIA	†ALL INDIA RADIO, Delhi	(D) • S ASIA • 100 kW / DS • 50 kW
	MALAYSIA	RTM-SARAWAK, Kuching-Stapok	DS-MALAY • 10 kW
	NIGERIA	KWARA STATE BROADCASTING, Ilorin	DS-ENGLISH, ETC • 10 kW
	POLAND	RADIO POLONIA, Warsaw	EUROPE • 100 kW / W EUROPE & W AFRICA • 100 kW
	SAUDI ARABIA	†BS OF THE KINGDOM, Riyadh	EAST USSR • 350 kW
	UNITED KINGDOM	†BBC WORLD SERVICE, Via Singapore	SE ASIA • 100 kW
	USA	†RFE-RL, Via Germany	WEST USSR • 100/250 kW
		†RFE-RL, Via Portugal	WEST USSR • 250 kW / E EUROPE • 250 kW
	USSR	†RADIO MOSCOW, Tula	(D) • DS-1 • 100 kW
		†TURKMEN RADIO, Tula	DS-1/RUSSIAN, ETC • 20 kW
7149v	SOUTH AFRICA	CAPITAL RADIO, Umtata	DS • 20 kW
7150	ALBANIA	†RADIO TIRANA, Lushnjë	EUROPE • 50 kW
	BULGARIA	†RADIO SOFIA, Plovdiv	(D) • MIDEAST • 500 kW
	CAMEROON	CAMEROON RTV CORP, Douala	FRENCH & ENGLISH • DS • 100 kW
	CHINA (TAIWAN)		
(con'd)	CENTRAL BC SYSTEM, T'ai-pei	PRC-1 • 100 kW

FREQUENCY	COUNTRY, STATION, LOCATION	TARGET • NETWORK • POWER (kW)	World Time

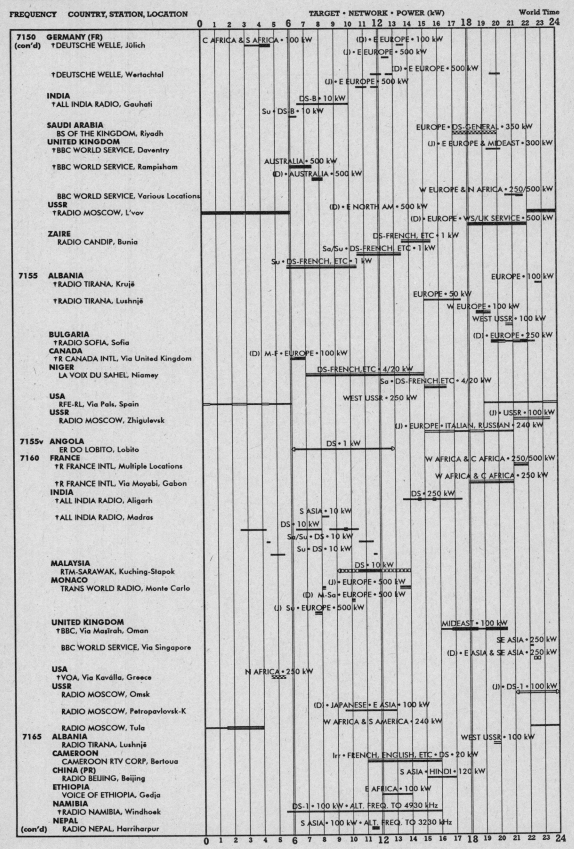

7150 **GERMANY (FR)**
(con'd) †DEUTSCHE WELLE, Jülich — C AFRICA & S AFRICA • 100 kW / (D) • E EUROPE • 100 kW / (J) • E EUROPE • 500 kW

†DEUTSCHE WELLE, Wertachtal — (D) • E EUROPE • 500 kW / (J) • E EUROPE • 500 kW

INDIA
†ALL INDIA RADIO, Gauhati — DS-B • 10 kW / Su • DS-B • 10 kW

SAUDI ARABIA
BS OF THE KINGDOM, Riyadh — EUROPE • DS-GENERAL • 350 kW
UNITED KINGDOM
†BBC WORLD SERVICE, Daventry — (J) • E EUROPE & MIDEAST • 300 kW

†BBC WORLD SERVICE, Rampisham — AUSTRALIA • 500 kW / (D) • AUSTRALIA • 500 kW

BBC WORLD SERVICE, Various Locations — W EUROPE & N AFRICA • 250/500 kW
USSR
†RADIO MOSCOW, L'vov — (D) • E NORTH AM • 500 kW / (D) • EUROPE • WS/UK SERVICE • 500 kW

ZAIRE
RADIO CANDIP, Bunia — DS-FRENCH, ETC • 1 kW / Sa/Su • DS-FRENCH, ETC • 1 kW / Su • DS-FRENCH, ETC • 1 kW

7155 **ALBANIA**
†RADIO TIRANA, Krujë — EUROPE • 100 kW

†RADIO TIRANA, Lushnjë — EUROPE • 50 kW / W EUROPE • 100 kW / WEST USSR • 100 kW

BULGARIA
†RADIO SOFIA, Sofia — (D) • EUROPE • 250 kW
CANADA
†R CANADA INTL, Via United Kingdom — (D) M-F • EUROPE • 100 kW
NIGER
LA VOIX DU SAHEL, Niamey — DS-FRENCH, ETC • 4/20 kW / Sa • DS-FRENCH, ETC • 4/20 kW

USA
RFE-RL, Via Pals, Spain — WEST USSR • 250 kW
USSR
RADIO MOSCOW, Zhigulevsk — (J) • USSR • 100 kW / (J) • EUROPE • ITALIAN, RUSSIAN • 240 kW

7155v **ANGOLA**
ER DO LOBITO, Lobito — DS • 1 kW
7160 **FRANCE**
†R FRANCE INTL, Multiple Locations — W AFRICA & C AFRICA • 250/500 kW

†R FRANCE INTL, Via Moyabi, Gabon — W AFRICA & C AFRICA • 250 kW
INDIA
†ALL INDIA RADIO, Aligarh — DS • 250 kW

†ALL INDIA RADIO, Madras — S ASIA • 10 kW / DS • 10 kW / Sa/Su • DS • 10 kW / Su • DS • 10 kW

MALAYSIA
RTM-SARAWAK, Kuching-Stapok — DS • 10 kW
MONACO
TRANS WORLD RADIO, Monte Carlo — (J) • EUROPE • 500 kW / (D) M-Sa • EUROPE • 500 kW / (J) Su • EUROPE • 500 kW

UNITED KINGDOM
†BBC, Via Maşïrah, Oman — MIDEAST • 100 kW

BBC WORLD SERVICE, Via Singapore — SE ASIA • 250 kW / (D) • E ASIA & SE ASIA • 250 kW

USA
†VOA, Via Kaválla, Greece — N AFRICA • 250 kW
USSR
RADIO MOSCOW, Omsk — (J) • DS-1 • 100 kW

RADIO MOSCOW, Petropavlovsk-K — (D) • JAPANESE • E ASIA • 100 kW

RADIO MOSCOW, Tula — W AFRICA & S AMERICA • 240 kW
7165 **ALBANIA**
RADIO TIRANA, Lushnjë — WEST USSR • 100 kW
CAMEROON
CAMEROON RTV CORP, Bertoua — Irr • FRENCH, ENGLISH, ETC • DS • 20 kW
CHINA (PR)
RADIO BEIJING, Beijing — S ASIA • HINDI • 120 kW
ETHIOPIA
VOICE OF ETHIOPIA, Gedja — E AFRICA • 100 kW
NAMIBIA
†RADIO NAMIBIA, Windhoek — DS-1 • 100 kW • ALT. FREQ. TO 4930 kHz
NEPAL
(con'd) RADIO NEPAL, Harriharpur — S ASIA • 100 kW • ALT. FREQ. TO 3230 kHz

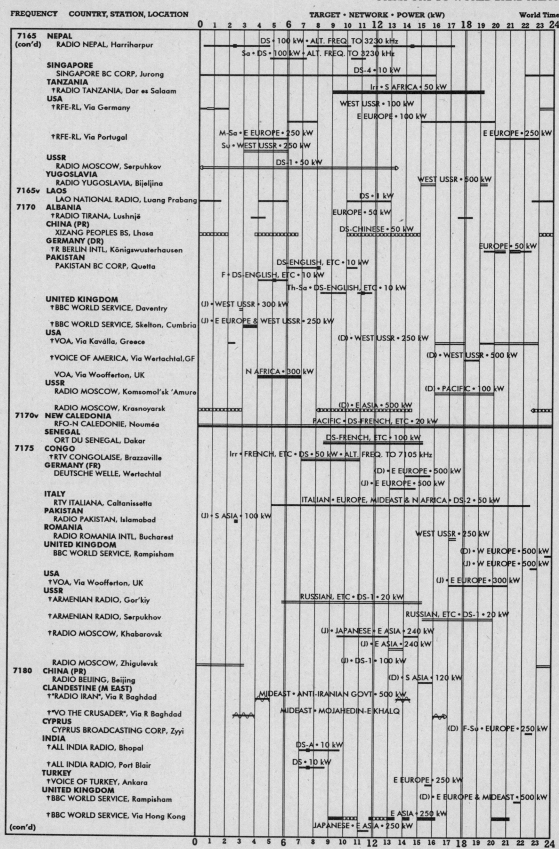

FREQUENCY	COUNTRY, STATION, LOCATION

TARGET • NETWORK • POWER (kW)   **World Time**

7165 (con'd)	**NEPAL** RADIO NEPAL, Harriharpur
	DS • 100 kW • ALT. FREQ. TO 3230 kHz
	Sa • DS • 100 kW • ALT. FREQ. TO 3230 kHz
	SINGAPORE SINGAPORE BC CORP, Jurong
	DS-4 • 10 kW
	TANZANIA †RADIO TANZANIA, Dar es Salaam
	Irr • S AFRICA • 50 kW
	USA †RFE-RL, Via Germany
	WEST USSR • 100 kW
	E EUROPE • 100 kW
	†RFE-RL, Via Portugal
	M-Sa • E EUROPE • 250 kW
	Su • WEST USSR • 250 kW
	E EUROPE • 250 kW
	USSR RADIO MOSCOW, Serpuhkov
	DS-1 • 50 kW
	YUGOSLAVIA RADIO YUGOSLAVIA, Bijeljina
	WEST USSR • 500 kW
7165v	**LAOS** LAO NATIONAL RADIO, Luang Prabang
	DS • 1 kW
7170	**ALBANIA** †RADIO TIRANA, Lushnjë
	EUROPE • 50 kW
	CHINA (PR) XIZANG PEOPLES BS, Lhasa
	DS-CHINESE • 50 kW
	GERMANY (DR) †R BERLIN INTL, Königswusterhausen
	EUROPE • 50 kW
	PAKISTAN PAKISTAN BC CORP, Quetta
	DS-ENGLISH, ETC • 10 kW
	F • DS-ENGLISH, ETC • 10 kW
	Th-Sa • DS-ENGLISH, ETC • 10 kW
	UNITED KINGDOM †BBC WORLD SERVICE, Daventry
	(J) • WEST USSR • 300 kW
	†BBC WORLD SERVICE, Skelton, Cumbria
	(J) • E EUROPE & WEST USSR • 250 kW
	USA †VOA, Via Kaválla, Greece
	(D) • WEST USSR • 250 kW
	†VOICE OF AMERICA, Via Wertachtal, GF
	(D) • WEST USSR • 500 kW
	VOA, Via Woofferton, UK
	N AFRICA • 300 kW
	USSR RADIO MOSCOW, Komsomol'sk 'Amure
	(D) • PACIFIC • 100 kW
	RADIO MOSCOW, Krasnoyarsk
	(D) • E ASIA • 500 kW
7170v	**NEW CALEDONIA** RFO-N CALEDONIE, Nouméa
	PACIFIC • DS-FRENCH, ETC • 20 kW
	SENEGAL ORT DU SENEGAL, Dakar
	DS-FRENCH, ETC • 100 kW
7175	**CONGO** †RTV CONGOLAISE, Brazzaville
	Irr • FRENCH, ETC • DS • 50 kW • ALT. FREQ. TO 7105 kHz
	GERMANY (FR) DEUTSCHE WELLE, Wertachtal
	(D) • E EUROPE • 500 kW
	(J) • E EUROPE • 500 kW
	ITALY RTV ITALIANA, Caltanissetta
	ITALIAN • EUROPE, MIDEAST & N AFRICA • DS-2 • 50 kW
	PAKISTAN RADIO PAKISTAN, Islamabad
	(J) • S ASIA • 100 kW
	ROMANIA RADIO ROMANIA INTL, Bucharest
	WEST USSR • 250 kW
	UNITED KINGDOM BBC WORLD SERVICE, Rampisham
	(D) • W EUROPE • 500 kW
	(J) • W EUROPE • 500 kW
	USA †VOA, Via Woofferton, UK
	(J) • E EUROPE • 300 kW
	USSR †ARMENIAN RADIO, Gor'kiy
	RUSSIAN, ETC • DS-1 • 20 kW
	†ARMENIAN RADIO, Serpukhov
	RUSSIAN, ETC • DS-1 • 20 kW
	†RADIO MOSCOW, Khabarovsk
	(J) • JAPANESE • E ASIA • 240 kW
	(J) • E ASIA • 240 kW
	RADIO MOSCOW, Zhigulevsk
	(J) • DS-1 • 100 kW
7180	**CHINA (PR)** RADIO BEIJING, Beijing
	(D) • S ASIA • 120 kW
	CLANDESTINE (M EAST) †"RADIO IRAN", Via R Baghdad
	MIDEAST • ANTI-IRANIAN GOVT • 500 kW
	†"VO THE CRUSADER", Via R Baghdad
	MIDEAST • MOJAHEDIN-E KHALQ
	CYPRUS CYPRUS BROADCASTING CORP, Zyyi
	(D) F-Su • EUROPE • 250 kW
	INDIA †ALL INDIA RADIO, Bhopal
	DS-A • 10 kW
	†ALL INDIA RADIO, Port Blair
	DS • 10 kW
	TURKEY †VOICE OF TURKEY, Ankara
	E EUROPE • 250 kW
	UNITED KINGDOM †BBC WORLD SERVICE, Rampisham
	(D) • E EUROPE & MIDEAST • 500 kW
	†BBC WORLD SERVICE, Via Hong Kong
	E ASIA • 250 kW
(con'd)	JAPANESE • E ASIA • 250 kW

FREQUENCY   COUNTRY, STATION, LOCATION

TARGET • NETWORK • POWER (kW)

World Time

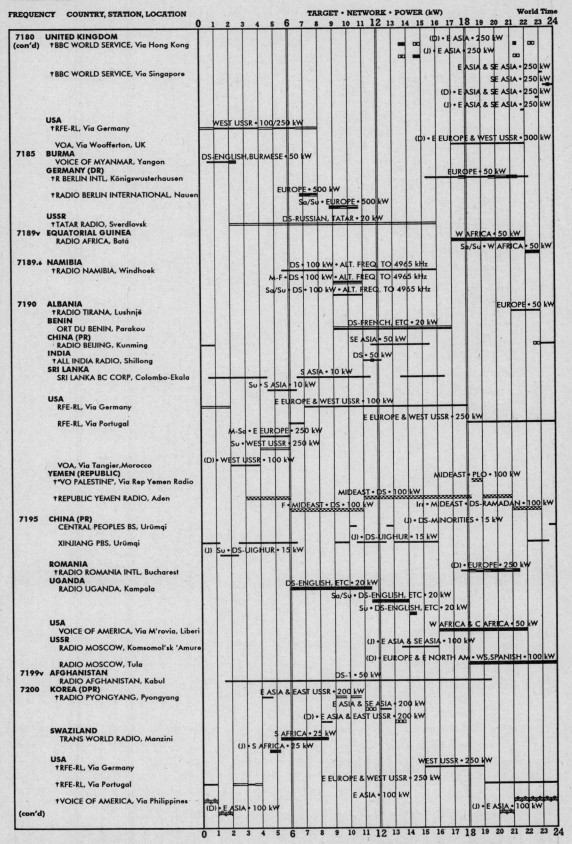

FREQUENCY	COUNTRY, STATION, LOCATION	Details
7180 (con'd)	UNITED KINGDOM †BBC WORLD SERVICE, Via Hong Kong	(D) • E ASIA • 250 kW; (J) • E ASIA • 250 kW
	†BBC WORLD SERVICE, Via Singapore	E ASIA & SE ASIA • 250 kW; SE ASIA • 250 kW; (D) • E ASIA & SE ASIA • 250 kW; (J) • E ASIA & SE ASIA • 250 kW
	USA †RFE-RL, Via Germany	WEST USSR • 100/250 kW
	VOA, Via Woofferton, UK	(D) • E EUROPE & WEST USSR • 300 kW
7185	BURMA VOICE OF MYANMAR, Yangon	DS-ENGLISH, BURMESE • 50 kW
	GERMANY (DR) †R BERLIN INTL, Königswusterhausen	EUROPE • 50 kW
	†RADIO BERLIN INTERNATIONAL, Nauen	EUROPE • 500 kW; Sa/Su • EUROPE • 500 kW
	USSR †TATAR RADIO, Sverdlovsk	DS-RUSSIAN, TATAR • 20 kW
7189v	EQUATORIAL GUINEA RADIO AFRICA, Batá	W AFRICA • 50 kW; Sa/Su • W AFRICA • 50 kW
7189.6	NAMIBIA †RADIO NAMIBIA, Windhoek	DS • 100 kW • ALT. FREQ. TO 4965 kHz; M-F • DS • 100 kW • ALT. FREQ. TO 4965 kHz; Sa/Su • DS • 100 kW • ALT. FREQ. TO 4965 kHz
7190	ALBANIA †RADIO TIRANA, Lushnjë	EUROPE • 50 kW
	BENIN ORT DU BENIN, Parakou	DS-FRENCH, ETC • 20 kW
	CHINA (PR) RADIO BEIJING, Kunming	SE ASIA • 50 kW
	INDIA †ALL INDIA RADIO, Shillong	DS • 50 kW
	SRI LANKA SRI LANKA BC CORP, Colombo-Ekala	S ASIA • 10 kW; Su • S ASIA • 10 kW
	USA RFE-RL, Via Germany	E EUROPE & WEST USSR • 100 kW
	RFE-RL, Via Portugal	E EUROPE & WEST USSR • 250 kW; M-Sa • E EUROPE • 250 kW; Su • WEST USSR • 250 kW
	VOA, Via Tangier, Morocco	(D) • WEST USSR • 100 kW
	YEMEN (REPUBLIC) †"VO PALESTINE", Via Rep Yemen Radio	MIDEAST • PLO • 100 kW
	†REPUBLIC YEMEN RADIO, Aden	MIDEAST • DS • 100 kW; F • MIDEAST • DS • 100 kW; Irr • MIDEAST • DS-RAMADAN • 100 kW
7195	CHINA (PR) CENTRAL PEOPLES BS, Urümqi	(J) • DS-MINORITIES • 15 kW
	XINJIANG PBS, Urümqi	(J) • DS-UIGHUR • 15 kW; (J) Su • DS-UIGHUR • 15 kW
	ROMANIA †RADIO ROMANIA INTL, Bucharest	(D) • EUROPE • 250 kW
	UGANDA RADIO UGANDA, Kampala	DS-ENGLISH, ETC • 20 kW; Sa/Su • DS-ENGLISH, ETC • 20 kW; Su • DS-ENGLISH, ETC • 20 kW
	USA VOICE OF AMERICA, Via M'rovia, Liberi	W AFRICA & C AFRICA • 50 kW
	USSR RADIO MOSCOW, Komsomol'sk 'Amure	(J) • E ASIA & SE ASIA • 100 kW
	RADIO MOSCOW, Tula	(D) • EUROPE & E NORTH AM • WS, SPANISH • 100 kW
7199v	AFGHANISTAN RADIO AFGHANISTAN, Kabul	DS-1 • 50 kW
7200	KOREA (DPR) †RADIO PYONGYANG, Pyongyang	E ASIA & EAST USSR • 200 kW; E ASIA & SE ASIA • 200 kW; (D) • E ASIA & EAST USSR • 200 kW
	SWAZILAND TRANS WORLD RADIO, Manzini	S AFRICA • 25 kW; (J) • S AFRICA • 25 kW
	USA †RFE-RL, Via Germany	WEST USSR • 250 kW
	†RFE-RL, Via Portugal	E EUROPE & WEST USSR • 250 kW
	†VOICE OF AMERICA, Via Philippines	E ASIA • 100 kW; (D) • E ASIA • 100 kW; (J) • E ASIA • 100 kW
(con'd)		

ENGLISH ▬   ARABIC ﹏   CHINESE ▭▭▭   FRENCH ═══   GERMAN ▭▭   RUSSIAN ═══   SPANISH ▬▬   OTHER ──

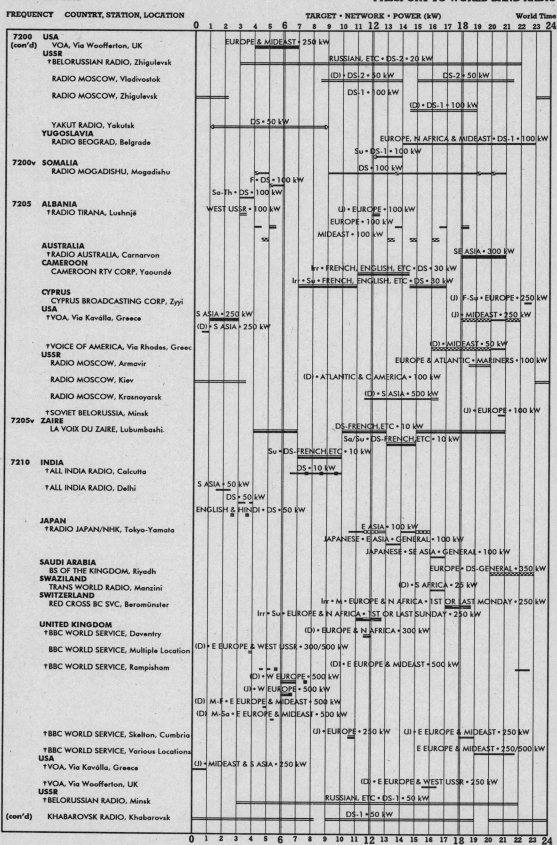

FREQUENCY	COUNTRY, STATION, LOCATION	TARGET • NETWORK • POWER (kW)

World Time: 0 1 2 3 4 5 6 7 8 9 10 11 12 13 14 15 16 17 18 19 20 21 22 23 24

7200 (con'd) USA
- VOA, Via Woofferton, UK — EUROPE & MIDEAST • 250 kW
- **USSR**
- †BELORUSSIAN RADIO, Zhigulevsk — RUSSIAN, ETC • DS-2 • 20 kW
- RADIO MOSCOW, Vladivostok — (D) • DS-2 • 50 kW / DS-2 • 50 kW
- RADIO MOSCOW, Zhigulevsk — DS-1 • 100 kW / (D) • DS-1 • 100 kW
- YAKUT RADIO, Yakutsk — DS • 50 kW
- **YUGOSLAVIA**
- RADIO BEOGRAD, Belgrade — EUROPE, N AFRICA & MIDEAST • DS-1 • 100 kW / Su • DS-1 • 100 kW

7200v SOMALIA
- RADIO MOGADISHU, Mogadishu — DS • 100 kW / F • DS • 100 kW / Sa-Th • DS • 100 kW

7205 ALBANIA
- †RADIO TIRANA, Lushnjë — WEST USSR • 100 kW / (J) • EUROPE • 100 kW / EUROPE • 100 kW / MIDEAST • 100 kW
- **AUSTRALIA**
- †RADIO AUSTRALIA, Carnarvon — SE ASIA • 300 kW
- **CAMEROON**
- CAMEROON RTV CORP, Yaoundé — Irr • FRENCH, ENGLISH, ETC • DS • 30 kW / Irr • Su • FRENCH, ENGLISH, ETC • DS • 30 kW
- **CYPRUS**
- CYPRUS BROADCASTING CORP, Zyyi — (J) F-Su • EUROPE • 250 kW
- **USA**
- †VOA, Via Kaválla, Greece — S ASIA • 250 kW / (J) • MIDEAST • 250 kW / (D) • S ASIA • 250 kW
- †VOICE OF AMERICA, Via Rhodes, Greec — (D) • MIDEAST • 50 kW
- **USSR**
- RADIO MOSCOW, Armavir — EUROPE & ATLANTIC • MARINERS • 100 kW
- RADIO MOSCOW, Kiev — (D) • ATLANTIC & C AMERICA • 100 kW
- RADIO MOSCOW, Krasnoyarsk — (D) • S ASIA • 500 kW
- †SOVIET BELORUSSIA, Minsk — (J) • EUROPE • 100 kW

7205v ZAIRE
- LA VOIX DU ZAIRE, Lubumbashi — DS-FRENCH, ETC • 10 kW / Sa/Su • DS-FRENCH, ETC • 10 kW / Su • DS-FRENCH, ETC • 10 kW

7210 INDIA
- †ALL INDIA RADIO, Calcutta — DS • 10 kW
- †ALL INDIA RADIO, Delhi — S ASIA • 50 kW / DS • 50 kW / ENGLISH & HINDI • DS • 50 kW
- **JAPAN**
- †RADIO JAPAN/NHK, Tokyo-Yamata — E ASIA • 100 kW / JAPANESE • E ASIA • GENERAL • 100 kW / JAPANESE • SE ASIA • GENERAL • 100 kW
- **SAUDI ARABIA**
- BS OF THE KINGDOM, Riyadh — EUROPE • DS-GENERAL • 350 kW
- **SWAZILAND**
- TRANS WORLD RADIO, Manzini — (D) • S AFRICA • 25 kW
- **SWITZERLAND**
- RED CROSS BC SVC, Beromünster — Irr • M • EUROPE & N AFRICA • 1ST OR LAST MONDAY • 250 kW / Irr • Su • EUROPE & N AFRICA • 1ST OR LAST SUNDAY • 250 kW
- **UNITED KINGDOM**
- †BBC WORLD SERVICE, Daventry — (D) • EUROPE & N AFRICA • 300 kW
- BBC WORLD SERVICE, Multiple Location — (D) • E EUROPE & WEST USSR • 300/500 kW
- †BBC WORLD SERVICE, Rampisham — (D) • E EUROPE & MIDEAST • 500 kW / (D) • W EUROPE • 500 kW / (J) • W EUROPE • 500 kW / (D) M-F • E EUROPE & MIDEAST • 500 kW / (D) M-Sa • E EUROPE & MIDEAST • 500 kW
- †BBC WORLD SERVICE, Skelton, Cumbria — (J) • EUROPE • 250 kW / (J) • E EUROPE & MIDEAST • 250 kW
- †BBC WORLD SERVICE, Various Locations — E EUROPE & MIDEAST • 250/500 kW
- **USA**
- †VOA, Via Kaválla, Greece — (J) • MIDEAST & S ASIA • 250 kW
- †VOA, Via Woofferton, UK — (D) • E EUROPE & WEST USSR • 250 kW
- **USSR**
- †BELORUSSIAN RADIO, Minsk — RUSSIAN, ETC • DS-1 • 50 kW
- **(con'd)** KHABAROVSK RADIO, Khabarovsk — DS-1 • 50 kW

World Time: 0 1 2 3 4 5 6 7 8 9 10 11 12 13 14 15 16 17 18 19 20 21 22 23 24

SUMMER ONLY (J)   WINTER ONLY (D)   JAMMING / OR ∧   EARLIEST HEARD ◁   LATEST HEARD ▷   NEW OR CHANGED FOR 1991 †

FREQUENCY   COUNTRY, STATION, LOCATION   TARGET • NETWORK • POWER (kW)   World Time

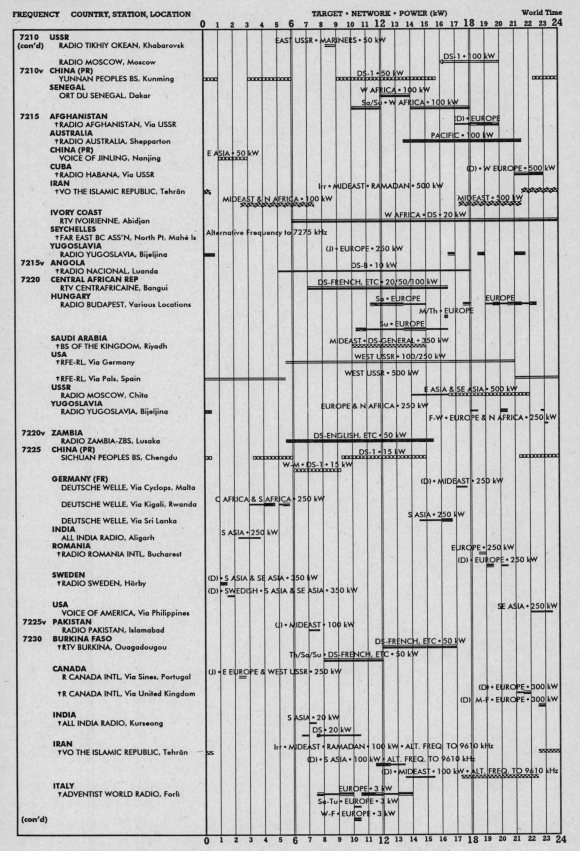

7210 USSR — RADIO TIKHIY OKEAN, Khabarovsk — EAST USSR • MARINERS • 50 kW
(con'd) — RADIO MOSCOW, Moscow — DS-1 • 100 kW
7210v CHINA (PR) — YUNNAN PEOPLES BS, Kunming — DS-1 • 50 kW
SENEGAL — ORT DU SENEGAL, Dakar — W AFRICA • 100 kW — Sa/Su • W AFRICA • 100 kW

7215 AFGHANISTAN — †RADIO AFGHANISTAN, Via USSR — (D) • EUROPE
AUSTRALIA — †RADIO AUSTRALIA, Shepparton — PACIFIC • 100 kW
CHINA (PR) — VOICE OF JINLING, Nanjing — E ASIA • 50 kW
CUBA — †RADIO HABANA, Via USSR — (D) • W EUROPE • 500 kW
IRAN — †VO THE ISLAMIC REPUBLIC, Tehrān — Irr • MIDEAST • RAMADAN • 500 kW — MIDEAST & N AFRICA • 100 kW — MIDEAST • 500 kW
IVORY COAST — RTV IVOIRIENNE, Abidjan — W AFRICA • DS • 20 kW
SEYCHELLES — †FAR EAST BC ASS'N, North Pt, Mahé Is — Alternative Frequency to 7275 kHz
YUGOSLAVIA — RADIO YUGOSLAVIA, Bijeljina — (J) • EUROPE • 250 kW
7215v ANGOLA — †RADIO NACIONAL, Luanda — DS-8 • 10 kW
7220 CENTRAL AFRICAN REP — RTV CENTRAFRICAINE, Bangui — DS-FRENCH, ETC • 20/50/100 kW
HUNGARY — RADIO BUDAPEST, Various Locations — Sa • EUROPE — EUROPE — M/Th • EUROPE — Su • EUROPE
SAUDI ARABIA — †BS OF THE KINGDOM, Riyadh — MIDEAST • DS-GENERAL • 350 kW
USA — †RFE-RL, Via Germany — WEST USSR • 100/250 kW
— †RFE-RL, Via Pals, Spain — WEST USSR • 500 kW
USSR — RADIO MOSCOW, Chita — E ASIA & SE ASIA • 500 kW
YUGOSLAVIA — RADIO YUGOSLAVIA, Bijeljina — EUROPE & N AFRICA • 250 kW — F-W • EUROPE & N AFRICA • 250 kW
7220v ZAMBIA — RADIO ZAMBIA-ZBS, Lusaka — DS-ENGLISH, ETC • 50 kW
7225 CHINA (PR) — SICHUAN PEOPLES BS, Chengdu — DS-1 • 15 kW — W-M • DS-1 • 15 kW
GERMANY (FR) — DEUTSCHE WELLE, Via Cyclops, Malta — (D) • MIDEAST • 250 kW
— DEUTSCHE WELLE, Via Kigali, Rwanda — C AFRICA & S AFRICA • 250 kW
— DEUTSCHE WELLE, Via Sri Lanka — S ASIA • 250 kW
INDIA — ALL INDIA RADIO, Aligarh — S ASIA • 250 kW
ROMANIA — †RADIO ROMANIA INTL, Bucharest — EUROPE • 250 kW — (D) • EUROPE • 250 kW
SWEDEN — †RADIO SWEDEN, Hörby — (D) • S ASIA & SE ASIA • 350 kW — (D) • SWEDISH • S ASIA & SE ASIA • 350 kW
USA — VOICE OF AMERICA, Via Philippines — SE ASIA • 250 kW
7225v PAKISTAN — RADIO PAKISTAN, Islamabad — (J) • MIDEAST • 100 kW
7230 BURKINA FASO — †RTV BURKINA, Ouagadougou — DS-FRENCH, ETC • 50 kW — Th/Sa/Su • DS-FRENCH, ETC • 50 kW
CANADA — R CANADA INTL, Via Sines, Portugal — (J) • E EUROPE & WEST USSR • 250 kW
— †R CANADA INTL, Via United Kingdom — (D) • EUROPE • 300 kW — (D) • M-F • EUROPE • 300 kW
INDIA — †ALL INDIA RADIO, Kurseong — S ASIA • 20 kW — DS • 20 kW
IRAN — †VO THE ISLAMIC REPUBLIC, Tehrān — Irr • MIDEAST • RAMADAN • 100 kW • ALT. FREQ TO 9610 kHz — (D) • S ASIA • 100 kW • ALT. FREQ. TO 9610 kHz — (D) • MIDEAST • 100 kW • ALT. FREQ. TO 9610 kHz
ITALY — †ADVENTIST WORLD RADIO, Forlì — EUROPE • 3 kW — Sa-Tu • EUROPE • 3 kW — W-F • EUROPE • 3 kW

(con'd)

ENGLISH ▬   ARABIC ▨   CHINESE ▭▭▭   FRENCH ▬   GERMAN ▬   RUSSIAN ═   SPANISH ▬   OTHER ─

FREQUENCY   COUNTRY, STATION, LOCATION   TARGET • NETWORK • POWER (kW)   World Time

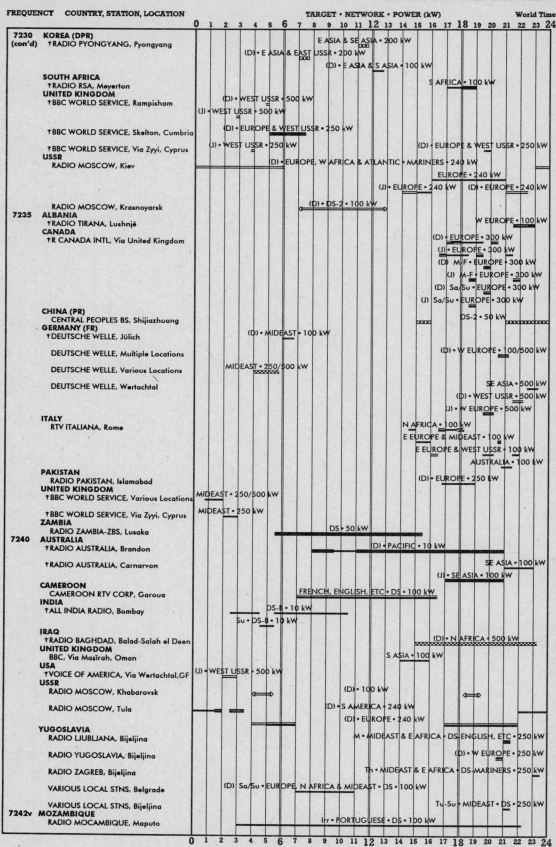

FREQUENCY	COUNTRY, STATION, LOCATION
7230 (con'd)	**KOREA (DPR)** †RADIO PYONGYANG, Pyongyang
	SOUTH AFRICA †RADIO RSA, Meyerton
	UNITED KINGDOM †BBC WORLD SERVICE, Rampisham
	†BBC WORLD SERVICE, Skelton, Cumbria
	†BBC WORLD SERVICE, Via Zyyi, Cyprus
	USSR RADIO MOSCOW, Kiev
	RADIO MOSCOW, Krasnoyarsk
7235	**ALBANIA** †RADIO TIRANA, Lushnjë
	CANADA †R CANADA INTL, Via United Kingdom
	CHINA (PR) CENTRAL PEOPLES BS, Shijiazhuang
	GERMANY (FR) †DEUTSCHE WELLE, Jülich
	DEUTSCHE WELLE, Multiple Locations
	DEUTSCHE WELLE, Various Locations
	DEUTSCHE WELLE, Wertachtal
	ITALY RTV ITALIANA, Rome
	PAKISTAN RADIO PAKISTAN, Islamabad
	UNITED KINGDOM †BBC WORLD SERVICE, Various Locations
	†BBC WORLD SERVICE, Via Zyyi, Cyprus
	ZAMBIA RADIO ZAMBIA-ZBS, Lusaka
7240	**AUSTRALIA** †RADIO AUSTRALIA, Brandon
	†RADIO AUSTRALIA, Carnarvon
	CAMEROON CAMEROON RTV CORP, Garoua
	INDIA †ALL INDIA RADIO, Bombay
	IRAQ †RADIO BAGHDAD, Balad-Salah el Deen
	UNITED KINGDOM BBC, Via Maşīrah, Oman
	USA †VOICE OF AMERICA, Via Wertachtal, GF
	USSR RADIO MOSCOW, Khabarovsk
	RADIO MOSCOW, Tula
	YUGOSLAVIA RADIO LJUBLJANA, Bijeljina
	RADIO YUGOSLAVIA, Bijeljina
	RADIO ZAGREB, Bijeljina
	VARIOUS LOCAL STNS, Belgrade
	VARIOUS LOCAL STNS, Bijeljina
7242v	**MOZAMBIQUE** RADIO MOCAMBIQUE, Maputo

Transmission data (target • network • power):

- RADIO PYONGYANG: E ASIA & SE ASIA • 200 kW; (D) • E ASIA & EAST USSR • 200 kW; (D) • E ASIA & S ASIA • 100 kW
- RADIO RSA: S AFRICA • 100 kW
- BBC WORLD SERVICE, Rampisham: (D) • WEST USSR • 500 kW; (J) • WEST USSR • 500 kW
- BBC WORLD SERVICE, Skelton: (D) • EUROPE & WEST USSR • 250 kW
- BBC WORLD SERVICE, Via Zyyi, Cyprus: (J) • WEST USSR • 250 kW; (D) • EUROPE & WEST USSR • 250 kW
- RADIO MOSCOW, Kiev: (D) • EUROPE, W AFRICA & ATLANTIC • MARINERS • 240 kW; EUROPE • 240 kW; (J) • EUROPE • 240 kW; (D) • EUROPE • 240 kW
- RADIO MOSCOW, Krasnoyarsk: (D) • DS-2 • 100 kW
- RADIO TIRANA: W EUROPE • 100 kW
- R CANADA INTL: (D) • EUROPE • 300 kW; (J) • EUROPE • 300 kW; (D) M-F • EUROPE • 300 kW; (J) M-F • EUROPE • 300 kW; (D) Sa/Su • EUROPE • 300 kW; (J) Sa/Su • EUROPE • 300 kW
- CENTRAL PEOPLES BS: DS-2 • 50 kW
- DEUTSCHE WELLE, Jülich: (D) • MIDEAST • 100 kW
- DEUTSCHE WELLE, Multiple Locations: (D) • W EUROPE • 100/500 kW
- DEUTSCHE WELLE, Various Locations: MIDEAST • 250/500 kW
- DEUTSCHE WELLE, Wertachtal: SE ASIA • 500 kW; (D) • WEST USSR • 500 kW; (J) • W EUROPE • 500 kW
- RTV ITALIANA: N AFRICA • 100 kW; E EUROPE & MIDEAST • 100 kW; E EUROPE & WEST USSR • 100 kW; AUSTRALIA • 100 kW
- RADIO PAKISTAN: (D) • EUROPE • 250 kW
- BBC WORLD SERVICE, Various Locations: MIDEAST • 250/500 kW
- BBC WORLD SERVICE, Via Zyyi, Cyprus: MIDEAST • 250 kW
- RADIO ZAMBIA-ZBS: DS • 50 kW
- RADIO AUSTRALIA, Brandon: (D) • PACIFIC • 10 kW
- RADIO AUSTRALIA, Carnarvon: SE ASIA • 100 kW; (J) • SE ASIA • 100 kW
- CAMEROON RTV CORP: FRENCH, ENGLISH, ETC • DS • 100 kW
- ALL INDIA RADIO: DS-B • 10 kW; Su • DS-B • 10 kW
- RADIO BAGHDAD: (D) • N AFRICA • 500 kW
- BBC, Via Maşīrah: S ASIA • 100 kW
- VOICE OF AMERICA: (J) • WEST USSR • 500 kW
- RADIO MOSCOW, Khabarovsk: (D) • 100 kW
- RADIO MOSCOW, Tula: (D) • S AMERICA • 240 kW; (D) • EUROPE • 240 kW
- RADIO LJUBLJANA: M • MIDEAST & E AFRICA • DS-ENGLISH, ETC • 250 kW
- RADIO YUGOSLAVIA: (D) • W EUROPE • 250 kW
- RADIO ZAGREB: Th • MIDEAST & E AFRICA • DS-MARINERS • 250 kW
- VARIOUS LOCAL STNS, Belgrade: (D) Sa/Su • EUROPE, N AFRICA & MIDEAST • DS • 100 kW
- VARIOUS LOCAL STNS, Bijeljina: Tu-Su • MIDEAST • DS • 250 kW
- RADIO MOCAMBIQUE: Irr • PORTUGUESE • DS • 100 kW

SUMMER ONLY (J)   WINTER ONLY (D)   JAMMING / OR ∧   EARLIEST HEARD ◁   LATEST HEARD ▷   NEW OR CHANGED FOR 1991 †

FREQUENCY   COUNTRY, STATION, LOCATION

TARGET • NETWORK • POWER (kW)

World Time

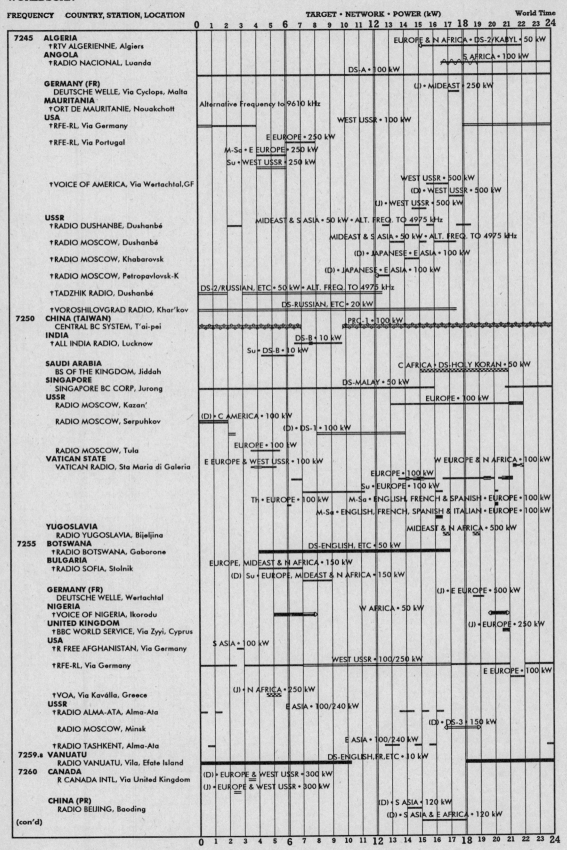

Freq	Country, Station, Location	Details
7245	**ALGERIA** †RTV ALGERIENNE, Algiers	EUROPE & N AFRICA • DS-2/KABYL • 50 kW
	ANGOLA †RADIO NACIONAL, Luanda	S AFRICA • 100 kW / DS-A • 100 kW
	GERMANY (FR) DEUTSCHE WELLE, Via Cyclops, Malta	(J) • MIDEAST • 250 kW
	MAURITANIA †ORT DE MAURITANIE, Nouakchott	Alternative Frequency to 9610 kHz
	USA †RFE-RL, Via Germany	WEST USSR • 100 kW
	†RFE-RL, Via Portugal	E EUROPE • 250 kW / M-Sa • E EUROPE • 250 kW / Su • WEST USSR • 250 kW
	†VOICE OF AMERICA, Via Wertachtal, GF	WEST USSR • 500 kW / (D) • WEST USSR • 500 kW / (J) • WEST USSR • 500 kW
	USSR †RADIO DUSHANBE, Dushanbé	MIDEAST & S ASIA • 50 kW • ALT. FREQ. TO 4975 kHz
	†RADIO MOSCOW, Dushanbé	MIDEAST & S ASIA • 50 kW • ALT. FREQ. TO 4975 kHz
	†RADIO MOSCOW, Khabarovsk	(D) • JAPANESE • E ASIA • 100 kW
	†RADIO MOSCOW, Petropavlovsk-K	(D) • JAPANESE • E ASIA • 100 kW
	†TADZHIK RADIO, Dushanbé	DS-2/RUSSIAN, ETC • 50 kW • ALT. FREQ. TO 4975 kHz
	†VOROSHILOVGRAD RADIO, Khar'kov	DS-RUSSIAN, ETC • 20 kW
7250	**CHINA (TAIWAN)** CENTRAL BC SYSTEM, T'ai-pei	PRC-1 • 100 kW
	INDIA †ALL INDIA RADIO, Lucknow	DS-B • 10 kW / Su • DS-B • 10 kW
	SAUDI ARABIA BS OF THE KINGDOM, Jiddah	C AFRICA • DS-HOLY KORAN • 50 kW
	SINGAPORE SINGAPORE BC CORP, Jurong	DS-MALAY • 50 kW
	USSR RADIO MOSCOW, Kazan'	EUROPE • 100 kW
	RADIO MOSCOW, Serpuhkov	(D) • C AMERICA • 100 kW / (D) • DS-1 • 100 kW
	RADIO MOSCOW, Tula	EUROPE • 100 kW
	VATICAN STATE VATICAN RADIO, Sta Maria di Galeria	E EUROPE & WEST USSR • 100 kW / W EUROPE & N AFRICA • 100 kW / EUROPE • 100 kW / Su • EUROPE • 100 kW / Th • EUROPE • 100 kW / M-Sa • ENGLISH, FRENCH & SPANISH • EUROPE • 100 kW / M-Sa • ENGLISH, FRENCH, SPANISH & ITALIAN • EUROPE • 100 kW
	YUGOSLAVIA RADIO YUGOSLAVIA, Bijeljina	MIDEAST & N AFRICA • 500 kW
7255	**BOTSWANA** †RADIO BOTSWANA, Gaborone	DS-ENGLISH, ETC • 50 kW
	BULGARIA †RADIO SOFIA, Stolnik	EUROPE, MIDEAST & N AFRICA • 150 kW / (D) Su • EUROPE, MIDEAST & N AFRICA • 150 kW
	GERMANY (FR) DEUTSCHE WELLE, Wertachtal	(J) • E EUROPE • 500 kW
	NIGERIA †VOICE OF NIGERIA, Ikorodu	W AFRICA • 50 kW
	UNITED KINGDOM †BBC WORLD SERVICE, Via Zyyi, Cyprus	(J) • EUROPE • 250 kW
	USA †R FREE AFGHANISTAN, Via Germany	S ASIA • 100 kW
	†RFE-RL, Via Germany	WEST USSR • 100/250 kW / E EUROPE • 100 kW
	†VOA, Via Kaválla, Greece	(J) • N AFRICA • 250 kW
	USSR †RADIO ALMA-ATA, Alma-Ata	E ASIA • 100/240 kW
	RADIO MOSCOW, Minsk	(D) • DS-3 • 150 kW
	†RADIO TASHKENT, Alma-Ata	E ASIA • 100/240 kW
7259.8	**VANUATU** RADIO VANUATU, Vila, Efate Island	DS-ENGLISH, FR, ETC • 10 kW
7260	**CANADA** R CANADA INTL, Via United Kingdom	(D) • EUROPE & WEST USSR • 300 kW / (J) • EUROPE & WEST USSR • 300 kW
	CHINA (PR) RADIO BEIJING, Baoding	(D) • S ASIA • 120 kW / (D) • S ASIA & E AFRICA • 120 kW

(con'd)

ENGLISH ▬ ARABIC ▨ CHINESE ▭▭▭ FRENCH ▬ GERMAN ▬ RUSSIAN ═ SPANISH ▬ OTHER ▬

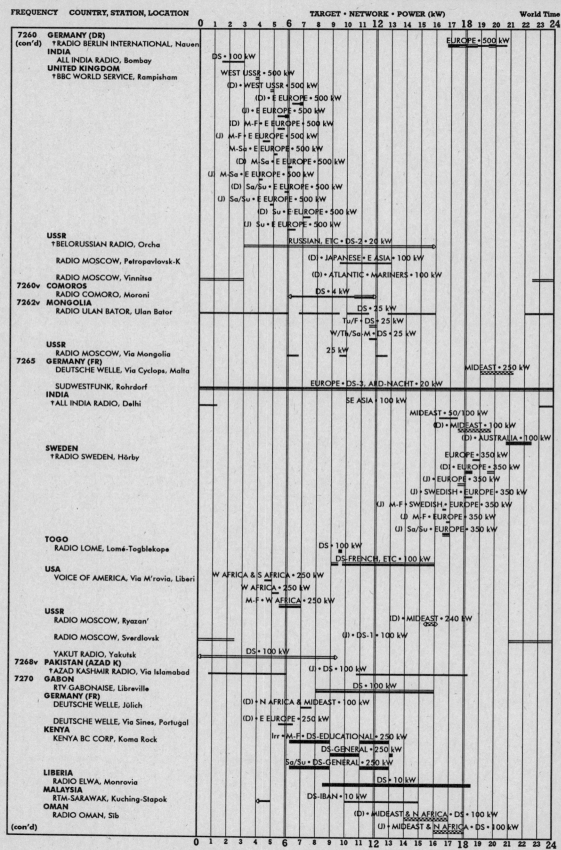

FREQUENCY   COUNTRY, STATION, LOCATION   TARGET • NETWORK • POWER (kW)   World Time

0 1 2 3 4 5 6 7 8 9 10 11 12 13 14 15 16 17 18 19 20 21 22 23 24

7270 (con'd)	POLAND
	RADIO POLONIA, Warsaw	EUROPE & ATLANTIC • 100 kW
		W EUROPE & N AFRICA • 100 kW
		EUROPE • 100 kW
	SOUTH AFRICA
	†RADIO RSA, Meyerton	S AFRICA • 250 kW
	SWAZILAND
	TRANS WORLD RADIO, Manzini	(D) • S AFRICA • 25 kW
		(D) Sa/Su • S AFRICA • 25 kW
	USA
	†VOA, Via Kaválla, Greece	(D) • WEST USSR • 250 kW
		(J) • WEST USSR • 250 kW
	†VOICE OF AMERICA, Via Wertachtal, GF	WEST USSR • 500 kW
		(J) • WEST USSR • 500 kW
	USSR
	†RADIO MOSCOW, Khabarovsk	(D) • JAPANESE • E ASIA • 100 kW
	†RADIO MOSCOW, Petropavlovsk-K	(D) • JAPANESE • E ASIA • 100 kW
7275	CHINA (PR)
	GUIZHOU PEOPLES BS, Guiyang	DS-1 • 50 kW
	GERMANY (FR)
	DEUTSCHE WELLE, Multiple Locations	(D) • MIDEAST & S ASIA • 100/500 kW
	ITALY
	†RTV ITALIANA, Rome	E EUROPE & WEST USSR • 100 kW
		EUROPE, N AFRICA & MIDEAST • 100 kW
		EUROPE • 100 kW
		N AFRICA • 100 kW
	KOREA (REPUBLIC)
	†RADIO KOREA, In-Kimjae	E ASIA • 250 kW
		JAPANESE • E ASIA • 250 kW
	SAUDI ARABIA
	BS OF THE KINGDOM, Riyadh	W AFRICA • 350 kW
		W AFRICA • DS HOLY KORAN • 350 kW
	SEYCHELLES
	†FAR EAST BC ASS'N, North Pt, Mahé Is	S ASIA • 100 kW • ALT. FREQ. TO 7215 kHz
		F-Tu • S ASIA • 100 kW • ALT. FREQ. TO 7215 kHz
	UNITED KINGDOM
	BBC WORLD SERVICE, Via Singapore	SE ASIA • 100 kW
	USA
	†RFE-RL, Via Portugal	WEST USSR • 250 kW
	USSR
	†RADIO TASHKENT, Tashkent	(D) • MIDEAST • 50 kW • ALT FREQ. TO 7285 kHz
7280	CHINA (PR)
	†VOICE OF THE STRAIT-PLA, Fuzhou	TAIWAN-1 • 50 kW
		(J) • TAIWAN-1 • 50 kW
	FRANCE
	†R FRANCE INTL, Issoudun-Allouis	E EUROPE • 100 kW
		(D) • E EUROPE • 100 kW
		(J) • E EUROPE • 100 kW
	INDIA
	†ALL INDIA RADIO, Delhi	(D) • DS • 20 kW
	†ALL INDIA RADIO, Gauhati	DS-A • 50 kW
		Su • DS-A • 50 kW
	SAUDI ARABIA
	BS OF THE KINGDOM, Jiddah	MIDEAST & E AFRICA • DS-GENERAL • 50 kW
	TANZANIA
	†RADIO TANZANIA, Dar es Salaam	Irr • S AFRICA • 50 kW
	UNITED ARAB EMIRATES
	VOICE OF THE UAE, Abu Dhabi	MIDEAST • 500 kW
	USA
	†VOA, Via Kaválla, Greece	MIDEAST • 250 kW
		WEST USSR • 250 kW
		(D) • MIDEAST • 250 kW
		(D) • WEST USSR • 250 kW
		(J) • WEST USSR • 250 kW
	VOICE OF AMERICA, Via M'rovia, Liberi	W AFRICA & C AFRICA • 250 kW
	USSR
	†KAZAKH RADIO	DS-2
	MARKOVSK RADIO, Ripov	DS • 20 kW
	†RADIO MOSCOW, Kenga	(D) • E ASIA • 50 kW
7285	CANADA
	R CANADA INTL, Via Sines, Portugal	(D) • EUROPE & WEST USSR • 250 kW
	CHINA (TAIWAN)
	VOICE OF ASIA, Kao-hsiung	SE ASIA • 100 kW
	GERMANY (FR)
	DEUTSCHE WELLE, Jülich	(J) • WEST USSR • 100 kW
	DEUTSCHE WELLE, Via Sines, Portugal	(D) • E EUROPE • 250 kW
	DEUTSCHE WELLE, Wertachtal	S ASIA • 500 kW
		(D) • WEST USSR • 500 kW
(con'd)	

0 1 2 3 4 5 6 7 8 9 10 11 12 13 14 15 16 17 18 19 20 21 22 23 24

ENGLISH ▬▬   ARABIC ░░░   CHINESE ▫▫▫   FRENCH ▭▭   GERMAN ▬▬   RUSSIAN ═══   SPANISH ▬▬   OTHER ——

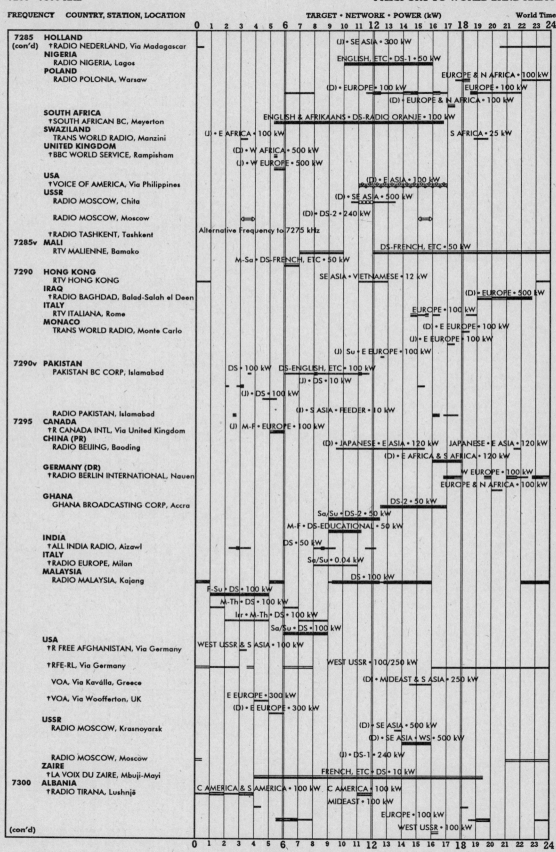

FREQUENCY   COUNTRY, STATION, LOCATION   TARGET • NETWORK • POWER (kW)   World Time

7285	**HOLLAND**
(con'd)	†RADIO NEDERLAND, Via Madagascar
	NIGERIA
	RADIO NIGERIA, Lagos
	POLAND
	RADIO POLONIA, Warsaw
	SOUTH AFRICA
	†SOUTH AFRICAN BC, Meyerton
	SWAZILAND
	TRANS WORLD RADIO, Manzini
	UNITED KINGDOM
	†BBC WORLD SERVICE, Rampisham
	USA
	†VOICE OF AMERICA, Via Philippines
	USSR
	RADIO MOSCOW, Chita
	RADIO MOSCOW, Moscow
	†RADIO TASHKENT, Tashkent
7285v	**MALI**
	RTV MALIENNE, Bamako
7290	**HONG KONG**
	RTV HONG KONG
	IRAQ
	†RADIO BAGHDAD, Balad-Salah el Deen
	ITALY
	RTV ITALIANA, Rome
	MONACO
	TRANS WORLD RADIO, Monte Carlo
7290v	**PAKISTAN**
	PAKISTAN BC CORP, Islamabad
	RADIO PAKISTAN, Islamabad
7295	**CANADA**
	†R CANADA INTL, Via United Kingdom
	CHINA (PR)
	RADIO BEIJING, Baoding
	GERMANY (DR)
	†RADIO BERLIN INTERNATIONAL, Nauen
	GHANA
	GHANA BROADCASTING CORP, Accra
	INDIA
	†ALL INDIA RADIO, Aizawl
	ITALY
	†RADIO EUROPE, Milan
	MALAYSIA
	RADIO MALAYSIA, Kajang
	USA
	†R FREE AFGHANISTAN, Via Germany
	†RFE-RL, Via Germany
	VOA, Via Kaválla, Greece
	†VOA, Via Woofferton, UK
	USSR
	RADIO MOSCOW, Krasnoyarsk
	RADIO MOSCOW, Moscow
	ZAIRE
	†LA VOIX DU ZAIRE, Mbuji-Mayi
7300	**ALBANIA**
	†RADIO TIRANA, Lushnjë
(con'd)	

Bardata / labels within grid:

(J) • SE ASIA • 300 kW
ENGLISH, ETC • DS-1 • 50 kW
EUROPE & N AFRICA • 100 kW
(D) • EUROPE • 100 kW
EUROPE • 100 kW
(D) • EUROPE & N AFRICA • 100 kW
ENGLISH & AFRIKAANS • DS-RADIO ORANJE • 100 kW
(J) • E AFRICA • 100 kW   S AFRICA • 25 kW
(D) • W AFRICA • 500 kW
(J) • W EUROPE • 500 kW
(D) • E ASIA • 100 kW
(D) • SE ASIA • 500 kW
(D) • DS-2 • 240 kW
Alternative Frequency to 7275 kHz
DS-FRENCH, ETC • 50 kW
M-Sa • DS-FRENCH, ETC • 50 kW
SE ASIA • VIETNAMESE • 12 kW
(D) • EUROPE • 500 kW
EUROPE • 100 kW
(D) • E EUROPE • 100 kW
(J) • E EUROPE • 100 kW
(J) • Su • E EUROPE • 100 kW
DS • 100 kW   DS-ENGLISH, ETC • 100 kW
(J) • DS • 10 kW
(J) • DS • 100 kW
(J) • S ASIA • FEEDER • 10 kW
(J) • M-F • EUROPE • 100 kW
(D) • JAPANESE • E ASIA • 120 kW   JAPANESE • E ASIA • 120 kW
(D) • E AFRICA & S AFRICA • 120 kW
W EUROPE • 100 kW
EUROPE & N AFRICA • 100 kW
DS-2 • 50 kW
Sa/Su • DS-2 • 50 kW
M-F • DS-EDUCATIONAL • 50 kW
DS • 50 kW
Sa/Su • 0.04 kW
DS • 100 kW
F-Su • DS • 100 kW
M-Th • DS • 100 kW
Irr • M-Th • DS • 100 kW
Sa/Su • DS • 100 kW
WEST USSR & S ASIA • 100 kW
WEST USSR • 100/250 kW
(D) • MIDEAST & S ASIA • 250 kW
E EUROPE • 300 kW
(D) • E EUROPE • 300 kW
(D) • SE ASIA • 500 kW
(D) • SE ASIA • WS • 500 kW
(J) • DS-1 • 240 kW
FRENCH, ETC • DS • 10 kW
C AMERICA & S AMERICA • 100 kW   C AMERICA • 100 kW
MIDEAST • 100 kW
EUROPE • 100 kW
WEST USSR • 100 kW

SUMMER ONLY (J)   WINTER ONLY (D)   JAMMING / OR ∧   EARLIEST HEARD ◁   LATEST HEARD ▷   NEW OR CHANGED FOR 1991 †

FREQUENCY	COUNTRY, STATION, LOCATION	TARGET • NETWORK • POWER (kW)

World Time
0 1 2 3 4 5 6 7 8 9 10 11 12 13 14 15 16 17 18 19 20 21 22 23 24

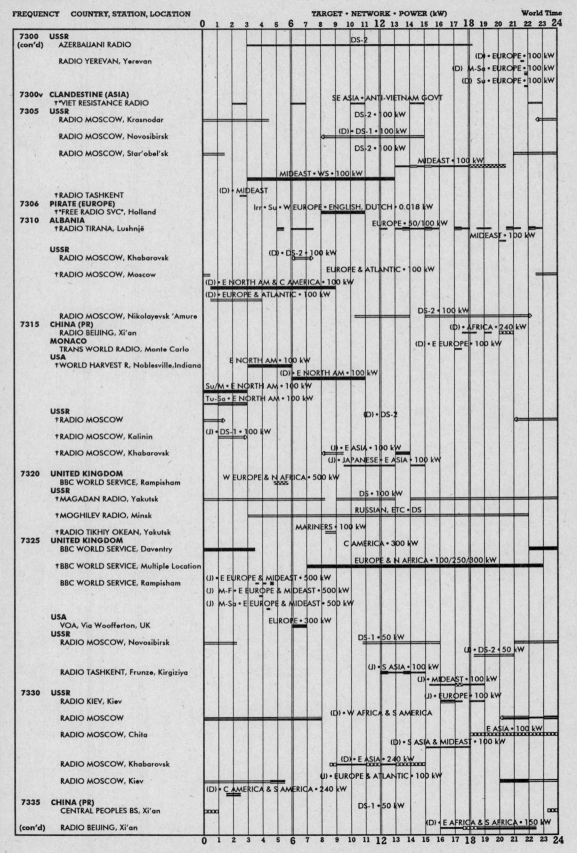

7300 (con'd)	USSR
	AZERBAIJANI RADIO — DS-2
	RADIO YEREVAN, Yerevan — (D) • EUROPE • 100 kW; (D) M-Sa • EUROPE • 100 kW; (D) Su • EUROPE • 100 kW
7300v	CLANDESTINE (ASIA) — SE ASIA • ANTI-VIETNAM GOVT
	†"VIET RESISTANCE RADIO"
7305	USSR
	RADIO MOSCOW, Krasnodar — DS-2 • 100 kW
	RADIO MOSCOW, Novosibirsk — (D) • DS-1 • 100 kW
	RADIO MOSCOW, Star'obel'sk — DS-2 • 100 kW; MIDEAST • 100 kW; MIDEAST • WS • 100 kW
	†RADIO TASHKENT — (D) • MIDEAST
7306	PIRATE (EUROPE) — Irr • Su • W EUROPE • ENGLISH, DUTCH • 0.018 kW
	†"FREE RADIO SVC", Holland
7310	ALBANIA — EUROPE • 50/100 kW; MIDEAST • 100 kW
	†RADIO TIRANA, Lushnjë
	USSR
	RADIO MOSCOW, Khabarovsk — (D) • DS-2 • 100 kW
	†RADIO MOSCOW, Moscow — EUROPE & ATLANTIC • 100 kW; (D) • E NORTH AM & C AMERICA • 100 kW; (D) • EUROPE & ATLANTIC • 100 kW
	RADIO MOSCOW, Nikolayevsk 'Amure — DS-2 • 100 kW
7315	CHINA (PR) — (D) • AFRICA • 240 kW
	RADIO BEIJING, Xi'an
	MONACO — (D) • E EUROPE • 100 kW
	TRANS WORLD RADIO, Monte Carlo
	USA — E NORTH AM • 100 kW; (D) • E NORTH AM • 100 kW; Su/M • E NORTH AM • 100 kW; Tu-Sa • E NORTH AM • 100 kW
	†WORLD HARVEST R, Noblesville, Indiana
	USSR — (D) • DS-2
	†RADIO MOSCOW
	†RADIO MOSCOW, Kalinin — (J) • DS-1 • 100 kW
	†RADIO MOSCOW, Khabarovsk — (J) • E ASIA • 100 kW; (J) • JAPANESE • E ASIA • 100 kW
7320	UNITED KINGDOM — W EUROPE & N AFRICA • 500 kW
	BBC WORLD SERVICE, Rampisham
	USSR — DS • 100 kW
	†MAGADAN RADIO, Yakutsk
	†MOGHILEV RADIO, Minsk — RUSSIAN, ETC • DS
	†RADIO TIKHIY OKEAN, Yakutsk — MARINERS • 100 kW
7325	UNITED KINGDOM — C AMERICA • 300 kW
	BBC WORLD SERVICE, Daventry — EUROPE & N AFRICA • 100/250/300 kW
	†BBC WORLD SERVICE, Multiple Location
	BBC WORLD SERVICE, Rampisham — (J) • E EUROPE & MIDEAST • 500 kW; (J) M-F • E EUROPE & MIDEAST • 500 kW; (J) M-Sa • E EUROPE & MIDEAST • 500 kW
	USA — EUROPE • 300 kW
	VOA, Via Woofferton, UK
	USSR — DS-1 • 50 kW
	RADIO MOSCOW, Novosibirsk — (J) • DS-2 • 50 kW
	RADIO TASHKENT, Frunze, Kirgiziya — (J) • S ASIA • 100 kW; (J) • MIDEAST • 100 kW
7330	USSR — (J) • EUROPE • 100 kW
	RADIO KIEV, Kiev
	RADIO MOSCOW — (D) • W AFRICA & S AMERICA; E ASIA • 100 kW
	RADIO MOSCOW, Chita — (D) • S ASIA & MIDEAST • 100 kW
	RADIO MOSCOW, Khabarovsk — (D) • E ASIA • 240 kW
	RADIO MOSCOW, Kiev — (J) • EUROPE & ATLANTIC • 100 kW; (D) • C AMERICA & S AMERICA • 240 kW
7335	CHINA (PR) — DS-1 • 50 kW
	CENTRAL PEOPLES BS, Xi'an
(con'd)	RADIO BEIJING, Xi'an — (D) • E AFRICA & S AFRICA • 150 kW

0 1 2 3 4 5 6 7 8 9 10 11 12 13 14 15 16 17 18 19 20 21 22 23 24

ENGLISH ▬   ARABIC ▩   CHINESE ▢▢▢   FRENCH ▬   GERMAN ▬   RUSSIAN =   SPANISH ▬   OTHER —

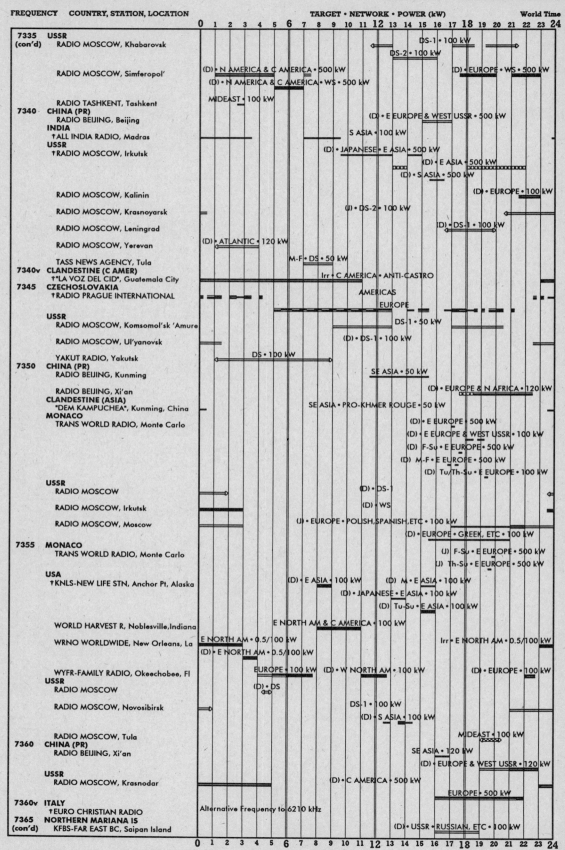

FREQUENCY   COUNTRY, STATION, LOCATION

TARGET • NETWORK • POWER (kW)   World Time

7335 **USSR**
(con'd)   RADIO MOSCOW, Khabarovsk
            RADIO MOSCOW, Simferopol'
            RADIO TASHKENT, Tashkent
7340 **CHINA (PR)**
            RADIO BEIJING, Beijing
        INDIA
            †ALL INDIA RADIO, Madras
        USSR
            †RADIO MOSCOW, Irkutsk
            RADIO MOSCOW, Kalinin
            RADIO MOSCOW, Krasnoyarsk
            RADIO MOSCOW, Leningrad
            RADIO MOSCOW, Yerevan
            TASS NEWS AGENCY, Tula
7340v **CLANDESTINE (C AMER)**
            †"LA VOZ DEL CID", Guatemala City
7345 **CZECHOSLOVAKIA**
            †RADIO PRAGUE INTERNATIONAL
        USSR
            RADIO MOSCOW, Komsomol'sk 'Amure
            RADIO MOSCOW, Ul'yanovsk
            YAKUT RADIO, Yakutsk
7350 **CHINA (PR)**
            RADIO BEIJING, Kunming
            RADIO BEIJING, Xi'an
        CLANDESTINE (ASIA)
            "DEM KAMPUCHEA", Kunming, China
        MONACO
            TRANS WORLD RADIO, Monte Carlo
        USSR
            RADIO MOSCOW
            RADIO MOSCOW, Irkutsk
            RADIO MOSCOW, Moscow
7355 **MONACO**
            TRANS WORLD RADIO, Monte Carlo
        USA
            †KNLS-NEW LIFE STN, Anchor Pt, Alaska
            WORLD HARVEST R, Noblesville, Indiana
            WRNO WORLDWIDE, New Orleans, La
            WYFR-FAMILY RADIO, Okeechobee, Fl
        USSR
            RADIO MOSCOW
            RADIO MOSCOW, Novosibirsk
            RADIO MOSCOW, Tula
7360 **CHINA (PR)**
            RADIO BEIJING, Xi'an
        USSR
            RADIO MOSCOW, Krasnodar
7360v **ITALY**
            †EURO CHRISTIAN RADIO
7365 **NORTHERN MARIANA IS**
(con'd)   KFBS-FAR EAST BC, Saipan Island

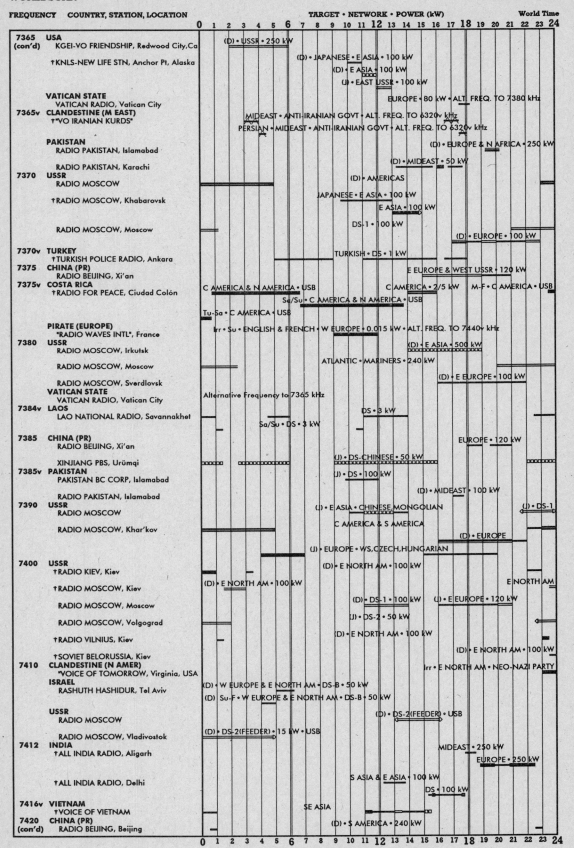

FREQUENCY   COUNTRY, STATION, LOCATION

TARGET • NETWORK • POWER (kW)

World Time

Frequency	Country, Station, Location	Target • Network • Power
7365 (con'd)	**USA** KGEI-VO FRIENDSHIP, Redwood City,Ca	(D) • USSR • 250 kW
	†KNLS-NEW LIFE STN, Anchor Pt, Alaska	(D) • JAPANESE • E ASIA • 100 kW / (D) • E ASIA • 100 kW / (J) • EAST USSR • 100 kW
	VATICAN STATE VATICAN RADIO, Vatican City	EUROPE • 80 kW • ALT. FREQ. TO 7380 kHz
7365v	**CLANDESTINE (M EAST)** †"VO IRANIAN KURDS"	MIDEAST • ANTI-IRANIAN GOVT • ALT. FREQ. TO 6320v kHz / PERSIAN • MIDEAST • ANTI-IRANIAN GOVT • ALT. FREQ. TO 6320v kHz
	PAKISTAN RADIO PAKISTAN, Islamabad	(D) • EUROPE & N AFRICA • 250 kW
	RADIO PAKISTAN, Karachi	(D) • MIDEAST • 50 kW
7370	**USSR** RADIO MOSCOW	(D) • AMERICAS
	†RADIO MOSCOW, Khabarovsk	JAPANESE • E ASIA • 100 kW / E ASIA • 100 kW
	RADIO MOSCOW, Moscow	DS-1 • 100 kW / (D) • EUROPE • 100 kW
7370v	**TURKEY** †TURKISH POLICE RADIO, Ankara	TURKISH • DS • 1 kW
7375	**CHINA (PR)** RADIO BEIJING, Xi'an	E EUROPE & WEST USSR • 120 kW
7375v	**COSTA RICA** †RADIO FOR PEACE, Ciudad Colón	C AMERICA & N AMERICA • USB / C AMERICA • 2/5 kW / M-F • C AMERICA • USB / Sa/Su • C AMERICA & N AMERICA • USB / Tu-Sa • C AMERICA • USB
	PIRATE (EUROPE) "RADIO WAVES INTL", France	Irr • Su • ENGLISH & FRENCH • W EUROPE • 0.015 kW • ALT. FREQ. TO 7440v kHz
7380	**USSR** RADIO MOSCOW, Irkutsk	(D) • E ASIA • 500 kW
	RADIO MOSCOW, Moscow	ATLANTIC • MARINERS • 240 kW
	RADIO MOSCOW, Sverdlovsk	(D) • E EUROPE • 100 kW
	VATICAN STATE VATICAN RADIO, Vatican City	Alternative Frequency to 7365 kHz
7384v	**LAOS** LAO NATIONAL RADIO, Savannakhet	DS • 3 kW / Sa/Su • DS • 3 kW
7385	**CHINA (PR)** RADIO BEIJING, Xi'an	EUROPE • 120 kW
	XINJIANG PBS, Urümqi	(J) • DS-CHINESE • 50 kW
7385v	**PAKISTAN** PAKISTAN BC CORP, Islamabad	(J) • DS • 100 kW
	RADIO PAKISTAN, Islamabad	(D) • MIDEAST • 100 kW
7390	**USSR** RADIO MOSCOW	(J) • E ASIA • CHINESE, MONGOLIAN / (J) • DS-1
	RADIO MOSCOW, Khar'kov	C AMERICA & S AMERICA / (D) • EUROPE
7400	**USSR** †RADIO KIEV, Kiev	(J) • EUROPE • WS, CZECH, HUNGARIAN / (D) • E NORTH AM • 100 kW
	†RADIO MOSCOW, Kiev	(D) • E NORTH AM • 100 kW / E NORTH AM
	RADIO MOSCOW, Moscow	(D) • DS-1 • 100 kW / (J) • E EUROPE • 120 kW
	RADIO MOSCOW, Volgograd	(J) • DS-2 • 50 kW
	†RADIO VILNIUS, Kiev	(D) • E NORTH AM • 100 kW
	†SOVIET BELORUSSIA, Kiev	(D) • E NORTH AM • 100 kW
7410	**CLANDESTINE (N AMER)** "VOICE OF TOMORROW", Virginia, USA	Irr • E NORTH AM • NEO-NAZI PARTY
	ISRAEL RASHUTH HASHIDUR, Tel Aviv	(D) • W EUROPE & E NORTH AM • DS-B • 50 kW / (D) Su-F • W EUROPE & E NORTH AM • DS-B • 50 kW
	USSR RADIO MOSCOW	(D) • DS-2(FEEDER) • USB
	RADIO MOSCOW, Vladivostok	(D) • DS-2(FEEDER) • 15 kW • USB
7412	**INDIA** †ALL INDIA RADIO, Aligarh	MIDEAST • 250 kW / EUROPE • 250 kW
	†ALL INDIA RADIO, Delhi	S ASIA & E ASIA • 100 kW / DS • 100 kW
7416v	**VIETNAM** †VOICE OF VIETNAM	SE ASIA
7420 (con'd)	**CHINA (PR)** RADIO BEIJING, Beijing	(D) • S AMERICA • 240 kW

ENGLISH ▬▬   **ARABIC** ▨▨▨   **CHINESE** ▫▫▫   **FRENCH** ▬▬   **GERMAN** ▬▬   **RUSSIAN** ▬▬   **SPANISH** ▬▬   **OTHER** ▬

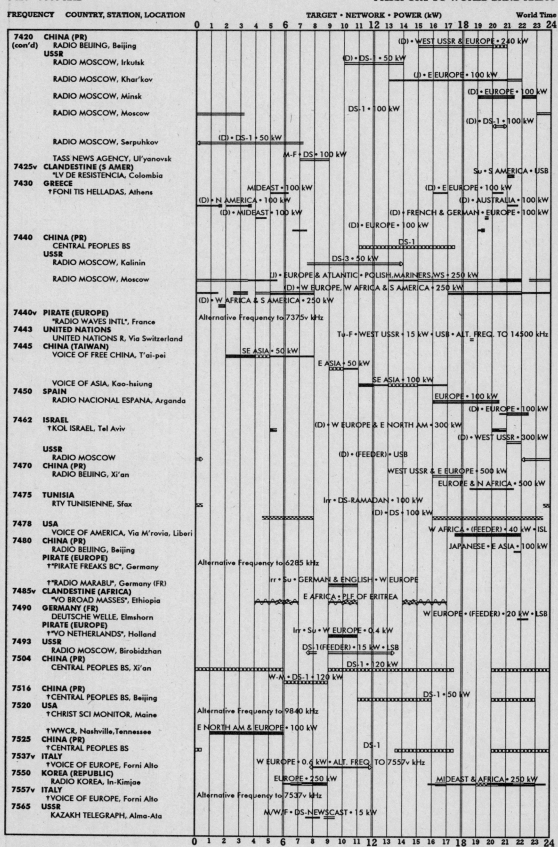

FREQUENCY	COUNTRY, STATION, LOCATION
7420 (con'd)	CHINA (PR) RADIO BEIJING, Beijing
	USSR RADIO MOSCOW, Irkutsk
	RADIO MOSCOW, Khar'kov
	RADIO MOSCOW, Minsk
	RADIO MOSCOW, Moscow
	RADIO MOSCOW, Serpuhkov
	TASS NEWS AGENCY, Ul'yanovsk
7425v	CLANDESTINE (S AMER) "LV DE RESISTENCIA, Colombia
7430	GREECE †FONI TIS HELLADAS, Athens
7440	CHINA (PR) CENTRAL PEOPLES BS
	USSR RADIO MOSCOW, Kalinin
	RADIO MOSCOW, Moscow
7440v	PIRATE (EUROPE) "RADIO WAVES INTL", France
7443	UNITED NATIONS UNITED NATIONS R, Via Switzerland
7445	CHINA (TAIWAN) VOICE OF FREE CHINA, T'ai-pei
	VOICE OF ASIA, Kao-hsiung
7450	SPAIN RADIO NACIONAL ESPANA, Arganda
7462	ISRAEL †KOL ISRAEL, Tel Aviv
	USSR RADIO MOSCOW
7470	CHINA (PR) RADIO BEIJING, Xi'an
7475	TUNISIA RTV TUNISIENNE, Sfax
7478	USA VOICE OF AMERICA, Via M'rovia, Liberi
7480	CHINA (PR) RADIO BEIJING, Beijing
	PIRATE (EUROPE) †"PIRATE FREAKS BC", Germany
	†"RADIO MARABU", Germany (FR)
7485v	CLANDESTINE (AFRICA) "VO BROAD MASSES", Ethiopia
7490	GERMANY (FR) DEUTSCHE WELLE, Elmshorn
	PIRATE (EUROPE) †"VO NETHERLANDS", Holland
7493	USSR RADIO MOSCOW, Birobidzhan
7504	CHINA (PR) CENTRAL PEOPLES BS, Xi'an
7516	CHINA (PR) †CENTRAL PEOPLES BS, Beijing
7520	USA †CHRIST SCI MONITOR, Maine
	†WWCR, Nashville, Tennessee
7525	CHINA (PR) †CENTRAL PEOPLES BS
7537v	ITALY †VOICE OF EUROPE, Forni Alto
7550	KOREA (REPUBLIC) RADIO KOREA, In-Kimjae
7557v	ITALY †VOICE OF EUROPE, Forni Alto
7565	USSR KAZAKH TELEGRAPH, Alma-Ata

TARGET • NETWORK • POWER (kW)   **World Time**

Chart annotations (left to right by frequency):

- RADIO BEIJING, Beijing: (D) • WEST USSR & EUROPE • 240 kW
- RADIO MOSCOW, Irkutsk: (D) • DS-1 • 50 kW
- RADIO MOSCOW, Khar'kov: (J) • E EUROPE • 100 kW
- RADIO MOSCOW, Minsk: (D) • EUROPE • 100 kW
- RADIO MOSCOW, Moscow: DS-1 • 100 kW ; (D) • DS-1 • 100 kW
- RADIO MOSCOW, Serpuhkov: (D) • DS-1 • 50 kW
- TASS NEWS AGENCY, Ul'yanovsk: M-F • DS • 100 kW
- "LV DE RESISTENCIA, Colombia: Su • S AMERICA • USB
- FONI TIS HELLADAS, Athens: MIDEAST • 100 kW ; (D) • E EUROPE • 100 kW ; (D) • N AMERICA • 100 kW ; (D) • AUSTRALIA • 100 kW ; (D) • MIDEAST • 100 kW ; (D) • FRENCH & GERMAN • EUROPE • 100 kW ; (D) • EUROPE • 100 kW
- CENTRAL PEOPLES BS: DS-1
- RADIO MOSCOW, Kalinin: DS-3 • 50 kW
- RADIO MOSCOW, Moscow: (J) • EUROPE & ATLANTIC • POLISH, MARINERS, WS • 250 kW ; (D) • W EUROPE, W AFRICA & S AMERICA • 250 kW ; (D) • W AFRICA & S AMERICA • 250 kW
- "RADIO WAVES INTL", France: Alternative Frequency to 7375v kHz
- UNITED NATIONS R: Tu-F • WEST USSR • 15 kW • USB • ALT. FREQ. TO 14500 kHz
- VOICE OF FREE CHINA, T'ai-pei: SE ASIA • 50 kW ; E ASIA • 50 kW
- VOICE OF ASIA, Kao-hsiung: SE ASIA • 100 kW
- RADIO NACIONAL ESPANA, Arganda: EUROPE • 100 kW ; (D) • EUROPE • 100 kW
- KOL ISRAEL, Tel Aviv: (D) • W EUROPE & E NORTH AM • 300 kW ; (D) • WEST USSR • 300 kW
- RADIO MOSCOW: (D) • (FEEDER) • USB
- RADIO BEIJING, Xi'an: WEST USSR & E EUROPE • 500 kW ; EUROPE & N AFRICA • 500 kW
- RTV TUNISIENNE, Sfax: Irr • DS-RAMADAN • 100 kW ; (D) • DS • 100 kW
- VOICE OF AMERICA, Via M'rovia, Liberi: W AFRICA • (FEEDER) • 40 kW • ISL
- RADIO BEIJING, Beijing: JAPANESE • E ASIA • 100 kW
- "PIRATE FREAKS BC", Germany: Alternative Frequency to 6285 kHz
- "RADIO MARABU", Germany (FR): Irr • Su • GERMAN & ENGLISH • W EUROPE
- "VO BROAD MASSES", Ethiopia: E AFRICA • PLF OF ERITREA
- DEUTSCHE WELLE, Elmshorn: W EUROPE • (FEEDER) • 20 kW • LSB
- "VO NETHERLANDS", Holland: Irr • Su • W EUROPE • 0.4 kW
- RADIO MOSCOW, Birobidzhan: DS-1 (FEEDER) • 15 kW • LSB
- CENTRAL PEOPLES BS, Xi'an: DS-1 • 120 kW ; W-M • DS-1 • 120 kW
- CENTRAL PEOPLES BS, Beijing: DS-1 • 50 kW
- CHRIST SCI MONITOR, Maine: Alternative Frequency to 9840 kHz
- WWCR, Nashville, Tennessee: E NORTH AM & EUROPE • 100 kW
- CENTRAL PEOPLES BS: DS-1
- VOICE OF EUROPE, Forni Alto: W EUROPE • 0.6 kW • ALT. FREQ. TO 7557v kHz
- RADIO KOREA, In-Kimjae: EUROPE • 250 kW ; MIDEAST & AFRICA • 250 kW
- VOICE OF EUROPE, Forni Alto: Alternative Frequency to 7537v kHz
- KAZAKH TELEGRAPH, Alma-Ata: M/W/F • DS-NEWSCAST • 15 kW

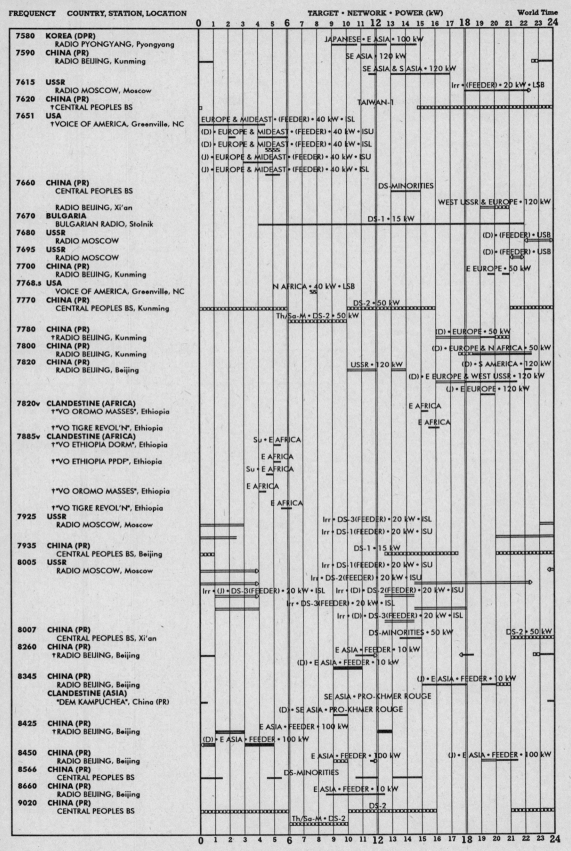

FREQUENCY	COUNTRY, STATION, LOCATION	TARGET • NETWORK • POWER (kW) / World Time
7580	**KOREA (DPR)** RADIO PYONGYANG, Pyongyang	JAPANESE • E ASIA • 100 kW
7590	**CHINA (PR)** RADIO BEIJING, Kunming	SE ASIA • 120 kW / SE ASIA & S ASIA • 120 kW
7615	**USSR** RADIO MOSCOW, Moscow	Irr • (FEEDER) • 20 kW • LSB
7620	**CHINA (PR)** †CENTRAL PEOPLES BS	TAIWAN-1
7651	**USA** †VOICE OF AMERICA, Greenville, NC	EUROPE & MIDEAST • (FEEDER) • 40 kW • ISL / (D) • EUROPE & MIDEAST • (FEEDER) • 40 kW • ISU / (D) • EUROPE & MIDEAST • (FEEDER) • 40 kW • ISL / (J) • EUROPE & MIDEAST • (FEEDER) • 40 kW • ISU / (J) • EUROPE & MIDEAST • (FEEDER) • 40 kW • ISL
7660	**CHINA (PR)** CENTRAL PEOPLES BS	DS-MINORITIES
	RADIO BEIJING, Xi'an	WEST USSR & EUROPE • 120 kW
7670	**BULGARIA** BULGARIAN RADIO, Stolnik	DS-1 • 15 kW
7680	**USSR** RADIO MOSCOW	(D) • (FEEDER) • USB
7695	**USSR** RADIO MOSCOW	(D) • (FEEDER) • USB
7700	**CHINA (PR)** RADIO BEIJING, Kunming	E EUROPE • 50 kW
7768.5	**USA** VOICE OF AMERICA, Greenville, NC	N AFRICA • 40 kW • LSB
7770	**CHINA (PR)** CENTRAL PEOPLES BS, Kunming	DS-2 • 50 kW / Th/Sa-M • DS-2 • 50 kW
7780	**CHINA (PR)** †RADIO BEIJING, Kunming	(D) • EUROPE • 50 kW
7800	**CHINA (PR)** RADIO BEIJING, Kunming	(D) • EUROPE & N AFRICA • 50 kW
7820	**CHINA (PR)** RADIO BEIJING, Beijing	USSR • 120 kW / (D) • S AMERICA • 120 kW / (D) • E EUROPE & WEST USSR • 120 kW / (J) • E EUROPE • 120 kW
7820v	**CLANDESTINE (AFRICA)** †"VO OROMO MASSES", Ethiopia	E AFRICA
	†"VO TIGRE REVOL'N", Ethiopia	E AFRICA
7885v	**CLANDESTINE (AFRICA)** †"VO ETHIOPIA DORM", Ethiopia	Su • E AFRICA / E AFRICA
	†"VO ETHIOPIA PPDF", Ethiopia	Su • E AFRICA
	†"VO OROMO MASSES", Ethiopia	E AFRICA
	†"VO TIGRE REVOL'N", Ethiopia	E AFRICA
7925	**USSR** RADIO MOSCOW, Moscow	Irr • DS-3(FEEDER) • 20 kW • ISL / Irr • DS-1(FEEDER) • 20 kW • ISU
7935	**CHINA (PR)** CENTRAL PEOPLES BS, Beijing	DS-1 • 15 kW
8005	**USSR** RADIO MOSCOW, Moscow	Irr • DS-1(FEEDER) • 20 kW • ISU / Irr • DS-2(FEEDER) • 20 kW • ISU / Irr • (J) • DS-3(FEEDER) • 20 kW • ISL • Irr • (D) • DS-2(FEEDER) • 20 kW • ISU / Irr • DS-3(FEEDER) • 20 kW • ISL / Irr • (D) • DS-3(FEEDER) • 20 kW • ISL
8007	**CHINA (PR)** CENTRAL PEOPLES BS, Xi'an	DS-MINORITIES • 50 kW / DS-2 • 50 kW
8260	**CHINA (PR)** †RADIO BEIJING, Beijing	E ASIA • FEEDER • 10 kW / (D) • E ASIA • FEEDER • 10 kW
8345	**CHINA (PR)** RADIO BEIJING, Beijing	(J) • E ASIA • FEEDER • 10 kW
	CLANDESTINE (ASIA) "DEM KAMPUCHEA", China (PR)	SE ASIA • PRO-KHMER ROUGE / (D) • SE ASIA • PRO-KHMER ROUGE
8425	**CHINA (PR)** †RADIO BEIJING, Beijing	E ASIA • FEEDER • 100 kW / (D) • E ASIA • FEEDER • 100 kW
8450	**CHINA (PR)** RADIO BEIJING, Beijing	E ASIA • FEEDER • 100 kW / (J) • E ASIA • FEEDER • 100 kW
8566	**CHINA (PR)** CENTRAL PEOPLES BS	DS-MINORITIES
8660	**CHINA (PR)** RADIO BEIJING, Beijing	E ASIA • FEEDER • 10 kW
9020	**CHINA (PR)** CENTRAL PEOPLES BS	DS-2 / Th/Sa-M • DS-2

ENGLISH ■■ ARABIC ⌇⌇⌇ CHINESE ▫▫▫ FRENCH ══ GERMAN ▬▬ RUSSIAN ══ SPANISH ▬▬ OTHER ▬

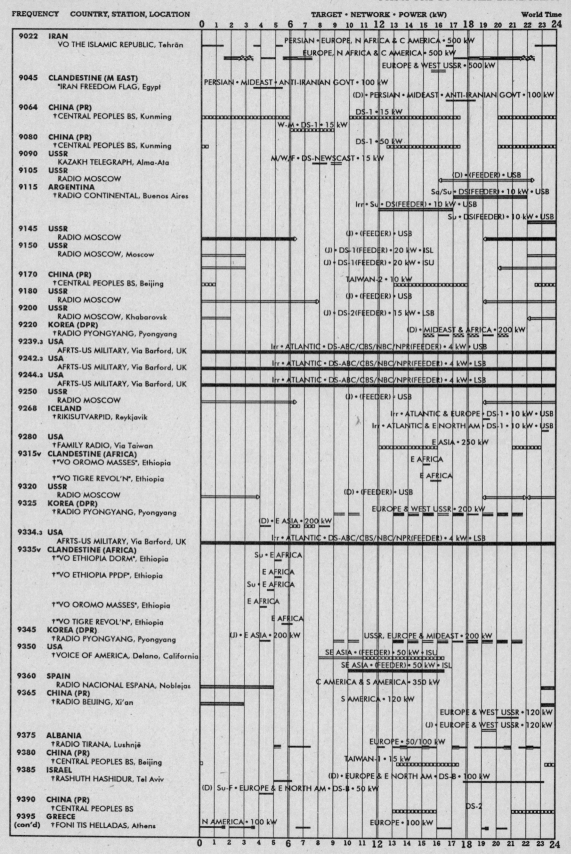

FREQUENCY   COUNTRY, STATION, LOCATION

TARGET • NETWORK • POWER (kW)

World Time

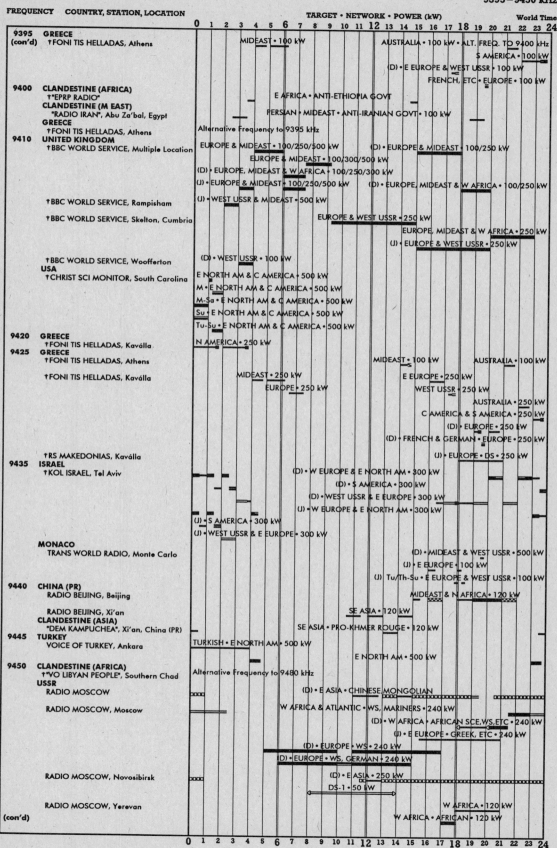

FREQUENCY	COUNTRY, STATION, LOCATION	Details
9395 (con'd)	GREECE †FONI TIS HELLADAS, Athens	MIDEAST • 100 kW; AUSTRALIA • 100 kW • ALT. FREQ. TO 9400 kHz; S AMERICA • 100 kW; (D) • E EUROPE & WEST USSR • 100 kW; FRENCH, ETC • EUROPE • 100 kW
9400	CLANDESTINE (AFRICA) †"EPRP RADIO"	E AFRICA • ANTI-ETHIOPIA GOVT
	CLANDESTINE (M EAST) "RADIO IRAN", Abu Za'bal, Egypt	PERSIAN • MIDEAST • ANTI-IRANIAN GOVT • 100 kW
	GREECE †FONI TIS HELLADAS, Athens	Alternative Frequency to 9395 kHz
9410	UNITED KINGDOM †BBC WORLD SERVICE, Multiple Location	EUROPE & MIDEAST • 100/250/500 kW; (D) • EUROPE & MIDEAST • 100/250 kW; EUROPE & MIDEAST • 100/300/500 kW; (D) • EUROPE, MIDEAST & W AFRICA • 100/250/300 kW; (J) • EUROPE & MIDEAST • 100/250/500 kW; (D) • EUROPE, MIDEAST & W AFRICA • 100/250 kW
	†BBC WORLD SERVICE, Rampisham	(J) • WEST USSR & MIDEAST • 500 kW
	†BBC WORLD SERVICE, Skelton, Cumbria	EUROPE & WEST USSR • 250 kW; EUROPE, MIDEAST & W AFRICA • 250 kW; (J) • EUROPE & WEST USSR • 250 kW
	†BBC WORLD SERVICE, Woofferton	(D) • WEST USSR • 100 kW
	USA †CHRIST SCI MONITOR, South Carolina	E NORTH AM & C AMERICA • 500 kW; M • E NORTH AM & C AMERICA • 500 kW; M-Sa • E NORTH AM & C AMERICA • 500 kW; Su • E NORTH AM & C AMERICA • 500 kW; Tu-Su • E NORTH AM & C AMERICA • 500 kW
9420	GREECE †FONI TIS HELLADAS, Kaválla.	N AMERICA • 250 kW
9425	GREECE †FONI TIS HELLADAS, Athens	MIDEAST • 100 kW; AUSTRALIA • 100 kW
	†FONI TIS HELLADAS, Kaválla	MIDEAST • 250 kW; E EUROPE • 250 kW; EUROPE • 250 kW; WEST USSR • 250 kW; AUSTRALIA • 250 kW; C AMERICA & S AMERICA • 250 kW; (D) • EUROPE • 250 kW; (D) • FRENCH & GERMAN • EUROPE • 250 kW
	†RS MAKEDONIAS, Kaválla	(J) • EUROPE • DS • 250 kW
9435	ISRAEL †KOL ISRAEL, Tel Aviv	(D) • W EUROPE & E NORTH AM • 300 kW; (D) • S AMERICA • 300 kW; (D) • WEST USSR & E EUROPE • 300 kW; (J) • W EUROPE & E NORTH AM • 300 kW; (J) • S AMERICA • 300 kW; (J) • WEST USSR & E EUROPE • 300 kW
	MONACO TRANS WORLD RADIO, Monte Carlo	(D) • MIDEAST & WEST USSR • 500 kW; (D) • E EUROPE • 100 kW; (J) Tu/Th-Su • E EUROPE & WEST USSR • 100 kW
9440	CHINA (PR) RADIO BEIJING, Beijing	MIDEAST & N AFRICA • 120 kW
	RADIO BEIJING, Xi'an	SE ASIA • 120 kW
	CLANDESTINE (ASIA) "DEM KAMPUCHEA", Xi'an, China (PR)	SE ASIA • PRO-KHMER ROUGE • 120 kW
9445	TURKEY VOICE OF TURKEY, Ankara	TURKISH • E NORTH AM • 500 kW; E NORTH AM • 500 kW
9450	CLANDESTINE (AFRICA) †"VO LIBYAN PEOPLE", Southern Chad	Alternative Frequency to 9480 kHz
	USSR RADIO MOSCOW	(D) • E ASIA • CHINESE MONGOLIAN
	RADIO MOSCOW, Moscow	W AFRICA & ATLANTIC • WS, MARINERS • 240 kW; (D) • W AFRICA • AFRICAN SCE, WS, ETC • 240 kW; (J) • E EUROPE • GREEK, ETC • 240 kW; (D) • EUROPE • WS • 240 kW; (D) • EUROPE • WS, GERMAN • 240 kW
	RADIO MOSCOW, Novosibirsk	(D) • E ASIA • 250 kW; DS-1 • 50 kW
	RADIO MOSCOW, Yerevan	W AFRICA • 120 kW; W AFRICA • AFRICAN • 120 kW
(con'd)		

ENGLISH ▬   ARABIC ≋   CHINESE ▭▭▭   FRENCH ▬   GERMAN ▬   RUSSIAN ═   SPANISH ▬   OTHER ▬

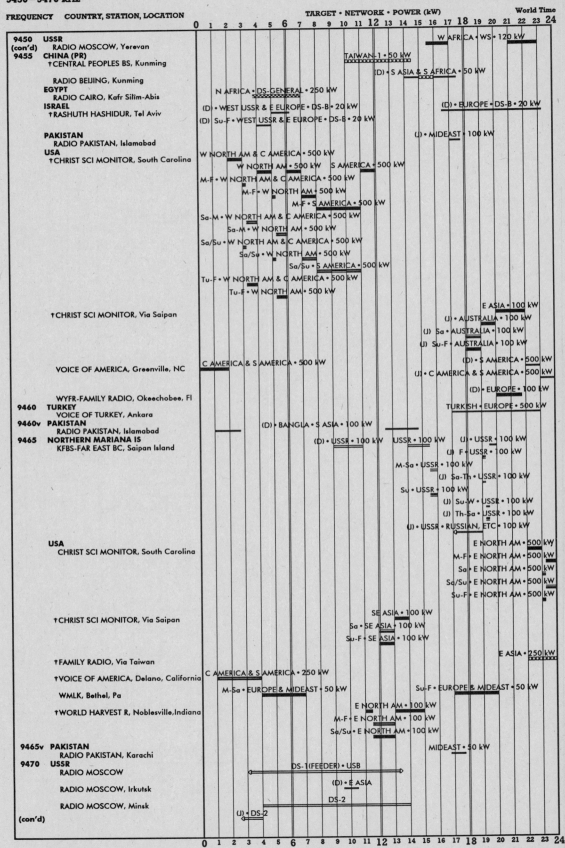

FREQUENCY   COUNTRY, STATION, LOCATION

9450 (con'd) **USSR** — RADIO MOSCOW, Yerevan
9455 **CHINA (PR)** — †CENTRAL PEOPLES BS, Kunming; RADIO BEIJING, Kunming
EGYPT — RADIO CAIRO, Kafr Silim-Abis
ISRAEL — †RASHUTH HASHIDUR, Tel Aviv
PAKISTAN — RADIO PAKISTAN, Islamabad
USA — †CHRIST SCI MONITOR, South Carolina; †CHRIST SCI MONITOR, Via Saipan; VOICE OF AMERICA, Greenville, NC; WYFR-FAMILY RADIO, Okeechobee, Fl
9460 **TURKEY** — VOICE OF TURKEY, Ankara
9460v **PAKISTAN** — RADIO PAKISTAN, Islamabad
9465 **NORTHERN MARIANA IS** — KFBS-FAR EAST BC, Saipan Island
USA — CHRIST SCI MONITOR, South Carolina; †CHRIST SCI MONITOR, Via Saipan; †FAMILY RADIO, Via Taiwan; †VOICE OF AMERICA, Delano, California; WMLK, Bethel, Pa; †WORLD HARVEST R, Noblesville, Indiana
9465v **PAKISTAN** — RADIO PAKISTAN, Karachi
9470 **USSR** — RADIO MOSCOW; RADIO MOSCOW, Irkutsk; RADIO MOSCOW, Minsk
(con'd)

SUMMER ONLY (J)   WINTER ONLY (D)   JAMMING / OR ∧   EARLIEST HEARD ◁   LATEST HEARD ▷   NEW OR CHANGED FOR 1991 †

FREQUENCY   COUNTRY, STATION, LOCATION

TARGET • NETWORK • POWER (kW)

World Time

0 1 2 3 4 5 6 7 8 9 10 11 12 13 14 15 16 17 18 19 20 21 22 23 24

Frequency	Country, Station, Location	Schedule details
9470 (con'd)	USSR RADIO MOSCOW, Ul'yanovsk	S AMERICA • 100 kW / (D) • S AMERICA • 100 kW / (J) • E EUROPE • 100 kW / (J) • S AMERICA • 100 kW / (D) • W AFRICA • AFRICAN SCE • 100 kW / S AMERICA • ARMENIAN, SPANISH • 100 kW
	RADIO YEREVAN, Ul'yanovsk	
9475	EGYPT RADIO CAIRO, Kafr Silim-Abis	N AMERICA & C AMERICA • 250 kW
	PAKISTAN PAKISTAN BC CORP, Islamabad	(J) • MIDEAST • DS • 100 kW
9475v	PAKISTAN RADIO PAKISTAN, Karachi	MIDEAST • 50 kW
9480	CHINA (PR) RADIO BEIJING, Beijing	SE ASIA & E ASIA • 120 kW
	RADIO BEIJING, Xi'an	MIDEAST • 120 kW / (D) • MIDEAST • 120 kW
	CLANDESTINE (AFRICA) †"VO LIBYAN PEOPLE", Southern Chad	Irr • N AFRICA • ANTI-QADDAFI • ALT. FREQ. TO 9450 kHz
	†"VO THE PEOPLE", Southern Chad	Irr • N AFRICA • ANTI-QADDAFI
	MONACO TRANS WORLD RADIO, Monte Carlo	(D) • W EUROPE • 100 kW / (D) Su • W EUROPE • 100 kW
	USSR RADIO MOSCOW	(D)
	RADIO MOSCOW, Novosibirsk	E ASIA • 250 kW / (D) • E ASIA • 250 kW / E ASIA • DS-2 • 250 kW
	RADIO MOSCOW, Yerevan	MIDEAST & E AFRICA • 120 kW / (D) • N AFRICA • 120 kW
	RADIO YEREVAN, Yerevan	(D) • S AMERICA • ARMENIAN, SPANISH • 120 kW
9480v	ALBANIA †RADIO TIRANA, Krujë	C AFRICA & S AFRICA • 100 kW / (D) • EUROPE • 100 kW / (J) • EUROPE • 100 kW
	†RADIO TIRANA, Lushnjë	C AFRICA & S AFRICA • 100 kW / WEST USSR • 100 kW / AUSTRALIA • 100 kW / (D) • EUROPE • 100 kW / MIDEAST • 100 kW / (D) • WEST USSR • 100 kW / (J) • WEST USSR • 100 kW / (J) • EUROPE • 100 kW
9485	MONACO TRANS WORLD RADIO, Monte Carlo	(J) • W EUROPE • 100 kW / (J) • WEST USSR • 100 kW / (J) • M • WEST USSR • 100 kW / (J) Su • W EUROPE • 100 kW / (J) Tu/W/F/Su • WEST USSR • 100 kW
9486	PERU †RADIO TACNA, Tacna	Su • DS • 0.18 kW
9490	CHINA (PR) RADIO BEIJING, Lhasa	S ASIA • 50 kW
	XIZANG PEOPLES BS, Lhasa	DS-CHINESE • 50 kW
	USSR RADIO MOSCOW, Nikolayev	S AMERICA • 500 kW / (J) • W AFRICA • 500 kW / (D) • W AFRICA • 500 kW / (D) • S AMERICA • 500 kW
	RADIO MOSCOW, Ul'yanovsk	DS-1/DS-2/POLAR • 240 kW
9495	GUAM †ADVENTIST WORLD RADIO, Agat	(D) • E ASIA • 100 kW
	MONACO TRANS WORLD RADIO, Monte Carlo	(D) • E EUROPE • 100 kW / (D) • WEST USSR • 500 kW / (J) • E EUROPE • 100 kW / (D) • WEST USSR • 100 kW / (J) F-Su • E EUROPE • 500 kW / (J) • E EUROPE • 500 kW / (J) Sa/Su • E EUROPE • 500 kW / (J) • WEST USSR • 500 kW / (J) M-F • E EUROPE • 500 kW / (D) M • W EUROPE • 100 kW / (J) M • W EUROPE • 100 kW / (D) Sa/Su • E EUROPE • 500 kW / (D) Tu/Sa/Su • E EUROPE • 100 kW / (D) Sa/Su • WEST USSR • 500 kW / (J) Tu/Sa/Su • E EUROPE • 100 kW / (J) Sa/Su • WEST USSR • 500 kW / (D) Su • E EUROPE • 100 kW

(con'd)

0 1 2 3 4 5 6 7 8 9 10 11 12 13 14 15 16 17 18 19 20 21 22 23 24

ENGLISH ▬   ARABIC ⧓⧓⧓   CHINESE ▭▭▭   FRENCH ▬▬   GERMAN ▬▬   RUSSIAN ▭▭   SPANISH ▬▬   OTHER ▬

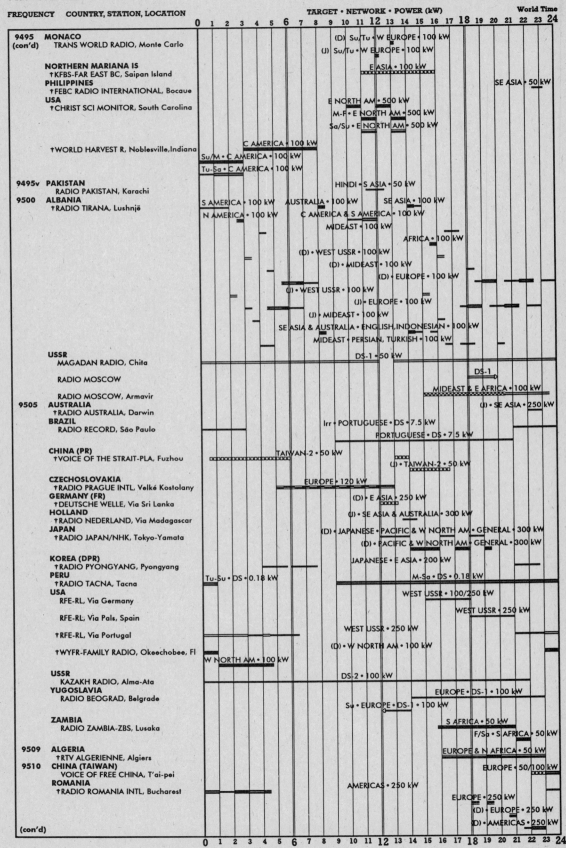

FREQUENCY   COUNTRY, STATION, LOCATION   TARGET • NETWORK • POWER (kW)   World Time

Partial transcription of chart entries:

9495 MONACO (con'd) — TRANS WORLD RADIO, Monte Carlo — (D) Su/Tu • W EUROPE • 100 kW; (J) Su/Tu • W EUROPE • 100 kW

NORTHERN MARIANA IS — †KFBS-FAR EAST BC, Saipan Island — E ASIA • 100 kW

PHILIPPINES — †FEBC RADIO INTERNATIONAL, Bocaue — SE ASIA • 50 kW

USA — †CHRIST SCI MONITOR, South Carolina — E NORTH AM • 500 kW; M-F • E NORTH AM • 500 kW; Sa/Su • E NORTH AM • 500 kW

†WORLD HARVEST R, Noblesville, Indiana — C AMERICA • 100 kW; Su/M • C AMERICA • 100 kW; Tu-Sa • C AMERICA • 100 kW

9495v PAKISTAN — RADIO PAKISTAN, Karachi — HINDI • S ASIA • 50 kW

9500 ALBANIA — †RADIO TIRANA, Lushnjë — S AMERICA • 100 kW; AUSTRALIA • 100 kW; SE ASIA • 100 kW; N AMERICA • 100 kW; C AMERICA & S AMERICA • 100 kW; MIDEAST • 100 kW; AFRICA • 100 kW; (D) • WEST USSR • 100 kW; (D) • MIDEAST • 100 kW; (D) • EUROPE • 100 kW; (J) • WEST USSR • 100 kW; (J) • EUROPE • 100 kW; (J) • MIDEAST • 100 kW; SE ASIA & AUSTRALIA • ENGLISH, INDONESIAN • 100 kW; MIDEAST • PERSIAN, TURKISH • 100 kW

USSR — MAGADAN RADIO, Chita — DS-1 • 50 kW

RADIO MOSCOW — DS-1

RADIO MOSCOW, Armavir — MIDEAST & E AFRICA • 100 kW

9505 AUSTRALIA — †RADIO AUSTRALIA, Darwin — (J) • SE ASIA • 250 kW

BRAZIL — RADIO RECORD, São Paulo — Irr • PORTUGUESE • DS • 7.5 kW; PORTUGUESE • DS • 7.5 kW

CHINA (PR) — †VOICE OF THE STRAIT-PLA, Fuzhou — TAIWAN-2 • 50 kW; (J) • TAIWAN-2 • 50 kW

CZECHOSLOVAKIA — †RADIO PRAGUE INTL, Velké Kostolany — EUROPE • 120 kW

GERMANY (FR) — †DEUTSCHE WELLE, Via Sri Lanka — (D) • E ASIA • 250 kW

HOLLAND — †RADIO NEDERLAND, Via Madagascar — (J) • SE ASIA & AUSTRALIA • 300 kW

JAPAN — †RADIO JAPAN/NHK, Tokyo-Yamata — (D) JAPANESE • PACIFIC & W NORTH AM • GENERAL • 300 kW; (D) • PACIFIC & W NORTH AM • GENERAL • 300 kW

KOREA (DPR) — †RADIO PYONGYANG, Pyongyang — JAPANESE • E ASIA • 200 kW

PERU — †RADIO TACNA, Tacna — Tu-Su • DS • 0.18 kW; M-Sa • DS • 0.18 kW

USA — RFE-RL, Via Germany — WEST USSR • 100/250 kW; WEST USSR • 250 kW

RFE-RL, Via Pals, Spain — WEST USSR • 250 kW

†RFE-RL, Via Portugal — (D) • W NORTH AM • 100 kW

†WYFR-FAMILY RADIO, Okeechobee, Fl — W NORTH AM • 100 kW

USSR — KAZAKH RADIO, Alma-Ata — DS-2 • 100 kW

YUGOSLAVIA — RADIO BEOGRAD, Belgrade — EUROPE • DS-1 • 100 kW; Su • EUROPE • DS-1 • 100 kW

ZAMBIA — RADIO ZAMBIA-ZBS, Lusaka — S AFRICA • 50 kW; F/Sa • S AFRICA • 50 kW

9509 ALGERIA — †RTV ALGERIENNE, Algiers — EUROPE & N AFRICA • 50 kW

9510 CHINA (TAIWAN) — VOICE OF FREE CHINA, T'ai-pei — EUROPE • 50/100 kW

ROMANIA — †RADIO ROMANIA INTL, Bucharest — AMERICAS • 250 kW; EUROPE • 250 kW; (D) • EUROPE • 250 kW; (D) • AMERICAS • 250 kW

(con'd)

FREQUENCY   COUNTRY, STATION, LOCATION

TARGET • NETWORK • POWER (kW)

World Time

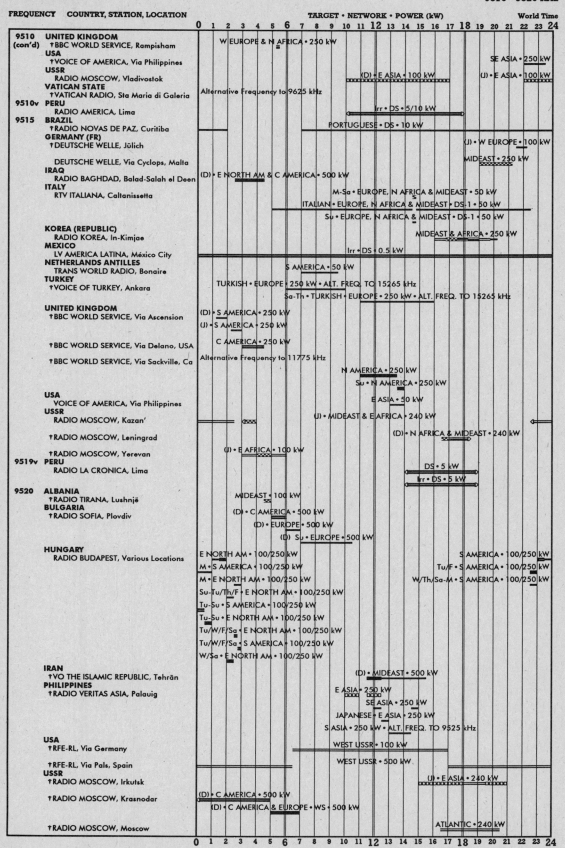

Frequency	Country, Station, Location	Details
9510 (con'd)	**UNITED KINGDOM** †BBC WORLD SERVICE, Rampisham	W EUROPE & N AFRICA • 250 kW
	USA †VOICE OF AMERICA, Via Philippines	SE ASIA • 250 kW
	USSR RADIO MOSCOW, Vladivostok	(D) • E ASIA • 100 kW (J) • E ASIA • 100 kW
	VATICAN STATE †VATICAN RADIO, Sta Maria di Galeria	Alternative Frequency to 9625 kHz
9510v	**PERU** RADIO AMERICA, Lima	Irr • DS • 5/10 kW
9515	**BRAZIL** †RADIO NOVAS DE PAZ, Curitiba	PORTUGUESE • DS • 10 kW
	GERMANY (FR) †DEUTSCHE WELLE, Jülich	(J) • W EUROPE • 100 kW MIDEAST • 250 kW
	DEUTSCHE WELLE, Via Cyclops, Malta	
	IRAQ RADIO BAGHDAD, Balad-Salah el Deen	(D) • E NORTH AM & C AMERICA • 500 kW
	ITALY RTV ITALIANA, Caltanissetta	M-Sa • EUROPE, N AFRICA & MIDEAST • 50 kW ITALIAN • EUROPE, N AFRICA & MIDEAST • DS-1 • 50 kW Su • EUROPE, N AFRICA & MIDEAST • DS-1 • 50 kW
	KOREA (REPUBLIC) RADIO KOREA, In-Kimjae	MIDEAST & AFRICA • 250 kW
	MEXICO LV AMERICA LATINA, México City	Irr • DS • 0.5 kW
	NETHERLANDS ANTILLES TRANS WORLD RADIO, Bonaire	S AMERICA • 50 kW
	TURKEY †VOICE OF TURKEY, Ankara	TURKISH • EUROPE • 250 kW • ALT. FREQ. TO 15265 kHz Sa-Th • TURKISH • EUROPE • 250 kW • ALT. FREQ. TO 15265 kHz
	UNITED KINGDOM †BBC WORLD SERVICE, Via Ascension	(D) • S AMERICA • 250 kW (J) • S AMERICA • 250 kW
	†BBC WORLD SERVICE, Via Delano, USA	C AMERICA • 250 kW
	†BBC WORLD SERVICE, Via Sackville, Ca	Alternative Frequency to 11775 kHz N AMERICA • 250 kW Su • N AMERICA • 250 kW
	USA VOICE OF AMERICA, Via Philippines	E ASIA • 50 kW
	USSR RADIO MOSCOW, Kazan'	(J) • MIDEAST & E AFRICA • 240 kW
	†RADIO MOSCOW, Leningrad	(D) • N AFRICA & MIDEAST • 240 kW
	†RADIO MOSCOW, Yerevan	(J) • E AFRICA • 100 kW
9519v	**PERU** RADIO LA CRONICA, Lima	DS • 5 kW Irr • DS • 5 kW
9520	**ALBANIA** †RADIO TIRANA, Lushnjë	MIDEAST • 100 kW
	BULGARIA †RADIO SOFIA, Plovdiv	(D) • C AMERICA • 500 kW (D) • EUROPE • 500 kW (D) • Su • EUROPE • 500 kW
	HUNGARY RADIO BUDAPEST, Various Locations	E NORTH AM • 100/250 kW S AMERICA • 100/250 kW M • S AMERICA • 100/250 kW Tu/F • S AMERICA • 100/250 kW M • E NORTH AM • 100/250 kW W/Th/Sa-M • S AMERICA • 100/250 kW Su-Tu/Th/F • E NORTH AM • 100/250 kW Tu-Su • S AMERICA • 100/250 kW Tu-Su • E NORTH AM • 100/250 kW Tu/W/F/Sa • E NORTH AM • 100/250 kW Tu/W/F/Sa • S AMERICA • 100/250 kW W/Sa • E NORTH AM • 100/250 kW
	IRAN †VO THE ISLAMIC REPUBLIC, Tehrān	(D) • MIDEAST • 500 kW
	PHILIPPINES †RADIO VERITAS ASIA, Palauig	E ASIA • 250 kW SE ASIA • 250 kW JAPANESE • E ASIA • 250 kW S ASIA • 250 kW • ALT. FREQ. TO 9525 kHz
	USA †RFE-RL, Via Germany	WEST USSR • 100 kW
	†RFE-RL, Via Pals, Spain	WEST USSR • 500 kW
	USSR †RADIO MOSCOW, Irkutsk	(J) • E ASIA • 240 kW
	†RADIO MOSCOW, Krasnodar	(D) • C AMERICA • 500 kW (D) • C AMERICA & EUROPE • WS • 500 kW
	†RADIO MOSCOW, Moscow	ATLANTIC • 240 kW

ENGLISH ▬▬ ARABIC ▧▧ CHINESE ▫▫▫ FRENCH ══ GERMAN ▬▬ RUSSIAN ══ SPANISH ▬▬ OTHER ▬

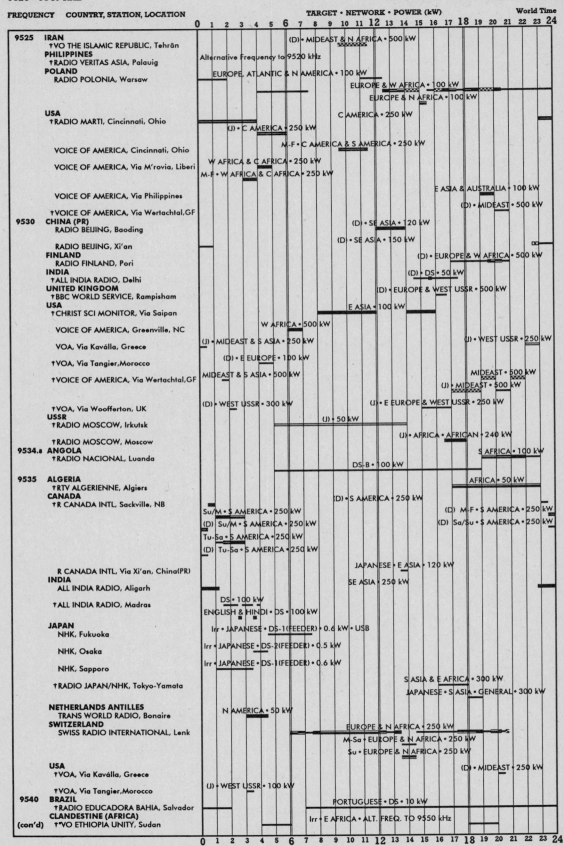

FREQUENCY   COUNTRY, STATION, LOCATION

TARGET • NETWORK • POWER (kW)   World Time

FREQUENCY	COUNTRY, STATION, LOCATION	Schedule details
9525	**IRAN**	
	†VO THE ISLAMIC REPUBLIC, Tehrān	(D) • MIDEAST & N AFRICA • 500 kW
	PHILIPPINES	
	†RADIO VERITAS ASIA, Palauig	Alternative Frequency to 9520 kHz
	POLAND	
	RADIO POLONIA, Warsaw	EUROPE, ATLANTIC & N AMERICA • 100 kW
		EUROPE & W AFRICA • 100 kW
		EUROPE & N AFRICA • 100 kW
	USA	
	†RADIO MARTI, Cincinnati, Ohio	C AMERICA • 250 kW
		(J) • C AMERICA • 250 kW
	VOICE OF AMERICA, Cincinnati, Ohio	M-F • C AMERICA & S AMERICA • 250 kW
	VOICE OF AMERICA, Via M'rovia, Liberi	W AFRICA & C AFRICA • 250 kW
		M-F • W AFRICA & C AFRICA • 250 kW
	VOICE OF AMERICA, Via Philippines	E ASIA & AUSTRALIA • 100 kW
	†VOICE OF AMERICA, Via Wertachtal, GF	(D) • MIDEAST • 500 kW
9530	**CHINA (PR)**	
	RADIO BEIJING, Baoding	(D) • SE ASIA • 120 kW
	RADIO BEIJING, Xi'an	(D) • SE ASIA • 150 kW
	FINLAND	
	RADIO FINLAND, Pori	(D) • EUROPE & W AFRICA • 500 kW
	INDIA	
	†ALL INDIA RADIO, Delhi	(D) • DS • 50 kW
	UNITED KINGDOM	
	†BBC WORLD SERVICE, Rampisham	(D) • EUROPE & WEST USSR • 500 kW
	USA	
	†CHRIST SCI MONITOR, Via Saipan	E ASIA • 100 kW
	VOICE OF AMERICA, Greenville, NC	W AFRICA • 500 kW
	VOA, Via Kaválla, Greece	(J) • MIDEAST & S ASIA • 250 kW
		(J) • WEST USSR • 250 kW
	†VOA, Via Tangier, Morocco	(D) • E EUROPE • 100 kW
	†VOICE OF AMERICA, Via Wertachtal, GF	MIDEAST & S ASIA • 500 kW
		MIDEAST • 500 kW
		(J) • MIDEAST • 500 kW
	†VOA, Via Woofferton, UK	(D) • WEST USSR • 300 kW
		(J) • E EUROPE & WEST USSR • 250 kW
	USSR	
	†RADIO MOSCOW, Irkutsk	(J) • 50 kW
	†RADIO MOSCOW, Moscow	(J) • AFRICA • AFRICAN • 240 kW
9534.8	**ANGOLA**	
	†RADIO NACIONAL, Luanda	S AFRICA • 100 kW
		DS-B • 100 kW
9535	**ALGERIA**	
	†RTV ALGERIENNE, Algiers	AFRICA • 50 kW
	CANADA	
	†R CANADA INTL, Sackville, NB	(D) • S AMERICA • 250 kW
		Su/M • S AMERICA • 250 kW
		(D) M-F • S AMERICA • 250 kW
		(D) Su/M • S AMERICA • 250 kW
		Tu-Sa • S AMERICA • 250 kW
		(D) Sa/Su • S AMERICA • 250 kW
		(D) Tu-Sa • S AMERICA • 250 kW
	R CANADA INTL, Via Xi'an, China(PR)	JAPANESE • E ASIA • 120 kW
	INDIA	
	ALL INDIA RADIO, Aligarh	SE ASIA • 250 kW
	†ALL INDIA RADIO, Madras	DS • 100 kW
		ENGLISH & HINDI • DS • 100 kW
	JAPAN	
	NHK, Fukuoka	Irr • JAPANESE • DS-1 (FEEDER) • 0.6 kW • USB
	NHK, Osaka	Irr • JAPANESE • DS-2 (FEEDER) • 0.5 kW
	NHK, Sapporo	Irr • JAPANESE • DS-1 (FEEDER) • 0.6 kW
	†RADIO JAPAN/NHK, Tokyo-Yamata	S ASIA & E AFRICA • 300 kW
		JAPANESE • S ASIA • GENERAL • 300 kW
	NETHERLANDS ANTILLES	
	TRANS WORLD RADIO, Bonaire	N AMERICA • 50 kW
	SWITZERLAND	
	SWISS RADIO INTERNATIONAL, Lenk	EUROPE & N AFRICA • 250 kW
		M-Sa • EUROPE & N AFRICA • 250 kW
		Su • EUROPE & N AFRICA • 250 kW
	USA	
	†VOA, Via Kaválla, Greece	(D) • MIDEAST • 250 kW
	†VOA, Via Tangier, Morocco	(J) • WEST USSR • 100 kW
9540	**BRAZIL**	
	†RADIO EDUCADORA BAHIA, Salvador	PORTUGUESE • DS • 10 kW
	CLANDESTINE (AFRICA)	
(con'd)	†•VO ETHIOPIA UNITY, Sudan	Irr • E AFRICA • ALT. FREQ. TO 9550 kHz

0 1 2 3 4 5 6 7 8 9 10 11 12 13 14 15 16 17 18 19 20 21 22 23 24

SUMMER ONLY (J)   WINTER ONLY (D)   JAMMING / OR ∧   EARLIEST HEARD ◁   LATEST HEARD ▷   NEW OR CHANGED FOR 1991 †

FREQUENCY   COUNTRY, STATION, LOCATION

TARGET • NETWORK • POWER (kW)

World Time

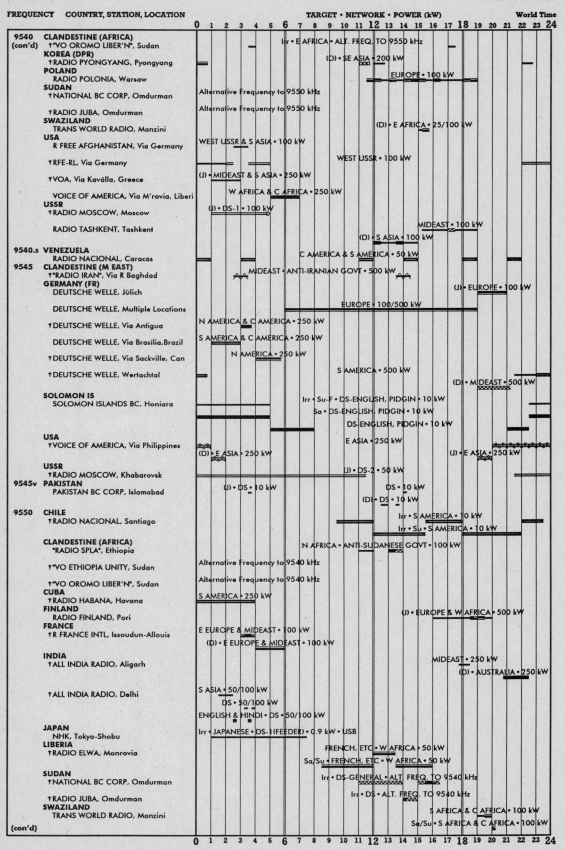

Frequency	Country, Station, Location	Target • Network • Power
9540 (con'd)	**CLANDESTINE (AFRICA)** †"VO OROMO LIBER'N", Sudan	Irr • E AFRICA • ALT. FREQ. TO 9550 kHz
	KOREA (DPR) †RADIO PYONGYANG, Pyongyang	(D) • SE ASIA • 200 kW
	POLAND RADIO POLONIA, Warsaw	EUROPE • 100 kW
	SUDAN †NATIONAL BC CORP, Omdurman	Alternative Frequency to 9550 kHz
	†RADIO JUBA, Omdurman	Alternative Frequency to 9550 kHz
	SWAZILAND TRANS WORLD RADIO, Manzini	(D) • E AFRICA • 25/100 kW
	USA R FREE AFGHANISTAN, Via Germany	WEST USSR & S ASIA • 100 kW
	†RFE-RL, Via Germany	WEST USSR • 100 kW
	†VOA, Via Kaválla, Greece	(J) • MIDEAST & S ASIA • 250 kW
	VOICE OF AMERICA, Via M'rovia, Liberi	W AFRICA & C AFRICA • 250 kW
	USSR †RADIO MOSCOW, Moscow	(J) • DS-1 • 100 kW
	RADIO TASHKENT, Tashkent	MIDEAST • 100 kW
		(D) • S ASIA • 100 kW
9540.5	**VENEZUELA** RADIO NACIONAL, Caracas	C AMERICA & S AMERICA • 50 kW
9545	**CLANDESTINE (M EAST)** †"RADIO IRAN", Via R Baghdad	MIDEAST • ANTI-IRANIAN GOVT • 500 kW
	GERMANY (FR) DEUTSCHE WELLE, Jülich	(J) • EUROPE • 100 kW
	DEUTSCHE WELLE, Multiple Locations	EUROPE • 100/500 kW
	†DEUTSCHE WELLE, Via Antigua	N AMERICA & C AMERICA • 250 kW
	DEUTSCHE WELLE, Via Brasília, Brazil	S AMERICA & C AMERICA • 250 kW
	†DEUTSCHE WELLE, Via Sackville, Can	N AMERICA • 250 kW
	†DEUTSCHE WELLE, Wertachtal	S AMERICA • 500 kW
		(D) • MIDEAST • 500 kW
	SOLOMON IS SOLOMON ISLANDS BC, Honiara	Irr • Su-F • DS-ENGLISH, PIDGIN • 10 kW
		Sa • DS-ENGLISH, PIDGIN • 10 kW
		DS-ENGLISH, PIDGIN • 10 kW
	USA †VOICE OF AMERICA, Via Philippines	E ASIA • 250 kW
		(D) • E ASIA • 250 kW
		(J) • E ASIA • 250 kW
	USSR †RADIO MOSCOW, Khabarovsk	(J) • DS-2 • 50 kW
9545v	**PAKISTAN** PAKISTAN BC CORP, Islamabad	(J) • DS • 10 kW
		DS • 10 kW
		(D) • DS • 10 kW
9550	**CHILE** †RADIO NACIONAL, Santiago	Irr • S AMERICA • 10 kW
		Irr • Su • S AMERICA • 10 kW
	CLANDESTINE (AFRICA) "RADIO SPLA", Ethiopia	N AFRICA • ANTI-SUDANESE GOVT • 100 kW
	†"VO ETHIOPIA UNITY, Sudan	Alternative Frequency to 9540 kHz
	†"VO OROMO LIBER'N", Sudan	Alternative Frequency to 9540 kHz
	CUBA †RADIO HABANA, Havana	S AMERICA • 250 kW
	FINLAND RADIO FINLAND, Pori	(J) • EUROPE & W AFRICA • 500 kW
	FRANCE †R FRANCE INTL, Issoudun-Allouis	E EUROPE & MIDEAST • 100 kW
		(D) • E EUROPE & MIDEAST • 100 kW
	INDIA †ALL INDIA RADIO, Aligarh	MIDEAST • 250 kW
		(D) • AUSTRALIA • 250 kW
	†ALL INDIA RADIO, Delhi	S ASIA • 50/100 kW
		DS • 50/100 kW
		ENGLISH & HINDI • DS • 50/100 kW
	JAPAN NHK, Tokyo-Shobu	Irr • JAPANESE • DS-1 (FEEDER) • 0.9 kW • USB
	LIBERIA †RADIO ELWA, Monrovia	FRENCH, ETC • W AFRICA • 50 kW
		Sa/Su • FRENCH, ETC • W AFRICA • 50 kW
	SUDAN †NATIONAL BC CORP, Omdurman	Irr • DS-GENERAL • ALT. FREQ. TO 9540 kHz
	†RADIO JUBA, Omdurman	Irr • DS • ALT. FREQ. TO 9540 kHz
	SWAZILAND TRANS WORLD RADIO, Manzini	S AFRICA & C AFRICA • 100 kW
		Sa/Su • S AFRICA & C AFRICA • 100 kW
(con'd)		

ENGLISH ▬▬   ARABIC ▨▨   CHINESE ▭▭   FRENCH ▬▬   GERMAN ▬▬   RUSSIAN ═══   SPANISH ▬▬   OTHER ▬▬

FREQUENCY　COUNTRY, STATION, LOCATION　　　　　　　TARGET • NETWORK • POWER (kW)　　　World Time

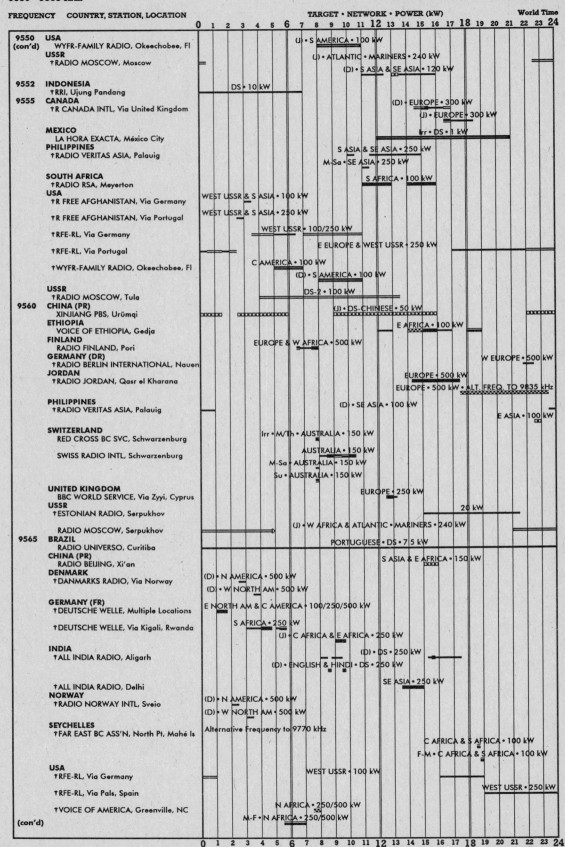

Frequency	Country, Station, Location	Target • Network • Power
9550 (con'd)	USA — WYFR-FAMILY RADIO, Okeechobee, Fl	(J) • S AMERICA • 100 kW
	USSR — †RADIO MOSCOW, Moscow	(J) • ATLANTIC • MARINERS • 240 kW / (D) • S ASIA & SE ASIA • 120 kW
9552	INDONESIA — †RRI, Ujung Pandang	DS • 10 kW
9555	CANADA — †R CANADA INTL, Via United Kingdom	(D) • EUROPE • 300 kW / (J) • EUROPE • 300 kW
	MEXICO — LA HORA EXACTA, México City	Irr • DS • 1 kW
	PHILIPPINES — †RADIO VERITAS ASIA, Palauig	S ASIA & SE ASIA • 250 kW / M-Sa • SE ASIA • 250 kW
	SOUTH AFRICA — †RADIO RSA, Meyerton	S AFRICA • 100 kW
	USA — †R FREE AFGHANISTAN, Via Germany	WEST USSR & S ASIA • 100 kW
	†R FREE AFGHANISTAN, Via Portugal	WEST USSR & S ASIA • 250 kW
	†RFE-RL, Via Germany	WEST USSR • 100/250 kW
	†RFE-RL, Via Portugal	E EUROPE & WEST USSR • 250 kW
	†WYFR-FAMILY RADIO, Okeechobee, Fl	C AMERICA • 100 kW / (D) • S AMERICA • 100 kW
	USSR — †RADIO MOSCOW, Tula	DS-2 • 100 kW
9560	CHINA (PR) — XINJIANG PBS, Urümqi	(J) • DS-CHINESE • 50 kW
	ETHIOPIA — VOICE OF ETHIOPIA, Gedja	E AFRICA • 100 kW
	FINLAND — RADIO FINLAND, Pori	EUROPE & W AFRICA • 500 kW
	GERMANY (DR) — †RADIO BERLIN INTERNATIONAL, Nauen	W EUROPE • 500 kW
	JORDAN — †RADIO JORDAN, Qasr el Kharana	EUROPE • 500 kW / EUROPE • 500 kW • ALT. FREQ. TO 9835 kHz
	PHILIPPINES — †RADIO VERITAS ASIA, Palauig	(D) • SE ASIA • 100 kW / E ASIA • 100 kW
	SWITZERLAND — RED CROSS BC SVC, Schwarzenburg	Irr • M/Th • AUSTRALIA • 150 kW
	SWISS RADIO INTL, Schwarzenburg	AUSTRALIA • 150 kW / M-Sa • AUSTRALIA • 150 kW / Su • AUSTRALIA • 150 kW
	UNITED KINGDOM — BBC WORLD SERVICE, Via Zyyi, Cyprus	EUROPE • 250 kW
	USSR — †ESTONIAN RADIO, Serpukhov	20 kW
	RADIO MOSCOW, Serpukhov	(J) • W AFRICA & ATLANTIC • MARINERS • 240 kW
9565	BRAZIL — RADIO UNIVERSO, Curitiba	PORTUGUESE • DS • 7.5 kW
	CHINA (PR) — RADIO BEIJING, Xi'an	S ASIA & E AFRICA • 150 kW
	DENMARK — †DANMARKS RADIO, Via Norway	(D) • N AMERICA • 500 kW / (D) • W NORTH AM • 500 kW
	GERMANY (FR) — †DEUTSCHE WELLE, Multiple Locations	E NORTH AM & C AMERICA • 100/250/500 kW
	†DEUTSCHE WELLE, Via Kigali, Rwanda	S AFRICA • 250 kW / (J) • C AFRICA & E AFRICA • 250 kW
	INDIA — †ALL INDIA RADIO, Aligarh	(D) • DS • 250 kW / (D) • ENGLISH & HINDI • DS • 250 kW
	†ALL INDIA RADIO, Delhi	SE ASIA • 250 kW
	NORWAY — †RADIO NORWAY INTL, Sveio	(D) • N AMERICA • 500 kW / (D) • W NORTH AM • 500 kW
	SEYCHELLES — †FAR EAST BC ASS'N, North Pt, Mahé Is	Alternative Frequency to 9770 kHz / C AFRICA & S AFRICA • 100 kW / F-M • C AFRICA & S AFRICA • 100 kW
	USA — †RFE-RL, Via Germany	WEST USSR • 100 kW
	†RFE-RL, Via Pals, Spain	WEST USSR • 250 kW
	†VOICE OF AMERICA, Greenville, NC	N AFRICA • 250/500 kW / M-F • N AFRICA • 250/500 kW
(con'd)		

FREQUENCY	COUNTRY, STATION, LOCATION	TARGET • NETWORK • POWER (kW) / World Time

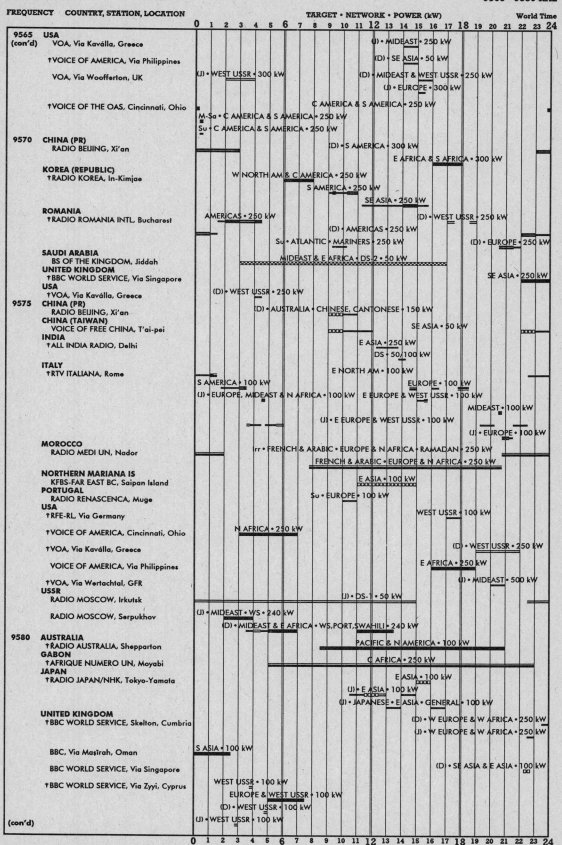

9565 USA
(con'd)
- VOA, Via Kaválla, Greece — (J) • MIDEAST • 250 kW
- †VOICE OF AMERICA, Via Philippines — (D) • SE ASIA • 50 kW
- VOA, Via Woofferton, UK — (J) • WEST USSR • 300 kW · (D) • MIDEAST & WEST USSR • 250 kW · (J) • EUROPE • 300 kW
- †VOICE OF THE OAS, Cincinnati, Ohio — C AMERICA & S AMERICA • 250 kW · M-Sa • C AMERICA & S AMERICA • 250 kW · Su • C AMERICA & S AMERICA • 250 kW

9570 CHINA (PR)
- RADIO BEIJING, Xi'an — (D) • S AMERICA • 300 kW · E AFRICA & S AFRICA • 300 kW

KOREA (REPUBLIC)
- †RADIO KOREA, In-Kimjae — W NORTH AM & C AMERICA • 250 kW · S AMERICA • 250 kW · SE ASIA • 250 kW

ROMANIA
- †RADIO ROMANIA INTL, Bucharest — AMERICAS • 250 kW · (D) • WEST USSR • 250 kW · (D) • AMERICAS • 250 kW · Su • ATLANTIC • MARINERS • 250 kW · (D) • EUROPE • 250 kW

SAUDI ARABIA
- BS OF THE KINGDOM, Jiddah — MIDEAST & E AFRICA • DS-2 • 50 kW

UNITED KINGDOM
- †BBC WORLD SERVICE, Via Singapore — SE ASIA • 250 kW

USA
- †VOA, Via Kaválla, Greece — (D) • WEST USSR • 250 kW

9575 CHINA (PR)
- RADIO BEIJING, Xi'an — (D) • AUSTRALIA • CHINESE, CANTONESE • 150 kW

CHINA (TAIWAN)
- VOICE OF FREE CHINA, T'ai-pei — SE ASIA • 50 kW

INDIA
- †ALL INDIA RADIO, Delhi — E ASIA • 250 kW · DS • 50/100 kW · E NORTH AM • 100 kW

ITALY
- †RTV ITALIANA, Rome — S AMERICA • 100 kW · EUROPE • 100 kW · (J) • EUROPE, MIDEAST & N AFRICA • 100 kW · E EUROPE & WEST USSR • 100 kW · MIDEAST • 100 kW · (J) • E EUROPE & WEST USSR • 100 kW · (J) • EUROPE • 100 kW

MOROCCO
- RADIO MEDI UN, Nador — Irr • FRENCH & ARABIC • EUROPE & N AFRICA • RAMADAN • 250 kW · FRENCH & ARABIC • EUROPE & N AFRICA • 250 kW

NORTHERN MARIANA IS
- KFBS-FAR EAST BC, Saipan Island — E ASIA • 100 kW

PORTUGAL
- RADIO RENASCENCA, Muge — Su • EUROPE • 100 kW

USA
- †RFE-RL, Via Germany — WEST USSR • 100 kW
- †VOICE OF AMERICA, Cincinnati, Ohio — N AFRICA • 250 kW
- †VOA, Via Kaválla, Greece — (D) • WEST USSR • 250 kW
- VOICE OF AMERICA, Via Philippines — E AFRICA • 250 kW
- †VOA, Via Wertachtal, GFR — (J) • MIDEAST • 500 kW

USSR
- RADIO MOSCOW, Irkutsk — (J) • DS-1 • 50 kW
- RADIO MOSCOW, Serpukhov — (J) • MIDEAST • WS • 240 kW · (D) • MIDEAST & E AFRICA • WS, PORT, SWAHILI • 240 kW

9580 AUSTRALIA
- †RADIO AUSTRALIA, Shepparton — PACIFIC & N AMERICA • 100 kW

GABON
- †AFRIQUE NUMERO UN, Moyabi — C AFRICA • 250 kW

JAPAN
- †RADIO JAPAN/NHK, Tokyo-Yamata — E ASIA • 100 kW · (J) • E ASIA • 100 kW · (J) • JAPANESE • E ASIA • GENERAL • 100 kW

UNITED KINGDOM
- †BBC WORLD SERVICE, Skelton, Cumbria — (D) • W EUROPE & W AFRICA • 250 kW · (J) • W EUROPE & W AFRICA • 250 kW
- BBC, Via Maşīrah, Oman — S ASIA • 100 kW
- BBC WORLD SERVICE, Via Singapore — (D) • SE ASIA & E ASIA • 100 kW
- †BBC WORLD SERVICE, Via Zyyi, Cyprus — WEST USSR • 100 kW · EUROPE & WEST USSR • 100 kW · (D) • WEST USSR • 100 kW · (J) • WEST USSR • 100 kW

(con'd)

ENGLISH ▬ ARABIC ▨ CHINESE ▭▭ FRENCH ▬ GERMAN ▬ RUSSIAN ═ SPANISH ▬ OTHER —

FREQUENCY   COUNTRY, STATION, LOCATION

TARGET • NETWORK • POWER (kW)

World Time

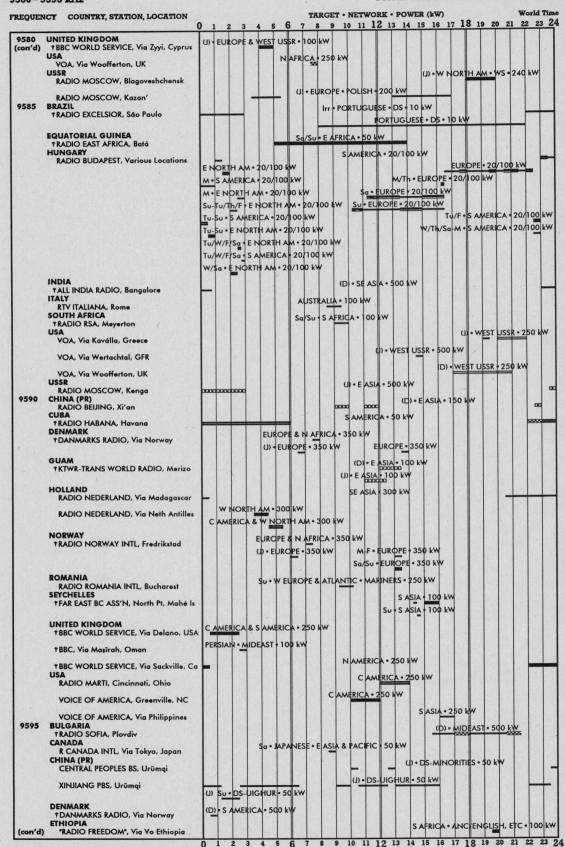

Frequency	Country / Station / Location	Target • Network • Power
9580 (con'd)	UNITED KINGDOM †BBC WORLD SERVICE, Via Zyyi, Cyprus	(J) • EUROPE & WEST USSR • 100 kW
	USA VOA, Via Woofferton, UK	N AFRICA • 250 kW
	USSR RADIO MOSCOW, Blagoveshchensk	(J) • W NORTH AM • WS • 240 kW
	RADIO MOSCOW, Kazan'	(J) • EUROPE • POLISH • 200 kW
9585	BRAZIL †RADIO EXCELSIOR, São Paulo	Irr • PORTUGUESE • DS • 10 kW / PORTUGUESE • DS • 10 kW
	EQUATORIAL GUINEA †RADIO EAST AFRICA, Batá	Sa/Su • E AFRICA • 50 kW
	HUNGARY RADIO BUDAPEST, Various Locations	S AMERICA • 20/100 kW; E NORTH AM • 20/100 kW; EUROPE • 20/100 kW; M • S AMERICA • 20/100 kW; M/Th • EUROPE • 20/100 kW; M • E NORTH AM • 20/100 kW; Sa • EUROPE • 20/100 kW; Su-Tu/Th/F • E NORTH AM • 20/100 kW; Su • EUROPE • 20/100 kW; Tu-Su • S AMERICA • 20/100 kW; Tu/F • S AMERICA • 20/100 kW; Tu-Su • E NORTH AM • 20/100 kW; W/Th/Sa-M • S AMERICA • 20/100 kW; Tu/W/F/Sa • E NORTH AM • 20/100 kW; Tu/W/F/Sa • S AMERICA • 20/100 kW; W/Sa • E NORTH AM • 20/100 kW
	INDIA †ALL INDIA RADIO, Bangalore	(D) • SE ASIA • 500 kW
	ITALY RTV ITALIANA, Rome	AUSTRALIA • 100 kW
	SOUTH AFRICA †RADIO RSA, Meyerton	Sa/Su • S AFRICA • 100 kW
	USA VOA, Via Kaválla, Greece	(J) • WEST USSR • 250 kW
	VOA, Via Wertachtal, GFR	(J) • WEST USSR • 500 kW
	VOA, Via Woofferton, UK	(D) • WEST USSR • 250 kW
	USSR RADIO MOSCOW, Kenga	(J) • E ASIA • 500 kW
9590	CHINA (PR) RADIO BEIJING, Xi'an	(D) • E ASIA • 150 kW
	CUBA †RADIO HABANA, Havana	S AMERICA • 50 kW
	DENMARK †DANMARKS RADIO, Via Norway	EUROPE & N AFRICA • 350 kW; (J) • EUROPE • 350 kW; EUROPE • 350 kW
	GUAM †KTWR-TRANS WORLD RADIO, Merizo	(D) • E ASIA • 100 kW; (J) • E ASIA • 100 kW
	HOLLAND RADIO NEDERLAND, Via Madagascar	SE ASIA • 300 kW
	RADIO NEDERLAND, Via Neth Antilles	W NORTH AM • 300 kW; C AMERICA & W NORTH AM • 300 kW
	NORWAY †RADIO NORWAY INTL, Fredrikstad	EUROPE & N AFRICA • 350 kW; (J) • EUROPE • 350 kW; M-F • EUROPE • 350 kW; Sa/Su • EUROPE • 350 kW
	ROMANIA RADIO ROMANIA INTL, Bucharest	Su • W EUROPE & ATLANTIC • MARINERS • 250 kW
	SEYCHELLES †FAR EAST BC ASS'N, North Pt, Mahé Is	S ASIA • 100 kW; Su • S ASIA • 100 kW
	UNITED KINGDOM †BBC WORLD SERVICE, Via Delano, USA	C AMERICA & S AMERICA • 250 kW
	†BBC, Via Maşirah, Oman	PERSIAN • MIDEAST • 100 kW
	†BBC WORLD SERVICE, Via Sackville, Ca	N AMERICA • 250 kW
	USA RADIO MARTI, Cincinnati, Ohio	C AMERICA • 250 kW
	VOICE OF AMERICA, Greenville, NC	C AMERICA • 250 kW
	VOICE OF AMERICA, Via Philippines	S ASIA • 250 kW
9595	BULGARIA †RADIO SOFIA, Plovdiv	(D) • MIDEAST • 500 kW
	CANADA R CANADA INTL, Via Tokyo, Japan	Sa • JAPANESE • E ASIA & PACIFIC • 50 kW
	CHINA (PR) CENTRAL PEOPLES BS, Urūmqi	(J) • DS • MINORITIES • 50 kW
	XINJIANG PBS, Urūmqi	(J) • DS • UIGHUR • 50 kW; (J) Su • DS • UIGHUR • 50 kW
	DENMARK †DANMARKS RADIO, Via Norway	(D) • S AMERICA • 500 kW
(con'd)	ETHIOPIA "RADIO FREEDOM", Via Vo Ethiopia	S AFRICA • ANC • ENGLISH, ETC • 100 kW

FREQUENCY   COUNTRY, STATION, LOCATION   TARGET • NETWORK • POWER (kW)   World Time

		0 1 2 3 4 5 6 7 8 9 10 11 12 13 14 15 16 17 18 19 20 21 22 23 24

9595 **ETHIOPIA**
(con'd)   "VOICE OF NAMIBIA", Via Vo Ethiopia — S AFRICA • SWAPO/ENGLISH, ETC • 100 kW
   JAPAN
      RADIO TANPA, Tokyo-Nagara — JAPANESE • DS-1 • 50 kW
      Su-F • JAPANESE • DS-1 • 50 kW
   NORWAY
      †RADIO NORWAY INTL, Sveio — (D) M-F • S AMERICA • 500 kW
      (D) Sa/Su • S AMERICA • 500 kW
   UNITED KINGDOM
      †BBC WORLD SERVICE, Via Seychelles — S AFRICA • 250 kW
   URUGUAY
      RADIO MONTE CARLO, Montevideo — DS • 1.5 kW
   USA
      †RFE-RL, Via Germany — E EUROPE • 100 kW
      †RFE-RL, Via Portugal — E EUROPE • 250 kW
      M-Sa • E EUROPE • 250 kW
      Su • WEST USSR • 250 kW
   USSR
      †KAZAKH RADIO — DS-2
      RADIO MOSCOW, Novosibirsk — E ASIA • 100 kW / (J) • E ASIA • CHINESE, MONGOLIAN • 100 kW
      †UZBEK RADIO, Serpukhov — DS-2/RUSSIAN, UZBEK • 20 kW
9599.7 **BRAZIL**
      †RADIO MEC, Rio de Janeiro — Irr • PORTUGUESE • DS • 7.5 kW
9600 **ALBANIA**
      RADIO TIRANA, Lushnjë — SE ASIA • 100 kW
   GERMANY (FR)
      †DEUTSCHE WELLE, Via Sri Lanka — (D) • MIDEAST • 250 kW
   KOREA (DPR)
      †RADIO PYONGYANG, Pyongyang — (D) • EAST USSR • 200 kW
      (D) • C AMERICA • 400 kW
      (D) • SE ASIA • 200 kW
   LIBYA
      RADIO JAMAHIRIYA, Benghazi — MIDEAST • DS • 100 kW
   PORTUGAL
      R PORTUGAL INTERNATIONAL, Lisbon — S AMERICA • 100 kW
      Su/M • S AMERICA • 100 kW
      Tu-Sa • S AMERICA • 100 kW
      RADIO RENASCENCA, Muge — S AMERICA • 100 kW
   SWAZILAND
      TRANS WORLD RADIO, Manzini — (D) • E AFRICA • 25 kW
   UNITED ARAB EMIRATES
      †VOICE OF THE UAE, Abu Dhabi — E NORTH AM • 500 kW
   UNITED KINGDOM
      †BBC WORLD SERVICE, Daventry — (J) • EUROPE & N AFRICA • 300 kW
      (J) • EUROPE • 300 kW
      †BBC WORLD SERVICE, Skelton, Cumbria — (D) • EUROPE & N AFRICA • 250 kW
      †BBC WORLD SERVICE, Via Ascension — S AFRICA • 250 kW
      W AFRICA • 250 kW
      BBC, Via Maṣīrah, Oman — S ASIA • 100 kW
      BBC WORLD SERVICE, Via Singapore — SE ASIA & S ASIA • 100 kW
   USSR
      †MAGADAN RADIO, Okhotsk — DS • 50/100 kW
      RADIO MOSCOW, Moscow — (J) • W EUROPE • 240 kW
      RADIO MOSCOW, Via Havana, Cuba — (J) • N AMERICA • 100 kW
      †RADIO TASHKENT, Tashkent — (D) • S ASIA • 100 kW
9600v **MEXICO**
      RADIO UNIVERSIDAD, México City — Irr • DS • 0.25/1 kW
9605 **CHINA (PR)**
      RADIO BEIJING, Kunming — SE ASIA • 50 kW
   CZECHOSLOVAKIA
      †RADIO PRAGUE INTL, Litomyšl — EUROPE • 120 kW
   DENMARK
      †DANMARKS RADIO, Via Norway — (D) • MIDEAST & S ASIA • 500 kW
      (D) • E ASIA & AUSTRALIA • 500 kW
      (D) • E NORTH AM • 500 kW
   FRANCE
      †R FRANCE INTL, Issoudun-Allouis — (D) • E EUROPE • 100 kW
      (J) • E EUROPE • 100 kW
   GERMANY (FR)
      †DEUTSCHE WELLE, Jülich — (D) • MIDEAST • 100 kW
      (J) • WEST USSR • 100 kW
      DEUTSCHE WELLE, Multiple Locations — SE ASIA • 100/500 kW
      †DEUTSCHE WELLE, Via Cyclops, Malta — (D) • N AMERICA • 250 kW
      DEUTSCHE WELLE, Wertachtal — (D) • E EUROPE • 500 kW
      (D) • WEST USSR • 500 kW
   IRAQ
(con'd)   †RADIO BAGHDAD, Balad-Salah el Deen — (D) • EUROPE & N AFRICA • 500 kW

		0 1 2 3 4 5 6 7 8 9 10 11 12 13 14 15 16 17 18 19 20 21 22 23 24

ENGLISH ▬▬   ARABIC ⸼⸼⸼   CHINESE □□□   FRENCH ══   GERMAN ▬▬   RUSSIAN ══   SPANISH ▬▬   OTHER ——

FREQUENCY   COUNTRY, STATION, LOCATION   TARGET • NETWORK • POWER (kW)   World Time

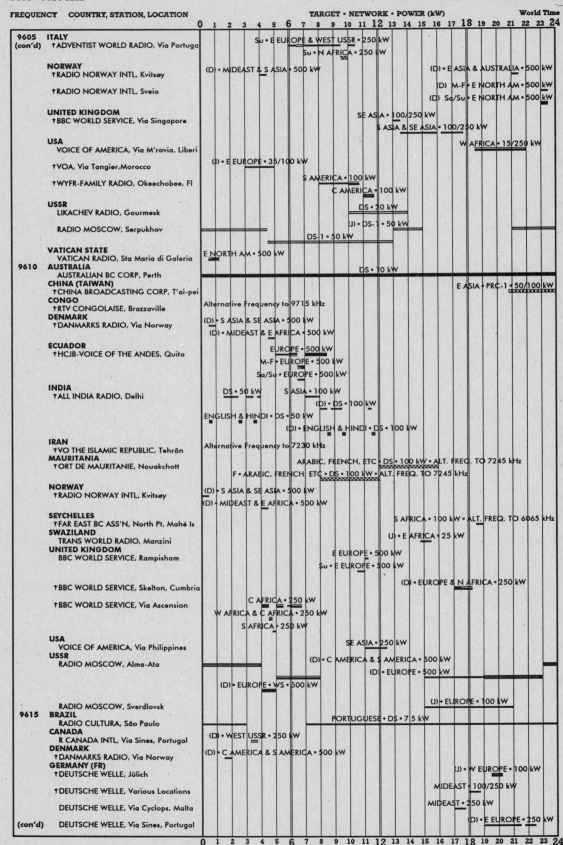

9605 (con'd)	**ITALY** †ADVENTIST WORLD RADIO, Via Portugal — Su • E EUROPE & WEST USSR • 250 kW / Su • N AFRICA • 250 kW
	NORWAY †RADIO NORWAY INTL, Kvitsøy — (D) • MIDEAST & S ASIA • 500 kW / (D) • E ASIA & AUSTRALIA • 500 kW
	†RADIO NORWAY INTL, Sveio — (D) • M-F • E NORTH AM • 500 kW / (D) • Sa/Su • E NORTH AM • 500 kW
	UNITED KINGDOM †BBC WORLD SERVICE, Via Singapore — SE ASIA • 100/250 kW / S ASIA & SE ASIA • 100/250 kW
	USA VOICE OF AMERICA, Via M'rovia, Liberi — W AFRICA • 15/250 kW
	†VOA, Via Tangier, Morocco — (J) • E EUROPE • 35/100 kW
	†WYFR-FAMILY RADIO, Okeechobee, Fl — S AMERICA • 100 kW / C AMERICA • 100 kW
	USSR LIKACHEV RADIO, Gourmesk — DS • 20 kW
	RADIO MOSCOW, Serpukhov — (J) • DS-1 • 50 kW / DS-1 • 50 kW
	VATICAN STATE VATICAN RADIO, Sta Maria di Galeria — E NORTH AM • 500 kW
9610	**AUSTRALIA** AUSTRALIAN BC CORP, Perth — DS • 10 kW
	CHINA (TAIWAN) †CHINA BROADCASTING CORP, T'ai-pei — E ASIA • PRC-1 • 50/100 kW
	CONGO †RTV CONGOLAISE, Brazzaville — Alternative Frequency to 9715 kHz
	DENMARK †DANMARKS RADIO, Via Norway — (D) • S ASIA & SE ASIA • 500 kW / (D) • MIDEAST & E AFRICA • 500 kW
	ECUADOR †HCJB-VOICE OF THE ANDES, Quito — EUROPE • 500 kW / M-F • EUROPE • 500 kW / Sa/Su • EUROPE • 500 kW
	INDIA †ALL INDIA RADIO, Delhi — DS • 50 kW / S ASIA • 100 kW / (D) • DS • 100 kW / ENGLISH & HINDI • DS • 50 kW / (D) • ENGLISH & HINDI • DS • 100 kW
	IRAN †VO THE ISLAMIC REPUBLIC, Tehrān — Alternative Frequency to 7230 kHz
	MAURITANIA †ORT DE MAURITANIE, Nouakchott — ARABIC, FRENCH, ETC • DS • 100 kW • ALT. FREQ. TO 7245 kHz / F • ARABIC, FRENCH, ETC • DS • 100 kW • ALT. FREQ. TO 7245 kHz
	NORWAY †RADIO NORWAY INTL, Kvitsøy — (D) • S ASIA & SE ASIA • 500 kW / (D) • MIDEAST & E AFRICA • 500 kW
	SEYCHELLES †FAR EAST BC ASS'N, North Pt, Mahé Is — S AFRICA • 100 kW • ALT. FREQ. TO 6065 kHz
	SWAZILAND TRANS WORLD RADIO, Manzini — (J) • E AFRICA • 25 kW
	UNITED KINGDOM BBC WORLD SERVICE, Rampisham — E EUROPE • 500 kW / Su • E EUROPE • 500 kW
	†BBC WORLD SERVICE, Skelton, Cumbria — (D) • EUROPE & N AFRICA • 250 kW
	†BBC WORLD SERVICE, Via Ascension — C AFRICA • 250 kW / W AFRICA & C AFRICA • 250 kW / S AFRICA • 250 kW
	USA VOICE OF AMERICA, Via Philippines — SE ASIA • 250 kW
	USSR RADIO MOSCOW, Alma-Ata — (D) • C AMERICA & S AMERICA • 500 kW / (D) • EUROPE • 500 kW / (D) • EUROPE • WS • 500 kW
	RADIO MOSCOW, Sverdlovsk — (J) • EUROPE • 100 kW
9615	**BRAZIL** RADIO CULTURA, São Paulo — PORTUGUESE • DS • 7.5 kW
	CANADA R CANADA INTL, Via Sines, Portugal — (D) • WEST USSR • 250 kW
	DENMARK †DANMARKS RADIO, Via Norway — (D) • C AMERICA & S AMERICA • 500 kW
	GERMANY (FR) †DEUTSCHE WELLE, Jülich — (J) • W EUROPE • 100 kW
	†DEUTSCHE WELLE, Various Locations — MIDEAST • 100/250 kW
	DEUTSCHE WELLE, Via Cyclops, Malta — MIDEAST • 250 kW
(con'd)	DEUTSCHE WELLE, Via Sines, Portugal — (D) • E EUROPE • 250 kW

FREQUENCY   COUNTRY, STATION, LOCATION

TARGET • NETWORK • POWER (kW)

World Time

0 1 2 3 4 5 6 7 8 9 10 11 12 13 14 15 16 17 18 19 20 21 22 23 24

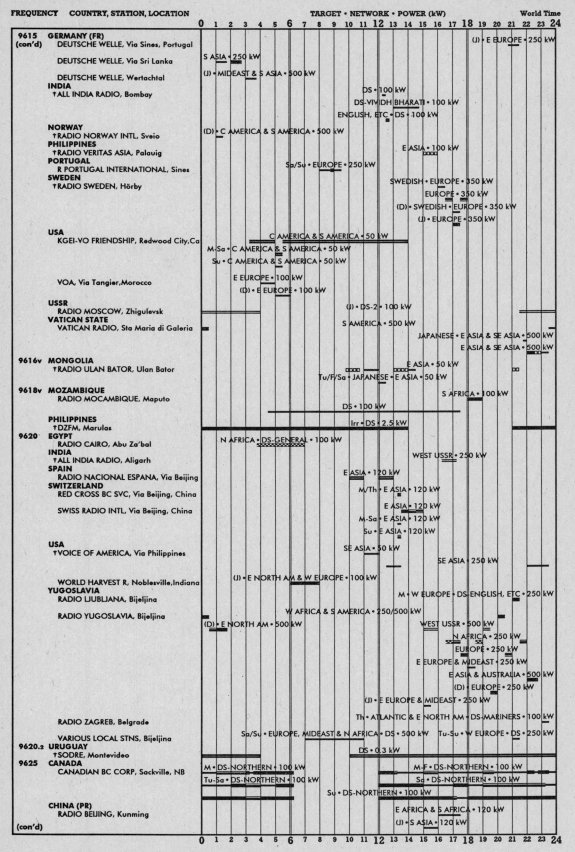

Frequency	Country, Station, Location	Target • Network • Power
9615 (con'd)	**GERMANY (FR)**	
	DEUTSCHE WELLE, Via Sines, Portugal	(J) • E EUROPE • 250 kW
	DEUTSCHE WELLE, Via Sri Lanka	S ASIA • 250 kW
	DEUTSCHE WELLE, Wertachtal	(J) • MIDEAST & S ASIA • 500 kW
	INDIA	
	†ALL INDIA RADIO, Bombay	DS • 100 kW
		DS-VIVIDH BHARATI • 100 kW
		ENGLISH, ETC • DS • 100 kW
	NORWAY	
	†RADIO NORWAY INTL, Sveio	(D) • C AMERICA & S AMERICA • 500 kW
	PHILIPPINES	
	†RADIO VERITAS ASIA, Palauig	E ASIA • 100 kW
	PORTUGAL	
	R PORTUGAL INTERNATIONAL, Sines	Sa/Su • EUROPE • 250 kW
	SWEDEN	
	†RADIO SWEDEN, Hörby	SWEDISH • EUROPE • 350 kW
		EUROPE • 350 kW
		(D) • SWEDISH • EUROPE • 350 kW
		(J) • EUROPE • 350 kW
	USA	
	KGEI-VO FRIENDSHIP, Redwood City, Ca	C AMERICA & S AMERICA • 50 kW
		M-Sa • C AMERICA & S AMERICA • 50 kW
		Su • C AMERICA & S AMERICA • 50 kW
	VOA, Via Tangier, Morocco	E EUROPE • 100 kW
		(D) • E EUROPE • 100 kW
	USSR	
	RADIO MOSCOW, Zhigulevsk	(J) • DS-2 • 100 kW
	VATICAN STATE	
	VATICAN RADIO, Sta Maria di Galeria	S AMERICA • 500 kW
		JAPANESE • E ASIA & SE ASIA • 500 kW
		E ASIA & SE ASIA • 500 kW
9616v	**MONGOLIA**	
	†RADIO ULAN BATOR, Ulan Bator	E ASIA • 50 kW
		Tu/F/Sa • JAPANESE • E ASIA • 50 kW
9618v	**MOZAMBIQUE**	
	RADIO MOCAMBIQUE, Maputo	S AFRICA • 100 kW
		DS • 100 kW
	PHILIPPINES	
	†DZFM, Marulas	Irr • DS • 2.5 kW
9620	**EGYPT**	
	RADIO CAIRO, Abu Za'bal	N AFRICA • DS-GENERAL • 100 kW
	INDIA	
	†ALL INDIA RADIO, Aligarh	WEST USSR • 250 kW
	SPAIN	
	RADIO NACIONAL ESPANA, Via Beijing	E ASIA • 120 kW
	SWITZERLAND	
	RED CROSS BC SVC, Via Beijing, China	M/Th • E ASIA • 120 kW
	SWISS RADIO INTL, Via Beijing, China	E ASIA • 120 kW
		M-Sa • E ASIA • 120 kW
		Su • E ASIA • 120 kW
	USA	
	†VOICE OF AMERICA, Via Philippines	SE ASIA • 50 kW
		SE ASIA • 250 kW
	WORLD HARVEST R, Noblesville, Indiana	(J) • E NORTH AM & W EUROPE • 100 kW
	YUGOSLAVIA	
	RADIO LJUBLJANA, Bijeljina	M • W EUROPE • DS-ENGLISH, ETC • 250 kW
	RADIO YUGOSLAVIA, Bijeljina	W AFRICA & S AMERICA • 250/500 kW
		(D) • E NORTH AM • 500 kW
		WEST USSR • 500 kW
		N AFRICA • 250 kW
		EUROPE • 250 kW
		E EUROPE & MIDEAST • 250 kW
		E ASIA & AUSTRALIA • 500 kW
		(D) • EUROPE • 250 kW
		(J) • E EUROPE & MIDEAST • 250 kW
	RADIO ZAGREB, Belgrade	Th • ATLANTIC & E NORTH AM • DS-MARINERS • 100 kW
	VARIOUS LOCAL STNS, Bijeljina	Sa/Su • EUROPE, MIDEAST & N AFRICA • DS • 500 kW Tu-Su • W EUROPE • DS • 250 kW
9620.2	**URUGUAY**	
	†SODRE, Montevideo	DS • 0.3 kW
9625	**CANADA**	
	CANADIAN BC CORP, Sackville, NB	M • DS-NORTHERN • 100 kW M-F • DS-NORTHERN • 100 kW
		Tu-Sa • DS-NORTHERN • 100 kW Sa • DS-NORTHERN • 100 kW
		Su • DS-NORTHERN • 100 kW
	CHINA (PR)	
	RADIO BEIJING, Kunming	E AFRICA & S AFRICA • 120 kW
		(J) • S ASIA • 120 kW
(con'd)		

0 1 2 3 4 5 6 7 8 9 10 11 12 13 14 15 16 17 18 19 20 21 22 23 24

ENGLISH ▬▬   ARABIC ⨯⨯⨯   CHINESE □□□   FRENCH ▬▬   GERMAN ▬▬   RUSSIAN ══   SPANISH ▬▬   OTHER ──

FREQUENCY   COUNTRY, STATION, LOCATION   TARGET • NETWORK • POWER (kW)   World Time
                                          0 1 2 3 4 5 6 7 8 9 10 11 12 13 14 15 16 17 18 19 20 21 22 23 24

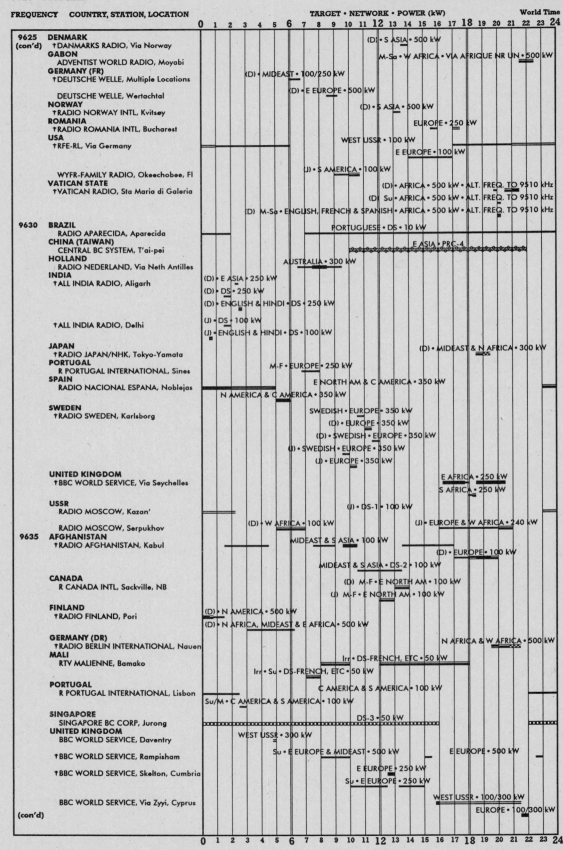

9625 **DENMARK**
(con'd)   †DANMARKS RADIO, Via Norway   (D) • S ASIA • 500 kW
          GABON
          ADVENTIST WORLD RADIO, Moyabi   M-Sa • W AFRICA • VIA AFRIQUE NR UN • 500 kW
          GERMANY (FR)
          †DEUTSCHE WELLE, Multiple Locations   (D) • MIDEAST • 100/250 kW
          DEUTSCHE WELLE, Wertachtal   (D) • E EUROPE • 500 kW
          NORWAY
          †RADIO NORWAY INTL, Kvitsøy   (D) • S ASIA • 500 kW
          ROMANIA
          †RADIO ROMANIA INTL, Bucharest   EUROPE • 250 kW
          USA
          †RFE-RL, Via Germany   WEST USSR • 100 kW
                                                E EUROPE • 100 kW
          WYFR-FAMILY RADIO, Okeechobee, Fl   (J) • S AMERICA • 100 kW
          VATICAN STATE
          †VATICAN RADIO, Sta Maria di Galeria   (D) • AFRICA • 500 kW • ALT. FREQ. TO 9510 kHz
                                                (D) Su • AFRICA • 500 kW • ALT. FREQ. TO 9510 kHz
                                        (D) M-Sa • ENGLISH, FRENCH & SPANISH • AFRICA • 500 kW • ALT. FREQ. TO 9510 kHz

9630 **BRAZIL**
          RADIO APARECIDA, Aparecida   PORTUGUESE • DS • 10 kW
          CHINA (TAIWAN)
          CENTRAL BC SYSTEM, T'ai-pei   E ASIA • PRC-4
          HOLLAND
          RADIO NEDERLAND, Via Neth Antilles   AUSTRALIA • 300 kW
          INDIA
          †ALL INDIA RADIO, Aligarh   (D) • E ASIA • 250 kW
                                               (D) • DS • 250 kW
                                               (D) • ENGLISH & HINDI • DS • 250 kW
          †ALL INDIA RADIO, Delhi   (J) • DS • 100 kW
                                               (J) • ENGLISH & HINDI • DS • 100 kW
          JAPAN
          †RADIO JAPAN/NHK, Tokyo-Yamata   (D) • MIDEAST & N AFRICA • 300 kW
          PORTUGAL
          R PORTUGAL INTERNATIONAL, Sines   M-F • EUROPE • 250 kW
          SPAIN
          RADIO NACIONAL ESPANA, Noblejas   E NORTH AM & C AMERICA • 350 kW
                                               N AMERICA & C AMERICA • 350 kW
          SWEDEN
          †RADIO SWEDEN, Karlsborg   SWEDISH • EUROPE • 350 kW
                                               (D) • EUROPE • 350 kW
                                               (D) • SWEDISH • EUROPE • 350 kW
                                               (J) • SWEDISH • EUROPE • 350 kW
                                               (J) • EUROPE • 350 kW
          UNITED KINGDOM
          †BBC WORLD SERVICE, Via Seychelles   E AFRICA • 250 kW
                                                S AFRICA • 250 kW
          USSR
          RADIO MOSCOW, Kazan'   (J) • DS-1 • 100 kW
          RADIO MOSCOW, Serpukhov   (D) • W AFRICA • 100 kW   (J) • EUROPE & W AFRICA • 240 kW
9635 **AFGHANISTAN**
          †RADIO AFGHANISTAN, Kabul   MIDEAST & S ASIA • 100 kW
                                               (D) • EUROPE • 100 kW
                                               MIDEAST & S ASIA • DS-2 • 100 kW
          CANADA
          R CANADA INTL, Sackville, NB   (D) M-F • E NORTH AM • 100 kW
                                               (J) M-F • E NORTH AM • 100 kW
          FINLAND
          †RADIO FINLAND, Pori   (D) • N AMERICA • 500 kW
                                               (D) • N AFRICA, MIDEAST & E AFRICA • 500 kW
          GERMANY (DR)
          †RADIO BERLIN INTERNATIONAL, Nauen   N AFRICA & W AFRICA • 500 kW
          MALI
          RTV MALIENNE, Bamako   Irr • DS-FRENCH, ETC • 50 kW
                                               Irr • Su • DS-FRENCH, ETC • 50 kW
          PORTUGAL
          R PORTUGAL INTERNATIONAL, Lisbon   C AMERICA & S AMERICA • 100 kW
                                               Su/M • C AMERICA & S AMERICA • 100 kW
          SINGAPORE
          SINGAPORE BC CORP, Jurong   DS-3 • 50 kW
          UNITED KINGDOM
          BBC WORLD SERVICE, Daventry   WEST USSR • 300 kW
          †BBC WORLD SERVICE, Rampisham   Su • E EUROPE & MIDEAST • 500 kW   E EUROPE • 500 kW
          †BBC WORLD SERVICE, Skelton, Cumbria E EUROPE • 250 kW
                                               Su • E EUROPE • 250 kW
          BBC WORLD SERVICE, Via Zyyi, Cyprus WEST USSR • 100/300 kW
                                               EUROPE • 100/300 kW
(con'd)

                                          0 1 2 3 4 5 6 7 8 9 10 11 12 13 14 15 16 17 18 19 20 21 22 23 24

SUMMER ONLY (J)   WINTER ONLY (D)   JAMMING / OR ∧   EARLIEST HEARD ◁   LATEST HEARD ▷   NEW OR CHANGED FOR 1991 †

FREQUENCY	COUNTRY, STATION, LOCATION	TARGET • NETWORK • POWER (kW)	World Time

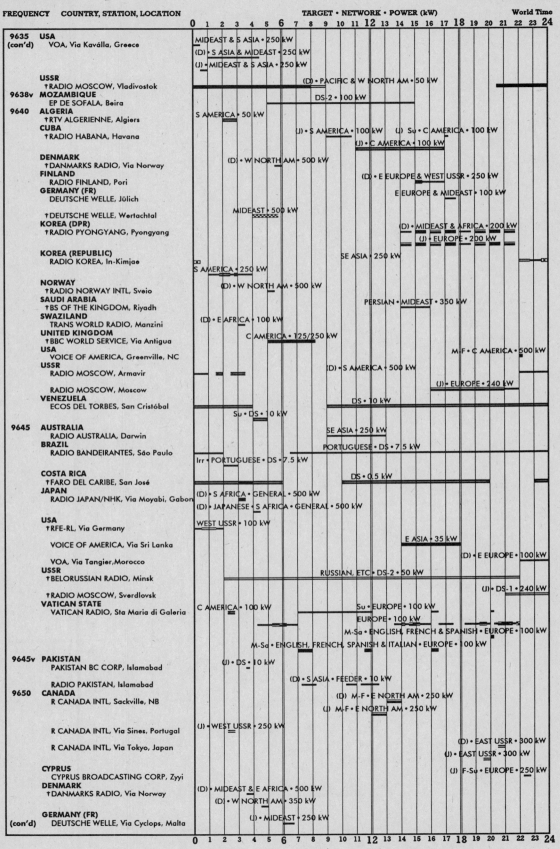

9635 **USA**
(con'd)   VOA, Via Kaválla, Greece — MIDEAST & S ASIA • 250 kW; (D) • S ASIA & MIDEAST • 250 kW; (J) • MIDEAST & S ASIA • 250 kW

USSR
†RADIO MOSCOW, Vladivostok — (D) • PACIFIC & W NORTH AM • 50 kW

9638v MOZAMBIQUE
EP DE SOFALA, Beira — DS-2 • 100 kW

9640 ALGERIA
†RTV ALGERIENNE, Algiers — S AMERICA • 50 kW

CUBA
†RADIO HABANA, Havana — (J) • S AMERICA • 100 kW; (J) Su • C AMERICA • 100 kW; (J) • C AMERICA • 100 kW

DENMARK
†DANMARKS RADIO, Via Norway — (D) • W NORTH AM • 500 kW

FINLAND
RADIO FINLAND, Pori — (D) • E EUROPE & WEST USSR • 250 kW

GERMANY (FR)
DEUTSCHE WELLE, Jülich — E EUROPE & MIDEAST • 100 kW

†DEUTSCHE WELLE, Wertachtal — MIDEAST • 500 kW

KOREA (DPR)
†RADIO PYONGYANG, Pyongyang — (D) • MIDEAST & AFRICA • 200 kW; (J) • EUROPE • 200 kW

KOREA (REPUBLIC)
RADIO KOREA, In-Kimjae — SE ASIA • 250 kW

NORWAY
†RADIO NORWAY INTL, Sveio — S AMERICA • 250 kW; (D) • W NORTH AM • 500 kW

SAUDI ARABIA
†BS OF THE KINGDOM, Riyadh — PERSIAN • MIDEAST • 350 kW

SWAZILAND
TRANS WORLD RADIO, Manzini — (D) • E AFRICA • 100 kW

UNITED KINGDOM
†BBC WORLD SERVICE, Via Antigua — C AMERICA • 125/250 kW

USA
VOICE OF AMERICA, Greenville, NC — M-F • C AMERICA • 500 kW

USSR
RADIO MOSCOW, Armavir — (D) • S AMERICA • 500 kW

RADIO MOSCOW, Moscow — (J) • EUROPE • 240 kW

VENEZUELA
ECOS DEL TORBES, San Cristóbal — DS • 10 kW; Su • DS • 10 kW

9645 AUSTRALIA
RADIO AUSTRALIA, Darwin — SE ASIA • 250 kW

BRAZIL
RADIO BANDEIRANTES, São Paulo — PORTUGUESE • DS • 7.5 kW; Irr • PORTUGUESE • DS • 7.5 kW

COSTA RICA
†FARO DEL CARIBE, San José — DS • 0.5 kW

JAPAN
RADIO JAPAN/NHK, Via Moyabi, Gabon — (D) • S AFRICA • GENERAL • 500 kW; (D) • JAPANESE • S AFRICA • GENERAL • 500 kW

USA
†RFE-RL, Via Germany — WEST USSR • 100 kW

VOICE OF AMERICA, Via Sri Lanka — E ASIA • 35 kW

VOA, Via Tangier, Morocco — (D) • E EUROPE • 100 kW

USSR
†BELORUSSIAN RADIO, Minsk — RUSSIAN, ETC • DS-2 • 50 kW

†RADIO MOSCOW, Sverdlovsk — (J) • DS-1 • 240 kW

VATICAN STATE
VATICAN RADIO, Sta Maria di Galeria — C AMERICA • 100 kW; Su • EUROPE • 100 kW; EUROPE • 100 kW; M-Sa • ENGLISH, FRENCH & SPANISH • EUROPE • 100 kW; M-Sa • ENGLISH, FRENCH, SPANISH & ITALIAN • EUROPE • 100 kW

9645v PAKISTAN
PAKISTAN BC CORP, Islamabad — (J) • DS • 10 kW

RADIO PAKISTAN, Islamabad — (D) • S ASIA • FEEDER • 10 kW

9650 CANADA
R CANADA INTL, Sackville, NB — (D) M-F • E NORTH AM • 250 kW; (J) M-F • E NORTH AM • 250 kW

R CANADA INTL, Via Sines, Portugal — (J) • WEST USSR • 250 kW

R CANADA INTL, Via Tokyo, Japan — (D) • EAST USSR • 300 kW; (J) • EAST USSR • 300 kW

CYPRUS
CYPRUS BROADCASTING CORP, Zyyi — (J) F-Su • EUROPE • 250 kW

DENMARK
†DANMARKS RADIO, Via Norway — (D) • MIDEAST & E AFRICA • 500 kW; (D) • W NORTH AM • 350 kW

GERMANY (FR)
(con'd)   DEUTSCHE WELLE, Via Cyclops, Malta — (J) • MIDEAST • 250 kW

ENGLISH ▬ ARABIC ⁓ CHINESE ∞ FRENCH ▬ GERMAN ▬ RUSSIAN ═ SPANISH ▬ OTHER —

FREQUENCY   COUNTRY, STATION, LOCATION   TARGET • NETWORK • POWER (kW)   World Time

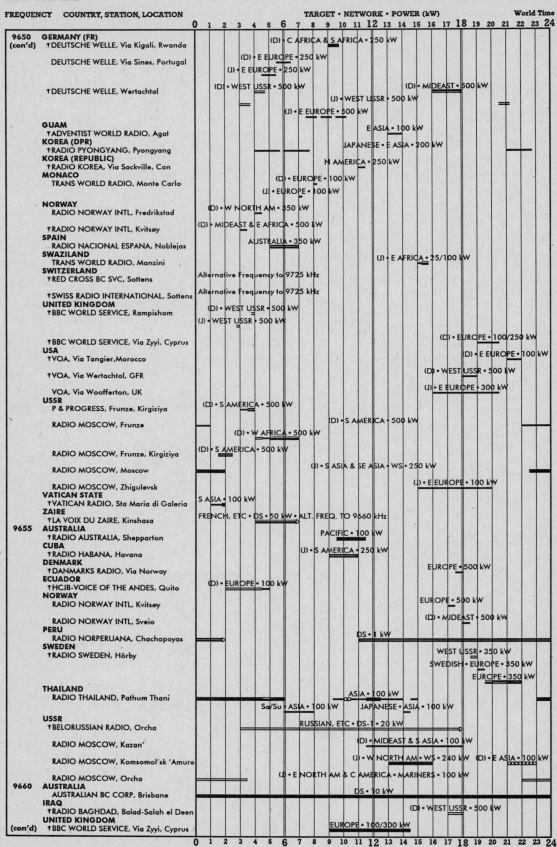

0 1 2 3 4 5 6 7 8 9 10 11 12 13 14 15 16 17 18 19 20 21 22 23 24

9650 (con'd)
GERMANY (FR)
 †DEUTSCHE WELLE, Via Kigali, Rwanda — (D) • C AFRICA & S AFRICA • 250 kW
 DEUTSCHE WELLE, Via Sines, Portugal — (D) • E EUROPE • 250 kW / (J) • E EUROPE • 250 kW
 †DEUTSCHE WELLE, Wertachtal — (D) • WEST USSR • 500 kW / (D) • MIDEAST • 500 kW / (J) • WEST USSR • 500 kW / (J) • E EUROPE • 500 kW

GUAM
 †ADVENTIST WORLD RADIO, Agat — E ASIA • 100 kW
KOREA (DPR)
 †RADIO PYONGYANG, Pyongyang — JAPANESE • E ASIA • 200 kW
KOREA (REPUBLIC)
 †RADIO KOREA, Via Sackville, Can — N AMERICA • 250 kW
MONACO
 TRANS WORLD RADIO, Monte Carlo — (D) • EUROPE • 100 kW / (J) • EUROPE • 100 kW

NORWAY
 RADIO NORWAY INTL, Fredrikstad — (D) • W NORTH AM • 350 kW
 †RADIO NORWAY INTL, Kvitsøy — (D) • MIDEAST & E AFRICA • 500 kW
SPAIN
 RADIO NACIONAL ESPANA, Noblejas — AUSTRALIA • 350 kW
SWAZILAND
 TRANS WORLD RADIO, Manzini — (J) • E AFRICA • 25/100 kW
SWITZERLAND
 †RED CROSS BC SVC, Sottens — Alternative Frequency to 9725 kHz
 †SWISS RADIO INTERNATIONAL, Sottens — Alternative Frequency to 9725 kHz
UNITED KINGDOM
 †BBC WORLD SERVICE, Rampisham — (D) • WEST USSR • 500 kW / (J) • WEST USSR • 500 kW
 †BBC WORLD SERVICE, Via Zyyi, Cyprus — (D) • EUROPE • 100/250 kW / (D) • E EUROPE • 100 kW
USA
 †VOA, Via Tangier, Morocco — (D) • WEST USSR • 500 kW
 †VOA, Via Wertachtal, GFR — (J) • E EUROPE • 300 kW
 VOA, Via Woofferton, UK
USSR
 P & PROGRESS, Frunze, Kirgiziya — (D) • S AMERICA • 500 kW
 RADIO MOSCOW, Frunze — (D) • S AMERICA • 500 kW
 — (D) • W AFRICA • 500 kW
 RADIO MOSCOW, Frunze, Kirgiziya — (D) • S AMERICA • 500 kW
 RADIO MOSCOW, Moscow — (J) • S ASIA & SE ASIA • WS • 250 kW
 RADIO MOSCOW, Zhigulevsk — (J) • E EUROPE • 100 kW
VATICAN STATE
 †VATICAN RADIO, Sta Maria di Galeria — S ASIA • 100 kW
ZAIRE
 †LA VOIX DU ZAIRE, Kinshasa — FRENCH, ETC • DS • 50 kW • ALT. FREQ. TO 9660 kHz
9655 AUSTRALIA
 †RADIO AUSTRALIA, Shepparton — PACIFIC • 100 kW
CUBA
 †RADIO HABANA, Havana — (J) • S AMERICA • 250 kW
DENMARK
 †DANMARKS RADIO, Via Norway — EUROPE • 500 kW
ECUADOR
 †HCJB-VOICE OF THE ANDES, Quito — (D) • EUROPE • 100 kW
NORWAY
 RADIO NORWAY INTL, Kvitsøy — EUROPE • 500 kW
 RADIO NORWAY INTL, Sveio — (D) • MIDEAST • 500 kW
PERU
 RADIO NORPERUANA, Chachapoyas — DS • 1 kW
SWEDEN
 †RADIO SWEDEN, Hörby — WEST USSR • 350 kW / SWEDISH • EUROPE • 350 kW / EUROPE • 350 kW

THAILAND
 RADIO THAILAND, Pathum Thani — ASIA • 100 kW / Sa/Su • ASIA • 100 kW / JAPANESE • ASIA • 100 kW

USSR
 †BELORUSSIAN RADIO, Orcha — RUSSIAN, ETC • DS-1 • 20 kW
 RADIO MOSCOW, Kazan' — (D) • MIDEAST & S ASIA • 100 kW
 RADIO MOSCOW, Komsomol'sk 'Amure — (J) • W NORTH AM • WS • 240 kW / (D) • E ASIA • 100 kW
 RADIO MOSCOW, Orcha — (J) • E NORTH AM & C AMERICA • MARINERS • 100 kW
9660 AUSTRALIA
 AUSTRALIAN BC CORP, Brisbane — DS • 10 kW
IRAQ
 †RADIO BAGHDAD, Balad-Salah el Deen — (D) • WEST USSR • 500 kW
UNITED KINGDOM
(con'd) †BBC WORLD SERVICE, Via Zyyi, Cyprus — EUROPE • 100/300 kW

0 1 2 3 4 5 6 7 8 9 10 11 12 13 14 15 16 17 18 19 20 21 22 23 24

SUMMER ONLY (J)   WINTER ONLY (D)   JAMMING / OR ⋀   EARLIEST HEARD ◁   LATEST HEARD ▷   NEW OR CHANGED FOR 1991 †

FREQUENCY   COUNTRY, STATION, LOCATION   TARGET • NETWORK • POWER (kW)   World Time

0 1 2 3 4 5 6 7 8 9 10 11 12 13 14 15 16 17 18 19 20 21 22 23 24

FREQUENCY	COUNTRY, STATION, LOCATION	TARGET • NETWORK • POWER (kW)
9660 (con'd)	UNITED KINGDOM †BBC WORLD SERVICE, Via Zyyi, Cyprus	(D) Sa/Su • EUROPE • 300 kW (D) • EUROPE • 300 kW Sa/Su • EUROPE • 100/300 kW
	USA †RFE-RL, Via Germany	WEST USSR • 250 kW
	†RFE-RL, Via Pals, Spain	WEST USSR • 250 kW
	VOICE OF AMERICA, Via Wertachtal, GF	(J) • WEST USSR • 500 kW
	VOA, Via Woofferton, UK	(D) • E EUROPE & WEST USSR • 300 kW
	VENEZUELA †RADIO RUMBOS, Caracas	DS • 10 kW Tu-Su • DS • 10 kW M-Sa • DS • 10 kW
	YUGOSLAVIA RADIO YUGOSLAVIA, Bijeljina	(D) • E NORTH AM • 500 kW (D) • EUROPE • 250 kW (D) • EUROPE & E NORTH AM • 500 kW (J) • EUROPE • 250 kW
	ZAIRE †LA VOIX DU ZAIRE, Kinshasa	Alternative Frequency to 9650 kHz
9665	CHINA (PR) RADIO BEIJING, Shijiazhuang	(D) • E NORTH AM, C AMERICA & S AMERICA • 500 kW
	GERMANY (DR) †R BERLIN INTL, Königswusterhausen	EUROPE • 100 kW
	INDIA †ALL INDIA RADIO, Aligarh	EUROPE • 250 kW
	†ALL INDIA RADIO, Delhi	(D) • DS • 50 kW (D) • ENGLISH & HINDI • DS • 50 kW
	KOREA (DPR) KOREAN CENTRAL BS, Pyongyang	DS • 200 kW
	ROMANIA RADIO ROMANIA INTL, Bucharest	Su • ATLANTIC • MARINERS • 250 kW
	SOUTH AFRICA †SOUTH AFRICAN BC, Meyerton	RADIO SUID-AFRIKA • 100 kW
	SWEDEN †IBRA RADIO, Via Cyclops, Malta	Sa/Su • E EUROPE & WEST USSR • 250 kW Sa/Su • W EUROPE • 250 kW
	†IBRA RADIO, Via Sines, Portugal	(D) • MIDEAST • 250 kW • ALT. FREQ. TO 9685 kHz (D) • E EUROPE & WEST USSR • RUSSIAN, ETC • 250 kW • ALT. FREQ. TO 9685 kHz
	TURKEY VOICE OF TURKEY, Ankara	MIDEAST • 500 kW MIDEAST • 250 kW
	USSR RADIO MOSCOW, Dushanbé	(J) • S AMERICA • 500 kW (D) • S AMERICA • 500 kW (J) Su-Tu • S AMERICA • 500 kW (J) W-Sa • S AMERICA • 500 kW
	RADIO MOSCOW, Voronezh, RSFSR	(D) • MIDEAST & E AFRICA • ARABIC, PERSIAN, ETC • 240 kW
9665v	BRAZIL RADIO MARUMBI, Florianópolis	PORTUGUESE • DS • 10 kW
9670	CANADA †R CANADA INTL, Via United Kingdom	(J) • EUROPE • 300 kW
	CHINA (PR) RADIO BEIJING, Kunming	S ASIA • 50 kW S AFRICA • 50 kW (D) • C AFRICA • 50 kW
	ECUADOR HCJB-VOICE OF THE ANDES, Quito	S AMERICA • 100 kW
	EGYPT †RADIO CAIRO, Kafr Silim-Abis	EUROPE • DS-GENERAL • 250 kW
	FINLAND †RADIO FINLAND, Pori	(J) • E EUROPE • 250 kW (D) • E ASIA • 500 kW
	GERMANY (FR) DEUTSCHE WELLE, Via Antigua	N AMERICA • 250 kW
	DEUTSCHE WELLE, Via Sri Lanka	SE ASIA & AUSTRALIA • 250 kW
	ITALY ADVENTIST WORLD RADIO, Via Portugal	Su • E EUROPE & WEST USSR • 250 kW Su • W EUROPE • 250 kW
	PHILIPPINES †FEBC RADIO INTERNATIONAL, Bocaue	SE ASIA & S ASIA • 50 kW
	SWAZILAND TRANS WORLD RADIO, Manzini	(J) • S AFRICA • 25 kW (J) Sa/Su • S AFRICA • 25 kW
	UNITED KINGDOM †BBC WORLD SERVICE, Daventry	(D) • E EUROPE & WEST USSR • 300 kW (D) • EUROPE & WEST USSR • 300 kW (D) • W AFRICA • 300 kW (D) • EUROPE, N AFRICA & W AFRICA • 250 kW (J) • EUROPE & WEST USSR • 300 kW
(con'd)	†BBC WORLD SERVICE, Skelton, Cumbria	(J) • EUROPE • 250 kW

0 1 2 3 4 5 6 7 8 9 10 11 12 13 14 15 16 17 18 19 20 21 22 23 24

ENGLISH ▬▬   ARABIC ▧▧▧   CHINESE ▫▫▫   FRENCH ▭▭   GERMAN ▬▬   RUSSIAN ▭▭   SPANISH ▬▬   OTHER ▬▬

FREQUENCY   COUNTRY, STATION, LOCATION   TARGET • NETWORK • POWER (kW)   World Time

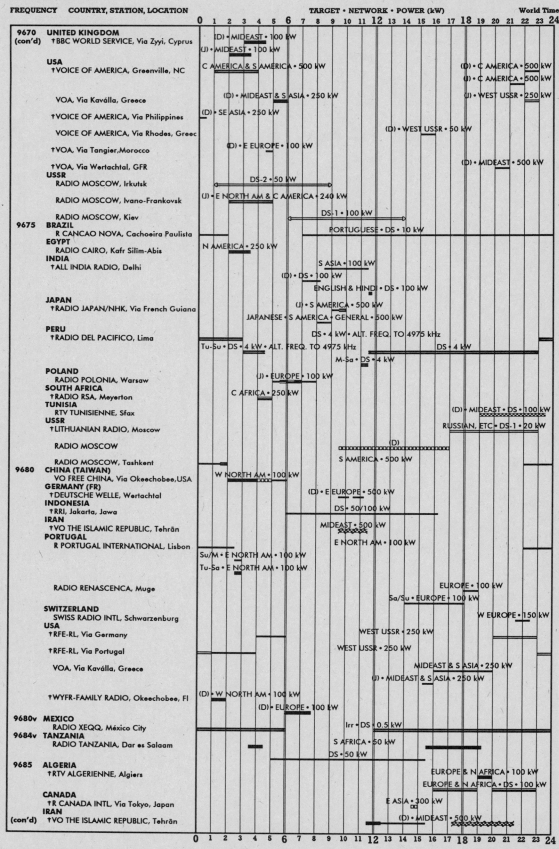

FREQUENCY	COUNTRY, STATION, LOCATION	TARGET • NETWORK • POWER (kW)
9670 (con'd)	UNITED KINGDOM †BBC WORLD SERVICE, Via Zyyi, Cyprus	(D) • MIDEAST • 100 kW / (J) • MIDEAST • 100 kW
	USA †VOICE OF AMERICA, Greenville, NC	C AMERICA & S AMERICA • 500 kW / (D) • C AMERICA • 500 kW / (J) • C AMERICA • 500 kW
	VOA, Via Kaválla, Greece	(D) • MIDEAST & S ASIA • 250 kW / (J) • WEST USSR • 250 kW
	†VOICE OF AMERICA, Via Philippines	(D) • SE ASIA • 250 kW
	VOICE OF AMERICA, Via Rhodes, Greec	(D) • WEST USSR • 50 kW
	†VOA, Via Tangier, Morocco	(D) • E EUROPE • 100 kW
	†VOA, Via Wertachtal, GFR	(D) • MIDEAST • 500 kW
	USSR RADIO MOSCOW, Irkutsk	DS-2 • 50 kW
	RADIO MOSCOW, Ivano-Frankovsk	(J) • E NORTH AM & C AMERICA • 240 kW
	RADIO MOSCOW, Kiev	DS-1 • 100 kW
9675	BRAZIL R CANCAO NOVA, Cachoeira Paulista	PORTUGUESE • DS • 10 kW
	EGYPT RADIO CAIRO, Kafr Silim-Abis	N AMERICA • 250 kW
	INDIA †ALL INDIA RADIO, Delhi	S ASIA • 100 kW / (D) • DS • 100 kW / ENGLISH & HINDI • DS • 100 kW
	JAPAN †RADIO JAPAN/NHK, Via French Guiana	(J) • S AMERICA • 500 kW / JAPANESE • S AMERICA • GENERAL • 500 kW
	PERU †RADIO DEL PACIFICO, Lima	DS • 4 kW • ALT. FREQ. TO 4975 kHz / Tu–Su • DS • 4 kW • ALT. FREQ. TO 4975 kHz / DS • 4 kW / M–Sa • DS • 4 kW
	POLAND RADIO POLONIA, Warsaw	(J) • EUROPE • 100 kW
	SOUTH AFRICA †RADIO RSA, Meyerton	C AFRICA • 250 kW
	TUNISIA RTV TUNISIENNE, Sfax	(D) • MIDEAST • DS • 100 kW
	USSR †LITHUANIAN RADIO, Moscow	RUSSIAN, ETC • DS-1 • 20 kW
	RADIO MOSCOW	(D)
	RADIO MOSCOW, Tashkent	S AMERICA • 500 kW
9680	CHINA (TAIWAN) VO FREE CHINA, Via Okeechobee, USA	W NORTH AM • 100 kW
	GERMANY (FR) †DEUTSCHE WELLE, Wertachtal	(D) • E EUROPE • 500 kW
	INDONESIA †RRI, Jakarta, Jawa	DS • 50/100 kW
	IRAN †VO THE ISLAMIC REPUBLIC, Tehrān	MIDEAST • 500 kW
	PORTUGAL R PORTUGAL INTERNATIONAL, Lisbon	E NORTH AM • 100 kW / Su/M • E NORTH AM • 100 kW / Tu–Sa • E NORTH AM • 100 kW
	RADIO RENASCENCA, Muge	EUROPE • 100 kW / Sa/Su • EUROPE • 100 kW
	SWITZERLAND SWISS RADIO INTL, Schwarzenburg	W EUROPE • 150 kW
	USA †RFE-RL, Via Germany	WEST USSR • 250 kW
	†RFE-RL, Via Portugal	WEST USSR • 250 kW
	VOA, Via Kaválla, Greece	MIDEAST & S ASIA • 250 kW / (J) • MIDEAST & S ASIA • 250 kW
	†WYFR-FAMILY RADIO, Okeechobee, Fl	(D) • W NORTH AM • 100 kW / (D) • EUROPE • 100 kW
9680v	MEXICO RADIO XEQQ, México City	Irr • DS • 0.5 kW
9684v	TANZANIA RADIO TANZANIA, Dar es Salaam	S AFRICA • 50 kW / DS • 50 kW
9685	ALGERIA †RTV ALGERIENNE, Algiers	EUROPE & N AFRICA • 100 kW / EUROPE & N AFRICA • DS • 100 kW
	CANADA †R CANADA INTL, Via Tokyo, Japan	E ASIA • 300 kW
(con'd)	IRAN †VO THE ISLAMIC REPUBLIC, Tehrān	(D) • MIDEAST • 500 kW

FREQUENCY   COUNTRY, STATION, LOCATION

TARGET • NETWORK • POWER (kW)

World Time

0 1 2 3 4 5 6 7 8 9 10 11 12 13 14 15 16 17 18 19 20 21 22 23 24

Frequency	Country, Station, Location	Schedule
9685 (con'd)	**JAPAN** RADIO JAPAN/NHK, Via French Guiana	JAPANESE • S AMERICA • GENERAL • 500 kW
	SWEDEN †IBRA RADIO, Via Sines, Portugal	Alternative Frequency to 9665 kHz
	TURKEY VOICE OF TURKEY, Ankara	(J) • TURKISH • EUROPE • 250 kW / (J) • EUROPE • 250 kW
	USSR RADIO MOSCOW, Irkutsk	(D) E ASIA & SE ASIA • 500 kW / (J) • SE ASIA • 500 kW / (J) • E ASIA & SE ASIA • 500 kW
	†RADIO MOSCOW, Moscow	(D) • E NORTH AM & C AMERICA • 100 kW / (D) • W EUROPE • 100 kW
9685v	**BRAZIL** †RADIO GAZETA, São Paulo	PORTUGUESE • DS • 7.5 kW
9688.8	**MADAGASCAR** RADIO MADAGASIKARA, Antananarivo	DS-FRENCH, ETC • 10 kW
9690	**ARGENTINA** †RADIO ARGENTINA-RAE, Buenos Aires	Tu-Sa • S AMERICA • 25 kW
		S AMERICA • DS • 25 kW
	†RADIO NACIONAL, Buenos Aires	Su/M • S AMERICA • DS • 25 kW
	CHINA (PR) RADIO BEIJING, Kunming	W EUROPE • 120 kW
	RADIO BEIJING, Via Noblejas, Spain	N AMERICA & C AMERICA • 350 kW
	CHINA (TAIWAN) †CENTRAL BC SYSTEM, T'ai-pei	E ASIA • PRC-1 • 10 kW / E ASIA • PRC-5 • 10 kW
	GERMANY (FR) DEUTSCHE WELLE, Jülich	(D) • WEST USSR • 100 kW / (J) • WEST USSR • 100 kW / (J) • MIDEAST & N AFRICA • 100/500 kW
	DEUTSCHE WELLE, Multiple Locations	AUSTRALIA & C AMERICA • 250 kW
	DEUTSCHE WELLE, Via Antigua	(J) • MIDEAST • 250 kW
	DEUTSCHE WELLE, Via Cyclops, Malta	S ASIA & SE ASIA • 500 kW
	†DEUTSCHE WELLE, Wertachtal	(D) • MIDEAST & S ASIA • 500 kW
	ROMANIA †RADIO ROMANIA INTL, Bucharest	EUROPE • 250 kW / MIDEAST • 250 kW / WEST USSR • 250 kW / (D) • MIDEAST • 250 kW / (D) • EUROPE • 250 kW / (J) • WEST USSR • 250 kW
	UNITED KINGDOM †BBC WORLD SERVICE, Via Delano, USA	C AMERICA • 250 kW / (J) • C AMERICA • 250 kW
	USA †VOA, Via Kaválla, Greece	WEST USSR • 250 kW / E AFRICA • 250 kW / (D) • USSR • 250 kW
	†VOICE OF AMERICA, Via Philippines	(J) • SE ASIA • 250 kW
	USSR †KAZAKH RADIO, Tula	DS-2 • 20 kW
9695	**BRAZIL** †RADIO RIO MAR, Manaus	Irr • PORTUGUESE • DS • 7.5 kW / Irr • Sa • DS • 7.5 kW / Irr • Su-F • DS • 7.5 kW
	CAMBODIA VOICE OF THE PEOPLE, Phnom Penh	SE ASIA
	JAPAN RADIO JAPAN/NHK, Tokyo-Yamata	(J) • JAPANESE • E ASIA • GENERAL • 300 kW / (J) • E ASIA • GENERAL • 300 kW
	SWEDEN †RADIO SWEDEN, Hörby	(D) • S AMERICA • 350 kW / (D) • SWEDISH • S AMERICA • 350 kW / (D) • N AMERICA • 350 kW / (D) • WEST USSR • 350 kW / (D) • SWEDISH • N AMERICA • 350 kW / (J) • WEST USSR • 350 kW
	UNITED ARAB EMIRATES †VOICE OF THE UAE, Abu Dhabi	S ASIA • 120 kW
	USA †RFE-RL, Via Germany	E EUROPE • 100 kW
	†RFE-RL, Via Portugal	E EUROPE • 250 kW / M-F • E EUROPE • 250 kW / Sa/Su • WEST USSR • 250 kW

(con'd)

0 1 2 3 4 5 6 7 8 9 10 11 12 13 14 15 16 17 18 19 20 21 22 23 24

ENGLISH ▬   ARABIC ▨   CHINESE ▭▭   FRENCH ▬▬   GERMAN ▬   RUSSIAN ═   SPANISH ▬   OTHER ▬

FREQUENCY   COUNTRY, STATION, LOCATION — TARGET • NETWORK • POWER (kW) — World Time

0 1 2 3 4 5 6 7 8 9 10 11 12 13 14 15 16 17 18 19 20 21 22 23 24

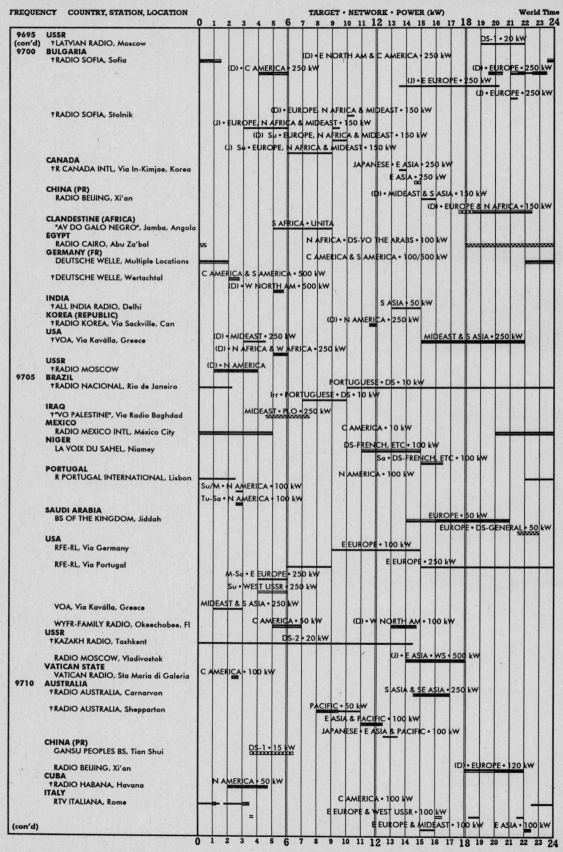

Frequency	Country / Station / Location	Schedule detail
9695 (con'd)	USSR †LATVIAN RADIO, Moscow	DS-1 • 20 kW
9700	BULGARIA †RADIO SOFIA, Sofia	(D) • E NORTH AM & C AMERICA • 250 kW
		(D) • C AMERICA • 250 kW
		(D) • EUROPE • 250 kW
		(J) • E EUROPE • 250 kW
		(J) • EUROPE • 250 kW
	†RADIO SOFIA, Stolnik	(D) • EUROPE, N AFRICA & MIDEAST • 150 kW
		(J) • EUROPE, N AFRICA & MIDEAST • 150 kW
		(D) Su • EUROPE, N AFRICA & MIDEAST • 150 kW
		(J) Su • EUROPE, N AFRICA & MIDEAST • 150 kW
	CANADA †R CANADA INTL, Via In-Kimjae, Korea	JAPANESE • E ASIA • 250 kW
		E ASIA • 250 kW
	CHINA (PR) RADIO BEIJING, Xi'an	(D) • MIDEAST & S ASIA • 150 kW
		(D) • EUROPE & N AFRICA • 150 kW
	CLANDESTINE (AFRICA) "AV DO GALO NEGRO", Jamba, Angola	S AFRICA • UNITA
	EGYPT RADIO CAIRO, Abu Za'bal	N AFRICA • DS-VO THE ARABS • 100 kW
	GERMANY (FR) DEUTSCHE WELLE, Multiple Locations	C AMERICA & S AMERICA • 100/500 kW
	†DEUTSCHE WELLE, Wertachtal	C AMERICA & S AMERICA • 500 kW
		(D) • W NORTH AM • 500 kW
	INDIA †ALL INDIA RADIO, Delhi	S ASIA • 50 kW
	KOREA (REPUBLIC) †RADIO KOREA, Via Sackville, Can	(D) • N AMERICA • 250 kW
	USA †VOA, Via Kaválla, Greece	(D) • MIDEAST • 250 kW
		MIDEAST & S ASIA • 250 kW
		(D) • N AFRICA & W AFRICA • 250 kW
	USSR †RADIO MOSCOW	(D) • N AMERICA
9705	BRAZIL †RADIO NACIONAL, Rio de Janeiro	PORTUGUESE • DS • 10 kW
		Irr • PORTUGUESE • DS • 10 kW
	IRAQ †"VO PALESTINE", Via Radio Baghdad	MIDEAST • PLO • 250 kW
	MEXICO RADIO MEXICO INTL, México City	C AMERICA • 10 kW
	NIGER LA VOIX DU SAHEL, Niamey	DS-FRENCH, ETC • 100 kW
		Sa • DS-FRENCH, ETC • 100 kW
	PORTUGAL R PORTUGAL INTERNATIONAL, Lisbon	N AMERICA • 100 kW
		Su/M • N AMERICA • 100 kW
		Tu-Sa • N AMERICA • 100 kW
	SAUDI ARABIA BS OF THE KINGDOM, Jiddah	EUROPE • 50 kW
		EUROPE • DS-GENERAL • 50 kW
	USA RFE-RL, Via Germany	E EUROPE • 100 kW
	RFE-RL, Via Portugal	E EUROPE • 250 kW
		M-Sa • E EUROPE • 250 kW
		Su • WEST USSR • 250 kW
	VOA, Via Kaválla, Greece	MIDEAST & S ASIA • 250 kW
	WYFR-FAMILY RADIO, Okeechobee, Fl	C AMERICA • 50 kW
		(D) • W NORTH AM • 100 kW
	USSR †KAZAKH RADIO, Tashkent	DS-2 • 20 kW
	RADIO MOSCOW, Vladivostok	(J) • E ASIA • WS • 500 kW
	VATICAN STATE VATICAN RADIO, Sta Maria di Galeria	C AMERICA • 100 kW
9710	AUSTRALIA †RADIO AUSTRALIA, Carnarvon	S ASIA & SE ASIA • 250 kW
	†RADIO AUSTRALIA, Shepparton	PACIFIC • 50 kW
		E ASIA & PACIFIC • 100 kW
		JAPANESE • E ASIA & PACIFIC • 100 kW
	CHINA (PR) GANSU PEOPLES BS, Tian Shui	DS-1 • 15 kW
	RADIO BEIJING, Xi'an	(D) • EUROPE • 120 kW
	CUBA †RADIO HABANA, Havana	N AMERICA • 50 kW
	ITALY RTV ITALIANA, Rome	C AMERICA • 100 kW
		E EUROPE & WEST USSR • 100 kW
	(con'd)	E EUROPE & MIDEAST • 100 kW E ASIA • 100 kW

0 1 2 3 4 5 6 7 8 9 10 11 12 13 14 15 16 17 18 19 20 21 22 23 24

SUMMER ONLY (J)   WINTER ONLY (D)   JAMMING / OR ∧   EARLIEST HEARD ◁   LATEST HEARD ▷   NEW OR CHANGED FOR 1991 †

FREQUENCY   COUNTRY, STATION, LOCATION   TARGET • NETWORK • POWER (kW)   World Time

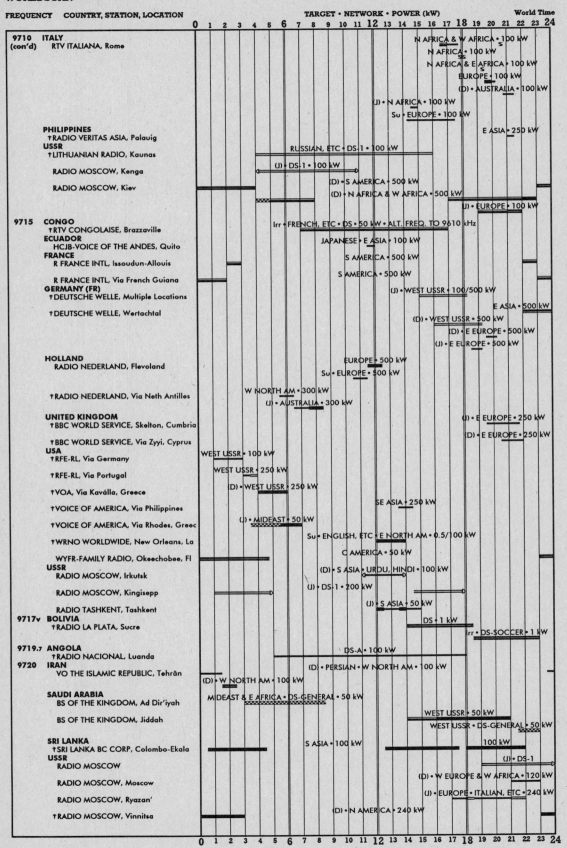

Freq	Country, Station, Location	Target • Network • Power
9710 (con'd)	**ITALY** RTV ITALIANA, Rome	N AFRICA & W AFRICA • 100 kW
		N AFRICA • 100 kW
		N AFRICA & E AFRICA • 100 kW
		EUROPE • 100 kW
		(D) • AUSTRALIA • 100 kW
		(J) • N AFRICA • 100 kW
		Su • EUROPE • 100 kW
		E ASIA • 250 kW
	PHILIPPINES †RADIO VERITAS ASIA, Palauig	
	USSR †LITHUANIAN RADIO, Kaunas	RUSSIAN, ETC • DS-1 • 100 kW
	RADIO MOSCOW, Kenga	(J) • DS-1 • 100 kW
	RADIO MOSCOW, Kiev	(D) • S AMERICA • 500 kW
		(D) • N AFRICA & W AFRICA • 500 kW
		(J) • EUROPE • 100 kW
9715	**CONGO** †RTV CONGOLAISE, Brazzaville	Irr • FRENCH, ETC • DS • 50 kW • ALT. FREQ. TO 9610 kHz
	ECUADOR HCJB-VOICE OF THE ANDES, Quito	JAPANESE • E ASIA • 100 kW
	FRANCE R FRANCE INTL, Issoudun-Allouis	S AMERICA • 500 kW
	R FRANCE INTL, Via French Guiana	S AMERICA • 500 kW
	GERMANY (FR) †DEUTSCHE WELLE, Multiple Locations	(J) • WEST USSR • 100/500 kW
	†DEUTSCHE WELLE, Wertachtal	E ASIA • 500 kW
		(D) • WEST USSR • 500 kW
		(D) • E EUROPE • 500 kW
		(J) • E EUROPE • 500 kW
	HOLLAND RADIO NEDERLAND, Flevoland	EUROPE • 500 kW
		Su • EUROPE • 500 kW
	†RADIO NEDERLAND, Via Neth Antilles	W NORTH AM • 300 kW
		(J) • AUSTRALIA • 300 kW
	UNITED KINGDOM †BBC WORLD SERVICE, Skelton, Cumbria	(J) • E EUROPE • 250 kW
	†BBC WORLD SERVICE, Via Zyyi, Cyprus	(D) • E EUROPE • 250 kW
	USA †RFE-RL, Via Germany	WEST USSR • 100 kW
	†RFE-RL, Via Portugal	WEST USSR • 250 kW
	†VOA, Via Kaválla, Greece	(D) • WEST USSR • 250 kW
	†VOICE OF AMERICA, Via Philippines	SE ASIA • 250 kW
	†VOICE OF AMERICA, Via Rhodes, Greec	(J) • MIDEAST • 50 kW
	†WRNO WORLDWIDE, New Orleans, La	Su • ENGLISH, ETC • E NORTH AM • 0.5/100 kW
	WYFR-FAMILY RADIO, Okeechobee, Fl	C AMERICA • 50 kW
	USSR RADIO MOSCOW, Irkutsk	(D) • S ASIA • URDU, HINDI • 100 kW
	RADIO MOSCOW, Kingisepp	(J) • DS-1 • 200 kW
	RADIO TASHKENT, Tashkent	(J) • S ASIA • 50 kW
9717v	**BOLIVIA** †RADIO LA PLATA, Sucre	DS • 1 kW
		Irr • DS-SOCCER • 1 kW
9719.7	**ANGOLA** †RADIO NACIONAL, Luanda	DS-A • 100 kW
9720	**IRAN** VO THE ISLAMIC REPUBLIC, Tehrān	(D) • PERSIAN • W NORTH AM • 100 kW
		(D) • W NORTH AM • 100 kW
	SAUDI ARABIA BS OF THE KINGDOM, Ad Dir'iyah	MIDEAST & E AFRICA • DS-GENERAL • 50 kW
	BS OF THE KINGDOM, Jiddah	WEST USSR • 50 kW
		WEST USSR • DS-GENERAL • 50 kW
	SRI LANKA †SRI LANKA BC CORP, Colombo-Ekala	S ASIA • 100 kW 100 kW
	USSR RADIO MOSCOW	(J) • DS-1
	RADIO MOSCOW, Moscow	(D) • W EUROPE & W AFRICA • 120 kW
	RADIO MOSCOW, Ryazan'	(J) • EUROPE • ITALIAN, ETC • 240 kW
	†RADIO MOSCOW, Vinnitsa	(D) • N AMERICA • 240 kW

ENGLISH ■■■   ARABIC ※※※   CHINESE □□□   FRENCH ══   GERMAN ▬▬   RUSSIAN ══   SPANISH ══   OTHER ──

FREQUENCY COUNTRY, STATION, LOCATION   TARGET • NETWORK • POWER (kW)   World Time

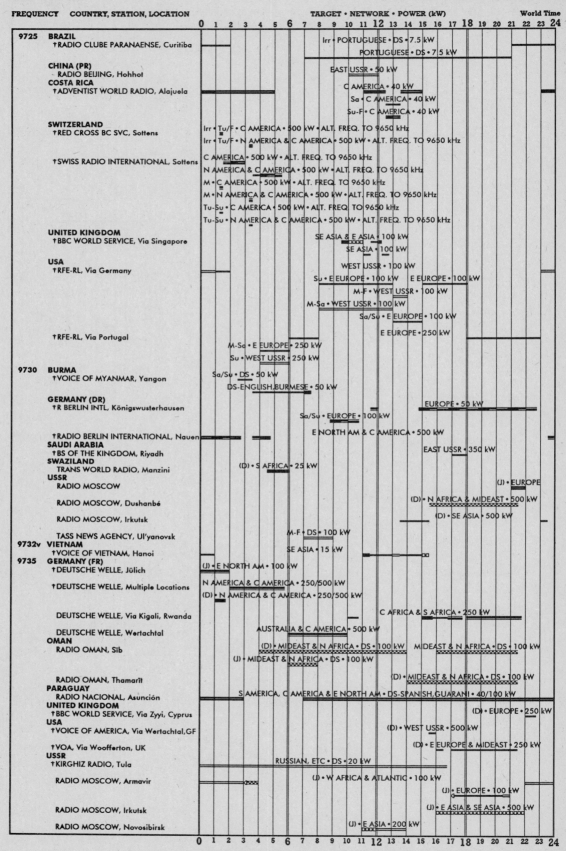

		World Time 0–24
9725	**BRAZIL**	
	†RADIO CLUBE PARANAENSE, Curitiba	Irr • PORTUGUESE • DS • 7.5 kW
		PORTUGUESE • DS • 7.5 kW
	CHINA (PR)	
	RADIO BEIJING, Hohhot	EAST USSR • 50 kW
	COSTA RICA	
	†ADVENTIST WORLD RADIO, Alajuela	C AMERICA • 40 kW
		Sa • C AMERICA • 40 kW
		Su-F • C AMERICA • 40 kW
	SWITZERLAND	
	†RED CROSS BC SVC, Sottens	Irr • Tu/F • C AMERICA • 500 kW • ALT. FREQ. TO 9650 kHz
		Irr • Tu/F • N AMERICA & C AMERICA • 500 kW • ALT. FREQ. TO 9650 kHz
	†SWISS RADIO INTERNATIONAL, Sottens	C AMERICA • 500 kW • ALT. FREQ. TO 9650 kHz
		N AMERICA & C AMERICA • 500 kW • ALT. FREQ. TO 9650 kHz
		M • C AMERICA • 500 kW • ALT. FREQ. TO 9650 kHz
		M • N AMERICA & C AMERICA • 500 kW • ALT. FREQ. TO 9650 kHz
		Tu-Su • C AMERICA • 500 kW • ALT. FREQ. TO 9650 kHz
		Tu-Su • N AMERICA & C AMERICA • 500 kW • ALT. FREQ. TO 9650 kHz
	UNITED KINGDOM	
	†BBC WORLD SERVICE, Via Singapore	SE ASIA & E ASIA • 100 kW
		SE ASIA • 100 kW
	USA	
	†RFE-RL, Via Germany	WEST USSR • 100 kW
		Su • E EUROPE • 100 kW E EUROPE • 100 kW
		M-F • WEST USSR • 100 kW
		M-Sa • WEST USSR • 100 kW
		Sa/Su • E EUROPE • 100 kW
		E EUROPE • 250 kW
	†RFE-RL, Via Portugal	M-Sa • E EUROPE • 250 kW
		Su • WEST USSR • 250 kW
9730	**BURMA**	
	†VOICE OF MYANMAR, Yangon	Sa/Su • DS • 50 kW
		DS-ENGLISH, BURMESE • 50 kW
	GERMANY (DR)	
	†R BERLIN INTL, Königswusterhausen	EUROPE • 50 kW
		Sa/Su • EUROPE • 100 kW
	†RADIO BERLIN INTERNATIONAL, Nauen	E NORTH AM & C AMERICA • 500 kW
	SAUDI ARABIA	
	†BS OF THE KINGDOM, Riyadh	EAST USSR • 350 kW
	SWAZILAND	
	TRANS WORLD RADIO, Manzini	(D) • S AFRICA • 25 kW
	USSR	
	RADIO MOSCOW	(J) • EUROPE
	RADIO MOSCOW, Dushanbé	(D) • N AFRICA & MIDEAST • 500 kW
	RADIO MOSCOW, Irkutsk	(D) • SE ASIA • 500 kW
	TASS NEWS AGENCY, Ul'yanovsk	M-F • DS • 100 kW
9732v	**VIETNAM**	
	†VOICE OF VIETNAM, Hanoi	SE ASIA • 15 kW
9735	**GERMANY (FR)**	
	†DEUTSCHE WELLE, Jülich	(J) • E NORTH AM • 100 kW
	†DEUTSCHE WELLE, Multiple Locations	N AMERICA & C AMERICA • 250/500 kW
		(D) • N AMERICA & C AMERICA • 250/500 kW
	DEUTSCHE WELLE, Via Kigali, Rwanda	C AFRICA & S AFRICA • 250 kW
	DEUTSCHE WELLE, Wertachtal	AUSTRALIA & C AMERICA • 500 kW
	OMAN	
	RADIO OMAN, Sīb	(D) • MIDEAST & N AFRICA • DS • 100 kW MIDEAST & N AFRICA • DS • 100 kW
		(J) • MIDEAST & N AFRICA • DS • 100 kW
	RADIO OMAN, Thamarīt	(D) • MIDEAST & N AFRICA • DS • 100 kW
	PARAGUAY	
	RADIO NACIONAL, Asunción	S AMERICA, C AMERICA & E NORTH AM • DS-SPANISH, GUARANI • 40/100 kW
	UNITED KINGDOM	
	†BBC WORLD SERVICE, Via Zyyi, Cyprus	(D) • EUROPE • 250 kW
	USA	
	†VOICE OF AMERICA, Via Wertachtal, GF	(D) • WEST USSR • 500 kW
	†VOA, Via Woofferton, UK	(D) • E EUROPE & MIDEAST • 250 kW
	USSR	
	†KIRGHIZ RADIO, Tula	RUSSIAN, ETC • DS • 20 kW
	RADIO MOSCOW, Armavir	(J) • W AFRICA & ATLANTIC • 100 kW
		(J) • EUROPE • 100 kW
	RADIO MOSCOW, Irkutsk	(J) • E ASIA & SE ASIA • 500 kW
	RADIO MOSCOW, Novosibirsk	(J) • E ASIA • 200 kW

0 1 2 3 4 5 6 7 8 9 10 11 12 13 14 15 16 17 18 19 20 21 22 23 24

SUMMER ONLY (J) WINTER ONLY (D) JAMMING / OR ∧ EARLIEST HEARD ◁ LATEST HEARD ▷ NEW OR CHANGED FOR 1991 †

FREQUENCY   COUNTRY, STATION, LOCATION

TARGET • NETWORK • POWER (kW)

World Time
0 1 2 3 4 5 6 7 8 9 10 11 12 13 14 15 16 17 18 19 20 21 22 23 24

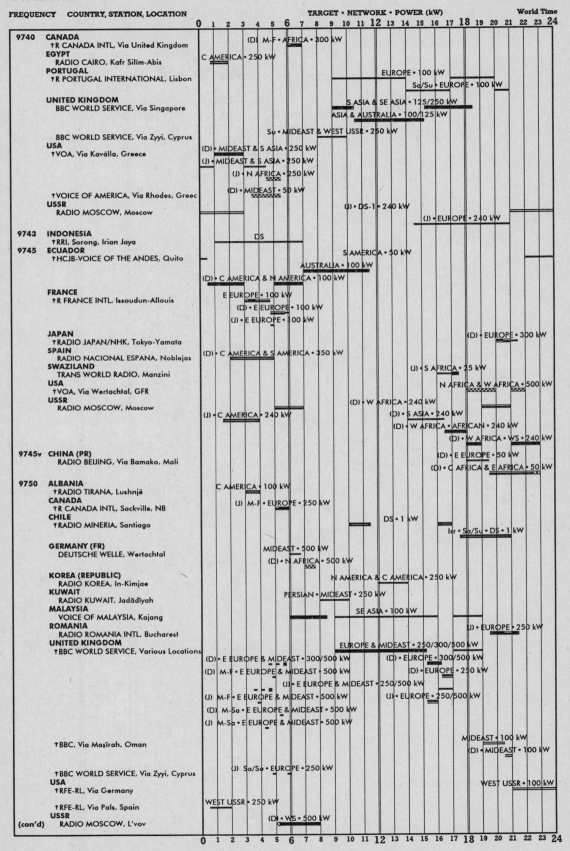

9740 CANADA
  ↑R CANADA INTL, Via United Kingdom — (D) M-F • AFRICA • 300 kW
EGYPT
  RADIO CAIRO, Kafr Silim-Abis — C AMERICA • 250 kW
PORTUGAL
  ↑R PORTUGAL INTERNATIONAL, Lisbon — EUROPE • 100 kW / Sa/Su • EUROPE • 100 kW

UNITED KINGDOM
  BBC WORLD SERVICE, Via Singapore — S ASIA & SE ASIA • 125/250 kW / ASIA & AUSTRALIA • 100/125 kW

  BBC WORLD SERVICE, Via Zyyi, Cyprus — Su • MIDEAST & WEST USSR • 250 kW
USA
  ↑VOA, Via Kaválla, Greece — (D) • MIDEAST & S ASIA • 250 kW / (J) • MIDEAST & S ASIA • 250 kW / (J) • N AFRICA • 250 kW

  ↑VOICE OF AMERICA, Via Rhodes, Greec — (D) • MIDEAST • 50 kW
USSR
  RADIO MOSCOW, Moscow — (J) • DS-1 • 240 kW / (J) • EUROPE • 240 kW

9743 INDONESIA
  ↑RRI, Sorong, Irian Jaya — DS
9745 ECUADOR
  ↑HCJB-VOICE OF THE ANDES, Quito — S AMERICA • 50 kW / AUSTRALIA • 100 kW / (D) • C AMERICA & N AMERICA • 100 kW

FRANCE
  ↑R FRANCE INTL, Issoudun-Allouis — E EUROPE • 100 kW / (D) • E EUROPE • 100 kW / (J) • E EUROPE • 100 kW

JAPAN
  ↑RADIO JAPAN/NHK, Tokyo-Yamata — (D) • EUROPE • 300 kW
SPAIN
  RADIO NACIONAL ESPANA, Noblejas — (D) • C AMERICA & S AMERICA • 350 kW
SWAZILAND
  TRANS WORLD RADIO, Manzini — (J) • S AFRICA • 25 kW
USA
  ↑VOA, Via Wertachtal, GFR — N AFRICA & W AFRICA • 500 kW
USSR
  RADIO MOSCOW, Moscow — (D) • W AFRICA • 240 kW / (J) • C AMERICA • 240 kW / (D) • S ASIA • 240 kW / (D) • W AFRICA • AFRICAN • 240 kW / (D) • W AFRICA • WS • 240 kW

9745v CHINA (PR)
  RADIO BEIJING, Via Bamako, Mali — (D) • E EUROPE • 50 kW / (D) • C AFRICA & E AFRICA • 50 kW

9750 ALBANIA
  ↑RADIO TIRANA, Lushnjë — C AMERICA • 100 kW
CANADA
  ↑R CANADA INTL, Sackville, NB — (J) M-F • EUROPE • 250 kW
CHILE
  ↑RADIO MINERIA, Santiago — DS • 1 kW / Irr • Sa/Su • DS • 1 kW

GERMANY (FR)
  DEUTSCHE WELLE, Wertachtal — MIDEAST • 500 kW / (D) • N AFRICA • 500 kW

KOREA (REPUBLIC)
  RADIO KOREA, In-Kimjae — N AMERICA & C AMERICA • 250 kW
KUWAIT
  RADIO KUWAIT, Jadādīyah — PERSIAN • MIDEAST • 250 kW
MALAYSIA
  VOICE OF MALAYSIA, Kajang — SE ASIA • 100 kW
ROMANIA
  RADIO ROMANIA INTL, Bucharest — (J) • EUROPE • 250 kW
UNITED KINGDOM
  ↑BBC WORLD SERVICE, Various Locations — EUROPE & MIDEAST • 250/300/500 kW / (D) • E EUROPE & MIDEAST • 300/500 kW / (D) • EUROPE • 300/500 kW / (D) M-F • E EUROPE & MIDEAST • 500 kW / (D) • EUROPE • 250 kW / (J) • E EUROPE & MIDEAST • 250/500 kW / (J) M-F • E EUROPE & MIDEAST • 500 kW / (J) • EUROPE • 250/500 kW / (D) M-Sa • E EUROPE & MIDEAST • 500 kW / (J) M-Sa • E EUROPE & MIDEAST • 500 kW

  ↑BBC, Via Maṣīrah, Oman — MIDEAST • 100 kW / (D) • MIDEAST • 100 kW

  ↑BBC WORLD SERVICE, Via Zyyi, Cyprus — (J) Sa/Su • EUROPE • 250 kW
USA
  ↑RFE-RL, Via Germany — WEST USSR • 100 kW

  ↑RFE-RL, Via Pals, Spain — WEST USSR • 250 kW
USSR
(con'd) RADIO MOSCOW, L'vov — (D) • WS • 500 kW

0 1 2 3 4 5 6 7 8 9 10 11 12 13 14 15 16 17 18 19 20 21 22 23 24

ENGLISH ▬▬   ARABIC ▨▨   CHINESE ▭▭   FRENCH ▭▭   GERMAN ▬▬   RUSSIAN ══   SPANISH ▬▬   OTHER ──

FREQUENCY   COUNTRY, STATION, LOCATION   TARGET • NETWORK • POWER (kW)   World Time

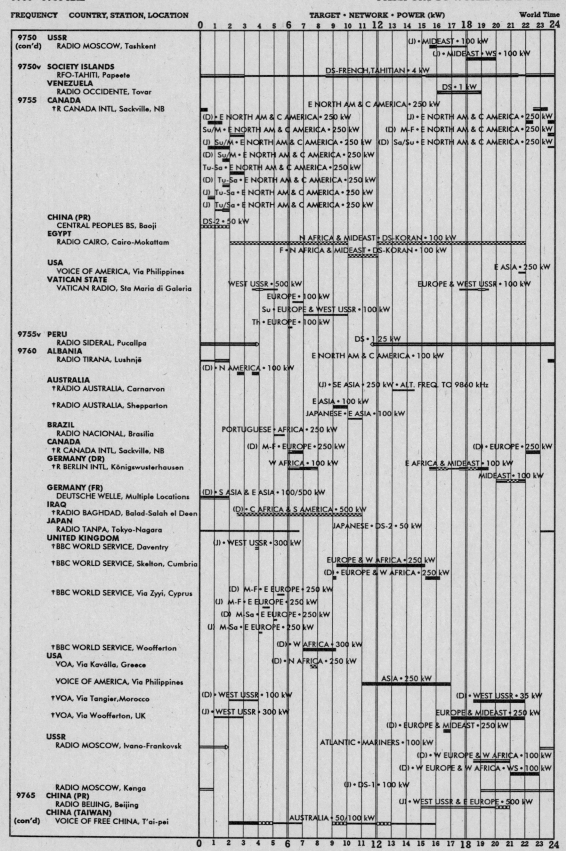

FREQUENCY	COUNTRY, STATION, LOCATION	Schedule
9750 (con'd)	USSR / RADIO MOSCOW, Tashkent	(J) • MIDEAST • 100 kW / (J) • MIDEAST • WS • 100 kW
9750v	SOCIETY ISLANDS / RFO-TAHITI, Papeete	DS-FRENCH, TAHITIAN • 4 kW
	VENEZUELA / RADIO OCCIDENTE, Tovar	DS • 1 kW
9755	CANADA / ↑R CANADA INTL, Sackville, NB	E NORTH AM & C AMERICA • 250 kW / (D) • E NORTH AM & C AMERICA • 250 kW / (J) • E NORTH AM & C AMERICA • 250 kW / Su/M • E NORTH AM & C AMERICA • 250 kW / (D) M-F • E NORTH AM & C AMERICA • 250 kW / (J) Su/M • E NORTH AM & C AMERICA • 250 kW / (D) Sa/Su • E NORTH AM & C AMERICA • 250 kW / (D) Su/M • E NORTH AM & C AMERICA • 250 kW / Tu-Sa • E NORTH AM & C AMERICA • 250 kW / (D) Tu-Sa • E NORTH AM & C AMERICA • 250 kW / (J) Tu-Sa • E NORTH AM & C AMERICA • 250 kW / (J) Tu/Sa • E NORTH AM & C AMERICA • 250 kW
	CHINA (PR) / CENTRAL PEOPLES BS, Baoji	DS-2 • 50 kW
	EGYPT / RADIO CAIRO, Cairo-Mokattam	N AFRICA & MIDEAST • DS-KORAN • 100 kW / F • N AFRICA & MIDEAST • DS-KORAN • 100 kW
	USA / VOICE OF AMERICA, Via Philippines	E ASIA • 250 kW
	VATICAN STATE / VATICAN RADIO, Sta Maria di Galeria	WEST USSR • 500 kW / EUROPE & WEST USSR • 100 kW / EUROPE • 100 kW / Su • EUROPE & WEST USSR • 100 kW / Th • EUROPE • 100 kW
9755v	PERU / RADIO SIDERAL, Pucallpa	DS • 1.25 kW
9760	ALBANIA / RADIO TIRANA, Lushnjë	E NORTH AM & C AMERICA • 100 kW / (D) • N AMERICA • 100 kW
	AUSTRALIA / ↑RADIO AUSTRALIA, Carnarvon	(J) • SE ASIA • 250 kW • ALT. FREQ. TO 9860 kHz
	↑RADIO AUSTRALIA, Shepparton	E ASIA • 100 kW / JAPANESE • E ASIA • 100 kW
	BRAZIL / RADIO NACIONAL, Brasília	PORTUGUESE • AFRICA • 250 kW
	CANADA / ↑R CANADA INTL, Sackville, NB	(D) M-F • EUROPE • 250 kW / (D) • EUROPE • 250 kW
	GERMANY (DR) / ↑R BERLIN INTL, Königswusterhausen	W AFRICA • 100 kW / E AFRICA & MIDEAST • 100 kW / MIDEAST • 100 kW
	GERMANY (FR) / DEUTSCHE WELLE, Multiple Locations	(D) • S ASIA & E ASIA • 100/500 kW
	IRAQ / ↑RADIO BAGHDAD, Balad-Salah el Deen	(D) • C AFRICA & S AMERICA • 500 kW
	JAPAN / RADIO TANPA, Tokyo-Nagara	JAPANESE • DS-2 • 50 kW
	UNITED KINGDOM / ↑BBC WORLD SERVICE, Daventry	(J) • WEST USSR • 300 kW
	↑BBC WORLD SERVICE, Skelton, Cumbria	EUROPE & W AFRICA • 250 kW / (D) • EUROPE & W AFRICA • 250 kW
	↑BBC WORLD SERVICE, Via Zyyi, Cyprus	(D) M-F • E EUROPE • 250 kW / (J) M-F • E EUROPE • 250 kW / (D) M-Sa • E EUROPE • 250 kW / (J) M-Sa • E EUROPE • 250 kW
	↑BBC WORLD SERVICE, Woofferton	(D) • W AFRICA • 300 kW
	USA / VOA, Via Kaválla, Greece	(D) • N AFRICA • 250 kW
	VOICE OF AMERICA, Via Philippines	ASIA • 250 kW
	↑VOA, Via Tangier, Morocco	(D) • WEST USSR • 100 kW / (D) • WEST USSR • 35 kW
	↑VOA, Via Woofferton, UK	(J) • WEST USSR • 300 kW / EUROPE & MIDEAST • 250 kW / (D) • EUROPE & MIDEAST • 250 kW
	USSR / RADIO MOSCOW, Ivano-Frankovsk	ATLANTIC • MARINERS • 100 kW / (D) • W EUROPE & W AFRICA • 100 kW / (D) • W EUROPE & W AFRICA • WS • 100 kW
	RADIO MOSCOW, Kenga	(J) • DS-1 • 100 kW
9765	CHINA (PR) / RADIO BEIJING, Beijing	(J) • WEST USSR & E EUROPE • 500 kW
(con'd)	CHINA (TAIWAN) / VOICE OF FREE CHINA, T'ai-pei	AUSTRALIA • 50/100 kW

FREQUENCY   COUNTRY, STATION, LOCATION   TARGET • NETWORK • POWER (kW)   World Time

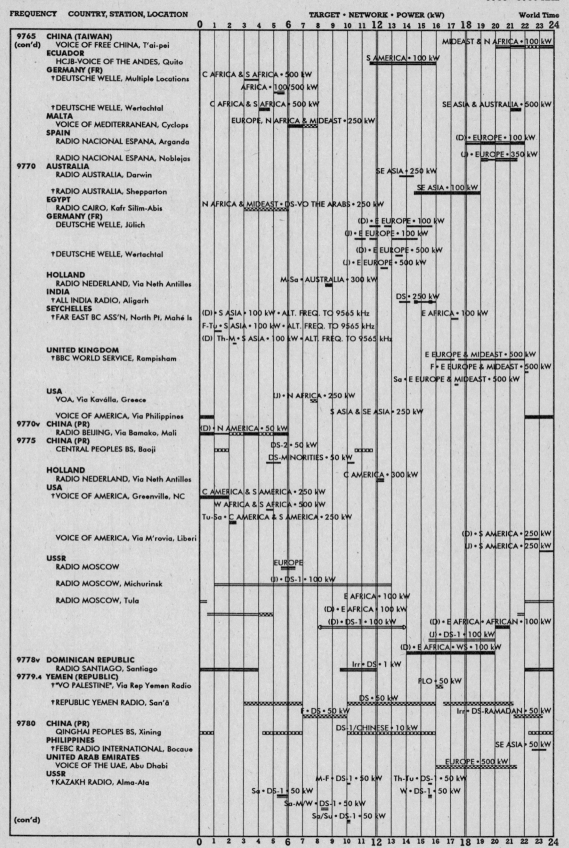

9765 CHINA (TAIWAN)
(con'd)   VOICE OF FREE CHINA, T'ai-pei — MIDEAST & N AFRICA • 100 kW
ECUADOR
  HCJB-VOICE OF THE ANDES, Quito — S AMERICA • 100 kW
GERMANY (FR)
  †DEUTSCHE WELLE, Multiple Locations — C AFRICA & S AFRICA • 500 kW
  AFRICA • 100/500 kW

  †DEUTSCHE WELLE, Wertachtal — C AFRICA & S AFRICA • 500 kW   SE ASIA & AUSTRALIA • 500 kW
MALTA
  VOICE OF MEDITERRANEAN, Cyclops — EUROPE, N AFRICA & MIDEAST • 250 kW
SPAIN
  RADIO NACIONAL ESPANA, Arganda — (D) • EUROPE • 100 kW

  RADIO NACIONAL ESPANA, Noblejas — (J) • EUROPE • 350 kW
9770 AUSTRALIA
  RADIO AUSTRALIA, Darwin — SE ASIA • 250 kW

  †RADIO AUSTRALIA, Shepparton — SE ASIA • 100 kW
EGYPT
  RADIO CAIRO, Kafr Silim-Abis — N AFRICA & MIDEAST • DS-VO THE ARABS • 250 kW
GERMANY (FR)
  DEUTSCHE WELLE, Jülich — (D) • E EUROPE • 100 kW
  (J) • E EUROPE • 100 kW

  †DEUTSCHE WELLE, Wertachtal — (D) • E EUROPE • 500 kW
  (J) • E EUROPE • 500 kW

HOLLAND
  RADIO NEDERLAND, Via Neth Antilles — M-Sa • AUSTRALIA • 300 kW
INDIA
  †ALL INDIA RADIO, Aligarh — DS • 250 kW
SEYCHELLES
  †FAR EAST BC ASS'N, North Pt, Mahé Is — (D) • S ASIA • 100 kW • ALT. FREQ. TO 9565 kHz   E AFRICA • 100 kW
  F-Tu • S ASIA • 100 kW • ALT. FREQ. TO 9565 kHz
  (D) Th-M • S ASIA • 100 kW • ALT. FREQ. TO 9565 kHz

UNITED KINGDOM
  †BBC WORLD SERVICE, Rampisham — E EUROPE & MIDEAST • 500 kW
  F • E EUROPE & MIDEAST • 500 kW
  Sa • E EUROPE & MIDEAST • 500 kW

USA
  VOA, Via Kaválla, Greece — (J) • N AFRICA • 250 kW

  VOICE OF AMERICA, Via Philippines — S ASIA & SE ASIA • 250 kW
9770v CHINA (PR)
  RADIO BEIJING, Via Bamako, Mali — (D) • N AMERICA • 50 kW
9775 CHINA (PR)
  CENTRAL PEOPLES BS, Baoji — DS-2 • 50 kW
  DS-MINORITIES • 50 kW

HOLLAND
  RADIO NEDERLAND, Via Neth Antilles — C AMERICA • 300 kW
USA
  †VOICE OF AMERICA, Greenville, NC — C AMERICA & S AMERICA • 250 kW
  W AFRICA & S AFRICA • 500 kW
  Tu-Sa • C AMERICA & S AMERICA • 250 kW

  VOICE OF AMERICA, Via M'rovia, Liberi — (D) • S AMERICA • 250 kW
  (J) • S AMERICA • 250 kW

USSR
  RADIO MOSCOW — EUROPE

  RADIO MOSCOW, Michurinsk — (J) • DS-1 • 100 kW

  RADIO MOSCOW, Tula — E AFRICA • 100 kW
  (D) • E AFRICA • 100 kW
  (D) • DS-1 • 100 kW   (D) • E AFRICA • AFRICAN • 100 kW
  (J) • DS-1 • 100 kW
  (D) • E AFRICA • WS • 100 kW

9778v DOMINICAN REPUBLIC
  RADIO SANTIAGO, Santiago — Irr • DS • 1 kW
9779.4 YEMEN (REPUBLIC)
  †"VO PALESTINE", Via Rep Yemen Radio — FLO • 50 kW

  †REPUBLIC YEMEN RADIO, San'ã — DS • 50 kW
  F • DS • 50 kW   Irr • DS-RAMADAN • 50 kW

9780 CHINA (PR)
  QINGHAI PEOPLES BS, Xining — DS-1/CHINESE • 10 kW
PHILIPPINES
  †FEBC RADIO INTERNATIONAL, Bocaue — SE ASIA • 50 kW
UNITED ARAB EMIRATES
  VOICE OF THE UAE, Abu Dhabi — EUROPE • 500 kW
USSR
  †KAZAKH RADIO, Alma-Ata — M-F • DS-1 • 50 kW   Th-Tu • DS-1 • 50 kW
  Sa • DS-1 • 50 kW   W • DS-1 • 50 kW
  Sa-M/W • DS-1 • 50 kW
  Sa/Su • DS-1 • 50 kW

(con'd)

FREQUENCY   COUNTRY, STATION, LOCATION   TARGET • NETWORK • POWER (kW)   World Time

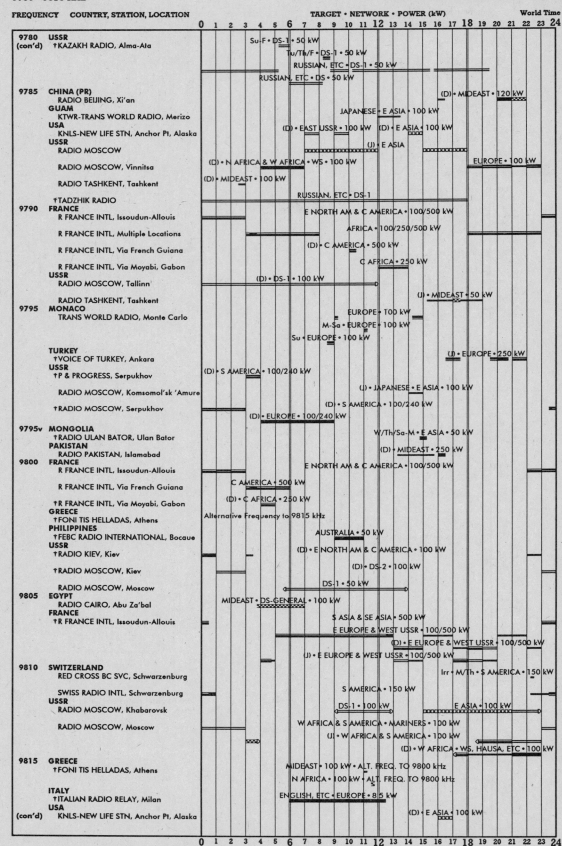

FREQUENCY	COUNTRY, STATION, LOCATION	TARGET • NETWORK • POWER (kW)
9780 (con'd)	USSR †KAZAKH RADIO, Alma-Ata	Su-F • DS-1 • 50 kW; Tu/Th/F • DS-1 • 50 kW; RUSSIAN, ETC • DS-1 • 50 kW; RUSSIAN, ETC • DS • 50 kW
9785	CHINA (PR) RADIO BEIJING, Xi'an	(D) • MIDEAST • 120 kW
	GUAM KTWR-TRANS WORLD RADIO, Merizo	JAPANESE • E ASIA • 100 kW
	USA KNLS-NEW LIFE STN, Anchor Pt, Alaska	(D) • EAST USSR • 100 kW; (D) • E ASIA • 100 kW
	USSR RADIO MOSCOW	(J) • E ASIA
	RADIO MOSCOW, Vinnitsa	(D) • N AFRICA & W AFRICA • WS • 100 kW; EUROPE • 100 kW
	RADIO TASHKENT, Tashkent	(D) • MIDEAST • 100 kW
	†TADZHIK RADIO	RUSSIAN, ETC • DS-1
9790	FRANCE R FRANCE INTL, Issoudun-Allouis	E NORTH AM & C AMERICA • 100/500 kW
	R FRANCE INTL, Multiple Locations	AFRICA • 100/250/500 kW
	R FRANCE INTL, Via French Guiana	(D) • C AMERICA • 500 kW
	R FRANCE INTL, Via Moyabi, Gabon	C AFRICA • 250 kW
	USSR RADIO MOSCOW, Tallinn	(D) • DS-1 • 100 kW
	RADIO TASHKENT, Tashkent	(J) • MIDEAST • 50 kW
9795	MONACO TRANS WORLD RADIO, Monte Carlo	EUROPE • 100 kW; M-Sa • EUROPE • 100 kW; Su • EUROPE • 100 kW
	TURKEY †VOICE OF TURKEY, Ankara	(J) • EUROPE • 250 kW
	USSR †P & PROGRESS, Serpukhov	(D) • S AMERICA • 100/240 kW
	RADIO MOSCOW, Komsomol'sk 'Amure	(J) • JAPANESE • E ASIA • 100 kW
	†RADIO MOSCOW, Serpukhov	(D) • S AMERICA • 100/240 kW; (D) • EUROPE • 100/240 kW
9795v	MONGOLIA †RADIO ULAN BATOR, Ulan Bator	W/Th/Sa-M • E ASIA • 50 kW
	PAKISTAN RADIO PAKISTAN, Islamabad	(D) • MIDEAST • 250 kW
9800	FRANCE R FRANCE INTL, Issoudun-Allouis	E NORTH AM & C AMERICA • 100/500 kW
	R FRANCE INTL, Via French Guiana	C AMERICA • 500 kW
	†R FRANCE INTL, Via Moyabi, Gabon	(D) • C AFRICA • 250 kW
	GREECE †FONI TIS HELLADAS, Athens	Alternative Frequency to 9815 kHz
	PHILIPPINES †FEBC RADIO INTERNATIONAL, Bocaue	AUSTRALIA • 50 kW
	USSR †RADIO KIEV, Kiev	(D) • E NORTH AM & C AMERICA • 100 kW
	†RADIO MOSCOW, Kiev	(D) • DS-2 • 100 kW
	RADIO MOSCOW, Moscow	DS-1 • 50 kW
9805	EGYPT RADIO CAIRO, Abu Za'bal	MIDEAST • DS-GENERAL • 100 kW
	FRANCE †R FRANCE INTL, Issoudun-Allouis	S ASIA & SE ASIA • 500 kW; E EUROPE & WEST USSR • 100/500 kW; (D) • E EUROPE & WEST USSR • 100/500 kW; (J) • E EUROPE & WEST USSR • 100/500 kW
9810	SWITZERLAND RED CROSS BC SVC, Schwarzenburg	Irr • M/Th • S AMERICA • 150 kW
	SWISS RADIO INTL, Schwarzenburg	S AMERICA • 150 kW
	USSR RADIO MOSCOW, Khabarovsk	DS-1 • 100 kW; E ASIA • 100 kW
	RADIO MOSCOW, Moscow	W AFRICA & S AMERICA • MARINERS • 100 kW; (J) • W AFRICA & S AMERICA • 100 kW; (D) • W AFRICA • WS, HAUSA, ETC • 100 kW
9815	GREECE †FONI TIS HELLADAS, Athens	MIDEAST • 100 kW • ALT. FREQ. TO 9800 kHz; N AFRICA • 100 kW • ALT. FREQ. TO 9800 kHz
	ITALY †ITALIAN RADIO RELAY, Milan	ENGLISH, ETC • EUROPE • 8.5 kW
(con'd)	USA KNLS-NEW LIFE STN, Anchor Pt, Alaska	(D) • E ASIA • 100 kW

FREQUENCY　　COUNTRY, STATION, LOCATION　　　　　　　TARGET • NETWORK • POWER (kW)　　　　World Time

0　1　2　3　4　5　6　7　8　9　10　11　12　13　14　15　16　17　18　19　20　21　22　23　24

Freq	Country / Station / Location	Schedule
9815 (con'd)	**USA** †KUSW, Salt Lake City, Utah	Su • E NORTH AM • 100 kW
		Th-Su • E NORTH AM • 100 kW
	VOICE OF AMERICA, Delano, California	C AMERICA & S AMERICA • 250 kW
		Tu-Sa • C AMERICA & S AMERICA • 250 kW
9820	**CHINA (PR)** RADIO BEIJING, Xi'an	(J) • EUROPE • 120 kW
	GUAM †KHBN, Piti	E ASIA • TO START 1/1/91 • 100 kW • ALT. FREQ. TO 9840 kHz
	†KTWR-TRANS WORLD RADIO, Merizo	(D) • E ASIA • 100 kW
	USSR RADIO MOSCOW, Irkutsk	DS-1 • 100 kW
	RADIO MOSCOW, Kalinin	(J) • EUROPE • 100 kW
9825	**UNITED KINGDOM** †BBC WORLD SERVICE, Daventry	(D) • C AMERICA • 300 kW
		(D) • WEST USSR • 300 kW
		(D) • S AMERICA • 300 kW
		(J) • S AMERICA • 300 kW
		(J) • MIDEAST • 300 kW
		(J) • W AFRICA • 300 kW
	†BBC WORLD SERVICE, Multiple Location	C AMERICA & S AMERICA • 100/300/500 kW
	†BBC WORLD SERVICE, Rampisham	(D) • W EUROPE & N AFRICA • 500 kW
		(D) • WEST USSR • 500 kW
		(J) • E NORTH AM • 500 kW
		(J) • WEST USSR • 500 kW
		(J) • W EUROPE & N AFRICA • 500 kW
		(D) • Su • E EUROPE • 500 kW
		(J) • Su • E EUROPE • 500 kW
	†BBC WORLD SERVICE, Skelton, Cumbria	W EUROPE & N AFRICA • 250 kW
		(J) • EUROPE & N AFRICA • 250 kW
9830	**FRANCE** †R FRANCE INTL, Issoudun-Allouis	E EUROPE • 100 kW
		(D) • E EUROPE • 100 kW
	GUAM †KHBN, Piti	E ASIA • TO START 1/1/91 • 100 kW
	NORTHERN MARIANA IS KFBS-FAR EAST BC, Saipan Island	E ASIA • 100 kW
		(J) • F • USSR • 100 kW
		(J) • USSR • 100 kW
		(J) • Sa-Th • USSR • 100 kW
		(J) • Su-W • USSR • 100 kW
		(J) • Th-Sa • USSR • 100 kW
		(J) • USSR • RUSSIAN, ETC • 100 kW
	PHILIPPINES FEBC RADIO INTERNATIONAL, Iba	E ASIA • 100 kW
	USSR RADIO MOSCOW, Krasnodar	(D) • AFRICA • 100 kW
9835	**HUNGARY** RADIO BUDAPEST, Various Locations	E NORTH AM • 100/250 kW
		EUROPE • 100 kW
		M • S AMERICA • 100/250 kW
		Sa • EUROPE • 100 kW
		S AMERICA • 100/250 kW
		M • E NORTH AM • 100/250 kW
		M/Th • EUROPE • 100 kW
		Tu-Su • S AMERICA • 100/250 kW
		Su • EUROPE • 100 kW
		Su-Tu/Th/F • E NORTH AM • 100/250 kW
		Tu/F • S AMERICA • 100/250 kW
		Tu-Su • E NORTH AM • 100/250 kW
		W/Th/Sa-M • S AMERICA • 100/250 kW
		Tu/W/F/Sa • E NORTH AM • 100/250 kW
		Tu/W/F/Sa • S AMERICA • 100/250 kW
		W/Sa • E NORTH AM • 100/250 kW
	JORDAN †RADIO JORDAN, Qasr el Kharana	Alternative Frequency to 9560 kHz
	PHILIPPINES †FEBC RADIO INTERNATIONAL, Bocaue	E ASIA • 50 kW
9840	**GUAM** †KHBN, Piti	Alternative Frequency to 9820 kHz
	HOLLAND †RADIO NEDERLAND, Flevoland	(D) • N AFRICA • 500 kW
	NORTHERN MARIANA IS KFBS-FAR EAST BC, Saipan Island	(D) • SE ASIA • 100 kW
	USA †CHRIST SCI MONITOR, Maine	W AFRICA & S AFRICA • 500 kW
		EUROPE • 500 kW • ALT. FREQ. TO 7520 kHz
		(D) • EUROPE • 500 kW
		M-F • W AFRICA & S AFRICA • 500 kW
		M-F • EUROPE • 500 kW • ALT. FREQ. TO 7520 kHz
		(D) • M-F • EUROPE • 500 kW
		Sa/Su • W AFRICA & S AFRICA • 500 kW
		Sa/Su • EUROPE • 500 kW • ALT. FREQ. TO 7520 kHz
		(D) • Sa/Su • EUROPE • 500 kW
(con'd)		

0　1　2　3　4　5　6　7　8　9　10　11　12　13　14　15　16　17　18　19　20　21　22　23　24

ENGLISH ▬　ARABIC ≋　CHINESE ▭▭▭　FRENCH ▬▬　GERMAN ▬　RUSSIAN ═　SPANISH ▬　OTHER ▬

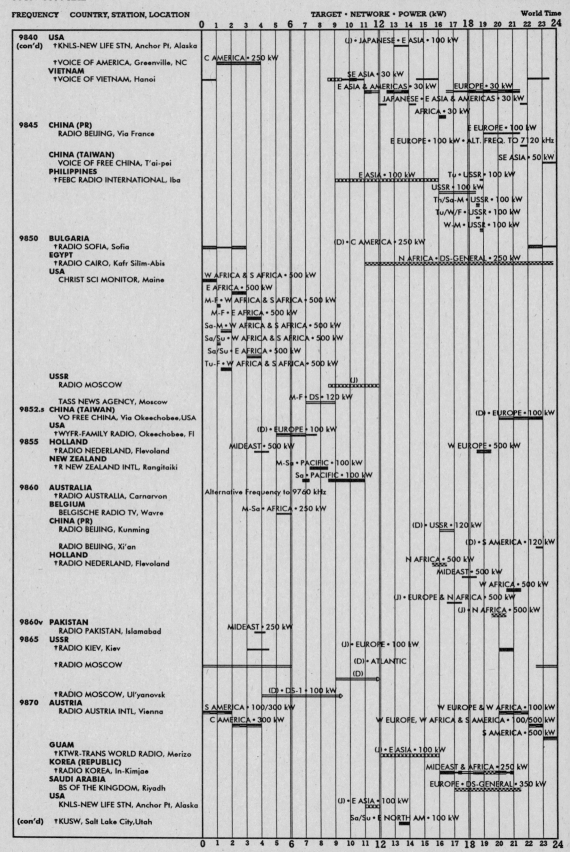

FREQUENCY	COUNTRY, STATION, LOCATION
9840 (con'd)	USA †KNLS-NEW LIFE STN, Anchor Pt, Alaska — (J) • JAPANESE • E ASIA • 100 kW
	†VOICE OF AMERICA, Greenville, NC — C AMERICA • 250 kW
	VIETNAM †VOICE OF VIETNAM, Hanoi — SE ASIA • 30 kW / E ASIA & AMERICAS • 30 kW / EUROPE • 30 kW / JAPANESE • E ASIA & AMERICAS • 30 kW / AFRICA • 30 kW
9845	CHINA (PR) RADIO BEIJING, Via France — E EUROPE • 100 kW / E EUROPE • 100 kW • ALT. FREQ. TO 7120 kHz
	CHINA (TAIWAN) VOICE OF FREE CHINA, T'ai-pei — SE ASIA • 50 kW
	PHILIPPINES †FEBC RADIO INTERNATIONAL, Iba — E ASIA • 100 kW / Tu • USSR • 100 kW / USSR • 100 kW / Th/Sa-M • USSR • 100 kW / Tu/W/F • USSR • 100 kW / W-M • USSR • 100 kW
9850	BULGARIA †RADIO SOFIA, Sofia — (D) • C AMERICA • 250 kW
	EGYPT †RADIO CAIRO, Kafr Silim-Abis — N AFRICA • DS-GENERAL • 250 kW
	USA CHRIST SCI MONITOR, Maine — W AFRICA & S AFRICA • 500 kW / E AFRICA • 500 kW / M-F • W AFRICA & S AFRICA • 500 kW / M-F • E AFRICA • 500 kW / Sa-M • W AFRICA & S AFRICA • 500 kW / Sa/Su • W AFRICA & S AFRICA • 500 kW / Sa/Su • E AFRICA • 500 kW / Tu-F • W AFRICA & S AFRICA • 500 kW
	USSR RADIO MOSCOW — (J)
	TASS NEWS AGENCY, Moscow — M-F • DS • 120 kW
9852.5	CHINA (TAIWAN) VO FREE CHINA, Via Okeechobee, USA — (D) • EUROPE • 100 kW
	USA †WYFR-FAMILY RADIO, Okeechobee, Fl — (D) • EUROPE • 100 kW
9855	HOLLAND †RADIO NEDERLAND, Flevoland — MIDEAST • 500 kW / W EUROPE • 500 kW
	NEW ZEALAND †R NEW ZEALAND INTL, Rangitaiki — M-Sa • PACIFIC • 100 kW / Sa • PACIFIC • 100 kW
9860	AUSTRALIA †RADIO AUSTRALIA, Carnarvon — Alternative Frequency to 9760 kHz
	BELGIUM BELGISCHE RADIO TV, Wavre — M-Sa • AFRICA • 250 kW
	CHINA (PR) RADIO BEIJING, Kunming — (D) • USSR • 120 kW
	RADIO BEIJING, Xi'an — (D) • S AMERICA • 120 kW
	HOLLAND †RADIO NEDERLAND, Flevoland — N AFRICA • 500 kW / MIDEAST • 500 kW / W AFRICA • 500 kW / (J) • EUROPE & N AFRICA • 500 kW / (J) • N AFRICA • 500 kW
9860v	PAKISTAN RADIO PAKISTAN, Islamabad — MIDEAST • 250 kW
9865	USSR †RADIO KIEV, Kiev — (J) • EUROPE • 100 kW
	†RADIO MOSCOW — (D) • ATLANTIC / (D)
	†RADIO MOSCOW, Ul'yanovsk — (D) • DS-1 • 100 kW
9870	AUSTRIA RADIO AUSTRIA INTL, Vienna — S AMERICA • 100/300 kW / C AMERICA • 300 kW / W EUROPE & W AFRICA • 100 kW / W EUROPE, W AFRICA & S AMERICA • 100/500 kW / S AMERICA • 500 kW
	GUAM †KTWR-TRANS WORLD RADIO, Merizo — (J) • E ASIA • 100 kW
	KOREA (REPUBLIC) †RADIO KOREA, In-Kimjae — MIDEAST & AFRICA • 250 kW
	SAUDI ARABIA BS OF THE KINGDOM, Riyadh — EUROPE • DS-GENERAL • 350 kW
	USA KNLS-NEW LIFE STN, Anchor Pt, Alaska — (J) • E ASIA • 100 kW
(con'd)	†KUSW, Salt Lake City, Utah — Sa/Su • E NORTH AM • 100 kW

FREQUENCY   COUNTRY, STATION, LOCATION

TARGET • NETWORK • POWER (kW)

World Time

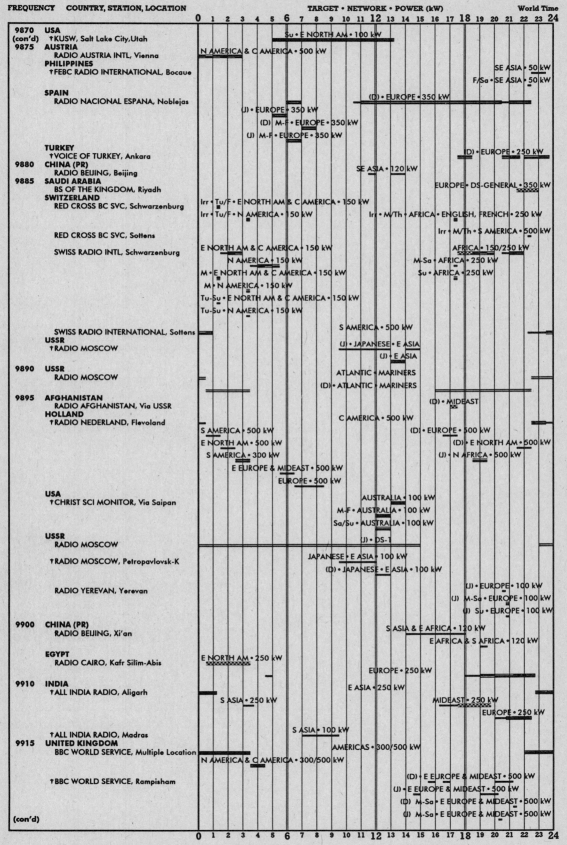

9870 (con'd)	USA	†KUSW, Salt Lake City, Utah — Su • E NORTH AM • 100 kW
9875	AUSTRIA	RADIO AUSTRIA INTL, Vienna — N AMERICA & C AMERICA • 500 kW
	PHILIPPINES	†FEBC RADIO INTERNATIONAL, Bocaue — SE ASIA • 50 kW / F/Sa • SE ASIA • 50 kW
	SPAIN	RADIO NACIONAL ESPANA, Noblejas — (D) • EUROPE • 350 kW / (J) • EUROPE • 350 kW / (D) M-F • EUROPE • 350 kW / (J) M-F • EUROPE • 350 kW
	TURKEY	†VOICE OF TURKEY, Ankara — (D) • EUROPE • 250 kW
9880	CHINA (PR)	RADIO BEIJING, Beijing — SE ASIA • 120 kW
9885	SAUDI ARABIA	BS OF THE KINGDOM, Riyadh — EUROPE • DS-GENERAL • 350 kW
	SWITZERLAND	RED CROSS BC SVC, Schwarzenburg — Irr • Tu/F • E NORTH AM & C AMERICA • 150 kW / Irr • Tu/F • N AMERICA • 150 kW / Irr • M/Th • AFRICA • ENGLISH, FRENCH • 250 kW
		RED CROSS BC SVC, Sottens — Irr • M/Th • S AMERICA • 500 kW
		SWISS RADIO INTL, Schwarzenburg — E NORTH AM & C AMERICA • 150 kW / AFRICA • 150/250 kW / N AMERICA • 150 kW / M-Sa • AFRICA • 250 kW / M • E NORTH AM & C AMERICA • 150 kW / Su • AFRICA • 250 kW / M • N AMERICA • 150 kW / Tu-Su • E NORTH AM & C AMERICA • 150 kW / Tu-Su • N AMERICA • 150 kW
		SWISS RADIO INTERNATIONAL, Sottens — S AMERICA • 500 kW
	USSR	†RADIO MOSCOW — (J) • JAPANESE • E ASIA / (J) • E ASIA
9890	USSR	RADIO MOSCOW — ATLANTIC • MARINERS / (D) • ATLANTIC • MARINERS
9895	AFGHANISTAN	RADIO AFGHANISTAN, Via USSR — (D) • MIDEAST
	HOLLAND	†RADIO NEDERLAND, Flevoland — C AMERICA • 500 kW / S AMERICA • 500 kW / (D) • EUROPE • 500 kW / E NORTH AM • 500 kW / (D) • E NORTH AM • 500 kW / S AMERICA • 300 kW / (J) • N AFRICA • 500 kW / E EUROPE & MIDEAST • 500 kW / EUROPE • 500 kW
	USA	†CHRIST SCI MONITOR, Via Saipan — AUSTRALIA • 100 kW / M-F • AUSTRALIA • 100 kW / Sa/Su • AUSTRALIA • 100 kW
	USSR	RADIO MOSCOW — (J) • DS-1 / †RADIO MOSCOW, Petropavlovsk-K — JAPANESE • E ASIA • 100 kW / (D) • JAPANESE • E ASIA • 100 kW / RADIO YEREVAN, Yerevan — (J) • EUROPE • 100 kW / (J) M-Sa • EUROPE • 100 kW / (J) Su • EUROPE • 100 kW
9900	CHINA (PR)	RADIO BEIJING, Xi'an — S ASIA & E AFRICA • 120 kW / E AFRICA & S AFRICA • 120 kW
	EGYPT	RADIO CAIRO, Kafr Silim-Abis — E NORTH AM • 250 kW / EUROPE • 250 kW
9910	INDIA	†ALL INDIA RADIO, Aligarh — E ASIA • 250 kW / S ASIA • 250 kW / MIDEAST • 250 kW / EUROPE • 250 kW
		†ALL INDIA RADIO, Madras — S ASIA • 100 kW
9915	UNITED KINGDOM	BBC WORLD SERVICE, Multiple Location — AMERICAS • 300/500 kW / N AMERICA & C AMERICA • 300/500 kW
		†BBC WORLD SERVICE, Rampisham — (D) • E EUROPE & MIDEAST • 500 kW / (J) • E EUROPE & MIDEAST • 500 kW / (D) M-Sa • E EUROPE & MIDEAST • 500 kW / (J) M-Sa • E EUROPE & MIDEAST • 500 kW

(con'd)

ENGLISH ▬   ARABIC ⋙   CHINESE ▭▭▭   FRENCH ▭▭   GERMAN ▬   RUSSIAN ═   SPANISH ▬   OTHER ▬

FREQUENCY	COUNTRY, STATION, LOCATION	TARGET • NETWORK • POWER (kW)	World Time

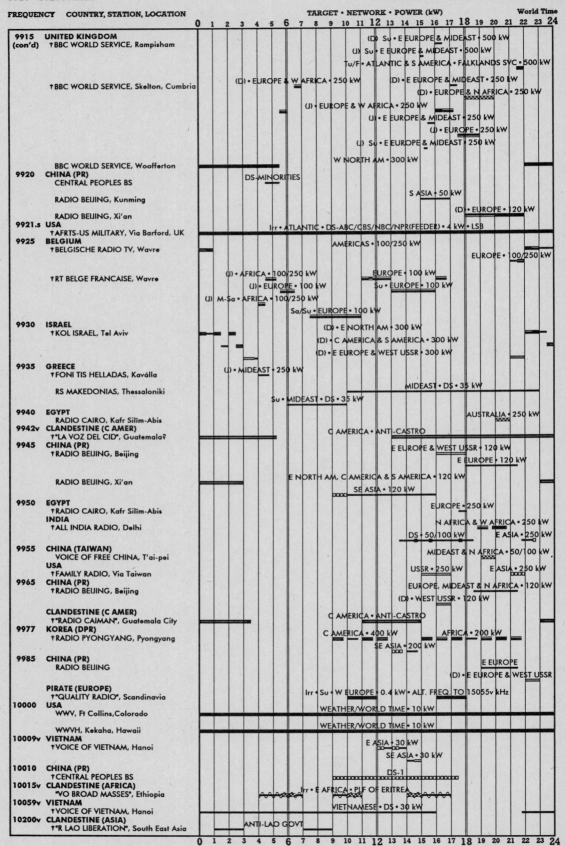

9915 UNITED KINGDOM
(con'd) †BBC WORLD SERVICE, Rampisham
(D) Su • E EUROPE & MIDEAST • 500 kW
(J) Su • E EUROPE & MIDEAST • 500 kW
Tu/F • ATLANTIC & S AMERICA • FALKLANDS SVC • 500 kW

†BBC WORLD SERVICE, Skelton, Cumbria
(D) • EUROPE & W AFRICA • 250 kW
(D) E EUROPE & MIDEAST • 250 kW
(D) • EUROPE & N AFRICA • 250 kW
(J) • EUROPE & W AFRICA • 250 kW
(J) • E EUROPE & MIDEAST • 250 kW
(J) • EUROPE • 250 kW
(J) Su • E EUROPE & MIDEAST • 250 kW

BBC WORLD SERVICE, Woofferton
W NORTH AM • 300 kW

9920 CHINA (PR)
CENTRAL PEOPLES BS
DS-MINORITIES

RADIO BEIJING, Kunming
S ASIA • 50 kW

RADIO BEIJING, Xi'an
(D) • EUROPE • 120 kW

9921.5 USA
†AFRTS-US MILITARY, Via Barford, UK
Irr • ATLANTIC • DS-ABC/CBS/NBC/NPR(FEEDER) • 4 kW • LSB

9925 BELGIUM
†BELGISCHE RADIO TV, Wavre
AMERICAS • 100/250 kW
EUROPE • 100/250 kW

†RT BELGE FRANCAISE, Wavre
(J) • AFRICA • 100/250 kW
EUROPE • 100 kW
(J) • EUROPE • 100 kW
Su • EUROPE • 100 kW
(J) M-Sa • AFRICA • 100/250 kW
Sa/Su • EUROPE • 100 kW

9930 ISRAEL
†KOL ISRAEL, Tel Aviv
(D) • E NORTH AM • 300 kW
(D) • C AMERICA & S AMERICA • 300 kW
(D) • E EUROPE & WEST USSR • 300 kW

9935 GREECE
†FONI TIS HELLADAS, Kaválla
(J) • MIDEAST • 250 kW

RS MAKEDONIAS, Thessaloniki
MIDEAST • DS • 35 kW
Su • MIDEAST • DS • 35 kW

9940 EGYPT
RADIO CAIRO, Kafr Silim-Abis
AUSTRALIA • 250 kW

9942v CLANDESTINE (C AMER)
†"LA VOZ DEL CID", Guatemala?
C AMERICA • ANTI-CASTRO

9945 CHINA (PR)
†RADIO BEIJING, Beijing
E EUROPE & WEST USSR • 120 kW
E EUROPE • 120 kW

RADIO BEIJING, Xi'an
E NORTH AM, C AMERICA & S AMERICA • 120 kW
SE ASIA • 120 kW

9950 EGYPT
†RADIO CAIRO, Kafr Silim-Abis
EUROPE • 250 kW
INDIA
†ALL INDIA RADIO, Delhi
N AFRICA & W AFRICA • 250 kW
DS • 50/100 kW
E ASIA • 250 kW

9955 CHINA (TAIWAN)
VOICE OF FREE CHINA, T'ai-pei
MIDEAST & N AFRICA • 50/100 kW
USA
†FAMILY RADIO, Via Taiwan
USSR • 250 kW
E ASIA • 250 kW

9965 CHINA (PR)
†RADIO BEIJING, Beijing
EUROPE, MIDEAST & N AFRICA • 120 kW
(D) • WEST USSR • 120 kW

CLANDESTINE (C AMER)
†"RADIO CAIMAN", Guatemala City
C AMERICA • ANTI-CASTRO

9977 KOREA (DPR)
†RADIO PYONGYANG, Pyongyang
C AMERICA • 400 kW
AFRICA • 200 kW
SE ASIA • 200 kW

9985 CHINA (PR)
RADIO BEIJING
E EUROPE
(D) • E EUROPE & WEST USSR

PIRATE (EUROPE)
†"QUALITY RADIO", Scandinavia
Irr • Su • W EUROPE • 0.4 kW • ALT. FREQ. TO 15055v kHz

10000 USA
WWV, Ft Collins, Colorado
WEATHER/WORLD TIME • 10 kW

WWVH, Kekaha, Hawaii
WEATHER/WORLD TIME • 10 kW

10009v VIETNAM
†VOICE OF VIETNAM, Hanoi
E ASIA • 30 kW
SE ASIA • 30 kW

10010 CHINA (PR)
†CENTRAL PEOPLES BS
DS-1

10015v CLANDESTINE (AFRICA)
"VO BROAD MASSES", Ethiopia
Irr • E AFRICA • PLF OF ERITREA

10059v VIETNAM
†VOICE OF VIETNAM, Hanoi
VIETNAMESE • DS • 30 kW

10200v CLANDESTINE (ASIA)
†"R LAO LIBERATION", South East Asia
ANTI-LAO GOVT

0 1 2 3 4 5 6 7 8 9 10 11 12 13 14 15 16 17 18 19 20 21 22 23 24

SUMMER ONLY (J)   WINTER ONLY (D)   JAMMING / OR ∧   EARLIEST HEARD ◁   LATEST HEARD ▷   NEW OR CHANGED FOR 1991 †

FREQUENCY	COUNTRY, STATION, LOCATION	TARGET • NETWORK • POWER (kW) — World Time

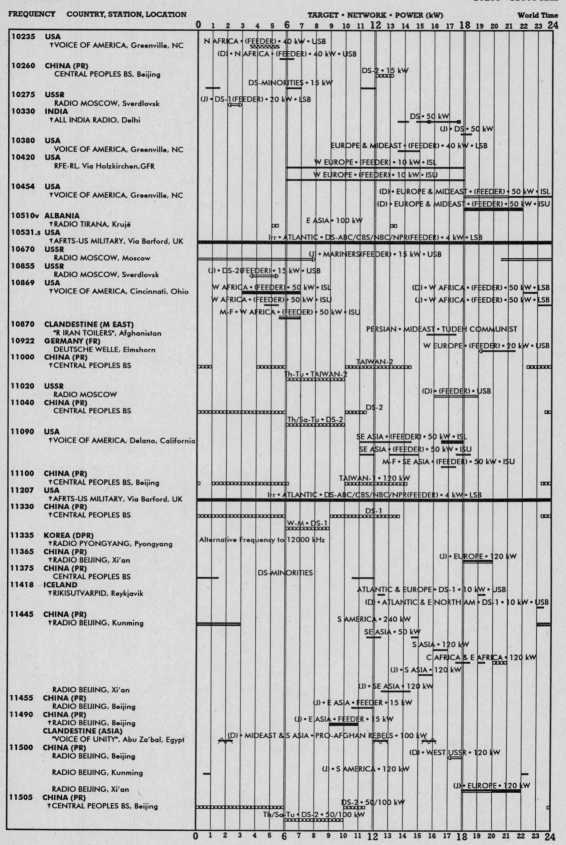

10235 USA
†VOICE OF AMERICA, Greenville, NC
- N AFRICA • (FEEDER) • 40 kW • USB
- (D) • N AFRICA • (FEEDER) • 40 kW • USB

10260 CHINA (PR)
CENTRAL PEOPLES BS, Beijing
- DS-2 • 15 kW
- DS-MINORITIES • 15 kW

10275 USSR
RADIO MOSCOW, Sverdlovsk
- (J) • DS-1 (FEEDER) • 20 kW • LSB

10330 INDIA
†ALL INDIA RADIO, Delhi
- DS • 50 kW
- (J) • DS • 50 kW

10380 USA
VOICE OF AMERICA, Greenville, NC
- EUROPE & MIDEAST • (FEEDER) • 40 kW • LSB

10420 USA
RFE-RL, Via Holzkirchen, GFR
- W EUROPE • (FEEDER) • 10 kW • ISL
- W EUROPE • (FEEDER) • 10 kW • ISU

10454 USA
†VOICE OF AMERICA, Greenville, NC
- (D) • EUROPE & MIDEAST • (FEEDER) • 50 kW • ISL
- (D) • EUROPE & MIDEAST • (FEEDER) • 50 kW • ISU

10510v ALBANIA
†RADIO TIRANA, Krujë
- E ASIA • 100 kW

10531.s USA
†AFRTS-US MILITARY, Via Barford, UK
- Irr • ATLANTIC • DS-ABC/CBS/NBC/NPR (FEEDER) • 4 kW • LSB

10670 USSR
RADIO MOSCOW, Moscow
- (J) • MARINERS (FEEDER) • 15 kW • USB

10855 USSR
RADIO MOSCOW, Sverdlovsk
- (J) • DS-2 (FEEDER) • 15 kW • USB

10869 USA
†VOICE OF AMERICA, Cincinnati, Ohio
- W AFRICA • (FEEDER) • 50 kW • ISL
- (D) • W AFRICA • (FEEDER) • 50 kW • LSB
- W AFRICA • (FEEDER) • 50 kW • ISU
- (J) • W AFRICA • (FEEDER) • 50 kW • LSB
- M-F • W AFRICA • (FEEDER) • 50 kW • ISU

10870 CLANDESTINE (M EAST)
"R IRAN TOILERS", Afghanistan
- PERSIAN • MIDEAST • TUDEH COMMUNIST

10922 GERMANY (FR)
DEUTSCHE WELLE, Elmshorn
- W EUROPE • (FEEDER) • 20 kW • USB

11000 CHINA (PR)
†CENTRAL PEOPLES BS
- TAIWAN-2
- Th-Tu • TAIWAN-2

11020 USSR
RADIO MOSCOW
- (D) • (FEEDER) • USB

11040 CHINA (PR)
CENTRAL PEOPLES BS
- DS-2
- Th/Sa-Tu • DS-2

11090 USA
†VOICE OF AMERICA, Delano, California
- SE ASIA • (FEEDER) • 50 kW • ISL
- SE ASIA • (FEEDER) • 50 kW • ISU
- M-F • SE ASIA • (FEEDER) • 50 kW • ISU

11100 CHINA (PR)
†CENTRAL PEOPLES BS, Beijing
- TAIWAN-1 • 120 kW

11207 USA
†AFRTS-US MILITARY, Via Barford, UK
- Irr • ATLANTIC • DS-ABC/CBS/NBC/NPR (FEEDER) • 4 kW • LSB

11330 CHINA (PR)
†CENTRAL PEOPLES BS
- DS-1
- W-M • DS-1

11335 KOREA (DPR)
†RADIO PYONGYANG, Pyongyang
- Alternative Frequency to 12000 kHz

11365 CHINA (PR)
†RADIO BEIJING, Xi'an
- (J) • EUROPE • 120 kW

11375 CHINA (PR)
CENTRAL PEOPLES BS
- DS-MINORITIES

11418 ICELAND
†RIKISUTVARPID, Reykjavik
- ATLANTIC & EUROPE • DS-1 • 10 kW • USB
- (D) • ATLANTIC & E NORTH AM • DS-1 • 10 kW • USB

11445 CHINA (PR)
†RADIO BEIJING, Kunming
- S AMERICA • 240 kW
- SE ASIA • 50 kW
- S ASIA • 120 kW
- C AFRICA & E AFRICA • 120 kW
- (J) • S ASIA • 120 kW

RADIO BEIJING, Xi'an
- (J) • SE ASIA • 120 kW

11455 CHINA (PR)
RADIO BEIJING, Beijing
- (J) • E ASIA • FEEDER • 15 kW

11490 CHINA (PR)
†RADIO BEIJING, Beijing
- (J) • E ASIA • FEEDER • 15 kW

CLANDESTINE (ASIA)
"VOICE OF UNITY", Abu Za'bal, Egypt
- (D) • MIDEAST & S ASIA • PRO-AFGHAN REBELS • 100 kW

11500 CHINA (PR)
RADIO BEIJING, Beijing
- (D) • WEST USSR • 120 kW

RADIO BEIJING, Kunming
- (J) • S AMERICA • 120 kW

RADIO BEIJING, Xi'an
- (J) • EUROPE • 120 kW

11505 CHINA (PR)
†CENTRAL PEOPLES BS, Beijing
- DS-2 • 50/100 kW
- Th/Sa-Tu • DS-2 • 50/100 kW

ENGLISH ▬ ARABIC ≋ CHINESE ▫▫▫ FRENCH ▭ GERMAN ═ RUSSIAN ═ SPANISH ▬ OTHER ▬

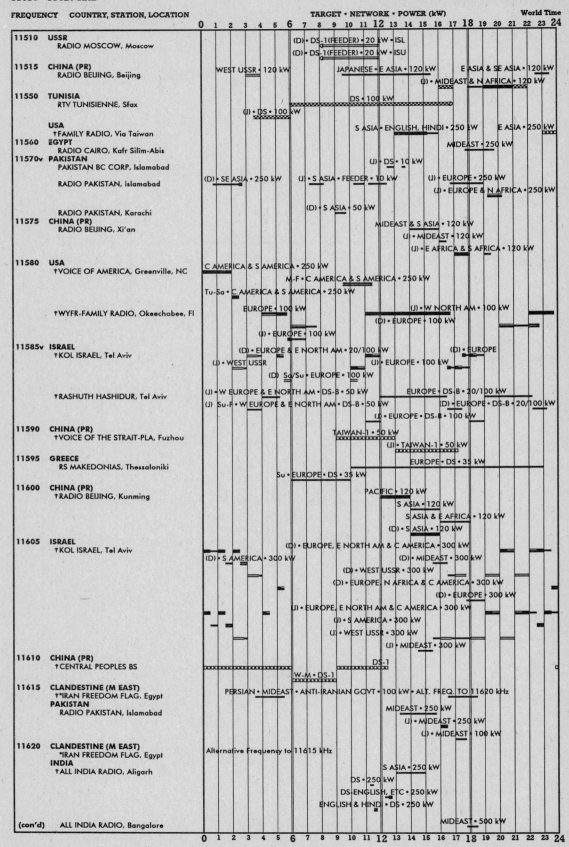

FREQUENCY   COUNTRY, STATION, LOCATION   TARGET • NETWORK • POWER (kW)   World Time

0 1 2 3 4 5 6 7 8 9 10 11 12 13 14 15 16 17 18 19 20 21 22 23 24

11510 USSR
RADIO MOSCOW, Moscow
- (D) • DS-1 (FEEDER) • 20 kW • ISL
- (D) • DS-1 (FEEDER) • 20 kW • ISU

11515 CHINA (PR)
RADIO BEIJING, Beijing
- WEST USSR • 120 kW
- JAPANESE • E ASIA • 120 kW
- E ASIA & SE ASIA • 120 kW
- (J) • MIDEAST & N AFRICA • 120 kW

11550 TUNISIA
RTV TUNISIENNE, Sfax
- DS • 100 kW
- (J) • DS • 100 kW

USA
†FAMILY RADIO, Via Taiwan
- S ASIA • ENGLISH, HINDI • 250 kW
- E ASIA • 250 kW

11560 EGYPT
RADIO CAIRO, Kafr Silim-Abis
- MIDEAST • 250 kW

11570v PAKISTAN
PAKISTAN BC CORP, Islamabad
- (J) • DS • 10 kW

RADIO PAKISTAN, Islamabad
- (D) • SE ASIA • 250 kW
- (J) • S ASIA • FEEDER • 10 kW
- (J) • EUROPE • 250 kW
- (J) • EUROPE & N AFRICA • 250 kW

RADIO PAKISTAN, Karachi
- (D) • S ASIA • 50 kW

11575 CHINA (PR)
RADIO BEIJING, Xi'an
- MIDEAST & S ASIA • 120 kW
- (J) • MIDEAST • 120 kW
- (J) • E AFRICA & S AFRICA • 120 kW

11580 USA
†VOICE OF AMERICA, Greenville, NC
- C AMERICA & S AMERICA • 250 kW
- M-F • C AMERICA & S AMERICA • 250 kW
- Tu-Sa • C AMERICA & S AMERICA • 250 kW

†WYFR-FAMILY RADIO, Okeechobee, Fl
- EUROPE • 100 kW
- (J) • W NORTH AM • 100 kW
- (D) • EUROPE • 100 kW
- (J) • EUROPE • 100 kW

11585v ISRAEL
†KOL ISRAEL, Tel Aviv
- (D) • EUROPE & E NORTH AM • 20/100 kW
- (D) • EUROPE
- (J) • WEST USSR
- (J) • EUROPE • 100 kW
- (D) Sa/Su • EUROPE • 100 kW

†RASHUTH HASHIDUR, Tel Aviv
- (J) • W EUROPE & E NORTH AM • DS-B • 50 kW
- EUROPE • DS-B • 20/100 kW
- (J) Su-F • W EUROPE & E NORTH AM • DS-B • 50 kW
- (D) • EUROPE • DS-B • 20/100 kW
- (J) • EUROPE • DS-B • 100 kW

11590 CHINA (PR)
†VOICE OF THE STRAIT-PLA, Fuzhou
- TAIWAN-1 • 50 kW
- (J) • TAIWAN-1 • 50 kW

11595 GREECE
RS MAKEDONIAS, Thessaloniki
- EUROPE • DS • 35 kW
- Su • EUROPE • DS • 35 kW

11600 CHINA (PR)
†RADIO BEIJING, Kunming
- PACIFIC • 120 kW
- S ASIA • 120 kW
- S ASIA & E AFRICA • 120 kW
- (D) • S ASIA • 120 kW

11605 ISRAEL
†KOL ISRAEL, Tel Aviv
- (D) • EUROPE, E NORTH AM & C AMERICA • 300 kW
- (D) • S AMERICA • 300 kW
- (D) • MIDEAST • 300 kW
- (D) • WEST USSR • 300 kW
- (D) • EUROPE, N AFRICA & C AMERICA • 300 kW
- (D) • EUROPE • 300 kW
- (J) • EUROPE, E NORTH AM & C AMERICA • 300 kW
- (J) • S AMERICA • 300 kW
- (J) • WEST USSR • 300 kW
- (J) • MIDEAST • 300 kW

11610 CHINA (PR)
†CENTRAL PEOPLES BS
- DS-1
- W-M • DS-1

11615 CLANDESTINE (M EAST)
†"IRAN FREEDOM FLAG, Egypt
- PERSIAN • MIDEAST • ANTI-IRANIAN GOVT • 100 kW • ALT. FREQ. TO 11620 kHz

PAKISTAN
RADIO PAKISTAN, Islamabad
- MIDEAST • 250 kW
- (J) • MIDEAST • 250 kW
- (J) • MIDEAST • 100 kW

11620 CLANDESTINE (M EAST)
"IRAN FREEDOM FLAG, Egypt
- Alternative Frequency to 11615 kHz

INDIA
†ALL INDIA RADIO, Aligarh
- S ASIA • 250 kW
- DS • 250 kW
- DS-ENGLISH, ETC • 250 kW
- ENGLISH & HINDI • DS • 250 kW

(con'd)   ALL INDIA RADIO, Bangalore
- MIDEAST • 500 kW

0 1 2 3 4 5 6 7 8 9 10 11 12 13 14 15 16 17 18 19 20 21 22 23 24

SUMMER ONLY (J)   WINTER ONLY (D)   JAMMING / OR ∧   EARLIEST HEARD ◁   LATEST HEARD ▷   NEW OR CHANGED FOR 1991 †

FREQUENCY   COUNTRY, STATION, LOCATION   TARGET • NETWORK • POWER (kW)   World Time

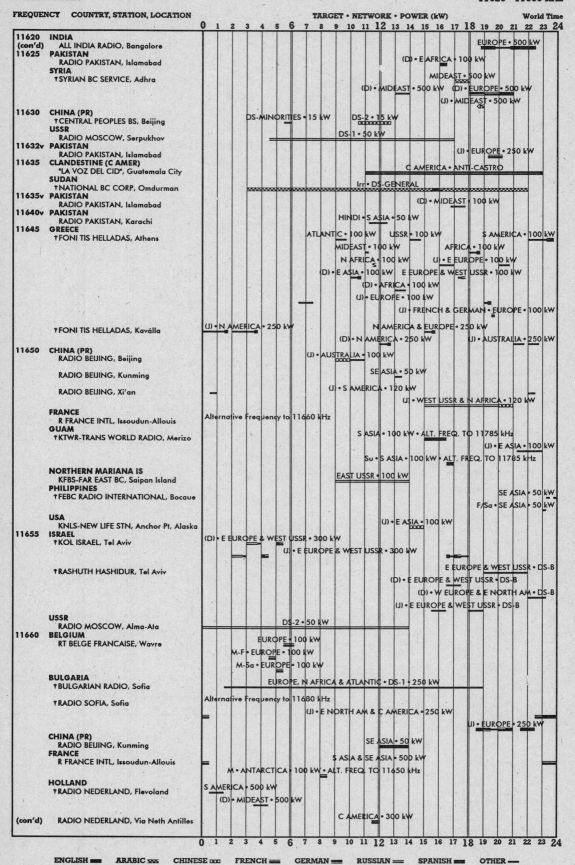

FREQUENCY	COUNTRY, STATION, LOCATION	TARGET • NETWORK • POWER (kW)
11620 (con'd)	INDIA — ALL INDIA RADIO, Bangalore	EUROPE • 500 kW
11625	PAKISTAN — RADIO PAKISTAN, Islamabad	(D) • E AFRICA • 100 kW
	SYRIA — †SYRIAN BC SERVICE, Adhra	MIDEAST • 500 kW / (D) • MIDEAST • 500 kW / (D) • EUROPE • 500 kW / (J) • MIDEAST • 500 kW
11630	CHINA (PR) — †CENTRAL PEOPLES BS, Beijing	DS-MINORITIES • 15 kW / DS-2 • 15 kW
	USSR — RADIO MOSCOW, Serpukhov	DS-1 • 50 kW
11632v	PAKISTAN — RADIO PAKISTAN, Islamabad	(J) • EUROPE • 250 kW
11635	CLANDESTINE (C AMER) — "LA VOZ DEL CID", Guatemala City	C AMERICA • ANTI-CASTRO
	SUDAN — †NATIONAL BC CORP, Omdurman	Irr • DS-GENERAL
11635v	PAKISTAN — RADIO PAKISTAN, Islamabad	(D) • MIDEAST • 100 kW
11640v	PAKISTAN — RADIO PAKISTAN, Karachi	HINDI • S ASIA • 50 kW
11645	GREECE — †FONI TIS HELLADAS, Athens	ATLANTIC • 100 kW / USSR • 100 kW / S AMERICA • 100 kW / MIDEAST • 100 kW / AFRICA • 100 kW / N AFRICA • 100 kW / (J) • E EUROPE • 100 kW / (D) • E ASIA • 100 kW / E EUROPE & WEST USSR • 100 kW / (D) • AFRICA • 100 kW / (J) • EUROPE • 100 kW / (J) • FRENCH & GERMAN • EUROPE • 100 kW
	†FONI TIS HELLADAS, Kaválla	(J) • N AMERICA • 250 kW / N AMERICA & EUROPE • 250 kW / (D) • N AMERICA • 250 kW / (J) • AUSTRALIA • 250 kW
11650	CHINA (PR) — RADIO BEIJING, Beijing	(J) • AUSTRALIA • 100 kW
	RADIO BEIJING, Kunming	SE ASIA • 50 kW
	RADIO BEIJING, Xi'an	(J) • S AMERICA • 120 kW / (J) • WEST USSR & N AFRICA • 120 kW
	FRANCE — R FRANCE INTL, Issoudun-Allouis	Alternative Frequency to 11660 kHz
	GUAM — †KTWR-TRANS WORLD RADIO, Merizo	S ASIA • 100 kW • ALT. FREQ. TO 11785 kHz / (J) • E ASIA • 100 kW / Su • S ASIA • 100 kW • ALT. FREQ. TO 11785 kHz
	NORTHERN MARIANA IS — KFBS-FAR EAST BC, Saipan Island	EAST USSR • 100 kW
	PHILIPPINES — †FEBC RADIO INTERNATIONAL, Bocaue	SE ASIA • 50 kW / F/Sa • SE ASIA • 50 kW
	USA — KNLS-NEW LIFE STN, Anchor Pt, Alaska	(J) • E ASIA • 100 kW
11655	ISRAEL — †KOL ISRAEL, Tel Aviv	(D) • E EUROPE & WEST USSR • 300 kW / (J) • E EUROPE & WEST USSR • 300 kW
	†RASHUTH HASHIDUR, Tel Aviv	E EUROPE & WEST USSR • DS-B / (D) • E EUROPE & WEST USSR • DS-B / (D) • W EUROPE & E NORTH AM • DS-B / (J) • E EUROPE & WEST USSR • DS-B
	USSR — RADIO MOSCOW, Alma-Ata	DS-2 • 50 kW
11660	BELGIUM — RT BELGE FRANCAISE, Wavre	EUROPE • 100 kW / M-F • EUROPE • 100 kW / M-Sa • EUROPE • 100 kW
	BULGARIA — †BULGARIAN RADIO, Sofia	EUROPE, N AFRICA & ATLANTIC • DS-1 • 250 kW
	†RADIO SOFIA, Sofia	Alternative Frequency to 11680 kHz / (J) • E NORTH AM & C AMERICA • 250 kW / (J) • EUROPE • 250 kW
	CHINA (PR) — RADIO BEIJING, Kunming	SE ASIA • 50 kW
	FRANCE — R FRANCE INTL, Issoudun-Allouis	S ASIA & SE ASIA • 500 kW / M • ANTARCTICA • 100 kW • ALT. FREQ. TO 11650 kHz
	HOLLAND — †RADIO NEDERLAND, Flevoland	S AMERICA • 500 kW / (D) • MIDEAST • 500 kW
(con'd)	RADIO NEDERLAND, Via Neth Antilles	C AMERICA • 300 kW

ENGLISH ▬   ARABIC ▨   CHINESE ▫▫▫   FRENCH ▬▬   GERMAN ▬   RUSSIAN ═   SPANISH ▬   OTHER ▬

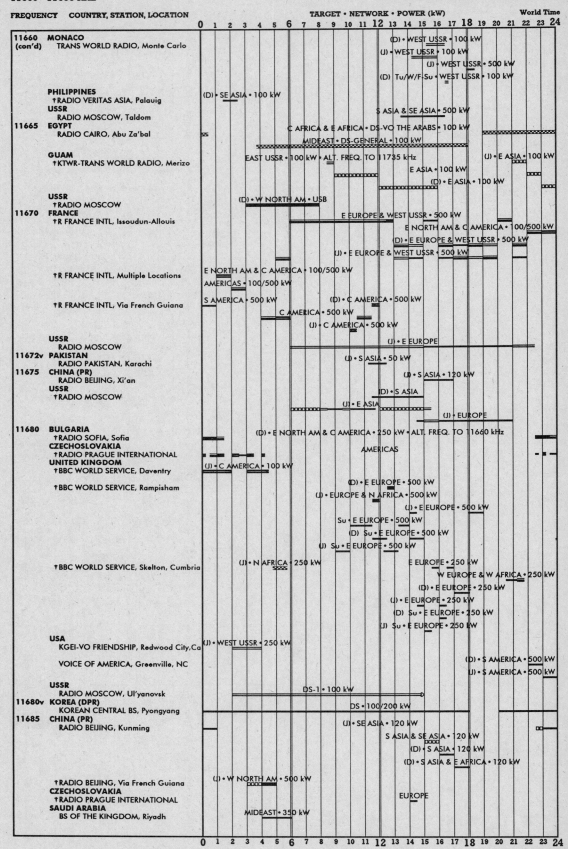

FREQUENCY   COUNTRY, STATION, LOCATION   TARGET • NETWORK • POWER (kW)   World Time

11660 **MONACO**
(con'd)   TRANS WORLD RADIO, Monte Carlo
- (D) • WEST USSR • 100 kW
- (J) • WEST USSR • 100 kW
- (J) • WEST USSR • 500 kW
- (D) • Tu/W/F-Su • WEST USSR • 100 kW

PHILIPPINES
†RADIO VERITAS ASIA, Palauig — (D) • SE ASIA • 100 kW
USSR
RADIO MOSCOW, Taldom — S ASIA & SE ASIA • 500 kW

11665 **EGYPT**
RADIO CAIRO, Abu Za'bal
- C AFRICA & E AFRICA • DS-VO THE ARABS • 100 kW
- MIDEAST • DS-GENERAL • 100 kW

GUAM
†KTWR-TRANS WORLD RADIO, Merizo
- EAST USSR • 100 kW • ALT. FREQ. TO 11735 kHz
- (J) • E ASIA • 100 kW
- E ASIA • 100 kW
- (D) • E ASIA • 100 kW

USSR
†RADIO MOSCOW — (D) • W NORTH AM • USB
11670 **FRANCE**
†R FRANCE INTL, Issoudun-Allouis
- E EUROPE & WEST USSR • 500 kW
- E NORTH AM & C AMERICA • 100/500 kW
- (D) • E EUROPE & WEST USSR • 500 kW
- (J) • E EUROPE & WEST USSR • 500 kW

†R FRANCE INTL, Multiple Locations
- E NORTH AM & C AMERICA • 100/500 kW
- AMERICAS • 100/500 kW

†R FRANCE INTL, Via French Guiana
- S AMERICA • 500 kW
- (D) • C AMERICA • 500 kW
- C AMERICA • 500 kW
- (J) • C AMERICA • 500 kW

USSR
RADIO MOSCOW — (J) • E EUROPE
11672v **PAKISTAN**
RADIO PAKISTAN, Karachi — (J) • S ASIA • 50 kW
11675 **CHINA (PR)**
RADIO BEIJING, Xi'an — (J) • S ASIA • 120 kW
USSR
†RADIO MOSCOW
- (D) • S ASIA
- (J) • E ASIA
- (J) • EUROPE

11680 **BULGARIA**
†RADIO SOFIA, Sofia — (D) • E NORTH AM & C AMERICA • 250 kW • ALT. FREQ. TO 11660 kHz
CZECHOSLOVAKIA
†RADIO PRAGUE INTERNATIONAL — AMERICAS
UNITED KINGDOM
†BBC WORLD SERVICE, Daventry — (J) • C AMERICA • 100 kW

†BBC WORLD SERVICE, Rampisham
- (D) • E EUROPE • 500 kW
- (J) • EUROPE & N AFRICA • 500 kW
- (J) • E EUROPE • 500 kW
- Su • E EUROPE • 500 kW
- (D) • Su • E EUROPE • 500 kW
- (J) • Su • E EUROPE • 500 kW

†BBC WORLD SERVICE, Skelton, Cumbria
- (J) • N AFRICA • 250 kW
- E EUROPE • 250 kW
- W EUROPE & W AFRICA • 250 kW
- (D) • E EUROPE • 250 kW
- (J) • E EUROPE • 250 kW
- (D) • Su • E EUROPE • 250 kW
- (J) • Su • E EUROPE • 250 kW

USA
KGEI-VO FRIENDSHIP, Redwood City, Ca — (J) • WEST USSR • 250 kW

VOICE OF AMERICA, Greenville, NC
- (D) • S AMERICA • 500 kW
- (J) • S AMERICA • 500 kW

USSR
RADIO MOSCOW, Ul'yanovsk — DS-1 • 100 kW
11680v **KOREA (DPR)**
KOREAN CENTRAL BS, Pyongyang — DS • 100/200 kW
11685 **CHINA (PR)**
RADIO BEIJING, Kunming
- (J) • SE ASIA • 120 kW
- S ASIA & SE ASIA • 120 kW
- (D) • S ASIA • 120 kW
- (D) • S ASIA & E AFRICA • 120 kW

†RADIO BEIJING, Via French Guiana — (J) • W NORTH AM • 500 kW
CZECHOSLOVAKIA
†RADIO PRAGUE INTERNATIONAL — EUROPE
SAUDI ARABIA
BS OF THE KINGDOM, Riyadh — MIDEAST • 350 kW

SUMMER ONLY (J)   WINTER ONLY (D)   JAMMING / OR ∧   EARLIEST HEARD ◁   LATEST HEARD ▷   NEW OR CHANGED FOR 1991 †

| FREQUENCY | COUNTRY, STATION, LOCATION | TARGET • NETWORK • POWER (kW) | World Time |

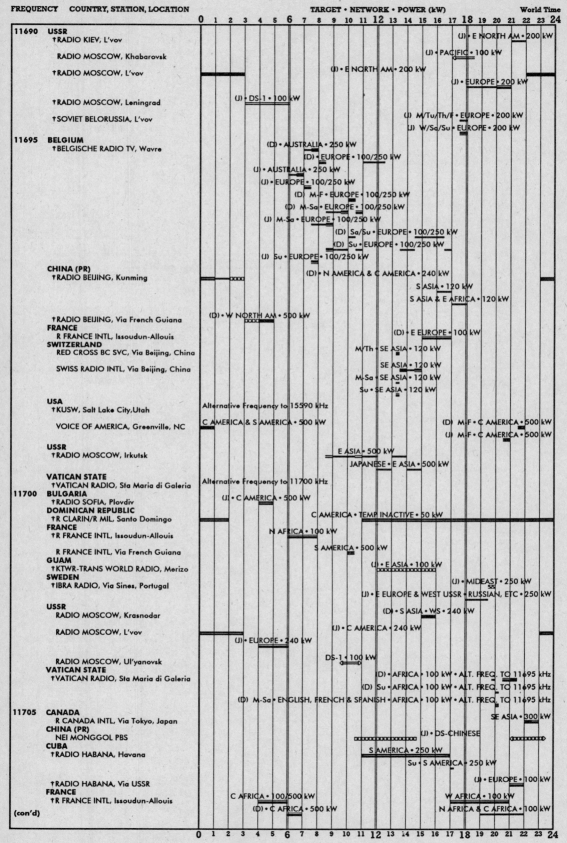

11690 USSR
  †RADIO KIEV, L'vov — (J) • E NORTH AM • 200 kW

  RADIO MOSCOW, Khabarovsk — (J) • PACIFIC • 100 kW

  †RADIO MOSCOW, L'vov — (J) • E NORTH AM • 200 kW
  — (J) • EUROPE • 200 kW

  †RADIO MOSCOW, Leningrad — (J) • DS-1 • 100 kW

  †SOVIET BELORUSSIA, L'vov — (J) • M/Tu/Th/F • EUROPE • 200 kW
  — (J) • W/Sa/Su • EUROPE • 200 kW

11695 BELGIUM
  †BELGISCHE RADIO TV, Wavre — (D) • AUSTRALIA • 250 kW
  — (D) • EUROPE • 100/250 kW
  — (J) • AUSTRALIA • 250 kW
  — (J) • EUROPE • 100/250 kW
  — (D) M-F • EUROPE • 100/250 kW
  — (D) M-Sa • EUROPE • 100/250 kW
  — (J) M-Sa • EUROPE • 100/250 kW
  — (D) Sa/Su • EUROPE • 100/250 kW
  — (D) Su • EUROPE • 100/250 kW
  — (J) Su • EUROPE • 100/250 kW

  CHINA (PR)
  †RADIO BEIJING, Kunming — (D) • N AMERICA & C AMERICA • 240 kW
  — S ASIA • 120 kW
  — S ASIA & E AFRICA • 120 kW

  †RADIO BEIJING, Via French Guiana — (D) • W NORTH AM • 500 kW
  FRANCE
    R FRANCE INTL, Issoudun-Allouis — (D) • E EUROPE • 100 kW
  SWITZERLAND
    RED CROSS BC SVC, Via Beijing, China — M/Th • SE ASIA • 120 kW

    SWISS RADIO INTL, Via Beijing, China — SE ASIA • 120 kW
    — M-Sa • SE ASIA • 120 kW
    — Su • SE ASIA • 120 kW

  USA
  †KUSW, Salt Lake City, Utah — Alternative Frequency to 15590 kHz

  VOICE OF AMERICA, Greenville, NC — C AMERICA & S AMERICA • 500 kW
  — (D) M-F • C AMERICA • 500 kW
  — (J) M-F • C AMERICA • 500 kW

  USSR
  †RADIO MOSCOW, Irkutsk — E ASIA • 500 kW
  — JAPANESE • E ASIA • 500 kW

  VATICAN STATE
  †VATICAN RADIO, Sta Maria di Galeria — Alternative Frequency to 11700 kHz
11700 BULGARIA
  †RADIO SOFIA, Plovdiv — (J) • C AMERICA • 500 kW
  DOMINICAN REPUBLIC
  †R CLARIN/R MIL, Santo Domingo — C AMERICA • TEMP INACTIVE • 50 kW
  FRANCE
  †R FRANCE INTL, Issoudun-Allouis — N AFRICA • 100 kW

    R FRANCE INTL, Via French Guiana — S AMERICA • 500 kW
  GUAM
  †KTWR-TRANS WORLD RADIO, Merizo — (J) • E ASIA • 100 kW
  SWEDEN
  †IBRA RADIO, Via Sines, Portugal — (J) • MIDEAST • 250 kW
  — (J) • E EUROPE & WEST USSR • RUSSIAN, ETC • 250 kW

  USSR
  RADIO MOSCOW, Krasnodar — (D) • S ASIA • WS • 240 kW

  RADIO MOSCOW, L'vov — (J) • C AMERICA • 240 kW
  — (J) • EUROPE • 240 kW

  RADIO MOSCOW, Ul'yanovsk — DS-1 • 100 kW
  VATICAN STATE
  †VATICAN RADIO, Sta Maria di Galeria — (D) • AFRICA • 100 kW • ALT. FREQ. TO 11695 kHz
  — (D) Su • AFRICA • 100 kW • ALT. FREQ. TO 11695 kHz
  — (D) M-Sa • ENGLISH, FRENCH & SPANISH • AFRICA • 100 kW • ALT. FREQ. TO 11695 kHz

11705 CANADA
  R CANADA INTL, Via Tokyo, Japan — SE ASIA • 300 kW
  CHINA (PR)
    NEI MONGGOL PBS — (J) • DS-CHINESE
  CUBA
  †RADIO HABANA, Havana — S AMERICA • 250 kW
  — Su • S AMERICA • 250 kW

  †RADIO HABANA, Via USSR — (J) • EUROPE • 100 kW
  FRANCE
  †R FRANCE INTL, Issoudun-Allouis — C AFRICA • 100/500 kW — W AFRICA • 100 kW
  — (D) • C AFRICA • 500 kW — N AFRICA & C AFRICA • 100 kW

(con'd)

ENGLISH ▬ ARABIC ≋ CHINESE ▭▭▭ FRENCH ══ GERMAN ▬▬ RUSSIAN ══ SPANISH ▬▪ OTHER ▬

FREQUENCY   COUNTRY, STATION, LOCATION   TARGET • NETWORK • POWER (kW)   World Time

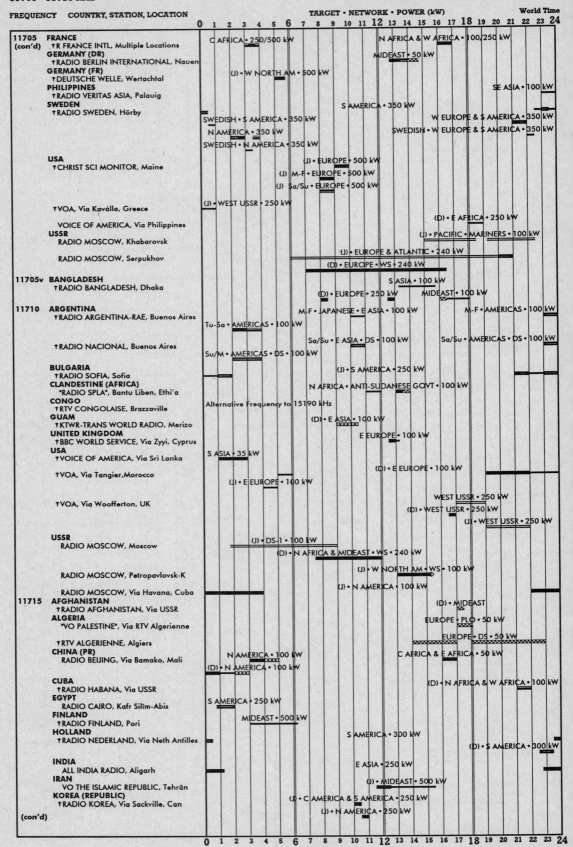

11705
(con'd) **FRANCE**
   ↑R FRANCE INTL, Multiple Locations   C AFRICA • 250/500 kW   N AFRICA & W AFRICA • 100/250 kW

  GERMANY (DR)
   ↑RADIO BERLIN INTERNATIONAL, Nauen   MIDEAST • 50 kW

  GERMANY (FR)
   ↑DEUTSCHE WELLE, Wertachtal   (J) • W NORTH AM • 500 kW

  PHILIPPINES
   ↑RADIO VERITAS ASIA, Palauig   SE ASIA • 100 kW

  SWEDEN
   ↑RADIO SWEDEN, Hörby   S AMERICA • 350 kW

                                            W EUROPE & S AMERICA • 350 kW

           SWEDISH • S AMERICA • 350 kW

           N AMERICA • 350 kW   SWEDISH • W EUROPE & S AMERICA • 350 kW

           SWEDISH • N AMERICA • 350 kW

  USA
   ↑CHRIST SCI MONITOR, Maine   (J) • EUROPE • 500 kW

                      (J) • M-F • EUROPE • 500 kW

                      (J) • Sa/Su • EUROPE • 500 kW

   ↑VOA, Via Kaválla, Greece   (J) • WEST USSR • 250 kW

                                  (D) • E AFRICA • 250 kW

   VOICE OF AMERICA, Via Philippines   (J) • PACIFIC • MARINERS • 100 kW

  USSR
   RADIO MOSCOW, Khabarovsk   (J) • EUROPE & ATLANTIC • 240 kW

   RADIO MOSCOW, Serpukhov   (D) • EUROPE • WS • 240 kW

11705v BANGLADESH
   ↑RADIO BANGLADESH, Dhaka   S ASIA • 100 kW

                     (D) • EUROPE • 250 kW   MIDEAST • 100 kW

11710 ARGENTINA
   ↑RADIO ARGENTINA-RAE, Buenos Aires   M-F • JAPANESE • E ASIA • 100 kW   M-F • AMERICAS • 100 kW

           Tu-Sa • AMERICAS • 100 kW

   ↑RADIO NACIONAL, Buenos Aires   Sa/Su • E ASIA • DS • 100 kW   Sa/Su • AMERICAS • DS • 100 kW

           Su/M • AMERICAS • DS • 100 kW

  BULGARIA
   ↑RADIO SOFIA, Sofia   (J) • S AMERICA • 250 kW

  CLANDESTINE (AFRICA)
   "RADIO SPLA", Bantu Liben, Ethi'a   N AFRICA • ANTI-SUDANESE GOVT • 100 kW

  CONGO
   ↑RTV CONGOLAISE, Brazzaville   Alternative Frequency to 15190 kHz

  GUAM
   ↑KTWR-TRANS WORLD RADIO, Merizo   (D) • E ASIA • 100 kW

  UNITED KINGDOM
   ↑BBC WORLD SERVICE, Via Zyyi, Cyprus   E EUROPE • 100 kW

  USA
   ↑VOICE OF AMERICA, Via Sri Lanka   S ASIA • 35 kW

   ↑VOA, Via Tangier, Morocco   (D) • E EUROPE • 100 kW

           (J) • E EUROPE • 100 kW

   ↑VOA, Via Woofferton, UK   WEST USSR • 250 kW

                            (D) • WEST USSR • 250 kW

                                (J) • WEST USSR • 250 kW

  USSR
   RADIO MOSCOW, Moscow   (J) • DS-1 • 100 kW

                (D) • N AFRICA & MIDEAST • WS • 240 kW

   RADIO MOSCOW, Petropavlovsk-K   (J) • W NORTH AM • WS • 100 kW

   RADIO MOSCOW, Via Havana, Cuba   (J) • N AMERICA • 100 kW

11715 AFGHANISTAN
   ↑RADIO AFGHANISTAN, Via USSR   (D) • MIDEAST

  ALGERIA
   "VO PALESTINE", Via RTV Algerienne   EUROPE • PLO • 50 kW

   ↑RTV ALGERIENNE, Algiers   EUROPE • DS • 50 kW

  CHINA (PR)
   RADIO BEIJING, Via Bamako, Mali   N AMERICA • 100 kW   C AFRICA & E AFRICA • 50 kW

          (D) • N AMERICA • 100 kW

  CUBA
   ↑RADIO HABANA, Via USSR   (D) • N AFRICA & W AFRICA • 100 kW

  EGYPT
   RADIO CAIRO, Kafr Silim-Abis   S AMERICA • 250 kW

  FINLAND
   ↑RADIO FINLAND, Pori   MIDEAST • 500 kW

  HOLLAND
   ↑RADIO NEDERLAND, Via Neth Antilles   S AMERICA • 300 kW

                                  (D) • S AMERICA • 300 kW

  INDIA
   ALL INDIA RADIO, Aligarh   E ASIA • 250 kW

  IRAN
   VO THE ISLAMIC REPUBLIC, Tehrān   (J) • MIDEAST • 500 kW

  KOREA (REPUBLIC)
   ↑RADIO KOREA, Via Sackville, Can   (J) • C AMERICA & S AMERICA • 250 kW

                   (J) • N AMERICA • 250 kW

(con'd)

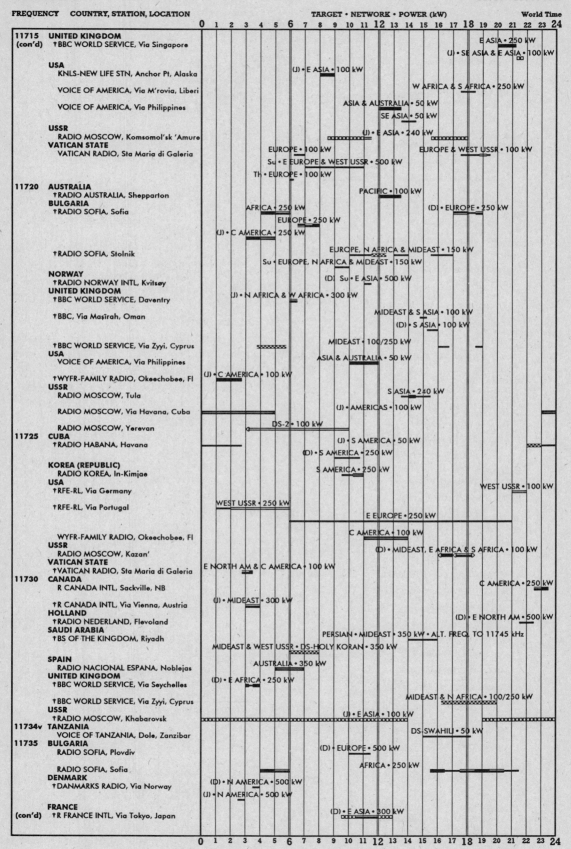

FREQUENCY   COUNTRY, STATION, LOCATION   TARGET • NETWORK • POWER (kW)   World Time

0 1 2 3 4 5 6 7 8 9 10 11 12 13 14 15 16 17 18 19 20 21 22 23 24

11715 **UNITED KINGDOM**
(con'd)   †BBC WORLD SERVICE, Via Singapore
     E ASIA • 250 kW
     (J) • SE ASIA & E ASIA • 100 kW

     USA
     KNLS-NEW LIFE STN, Anchor Pt, Alaska — (J) • E ASIA • 100 kW

     VOICE OF AMERICA, Via M'rovia, Liberi — W AFRICA & S AFRICA • 250 kW

     VOICE OF AMERICA, Via Philippines — ASIA & AUSTRALIA • 50 kW
     SE ASIA • 50 kW

     USSR
     RADIO MOSCOW, Komsomol'sk 'Amure — (J) • E ASIA • 240 kW
     VATICAN STATE
     VATICAN RADIO, Sta Maria di Galeria — EUROPE • 100 kW   EUROPE & WEST USSR • 100 kW
     Su • E EUROPE & WEST USSR • 500 kW
     Th • EUROPE • 100 kW

11720 **AUSTRALIA**
     †RADIO AUSTRALIA, Shepparton — PACIFIC • 100 kW
     BULGARIA
     †RADIO SOFIA, Sofia — AFRICA • 250 kW   (D) • EUROPE • 250 kW
     EUROPE • 250 kW
     (J) • C AMERICA • 250 kW

     †RADIO SOFIA, Stolnik — EUROPE, N AFRICA & MIDEAST • 150 kW
     Su • EUROPE, N AFRICA & MIDEAST • 150 kW

     NORWAY
     †RADIO NORWAY INTL, Kvitsøy — (D) Su • E ASIA • 500 kW
     UNITED KINGDOM
     †BBC WORLD SERVICE, Daventry — (J) • N AFRICA & W AFRICA • 300 kW

     †BBC, Via Maşīrah, Oman — MIDEAST & S ASIA • 100 kW
     (D) • S ASIA • 100 kW

     †BBC WORLD SERVICE, Via Zyyi, Cyprus — MIDEAST • 100/250 kW
     USA
     VOICE OF AMERICA, Via Philippines — ASIA & AUSTRALIA • 50 kW

     †WYFR-FAMILY RADIO, Okeechobee, Fl — (J) • C AMERICA • 100 kW
     USSR
     RADIO MOSCOW, Tula — S ASIA • 240 kW

     RADIO MOSCOW, Via Havana, Cuba — (J) • AMERICAS • 100 kW

     RADIO MOSCOW, Yerevan — DS-2 • 100 kW
11725 **CUBA**
     †RADIO HABANA, Havana — (J) • S AMERICA • 50 kW
     (D) • S AMERICA • 250 kW

     KOREA (REPUBLIC)
     RADIO KOREA, In-Kimjae — S AMERICA • 250 kW
     USA
     †RFE-RL, Via Germany — WEST USSR • 100 kW

     †RFE-RL, Via Portugal — WEST USSR • 250 kW
     E EUROPE • 250 kW

     WYFR-FAMILY RADIO, Okeechobee, Fl — C AMERICA • 100 kW
     USSR
     RADIO MOSCOW, Kazan' — (D) • MIDEAST, E AFRICA & S AFRICA • 100 kW
     VATICAN STATE
     †VATICAN RADIO, Sta Maria di Galeria — E NORTH AM & C AMERICA • 100 kW
11730 **CANADA**
     R CANADA INTL, Sackville, NB — C AMERICA • 250 kW

     †R CANADA INTL, Via Vienna, Austria — (J) • MIDEAST • 300 kW
     HOLLAND
     †RADIO NEDERLAND, Flevoland — (D) • E NORTH AM • 500 kW
     SAUDI ARABIA
     †BS OF THE KINGDOM, Riyadh — PERSIAN • MIDEAST • 350 kW • ALT. FREQ. TO 11745 kHz
     MIDEAST & WEST USSR • DS-HOLY KORAN • 350 kW

     SPAIN
     RADIO NACIONAL ESPANA, Noblejas — AUSTRALIA • 350 kW
     UNITED KINGDOM
     †BBC WORLD SERVICE, Via Seychelles — (D) • E AFRICA • 250 kW

     †BBC WORLD SERVICE, Via Zyyi, Cyprus — MIDEAST & N AFRICA • 100/250 kW
     USSR
     †RADIO MOSCOW, Khabarovsk — (J) • E ASIA • 100 kW
11734v **TANZANIA**
     VOICE OF TANZANIA, Dole, Zanzibar — DS-SWAHILI • 50 kW
11735 **BULGARIA**
     RADIO SOFIA, Plovdiv — (D) • EUROPE • 500 kW

     RADIO SOFIA, Sofia — AFRICA • 250 kW
     DENMARK
     †DANMARKS RADIO, Via Norway — (D) • N AMERICA • 500 kW
     (J) • N AMERICA • 500 kW

     FRANCE
(con'd)   †R FRANCE INTL, Via Tokyo, Japan — (D) • E ASIA • 300 kW

0 1 2 3 4 5 6 7 8 9 10 11 12 13 14 15 16 17 18 19 20 21 22 23 24

ENGLISH ▬   ARABIC ≋   CHINESE ▭▭   FRENCH ▬▬   GERMAN ▬   RUSSIAN ═   SPANISH ▬   OTHER —

FREQUENCY   COUNTRY, STATION, LOCATION

TARGET • NETWORK • POWER (kW)

World Time

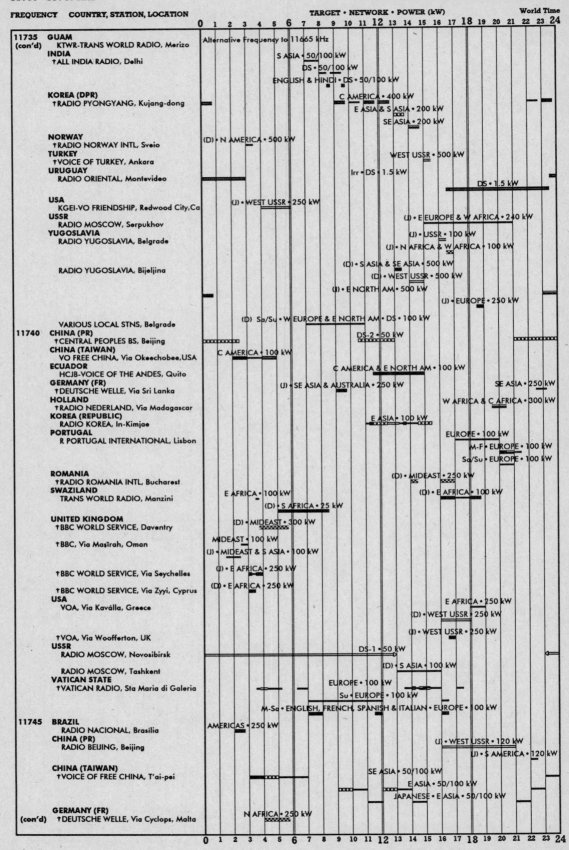

11735 (con'd)	GUAM	
	KTWR-TRANS WORLD RADIO, Merizo	Alternative Frequency to 11665 kHz
	INDIA	
	†ALL INDIA RADIO, Delhi	S ASIA • 50/100 kW
		DS • 50/100 kW
		ENGLISH & HINDI • DS • 50/100 kW
	KOREA (DPR)	
	†RADIO PYONGYANG, Kujang-dong	C AMERICA • 400 kW
		E ASIA & S ASIA • 200 kW
		SE ASIA • 200 kW
	NORWAY	
	†RADIO NORWAY INTL, Sveio	(D) • N AMERICA • 500 kW
	TURKEY	
	†VOICE OF TURKEY, Ankara	WEST USSR • 500 kW
	URUGUAY	
	RADIO ORIENTAL, Montevideo	Irr • DS • 1.5 kW
		DS • 1.5 kW
	USA	
	KGEI-VO FRIENDSHIP, Redwood City, Ca	(J) • WEST USSR • 250 kW
	USSR	
	RADIO MOSCOW, Serpukhov	(J) • E EUROPE & W AFRICA • 240 kW
	YUGOSLAVIA	
	RADIO YUGOSLAVIA, Belgrade	(J) • USSR • 100 kW
		(J) • N AFRICA & W AFRICA • 100 kW
	RADIO YUGOSLAVIA, Bijeljina	(D) • S ASIA & SE ASIA • 500 kW
		(D) • WEST USSR • 500 kW
		(J) • E NORTH AM • 500 kW
		(J) • EUROPE • 250 kW
	VARIOUS LOCAL STNS, Belgrade	(D) Sa/Su • W EUROPE & E NORTH AM • DS • 100 kW
11740	CHINA (PR)	
	†CENTRAL PEOPLES BS, Beijing	DS-2 • 50 kW
	CHINA (TAIWAN)	
	VO FREE CHINA, Via Okeechobee, USA	C AMERICA • 100 kW
	ECUADOR	
	HCJB-VOICE OF THE ANDES, Quito	C AMERICA & E NORTH AM • 100 kW
	GERMANY (FR)	
	†DEUTSCHE WELLE, Via Sri Lanka	(J) • SE ASIA & AUSTRALIA • 250 kW
		SE ASIA • 250 kW
	HOLLAND	
	†RADIO NEDERLAND, Via Madagascar	W AFRICA & C AFRICA • 300 kW
	KOREA (REPUBLIC)	
	RADIO KOREA, In-Kimjae	E ASIA • 100 kW
	PORTUGAL	
	R PORTUGAL INTERNATIONAL, Lisbon	EUROPE • 100 kW
		M-F • EUROPE • 100 kW
		Sa/Su • EUROPE • 100 kW
	ROMANIA	
	†RADIO ROMANIA INTL, Bucharest	(D) • MIDEAST • 250 kW
	SWAZILAND	
	TRANS WORLD RADIO, Manzini	E AFRICA • 100 kW
		(D) • E AFRICA • 100 kW
		(D) • S AFRICA • 25 kW
	UNITED KINGDOM	
	†BBC WORLD SERVICE, Daventry	(D) • MIDEAST • 300 kW
	†BBC, Via Maşîrah, Oman	MIDEAST • 100 kW
		(J) • MIDEAST & S ASIA • 100 kW
	†BBC WORLD SERVICE, Via Seychelles	(J) • E AFRICA • 250 kW
	†BBC WORLD SERVICE, Via Zyyi, Cyprus	(D) • E AFRICA • 250 kW
	USA	
	VOA, Via Kaválla, Greece	E AFRICA • 250 kW
		(D) • WEST USSR • 250 kW
	†VOA, Via Woofferton, UK	(J) • WEST USSR • 250 kW
	USSR	
	RADIO MOSCOW, Novosibirsk	DS-1 • 50 kW
	RADIO MOSCOW, Tashkent	(D) • S ASIA • 100 kW
	VATICAN STATE	
	†VATICAN RADIO, Sta Maria di Galeria	EUROPE • 100 kW
		Su • EUROPE • 100 kW
		M-Sa • ENGLISH, FRENCH, SPANISH & ITALIAN • EUROPE • 100 kW
11745	BRAZIL	
	RADIO NACIONAL, Brasília	AMERICAS • 250 kW
	CHINA (PR)	
	RADIO BEIJING, Beijing	(J) • WEST USSR • 120 kW
		(J) • S AMERICA • 120 kW
	CHINA (TAIWAN)	
	†VOICE OF FREE CHINA, T'ai-pei	SE ASIA • 50/100 kW
		E ASIA • 50/100 kW
		JAPANESE • E ASIA • 50/100 kW
(con'd)	GERMANY (FR)	
	†DEUTSCHE WELLE, Via Cyclops, Malta	N AFRICA • 250 kW

FREQUENCY	COUNTRY, STATION, LOCATION	TARGET • NETWORK • POWER (kW)	World Time

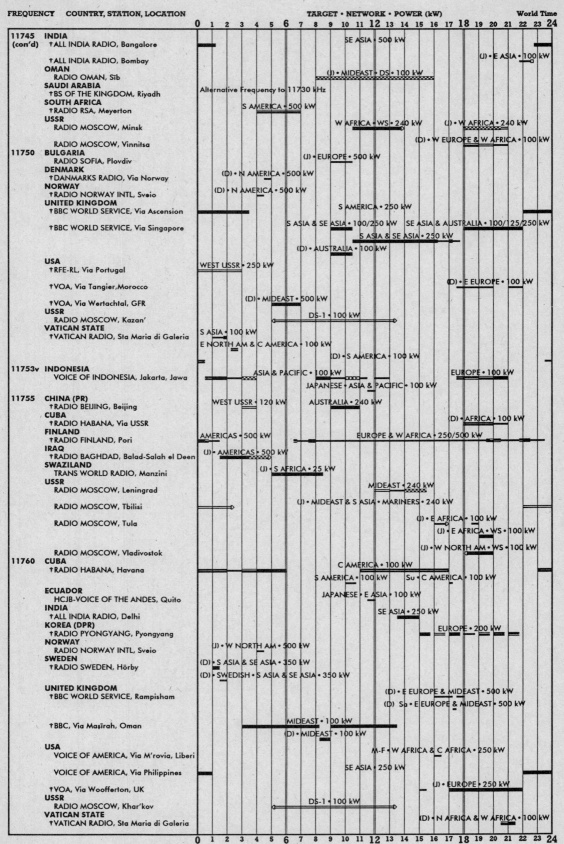

11745 (con'd) — **INDIA**
- †ALL INDIA RADIO, Bangalore — SE ASIA • 500 kW
- †ALL INDIA RADIO, Bombay — (J) • E ASIA • 100 kW

OMAN
- RADIO OMAN, Sīb — (J) • MIDEAST • DS • 100 kW

SAUDI ARABIA
- †BS OF THE KINGDOM, Riyadh — Alternative Frequency to 11730 kHz

SOUTH AFRICA
- †RADIO RSA, Meyerton — S AMERICA • 500 kW

USSR
- RADIO MOSCOW, Minsk — W AFRICA • WS • 240 kW / (J) • W AFRICA • 240 kW
- RADIO MOSCOW, Vinnitsa — (D) • W EUROPE & W AFRICA • 100 kW

11750 — **BULGARIA**
- RADIO SOFIA, Plovdiv — (J) • EUROPE • 500 kW

DENMARK
- †DANMARKS RADIO, Via Norway — (D) • N AMERICA • 500 kW

NORWAY
- †RADIO NORWAY INTL, Sveio — (D) • N AMERICA • 500 kW

UNITED KINGDOM
- †BBC WORLD SERVICE, Via Ascension — S AMERICA • 250 kW
- †BBC WORLD SERVICE, Via Singapore — S ASIA & SE ASIA • 100/250 kW   SE ASIA & AUSTRALIA • 100/125/250 kW / S ASIA & SE ASIA • 250 kW / (D) • AUSTRALIA • 100 kW

USA
- †RFE-RL, Via Portugal — WEST USSR • 250 kW
- †VOA, Via Tangier, Morocco — (D) • E EUROPE • 100 kW
- †VOA, Via Wertachtal, GFR — (D) • MIDEAST • 500 kW

USSR
- RADIO MOSCOW, Kazan' — DS-1 • 100 kW

VATICAN STATE
- †VATICAN RADIO, Sta Maria di Galeria — S ASIA • 100 kW / E NORTH AM & C AMERICA • 100 kW / (D) • S AMERICA • 100 kW

11753v — **INDONESIA**
- VOICE OF INDONESIA, Jakarta, Jawa — ASIA & PACIFIC • 100 kW / EUROPE • 100 kW / JAPANESE • ASIA & PACIFIC • 100 kW

11755 — **CHINA (PR)**
- †RADIO BEIJING, Beijing — WEST USSR • 120 kW / AUSTRALIA • 240 kW

CUBA
- †RADIO HABANA, Via USSR — (D) • AFRICA • 100 kW

FINLAND
- †RADIO FINLAND, Pori — AMERICAS • 500 kW / EUROPE & W AFRICA • 250/500 kW

IRAQ
- †RADIO BAGHDAD, Balad-Salah el Deen — (J) • AMERICAS • 500 kW

SWAZILAND
- TRANS WORLD RADIO, Manzini — (J) • S AFRICA • 25 kW

USSR
- RADIO MOSCOW, Leningrad — MIDEAST • 240 kW
- RADIO MOSCOW, Tbilisi — (J) • MIDEAST & S ASIA • MARINERS • 240 kW
- RADIO MOSCOW, Tula — (J) • E AFRICA • 100 kW / (J) • E AFRICA • WS • 100 kW
- RADIO MOSCOW, Vladivostok — (J) • W NORTH AM • WS • 100 kW

11760 — **CUBA**
- †RADIO HABANA, Havana — C AMERICA • 100 kW / S AMERICA • 100 kW   Su • C AMERICA • 100 kW

ECUADOR
- HCJB-VOICE OF THE ANDES, Quito — JAPANESE • E ASIA • 100 kW

INDIA
- †ALL INDIA RADIO, Delhi — SE ASIA • 250 kW

KOREA (DPR)
- †RADIO PYONGYANG, Pyongyang — EUROPE • 200 kW

NORWAY
- RADIO NORWAY INTL, Sveio — (J) • W NORTH AM • 500 kW

SWEDEN
- †RADIO SWEDEN, Hörby — (D) • S ASIA & SE ASIA • 350 kW / (D) • SWEDISH • S ASIA & SE ASIA • 350 kW

UNITED KINGDOM
- †BBC WORLD SERVICE, Rampisham — (D) • E EUROPE & MIDEAST • 500 kW / (D) • Sa • E EUROPE & MIDEAST • 500 kW
- †BBC, Via Maṣīrah, Oman — MIDEAST • 100 kW / (D) • MIDEAST • 100 kW

USA
- VOICE OF AMERICA, Via M'rovia, Liberi — M-F • W AFRICA & C AFRICA • 250 kW
- VOICE OF AMERICA, Via Philippines — SE ASIA • 250 kW
- †VOA, Via Woofferton, UK — (J) • EUROPE • 250 kW

USSR
- RADIO MOSCOW, Khar'kov — DS-1 • 100 kW

VATICAN STATE
- †VATICAN RADIO, Sta Maria di Galeria — (D) • N AFRICA & W AFRICA • 100 kW

FREQUENCY   COUNTRY, STATION, LOCATION

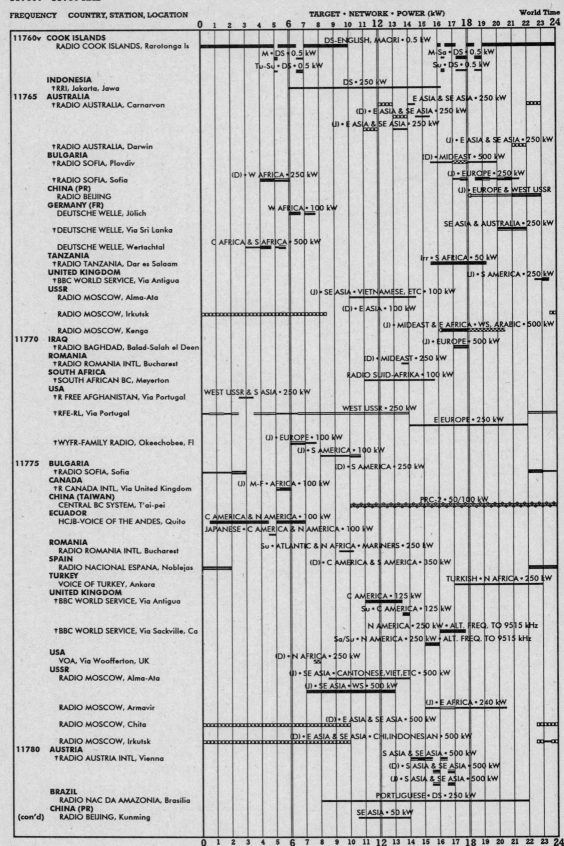

World Time
0 1 2 3 4 5 6 7 8 9 10 11 12 13 14 15 16 17 18 19 20 21 22 23 24

11760v COOK ISLANDS
  RADIO COOK ISLANDS, Rarotonga Is — DS-ENGLISH, MAORI • 0.5 kW
    M • DS • 0.5 kW / M-Sa • DS • 0.5 kW
    Tu-Su • DS • 0.5 kW / Su • DS • 0.5 kW

  INDONESIA
    †RRI, Jakarta, Jawa — DS • 250 kW
11765 AUSTRALIA
  †RADIO AUSTRALIA, Carnarvon — E ASIA & SE ASIA • 250 kW
    (D) • E ASIA & SE ASIA • 250 kW
    (J) • E ASIA & SE ASIA • 250 kW

  †RADIO AUSTRALIA, Darwin — (J) • E ASIA & SE ASIA • 250 kW
  BULGARIA
    †RADIO SOFIA, Plovdiv — (D) • MIDEAST • 500 kW

    †RADIO SOFIA, Sofia — (D) • W AFRICA • 250 kW / (J) • EUROPE • 250 kW
  CHINA (PR)
    RADIO BEIJING — (J) • EUROPE & WEST USSR
  GERMANY (FR)
    DEUTSCHE WELLE, Jülich — W AFRICA • 100 kW

    †DEUTSCHE WELLE, Via Sri Lanka — SE ASIA & AUSTRALIA • 250 kW

    DEUTSCHE WELLE, Wertachtal — C AFRICA & S AFRICA • 500 kW
  TANZANIA
    †RADIO TANZANIA, Dar es Salaam — Irr • S AFRICA • 50 kW
  UNITED KINGDOM
    †BBC WORLD SERVICE, Via Antigua — (J) • S AMERICA • 250 kW
  USSR
    RADIO MOSCOW, Alma-Ata — (J) • SE ASIA • VIETNAMESE, ETC • 100 kW

    RADIO MOSCOW, Irkutsk — (D) • E ASIA • 100 kW

    RADIO MOSCOW, Kenga — (J) • MIDEAST & E AFRICA • WS, ARABIC • 500 kW
11770 IRAQ
    †RADIO BAGHDAD, Balad-Salah el Deen — (J) • EUROPE • 500 kW
  ROMANIA
    †RADIO ROMANIA INTL, Bucharest — (D) • MIDEAST • 250 kW
  SOUTH AFRICA
    †SOUTH AFRICAN BC, Meyerton — RADIO SUID-AFRIKA • 100 kW
  USA
    †R FREE AFGHANISTAN, Via Portugal — WEST USSR & S ASIA • 250 kW

    †RFE-RL, Via Portugal — WEST USSR • 250 kW / E EUROPE • 250 kW

    †WYFR-FAMILY RADIO, Okeechobee, Fl — (J) • EUROPE • 100 kW
      (J) • S AMERICA • 100 kW

11775 BULGARIA
    †RADIO SOFIA, Sofia — (D) • S AMERICA • 250 kW
  CANADA
    †R CANADA INTL, Via United Kingdom — (J) • M-F • AFRICA • 100 kW
  CHINA (TAIWAN)
    CENTRAL BC SYSTEM, T'ai-pei — PRC-2 • 50/100 kW
  ECUADOR
    HCJB-VOICE OF THE ANDES, Quito — C AMERICA & N AMERICA • 100 kW
      JAPANESE • C AMERICA & N AMERICA • 100 kW

  ROMANIA
    RADIO ROMANIA INTL, Bucharest — Su • ATLANTIC & N AFRICA • MARINERS • 250 kW
  SPAIN
    RADIO NACIONAL ESPANA, Noblejas — (D) • C AMERICA & S AMERICA • 350 kW
  TURKEY
    VOICE OF TURKEY, Ankara — TURKISH • N AFRICA • 250 kW
  UNITED KINGDOM
    †BBC WORLD SERVICE, Via Antigua — C AMERICA • 125 kW
      Su • C AMERICA • 125 kW

    †BBC WORLD SERVICE, Via Sackville, Ca — N AMERICA • 250 kW • ALT. FREQ. TO 9515 kHz
      Sa/Su • N AMERICA • 250 kW • ALT. FREQ. TO 9515 kHz

  USA
    VOA, Via Woofferton, UK — (D) • N AFRICA • 250 kW
  USSR
    RADIO MOSCOW, Alma-Ata — (J) • SE ASIA • CANTONESE, VIET, ETC • 500 kW
      (J) • SE ASIA • WS • 500 kW

    RADIO MOSCOW, Armavir — (J) • E AFRICA • 240 kW

    RADIO MOSCOW, Chita — (D) • E ASIA & SE ASIA • 500 kW

    RADIO MOSCOW, Irkutsk — (D) • E ASIA & SE ASIA • CHI, INDONESIAN • 500 kW
11780 AUSTRIA
    †RADIO AUSTRIA INTL, Vienna — S ASIA & SE ASIA • 500 kW
      (D) • S ASIA & SE ASIA • 500 kW
      (J) • S ASIA & SE ASIA • 500 kW

  BRAZIL
    RADIO NAC DA AMAZONIA, Brasilia — PORTUGUESE • DS • 250 kW
  CHINA (PR)
(con'd)   RADIO BEIJING, Kunming — SE ASIA • 50 kW

0 1 2 3 4 5 6 7 8 9 10 11 12 13 14 15 16 17 18 19 20 21 22 23 24

FREQUENCY	COUNTRY, STATION, LOCATION	TARGET • NETWORK • POWER (kW)	World Time

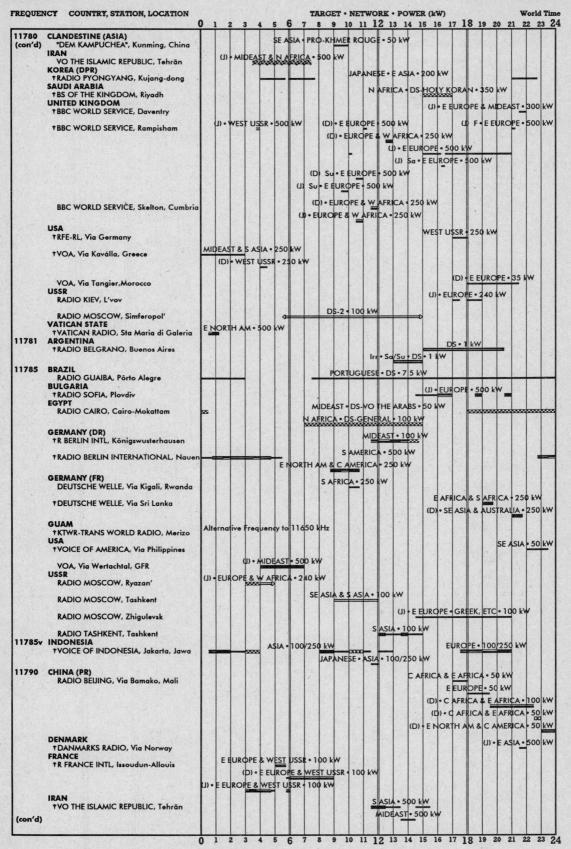

FREQUENCY	COUNTRY, STATION, LOCATION	TARGET • NETWORK • POWER (kW)
11780 (con'd)	**CLANDESTINE (ASIA)** "DEM KAMPUCHEA", Kunming, China	SE ASIA • PRO-KHMER ROUGE • 50 kW
	IRAN †VO THE ISLAMIC REPUBLIC, Tehrän	(J) • MIDEAST & N AFRICA • 500 kW
	KOREA (DPR) †RADIO PYONGYANG, Kujang-dong	JAPANESE • E ASIA • 200 kW
	SAUDI ARABIA †BS OF THE KINGDOM, Riyadh	N AFRICA • DS-HOLY KORAN • 350 kW
	UNITED KINGDOM †BBC WORLD SERVICE, Daventry	(J) • E EUROPE & MIDEAST • 300 kW
	†BBC WORLD SERVICE, Rampisham	(J) • WEST USSR • 500 kW (D) • E EUROPE • 500 kW (J) F • E EUROPE • 500 kW
		(D) • EUROPE & W AFRICA • 250 kW
		(J) • E EUROPE • 500 kW
		(J) Sa • E EUROPE • 500 kW
		(D) Su • E EUROPE • 500 kW
		(J) Su • E EUROPE • 500 kW
	BBC WORLD SERVICE, Skelton, Cumbria	(D) • EUROPE & W AFRICA • 250 kW
		(J) • EUROPE & W AFRICA • 250 kW
	USA †RFE-RL, Via Germany	WEST USSR • 250 kW
	†VOA, Via Kaválla, Greece	MIDEAST & S ASIA • 250 kW
		(D) • WEST USSR • 250 kW
	VOA, Via Tangier, Morocco	(D) • E EUROPE • 35 kW
	USSR RADIO KIEV, L'vov	(J) • EUROPE • 240 kW
	RADIO MOSCOW, Simferopol'	DS-2 • 100 kW
	VATICAN STATE †VATICAN RADIO, Sta Maria di Galeria	E NORTH AM • 500 kW
11781	**ARGENTINA** †RADIO BELGRANO, Buenos Aires	DS • 1 kW
		Irr • Sa/Su • DS • 1 kW
11785	**BRAZIL** RADIO GUAIBA, Pôrto Alegre	PORTUGUESE • DS • 7.5 kW
	BULGARIA †RADIO SOFIA, Plovdiv	(J) • EUROPE • 500 kW
	EGYPT RADIO CAIRO, Cairo-Mokattam	MIDEAST • DS-VO THE ARABS • 50 kW
		N AFRICA • DS-GENERAL • 100 kW
	GERMANY (DR) †R BERLIN INTL, Königswusterhausen	MIDEAST • 100 kW
	†RADIO BERLIN INTERNATIONAL, Nauen	S AMERICA • 500 kW
		E NORTH AM & C AMERICA • 250 kW
	GERMANY (FR) DEUTSCHE WELLE, Via Kigali, Rwanda	S AFRICA • 250 kW
	†DEUTSCHE WELLE, Via Sri Lanka	E AFRICA & S AFRICA • 250 kW
		(D) • SE ASIA & AUSTRALIA • 250 kW
	GUAM †KTWR-TRANS WORLD RADIO, Merizo	Alternative Frequency to 11650 kHz
	USA †VOICE OF AMERICA, Via Philippines	SE ASIA • 50 kW
	VOA, Via Wertachtal, GFR	(J) • MIDEAST • 500 kW
	USSR RADIO MOSCOW, Ryazan'	(J) • EUROPE & W AFRICA • 240 kW
	RADIO MOSCOW, Tashkent	SE ASIA & S ASIA • 100 kW
	RADIO MOSCOW, Zhigulevsk	(J) • E EUROPE • GREEK, ETC • 100 kW
	RADIO TASHKENT, Tashkent	S ASIA • 100 kW
11785v	**INDONESIA** †VOICE OF INDONESIA, Jakarta, Jawa	ASIA • 100/250 kW EUROPE • 100/250 kW
		JAPANESE • ASIA • 100/250 kW
11790	**CHINA (PR)** RADIO BEIJING, Via Bamako, Mali	C AFRICA & E AFRICA • 50 kW
		E EUROPE • 50 kW
		(D) • C AFRICA & E AFRICA • 100 kW
		(D) • C AFRICA & E AFRICA • 50 kW
		(D) • E NORTH AM & C AMERICA • 50 kW
	DENMARK †DANMARKS RADIO, Via Norway	(J) • E ASIA • 500 kW
	FRANCE †R FRANCE INTL, Issoudun-Allouis	E EUROPE & WEST USSR • 100 kW
		(D) • E EUROPE & WEST USSR • 100 kW
		(J) • E EUROPE & WEST USSR • 100 kW
	IRAN †VO THE ISLAMIC REPUBLIC, Tehrän	S ASIA • 500 kW
		MIDEAST • 500 kW
(con'd)		

ENGLISH ▬ ARABIC ∾∾∾ CHINESE □□□ FRENCH ═══ GERMAN ▬▬ RUSSIAN ══ SPANISH ▬▬ OTHER ──

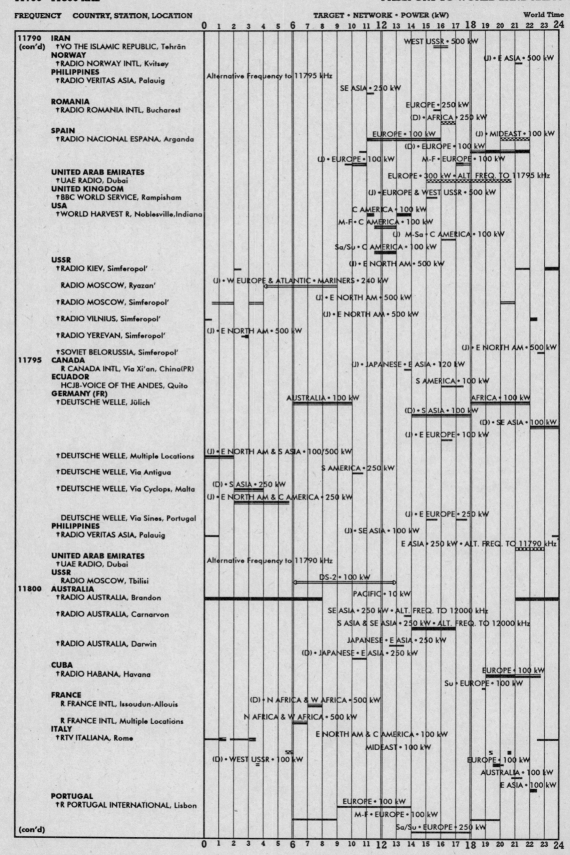

FREQUENCY   COUNTRY, STATION, LOCATION   TARGET • NETWORK • POWER (kW)   World Time

0 1 2 3 4 5 6 7 8 9 10 11 12 13 14 15 16 17 18 19 20 21 22 23 24

11790
(con'd) **IRAN**
   †VO THE ISLAMIC REPUBLIC, Tehrān — WEST USSR • 500 kW
  NORWAY
   †RADIO NORWAY INTL, Kvitsøy — (J) • E ASIA • 500 kW
  PHILIPPINES
   †RADIO VERITAS ASIA, Palauig — Alternative Frequency to 11795 kHz / SE ASIA • 250 kW

  ROMANIA
   †RADIO ROMANIA INTL, Bucharest — EUROPE • 250 kW / (D) • AFRICA • 250 kW

  SPAIN
   †RADIO NACIONAL ESPANA, Arganda — EUROPE • 100 kW / (J) • MIDEAST • 100 kW / (D) • EUROPE • 100 kW / (J) • EUROPE • 100 kW / M-F • EUROPE • 100 kW

  UNITED ARAB EMIRATES
   †UAE RADIO, Dubai — EUROPE • 300 kW • ALT. FREQ. TO 11795 kHz
  UNITED KINGDOM
   †BBC WORLD SERVICE, Rampisham — (J) • EUROPE & WEST USSR • 500 kW
  USA
   †WORLD HARVEST R, Noblesville, Indiana — C AMERICA • 100 kW / M-F • C AMERICA • 100 kW / (J) • M-Sa • C AMERICA • 100 kW / Sa/Su • C AMERICA • 100 kW

  USSR
   †RADIO KIEV, Simferopol' — (J) • E NORTH AM • 500 kW
   RADIO MOSCOW, Ryazan' — (J) • W EUROPE & ATLANTIC • MARINERS • 240 kW
   †RADIO MOSCOW, Simferopol' — (J) • E NORTH AM • 500 kW
   †RADIO VILNIUS, Simferopol' — (J) • E NORTH AM • 500 kW
   †RADIO YEREVAN, Simferopol' — (J) • E NORTH AM • 500 kW
   †SOVIET BELORUSSIA, Simferopol' — (J) • E NORTH AM • 500 kW

11795 **CANADA**
   R CANADA INTL, Via Xi'an, China(PR) — (J) • JAPANESE • E ASIA • 120 kW
  ECUADOR
   HCJB-VOICE OF THE ANDES, Quito — S AMERICA • 100 kW
  GERMANY (FR)
   †DEUTSCHE WELLE, Jülich — AUSTRALIA • 100 kW / AFRICA • 100 kW / (D) • S ASIA • 100 kW / (D) • SE ASIA • 100 kW / (J) • E EUROPE • 100 kW
   †DEUTSCHE WELLE, Multiple Locations — (J) • E NORTH AM & S ASIA • 100/500 kW
   †DEUTSCHE WELLE, Via Antigua — S AMERICA • 250 kW
   †DEUTSCHE WELLE, Via Cyclops, Malta — (D) • S ASIA • 250 kW / (J) • E NORTH AM & C AMERICA • 250 kW
   DEUTSCHE WELLE, Via Sines, Portugal — (J) • E EUROPE • 250 kW
  PHILIPPINES
   †RADIO VERITAS ASIA, Palauig — (J) • SE ASIA • 100 kW / E ASIA • 250 kW • ALT. FREQ. TO 11790 kHz

  UNITED ARAB EMIRATES
   †UAE RADIO, Dubai — Alternative Frequency to 11790 kHz
  USSR
   RADIO MOSCOW, Tbilisi — DS-2 • 100 kW

11800 **AUSTRALIA**
   †RADIO AUSTRALIA, Brandon — PACIFIC • 10 kW
   †RADIO AUSTRALIA, Carnarvon — SE ASIA • 250 kW • ALT. FREQ. TO 12000 kHz / S ASIA & SE ASIA • 250 kW • ALT. FREQ. TO 12000 kHz
   †RADIO AUSTRALIA, Darwin — JAPANESE • E ASIA • 250 kW / (D) • JAPANESE • E ASIA • 250 kW
  CUBA
   †RADIO HABANA, Havana — EUROPE • 100 kW / Su • EUROPE • 100 kW
  FRANCE
   R FRANCE INTL, Issoudun-Allouis — (D) • N AFRICA & W AFRICA • 500 kW
   R FRANCE INTL, Multiple Locations — N AFRICA & W AFRICA • 500 kW
  ITALY
   †RTV ITALIANA, Rome — E NORTH AM & C AMERICA • 100 kW / MIDEAST • 100 kW / (D) • WEST USSR • 100 kW / EUROPE • 100 kW / AUSTRALIA • 100 kW / E ASIA • 100 kW

  PORTUGAL
   †R PORTUGAL INTERNATIONAL, Lisbon — EUROPE • 100 kW / M-F • EUROPE • 100 kW / Sa/Su • EUROPE • 250 kW

(con'd)

0 1 2 3 4 5 6 7 8 9 10 11 12 13 14 15 16 17 18 19 20 21 22 23 24

SUMMER ONLY (J)   WINTER ONLY (D)   JAMMING / OR ∧   EARLIEST HEARD ◁   LATEST HEARD ▷   NEW OR CHANGED FOR 1991 †

FREQUENCY   COUNTRY, STATION, LOCATION   TARGET • NETWORK • POWER (kW)   World Time

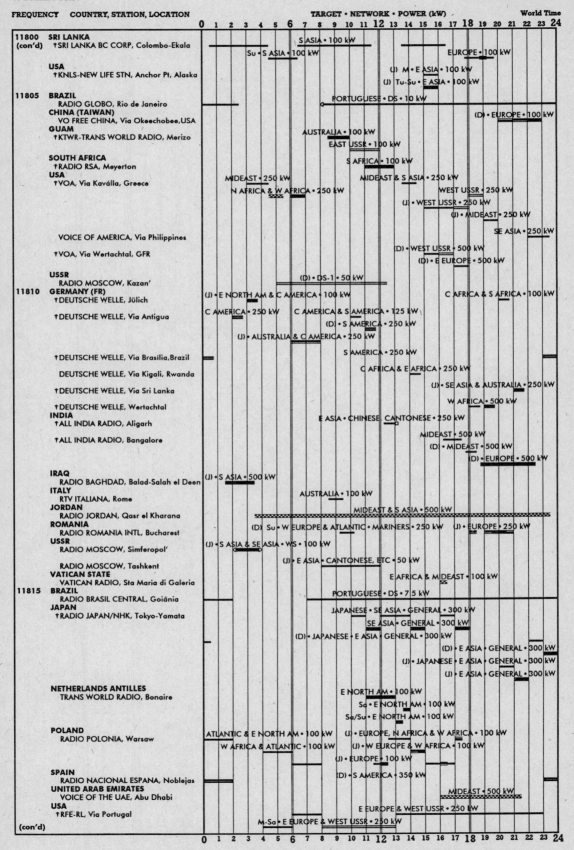

Frequency	Country, Station, Location
11800 (con'd)	**SRI LANKA** †SRI LANKA BC CORP, Colombo-Ekala
	USA †KNLS-NEW LIFE STN, Anchor Pt, Alaska
11805	**BRAZIL** RADIO GLOBO, Rio de Janeiro
	CHINA (TAIWAN) VO FREE CHINA, Via Okeechobee,USA
	GUAM †KTWR-TRANS WORLD RADIO, Merizo
	SOUTH AFRICA †RADIO RSA, Meyerton
	USA †VOA, Via Kaválla, Greece
	VOICE OF AMERICA, Via Philippines
	†VOA, Via Wertachtal, GFR
	USSR RADIO MOSCOW, Kazan'
11810	**GERMANY (FR)** †DEUTSCHE WELLE, Jülich
	†DEUTSCHE WELLE, Via Antigua
	†DEUTSCHE WELLE, Via Brasília,Brazil
	DEUTSCHE WELLE, Via Kigali, Rwanda
	†DEUTSCHE WELLE, Via Sri Lanka
	†DEUTSCHE WELLE, Wertachtal
	INDIA †ALL INDIA RADIO, Aligarh
	†ALL INDIA RADIO, Bangalore
	IRAQ RADIO BAGHDAD, Balad-Salah el Deen
	ITALY RTV ITALIANA, Rome
	JORDAN RADIO JORDAN, Qasr el Kharana
	ROMANIA RADIO ROMANIA INTL, Bucharest
	USSR RADIO MOSCOW, Simferopol'
	RADIO MOSCOW, Tashkent
	VATICAN STATE VATICAN RADIO, Sta Maria di Galeria
11815	**BRAZIL** RADIO BRASIL CENTRAL, Goiânia
	JAPAN †RADIO JAPAN/NHK, Tokyo-Yamata
	NETHERLANDS ANTILLES TRANS WORLD RADIO, Bonaire
	POLAND RADIO POLONIA, Warsaw
	SPAIN RADIO NACIONAL ESPANA, Noblejas
	UNITED ARAB EMIRATES VOICE OF THE UAE, Abu Dhabi
	USA †RFE-RL, Via Portugal
(con'd)	

Target/Network/Power entries:

- SRI LANKA BC CORP: S ASIA • 100 kW; Su • S ASIA • 100 kW; EUROPE • 100 kW
- KNLS-NEW LIFE STN: (J) M • E ASIA • 100 kW; (J) Tu-Su • E ASIA • 100 kW
- RADIO GLOBO: PORTUGUESE • DS • 10 kW
- VO FREE CHINA: (D) • EUROPE • 100 kW
- KTWR-TRANS WORLD RADIO: AUSTRALIA • 100 kW; EAST USSR • 100 kW
- RADIO RSA: S AFRICA • 100 kW
- VOA Via Kaválla: MIDEAST • 250 kW; MIDEAST & S ASIA • 250 kW; N AFRICA & W AFRICA • 250 kW; WEST USSR • 250 kW; (J) • WEST USSR • 250 kW; (J) • MIDEAST • 250 kW; SE ASIA • 250 kW
- VOA Via Wertachtal: (D) • WEST USSR • 500 kW; (D) • E EUROPE • 500 kW
- RADIO MOSCOW Kazan': (D) • DS-1 • 50 kW
- DEUTSCHE WELLE Jülich: (J) • E NORTH AM & C AMERICA • 100 kW; C AFRICA & S AFRICA • 100 kW
- DEUTSCHE WELLE Via Antigua: C AMERICA • 250 kW; C AMERICA & S AMERICA • 125 kW; (D) • S AMERICA • 250 kW; (J) • AUSTRALIA & C AMERICA • 250 kW
- DEUTSCHE WELLE Via Brasília: S AMERICA • 250 kW
- DEUTSCHE WELLE Via Kigali: C AFRICA & E AFRICA • 250 kW
- DEUTSCHE WELLE Via Sri Lanka: (J) • SE ASIA & AUSTRALIA • 250 kW
- DEUTSCHE WELLE Wertachtal: W AFRICA • 500 kW
- ALL INDIA RADIO Aligarh: E ASIA • CHINESE CANTONESE • 250 kW
- ALL INDIA RADIO Bangalore: MIDEAST • 500 kW; (D) • MIDEAST • 500 kW; (D) • EUROPE • 500 kW
- RADIO BAGHDAD: (J) • S ASIA • 500 kW
- RTV ITALIANA: AUSTRALIA • 100 kW
- RADIO JORDAN: MIDEAST & S ASIA • 500 kW
- RADIO ROMANIA INTL: (D) Su • W EUROPE & ATLANTIC • MARINERS • 250 kW; (J) • EUROPE • 250 kW
- RADIO MOSCOW Simferopol': (J) • S ASIA & SE ASIA • WS • 100 kW
- RADIO MOSCOW Tashkent: (J) • E ASIA • CANTONESE, ETC • 50 kW
- VATICAN RADIO: E AFRICA & MIDEAST • 100 kW
- RADIO BRASIL CENTRAL: PORTUGUESE • DS • 7.5 kW
- RADIO JAPAN/NHK: JAPANESE • SE ASIA • GENERAL • 300 kW; SE ASIA • GENERAL • 300 kW; (D) • JAPANESE • E ASIA • GENERAL • 300 kW; (D) • E ASIA • GENERAL • 300 kW; (J) • JAPANESE • E ASIA • GENERAL • 300 kW; (J) • E ASIA • GENERAL • 300 kW
- TRANS WORLD RADIO: E NORTH AM • 100 kW; Sa • E NORTH AM • 100 kW; Sa/Su • E NORTH AM • 100 kW
- RADIO POLONIA: ATLANTIC & E NORTH AM • 100 kW; (J) • EUROPE, N AFRICA & W AFRICA • 100 kW; W AFRICA & ATLANTIC • 100 kW; (J) • W EUROPE & W AFRICA • 100 kW; (J) • EUROPE • 100 kW
- RADIO NACIONAL ESPANA: (D) • S AMERICA • 350 kW
- VOICE OF THE UAE: MIDEAST • 500 kW
- RFE-RL Via Portugal: E EUROPE & WEST USSR • 250 kW; M-Sa • E EUROPE & WEST USSR • 250 kW

World Time scale: 0 1 2 3 4 5 6 7 8 9 10 11 12 13 14 15 16 17 18 19 20 21 22 23 24

ENGLISH ▬▬   ARABIC ▩▩   CHINESE ▭▭   FRENCH ▬▬   GERMAN ▬▬   RUSSIAN ══   SPANISH ▬▬   OTHER ──

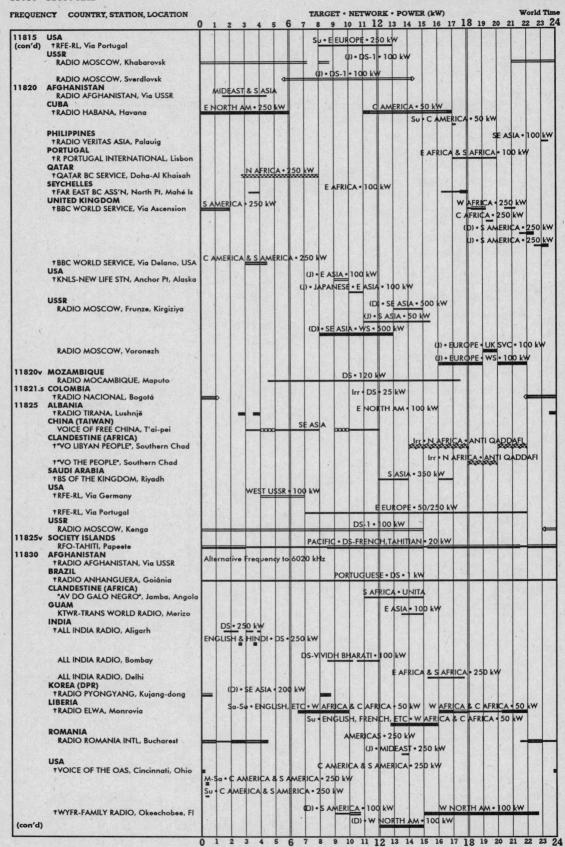

FREQUENCY   COUNTRY, STATION, LOCATION   TARGET • NETWORK • POWER (kW)   World Time

Freq	Country / Station
11815 (con'd)	**USA** †RFE-RL, Via Portugal — Su • E EUROPE • 250 kW
	USSR RADIO MOSCOW, Khabarovsk — (J) • DS-1 • 100 kW
	RADIO MOSCOW, Sverdlovsk — (J) • DS-1 • 100 kW
11820	**AFGHANISTAN** RADIO AFGHANISTAN, Via USSR — MIDEAST & S ASIA
	CUBA †RADIO HABANA, Havana — E NORTH AM • 250 kW / C AMERICA • 50 kW / Su • C AMERICA • 50 kW
	PHILIPPINES †RADIO VERITAS ASIA, Palauig — SE ASIA • 100 kW
	PORTUGAL †R PORTUGAL INTERNATIONAL, Lisbon — E AFRICA & S AFRICA • 100 kW
	QATAR †QATAR BC SERVICE, Doha-Al Khaisah — N AFRICA • 250 kW
	SEYCHELLES †FAR EAST BC ASS'N, North Pt, Mahé Is — E AFRICA • 100 kW
	UNITED KINGDOM †BBC WORLD SERVICE, Via Ascension — S AMERICA • 250 kW / W AFRICA • 250 kW / C AFRICA • 250 kW / (D) • S AMERICA • 250 kW / (J) • S AMERICA • 250 kW
	†BBC WORLD SERVICE, Via Delano, USA — C AMERICA & S AMERICA • 250 kW
	USA †KNLS-NEW LIFE STN, Anchor Pt, Alaska — (J) • E ASIA • 100 kW / (J) • JAPANESE • E ASIA • 100 kW
	USSR RADIO MOSCOW, Frunze, Kirgiziya — (D) • SE ASIA • 500 kW / (J) • S ASIA • 50 kW / (D) • SE ASIA • WS • 500 kW
	RADIO MOSCOW, Voronezh — (J) • EUROPE • UK SVC • 100 kW / (J) • EUROPE • WS • 100 kW
11820v	**MOZAMBIQUE** RADIO MOCAMBIQUE, Maputo — DS • 120 kW
11821.5	**COLOMBIA** †RADIO NACIONAL, Bogotá — Irr • DS • 25 kW
11825	**ALBANIA** †RADIO TIRANA, Lushnjë — E NORTH AM • 100 kW
	CHINA (TAIWAN) VOICE OF FREE CHINA, T'ai-pei — SE ASIA
	CLANDESTINE (AFRICA) †"VO LIBYAN PEOPLE", Southern Chad — Irr • N AFRICA • ANTI QADDAFI
	†"VO THE PEOPLE", Southern Chad — Irr • N AFRICA • ANTI QADDAFI
	SAUDI ARABIA †BS OF THE KINGDOM, Riyadh — S ASIA • 350 kW
	USA †RFE-RL, Via Germany — WEST USSR • 100 kW
	†RFE-RL, Via Portugal — E EUROPE • 50/250 kW
	USSR RADIO MOSCOW, Kenga — DS-1 • 100 kW
11825v	**SOCIETY ISLANDS** RFO-TAHITI, Papeete — PACIFIC • DS-FRENCH, TAHITIAN • 20 kW
11830	**AFGHANISTAN** †RADIO AFGHANISTAN, Via USSR — Alternative Frequency to 6020 kHz
	BRAZIL †RADIO ANHANGUERA, Goiânia — PORTUGUESE • DS • 1 kW
	CLANDESTINE (AFRICA) "AV DO GALO NEGRO", Jamba, Angola — S AFRICA • UNITA
	GUAM KTWR-TRANS WORLD RADIO, Merizo — E ASIA • 100 kW
	INDIA †ALL INDIA RADIO, Aligarh — DS • 250 kW / ENGLISH & HINDI • DS • 250 kW
	ALL INDIA RADIO, Bombay — DS-VIVIDH BHARATI • 100 kW
	ALL INDIA RADIO, Delhi — E AFRICA & S AFRICA • 250 kW
	KOREA (DPR) †RADIO PYONGYANG, Kujang-dong — (D) • SE ASIA • 200 kW
	LIBERIA †RADIO ELWA, Monrovia — Sa-Su • ENGLISH, ETC • W AFRICA & C AFRICA • 50 kW / W AFRICA & C AFRICA • 50 kW / Su • ENGLISH, FRENCH, ETC • W AFRICA & C AFRICA • 50 kW
	ROMANIA RADIO ROMANIA INTL, Bucharest — AMERICAS • 250 kW / (J) • MIDEAST • 250 kW
	USA †VOICE OF THE OAS, Cincinnati, Ohio — C AMERICA & S AMERICA • 250 kW / M-Sa • C AMERICA & S AMERICA • 250 kW / Su • C AMERICA & S AMERICA • 250 kW
	†WYFR-FAMILY RADIO, Okeechobee, Fl — (D) • S AMERICA • 100 kW / W NORTH AM • 100 kW / (D) • W NORTH AM • 100 kW
(con'd)	

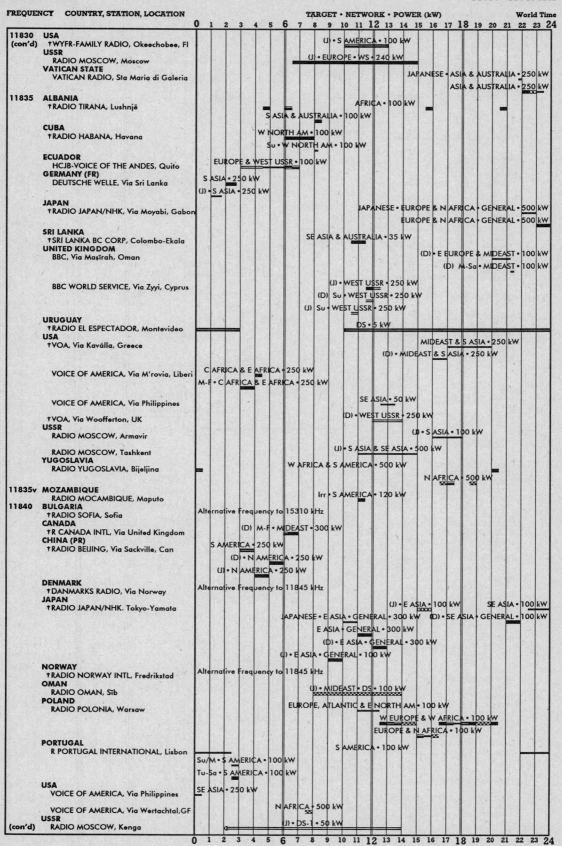

FREQUENCY   COUNTRY, STATION, LOCATION   TARGET • NETWORK • POWER (kW)   World Time

11830	**USA**
(con'd)	↑WYFR-FAMILY RADIO, Okeechobee, Fl — (J) • S AMERICA • 100 kW
	USSR
	RADIO MOSCOW, Moscow — (J) • EUROPE • WS • 240 kW
	VATICAN STATE
	VATICAN RADIO, Sta Maria di Galeria — JAPANESE • ASIA & AUSTRALIA • 250 kW / ASIA & AUSTRALIA • 250 kW
11835	**ALBANIA**
	↑RADIO TIRANA, Lushnjë — AFRICA • 100 kW / S ASIA & AUSTRALIA • 100 kW
	CUBA
	↑RADIO HABANA, Havana — W NORTH AM • 100 kW / Su • W NORTH AM • 100 kW
	ECUADOR
	HCJB-VOICE OF THE ANDES, Quito — EUROPE & WEST USSR • 100 kW
	GERMANY (FR)
	DEUTSCHE WELLE, Via Sri Lanka — S ASIA • 250 kW / (J) • S ASIA • 250 kW
	JAPAN
	↑RADIO JAPAN/NHK, Via Moyabi, Gabon — JAPANESE • EUROPE & N AFRICA • GENERAL • 500 kW / EUROPE & N AFRICA • GENERAL • 500 kW
	SRI LANKA
	↑SRI LANKA BC CORP, Colombo-Ekala — SE ASIA & AUSTRALIA • 35 kW
	UNITED KINGDOM
	BBC, Via Maṣīrah, Oman — (D) • E EUROPE & MIDEAST • 100 kW / (D) M-Sa • MIDEAST • 100 kW
	BBC WORLD SERVICE, Via Zyyi, Cyprus — (J) • WEST USSR • 250 kW / (D) Su • WEST USSR • 250 kW / (J) Su • WEST USSR • 250 kW
	URUGUAY
	↑RADIO EL ESPECTADOR, Montevideo — DS • 5 kW
	USA
	↑VOA, Via Kaválla, Greece — MIDEAST & S ASIA • 250 kW / (D) • MIDEAST & S ASIA • 250 kW
	VOICE OF AMERICA, Via M'rovia, Liberi — C AFRICA & E AFRICA • 250 kW / M-F • C AFRICA & E AFRICA • 250 kW
	VOICE OF AMERICA, Via Philippines — SE ASIA • 50 kW
	↑VOA, Via Woofferton, UK — (D) • WEST USSR • 250 kW
	USSR
	RADIO MOSCOW, Armavir — (J) • S ASIA • 100 kW
	RADIO MOSCOW, Tashkent — (J) • S ASIA & SE ASIA • 500 kW
	YUGOSLAVIA
	RADIO YUGOSLAVIA, Bijeljina — W AFRICA & S AMERICA • 500 kW / N AFRICA • 500 kW
11835v	**MOZAMBIQUE**
	RADIO MOCAMBIQUE, Maputo — Irr • S AMERICA • 120 kW
11840	**BULGARIA**
	↑RADIO SOFIA, Sofia — Alternative Frequency to 15310 kHz
	CANADA
	↑R CANADA INTL, Via United Kingdom — (D) M-F • MIDEAST • 300 kW
	CHINA (PR)
	↑RADIO BEIJING, Via Sackville, Can — S AMERICA • 250 kW / (D) • N AMERICA • 250 kW / (J) • N AMERICA • 250 kW
	DENMARK
	↑DANMARKS RADIO, Via Norway — Alternative Frequency to 11845 kHz
	JAPAN
	↑RADIO JAPAN/NHK, Tokyo-Yamata — (J) • E ASIA • 100 kW / SE ASIA • 100 kW / JAPANESE • E ASIA • GENERAL • 300 kW / (D) • SE ASIA • GENERAL • 100 kW / E ASIA • GENERAL • 300 kW / (D) • E ASIA • GENERAL • 300 kW / (J) • E ASIA • GENERAL • 100 kW
	NORWAY
	↑RADIO NORWAY INTL, Fredrikstad — Alternative Frequency to 11845 kHz
	OMAN
	RADIO OMAN, Sīb — (J) • MIDEAST • DS • 100 kW
	POLAND
	RADIO POLONIA, Warsaw — EUROPE, ATLANTIC & E NORTH AM • 100 kW / W EUROPE & W AFRICA • 100 kW / EUROPE & N AFRICA • 100 kW
	PORTUGAL
	R PORTUGAL INTERNATIONAL, Lisbon — S AMERICA • 100 kW / Su/M • S AMERICA • 100 kW / Tu-Sa • S AMERICA • 100 kW
	USA
	VOICE OF AMERICA, Via Philippines — SE ASIA • 250 kW
	VOICE OF AMERICA, Via Wertachtal, GF — N AFRICA • 500 kW
	USSR
(con'd)	RADIO MOSCOW, Kenga — (J) • DS-1 • 50 kW

ENGLISH ▬▬   ARABIC ⧖⧖⧖   CHINESE ▫▫▫   FRENCH ══   GERMAN ▬▬   RUSSIAN ══   SPANISH ▬▬   OTHER ▬▬

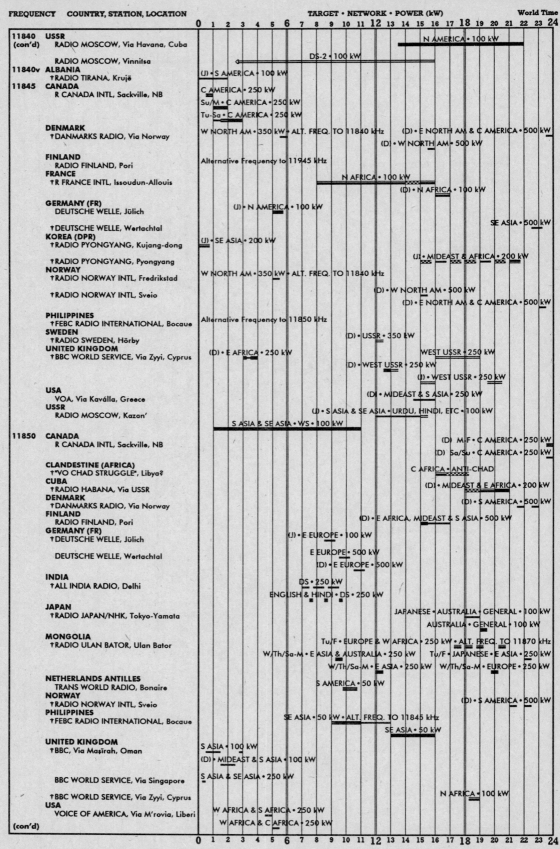

FREQUENCY	COUNTRY, STATION, LOCATION	TARGET • NETWORK • POWER (kW)	World Time

11840 (con'd) **USSR**
RADIO MOSCOW, Via Havana, Cuba — N AMERICA • 100 kW

RADIO MOSCOW, Vinnitsa — DS-2 • 100 kW

11840v ALBANIA
†RADIO TIRANA, Krujë — (J) • S AMERICA • 100 kW

11845 CANADA
R CANADA INTL, Sackville, NB — C AMERICA • 250 kW
Su/M • C AMERICA • 250 kW
Tu-Sa • C AMERICA • 250 kW

DENMARK
†DANMARKS RADIO, Via Norway — W NORTH AM • 350 kW • ALT. FREQ. TO 11840 kHz / (D) • E NORTH AM & C AMERICA • 500 kW / (D) • W NORTH AM • 500 kW

FINLAND
RADIO FINLAND, Pori — Alternative Frequency to 11945 kHz

FRANCE
†R FRANCE INTL, Issoudun-Allouis — N AFRICA • 100 kW / (D) • N AFRICA • 100 kW

GERMANY (FR)
DEUTSCHE WELLE, Jülich — (J) • N AMERICA • 100 kW

†DEUTSCHE WELLE, Wertachtal — SE ASIA • 500 kW

KOREA (DPR)
†RADIO PYONGYANG, Kujang-dong — (J) • SE ASIA • 200 kW

†RADIO PYONGYANG, Pyongyang — (J) • MIDEAST & AFRICA • 200 kW

NORWAY
†RADIO NORWAY INTL, Fredrikstad — W NORTH AM • 350 kW • ALT. FREQ. TO 11840 kHz

†RADIO NORWAY INTL, Sveio — (D) • W NORTH AM • 500 kW / (D) • E NORTH AM & C AMERICA • 500 kW

PHILIPPINES
†FEBC RADIO INTERNATIONAL, Bocaue — Alternative Frequency to 11850 kHz

SWEDEN
†RADIO SWEDEN, Hörby — (D) • USSR • 350 kW

UNITED KINGDOM
†BBC WORLD SERVICE, Via Zyyi, Cyprus — (D) • E AFRICA • 250 kW / WEST USSR • 250 kW / (D) • WEST USSR • 250 kW / (J) • WEST USSR • 250 kW

USA
VOA, Via Kaválla, Greece — (D) • MIDEAST & S ASIA • 250 kW

USSR
RADIO MOSCOW, Kazan' — (J) • S ASIA & SE ASIA • URDU, HINDI, ETC • 100 kW / S ASIA & SE ASIA • WS • 100 kW

11850 CANADA
R CANADA INTL, Sackville, NB — (D) • M-F • C AMERICA • 250 kW / (D) • Sa/Su • C AMERICA • 250 kW

CLANDESTINE (AFRICA)
†"VO CHAD STRUGGLE", Libya? — C AFRICA • ANTI-CHAD

CUBA
†RADIO HABANA, Via USSR — (D) • MIDEAST & E AFRICA • 200 kW

DENMARK
†DANMARKS RADIO, Via Norway — (D) • S AMERICA • 500 kW

FINLAND
RADIO FINLAND, Pori — (D) • E AFRICA, MIDEAST & S ASIA • 500 kW

GERMANY (FR)
†DEUTSCHE WELLE, Jülich — (J) • E EUROPE • 100 kW

DEUTSCHE WELLE, Wertachtal — E EUROPE • 500 kW / (D) • E EUROPE • 500 kW

INDIA
†ALL INDIA RADIO, Delhi — DS • 250 kW / ENGLISH & HINDI • DS • 250 kW

JAPAN
†RADIO JAPAN/NHK, Tokyo-Yamata — JAPANESE • AUSTRALIA • GENERAL • 100 kW / AUSTRALIA • GENERAL • 100 kW

MONGOLIA
†RADIO ULAN BATOR, Ulan Bator — Tu/F • EUROPE & W AFRICA • 250 kW • ALT. FREQ. TO 11870 kHz / W/Th/Sa-M • E ASIA & AUSTRALIA • 250 kW   Tu/F • JAPANESE • E ASIA • 250 kW / W/Th/Sa-M • E ASIA • 250 kW   W/Th/Sa-M • EUROPE • 250 kW

NETHERLANDS ANTILLES
TRANS WORLD RADIO, Bonaire — S AMERICA • 50 kW

NORWAY
†RADIO NORWAY INTL, Sveio — (D) • S AMERICA • 500 kW

PHILIPPINES
†FEBC RADIO INTERNATIONAL, Bocaue — SE ASIA • 50 kW • ALT. FREQ. TO 11845 kHz / SE ASIA • 50 kW

UNITED KINGDOM
†BBC, Via Maṣīrah, Oman — S ASIA • 100 kW / (D) • MIDEAST & S ASIA • 100 kW

BBC WORLD SERVICE, Via Singapore — S ASIA & SE ASIA • 250 kW

†BBC WORLD SERVICE, Via Zyyi, Cyprus — N AFRICA • 100 kW

USA
VOICE OF AMERICA, Via M'rovia, Liberi — W AFRICA & S AFRICA • 250 kW / W AFRICA & C AFRICA • 250 kW

(con'd)

SUMMER ONLY (J)   WINTER ONLY (D)   JAMMING / OR ∧   EARLIEST HEARD ◁   LATEST HEARD ▷   NEW OR CHANGED FOR 1991 †

FREQUENCY   COUNTRY, STATION, LOCATION | TARGET • NETWORK • POWER (kW) | World Time

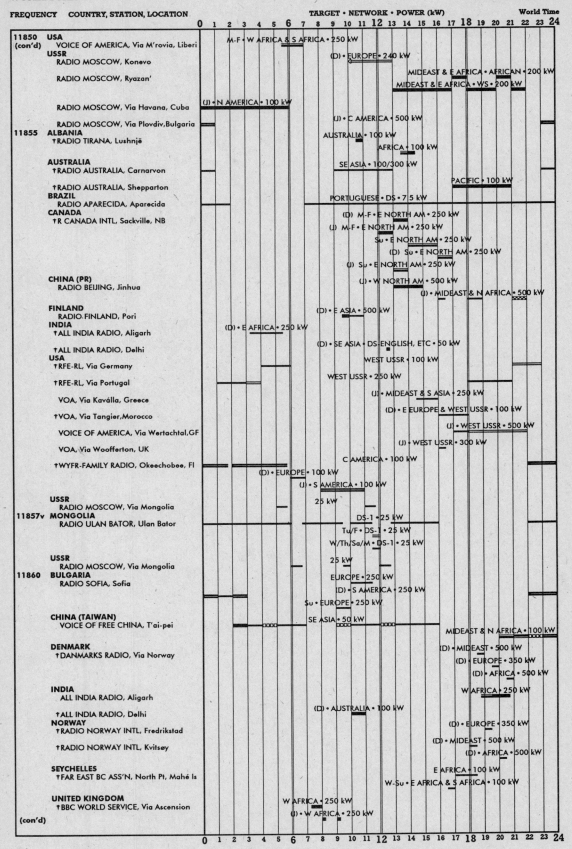

Frequency	Country, Station, Location	Target • Network • Power
11850 (con'd)	**USA** VOICE OF AMERICA, Via M'rovia, Liberi	M-F • W AFRICA & S AFRICA • 250 kW
	USSR RADIO MOSCOW, Konevo	(D) • EUROPE • 240 kW
	RADIO MOSCOW, Ryazan'	MIDEAST & E AFRICA • AFRICAN • 200 kW / MIDEAST & E AFRICA • WS • 200 kW
	RADIO MOSCOW, Via Havana, Cuba	(J) • N AMERICA • 100 kW
	RADIO MOSCOW, Via Plovdiv, Bulgaria	(J) • C AMERICA • 500 kW
11855	**ALBANIA** †RADIO TIRANA, Lushnjë	AUSTRALIA • 100 kW / AFRICA • 100 kW
	AUSTRALIA †RADIO AUSTRALIA, Carnarvon	SE ASIA • 100/300 kW
	†RADIO AUSTRALIA, Shepparton	PACIFIC • 100 kW
	BRAZIL RADIO APARECIDA, Aparecida	PORTUGUESE • DS • 7.5 kW
	CANADA †R CANADA INTL, Sackville, NB	(D) M-F • E NORTH AM • 250 kW / (J) M-F • E NORTH AM • 250 kW / Su • E NORTH AM • 250 kW / (D) Su • E NORTH AM • 250 kW / (J) Su • E NORTH AM • 250 kW
	CHINA (PR) RADIO BEIJING, Jinhua	(J) • W NORTH AM • 500 kW / (J) • MIDEAST & N AFRICA • 500 kW
	FINLAND RADIO FINLAND, Pori	(D) • E ASIA • 500 kW
	INDIA †ALL INDIA RADIO, Aligarh	(D) • E AFRICA • 250 kW
	†ALL INDIA RADIO, Delhi	(D) • SE ASIA • DS-ENGLISH, ETC • 50 kW
	USA †RFE-RL, Via Germany	WEST USSR • 100 kW
	†RFE-RL, Via Portugal	WEST USSR • 250 kW
	VOA, Via Kaválla, Greece	(J) • MIDEAST & S ASIA • 250 kW
	†VOA, Via Tangier, Morocco	(D) • E EUROPE & WEST USSR • 100 kW
	VOICE OF AMERICA, Via Wertachtal, GF	(J) • WEST USSR • 500 kW
	VOA, Via Woofferton, UK	(J) • WEST USSR • 300 kW
	†WYFR-FAMILY RADIO, Okeechobee, Fl	C AMERICA • 100 kW / (D) • EUROPE • 100 kW / (J) • S AMERICA • 100 kW
	USSR RADIO MOSCOW, Via Mongolia	25 kW
11857v	**MONGOLIA** RADIO ULAN BATOR, Ulan Bator	DS-1 • 25 kW / Tu/F • DS-1 • 25 kW / W/Th/Sa/M • DS-1 • 25 kW
	USSR RADIO MOSCOW, Via Mongolia	25 kW
11860	**BULGARIA** RADIO SOFIA, Sofia	EUROPE • 250 kW / (D) • S AMERICA • 250 kW / Su • EUROPE • 250 kW
	CHINA (TAIWAN) VOICE OF FREE CHINA, T'ai-pei	SE ASIA • 50 kW / MIDEAST & N AFRICA • 100 kW
	DENMARK †DANMARKS RADIO, Via Norway	(D) • MIDEAST • 500 kW / (D) • EUROPE • 350 kW / (D) • AFRICA • 500 kW
	INDIA ALL INDIA RADIO, Aligarh	W AFRICA • 250 kW
	†ALL INDIA RADIO, Delhi	(D) • AUSTRALIA • 100 kW
	NORWAY †RADIO NORWAY INTL, Fredrikstad	(D) • EUROPE • 350 kW
	†RADIO NORWAY INTL, Kvitsøy	(D) • MIDEAST • 500 kW / (D) • AFRICA • 500 kW
	SEYCHELLES †FAR EAST BC ASS'N, North Pt, Mahé Is	E AFRICA • 100 kW / W-Su • E AFRICA & S AFRICA • 100 kW
	UNITED KINGDOM †BBC WORLD SERVICE, Via Ascension	W AFRICA • 250 kW / (J) • W AFRICA • 250 kW
(con'd)		

ENGLISH ▬▬   ARABIC ⬚⬚⬚   CHINESE ▫▫▫   FRENCH ▬▬   GERMAN ▬▬   RUSSIAN ═══   SPANISH ▬▬   OTHER ──

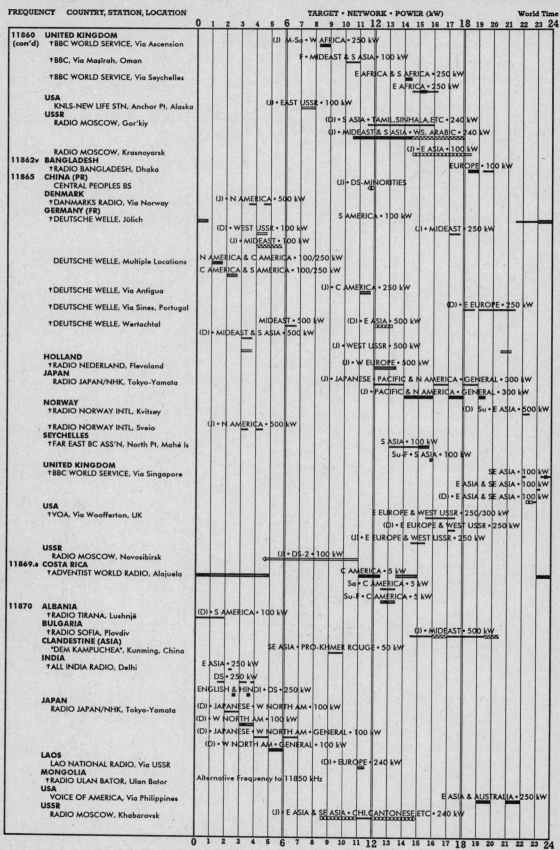

FREQUENCY   COUNTRY, STATION, LOCATION

TARGET • NETWORK • POWER (kW)   World Time

11860 (con'd)	**UNITED KINGDOM**
	†BBC WORLD SERVICE, Via Ascension
	†BBC, Via Maşīrah, Oman
	†BBC WORLD SERVICE, Via Seychelles
	USA
	KNLS-NEW LIFE STN, Anchor Pt, Alaska
	USSR
	RADIO MOSCOW, Gor'kiy
	RADIO MOSCOW, Krasnoyarsk
11862v	**BANGLADESH**
	†RADIO BANGLADESH, Dhaka
11865	**CHINA (PR)**
	CENTRAL PEOPLES BS
	DENMARK
	†DANMARKS RADIO, Via Norway
	GERMANY (FR)
	†DEUTSCHE WELLE, Jülich
	DEUTSCHE WELLE, Multiple Locations
	†DEUTSCHE WELLE, Via Antigua
	†DEUTSCHE WELLE, Via Sines, Portugal
	†DEUTSCHE WELLE, Wertachtal
	HOLLAND
	†RADIO NEDERLAND, Flevoland
	JAPAN
	RADIO JAPAN/NHK, Tokyo-Yamata
	NORWAY
	†RADIO NORWAY INTL, Kvitsøy
	†RADIO NORWAY INTL, Sveio
	SEYCHELLES
	†FAR EAST BC ASS'N, North Pt, Mahé Is
	UNITED KINGDOM
	†BBC WORLD SERVICE, Via Singapore
	USA
	†VOA, Via Woofferton, UK
	USSR
	RADIO MOSCOW, Novosibirsk
11869.8	**COSTA RICA**
	†ADVENTIST WORLD RADIO, Alajuela
11870	**ALBANIA**
	†RADIO TIRANA, Lushnjë
	BULGARIA
	†RADIO SOFIA, Plovdiv
	CLANDESTINE (ASIA)
	"DEM KAMPUCHEA", Kunming, China
	INDIA
	†ALL INDIA RADIO, Delhi
	JAPAN
	RADIO JAPAN/NHK, Tokyo-Yamata
	LAOS
	LAO NATIONAL RADIO, Via USSR
	MONGOLIA
	†RADIO ULAN BATOR, Ulan Bator
	USA
	VOICE OF AMERICA, Via Philippines
	USSR
	RADIO MOSCOW, Khabarovsk

Chart bar labels (left to right, by row):

- (J) • M-Sa • W AFRICA • 250 kW
- F • MIDEAST & S ASIA • 100 kW
- E AFRICA & S AFRICA • 250 kW
- E AFRICA • 250 kW
- (J) • EAST USSR • 100 kW
- (D) • S ASIA • TAMIL, SINHALA, ETC • 240 kW
- (J) • MIDEAST & S ASIA • WS, ARABIC • 240 kW
- (J) • E ASIA • 100 kW
- EUROPE • 100 kW
- (J) • DS-MINORITIES
- (J) • N AMERICA • 500 kW
- S AMERICA • 100 kW
- (D) • WEST USSR • 100 kW
- (J) • MIDEAST • 250 kW
- (J) • MIDEAST • 100 kW
- N AMERICA & C AMERICA • 100/250 kW
- C AMERICA & S AMERICA • 100/250 kW
- (J) • C AMERICA • 250 kW
- (D) • E EUROPE • 250 kW
- MIDEAST • 500 kW
- (D) • E ASIA • 500 kW
- (D) • MIDEAST & S ASIA • 500 kW
- (J) • WEST USSR • 500 kW
- (J) • W EUROPE • 500 kW
- (J) • JAPANESE • PACIFIC & N AMERICA • GENERAL • 300 kW
- (J) • PACIFIC & N AMERICA • GENERAL • 300 kW
- (D) • Su • E ASIA • 500 kW
- (J) • N AMERICA • 500 kW
- S ASIA • 100 kW
- Su-F • S ASIA • 100 kW
- SE ASIA • 100 kW
- E ASIA & SE ASIA • 100 kW
- (D) • E ASIA & SE ASIA • 100 kW
- E EUROPE & WEST USSR • 250/300 kW
- (D) • E EUROPE & WEST USSR • 250 kW
- (J) • E EUROPE & WEST USSR • 250 kW
- (J) • DS-2 • 100 kW
- C AMERICA • 5 kW
- Sa • C AMERICA • 5 kW
- Su-F • C AMERICA • 5 kW
- (D) • S AMERICA • 100 kW
- (J) • MIDEAST • 500 kW
- SE ASIA • PRO-KHMER ROUGE • 50 kW
- E ASIA • 250 kW
- DS • 250 kW
- ENGLISH & HINDI • DS • 250 kW
- (D) • JAPANESE • W NORTH AM • 100 kW
- (D) • W NORTH AM • 100 kW
- (D) • JAPANESE • W NORTH AM • GENERAL • 100 kW
- (D) • W NORTH AM • GENERAL • 100 kW
- (D) • EUROPE • 240 kW
- Alternative Frequency to 11850 kHz
- E ASIA & AUSTRALIA • 250 kW
- (J) • E ASIA & SE ASIA • CHI, CANTONESE, ETC • 240 kW

FREQUENCY   COUNTRY, STATION, LOCATION

TARGET • NETWORK • POWER (kW)

World Time

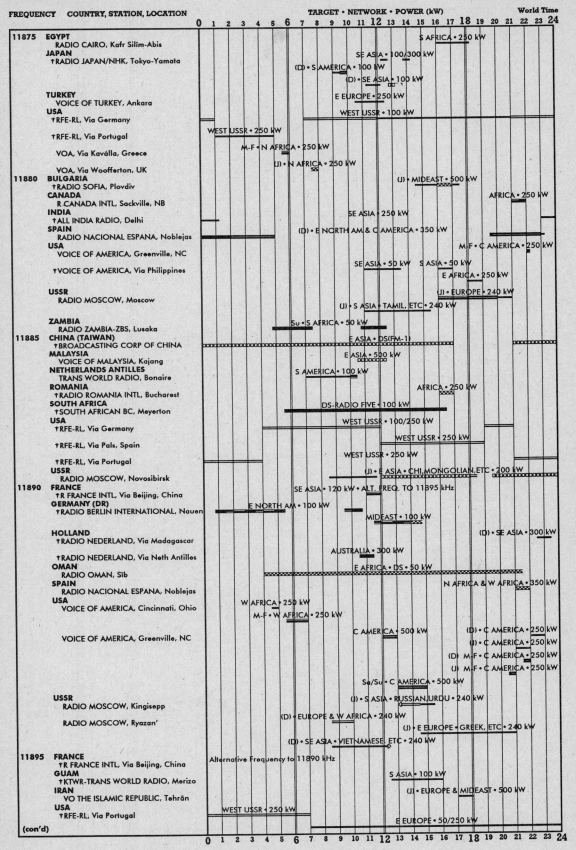

Frequency	Country, Station, Location	Target • Network • Power
11875	**EGYPT** RADIO CAIRO, Kafr Silim-Abis	S AFRICA • 250 kW
	JAPAN †RADIO JAPAN/NHK, Tokyo-Yamata	SE ASIA • 100/300 kW / (D) • S AMERICA • 100 kW / (D) • SE ASIA • 100 kW
	TURKEY VOICE OF TURKEY, Ankara	E EUROPE • 250 kW
	USA †RFE-RL, Via Germany	WEST USSR • 100 kW
	†RFE-RL, Via Portugal	WEST USSR • 250 kW
	VOA, Via Kaválla, Greece	M-F • N AFRICA • 250 kW
	VOA, Via Woofferton, UK	(J) • N AFRICA • 250 kW
11880	**BULGARIA** †RADIO SOFIA, Plovdiv	(J) • MIDEAST • 500 kW
	CANADA R CANADA INTL, Sackville, NB	AFRICA • 250 kW
	INDIA †ALL INDIA RADIO, Delhi	SE ASIA • 250 kW
	SPAIN RADIO NACIONAL ESPANA, Noblejas	(D) • E NORTH AM & C AMERICA • 350 kW
	USA VOICE OF AMERICA, Greenville, NC	M-F • C AMERICA • 250 kW
	†VOICE OF AMERICA, Via Philippines	SE ASIA • 50 kW / S ASIA • 50 kW / E AFRICA • 250 kW
	USSR RADIO MOSCOW, Moscow	(J) • EUROPE • 240 kW / (J) • S ASIA • TAMIL, ETC • 240 kW
	ZAMBIA RADIO ZAMBIA-ZBS, Lusaka	Su • S AFRICA • 50 kW
11885	**CHINA (TAIWAN)** †BROADCASTING CORP OF CHINA	E ASIA • DS(FM-1)
	MALAYSIA VOICE OF MALAYSIA, Kajang	E ASIA • 500 kW
	NETHERLANDS ANTILLES TRANS WORLD RADIO, Bonaire	S AMERICA • 100 kW
	ROMANIA †RADIO ROMANIA INTL, Bucharest	AFRICA • 250 kW
	SOUTH AFRICA †SOUTH AFRICAN BC, Meyerton	DS-RADIO FIVE • 100 kW
	USA †RFE-RL, Via Germany	WEST USSR • 100/250 kW
	†RFE-RL, Via Pals, Spain	WEST USSR • 250 kW
	†RFE-RL, Via Portugal	WEST USSR • 250 kW
	USSR RADIO MOSCOW, Novosibirsk	(J) • E ASIA • CHI, MONGOLIAN, ETC • 200 kW
11890	**FRANCE** †R FRANCE INTL, Via Beijing, China	SE ASIA • 120 kW • ALT. FREQ. TO 11895 kHz
	GERMANY (DR) †RADIO BERLIN INTERNATIONAL, Nauen	E NORTH AM • 100 kW / MIDEAST • 100 kW
	HOLLAND †RADIO NEDERLAND, Via Madagascar	(D) • SE ASIA • 300 kW
	†RADIO NEDERLAND, Via Neth Antilles	AUSTRALIA • 300 kW
	OMAN RADIO OMAN, Sīb	E AFRICA • DS • 50 kW
	SPAIN RADIO NACIONAL ESPANA, Noblejas	N AFRICA & W AFRICA • 350 kW
	USA VOICE OF AMERICA, Cincinnati, Ohio	W AFRICA • 250 kW / M-F • W AFRICA • 250 kW
	VOICE OF AMERICA, Greenville, NC	C AMERICA • 500 kW / (D) • C AMERICA • 250 kW / (J) • C AMERICA • 250 kW / (D) M-F • C AMERICA • 250 kW / (J) M-F • C AMERICA • 250 kW / Sa/Su • C AMERICA • 500 kW
	USSR RADIO MOSCOW, Kingisepp	(J) • S ASIA • RUSSIAN, URDU • 240 kW
	RADIO MOSCOW, Ryazan'	(D) • EUROPE & W AFRICA • 240 kW / (J) • E EUROPE • GREEK, ETC • 240 kW / (D) • SE ASIA • VIETNAMESE, ETC • 240 kW
11895	**FRANCE** †R FRANCE INTL, Via Beijing, China	Alternative Frequency to 11890 kHz
	GUAM †KTWR-TRANS WORLD RADIO, Merizo	S ASIA • 100 kW
	IRAN VO THE ISLAMIC REPUBLIC, Tehrān	(J) • EUROPE & MIDEAST • 500 kW
	USA †RFE-RL, Via Portugal	WEST USSR • 250 kW / E EUROPE • 50/250 kW

(con'd)

ENGLISH ▬ ARABIC ░ CHINESE ▭▭ FRENCH ▬ GERMAN ▬ RUSSIAN ═ SPANISH ▬ OTHER ▬

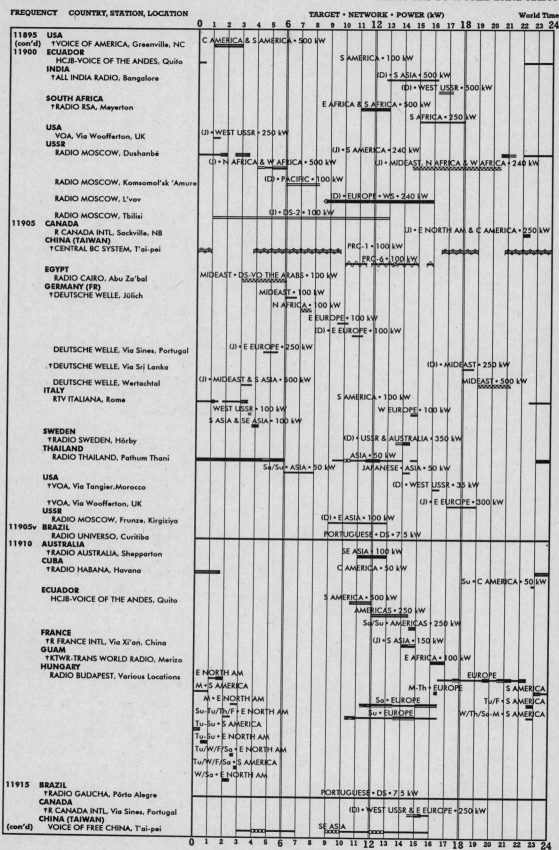

FREQUENCY   COUNTRY, STATION, LOCATION   TARGET • NETWORK • POWER (kW)   World Time

11895	USA
(con'd)	†VOICE OF AMERICA, Greenville, NC — C AMERICA & S AMERICA • 500 kW
11900	ECUADOR
	HCJB-VOICE OF THE ANDES, Quito — S AMERICA • 100 kW
	INDIA
	†ALL INDIA RADIO, Bangalore — (D) S ASIA • 500 kW
	(D) • WEST USSR • 500 kW
	SOUTH AFRICA
	†RADIO RSA, Meyerton — E AFRICA & S AFRICA • 500 kW
	S AFRICA • 250 kW
	USA
	VOA, Via Woofferton, UK — (J) • WEST USSR • 250 kW
	USSR
	RADIO MOSCOW, Dushanbé — (J) • S AMERICA • 240 kW
	(J) • N AFRICA & W AFRICA • 500 kW (J) • MIDEAST, N AFRICA & W AFRICA • 240 kW
	RADIO MOSCOW, Komsomol'sk 'Amure — (D) • PACIFIC • 100 kW
	RADIO MOSCOW, L'vov — (D) • EUROPE • WS • 240 kW
	RADIO MOSCOW, Tbilisi — (J) • DS-2 • 100 kW
11905	CANADA
	R CANADA INTL, Sackville, NB — (J) • E NORTH AM & C AMERICA • 250 kW
	CHINA (TAIWAN)
	†CENTRAL BC SYSTEM, T'ai-pei — PRC-1 • 100 kW
	PRC-6 • 100 kW
	EGYPT
	RADIO CAIRO, Abu Za'bal — MIDEAST • DS-VO THE ARABS • 100 kW
	GERMANY (FR)
	†DEUTSCHE WELLE, Jülich — MIDEAST • 100 kW
	N AFRICA • 100 kW
	E EUROPE • 100 kW
	(D) • E EUROPE • 100 kW
	DEUTSCHE WELLE, Via Sines, Portugal — (J) • E EUROPE • 250 kW
	†DEUTSCHE WELLE, Via Sri Lanka — (D) • MIDEAST • 250 kW
	DEUTSCHE WELLE, Wertachtal — (J) • MIDEAST & S ASIA • 500 kW MIDEAST • 500 kW
	ITALY
	RTV ITALIANA, Rome — S AMERICA • 100 kW
	WEST USSR • 100 kW W EUROPE • 100 kW
	S ASIA & SE ASIA • 100 kW
	SWEDEN
	†RADIO SWEDEN, Hörby — (D) • USSR & AUSTRALIA • 350 kW
	THAILAND
	RADIO THAILAND, Pathum Thani — ASIA • 50 kW
	Sa/Su • ASIA • 50 kW JAPANESE • ASIA • 50 kW
	USA
	†VOA, Via Tangier, Morocco — (D) • WEST USSR • 35 kW
	†VOA, Via Woofferton, UK — (J) • E EUROPE • 300 kW
	USSR
	RADIO MOSCOW, Frunze, Kirgiziya — (D) • E ASIA • 100 kW
11905v	BRAZIL
	RADIO UNIVERSO, Curitiba — PORTUGUESE • DS • 7.5 kW
11910	AUSTRALIA
	†RADIO AUSTRALIA, Shepparton — SE ASIA • 100 kW
	CUBA
	†RADIO HABANA, Havana — C AMERICA • 50 kW
	Su • C AMERICA • 50 kW
	ECUADOR
	HCJB-VOICE OF THE ANDES, Quito — S AMERICA • 500 kW
	AMERICAS • 250 kW
	Sa/Su • AMERICAS • 250 kW
	FRANCE
	†R FRANCE INTL, Via Xi'an, China — (J) • S ASIA • 150 kW
	GUAM
	†KTWR-TRANS WORLD RADIO, Merizo — E AFRICA • 100 kW
	HUNGARY
	RADIO BUDAPEST, Various Locations — E NORTH AM EUROPE
	M • S AMERICA M-Th • EUROPE S AMERICA
	M • E NORTH AM Sa • EUROPE Tu/F • S AMERICA
	Su-Tu/Th/F • E NORTH AM Su • EUROPE W/Th/Sa-M • S AMERICA
	Tu-Su • S AMERICA
	Tu-Su • E NORTH AM
	Tu/W/F/Sa • E NORTH AM
	Tu/W/F/Sa • S AMERICA
	W/Sa • E NORTH AM
11915	BRAZIL
	†RADIO GAUCHA, Pôrto Alegre — PORTUGUESE • DS • 7.5 kW
	CANADA
	†R CANADA INTL, Via Sines, Portugal — (D) • WEST USSR & E EUROPE • 250 kW
	CHINA (TAIWAN)
(con'd)	VOICE OF FREE CHINA, T'ai-pei — SE ASIA

FREQUENCY   COUNTRY, STATION, LOCATION

TARGET • NETWORK • POWER (kW)   World Time

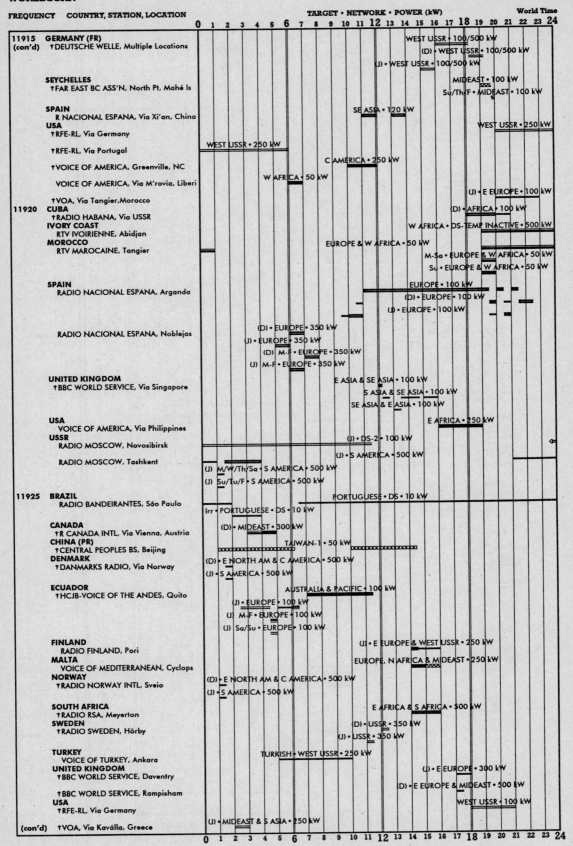

Frequency	Country, Station, Location	Target • Network • Power
11915 (con'd)	**GERMANY (FR)** †DEUTSCHE WELLE, Multiple Locations	WEST USSR • 100/500 kW; (D) • WEST USSR • 100/500 kW; (J) • WEST USSR • 100/500 kW
	SEYCHELLES †FAR EAST BC ASS'N, North Pt, Mahé Is	MIDEAST • 100 kW; Su/Th/F • MIDEAST • 100 kW
	SPAIN R NACIONAL ESPANA, Via Xi'an, China	SE ASIA • 120 kW
	USA †RFE-RL, Via Germany	WEST USSR • 250 kW
	†RFE-RL, Via Portugal	WEST USSR • 250 kW
	†VOICE OF AMERICA, Greenville, NC	C AMERICA • 250 kW
	VOICE OF AMERICA, Via M'rovia, Liberi	W AFRICA • 50 kW
	†VOA, Via Tangier, Morocco	(J) • E EUROPE • 100 kW
11920	**CUBA** †RADIO HABANA, Via USSR	(D) • AFRICA • 100 kW
	IVORY COAST RTV IVOIRIENNE, Abidjan	W AFRICA • DS-TEMP INACTIVE • 500 kW
	MOROCCO RTV MAROCAINE, Tangier	EUROPE & W AFRICA • 50 kW; M-Sa • EUROPE & W AFRICA • 50 kW; Su • EUROPE & W AFRICA • 50 kW
	SPAIN RADIO NACIONAL ESPANA, Arganda	EUROPE • 100 kW; (D) • EUROPE • 100 kW; (J) • EUROPE • 100 kW
	RADIO NACIONAL ESPANA, Noblejas	(D) • EUROPE • 350 kW; (J) • EUROPE • 350 kW; (D) • M-F • EUROPE • 350 kW; (J) • M-F • EUROPE • 350 kW
	UNITED KINGDOM †BBC WORLD SERVICE, Via Singapore	E ASIA & SE ASIA • 100 kW; S ASIA & SE ASIA • 100 kW; SE ASIA & E ASIA • 100 kW
	USA VOICE OF AMERICA, Via Philippines	E AFRICA • 250 kW
	USSR RADIO MOSCOW, Novosibirsk	(J) • DS-2 • 100 kW
	RADIO MOSCOW, Tashkent	(J) • S AMERICA • 500 kW; (J) • M/W/Th/Sa • S AMERICA • 500 kW; (J) • Su/Tu/F • S AMERICA • 500 kW
11925	**BRAZIL** RADIO BANDEIRANTES, São Paulo	PORTUGUESE • DS • 10 kW; Irr • PORTUGUESE • DS • 10 kW
	CANADA †R CANADA INTL, Via Vienna, Austria	(D) • MIDEAST • 300 kW
	CHINA (PR) †CENTRAL PEOPLES BS, Beijing	TAIWAN-1 • 50 kW
	DENMARK †DANMARKS RADIO, Via Norway	(D) • E NORTH AM & C AMERICA • 500 kW; (J) • S AMERICA • 500 kW
	ECUADOR †HCJB-VOICE OF THE ANDES, Quito	AUSTRALIA & PACIFIC • 100 kW; (J) • EUROPE • 100 kW; (J) • M-F • EUROPE • 100 kW; (J) • Sa/Su • EUROPE • 100 kW
	FINLAND RADIO FINLAND, Pori	(J) • E EUROPE & WEST USSR • 250 kW
	MALTA VOICE OF MEDITERRANEAN, Cyclops	EUROPE, N AFRICA & MIDEAST • 250 kW
	NORWAY †RADIO NORWAY INTL, Svoio	(D) • E NORTH AM & C AMERICA • 500 kW; (J) • S AMERICA • 500 kW
	SOUTH AFRICA †RADIO RSA, Meyerton	E AFRICA & S AFRICA • 500 kW
	SWEDEN †RADIO SWEDEN, Hörby	(D) • USSR • 350 kW; (J) • USSR • 350 kW
	TURKEY VOICE OF TURKEY, Ankara	TURKISH • WEST USSR • 250 kW
	UNITED KINGDOM †BBC WORLD SERVICE, Daventry	(J) • E EUROPE • 300 kW
	†BBC WORLD SERVICE, Rampisham	(D) • E EUROPE & MIDEAST • 500 kW
	USA †RFE-RL, Via Germany	WEST USSR • 100 kW
(con'd)	†VOA, Via Kaválla, Greece	(J) • MIDEAST & S ASIA • 250 kW

ENGLISH ▬▬ ARABIC ⧓⧓⧓ CHINESE ▭▭▭ FRENCH ▬▬ GERMAN ▬▬ RUSSIAN ══ SPANISH ▬▬ OTHER ▬▬

FREQUENCY   COUNTRY, STATION, LOCATION

TARGET • NETWORK • POWER (kW)   World Time

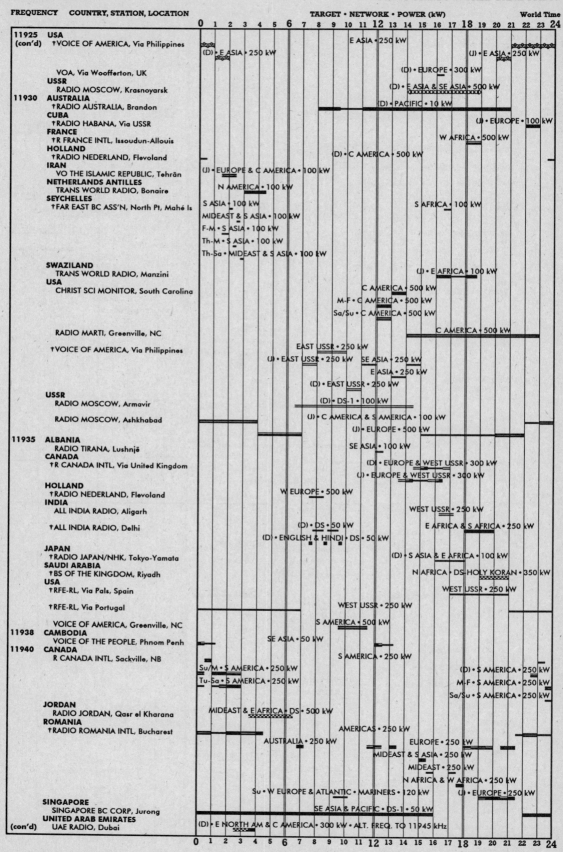

FREQUENCY	COUNTRY, STATION, LOCATION
11925 (con'd)	**USA**
	†VOICE OF AMERICA, Via Philippines
	VOA, Via Woofferton, UK
	USSR
	RADIO MOSCOW, Krasnoyarsk
11930	**AUSTRALIA**
	†RADIO AUSTRALIA, Brandon
	CUBA
	†RADIO HABANA, Via USSR
	FRANCE
	†R FRANCE INTL, Issoudun-Allouis
	HOLLAND
	†RADIO NEDERLAND, Flevoland
	IRAN
	VO THE ISLAMIC REPUBLIC, Tehrān
	NETHERLANDS ANTILLES
	TRANS WORLD RADIO, Bonaire
	SEYCHELLES
	†FAR EAST BC ASS'N, North Pt, Mahé Is
	SWAZILAND
	TRANS WORLD RADIO, Manzini
	USA
	CHRIST SCI MONITOR, South Carolina
	RADIO MARTI, Greenville, NC
	†VOICE OF AMERICA, Via Philippines
	USSR
	RADIO MOSCOW, Armavir
	RADIO MOSCOW, Ashkhabad
11935	**ALBANIA**
	RADIO TIRANA, Lushnjē
	CANADA
	†R CANADA INTL, Via United Kingdom
	HOLLAND
	†RADIO NEDERLAND, Flevoland
	INDIA
	ALL INDIA RADIO, Aligarh
	†ALL INDIA RADIO, Delhi
	JAPAN
	†RADIO JAPAN/NHK, Tokyo-Yamata
	SAUDI ARABIA
	†BS OF THE KINGDOM, Riyadh
	USA
	†RFE-RL, Via Pals, Spain
	†RFE-RL, Via Portugal
	VOICE OF AMERICA, Greenville, NC
11938	**CAMBODIA**
	VOICE OF THE PEOPLE, Phnom Penh
11940	**CANADA**
	R CANADA INTL, Sackville, NB
	JORDAN
	RADIO JORDAN, Qasr el Kharana
	ROMANIA
	†RADIO ROMANIA INTL, Bucharest
	SINGAPORE
	SINGAPORE BC CORP, Jurong
	UNITED ARAB EMIRATES
(con'd)	UAE RADIO, Dubai

Chart annotations:

- E ASIA • 250 kW
- (D) • E ASIA • 250 kW
- (J) • E ASIA • 250 kW
- (D) • EUROPE • 300 kW
- (D) • E ASIA & SE ASIA • 500 kW
- (D) • PACIFIC • 10 kW
- (J) • EUROPE • 100 kW
- W AFRICA • 500 kW
- (D) • C AMERICA • 500 kW
- (J) • EUROPE & C AMERICA • 100 kW
- N AMERICA • 100 kW
- S AFRICA • 100 kW
- S ASIA • 100 kW
- MIDEAST & S ASIA • 100 kW
- F-M • S ASIA • 100 kW
- Th-M • S ASIA • 100 kW
- Th-Sa • MIDEAST & S ASIA • 100 kW
- (J) • E AFRICA • 100 kW
- C AMERICA • 500 kW
- M-F • C AMERICA • 500 kW
- Sa/Su • C AMERICA • 500 kW
- C AMERICA • 500 kW
- EAST USSR • 250 kW
- (J) • EAST USSR • 250 kW
- SE ASIA • 250 kW
- E ASIA • 250 kW
- (D) • EAST USSR • 250 kW
- (D) • DS-1 • 100 kW
- (J) • C AMERICA & S AMERICA • 100 kW
- (J) • EUROPE • 500 kW
- SE ASIA • 100 kW
- (D) • EUROPE & WEST USSR • 300 kW
- (J) • EUROPE & WEST USSR • 300 kW
- W EUROPE • 500 kW
- WEST USSR • 250 kW
- (D) • DS • 50 kW
- E AFRICA & S AFRICA • 250 kW
- (D) • ENGLISH & HINDI • DS • 50 kW
- (D) • S ASIA & E AFRICA • 100 kW
- N AFRICA • DS-HOLY KORAN • 350 kW
- WEST USSR • 250 kW
- WEST USSR • 250 kW
- S AMERICA • 500 kW
- SE ASIA • 50 kW
- S AMERICA • 250 kW
- Su/M • S AMERICA • 250 kW
- (D) • S AMERICA • 250 kW
- Tu-Sa • S AMERICA • 250 kW
- M-F • S AMERICA • 250 kW
- Sa/Su • S AMERICA • 250 kW
- MIDEAST & E AFRICA • DS • 500 kW
- AMERICAS • 250 kW
- AUSTRALIA • 250 kW
- EUROPE • 250 kW
- MIDEAST & S ASIA • 250 kW
- MIDEAST • 250 kW
- N AFRICA & W AFRICA • 250 kW
- Su • W EUROPE & ATLANTIC • MARINERS • 120 kW
- (J) • EUROPE • 250 kW
- SE ASIA & PACIFIC • DS-1 • 50 kW
- (D) • E NORTH AM & C AMERICA • 300 kW • ALT. FREQ. TO 11945 kHz

FREQUENCY   COUNTRY, STATION, LOCATION

TARGET • NETWORK • POWER (kW)

World Time

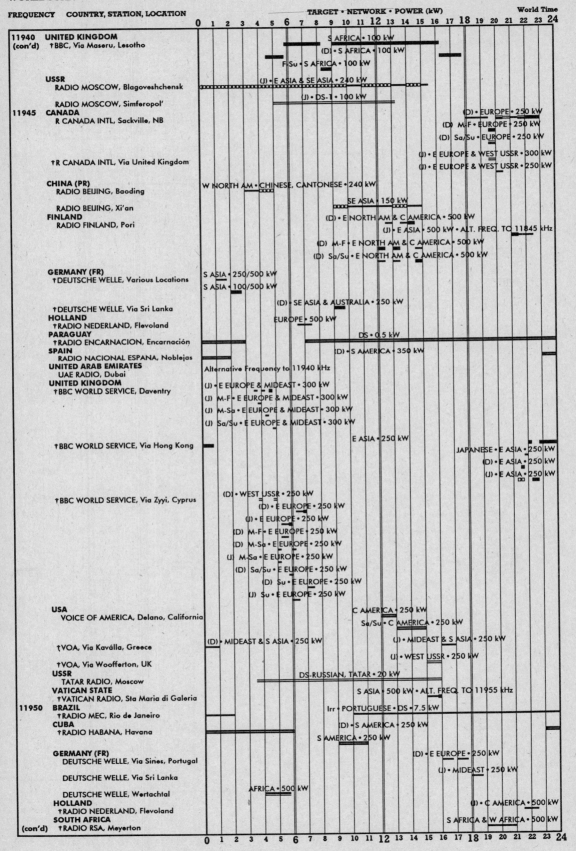

FREQUENCY	COUNTRY, STATION, LOCATION	TARGET • NETWORK • POWER (kW)
11940 (con'd)	**UNITED KINGDOM** †BBC, Via Maseru, Lesotho	S AFRICA • 100 kW (D) • S AFRICA • 100 kW F-Su • S AFRICA • 100 kW
	USSR RADIO MOSCOW, Blagoveshchensk	(J) • E ASIA & SE ASIA • 240 kW
	RADIO MOSCOW, Simferopol'	(J) • DS-1 • 100 kW
11945	**CANADA** R CANADA INTL, Sackville, NB	(D) • EUROPE • 250 kW (D) M-F • EUROPE • 250 kW (D) Sa/Su • EUROPE • 250 kW
	†R CANADA INTL, Via United Kingdom	(J) • E EUROPE & WEST USSR • 300 kW (J) • E EUROPE & WEST USSR • 250 kW
	CHINA (PR) RADIO BEIJING, Baoding	W NORTH AM • CHINESE, CANTONESE • 240 kW
	RADIO BEIJING, Xi'an	SE ASIA • 150 kW
	FINLAND RADIO FINLAND, Pori	(D) • E NORTH AM & C AMERICA • 500 kW (J) • E ASIA • 500 kW • ALT. FREQ. TO 11845 kHz (D) M-F • E NORTH AM & C AMERICA • 500 kW (D) Sa/Su • E NORTH AM & C AMERICA • 500 kW
	GERMANY (FR) †DEUTSCHE WELLE, Various Locations	S ASIA • 250/500 kW S ASIA • 100/500 kW
	†DEUTSCHE WELLE, Via Sri Lanka	(D) • SE ASIA & AUSTRALIA • 250 kW
	HOLLAND †RADIO NEDERLAND, Flevoland	EUROPE • 500 kW
	PARAGUAY †RADIO ENCARNACION, Encarnación	DS • 0.5 kW
	SPAIN RADIO NACIONAL ESPANA, Noblejas	(D) • S AMERICA • 350 kW
	UNITED ARAB EMIRATES UAE RADIO, Dubai	Alternative Frequency to 11940 kHz
	UNITED KINGDOM †BBC WORLD SERVICE, Daventry	(J) • E EUROPE & MIDEAST • 300 kW (J) M-F • E EUROPE & MIDEAST • 300 kW (J) M-Sa • E EUROPE & MIDEAST • 300 kW (J) Sa/Su • E EUROPE & MIDEAST • 300 kW
	†BBC WORLD SERVICE, Via Hong Kong	E ASIA • 250 kW JAPANESE • E ASIA • 250 kW (D) • E ASIA • 250 kW (J) • E ASIA • 250 kW
	†BBC WORLD SERVICE, Via Zyyi, Cyprus	(D) • WEST USSR • 250 kW (D) • E EUROPE • 250 kW (J) • E EUROPE • 250 kW (D) M-F • E EUROPE • 250 kW (D) M-Sa • E EUROPE • 250 kW (J) M-Sa • E EUROPE • 250 kW (D) Sa/Su • E EUROPE • 250 kW (D) Su • E EUROPE • 250 kW (J) Su • E EUROPE • 250 kW
	USA VOICE OF AMERICA, Delano, California	C AMERICA • 250 kW Sa/Su • C AMERICA • 250 kW
	†VOA, Via Kaválla, Greece	(D) • MIDEAST & S ASIA • 250 kW (J) • MIDEAST & S ASIA • 250 kW
	†VOA, Via Woofferton, UK	(J) • WEST USSR • 250 kW
	USSR TATAR RADIO, Moscow	DS-RUSSIAN, TATAR • 20 kW
	VATICAN STATE †VATICAN RADIO, Sta Maria di Galeria	S ASIA • 500 kW • ALT. FREQ. TO 11955 kHz
11950	**BRAZIL** †RADIO MEC, Rio de Janeiro	Irr • PORTUGUESE • DS • 7.5 kW
	CUBA †RADIO HABANA, Havana	(D) • S AMERICA • 250 kW S AMERICA • 250 kW
	GERMANY (FR) DEUTSCHE WELLE, Via Sines, Portugal	(D) • E EUROPE • 250 kW (J) • MIDEAST • 250 kW
	DEUTSCHE WELLE, Via Sri Lanka	
	DEUTSCHE WELLE, Wertachtal	AFRICA • 500 kW
	HOLLAND †RADIO NEDERLAND, Flevoland	(J) • C AMERICA • 500 kW
(con'd)	**SOUTH AFRICA** †RADIO RSA, Meyerton	S AFRICA & W AFRICA • 500 kW

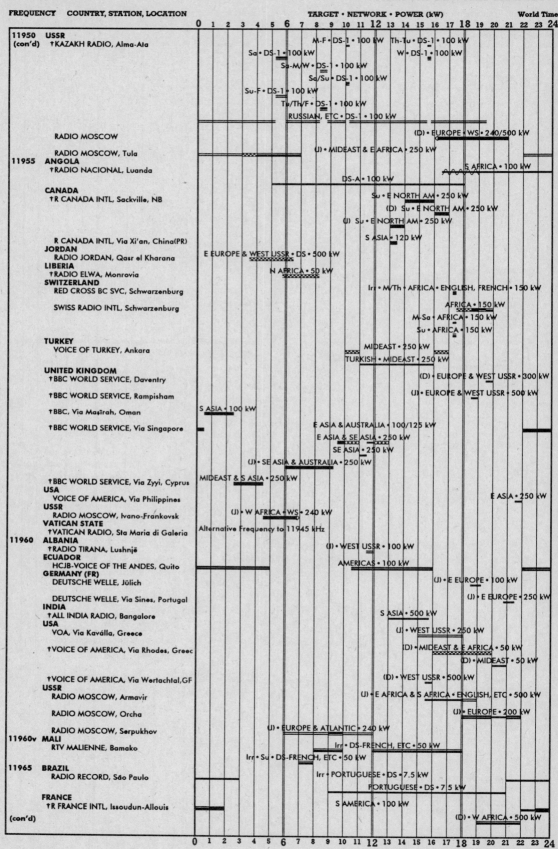

FREQUENCY   COUNTRY, STATION, LOCATION

TARGET • NETWORK • POWER (kW)   World Time

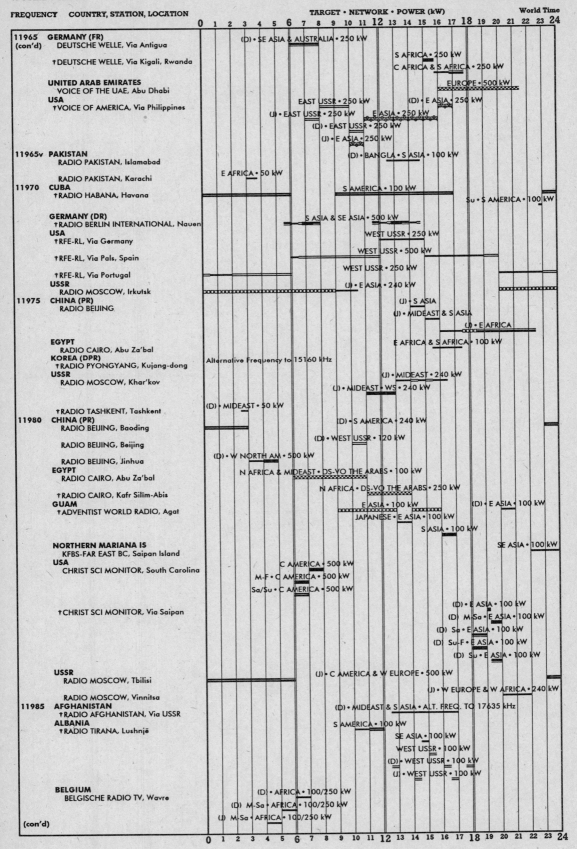

FREQUENCY	COUNTRY, STATION, LOCATION
11965 (con'd)	**GERMANY (FR)** DEUTSCHE WELLE, Via Antigua
	†DEUTSCHE WELLE, Via Kigali, Rwanda
	UNITED ARAB EMIRATES VOICE OF THE UAE, Abu Dhabi
	USA †VOICE OF AMERICA, Via Philippines
11965v	**PAKISTAN** RADIO PAKISTAN, Islamabad
	RADIO PAKISTAN, Karachi
11970	**CUBA** †RADIO HABANA, Havana
	GERMANY (DR) †RADIO BERLIN INTERNATIONAL, Nauen
	USA †RFE-RL, Via Germany
	†RFE-RL, Via Pals, Spain
	†RFE-RL, Via Portugal
	USSR RADIO MOSCOW, Irkutsk
11975	**CHINA (PR)** RADIO BEIJING
	EGYPT RADIO CAIRO, Abu Za'bal
	KOREA (DPR) †RADIO PYONGYANG, Kujang-dong
	USSR RADIO MOSCOW, Khar'kov
	†RADIO TASHKENT, Tashkent
11980	**CHINA (PR)** RADIO BEIJING, Baoding
	RADIO BEIJING, Beijing
	RADIO BEIJING, Jinhua
	EGYPT RADIO CAIRO, Abu Za'bal
	†RADIO CAIRO, Kafr Silim-Abis
	GUAM †ADVENTIST WORLD RADIO, Agat
	NORTHERN MARIANA IS KFBS-FAR EAST BC, Saipan Island
	USA CHRIST SCI MONITOR, South Carolina
	†CHRIST SCI MONITOR, Via Saipan
	USSR RADIO MOSCOW, Tbilisi
	RADIO MOSCOW, Vinnitsa
11985	**AFGHANISTAN** †RADIO AFGHANISTAN, Via USSR
	ALBANIA †RADIO TIRANA, Lushnjë
	BELGIUM BELGISCHE RADIO TV, Wavre
(con'd)	

Station program listings (TARGET • NETWORK • POWER):

- (D) • SE ASIA & AUSTRALIA • 250 kW
- S AFRICA • 250 kW
- C AFRICA & S AFRICA • 250 kW
- EUROPE • 500 kW
- EAST USSR • 250 kW
- (D) • E ASIA • 250 kW
- (J) • EAST USSR • 250 kW
- E ASIA • 250 kW
- (D) • EAST USSR • 250 kW
- (J) • E ASIA • 250 kW
- (D) • BANGLA • S ASIA • 100 kW
- E AFRICA • 50 kW
- S AMERICA • 100 kW
- Su • S AMERICA • 100 kW
- S ASIA & SE ASIA • 500 kW
- WEST USSR • 250 kW
- WEST USSR • 500 kW
- WEST USSR • 250 kW
- (J) • E ASIA • 240 kW
- (J) • S ASIA
- (J) • MIDEAST & S ASIA
- (J) • E AFRICA
- E AFRICA & S AFRICA • 100 kW
- Alternative Frequency to 15160 kHz
- (J) • MIDEAST • 240 kW
- (J) • MIDEAST • WS • 240 kW
- (D) • MIDEAST • 50 kW
- (D) • S AMERICA • 240 kW
- (D) • WEST USSR • 120 kW
- (D) • W NORTH AM • 500 kW
- N AFRICA & MIDEAST • DS-VO THE ARABS • 100 kW
- N AFRICA • DS-VO THE ARABS • 250 kW
- E ASIA • 100 kW
- (D) • E ASIA • 100 kW
- JAPANESE • E ASIA • 100 kW
- S ASIA • 100 kW
- SE ASIA • 100 kW
- C AMERICA • 500 kW
- M-F • C AMERICA • 500 kW
- Sa/Su • C AMERICA • 500 kW
- (D) • E ASIA • 100 kW
- (D) M-Sa • E ASIA • 100 kW
- (D) Sa • E ASIA • 100 kW
- (D) Su-F • E ASIA • 100 kW
- (D) Su • E ASIA • 100 kW
- (J) • C AMERICA & W EUROPE • 500 kW
- (J) • W EUROPE & W AFRICA • 240 kW
- (D) • MIDEAST & S ASIA • ALT. FREQ. TO 17635 kHz
- S AMERICA • 100 kW
- SE ASIA • 100 kW
- WEST USSR • 100 kW
- (D) • WEST USSR • 100 kW
- (J) • WEST USSR • 100 kW
- (D) • AFRICA • 100/250 kW
- (D) M-Sa • AFRICA • 100/250 kW
- (J) M-Sa • AFRICA • 100/250 kW

ENGLISH ▬   ARABIC ▨   CHINESE ▫▫▫   FRENCH ══   GERMAN ▬   RUSSIAN ═══   SPANISH ▬   OTHER ──

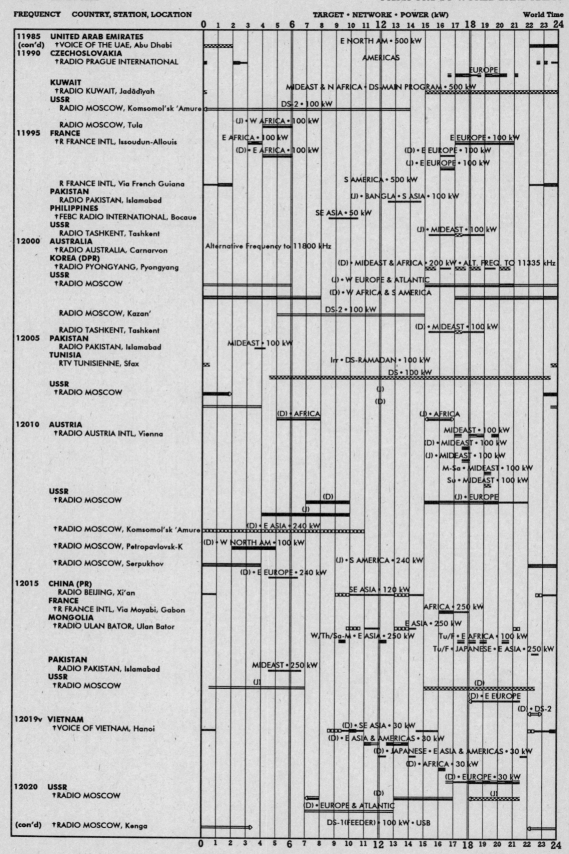

FREQUENCY   COUNTRY, STATION, LOCATION

TARGET • NETWORK • POWER (kW)

World Time

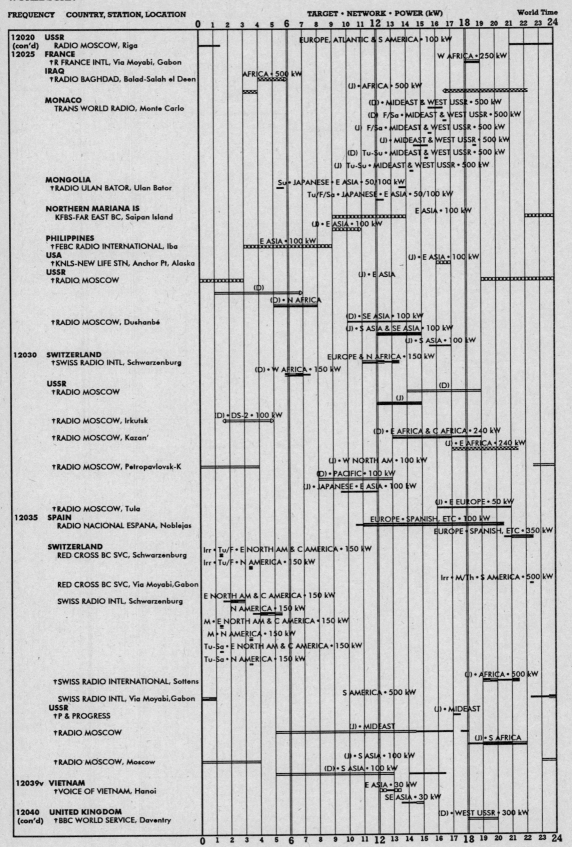

Frequency	Country, Station, Location	Target • Network • Power
12020 (con'd)	**USSR** RADIO MOSCOW, Riga	EUROPE, ATLANTIC & S AMERICA • 100 kW
12025	**FRANCE** †R FRANCE INTL, Via Moyabi, Gabon	W AFRICA • 250 kW
	IRAQ †RADIO BAGHDAD, Balad-Salah el Deen	AFRICA • 500 kW / (J) • AFRICA • 500 kW
	MONACO TRANS WORLD RADIO, Monte Carlo	(D) • MIDEAST & WEST USSR • 500 kW / (D) F/Sa • MIDEAST & WEST USSR • 500 kW / (J) F/Sa • MIDEAST & WEST USSR • 500 kW / (J) • MIDEAST & WEST USSR • 500 kW / (D) Tu-Su • MIDEAST & WEST USSR • 500 kW / (J) Tu-Su • MIDEAST & WEST USSR • 500 kW
	MONGOLIA †RADIO ULAN BATOR, Ulan Bator	Su • JAPANESE • E ASIA • 50/100 kW / Tu/F/Sa • JAPANESE • E ASIA • 50/100 kW
	NORTHERN MARIANA IS KFBS-FAR EAST BC, Saipan Island	E ASIA • 100 kW
	PHILIPPINES †FEBC RADIO INTERNATIONAL, Iba	(J) • E ASIA • 100 kW / E ASIA • 100 kW
	USA †KNLS-NEW LIFE STN, Anchor Pt, Alaska	(J) • E ASIA • 100 kW
	USSR †RADIO MOSCOW	(J) • E ASIA
		(D) / (D) • N AFRICA
	†RADIO MOSCOW, Dushanbé	(D) • SE ASIA • 100 kW / (J) • S ASIA & SE ASIA • 100 kW / (J) • S ASIA • 100 kW
12030	**SWITZERLAND** †SWISS RADIO INTL, Schwarzenburg	EUROPE & N AFRICA • 150 kW / (D) • W AFRICA • 150 kW
	USSR †RADIO MOSCOW	(D) / (J)
	†RADIO MOSCOW, Irkutsk	(D) • DS-2 • 100 kW
	†RADIO MOSCOW, Kazan'	(D) • E AFRICA & C AFRICA • 240 kW / (J) • E AFRICA • 240 kW
	†RADIO MOSCOW, Petropavlovsk-K	(J) • W NORTH AM • 100 kW / (D) • PACIFIC • 100 kW / (J) • JAPANESE • E ASIA • 100 kW
	†RADIO MOSCOW, Tula	(J) • E EUROPE • 50 kW
12035	**SPAIN** RADIO NACIONAL ESPANA, Noblejas	EUROPE • SPANISH, ETC • 100 kW / EUROPE • SPANISH, ETC • 350 kW
	SWITZERLAND RED CROSS BC SVC, Schwarzenburg	Irr • Tu/F • E NORTH AM & C AMERICA • 150 kW / Irr • Tu/F • N AMERICA • 150 kW
	RED CROSS BC SVC, Via Moyabi, Gabon	Irr • M/Th • S AMERICA • 500 kW
	SWISS RADIO INTL, Schwarzenburg	E NORTH AM & C AMERICA • 150 kW / N AMERICA • 150 kW / M • E NORTH AM & C AMERICA • 150 kW / M • N AMERICA • 150 kW / Tu-Sa • E NORTH AM & C AMERICA • 150 kW / Tu-Sa • N AMERICA • 150 kW
	†SWISS RADIO INTERNATIONAL, Sottens	(J) • AFRICA • 500 kW
	SWISS RADIO INTL, Via Moyabi, Gabon	S AMERICA • 500 kW
	USSR †P & PROGRESS	(J) • MIDEAST
	†RADIO MOSCOW	(J) • MIDEAST / (J) • S AFRICA
	†RADIO MOSCOW, Moscow	(J) • S ASIA • 100 kW / (D) • S ASIA • 100 kW
12039v	**VIETNAM** †VOICE OF VIETNAM, Hanoi	E ASIA • 30 kW / SE ASIA • 30 kW
12040 (con'd)	**UNITED KINGDOM** †BBC WORLD SERVICE, Daventry	(D) • WEST USSR • 300 kW

ENGLISH ▬▬   ARABIC ∼∼∼   CHINESE ▭▭▭   FRENCH ══   GERMAN ▬▬   RUSSIAN ▬▬   SPANISH ▬▬   OTHER ──

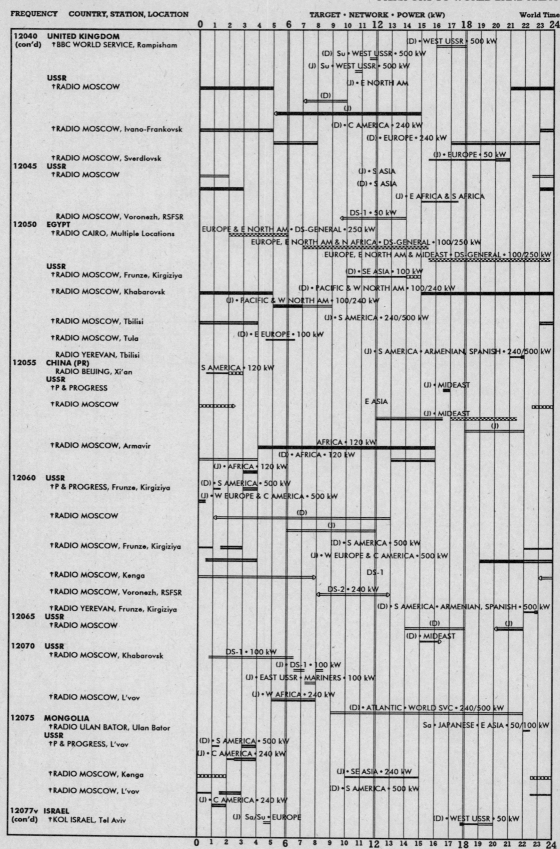

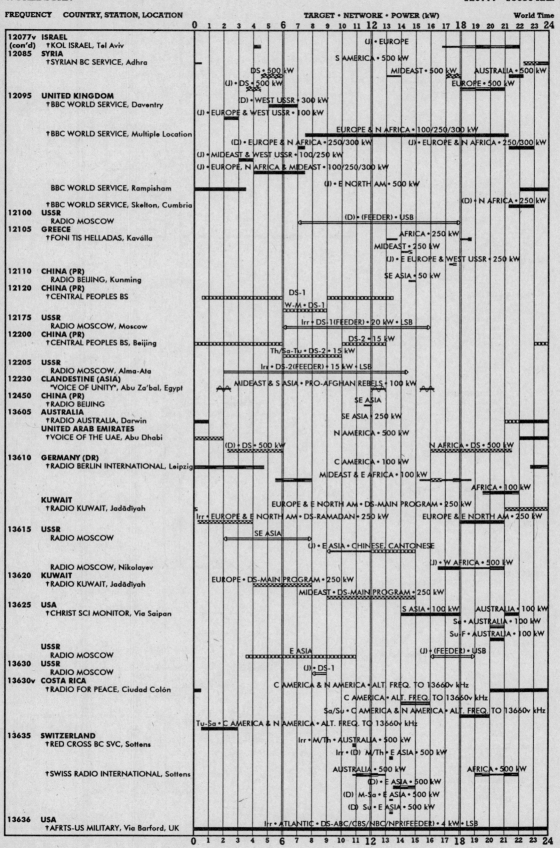

FREQUENCY   COUNTRY, STATION, LOCATION   TARGET • NETWORK • POWER (kW)   World Time

12077v	ISRAEL
(con'd)	↑KOL ISRAEL, Tel Aviv
12085	SYRIA
	↑SYRIAN BC SERVICE, Adhra
12095	UNITED KINGDOM
	↑BBC WORLD SERVICE, Daventry
	↑BBC WORLD SERVICE, Multiple Location
	BBC WORLD SERVICE, Rampisham
	↑BBC WORLD SERVICE, Skelton, Cumbria
12100	USSR
	RADIO MOSCOW
12105	GREECE
	↑FONI TIS HELLADAS, Kavála
12110	CHINA (PR)
	RADIO BEIJING, Kunming
12120	CHINA (PR)
	↑CENTRAL PEOPLES BS
12175	USSR
	RADIO MOSCOW, Moscow
12200	CHINA (PR)
	↑CENTRAL PEOPLES BS, Beijing
12205	USSR
	RADIO MOSCOW, Alma-Ata
12230	CLANDESTINE (ASIA)
	"VOICE OF UNITY", Abu Za'bal, Egypt
12450	CHINA (PR)
	↑RADIO BEIJING
13605	AUSTRALIA
	↑RADIO AUSTRALIA, Darwin
	UNITED ARAB EMIRATES
	↑VOICE OF THE UAE, Abu Dhabi
13610	GERMANY (DR)
	↑RADIO BERLIN INTERNATIONAL, Leipzig
	KUWAIT
	↑RADIO KUWAIT, Jadādīyah
13615	USSR
	RADIO MOSCOW
	RADIO MOSCOW, Nikolayev
13620	KUWAIT
	↑RADIO KUWAIT, Jadādīyah
13625	USA
	↑CHRIST SCI MONITOR, Via Saipan
	USSR
	RADIO MOSCOW
13630	USSR
	RADIO MOSCOW
13630v	COSTA RICA
	↑RADIO FOR PEACE, Ciudad Colón
13635	SWITZERLAND
	↑RED CROSS BC SVC, Sottens
	↑SWISS RADIO INTERNATIONAL, Sottens
13636	USA
	↑AFRTS-US MILITARY, Via Barford, UK

Schedule annotations (reading across the time grid):

- 12077v ISRAEL KOL ISRAEL, Tel Aviv: (J) • EUROPE
- 12085 SYRIA: S AMERICA • 500 kW; DS • 500 kW; (J) • DS • 500 kW; MIDEAST • 500 kW; AUSTRALIA • 500 kW; EUROPE • 500 kW
- 12095 UNITED KINGDOM BBC, Daventry: (D) • WEST USSR • 300 kW; (J) • EUROPE & WEST USSR • 100 kW
- BBC, Multiple Location: EUROPE & N AFRICA • 100/250/300 kW; (D) • EUROPE & N AFRICA • 250/300 kW; (J) • EUROPE & N AFRICA • 250/300 kW; (J) • MIDEAST & WEST USSR • 100/250 kW; (J) • EUROPE, N AFRICA & MIDEAST • 100/250/300 kW
- BBC, Rampisham: (J) • E NORTH AM • 500 kW
- BBC, Skelton, Cumbria: (D) • N AFRICA • 250 kW
- 12100 USSR RADIO MOSCOW: (D) • (FEEDER) • USB
- 12105 GREECE FONI TIS HELLADAS: AFRICA • 250 kW; MIDEAST • 250 kW; (J) • E EUROPE & WEST USSR • 250 kW
- 12110 CHINA (PR) RADIO BEIJING, Kunming: SE ASIA • 50 kW
- 12120 CHINA (PR) CENTRAL PEOPLES BS: DS-1; W-M • DS-1
- 12175 USSR RADIO MOSCOW, Moscow: Irr • DS-1 (FEEDER) • 20 kW • LSB
- 12200 CHINA (PR) CENTRAL PEOPLES BS, Beijing: DS-2 • 15 kW; Th/Sa-Tu • DS-2 • 15 kW
- 12205 USSR RADIO MOSCOW, Alma-Ata: Irr • DS-2 (FEEDER) • 15 kW • LSB
- 12230 CLANDESTINE (ASIA) "VOICE OF UNITY": MIDEAST & S ASIA • PRO-AFGHAN REBELS • 100 kW
- 12450 CHINA (PR) RADIO BEIJING: SE ASIA
- 13605 AUSTRALIA RADIO AUSTRALIA, Darwin: SE ASIA • 250 kW
- UNITED ARAB EMIRATES VOICE OF THE UAE: N AMERICA • 500 kW; (D) • DS • 500 kW; N AFRICA • DS • 500 kW
- 13610 GERMANY (DR) RADIO BERLIN INTERNATIONAL, Leipzig: C AMERICA • 100 kW; MIDEAST & E AFRICA • 100 kW; AFRICA • 100 kW
- KUWAIT RADIO KUWAIT, Jadādīyah: EUROPE & E NORTH AM • DS-MAIN PROGRAM • 250 kW; Irr • EUROPE & E NORTH AM • DS-RAMADAN • 250 kW; EUROPE & E NORTH AM • 250 kW
- 13615 USSR RADIO MOSCOW: SE ASIA; (J) • E ASIA • CHINESE, CANTONESE
- RADIO MOSCOW, Nikolayev: (J) • W AFRICA • 500 kW
- 13620 KUWAIT RADIO KUWAIT, Jadādīyah: EUROPE • DS-MAIN PROGRAM • 250 kW; MIDEAST • DS-MAIN PROGRAM • 250 kW
- 13625 USA CHRIST SCI MONITOR, Via Saipan: S ASIA • 100 kW; AUSTRALIA • 100 kW; Sa • AUSTRALIA • 100 kW; Su-F • AUSTRALIA • 100 kW
- USSR RADIO MOSCOW: E ASIA; (J) • (FEEDER) • USB
- 13630 USSR RADIO MOSCOW: (J) • DS-1
- 13630v COSTA RICA RADIO FOR PEACE: C AMERICA & N AMERICA • ALT. FREQ. TO 13660v kHz; C AMERICA • ALT. FREQ. TO 13660v kHz; Sa/Su • C AMERICA & N AMERICA • ALT. FREQ. TO 13660v kHz; Tu-Sa • C AMERICA & N AMERICA • ALT. FREQ. TO 13660v kHz
- 13635 SWITZERLAND RED CROSS BC SVC, Sottens: Irr • M/Th • AUSTRALIA • 500 kW; Irr • (D) M/Th • E ASIA • 500 kW
- SWISS RADIO INTERNATIONAL, Sottens: AUSTRALIA • 500 kW; AFRICA • 500 kW; (D) • E ASIA • 500 kW; (D) M-Sa • E ASIA • 500 kW; (D) Su • E ASIA • 500 kW
- 13636 USA AFRTS-US MILITARY, Via Barford, UK: Irr • ATLANTIC • DS-ABC/CBS/NBC/NPR (FEEDER) • 4 kW • LSB

ENGLISH ▬ ARABIC ▨ CHINESE ▢▢ FRENCH ▬ GERMAN ▬ RUSSIAN ═ SPANISH ▬ OTHER ▬

FREQUENCY   COUNTRY, STATION, LOCATION   TARGET • NETWORK • POWER (kW)   World Time

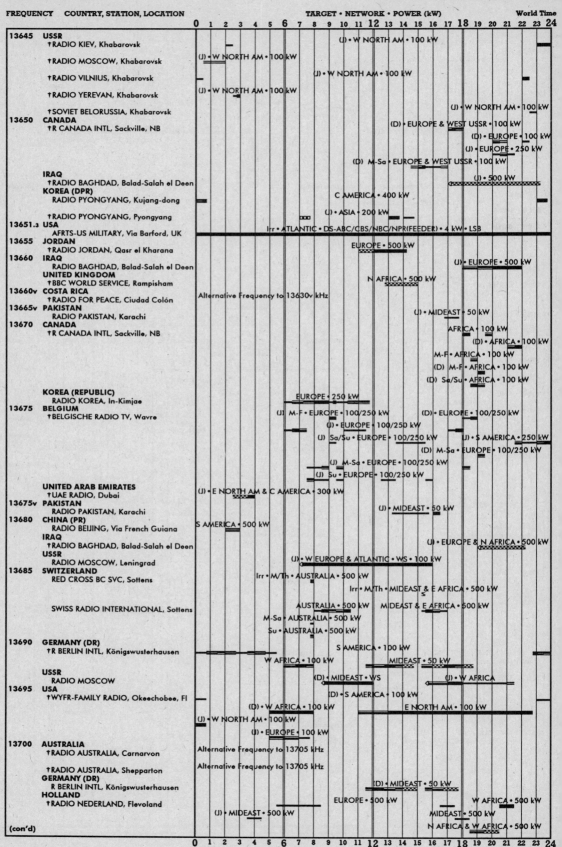

Frequency	Country, Station, Location	Target • Network • Power
13645	USSR	
	†RADIO KIEV, Khabarovsk	(J) • W NORTH AM • 100 kW
	†RADIO MOSCOW, Khabarovsk	(J) • W NORTH AM • 100 kW
	†RADIO VILNIUS, Khabarovsk	(J) • W NORTH AM • 100 kW
	†RADIO YEREVAN, Khabarovsk	(J) • W NORTH AM • 100 kW
	†SOVIET BELORUSSIA, Khabarovsk	(J) • W NORTH AM • 100 kW
13650	CANADA	
	†R CANADA INTL, Sackville, NB	(D) • EUROPE & WEST USSR • 100 kW
		(D) • EUROPE • 100 kW
		(J) • EUROPE • 250 kW
		(D) M-Sa • EUROPE & WEST USSR • 100 kW
	IRAQ	(J) • 500 kW
	†RADIO BAGHDAD, Balad-Salah el Deen	
	KOREA (DPR)	
	RADIO PYONGYANG, Kujang-dong	C AMERICA • 400 kW
	†RADIO PYONGYANG, Pyongyang	(J) • ASIA • 200 kW
13651.3	USA	
	AFRTS-US MILITARY, Via Barford, UK	Irr • ATLANTIC • DS-ABC/CBS/NBC/NPR(FEEDER) • 4 kW • LSB
13655	JORDAN	
	†RADIO JORDAN, Qasr el Kharana	EUROPE • 500 kW
13660	IRAQ	
	RADIO BAGHDAD, Balad-Salah el Deen	(J) • EUROPE • 500 kW
	UNITED KINGDOM	
	†BBC WORLD SERVICE, Rampisham	N AFRICA • 500 kW
13660v	COSTA RICA	
	†RADIO FOR PEACE, Ciudad Colón	Alternative Frequency to 13630v kHz
13665v	PAKISTAN	
	RADIO PAKISTAN, Karachi	(J) • MIDEAST • 50 kW
13670	CANADA	
	†R CANADA INTL, Sackville, NB	AFRICA • 100 kW
		(D) • AFRICA • 100 kW
		M-F • AFRICA • 100 kW
		(D) M-F • AFRICA • 100 kW
		(D) Sa/Su • AFRICA • 100 kW
	KOREA (REPUBLIC)	
	RADIO KOREA, In-Kimjae	EUROPE • 250 kW
13675	BELGIUM	
	†BELGISCHE RADIO TV, Wavre	(J) M-F • EUROPE • 100/250 kW
		(D) • EUROPE • 100/250 kW
		(J) • EUROPE • 100/250 kW
		(J) Sa/Su • EUROPE • 100/250 kW
		(J) • S AMERICA • 250 kW
		(D) M-Sa • EUROPE • 100/250 kW
		(J) M-Sa • EUROPE • 100/250 kW
		(J) Su • EUROPE • 100/250 kW
	UNITED ARAB EMIRATES	
	†UAE RADIO, Dubai	(J) • E NORTH AM & C AMERICA • 300 kW
13675v	PAKISTAN	
	RADIO PAKISTAN, Karachi	(J) • MIDEAST • 50 kW
13680	CHINA (PR)	
	RADIO BEIJING, Via French Guiana	S AMERICA • 500 kW
	IRAQ	
	†RADIO BAGHDAD, Balad-Salah el Deen	(J) • EUROPE & N AFRICA • 500 kW
	USSR	
	RADIO MOSCOW, Leningrad	(J) • W EUROPE & ATLANTIC • WS • 100 kW
13685	SWITZERLAND	
	RED CROSS BC SVC, Sottens	Irr • M/Th • AUSTRALIA • 500 kW
		Irr • M/Th • MIDEAST & E AFRICA • 500 kW
	SWISS RADIO INTERNATIONAL, Sottens	AUSTRALIA • 500 kW
		MIDEAST & E AFRICA • 500 kW
		M-Sa • AUSTRALIA • 500 kW
		Su • AUSTRALIA • 500 kW
13690	GERMANY (DR)	
	†R BERLIN INTL, Königswusterhausen	S AMERICA • 100 kW
		W AFRICA • 100 kW
		MIDEAST • 50 kW
	USSR	
	RADIO MOSCOW	(D) • MIDEAST • WS
		(J) • W AFRICA
13695	USA	
	†WYFR-FAMILY RADIO, Okeechobee, Fl	(D) • W AFRICA • 100 kW
		(D) • S AMERICA • 100 kW
		E NORTH AM • 100 kW
		(J) • W NORTH AM • 100 kW
		(J) • EUROPE • 100 kW
13700	AUSTRALIA	
	†RADIO AUSTRALIA, Carnarvon	Alternative Frequency to 13705 kHz
	†RADIO AUSTRALIA, Shepparton	Alternative Frequency to 13705 kHz
	GERMANY (DR)	
	R BERLIN INTL, Königswusterhausen	(D) • MIDEAST • 50 kW
	HOLLAND	
	†RADIO NEDERLAND, Flevoland	EUROPE • 500 kW
		W AFRICA • 500 kW
		(J) • MIDEAST • 500 kW
		MIDEAST • 500 kW
		N AFRICA & W AFRICA • 500 kW
(con'd)		

FREQUENCY   COUNTRY, STATION, LOCATION

TARGET • NETWORK • POWER (kW)

World Time

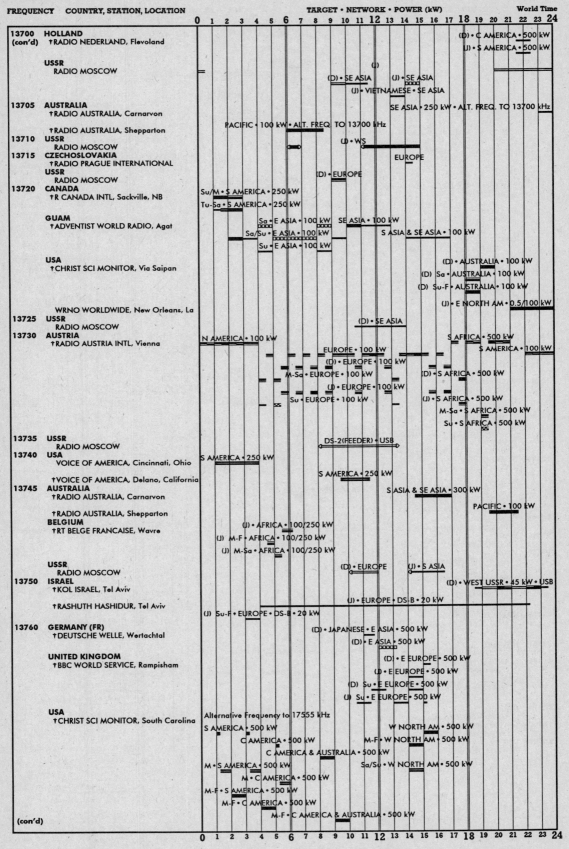

Frequency	Country, Station, Location
13700 (con'd)	**HOLLAND** †RADIO NEDERLAND, Flevoland
	USSR RADIO MOSCOW
13705	**AUSTRALIA** †RADIO AUSTRALIA, Carnarvon
	†RADIO AUSTRALIA, Shepparton
13710	**USSR** RADIO MOSCOW
13715	**CZECHOSLOVAKIA** †RADIO PRAGUE INTERNATIONAL
	USSR RADIO MOSCOW
13720	**CANADA** †R CANADA INTL, Sackville, NB
	GUAM †ADVENTIST WORLD RADIO, Agat
	USA †CHRIST SCI MONITOR, Via Saipan
	WRNO WORLDWIDE, New Orleans, La
13725	**USSR** RADIO MOSCOW
13730	**AUSTRIA** †RADIO AUSTRIA INTL, Vienna
13735	**USSR** RADIO MOSCOW
13740	**USA** VOICE OF AMERICA, Cincinnati, Ohio
	†VOICE OF AMERICA, Delano, California
13745	**AUSTRALIA** †RADIO AUSTRALIA, Carnarvon
	†RADIO AUSTRALIA, Shepparton
	BELGIUM †RT BELGE FRANCAISE, Wavre
	USSR RADIO MOSCOW
13750	**ISRAEL** †KOL ISRAEL, Tel Aviv
	†RASHUTH HASHIDUR, Tel Aviv
13760	**GERMANY (FR)** †DEUTSCHE WELLE, Wertachtal
	UNITED KINGDOM †BBC WORLD SERVICE, Rampisham
	USA †CHRIST SCI MONITOR, South Carolina
(con'd)	

Schedule annotations (by frequency):

- **13700 HOLLAND, RADIO NEDERLAND, Flevoland:** (D) • C AMERICA • 500 kW; (J) • S AMERICA • 500 kW
- **USSR, RADIO MOSCOW:** (D) • SE ASIA; (J) • SE ASIA; (J) • VIETNAMESE • SE ASIA
- **13705 AUSTRALIA, RADIO AUSTRALIA, Carnarvon:** SE ASIA • 250 kW • ALT. FREQ. TO 13700 kHz
- **RADIO AUSTRALIA, Shepparton:** PACIFIC • 100 kW • ALT. FREQ TO 13700 kHz
- **13710 USSR, RADIO MOSCOW:** (J) • WS
- **13715 CZECHOSLOVAKIA, RADIO PRAGUE INTERNATIONAL:** EUROPE
- **USSR, RADIO MOSCOW:** (D) • EUROPE
- **13720 CANADA, R CANADA INTL, Sackville, NB:** Su/M • S AMERICA • 250 kW; Tu-Sa • S AMERICA • 250 kW
- **GUAM, ADVENTIST WORLD RADIO, Agat:** Sa • E ASIA • 100 kW; SE ASIA • 100 kW; Sa/Su • E ASIA • 100 kW; S ASIA & SE ASIA • 100 kW; Su • E ASIA • 100 kW
- **USA, CHRIST SCI MONITOR, Via Saipan:** (D) • AUSTRALIA • 100 kW; (D) Sa • AUSTRALIA • 100 kW; (D) Su-F • AUSTRALIA • 100 kW
- **WRNO WORLDWIDE, New Orleans, La:** (J) • E NORTH AM • 0.5/100 kW
- **13725 USSR, RADIO MOSCOW:** (D) • SE ASIA
- **13730 AUSTRIA, RADIO AUSTRIA INTL, Vienna:** N AMERICA • 100 kW; EUROPE • 100 kW; S AFRICA • 500 kW; S AMERICA • 100 kW; (D) • EUROPE • 100 kW; M-Sa • EUROPE • 100 kW; (D) • S AFRICA • 500 kW; (J) • EUROPE • 100 kW; (J) • S AFRICA • 500 kW; Su • EUROPE • 100 kW; M-Sa • S AFRICA • 500 kW; Su • S AFRICA • 500 kW
- **13735 USSR, RADIO MOSCOW:** DS-2 (FEEDER) • USB
- **13740 USA, VOICE OF AMERICA, Cincinnati, Ohio:** S AMERICA • 250 kW
- **VOICE OF AMERICA, Delano, California:** S AMERICA • 250 kW
- **13745 AUSTRALIA, RADIO AUSTRALIA, Carnarvon:** S ASIA & SE ASIA • 300 kW
- **RADIO AUSTRALIA, Shepparton:** PACIFIC • 100 kW
- **BELGIUM, RT BELGE FRANCAISE, Wavre:** (J) • AFRICA • 100/250 kW; (J) M-F • AFRICA • 100/250 kW; (J) M-Sa • AFRICA • 100/250 kW
- **USSR, RADIO MOSCOW:** (D) • EUROPE; (J) • S ASIA
- **13750 ISRAEL, KOL ISRAEL, Tel Aviv:** (D) • WEST USSR • 45 kW • USB
- **RASHUTH HASHIDUR, Tel Aviv:** (J) • EUROPE • DS-B • 20 kW; (J) Su-F • EUROPE • DS-B • 20 kW
- **13760 GERMANY (FR), DEUTSCHE WELLE, Wertachtal:** (D) • JAPANESE • E ASIA • 500 kW; (D) • E ASIA • 500 kW
- **UNITED KINGDOM, BBC WORLD SERVICE, Rampisham:** (D) • E EUROPE • 500 kW; (J) • E EUROPE • 500 kW; (D) Su • E EUROPE • 500 kW; (J) Su • E EUROPE • 500 kW
- **USA, CHRIST SCI MONITOR, South Carolina:** Alternative Frequency to 17555 kHz; S AMERICA • 500 kW; W NORTH AM • 500 kW; C AMERICA • 500 kW; M-F • W NORTH AM • 500 kW; C AMERICA & AUSTRALIA • 500 kW; M • S AMERICA • 500 kW; Sa/Su • W NORTH AM • 500 kW; M • C AMERICA • 500 kW; M-F • S AMERICA • 500 kW; M-F • C AMERICA • 500 kW; M-F • C AMERICA & AUSTRALIA • 500 kW

FREQUENCY   COUNTRY, STATION, LOCATION   TARGET • NETWORK • POWER (kW)   World Time

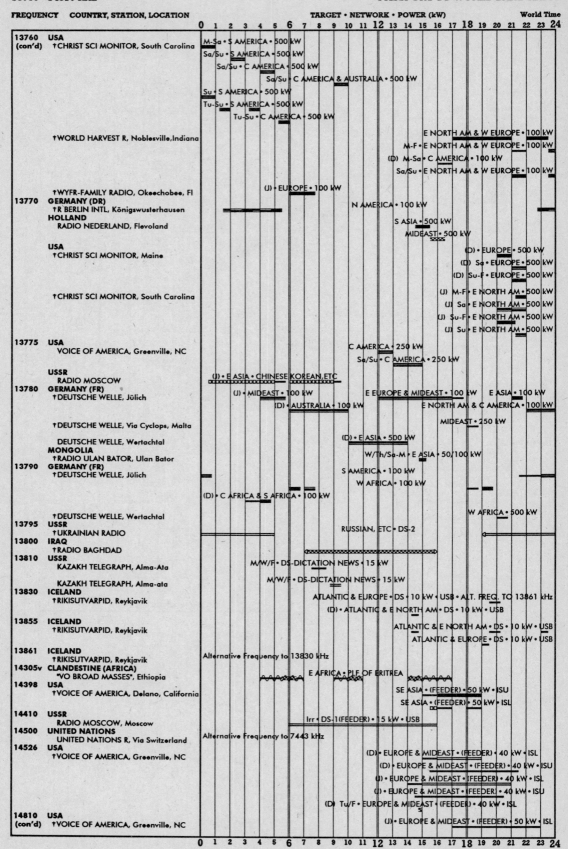

FREQUENCY	COUNTRY, STATION, LOCATION	TARGET • NETWORK • POWER (kW)
13760 (con'd)	USA †CHRIST SCI MONITOR, South Carolina	M-Sa • S AMERICA • 500 kW
		Sa/Su • S AMERICA • 500 kW
		Sa/Su • C AMERICA • 500 kW
		Sa/Su • C AMERICA & AUSTRALIA • 500 kW
		Su • S AMERICA • 500 kW
		Tu-Su • S AMERICA • 500 kW
		Tu-Su • C AMERICA • 500 kW
	†WORLD HARVEST R, Noblesville, Indiana	E NORTH AM & W EUROPE • 100 kW
		M-F • E NORTH AM & W EUROPE • 100 kW
		(D) M-Sa • C AMERICA • 100 kW
		Sa/Su • E NORTH AM & W EUROPE • 100 kW
	†WYFR-FAMILY RADIO, Okeechobee, Fl	(J) • EUROPE • 100 kW
13770	GERMANY (DR) †R BERLIN INTL, Königswusterhausen	N AMERICA • 100 kW
	HOLLAND RADIO NEDERLAND, Flevoland	S ASIA • 500 kW
		MIDEAST • 500 kW
	USA †CHRIST SCI MONITOR, Maine	(D) • EUROPE • 500 kW
		(D) Sa • EUROPE • 500 kW
		(D) Su-F • EUROPE • 500 kW
	†CHRIST SCI MONITOR, South Carolina	(J) M-F • E NORTH AM • 500 kW
		(J) Sa • E NORTH AM • 500 kW
		(J) Su-F • E NORTH AM • 500 kW
		(J) Su • E NORTH AM • 500 kW
13775	USA VOICE OF AMERICA, Greenville, NC	C AMERICA • 250 kW
		Sa/Su • C AMERICA • 250 kW
	USSR RADIO MOSCOW	(J) • E ASIA • CHINESE KOREAN, ETC
13780	GERMANY (FR) †DEUTSCHE WELLE, Jülich	(J) • MIDEAST • 100 kW E EUROPE & MIDEAST • 100 kW E ASIA • 100 kW
		(D) • AUSTRALIA • 100 kW E NORTH AM & C AMERICA • 100 kW
	†DEUTSCHE WELLE, Via Cyclops, Malta	MIDEAST • 250 kW
	DEUTSCHE WELLE, Wertachtal	(D) • E ASIA • 500 kW
	MONGOLIA †RADIO ULAN BATOR, Ulan Bator	W/Th/Sa-M • E ASIA • 50/100 kW
13790	GERMANY (FR) †DEUTSCHE WELLE, Jülich	S AMERICA • 100 kW
		W AFRICA • 100 kW
		(D) • C AFRICA & S AFRICA • 100 kW
	†DEUTSCHE WELLE, Wertachtal	W AFRICA • 500 kW
13795	USSR †UKRAINIAN RADIO	RUSSIAN, ETC • DS-2
13800	IRAQ †RADIO BAGHDAD	
13810	USSR KAZAKH TELEGRAPH, Alma-Ata	M/W/F • DS-DICTATION NEWS • 15 kW
	KAZAKH TELEGRAPH, Alma-ata	M/W/F • DS-DICTATION NEWS • 15 kW
13830	ICELAND †RIKISUTVARPID, Reykjavik	ATLANTIC & EUROPE • DS • 10 kW • USB • ALT. FREQ. TO 13861 kHz
		(D) • ATLANTIC & E NORTH AM • DS • 10 kW • USB
13855	ICELAND †RIKISUTVARPID, Reykjavik	ATLANTIC & E NORTH AM • DS • 10 kW • USB
		ATLANTIC & EUROPE • DS • 10 kW • USB
13861	ICELAND †RIKISUTVARPID, Reykjavik	Alternative Frequency to 13830 kHz
14305v	CLANDESTINE (AFRICA) "VO BROAD MASSES", Ethiopia	E AFRICA • PLF OF ERITREA
14398	USA †VOICE OF AMERICA, Delano, California	SE ASIA • (FEEDER) • 50 kW • ISU
		SE ASIA • (FEEDER) • 50 kW • ISL
14410	USSR RADIO MOSCOW, Moscow	Irr • DS-1(FEEDER) • 15 kW • USB
14500	UNITED NATIONS UNITED NATIONS R, Via Switzerland	Alternative Frequency to 7443 kHz
14526	USA †VOICE OF AMERICA, Greenville, NC	(D) • EUROPE & MIDEAST • (FEEDER) • 40 kW • ISL
		(D) • EUROPE & MIDEAST • (FEEDER) • 40 kW • ISU
		(J) • EUROPE & MIDEAST • (FEEDER) • 40 kW • ISL
		(J) • EUROPE & MIDEAST • (FEEDER) • 40 kW • ISU
		(D) Tu/F • EUROPE & MIDEAST • (FEEDER) • 40 kW • ISL
14810 (con'd)	USA †VOICE OF AMERICA, Greenville, NC	(J) • EUROPE & MIDEAST • (FEEDER) • 50 kW • ISL

SUMMER ONLY (J)   WINTER ONLY (D)   JAMMING / OR ∧   EARLIEST HEARD ◁   LATEST HEARD ▷   NEW OR CHANGED FOR 1991 †

FREQUENCY   COUNTRY, STATION, LOCATION

TARGET • NETWORK • POWER (kW)

World Time

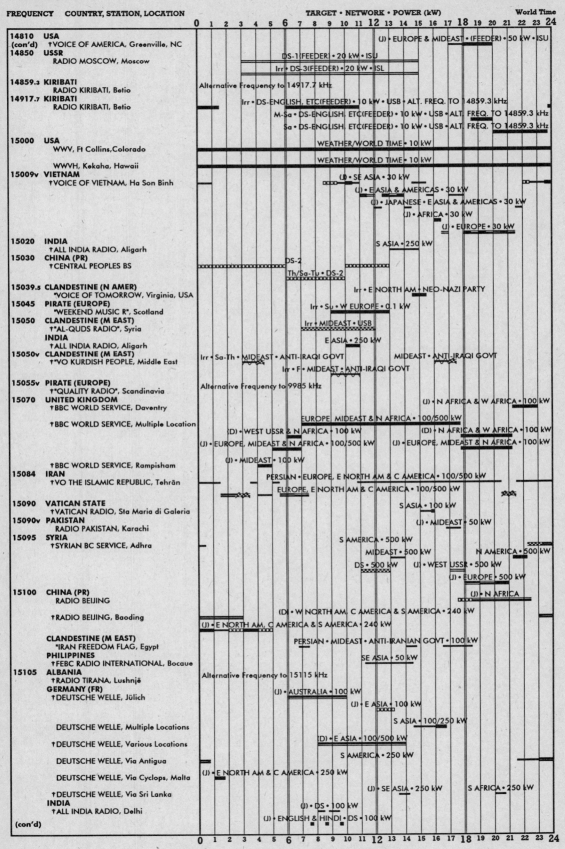

Frequency	Country, Station, Location	Details
14810 (con'd)	**USA** — †VOICE OF AMERICA, Greenville, NC	(J) • EUROPE & MIDEAST • (FEEDER) • 50 kW • ISU
14850	**USSR** — RADIO MOSCOW, Moscow	DS-1 (FEEDER) • 20 kW • ISU / Irr • DS-3 (FEEDER) • 20 kW • ISL
14859.3	**KIRIBATI** — RADIO KIRIBATI, Betio	Alternative Frequency to 14917.7 kHz
14917.7	**KIRIBATI** — RADIO KIRIBATI, Betio	Irr • DS-ENGLISH, ETC(FEEDER) • 10 kW • USB • ALT. FREQ. TO 14859.3 kHz / M-Sa • DS-ENGLISH, ETC(FEEDER) • 10 kW • USB • ALT. FREQ. TO 14859.3 kHz / Sa • DS-ENGLISH, ETC(FEEDER) • 10 kW • USB • ALT. FREQ. TO 14859.3 kHz
15000	**USA** — WWV, Ft Collins, Colorado	WEATHER/WORLD TIME • 10 kW
	WWVH, Kekaha, Hawaii	WEATHER/WORLD TIME • 10 kW
15009v	**VIETNAM** — †VOICE OF VIETNAM, Ha Son Binh	(J) • SE ASIA • 30 kW / (J) • E ASIA & AMERICAS • 30 kW / (J) • JAPANESE • E ASIA & AMERICAS • 30 kW / (J) • AFRICA • 30 kW / (J) • EUROPE • 30 kW
15020	**INDIA** — †ALL INDIA RADIO, Aligarh	S ASIA • 250 kW
15030	**CHINA (PR)** — †CENTRAL PEOPLES BS	DS-2 / Th/Sa-Tu • DS-2
15039.5	**CLANDESTINE (N AMER)** — "VOICE OF TOMORROW, Virginia, USA	Irr • E NORTH AM • NEO-NAZI PARTY
15045	**PIRATE (EUROPE)** — "WEEKEND MUSIC R", Scotland	Irr • Su • W EUROPE • 0.1 kW
15050	**CLANDESTINE (M EAST)** — †"AL-QUDS RADIO", Syria	Irr • MIDEAST • USB
	INDIA — †ALL INDIA RADIO, Aligarh	E ASIA • 250 kW
15050v	**CLANDESTINE (M EAST)** — †VO KURDISH PEOPLE, Middle East	Irr • Sa-Th • MIDEAST • ANTI-IRAQI GOVT / MIDEAST • ANTI-IRAQI GOVT / Irr • F • MIDEAST • ANTI-IRAQI GOVT
15055v	**PIRATE (EUROPE)** — †"QUALITY RADIO", Scandinavia	Alternative Frequency to 9985 kHz
15070	**UNITED KINGDOM** — †BBC WORLD SERVICE, Daventry	(J) • N AFRICA & W AFRICA • 100 kW
	†BBC WORLD SERVICE, Multiple Location	EUROPE, MIDEAST & N AFRICA • 100/500 kW / (D) • WEST USSR & N AFRICA • 100 kW / (D) • N AFRICA & W AFRICA • 100 kW / (J) • EUROPE, MIDEAST & N AFRICA • 100/500 kW / (J) • EUROPE, MIDEAST & N AFRICA • 100 kW
	†BBC WORLD SERVICE, Rampisham	(J) • MIDEAST • 100 kW
15084	**IRAN** — †VO THE ISLAMIC REPUBLIC, Tehrān	PERSIAN • EUROPE, E NORTH AM & C AMERICA • 100/500 kW / EUROPE, E NORTH AM & C AMERICA • 100/500 kW
15090	**VATICAN STATE** — †VATICAN RADIO, Sta Maria di Galeria	S ASIA • 100 kW
15090v	**PAKISTAN** — RADIO PAKISTAN, Karachi	(J) • MIDEAST • 50 kW
15095	**SYRIA** — †SYRIAN BC SERVICE, Adhra	S AMERICA • 500 kW / MIDEAST • 500 kW / N AMERICA • 500 kW / DS • 500 kW / (J) • WEST USSR • 500 kW / (J) • EUROPE • 500 kW
15100	**CHINA (PR)** — RADIO BEIJING	(J) • N AFRICA
	†RADIO BEIJING, Baoding	(D) • W NORTH AM, C AMERICA & S AMERICA • 240 kW / (J) • E NORTH AM, C AMERICA & S AMERICA • 240 kW
	CLANDESTINE (M EAST) — "IRAN FREEDOM FLAG, Egypt	PERSIAN • MIDEAST • ANTI-IRANIAN GOVT • 100 kW
	PHILIPPINES — †FEBC RADIO INTERNATIONAL, Bocaue	SE ASIA • 50 kW
15105	**ALBANIA** — †RADIO TIRANA, Lushnjë	Alternative Frequency to 15115 kHz
	GERMANY (FR) — †DEUTSCHE WELLE, Jülich	(J) • AUSTRALIA • 100 kW / (J) • E ASIA • 100 kW
	DEUTSCHE WELLE, Multiple Locations	S ASIA • 100/250 kW
	†DEUTSCHE WELLE, Various Locations	(D) • E ASIA • 100/500 kW
	DEUTSCHE WELLE, Via Antigua	S AMERICA • 250 kW
	DEUTSCHE WELLE, Via Cyclops, Malta	(J) • E NORTH AM & C AMERICA • 250 kW
	†DEUTSCHE WELLE, Via Sri Lanka	(J) • SE ASIA • 250 kW / S AFRICA • 250 kW
	INDIA — †ALL INDIA RADIO, Delhi	(J) • DS • 100 kW / (J) • ENGLISH & HINDI • DS • 100 kW
(con'd)		

ENGLISH ▰▰   ARABIC ⧓⧓   CHINESE ☐☐☐   FRENCH ▬▬   GERMAN ▭▭   RUSSIAN ══   SPANISH ▬▬   OTHER ──

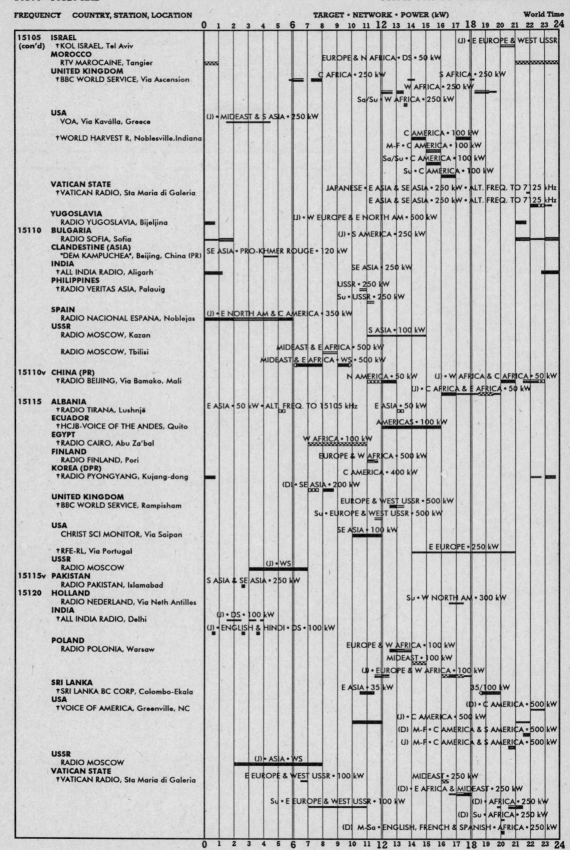

FREQUENCY   COUNTRY, STATION, LOCATION   TARGET • NETWORK • POWER (kW)   World Time

| | | | | | | | | | | | | | | | | | | | | | | | | |
| 0 | 1 | 2 | 3 | 4 | 5 | 6 | 7 | 8 | 9 | 10 | 11 | 12 | 13 | 14 | 15 | 16 | 17 | 18 | 19 | 20 | 21 | 22 | 23 | 24 |

15105
(con'd) ISRAEL
    †KOL ISRAEL, Tel Aviv — (J) • E EUROPE & WEST USSR
    MOROCCO
    RTV MAROCAINE, Tangier — EUROPE & N AFRICA • DS • 50 kW
    UNITED KINGDOM
    †BBC WORLD SERVICE, Via Ascension — C AFRICA • 250 kW / S AFRICA • 250 kW / W AFRICA • 250 kW / Sa/Su • W AFRICA • 250 kW
    USA
    VOA, Via Kaválla, Greece — (J) • MIDEAST & S ASIA • 250 kW
    †WORLD HARVEST R, Noblesville, Indiana — C AMERICA • 100 kW / M-F • C AMERICA • 100 kW / Sa/Su • C AMERICA • 100 kW / Su • C AMERICA • 100 kW
    VATICAN STATE
    †VATICAN RADIO, Sta Maria di Galeria — JAPANESE • E ASIA & SE ASIA • 250 kW • ALT. FREQ. TO 7125 kHz / E ASIA & SE ASIA • 250 kW • ALT. FREQ. TO 7125 kHz
    YUGOSLAVIA
    RADIO YUGOSLAVIA, Bijeljina — (J) • W EUROPE & E NORTH AM • 500 kW
15110 BULGARIA
    RADIO SOFIA, Sofia — (J) • S AMERICA • 250 kW
    CLANDESTINE (ASIA)
    "DEM KAMPUCHEA", Beijing, China (PR) — SE ASIA • PRO-KHMER ROUGE • 120 kW
    INDIA
    †ALL INDIA RADIO, Aligarh — SE ASIA • 250 kW
    PHILIPPINES
    †RADIO VERITAS ASIA, Palauig — USSR • 250 kW / Su • USSR • 250 kW
    SPAIN
    RADIO NACIONAL ESPANA, Noblejas — (J) • E NORTH AM & C AMERICA • 350 kW
    USSR
    RADIO MOSCOW, Kazan — S ASIA • 100 kW
    RADIO MOSCOW, Tbilisi — MIDEAST & E AFRICA • 500 kW / MIDEAST & E AFRICA • WS • 500 kW
15110v CHINA (PR)
    †RADIO BEIJING, Via Bamako, Mali — N AMERICA • 50 kW / (J) • W AFRICA & C AFRICA • 50 kW / (J) • C AFRICA & E AFRICA • 50 kW
15115 ALBANIA
    †RADIO TIRANA, Lushnjë — E ASIA • 50 kW • ALT. FREQ. TO 15105 kHz / E ASIA • 50 kW
    ECUADOR
    †HCJB-VOICE OF THE ANDES, Quito — AMERICAS • 100 kW
    EGYPT
    †RADIO CAIRO, Abu Za'bal — W AFRICA • 100 kW
    FINLAND
    RADIO FINLAND, Pori — EUROPE & W AFRICA • 500 kW
    KOREA (DPR)
    †RADIO PYONGYANG, Kujang-dong — C AMERICA • 400 kW / (D) • SE ASIA • 200 kW
    UNITED KINGDOM
    †BBC WORLD SERVICE, Rampisham — EUROPE & WEST USSR • 500 kW / Su • EUROPE & WEST USSR • 500 kW
    USA
    CHRIST SCI MONITOR, Via Saipan — SE ASIA • 100 kW
    †RFE-RL, Via Portugal — E EUROPE • 250 kW
    USSR
    RADIO MOSCOW — (J) • WS
15115v PAKISTAN
    RADIO PAKISTAN, Islamabad — S ASIA & SE ASIA • 250 kW
15120 HOLLAND
    RADIO NEDERLAND, Via Neth Antilles — Su • W NORTH AM • 300 kW
    INDIA
    †ALL INDIA RADIO, Delhi — (J) • DS • 100 kW / (J) • ENGLISH & HINDI • DS • 100 kW
    POLAND
    RADIO POLONIA, Warsaw — EUROPE & W AFRICA • 100 kW / MIDEAST • 100 kW / (J) • EUROPE & W AFRICA • 100 kW
    SRI LANKA
    †SRI LANKA BC CORP, Colombo-Ekala — E ASIA • 35 kW / 35/100 kW
    USA
    †VOICE OF AMERICA, Greenville, NC — (D) • C AMERICA • 500 kW / (J) • C AMERICA • 500 kW / (D) M-F • C AMERICA & S AMERICA • 500 kW / (J) M-F • C AMERICA & S AMERICA • 500 kW
    USSR
    RADIO MOSCOW — (J) • ASIA • WS
    VATICAN STATE
    †VATICAN RADIO, Sta Maria di Galeria — E EUROPE & WEST USSR • 100 kW / MIDEAST • 250 kW / (D) • E AFRICA & MIDEAST • 250 kW / Su • E EUROPE & WEST USSR • 100 kW / (D) • AFRICA • 250 kW / (D) Su • AFRICA • 250 kW / (D) M-Sa • ENGLISH, FRENCH & SPANISH • AFRICA • 250 kW

| | | | | | | | | | | | | | | | | | | | | | | | | |
| 0 | 1 | 2 | 3 | 4 | 5 | 6 | 7 | 8 | 9 | 10 | 11 | 12 | 13 | 14 | 15 | 16 | 17 | 18 | 19 | 20 | 21 | 22 | 23 | 24 |

SUMMER ONLY (J)   WINTER ONLY (D)   JAMMING / OR ∧   EARLIEST HEARD ◁   LATEST HEARD ▷   NEW OR CHANGED FOR 1991 †

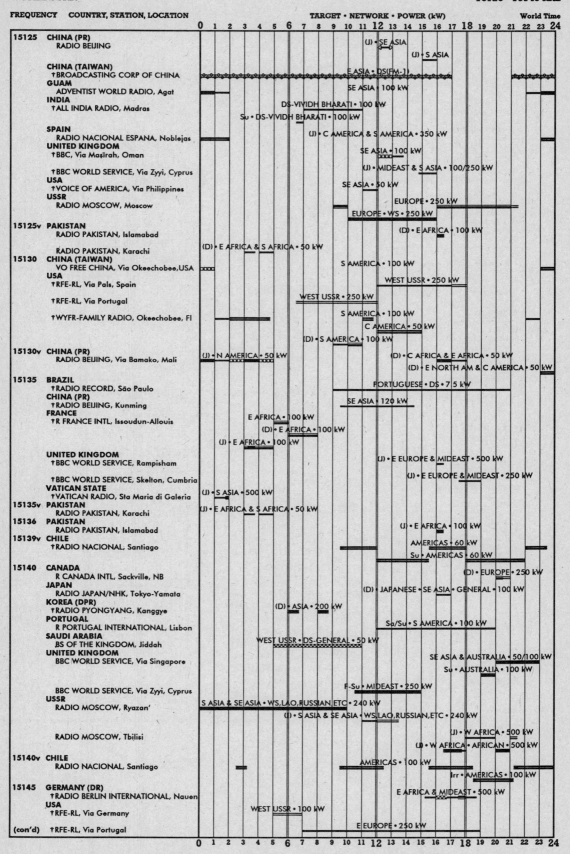

FREQUENCY   COUNTRY, STATION, LOCATION
TARGET • NETWORK • POWER (kW)
World Time

0 1 2 3 4 5 6 7 8 9 10 11 12 13 14 15 16 17 18 19 20 21 22 23 24

15125 CHINA (PR)
RADIO BEIJING — (J) • SE ASIA ; (J) • S ASIA

CHINA (TAIWAN)
↑BROADCASTING CORP OF CHINA — E ASIA • DS(FM-1)

GUAM
ADVENTIST WORLD RADIO, Agat — SE ASIA • 100 kW

INDIA
↑ALL INDIA RADIO, Madras — DS-VIVIDH BHARATI • 100 kW ; Su • DS-VIVIDH BHARATI • 100 kW

SPAIN
RADIO NACIONAL ESPANA, Noblejas — (J) • C AMERICA & S AMERICA • 350 kW

UNITED KINGDOM
↑BBC, Via Maṣīrah, Oman — SE ASIA • 100 kW

↑BBC WORLD SERVICE, Via Zyyi, Cyprus — (J) • MIDEAST & S ASIA • 100/250 kW

USA
↑VOICE OF AMERICA, Via Philippines — SE ASIA • 50 kW

USSR
RADIO MOSCOW, Moscow — EUROPE • 250 kW ; EUROPE • WS • 250 kW

15125v PAKISTAN
RADIO PAKISTAN, Islamabad — (D) • E AFRICA • 100 kW

RADIO PAKISTAN, Karachi — (D) • E AFRICA & S AFRICA • 50 kW

15130 CHINA (TAIWAN)
VO FREE CHINA, Via Okeechobee, USA — S AMERICA • 100 kW

USA
↑RFE-RL, Via Pals, Spain — WEST USSR • 250 kW

↑RFE-RL, Via Portugal — WEST USSR • 250 kW

↑WYFR-FAMILY RADIO, Okeechobee, Fl — S AMERICA • 100 kW ; C AMERICA • 50 kW ; (D) • S AMERICA • 100 kW

15130v CHINA (PR)
RADIO BEIJING, Via Bamako, Mali — (J) • N AMERICA • 50 kW ; (D) • C AFRICA & E AFRICA • 50 kW ; (D) • E NORTH AM & C AMERICA • 50 kW

15135 BRAZIL
↑RADIO RECORD, São Paulo — PORTUGUESE • DS • 7.5 kW

CHINA (PR)
↑RADIO BEIJING, Kunming — SE ASIA • 120 kW

FRANCE
↑R FRANCE INTL, Issoudun-Allouis — E AFRICA • 100 kW ; (D) • E AFRICA • 100 kW ; (J) • E AFRICA • 100 kW

UNITED KINGDOM
↑BBC WORLD SERVICE, Rampisham — (J) • E EUROPE & MIDEAST • 500 kW

↑BBC WORLD SERVICE, Skelton, Cumbria — (J) • E EUROPE & MIDEAST • 250 kW

VATICAN STATE
↑VATICAN RADIO, Sta Maria di Galeria — (J) • S ASIA • 500 kW

15135v PAKISTAN
RADIO PAKISTAN, Karachi — (J) • E AFRICA & S AFRICA • 50 kW

15136 PAKISTAN
RADIO PAKISTAN, Islamabad — (J) • E AFRICA • 100 kW

15139v CHILE
↑RADIO NACIONAL, Santiago — AMERICAS • 60 kW ; Su • AMERICAS • 60 kW

15140 CANADA
R CANADA INTL, Sackville, NB — (D) • EUROPE • 250 kW

JAPAN
RADIO JAPAN/NHK, Tokyo-Yamata — (D) JAPANESE • SE ASIA • GENERAL • 100 kW

KOREA (DPR)
↑RADIO PYONGYANG, Kanggye — (D) • ASIA • 200 kW

PORTUGAL
R PORTUGAL INTERNATIONAL, Lisbon — Sa/Su • S AMERICA • 100 kW

SAUDI ARABIA
BS OF THE KINGDOM, Jiddah — WEST USSR • DS-GENERAL • 50 kW

UNITED KINGDOM
BBC WORLD SERVICE, Via Singapore — SE ASIA & AUSTRALIA • 50/100 kW ; Su • AUSTRALIA • 100 kW

BBC WORLD SERVICE, Via Zyyi, Cyprus — F-Su • MIDEAST • 250 kW

USSR
RADIO MOSCOW, Ryazan' — S ASIA & SE ASIA • WS,LAO,RUSSIAN,ETC • 240 kW ; (J) • S ASIA & SE ASIA • WS,LAO,RUSSIAN,ETC • 240 kW

RADIO MOSCOW, Tbilisi — (J) • W AFRICA • 500 kW ; (J) • W AFRICA • AFRICAN • 500 kW

15140v CHILE
RADIO NACIONAL, Santiago — AMERICAS • 100 kW ; Irr • AMERICAS • 100 kW

15145 GERMANY (DR)
↑RADIO BERLIN INTERNATIONAL, Nauen — E AFRICA & MIDEAST • 500 kW

USA
↑RFE-RL, Via Germany — WEST USSR • 100 kW

(con'd) ↑RFE-RL, Via Portugal — E EUROPE • 250 kW

0 1 2 3 4 5 6 7 8 9 10 11 12 13 14 15 16 17 18 19 20 21 22 23 24

ENGLISH ▬   ARABIC ░░   CHINESE ☐☐☐   FRENCH ▬   GERMAN ▬   RUSSIAN ═══   SPANISH ▬   OTHER ▬

FREQUENCY   COUNTRY, STATION, LOCATION

TARGET • NETWORK • POWER (kW)   World Time
0 1 2 3 4 5 6 7 8 9 10 11 12 13 14 15 16 17 18 19 20 21 22 23 24

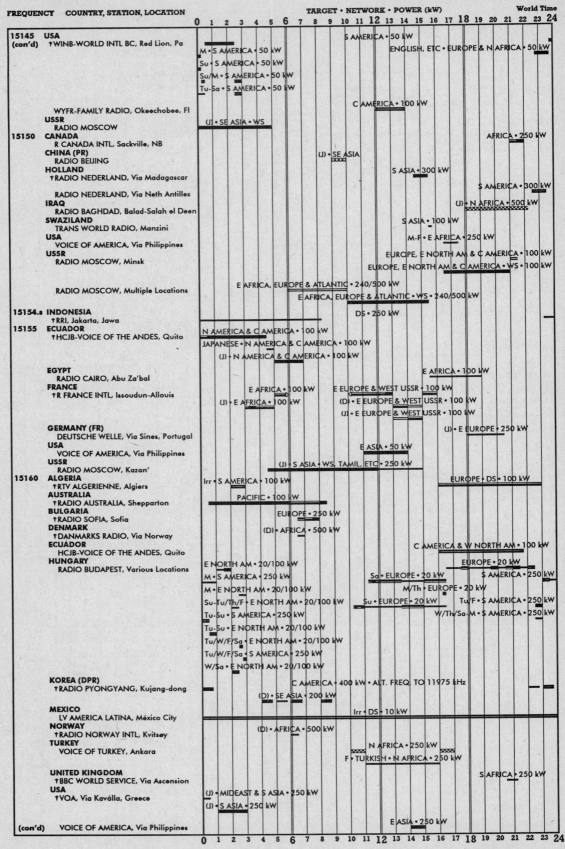

15145 **USA**
(con'd) †WINB-WORLD INTL BC, Red Lion, Pa
  S AMERICA • 50 kW
  M • S AMERICA • 50 kW
  Su • S AMERICA • 50 kW
  Su/M • S AMERICA • 50 kW
  Tu-Sa • S AMERICA • 50 kW
  ENGLISH, ETC • EUROPE & N AFRICA • 50 kW

  WYFR-FAMILY RADIO, Okeechobee, Fl
  C AMERICA • 100 kW
USSR
  RADIO MOSCOW
  (J) • SE ASIA • WS
15150 **CANADA**
  R CANADA INTL, Sackville, NB
  AFRICA • 250 kW
CHINA (PR)
  RADIO BEIJING
  (J) • SE ASIA
HOLLAND
  †RADIO NEDERLAND, Via Madagascar
  S ASIA • 300 kW

  RADIO NEDERLAND, Via Neth Antilles
  S AMERICA • 300 kW
IRAQ
  RADIO BAGHDAD, Balad-Salah el Deen
  (J) • N AFRICA • 500 kW
SWAZILAND
  TRANS WORLD RADIO, Manzini
  S ASIA • 100 kW
USA
  VOICE OF AMERICA, Via Philippines
  M-F • E AFRICA • 250 kW
USSR
  RADIO MOSCOW, Minsk
  EUROPE, E NORTH AM & C AMERICA • 100 kW
  EUROPE, E NORTH AM & C AMERICA • WS • 100 kW

  RADIO MOSCOW, Multiple Locations
  E AFRICA, EUROPE & ATLANTIC • 240/500 kW
  E AFRICA, EUROPE & ATLANTIC • WS • 240/500 kW

15154.8 **INDONESIA**
  †RRI, Jakarta, Jawa
  DS • 250 kW
15155 **ECUADOR**
  †HCJB-VOICE OF THE ANDES, Quito
  N AMERICA & C AMERICA • 100 kW
  JAPANESE • N AMERICA & C AMERICA • 100 kW
  (J) • N AMERICA & C AMERICA • 100 kW

EGYPT
  RADIO CAIRO, Abu Za'bal
  E AFRICA • 100 kW
FRANCE
  †R FRANCE INTL, Issoudun-Allouis
  E AFRICA • 100 kW   E EUROPE & WEST USSR • 100 kW
  (J) • E AFRICA • 100 kW   (D) • E EUROPE & WEST USSR • 100 kW
  (J) • E EUROPE & WEST USSR • 100 kW

GERMANY (FR)
  DEUTSCHE WELLE, Via Sines, Portugal
  (J) • E EUROPE • 250 kW
USA
  VOICE OF AMERICA, Via Philippines
  E ASIA • 50 kW
USSR
  RADIO MOSCOW, Kazan'
  (J) • S ASIA • WS, TAMIL, ETC • 250 kW
15160 **ALGERIA**
  †RTV ALGERIENNE, Algiers
  Irr • S AMERICA • 100 kW   EUROPE • DS • 100 kW
AUSTRALIA
  †RADIO AUSTRALIA, Shepparton
  PACIFIC • 100 kW
BULGARIA
  †RADIO SOFIA, Sofia
  EUROPE • 250 kW
DENMARK
  †DANMARKS RADIO, Via Norway
  (D) • AFRICA • 500 kW
ECUADOR
  HCJB-VOICE OF THE ANDES, Quito
  C AMERICA & W NORTH AM • 100 kW
HUNGARY
  RADIO BUDAPEST, Various Locations
  E NORTH AM • 20/100 kW   EUROPE • 20 kW
  M • S AMERICA • 250 kW   Sa • EUROPE • 20 kW   S AMERICA • 250 kW
  M • E NORTH AM • 20/100 kW   M/Th • EUROPE • 20 kW
  Su-Tu/Th/F • E NORTH AM • 20/100 kW   Su • EUROPE • 20 kW   Tu/F • S AMERICA • 250 kW
  Tu-Su • S AMERICA • 250 kW   W/Th/Sa-M • S AMERICA • 250 kW
  Tu-Su • E NORTH AM • 20/100 kW
  Tu/W/F/Sa • E NORTH AM • 20/100 kW
  Tu/W/F/Sa • S AMERICA • 250 kW
  W/Sa • E NORTH AM • 20/100 kW

KOREA (DPR)
  †RADIO PYONGYANG, Kujang-dong
  C AMERICA • 400 kW • ALT. FREQ TO 11975 kHz
  (D) • SE ASIA • 200 kW

MEXICO
  LV AMERICA LATINA, México City
  Irr • DS • 10 kW
NORWAY
  †RADIO NORWAY INTL, Kvitsøy
  (D) • AFRICA • 500 kW
TURKEY
  VOICE OF TURKEY, Ankara
  N AFRICA • 250 kW
  F • TURKISH • N AFRICA • 250 kW

UNITED KINGDOM
  †BBC WORLD SERVICE, Via Ascension
  S AFRICA • 250 kW
USA
  †VOA, Via Kaválla, Greece
  (J) • MIDEAST & S ASIA • 250 kW
  (J) • S ASIA • 250 kW

(con'd) VOICE OF AMERICA, Via Philippines
  E ASIA • 250 kW

0 1 2 3 4 5 6 7 8 9 10 11 12 13 14 15 16 17 18 19 20 21 22 23 24

SUMMER ONLY (J)   WINTER ONLY (D)   JAMMING / OR ∧   EARLIEST HEARD ◁   LATEST HEARD ▷   NEW OR CHANGED FOR 1991 †

FREQUENCY	COUNTRY, STATION, LOCATION	TARGET • NETWORK • POWER (kW)	World Time

0 1 2 3 4 5 6 7 8 9 10 11 12 13 14 15 16 17 18 19 20 21 22 23 24

15160
(con'd) USA
  †VOICE OF THE OAS, Cincinnati, Ohio
    C AMERICA & S AMERICA • 250 kW
    M-Sa • C AMERICA & S AMERICA • 250 kW
    Su • C AMERICA & S AMERICA • 250 kW

15165 CHINA (PR)
  RADIO BEIJING
    (J) • E AFRICA & S AFRICA
    (J) • C AFRICA & W AFRICA
    (J) • EUROPE
  RADIO BEIJING, Xi'an
    SE ASIA • 150 kW
    S ASIA • 150 kW
    AUSTRALIA • CHINESE, CANTONESE • 150 kW

  DENMARK
  †DANMARKS RADIO, Via Norway
    W NORTH AM & PACIFIC • 500 kW   (J) • EUROPE & AFRICA • 350 kW
    (J) • W AFRICA & S AMERICA • 500 kW   N AMERICA • 350 kW   (J) • S AMERICA • 500 kW
    (D) • EUROPE & W AFRICA • 500 kW   (J) • EUROPE & W AFRICA • 500 kW
    (J) • ATLANTIC • 350 kW
    (J) • E NORTH AM & C AMERICA • 500 kW

  INDIA
  ALL INDIA RADIO, Bombay
    E AFRICA • 100 kW
  †ALL INDIA RADIO, Delhi
    SE ASIA • 50 kW
    (D) • DS • 100 kW

  NORWAY
  †RADIO NORWAY INTL, Fredrikstad
    (J) • ATLANTIC • 350 kW
    M-F • N AMERICA • 350 kW
    (J) M-F • EUROPE & AFRICA • 350 kW
    Sa/Su • N AMERICA • 350 kW
    (J) Sa/Su • EUROPE & AFRICA • 350 kW
  †RADIO NORWAY INTL, Kvitsøy
    (J) M-F • W AFRICA & S AMERICA • 500 kW   (J) • EUROPE & W AFRICA • 500 kW
    (J) Sa/Su • W AFRICA & S AMERICA • 500 kW
  †RADIO NORWAY INTL, Sveio
    (D) • EUROPE & W AFRICA • 500 kW   (J) • S AMERICA • 500 kW
    M-F • W NORTH AM & PACIFIC • 500 kW   (J) M-F • E NORTH AM & C AMERICA • 500 kW
    Sa/Su • W NORTH AM & PACIFIC • 500 kW
    (J) Sa/Su • E NORTH AM & C AMERICA • 500 kW

  UNITED KINGDOM
  BBC WORLD SERVICE, Via Zyyi, Cyprus
    MIDEAST & E AFRICA • 100 kW
  USA
  VOICE OF AMERICA, Via Philippines
    E AFRICA • 250 kW

15170 AUSTRALIA
  †RADIO AUSTRALIA, Various Locations
    E ASIA & SE ASIA • 250/300 kW
    (D) • E ASIA & SE ASIA • 250/300 kW
    (J) • E ASIA & SE ASIA • 250/300 kW

  IRAQ
  †RADIO BAGHDAD, Balad-Salah el Deen
    (D) • W AFRICA • 500 kW
  SAUDI ARABIA
  BS OF THE KINGDOM, Jiddah
    C AFRICA • DS-HOLY KORAN • 50 kW
  USA
  †RFE-RL, Via Portugal
    E EUROPE • 50/250 kW
  †WYFR-FAMILY RADIO, Okeechobee, Fl
    (J) • C AMERICA • 100 kW
    (D) • S AMERICA • 100 kW
    C AMERICA • 50 kW

  USSR
  RADIO MOSCOW, Irkutsk
    SE ASIA • WS • 50 kW
    (J) • SE ASIA • WS • 50 kW

15170.8 SOCIETY ISLANDS
  RFO-TAHITI, Papeete
    PACIFIC • DS-FRENCH, TAHITIAN • 20 kW

15175 DENMARK
  †DANMARKS RADIO, Via Norway
    (J) • MIDEAST & S ASIA • 500 kW
  EGYPT
  RADIO CAIRO, Abu Za'bal
    MIDEAST • DS-GENERAL • 100 kW
  RADIO CAIRO, Kafr Silim-Abis
    MIDEAST & S ASIA • 250 kW
  HOLLAND
  †RADIO NEDERLAND, Via Madagascar
    (D) • SE ASIA • 300 kW
  INDIA
  ALL INDIA RADIO, Aligarh
    SE ASIA • 250 kW
  NORWAY
  †RADIO NORWAY INTL, Kvitsøy
    (J) • MIDEAST & S ASIA • 500 kW
  SEYCHELLES
  †FAR EAST BC ASS'N, North Pt, Mahé Is
    Alternative Frequency to 15205 kHz
  USSR
  RADIO MOSCOW, Armavir
    (J) • W EUROPE • 500 kW
    (J) • EUROPE, ATLANTIC & E NORTH AM • MARINERS • 500 kW
    (J) • W EUROPE • WS • 500 kW

  YUGOSLAVIA
  RADIO YUGOSLAVIA, Bijeljina
    (J) • WEST USSR • 500 kW
15180 FRANCE
(con'd) †R FRANCE INTL, Issoudun-Allouis
    E EUROPE & WEST USSR • 500 kW

0 1 2 3 4 5 6 7 8 9 10 11 12 13 14 15 16 17 18 19 20 21 22 23 24

ENGLISH ▬ ARABIC ≋ CHINESE ▭ FRENCH ═ GERMAN ▬ RUSSIAN ═ SPANISH ▬ OTHER ▬

FREQUENCY   COUNTRY, STATION, LOCATION   TARGET • NETWORK • POWER (kW)   World Time

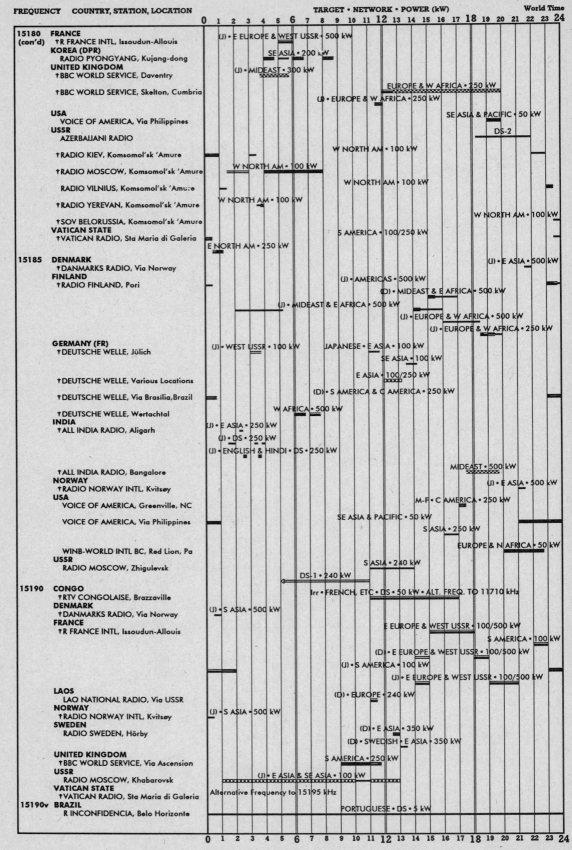

15180
(con'd)   **FRANCE**
        †R FRANCE INTL, Issoudun-Allouis   (J) • E EUROPE & WEST USSR • 500 kW
     KOREA (DPR)
        RADIO PYONGYANG, Kujang-dong   SE ASIA • 200 kW
     UNITED KINGDOM
        †BBC WORLD SERVICE, Daventry   (J) • MIDEAST • 300 kW

        †BBC WORLD SERVICE, Skelton, Cumbria   EUROPE & W AFRICA • 250 kW
                                     (J) • EUROPE & W AFRICA • 250 kW

     USA
        VOICE OF AMERICA, Via Philippines   SE ASIA & PACIFIC • 50 kW
     USSR
        AZERBAIJANI RADIO   DS-2

        †RADIO KIEV, Komsomol'sk 'Amure   W NORTH AM • 100 kW

        †RADIO MOSCOW, Komsomol'sk 'Amure   W NORTH AM • 100 kW

        RADIO VILNIUS, Komsomol'sk 'Amure   W NORTH AM • 100 kW

        †RADIO YEREVAN, Komsomol'sk 'Amure   W NORTH AM • 100 kW

        †SOV BELORUSSIA, Komsomol'sk 'Amure   W NORTH AM • 100 kW
     VATICAN STATE
        †VATICAN RADIO, Sta Maria di Galeria   S AMERICA • 100/250 kW
                    E NORTH AM • 250 kW

15185   **DENMARK**
        †DANMARKS RADIO, Via Norway   (J) • E ASIA • 500 kW
     FINLAND
        †RADIO FINLAND, Pori   (J) • AMERICAS • 500 kW
                      (D) • MIDEAST & E AFRICA • 500 kW
                      (J) • MIDEAST & E AFRICA • 500 kW
                      (J) • EUROPE & W AFRICA • 500 kW
                      (J) • EUROPE & W AFRICA • 250 kW

     GERMANY (FR)
        †DEUTSCHE WELLE, Jülich   (J) • WEST USSR • 100 kW   JAPANESE • E ASIA • 100 kW
                      SE ASIA • 100 kW

        †DEUTSCHE WELLE, Various Locations   E ASIA • 100/250 kW

        †DEUTSCHE WELLE, Via Brasilia, Brazil   (D) • S AMERICA & C AMERICA • 250 kW

        †DEUTSCHE WELLE, Wertachtal   W AFRICA • 500 kW
     INDIA
        †ALL INDIA RADIO, Aligarh   (J) • E ASIA • 250 kW
                      (J) • DS • 250 kW
                      (J) • ENGLISH & HINDI • DS • 250 kW

        †ALL INDIA RADIO, Bangalore   MIDEAST • 500 kW
     NORWAY
        †RADIO NORWAY INTL, Kvitsøy   (J) • E ASIA • 500 kW
     USA
        VOICE OF AMERICA, Greenville, NC   M-F • C AMERICA • 250 kW

        VOICE OF AMERICA, Via Philippines   SE ASIA & PACIFIC • 50 kW
                      S ASIA • 250 kW

        WINB-WORLD INTL BC, Red Lion, Pa   EUROPE & N AFRICA • 50 kW
     USSR
        RADIO MOSCOW, Zhigulevsk   S ASIA • 240 kW
                      DS-1 • 240 kW

15190   **CONGO**
        †RTV CONGOLAISE, Brazzaville   Irr • FRENCH, ETC • DS • 50 kW • ALT. FREQ. TO 11710 kHz
     DENMARK
        †DANMARKS RADIO, Via Norway   (J) • S ASIA • 500 kW
     FRANCE
        †R FRANCE INTL, Issoudun-Allouis   E EUROPE & WEST USSR • 100/500 kW
                      S AMERICA • 100 kW
                      (D) • E EUROPE & WEST USSR • 100/500 kW
                      (J) • S AMERICA • 100 kW
                      (J) • E EUROPE & WEST USSR • 100/500 kW

     LAOS
        LAO NATIONAL RADIO, Via USSR   (D) • EUROPE • 240 kW
     NORWAY
        †RADIO NORWAY INTL, Kvitsøy   (J) • S ASIA • 500 kW
     SWEDEN
        RADIO SWEDEN, Hörby   (D) • E ASIA • 350 kW
                      (D) • SWEDISH • E ASIA • 350 kW

     UNITED KINGDOM
        †BBC WORLD SERVICE, Via Ascension   S AMERICA • 250 kW
     USSR
        RADIO MOSCOW, Khabarovsk   (J) • E ASIA & SE ASIA • 100 kW
     VATICAN STATE
        †VATICAN RADIO, Sta Maria di Galeria   Alternative Frequency to 15195 kHz
15190v   **BRAZIL**
        R INCONFIDENCIA, Belo Horizonte   PORTUGUESE • DS • 5 kW

FREQUENCY	COUNTRY, STATION, LOCATION	TARGET • NETWORK • POWER (kW) — World Time

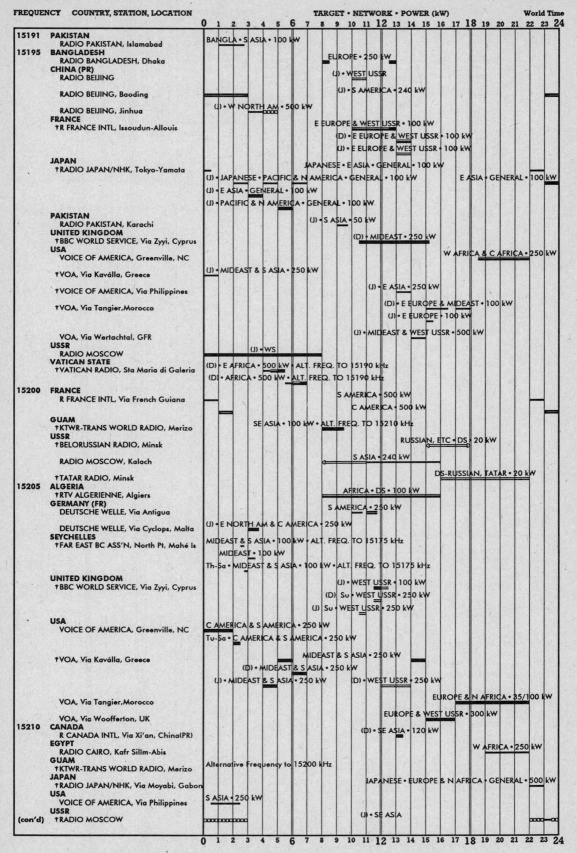

15191 PAKISTAN
  RADIO PAKISTAN, Islamabad — BANGLA • S ASIA • 100 kW

15195 BANGLADESH
  RADIO BANGLADESH, Dhaka — EUROPE • 250 kW
  CHINA (PR)
  RADIO BEIJING — (J) • WEST USSR
  RADIO BEIJING, Baoding — (J) • S AMERICA • 240 kW
  RADIO BEIJING, Jinhua — (J) • W NORTH AM • 500 kW
  FRANCE
  ↑R FRANCE INTL, Issoudun-Allouis — E EUROPE & WEST USSR • 100 kW
    (D) • E EUROPE & WEST USSR • 100 kW
    (J) • E EUROPE & WEST USSR • 100 kW
  JAPAN
  ↑RADIO JAPAN/NHK, Tokyo-Yamata — JAPANESE • E ASIA • GENERAL • 100 kW
    (J) • JAPANESE • PACIFIC & N AMERICA • GENERAL • 100 kW   E ASIA • GENERAL • 100 kW
    (J) • E ASIA • GENERAL • 100 kW
    (J) • PACIFIC & N AMERICA • GENERAL • 100 kW
  PAKISTAN
  RADIO PAKISTAN, Karachi — (J) • S ASIA • 50 kW
  UNITED KINGDOM
  ↑BBC WORLD SERVICE, Via Zyyi, Cyprus — (D) • MIDEAST • 250 kW
  USA
  VOICE OF AMERICA, Greenville, NC — W AFRICA & C AFRICA • 250 kW
  ↑VOA, Via Kaválla, Greece — (J) • MIDEAST & S ASIA • 250 kW
  ↑VOICE OF AMERICA, Via Philippines — (J) • E ASIA • 250 kW
  ↑VOA, Via Tangier, Morocco — (D) • E EUROPE & MIDEAST • 100 kW
    (J) • E EUROPE • 100 kW
  VOA, Via Wertachtal, GFR — (J) • MIDEAST & WEST USSR • 500 kW
  USSR
  RADIO MOSCOW — (J) • WS
  VATICAN STATE
  ↑VATICAN RADIO, Sta Maria di Galeria — (D) • E AFRICA • 500 kW • ALT. FREQ. TO 15190 kHz
    (D) • AFRICA • 500 kW • ALT. FREQ. TO 15190 kHz

15200 FRANCE
  R FRANCE INTL, Via French Guiana — S AMERICA • 500 kW
    C AMERICA • 500 kW
  GUAM
  ↑KTWR-TRANS WORLD RADIO, Merizo — SE ASIA • 100 kW • ALT. FREQ. TO 15210 kHz
  USSR
  ↑BELORUSSIAN RADIO, Minsk — RUSSIAN, ETC • DS • 20 kW
  RADIO MOSCOW, Kalach — S ASIA • 240 kW
  ↑TATAR RADIO, Minsk — DS-RUSSIAN, TATAR • 20 kW

15205 ALGERIA
  ↑RTV ALGERIENNE, Algiers — AFRICA • DS • 100 kW
  GERMANY (FR)
  DEUTSCHE WELLE, Via Antigua — S AMERICA • 250 kW
  DEUTSCHE WELLE, Via Cyclops, Malta — (J) • E NORTH AM & C AMERICA • 250 kW
  SEYCHELLES
  ↑FAR EAST BC ASS'N, North Pt, Mahé Is — MIDEAST & S ASIA • 100 kW • ALT. FREQ. TO 15175 kHz
    MIDEAST • 100 kW
    Th-Sa • MIDEAST & S ASIA • 100 kW • ALT. FREQ. TO 15175 kHz
  UNITED KINGDOM
  ↑BBC WORLD SERVICE, Via Zyyi, Cyprus — (J) • WEST USSR • 100 kW
    (D) Su • WEST USSR • 250 kW
    (J) Su • WEST USSR • 250 kW
  USA
  VOICE OF AMERICA, Greenville, NC — C AMERICA & S AMERICA • 250 kW
    Tu-Sa • C AMERICA & S AMERICA • 250 kW
  ↑VOA, Via Kaválla, Greece — MIDEAST & S ASIA • 250 kW
    (D) • MIDEAST & S ASIA • 250 kW
    (J) • MIDEAST & S ASIA • 250 kW   (D) • WEST USSR • 250 kW
  VOA, Via Tangier, Morocco — EUROPE & N AFRICA • 35/100 kW
  VOA, Via Woofferton, UK — EUROPE & WEST USSR • 300 kW

15210 CANADA
  R CANADA INTL, Via Xi'an, China(PR) — (D) • SE ASIA • 120 kW
  EGYPT
  RADIO CAIRO, Kafr Silim-Abis — W AFRICA • 250 kW
  GUAM
  ↑KTWR-TRANS WORLD RADIO, Merizo — Alternative Frequency to 15200 kHz
  JAPAN
  ↑RADIO JAPAN/NHK, Via Moyabi, Gabon — JAPANESE • EUROPE & N AFRICA • GENERAL • 500 kW
  USA
  VOICE OF AMERICA, Via Philippines — S ASIA • 250 kW
  USSR
  (con'd) ↑RADIO MOSCOW — (J) • SE ASIA

ENGLISH ▬▬ ARABIC ▨▨ CHINESE ▫▫▫ FRENCH ══ GERMAN ▬▬ RUSSIAN ══ SPANISH ▬▬ OTHER ▬

FREQUENCY   COUNTRY, STATION, LOCATION   TARGET • NETWORK • POWER (kW)   World Time

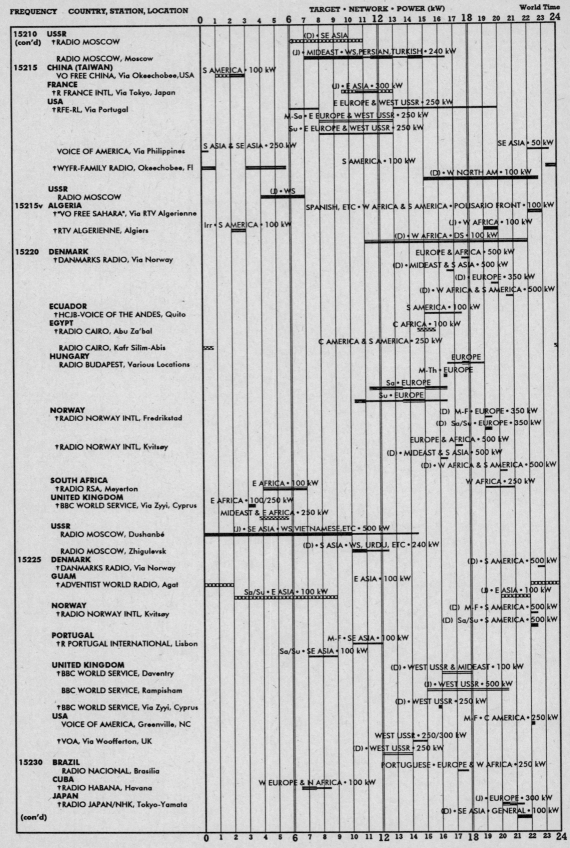

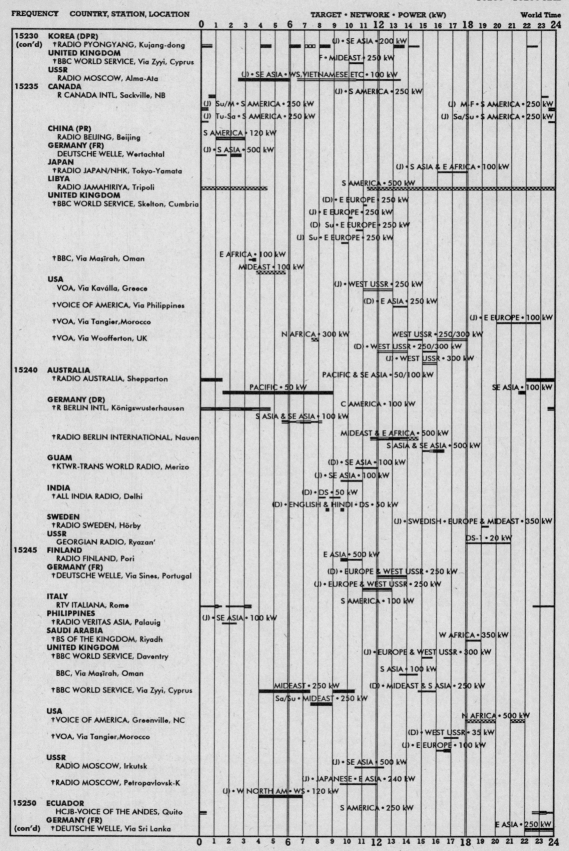

FREQUENCY   COUNTRY, STATION, LOCATION   TARGET • NETWORK • POWER (kW)   World Time

FREQUENCY	COUNTRY, STATION, LOCATION	TARGET • NETWORK • POWER (kW)
15230 (con'd)	KOREA (DPR)	
	†RADIO PYONGYANG, Kujang-dong	(J) • SE ASIA • 200 kW
	UNITED KINGDOM	
	†BBC WORLD SERVICE, Via Zyyi, Cyprus	F • MIDEAST • 250 kW
	USSR	
	RADIO MOSCOW, Alma-Ata	(J) • SE ASIA • WS, VIETNAMESE ETC • 100 kW
15235	CANADA	
	R CANADA INTL, Sackville, NB	(J) • S AMERICA • 250 kW
		(J) Su/M • S AMERICA • 250 kW (J) M-F • S AMERICA • 250 kW
		(J) Tu-Sa • S AMERICA • 250 kW (J) Sa/Su • S AMERICA • 250 kW
	CHINA (PR)	
	RADIO BEIJING, Beijing	S AMERICA • 120 kW
	GERMANY (FR)	
	DEUTSCHE WELLE, Wertachtal	(J) • S ASIA • 500 kW
	JAPAN	
	†RADIO JAPAN/NHK, Tokyo-Yamata	(J) • S ASIA & E AFRICA • 100 kW
	LIBYA	
	RADIO JAMAHIRIYA, Tripoli	S AMERICA • 500 kW
	UNITED KINGDOM	
	†BBC WORLD SERVICE, Skelton, Cumbria	(D) • E EUROPE • 250 kW
		(J) • E EUROPE • 250 kW
		(D) Su • E EUROPE • 250 kW
		(J) Su • E EUROPE • 250 kW
	†BBC, Via Maṣīrah, Oman	E AFRICA • 100 kW
		MIDEAST • 100 kW
	USA	
	VOA, Via Kaválla, Greece	(J) • WEST USSR • 250 kW
	†VOICE OF AMERICA, Via Philippines	(D) • E ASIA • 250 kW
	†VOA, Via Tangier, Morocco	(J) • E EUROPE • 100 kW
	†VOA, Via Woofferton, UK	N AFRICA • 300 kW WEST USSR • 250/300 kW
		(D) • WEST USSR • 250/300 kW
		(J) • WEST USSR • 300 kW
15240	AUSTRALIA	
	†RADIO AUSTRALIA, Shepparton	PACIFIC & SE ASIA • 50/100 kW
		PACIFIC • 50 kW SE ASIA • 100 kW
	GERMANY (DR)	
	†R BERLIN INTL, Königswusterhausen	C AMERICA • 100 kW
		S ASIA & SE ASIA • 100 kW
	†RADIO BERLIN INTERNATIONAL, Nauen	MIDEAST & E AFRICA • 500 kW
		S ASIA & SE ASIA • 500 kW
	GUAM	
	†KTWR-TRANS WORLD RADIO, Merizo	(D) • SE ASIA • 100 kW
		(J) • SE ASIA • 100 kW
	INDIA	
	†ALL INDIA RADIO, Delhi	(D) • DS • 50 kW
		(D) • ENGLISH & HINDI • DS • 50 kW
	SWEDEN	
	†RADIO SWEDEN, Hörby	(J) • SWEDISH • EUROPE & MIDEAST • 350 kW
	USSR	
	GEORGIAN RADIO, Ryazan'	DS-1 • 20 kW
15245	FINLAND	
	RADIO FINLAND, Pori	E ASIA • 500 kW
	GERMANY (FR)	
	†DEUTSCHE WELLE, Via Sines, Portugal	(D) • EUROPE & WEST USSR • 250 kW
		(J) • EUROPE & WEST USSR • 250 kW
	ITALY	
	RTV ITALIANA, Rome	S AMERICA • 100 kW
	PHILIPPINES	
	†RADIO VERITAS ASIA, Palauig	(J) • SE ASIA • 100 kW
	SAUDI ARABIA	
	†BS OF THE KINGDOM, Riyadh	W AFRICA • 350 kW
	UNITED KINGDOM	
	†BBC WORLD SERVICE, Daventry	(J) • EUROPE & WEST USSR • 300 kW
	BBC, Via Maṣīrah, Oman	S ASIA • 100 kW
	†BBC WORLD SERVICE, Via Zyyi, Cyprus	MIDEAST • 250 kW (D) • MIDEAST & S ASIA • 250 kW
		Sa/Su • MIDEAST • 250 kW
	USA	
	†VOICE OF AMERICA, Greenville, NC	N AFRICA • 500 kW
	†VOA, Via Tangier, Morocco	(D) • WEST USSR • 35 kW
		(J) • E EUROPE • 100 kW
	USSR	
	RADIO MOSCOW, Irkutsk	(J) • SE ASIA • 500 kW
	†RADIO MOSCOW, Petropavlovsk-K	(J) • JAPANESE • E ASIA • 240 kW
		(J) • W NORTH AM • WS • 120 kW
15250	ECUADOR	
	HCJB-VOICE OF THE ANDES, Quito	S AMERICA • 250 kW
	GERMANY (FR)	
(con'd)	†DEUTSCHE WELLE, Via Sri Lanka	E ASIA • 250 kW

FREQUENCY   COUNTRY, STATION, LOCATION   TARGET • NETWORK • POWER (kW)   World Time

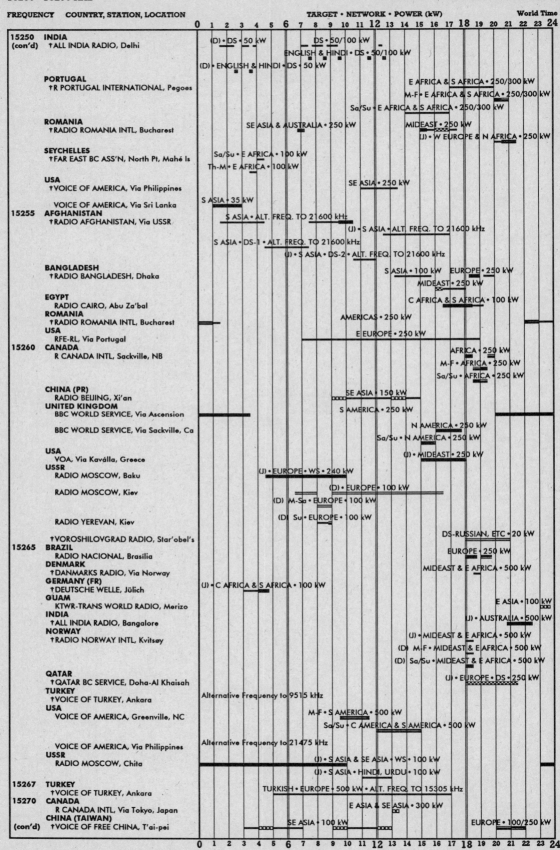

FREQUENCY	COUNTRY, STATION, LOCATION	TARGET • NETWORK • POWER (kW)
15250 (con'd)	**INDIA** †ALL INDIA RADIO, Delhi	(D) • DS • 50 kW / DS • 50/100 kW / ENGLISH & HINDI • DS • 50/100 kW / (D) • ENGLISH & HINDI • DS • 50 kW
	PORTUGAL †R PORTUGAL INTERNATIONAL, Pegoes	E AFRICA & S AFRICA • 250/300 kW / M-F • E AFRICA & S AFRICA • 250/300 kW / Sa/Su • E AFRICA & S AFRICA • 250/300 kW
	ROMANIA †RADIO ROMANIA INTL, Bucharest	SE ASIA & AUSTRALIA • 250 kW / MIDEAST • 250 kW / (J) • W EUROPE & N AFRICA • 250 kW
	SEYCHELLES †FAR EAST BC ASS'N, North Pt, Mahé Is	Sa/Su • E AFRICA • 100 kW / Th-M • E AFRICA • 100 kW
	USA †VOICE OF AMERICA, Via Philippines	SE ASIA • 250 kW
	VOICE OF AMERICA, Via Sri Lanka	S ASIA • 35 kW
15255	**AFGHANISTAN** †RADIO AFGHANISTAN, Via USSR	S ASIA • ALT. FREQ. TO 21600 kHz / (J) • S ASIA • ALT. FREQ. TO 21600 kHz / S ASIA • DS-1 • ALT. FREQ. TO 21600 kHz / (J) • S ASIA • DS-2 • ALT. FREQ. TO 21600 kHz
	BANGLADESH †RADIO BANGLADESH, Dhaka	S ASIA • 100 kW EUROPE • 250 kW / MIDEAST • 250 kW
	EGYPT RADIO CAIRO, Abu Za'bal	C AFRICA & S AFRICA • 100 kW
	ROMANIA †RADIO ROMANIA INTL, Bucharest	AMERICAS • 250 kW
	USA RFE-RL, Via Portugal	E EUROPE • 250 kW
15260	**CANADA** R CANADA INTL, Sackville, NB	AFRICA • 250 kW / M-F • AFRICA • 250 kW / Sa/Su • AFRICA • 250 kW
	CHINA (PR) RADIO BEIJING, Xi'an	SE ASIA • 150 kW
	UNITED KINGDOM BBC WORLD SERVICE, Via Ascension	S AMERICA • 250 kW
	BBC WORLD SERVICE, Via Sackville, Ca	N AMERICA • 250 kW / Sa/Su • N AMERICA • 250 kW / (J) • MIDEAST • 250 kW
	USA VOA, Via Kaválla, Greece	
	USSR RADIO MOSCOW, Baku	(J) • EUROPE • WS • 240 kW
	RADIO MOSCOW, Kiev	(D) • EUROPE • 100 kW / (D) M-Sa • EUROPE • 100 kW
	RADIO YEREVAN, Kiev	(D) Su • EUROPE • 100 kW
	†VOROSHILOVGRAD RADIO, Star'obel's	DS-RUSSIAN, ETC • 20 kW
15265	**BRAZIL** RADIO NACIONAL, Brasilia	EUROPE • 250 kW
	DENMARK †DANMARKS RADIO, Via Norway	MIDEAST & E AFRICA • 500 kW
	GERMANY (FR) †DEUTSCHE WELLE, Jülich	(J) • C AFRICA & S AFRICA • 100 kW
	GUAM KTWR-TRANS WORLD RADIO, Merizo	E ASIA • 100 kW
	INDIA †ALL INDIA RADIO, Bangalore	(J) • AUSTRALIA • 500 kW
	NORWAY †RADIO NORWAY INTL, Kvitsøy	(J) • MIDEAST & E AFRICA • 500 kW / (D) M-F • MIDEAST & E AFRICA • 500 kW / (D) Sa/Su • MIDEAST & E AFRICA • 500 kW
	QATAR †QATAR BC SERVICE, Doha-Al Khaisah	(J) • EUROPE • DS • 250 kW
	TURKEY †VOICE OF TURKEY, Ankara	Alternative Frequency to 9515 kHz
	USA VOICE OF AMERICA, Greenville, NC	M-F • S AMERICA • 500 kW / Sa/Su • C AMERICA & S AMERICA • 500 kW
	VOICE OF AMERICA, Via Philippines	Alternative Frequency to 21475 kHz
	USSR RADIO MOSCOW, Chita	(J) • S ASIA & SE ASIA • WS • 100 kW / (J) • S ASIA • HINDI, URDU • 100 kW
15267	**TURKEY** †VOICE OF TURKEY, Ankara	TURKISH • EUROPE • 500 kW • ALT. FREQ. TO 15305 kHz
15270	**CANADA** R CANADA INTL, Via Tokyo, Japan	E ASIA & SE ASIA • 300 kW
(con'd)	**CHINA (TAIWAN)** †VOICE OF FREE CHINA, T'ai-pei	SE ASIA • 100 kW EUROPE • 100/250 kW

SUMMER ONLY (J)   WINTER ONLY (D)   JAMMING / OR ∧   EARLIEST HEARD ◁   LATEST HEARD ▷   NEW OR CHANGED FOR 1991 †

FREQUENCY   COUNTRY, STATION, LOCATION

TARGET • NETWORK • POWER (kW)   World Time

0 1 2 3 4 5 6 7 8 9 10 11 12 13 14 15 16 17 18 19 20 21 22 23 24

Frequency	Country, Station, Location	Target • Network • Power
15270 (con'd)	**ECUADOR** †HCJB-VOICE OF THE ANDES, Quito	(J) • EUROPE • 500 kW / (J) M-F • EUROPE • 500 kW / (J) Sa/Su • EUROPE • 500 kW / EUROPE • 500 kW
	GERMANY (FR) †DEUTSCHE WELLE, Jülich	(J) • S ASIA • 100 kW
	DEUTSCHE WELLE, Via Kigali, Rwanda	W AFRICA & AMERICAS • 250 kW
	JAPAN †RADIO JAPAN/NHK, Tokyo-Yamata	AUSTRALIA • 100 kW / AUSTRALIA • GENERAL • 100 kW / (D) • SE ASIA • 300 kW / JAPANESE • AUSTRALIA • GENERAL • 100 kW
	NORWAY †RADIO NORWAY INTL, Kvitsøy	(J) • Su • E ASIA • 500 kW
	PAKISTAN RADIO PAKISTAN, Islamabad	(J) • EUROPE • 250 kW
	PHILIPPINES †RADIO VERITAS ASIA, Palauig	(D) • JAPANESE • E ASIA • 100 kW
	SOUTH AFRICA †RADIO RSA, Meyerton	E AFRICA & MIDEAST • 250 kW
	USA †VOA, Via Tangier, Morocco	(J) • E EUROPE & WEST USSR • 100 kW
	VOA, Via Wertachtal, GFR	(J) • WEST USSR • 500 kW
	VOA, Via Woofferton, UK	(J) • WEST USSR • 300 kW
	USSR †BELORUSSIAN RADIO, Minsk	RUSSIAN, ETC • DS-1 • 20 kW
	†KAZAKH RADIO, Moscow	DS-2 • 20 kW • ALT. FREQ. TO 15360 kHz
15275	**CANADA** †R CANADA INTL, Via Vienna, Austria	(J) • MIDEAST • 300 kW
	FRANCE R FRANCE INTL, Via Beijing, China	S ASIA • 120 kW
	GERMANY (FR) DEUTSCHE WELLE, Jülich	C AFRICA & S AFRICA • 100 kW / MIDEAST • 100 kW / (J) • MIDEAST • 100 kW
	DEUTSCHE WELLE, Multiple Locations	MIDEAST • 100/500 kW / AFRICA • 100/500 kW / MIDEAST & S ASIA • 100/500 kW
	†DEUTSCHE WELLE, Via Antigua	(D) • N AMERICA • 250 kW
	DEUTSCHE WELLE, Wertachtal	(J) • MIDEAST & S ASIA • 500 kW
	INDIA †ALL INDIA RADIO, Aligarh	SE ASIA • 250 kW / DS-ENGLISH, ETC • 250 kW
	SAUDI ARABIA †BS OF THE KINGDOM, Riyadh	MIDEAST • 350 kW
	SEYCHELLES †FAR EAST BC ASS'N, North Pt, Mahé Is	Alternative Frequency to 15415 kHz / Alternative Frequency to 15325 kHz
	USA CHRIST SCI MONITOR, Via Saipan	SE ASIA • 100 kW
15280	**HOLLAND** RADIO NEDERLAND, Flevoland	N AFRICA & W AFRICA • 500 kW
	INDIA ALL INDIA RADIO, Bombay	E AFRICA • 100 kW
	SPAIN †RADIO NACIONAL ESPANA, Arganda	(J) • EUROPE • 100 kW / (J) M-F • EUROPE • 100 kW
	UNITED KINGDOM †BBC WORLD SERVICE, Via Hong Kong	E ASIA • 250 kW / JAPANESE • E ASIA • 250 kW / (J) • E ASIA • 250 kW / (D) • E ASIA • 250 kW
	†BBC WORLD SERVICE, Via Singapore	E ASIA • 100 kW
	USA KGEI-VO FRIENDSHIP, Redwood City, Ca	C AMERICA & S AMERICA • 50 kW / (J) • E EUROPE • 100 kW
	†VOA, Via Tangier, Morocco	(D) • WEST USSR • 500 kW
	†VOA, Via Wertachtal, GFR	(J) • WEST USSR • 300 kW
	†VOA, Via Woofferton, UK	
	USSR RADIO MOSCOW, Armavir	(J) • W EUROPE & ATLANTIC • 500 kW
	RADIO MOSCOW, Serpukhov	(J) • S ASIA • WS • 240 kW
15285	**CANADA** R CANADA INTL, Via Xi'an, China(PR)	(J) • SE ASIA • 120 kW
	CHINA (PR) †RADIO BEIJING, Beijing	(J) • AUSTRALIA • 120 kW
	CUBA †RADIO HABANA, Havana	S AMERICA • 50 kW / (D) • W EUROPE & N AFRICA • 50 kW / Su • S AMERICA • 50 kW
(con'd)		

0 1 2 3 4 5 6 7 8 9 10 11 12 13 14 15 16 17 18 19 20 21 22 23 24

ENGLISH ▬▬   ARABIC ⌇⌇⌇   CHINESE ▭▭▭   FRENCH ═══   GERMAN ▬▬▬   RUSSIAN ═══   SPANISH ▬▬▬   OTHER ───

FREQUENCY   COUNTRY, STATION, LOCATION   TARGET • NETWORK • POWER (kW)   World Time

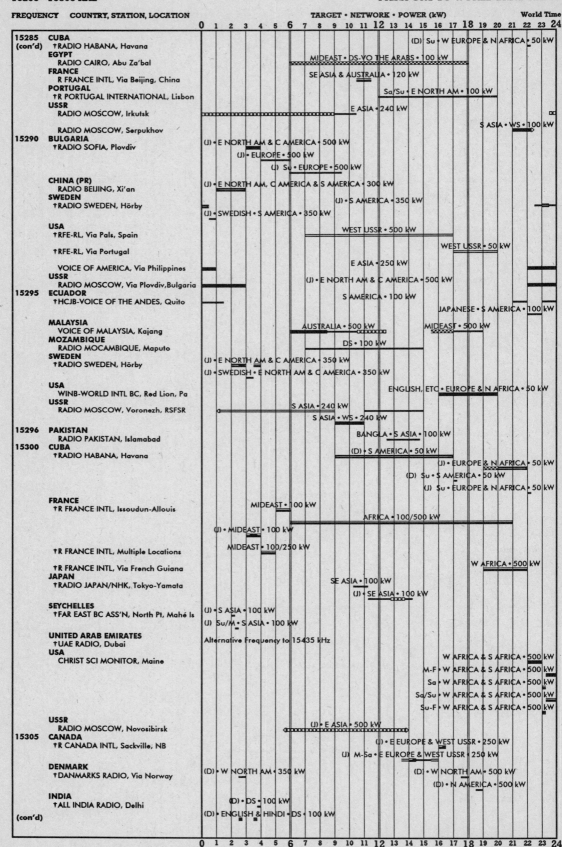

15285 (con'd)	**CUBA** †RADIO HABANA, Havana	(D) • Su • W EUROPE & N AFRICA • 50 kW
	EGYPT RADIO CAIRO, Abu Za'bal	MIDEAST • DS-VO THE ARABS • 100 kW
	FRANCE R FRANCE INTL, Via Beijing, China	SE ASIA & AUSTRALIA • 120 kW
	PORTUGAL †R PORTUGAL INTERNATIONAL, Lisbon	Sa/Su • E NORTH AM • 100 kW
	USSR RADIO MOSCOW, Irkutsk	E ASIA • 240 kW
	RADIO MOSCOW, Serpukhov	S ASIA • WS • 100 kW
15290	**BULGARIA** †RADIO SOFIA, Plovdiv	(J) • E NORTH AM & C AMERICA • 500 kW
		(J) • EUROPE • 500 kW
		(J) • Su • EUROPE • 500 kW
	CHINA (PR) RADIO BEIJING, Xi'an	(J) • E NORTH AM, C AMERICA & S AMERICA • 300 kW
	SWEDEN †RADIO SWEDEN, Hörby	(J) • S AMERICA • 350 kW
		(J) • SWEDISH • S AMERICA • 350 kW
	USA †RFE-RL, Via Pals, Spain	WEST USSR • 500 kW
	†RFE-RL, Via Portugal	WEST USSR • 50 kW
	VOICE OF AMERICA, Via Philippines	E ASIA • 250 kW
	USSR RADIO MOSCOW, Via Plovdiv, Bulgaria	(J) • E NORTH AM & C AMERICA • 500 kW
15295	**ECUADOR** †HCJB-VOICE OF THE ANDES, Quito	S AMERICA • 100 kW
		JAPANESE • S AMERICA • 100 kW
	MALAYSIA VOICE OF MALAYSIA, Kajang	AUSTRALIA • 500 kW MIDEAST • 500 kW
	MOZAMBIQUE RADIO MOCAMBIQUE, Maputo	DS • 100 kW
	SWEDEN †RADIO SWEDEN, Hörby	(J) • E NORTH AM & C AMERICA • 350 kW
		(J) • SWEDISH • E NORTH AM & C AMERICA • 350 kW
	USA WINB-WORLD INTL BC, Red Lion, Pa	ENGLISH, ETC • EUROPE & N AFRICA • 50 kW
	USSR RADIO MOSCOW, Voronezh, RSFSR	S ASIA • 240 kW
		S ASIA • WS • 240 kW
15296	**PAKISTAN** RADIO PAKISTAN, Islamabad	BANGLA • S ASIA • 100 kW
15300	**CUBA** †RADIO HABANA, Havana	(D) • S AMERICA • 50 kW
		(J) • EUROPE & N AFRICA • 50 kW
		(D) • Su • S AMERICA • 50 kW
		(J) • Su • EUROPE & N AFRICA • 50 kW
	FRANCE †R FRANCE INTL, Issoudun-Allouis	MIDEAST • 100 kW
		AFRICA • 100/500 kW
		(J) • MIDEAST • 100 kW
	†R FRANCE INTL, Multiple Locations	MIDEAST • 100/250 kW
	†R FRANCE INTL, Via French Guiana	W AFRICA • 500 kW
	JAPAN †RADIO JAPAN/NHK, Tokyo-Yamata	SE ASIA • 100 kW
		(J) • SE ASIA • 100 kW
	SEYCHELLES †FAR EAST BC ASS'N, North Pt, Mahé Is	(J) • S ASIA • 100 kW
		(J) • Su/M • S ASIA • 100 kW
	UNITED ARAB EMIRATES †UAE RADIO, Dubai	Alternative Frequency to 15435 kHz
	USA CHRIST SCI MONITOR, Maine	W AFRICA & S AFRICA • 500 kW
		M-F • W AFRICA & S AFRICA • 500 kW
		Sa • W AFRICA & S AFRICA • 500 kW
		Sa/Su • W AFRICA & S AFRICA • 500 kW
		Su-F • W AFRICA & S AFRICA • 500 kW
	USSR RADIO MOSCOW, Novosibirsk	(J) • E ASIA • 500 kW
15305	**CANADA** †R CANADA INTL, Sackville, NB	(J) • E EUROPE & WEST USSR • 250 kW
		(J) M-Sa • E EUROPE & WEST USSR • 250 kW
	DENMARK †DANMARKS RADIO, Via Norway	(D) • W NORTH AM • 350 kW (D) • W NORTH AM • 500 kW
		(D) • N AMERICA • 500 kW
	INDIA †ALL INDIA RADIO, Delhi	(D) • DS • 100 kW
(con'd)		(D) • ENGLISH & HINDI • DS • 100 kW

SUMMER ONLY (J)   WINTER ONLY (D)   JAMMING / OR ∧   EARLIEST HEARD ◁   LATEST HEARD ▷   NEW OR CHANGED FOR 1991 †

FREQUENCY   COUNTRY, STATION, LOCATION   TARGET • NETWORK • POWER (kW)   World Time

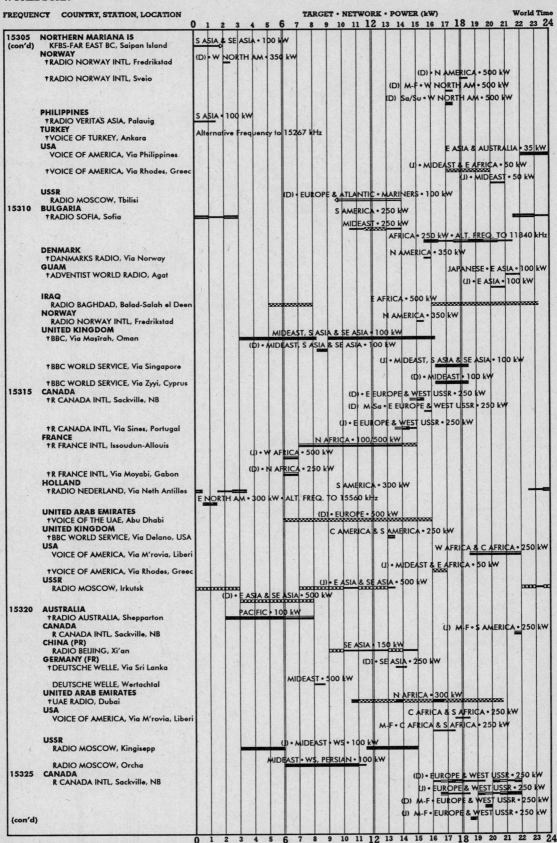

15305	NORTHERN MARIANA IS
(con'd)	KFBS-FAR EAST BC, Saipan Island — S ASIA & SE ASIA • 100 kW
	NORWAY
	↑RADIO NORWAY INTL, Fredrikstad — (D) • W NORTH AM • 350 kW
	↑RADIO NORWAY INTL, Sveio — (D) • N AMERICA • 500 kW
	(D) M-F • W NORTH AM • 500 kW
	(D) Sa/Su • W NORTH AM • 500 kW
	PHILIPPINES
	↑RADIO VERITAS ASIA, Palauig — S ASIA • 100 kW
	TURKEY
	↑VOICE OF TURKEY, Ankara — Alternative Frequency to 15267 kHz
	USA
	VOICE OF AMERICA, Via Philippines — E ASIA & AUSTRALIA • 35 kW
	↑VOICE OF AMERICA, Via Rhodes, Greec — (J) • MIDEAST & E AFRICA • 50 kW
	(J) • MIDEAST • 50 kW
	USSR
	RADIO MOSCOW, Tbilisi — (D) • EUROPE & ATLANTIC • MARINERS • 100 kW
15310	BULGARIA
	↑RADIO SOFIA, Sofia — S AMERICA • 250 kW
	MIDEAST • 250 kW
	AFRICA • 250 kW • ALT. FREQ. TO 11840 kHz
	DENMARK
	↑DANMARKS RADIO, Via Norway — N AMERICA • 350 kW
	GUAM
	↑ADVENTIST WORLD RADIO, Agat — JAPANESE • E ASIA • 100 kW
	(J) • E ASIA • 100 kW
	IRAQ
	RADIO BAGHDAD, Balad-Salah el Deen — E AFRICA • 500 kW
	NORWAY
	RADIO NORWAY INTL, Fredrikstad — N AMERICA • 350 kW
	UNITED KINGDOM
	↑BBC, Via Maṣīrah, Oman — MIDEAST, S ASIA & SE ASIA • 100 kW
	(D) • MIDEAST, S ASIA & SE ASIA • 100 kW
	↑BBC WORLD SERVICE, Via Singapore — (J) • MIDEAST, S ASIA & SE ASIA • 100 kW
	↑BBC WORLD SERVICE, Via Zyyi, Cyprus — (D) • MIDEAST • 100 kW
15315	CANADA
	↑R CANADA INTL, Sackville, NB — (D) • E EUROPE & WEST USSR • 250 kW
	(D) M-Sa • E EUROPE & WEST USSR • 250 kW
	(J) • E EUROPE & WEST USSR • 250 kW
	↑R CANADA INTL, Via Sines, Portugal — N AFRICA • 100/500 kW
	FRANCE
	↑R FRANCE INTL, Issoudun-Allouis — (J) • W AFRICA • 500 kW
	↑R FRANCE INTL, Via Moyabi, Gabon — (D) • N AFRICA • 250 kW
	HOLLAND
	↑RADIO NEDERLAND, Via Neth Antilles — S AMERICA • 300 kW
	E NORTH AM • 300 kW • ALT. FREQ. TO 15560 kHz
	UNITED ARAB EMIRATES
	↑VOICE OF THE UAE, Abu Dhabi — (D) • EUROPE • 500 kW
	UNITED KINGDOM
	↑BBC WORLD SERVICE, Via Delano, USA — C AMERICA & S AMERICA • 250 kW
	USA
	VOICE OF AMERICA, Via M'rovia, Liberi — W AFRICA & C AFRICA • 250 kW
	↑VOICE OF AMERICA, Via Rhodes, Greec — (J) • MIDEAST & E AFRICA • 50 kW
	USSR
	RADIO MOSCOW, Irkutsk — (J) • E ASIA & SE ASIA • 500 kW
	(D) • E ASIA & SE ASIA • 500 kW
15320	AUSTRALIA
	↑RADIO AUSTRALIA, Shepparton — PACIFIC • 100 kW
	CANADA
	R CANADA INTL, Sackville, NB — (J) • M-F • S AMERICA • 250 kW
	CHINA (PR)
	RADIO BEIJING, Xi'an — SE ASIA • 150 kW
	GERMANY (FR)
	↑DEUTSCHE WELLE, Via Sri Lanka — (D) • SE ASIA • 250 kW
	DEUTSCHE WELLE, Wertachtal — MIDEAST • 500 kW
	UNITED ARAB EMIRATES
	↑UAE RADIO, Dubai — N AFRICA • 300 kW
	USA
	VOICE OF AMERICA, Via M'rovia, Liberi — C AFRICA & S AFRICA • 250 kW
	M-F • C AFRICA & S AFRICA • 250 kW
	USSR
	RADIO MOSCOW, Kingisepp — (J) • MIDEAST • WS • 100 kW
	RADIO MOSCOW, Orcha — MIDEAST • WS, PERSIAN • 100 kW
15325	CANADA
	R CANADA INTL, Sackville, NB — (D) • EUROPE & WEST USSR • 250 kW
	(J) • EUROPE & WEST USSR • 250 kW
	(D) M-F • EUROPE & WEST USSR • 250 kW
	(J) M-F • EUROPE & WEST USSR • 250 kW
(con'd)	

ENGLISH ▬   ARABIC ⧉   CHINESE ▭▭▭   FRENCH ▬   GERMAN ▬   RUSSIAN ═   SPANISH ▬   OTHER ▬

FREQUENCY   COUNTRY, STATION, LOCATION   TARGET • NETWORK • POWER (kW)   World Time

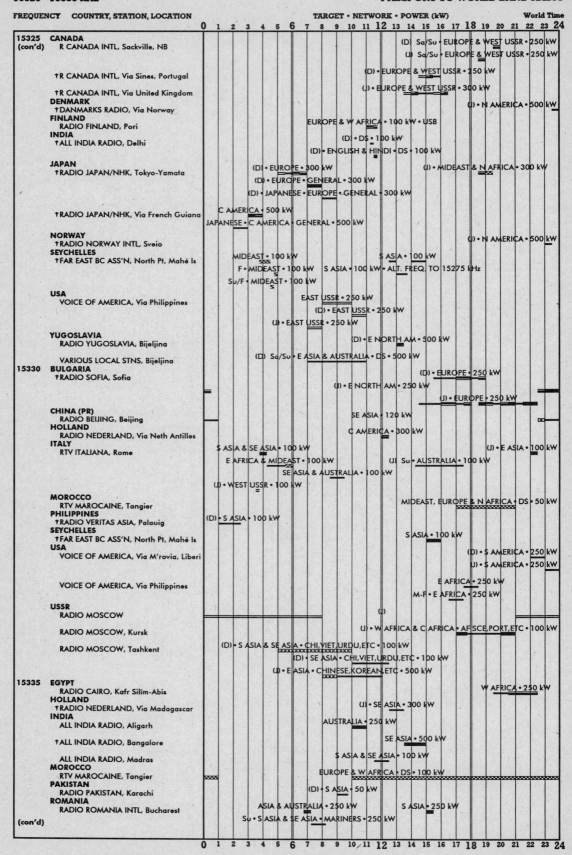

FREQUENCY	COUNTRY, STATION, LOCATION	TARGET • NETWORK • POWER (kW)
15325 (con'd)	**CANADA** R CANADA INTL, Sackville, NB	(D) Sa/Su • EUROPE & WEST USSR • 250 kW
		(J) Sa/Su • EUROPE & WEST USSR • 250 kW
	†R CANADA INTL, Via Sines, Portugal	(D) • EUROPE & WEST USSR • 250 kW
	†R CANADA INTL, Via United Kingdom	(J) • EUROPE & WEST USSR • 300 kW
	DENMARK †DANMARKS RADIO, Via Norway	(J) • N AMERICA • 500 kW
	FINLAND RADIO FINLAND, Pori	EUROPE & W AFRICA • 100 kW • USB
	INDIA †ALL INDIA RADIO, Delhi	(D) • DS • 100 kW
		(D) • ENGLISH & HINDI • DS • 100 kW
	JAPAN †RADIO JAPAN/NHK, Tokyo-Yamata	(D) • EUROPE • 300 kW
		(J) • MIDEAST & N AFRICA • 300 kW
		(D) • EUROPE • GENERAL • 300 kW
		(D) • JAPANESE • EUROPE • GENERAL • 300 kW
	†RADIO JAPAN/NHK, Via French Guiana	C AMERICA • 500 kW
		JAPANESE • C AMERICA • GENERAL • 500 kW
	NORWAY †RADIO NORWAY INTL, Sveio	(J) • N AMERICA • 500 kW
	SEYCHELLES †FAR EAST BC ASS'N, North Pt, Mahé Is	MIDEAST • 100 kW S ASIA • 100 kW
		F • MIDEAST • 100 kW S ASIA • 100 kW • ALT. FREQ. TO 15275 kHz
		Su/F • MIDEAST • 100 kW
	USA VOICE OF AMERICA, Via Philippines	EAST USSR • 250 kW
		(D) • EAST USSR • 250 kW
		(J) • EAST USSR • 250 kW
	YUGOSLAVIA RADIO YUGOSLAVIA, Bijeljina	(D) • E NORTH AM • 500 kW
	VARIOUS LOCAL STNS, Bijeljina	(D) Sa/Su • E ASIA & AUSTRALIA • DS • 500 kW
15330	**BULGARIA** †RADIO SOFIA, Sofia	(D) • EUROPE • 250 kW
		(J) • E NORTH AM • 250 kW
		(J) • EUROPE • 250 kW
	CHINA (PR) RADIO BEIJING, Beijing	SE ASIA • 120 kW
	HOLLAND RADIO NEDERLAND, Via Neth Antilles	C AMERICA • 300 kW
	ITALY RTV ITALIANA, Rome	S ASIA & SE ASIA • 100 kW (J) • E ASIA • 100 kW
		E AFRICA & MIDEAST • 100 kW (J) Su • AUSTRALIA • 100 kW
		SE ASIA & AUSTRALIA • 100 kW
		(J) • WEST USSR • 100 kW
	MOROCCO RTV MAROCAINE, Tangier	MIDEAST, EUROPE & N AFRICA • DS • 50 kW
	PHILIPPINES †RADIO VERITAS ASIA, Palauig	(D) • S ASIA • 100 kW
	SEYCHELLES †FAR EAST BC ASS'N, North Pt, Mahé Is	S ASIA • 100 kW
	USA VOICE OF AMERICA, Via M'rovia, Liberi	(D) • S AMERICA • 250 kW
		(J) • S AMERICA • 250 kW
	VOICE OF AMERICA, Via Philippines	E AFRICA • 250 kW
		M-F • E AFRICA • 250 kW
	USSR RADIO MOSCOW	(J)
	RADIO MOSCOW, Kursk	(J) • W AFRICA & C AFRICA • AF SCE, PORT, ETC • 100 kW
	RADIO MOSCOW, Tashkent	(D) • S ASIA & SE ASIA • CHI, VIET, URDU, ETC • 100 kW
		(D) • SE ASIA • CHI, VIET, URDU, ETC • 100 kW
		(J) • E ASIA • CHINESE, KOREAN, ETC • 500 kW
15335	**EGYPT** RADIO CAIRO, Kafr Silīm-Abis	W AFRICA • 250 kW
	HOLLAND †RADIO NEDERLAND, Via Madagascar	(J) • SE ASIA • 300 kW
	INDIA ALL INDIA RADIO, Aligarh	AUSTRALIA • 250 kW
	†ALL INDIA RADIO, Bangalore	SE ASIA • 500 kW
	ALL INDIA RADIO, Madras	S ASIA & SE ASIA • 100 kW
	MOROCCO RTV MAROCAINE, Tangier	EUROPE & W AFRICA • DS • 100 kW
	PAKISTAN RADIO PAKISTAN, Karachi	(D) • S ASIA • 50 kW
	ROMANIA RADIO ROMANIA INTL, Bucharest	ASIA & AUSTRALIA • 250 kW S ASIA • 250 kW
(con'd)		Su • S ASIA & SE ASIA • MARINERS • 250 kW

0 1 2 3 4 5 6 7 8 9 10 11 12 13 14 15 16 17 18 19 20 21 22 23 24

SUMMER ONLY (J)   WINTER ONLY (D)   JAMMING / OR ∧   EARLIEST HEARD ◁   LATEST HEARD ▷   NEW OR CHANGED FOR 1991 †

FREQUENCY	COUNTRY, STATION, LOCATION	TARGET • NETWORK • POWER (kW)	World Time

0 1 2 3 4 5 6 7 8 9 10 11 12 13 14 15 16 17 18 19 20 21 22 23 24

15335 (con'd)	**ROMANIA**
	RADIO ROMANIA INTL, Bucharest	Su • W AFRICA & ATLANTIC • MARINERS • 250 kW
	SAUDI ARABIA
	↑BS OF THE KINGDOM, Riyadh	E AFRICA • 350 kW
15340	**CUBA**
	↑RADIO HABANA, Havana	(D) • S AMERICA • 50 kW
		S AMERICA • 50 kW
		Su • S AMERICA • 50 kW
	ITALY
	↑RTV ITALIANA, Rome	MIDEAST • 100 kW
	KOREA (DPR)
	RADIO PYONGYANG, Kujang-dong	E AFRICA • 200 kW
	ROMANIA
	↑RADIO ROMANIA INTL, Bucharest	W AFRICA • 250 kW
		SE ASIA • 250 kW
		AFRICA • 250 kW
	USA
	↑RFE-RL, Via Germany	WEST USSR • 100 kW
	USSR
	RADIO MOSCOW, Khabarovsk	(J) • E ASIA & SE ASIA • 100 kW
15345	**ARGENTINA**
	↑RADIO ARGENTINA-RAE, Buenos Aires	Tu-Sa • AMERICAS • 50/100 kW
		M-F • S AMERICA • 50/100 kW
		M-F • EUROPE & N AFRICA • 50 kW
	↑RADIO NACIONAL, Buenos Aires	Sa/Su • S AMERICA • DS • 50/100 kW
		Su/M • AMERICAS • DS • 50/100 kW
		Sa/Su • EUROPE & N AFRICA • DS • 50 kW
	CHINA (TAIWAN)
	VOICE OF FREE CHINA, T'ai-pei	E ASIA • 100 kW
		SE ASIA • 50/100 kW
		E ASIA & N AMERICA • 100 kW
	INDIA
	↑ALL INDIA RADIO, Bangalore	AUSTRALIA • 500 kW
	KUWAIT
	RADIO KUWAIT, Jadādīyah	S ASIA • 250 kW
		S ASIA • DS-KORAN • 250 kW
	NETHERLANDS ANTILLES
	TRANS WORLD RADIO, Bonaire	E NORTH AM • 50 kW
		Sa • E NORTH AM • 50 kW
		Sa/Su • E NORTH AM • 50 kW
	SAUDI ARABIA
	↑BS OF THE KINGDOM, Riyadh	S ASIA • 350 kW
15350	**AFGHANISTAN**
	↑RADIO AFGHANISTAN, Via USSR	(D) • S ASIA • ALT. FREQ. TO 15435 kHz
		(D) • S ASIA • DS-1 • ALT. FREQ. TO 15435 kHz
		(D) • S ASIA • DS-2 • ALT. FREQ. TO 15435 kHz
	CUBA
	↑RADIO HABANA, Via USSR	W EUROPE & N AFRICA • 100 kW
	GERMANY (DR)
	↑RADIO BERLIN INTERNATIONAL, Nauen	W AFRICA & S AFRICA • 500 kW
	JAPAN
	↑RADIO JAPAN/NHK, Via French Guiana	S AMERICA • 500 kW
		JAPANESE • S AMERICA • GENERAL • 500 kW
		(J) • JAPANESE • S AMERICA • GENERAL • 500 kW
	LUXEMBOURG
	RADIO LUXEMBOURG, Junglinster	E NORTH AM • 10 kW
	USSR
	RADIO MOSCOW, Irkutsk	(J) • SE ASIA • 250 kW
	RADIO MOSCOW, Kazan'	(J) • E AFRICA • SOMALI, ETC • 240 kW
15355	**DENMARK**
	↑DANMARKS RADIO, Via Norway	(J) • E AFRICA • 500 kW
	NETHERLANDS ANTILLES
	TRANS WORLD RADIO, Bonaire	S AMERICA • 100 kW
	NORWAY
	↑RADIO NORWAY INTL, Kvitsøy	(J) • E AFRICA • 500 kW
	USA
	KGEI-VO FRIENDSHIP, Redwood City, Ca	C AMERICA & S AMERICA • 50 kW
	↑RFE-RL, Via Portugal	E EUROPE • 250 kW
15360	**DENMARK**
	↑DANMARKS RADIO, Via Norway	(J) • W NORTH AM • 500 kW
		(J) • W NORTH AM • 350 kW
	FRANCE
	↑R FRANCE INTL, Issoudun-Allouis	MIDEAST • 100 kW
		E NORTH AM • 100 kW
		(J) • E NORTH AM • 100 kW
	INDIA
	ALL INDIA RADIO, Bombay	E AFRICA & S AFRICA • 100 kW
	MOROCCO
	RTV MAROCAINE, Tangier	MIDEAST, EUROPE & N AFRICA • 50 kW
	NORWAY
	↑RADIO NORWAY INTL, Fredrikstad	(J) • W NORTH AM • 350 kW
	↑RADIO NORWAY INTL, Sveio	(J) • W NORTH AM • 500 kW
	UNITED KINGDOM
	↑BBC WORLD SERVICE, Via Singapore	SE ASIA • 100 kW
		E ASIA • 250 kW
		E ASIA & AUSTRALIA • 125 kW
		E ASIA & SE ASIA • 100 kW
(con'd)	

0 1 2 3 4 5 6 7 8 9 10 11 12 13 14 15 16 17 18 19 20 21 22 23 24

ENGLISH ▬   ARABIC ░   CHINESE ▫▫▫   FRENCH ═══   GERMAN ▬   RUSSIAN ══   SPANISH ▬   OTHER ▬

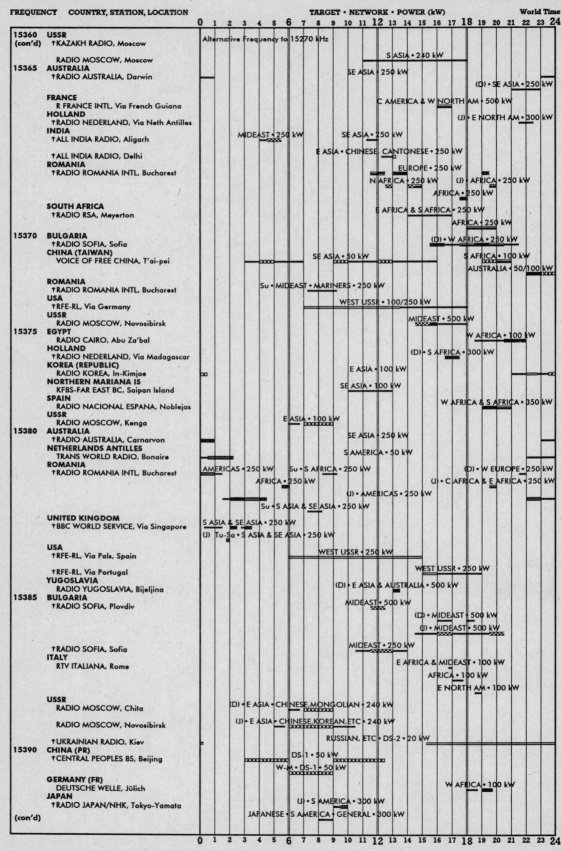

FREQUENCY   COUNTRY, STATION, LOCATION   TARGET • NETWORK • POWER (kW)   World Time

World Time scale: 0 1 2 3 4 5 6 7 8 9 10 11 12 13 14 15 16 17 18 19 20 21 22 23 24

Frequency	Country, Station, Location	Target • Network • Power
15360 (con'd)	USSR — †KAZAKH RADIO, Moscow	Alternative Frequency to 15270 kHz
	RADIO MOSCOW, Moscow	S ASIA • 240 kW
15365	AUSTRALIA — †RADIO AUSTRALIA, Darwin	SE ASIA • 250 kW; (D) • SE ASIA • 250 kW
	FRANCE — R FRANCE INTL, Via French Guiana	C AMERICA & W NORTH AM • 500 kW
	HOLLAND — †RADIO NEDERLAND, Via Neth Antilles	(J) • E NORTH AM • 300 kW
	INDIA — †ALL INDIA RADIO, Aligarh	MIDEAST • 250 kW; SE ASIA • 250 kW
	†ALL INDIA RADIO, Delhi	E ASIA • CHINESE, CANTONESE • 250 kW
	ROMANIA — †RADIO ROMANIA INTL, Bucharest	EUROPE • 250 kW; N AFRICA • 250 kW; (J) • AFRICA • 250 kW; AFRICA • 250 kW
	SOUTH AFRICA — †RADIO RSA, Meyerton	E AFRICA & S AFRICA • 250 kW; AFRICA • 250 kW
15370	BULGARIA — †RADIO SOFIA, Sofia	(D) • W AFRICA • 250 kW
	CHINA (TAIWAN) — VOICE OF FREE CHINA, T'ai-pei	SE ASIA • 50 kW; S AFRICA • 100 kW; AUSTRALIA • 50/100 kW
	ROMANIA — †RADIO ROMANIA INTL, Bucharest	Su • MIDEAST • MARINERS • 250 kW
	USA — †RFE-RL, Via Germany	WEST USSR • 100/250 kW
	USSR — RADIO MOSCOW, Novosibirsk	MIDEAST • 500 kW
15375	EGYPT — RADIO CAIRO, Abu Za'bal	W AFRICA • 100 kW
	HOLLAND — †RADIO NEDERLAND, Via Madagascar	(D) • S AFRICA • 300 kW
	KOREA (REPUBLIC) — RADIO KOREA, In-Kimjae	E ASIA • 100 kW
	NORTHERN MARIANA IS — KFBS-FAR EAST BC, Saipan Island	SE ASIA • 100 kW
	SPAIN — RADIO NACIONAL ESPANA, Noblejas	W AFRICA & S AFRICA • 350 kW
	USSR — RADIO MOSCOW, Kenga	E ASIA • 100 kW
15380	AUSTRALIA — †RADIO AUSTRALIA, Carnarvon	SE ASIA • 250 kW
	NETHERLANDS ANTILLES — TRANS WORLD RADIO, Bonaire	S AMERICA • 50 kW
	ROMANIA — †RADIO ROMANIA INTL, Bucharest	AMERICAS • 250 kW; Su • S AFRICA • 250 kW; (D) • W EUROPE • 250 kW; AFRICA • 250 kW; (J) • C AFRICA & E AFRICA • 250 kW; (J) • AMERICAS • 250 kW; Su • S ASIA & SE ASIA • 250 kW
	UNITED KINGDOM — †BBC WORLD SERVICE, Via Singapore	S ASIA & SE ASIA • 250 kW; (J) Tu-Sa • S ASIA & SE ASIA • 250 kW
	USA — †RFE-RL, Via Pals, Spain	WEST USSR • 250 kW
	†RFE-RL, Via Portugal	WEST USSR • 250 kW
	YUGOSLAVIA — RADIO YUGOSLAVIA, Bijeljina	(D) • E ASIA & AUSTRALIA • 500 kW
15385	BULGARIA — †RADIO SOFIA, Plovdiv	MIDEAST • 500 kW; (D) • MIDEAST • 500 kW; (J) • MIDEAST • 500 kW
	†RADIO SOFIA, Sofia	MIDEAST • 250 kW
	ITALY — RTV ITALIANA, Rome	E AFRICA & MIDEAST • 100 kW; AFRICA • 100 kW; E NORTH AM • 100 kW
	USSR — RADIO MOSCOW, Chita	(D) • E ASIA • CHINESE, MONGOLIAN • 240 kW
	RADIO MOSCOW, Novosibirsk	(J) • E ASIA • CHINESE, KOREAN, ETC • 240 kW
	†UKRAINIAN RADIO, Kiev	RUSSIAN, ETC • DS-2 • 20 kW
15390	CHINA (PR) — †CENTRAL PEOPLES BS, Beijing	DS-1 • 50 kW; W-M • DS-1 • 50 kW
	GERMANY (FR) — DEUTSCHE WELLE, Jülich	W AFRICA • 100 kW
	JAPAN — †RADIO JAPAN/NHK, Tokyo-Yamata	(J) • S AMERICA • 300 kW; JAPANESE • S AMERICA • GENERAL • 300 kW
(con'd)		

World Time scale: 0 1 2 3 4 5 6 7 8 9 10 11 12 13 14 15 16 17 18 19 20 21 22 23 24

SUMMER ONLY (J)   WINTER ONLY (D)   JAMMING / OR ∧   EARLIEST HEARD ◁   LATEST HEARD ▷   NEW OR CHANGED FOR 1991 †

FREQUENCY   COUNTRY, STATION, LOCATION

TARGET • NETWORK • POWER (kW)   World Time

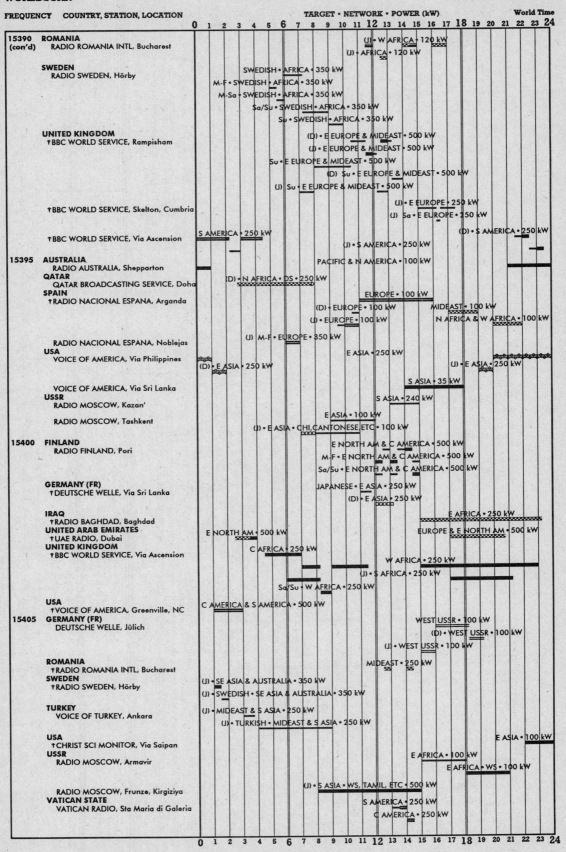

15390 (con'd)	ROMANIA
RADIO ROMANIA INTL, Bucharest	(J) • W AFRICA • 120 kW
	(J) • AFRICA • 120 kW
SWEDEN
RADIO SWEDEN, Hörby	SWEDISH • AFRICA • 350 kW
	M-F • SWEDISH • AFRICA • 350 kW
	M-Sa • SWEDISH • AFRICA • 350 kW
	Sa/Su • SWEDISH • AFRICA • 350 kW
	Su • SWEDISH • AFRICA • 350 kW
UNITED KINGDOM
†BBC WORLD SERVICE, Rampisham	(D) E EUROPE & MIDEAST • 500 kW
	(J) E EUROPE & MIDEAST • 500 kW
	Su • E EUROPE & MIDEAST • 500 kW
	(D) Su • E EUROPE & MIDEAST • 500 kW
	(J) Su • E EUROPE & MIDEAST • 500 kW
†BBC WORLD SERVICE, Skelton, Cumbria	(J) • E EUROPE • 250 kW
	(J) Sa • E EUROPE • 250 kW
†BBC WORLD SERVICE, Via Ascension	S AMERICA • 250 kW (D) • S AMERICA • 250 kW
	(J) • S AMERICA • 250 kW
15395	AUSTRALIA
RADIO AUSTRALIA, Shepparton	PACIFIC & N AMERICA • 100 kW
QATAR
QATAR BROADCASTING SERVICE, Doha	(D) • N AFRICA • DS 250 kW
SPAIN
†RADIO NACIONAL ESPANA, Arganda	EUROPE • 100 kW
	(D) • EUROPE • 100 kW MIDEAST • 100 kW
	(J) • EUROPE • 100 kW N AFRICA & W AFRICA • 100 kW
RADIO NACIONAL ESPANA, Noblejas	(J) M-F • EUROPE • 350 kW
USA
VOICE OF AMERICA, Via Philippines	E ASIA • 250 kW
	(D) • E ASIA • 250 kW (J) • E ASIA • 250 kW
VOICE OF AMERICA, Via Sri Lanka	S ASIA • 35 kW
USSR
RADIO MOSCOW, Kazan'	S ASIA • 240 kW
RADIO MOSCOW, Tashkent	E ASIA • 100 kW
	(J) • E ASIA • CHI, CANTONESE, ETC • 100 kW
15400	FINLAND
RADIO FINLAND, Pori	E NORTH AM & C AMERICA • 500 kW
	M-F • E NORTH AM & C AMERICA • 500 kW
	Sa/Su • E NORTH AM & C AMERICA • 500 kW
GERMANY (FR)
†DEUTSCHE WELLE, Via Sri Lanka	JAPANESE • E ASIA • 250 kW
	(D) • E ASIA • 250 kW
IRAQ
†RADIO BAGHDAD, Baghdad	E AFRICA • 250 kW
UNITED ARAB EMIRATES
†UAE RADIO, Dubai	E NORTH AM • 500 kW EUROPE & E NORTH AM • 500 kW
UNITED KINGDOM
†BBC WORLD SERVICE, Via Ascension	C AFRICA • 250 kW
	W AFRICA • 250 kW
	(J) • S AFRICA • 250 kW
	Sa/Su • W AFRICA • 250 kW
USA
†VOICE OF AMERICA, Greenville, NC	C AMERICA & S AMERICA • 500 kW
15405	GERMANY (FR)
DEUTSCHE WELLE, Jülich	WEST USSR • 100 kW
	(D) • WEST USSR • 100 kW
	(J) • WEST USSR • 100 kW
ROMANIA
†RADIO ROMANIA INTL, Bucharest	MIDEAST • 250 kW
SWEDEN
†RADIO SWEDEN, Hörby	(J) • SE ASIA & AUSTRALIA • 350 kW
	(J) • SWEDISH • SE ASIA & AUSTRALIA • 350 kW
TURKEY
VOICE OF TURKEY, Ankara	(J) • MIDEAST & S ASIA • 250 kW
	(J) • TURKISH • MIDEAST & S ASIA • 250 kW
USA
†CHRIST SCI MONITOR, Via Saipan	E ASIA • 100 kW
USSR
RADIO MOSCOW, Armavir	E AFRICA • 100 kW
	E AFRICA • WS • 100 kW
RADIO MOSCOW, Frunze, Kirgiziya	(J) • S ASIA • WS, TAMIL, ETC • 500 kW
VATICAN STATE
VATICAN RADIO, Sta Maria di Galeria	S AMERICA • 250 kW
	C AMERICA • 250 kW

ENGLISH ▬▬   ARABIC ∞∞   CHINESE ∞∞   FRENCH ▬▬   GERMAN ▬▬   RUSSIAN ══   SPANISH ▬▬   OTHER ──

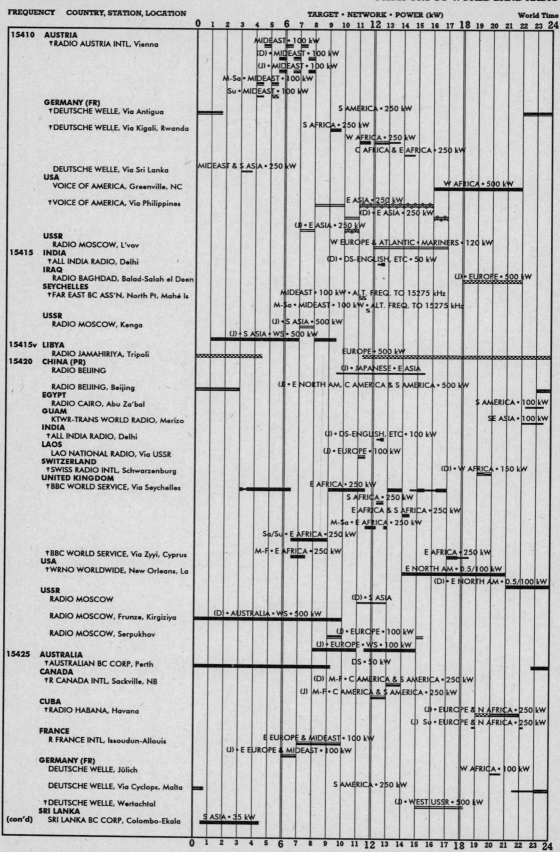

FREQUENCY	COUNTRY, STATION, LOCATION	TARGET • NETWORK • POWER (kW)	World Time

15410
AUSTRIA
†RADIO AUSTRIA INTL, Vienna — MIDEAST • 100 kW / (D) • MIDEAST • 100 kW / (J) • MIDEAST • 100 kW / M-Sa • MIDEAST • 100 kW / Su • MIDEAST • 100 kW

GERMANY (FR)
†DEUTSCHE WELLE, Via Antigua — S AMERICA • 250 kW
†DEUTSCHE WELLE, Via Kigali, Rwanda — S AFRICA • 250 kW / W AFRICA • 250 kW / C AFRICA & E AFRICA • 250 kW
DEUTSCHE WELLE, Via Sri Lanka — MIDEAST & S ASIA • 250 kW

USA
VOICE OF AMERICA, Greenville, NC — W AFRICA • 500 kW
†VOICE OF AMERICA, Via Philippines — E ASIA • 250 kW / (D) • E ASIA • 250 kW / (J) • E ASIA • 250 kW

USSR
RADIO MOSCOW, L'vov — W EUROPE & ATLANTIC • MARINERS • 120 kW

15415 INDIA
†ALL INDIA RADIO, Delhi — (D) • DS-ENGLISH, ETC • 50 kW

IRAQ
RADIO BAGHDAD, Balad-Salah el Deen — (J) • EUROPE • 500 kW

SEYCHELLES
†FAR EAST BC ASS'N, North Pt, Mahé Is — MIDEAST • 100 kW • ALT. FREQ. TO 15275 kHz / M-Sa • MIDEAST • 100 kW • ALT. FREQ. TO 15275 kHz

USSR
RADIO MOSCOW, Kenga — (J) • S ASIA • 500 kW / (J) • S ASIA • WS • 500 kW

15415v LIBYA
RADIO JAMAHIRIYA, Tripoli — EUROPE • 500 kW

15420 CHINA (PR)
RADIO BEIJING — (J) • JAPANESE • E ASIA
RADIO BEIJING, Beijing — (J) • E NORTH AM, C AMERICA & S AMERICA • 500 kW

EGYPT
RADIO CAIRO, Abu Za'bal — S AMERICA • 100 kW

GUAM
KTWR-TRANS WORLD RADIO, Merizo — SE ASIA • 100 kW

INDIA
†ALL INDIA RADIO, Delhi — (J) • DS-ENGLISH, ETC • 100 kW

LAOS
LAO NATIONAL RADIO, Via USSR — (J) • EUROPE • 100 kW

SWITZERLAND
†SWISS RADIO INTL, Schwarzenburg — (D) • W AFRICA • 150 kW

UNITED KINGDOM
†BBC WORLD SERVICE, Via Seychelles — E AFRICA • 250 kW / S AFRICA • 250 kW / E AFRICA & S AFRICA • 250 kW / M-Sa • E AFRICA • 250 kW / Sa/Su • E AFRICA • 250 kW
†BBC WORLD SERVICE, Via Zyyi, Cyprus — M-F • E AFRICA • 250 kW / E AFRICA • 250 kW

USA
†WRNO WORLDWIDE, New Orleans, La — E NORTH AM • 0.5/100 kW / (D) • E NORTH AM • 0.5/100 kW

USSR
RADIO MOSCOW — (D) • S ASIA
RADIO MOSCOW, Frunze, Kirgiziya — (D) • AUSTRALIA • WS • 500 kW
RADIO MOSCOW, Serpukhov — (J) • EUROPE • 100 kW / (J) • EUROPE • WS • 100 kW

15425 AUSTRALIA
†AUSTRALIAN BC CORP, Perth — DS • 50 kW

CANADA
†R CANADA INTL, Sackville, NB — (D) • M-F • C AMERICA & S AMERICA • 250 kW / (J) • M-F • C AMERICA & S AMERICA • 250 kW

CUBA
†RADIO HABANA, Havana — (J) • EUROPE & N AFRICA • 250 kW / (J) • Su • EUROPE & N AFRICA • 250 kW

FRANCE
R FRANCE INTL, Issoudun-Allouis — E EUROPE & MIDEAST • 100 kW / (J) • E EUROPE & MIDEAST • 100 kW

GERMANY (FR)
DEUTSCHE WELLE, Jülich — W AFRICA • 100 kW
DEUTSCHE WELLE, Via Cyclops, Malta — S AMERICA • 250 kW
†DEUTSCHE WELLE, Wertachtal — (J) • WEST USSR • 500 kW

SRI LANKA
(con'd) SRI LANKA BC CORP, Colombo-Ekala — S ASIA • 35 kW

SUMMER ONLY (J)   WINTER ONLY (D)   JAMMING / OR ∧   EARLIEST HEARD ◁   LATEST HEARD ▷   NEW OR CHANGED FOR 1991 †

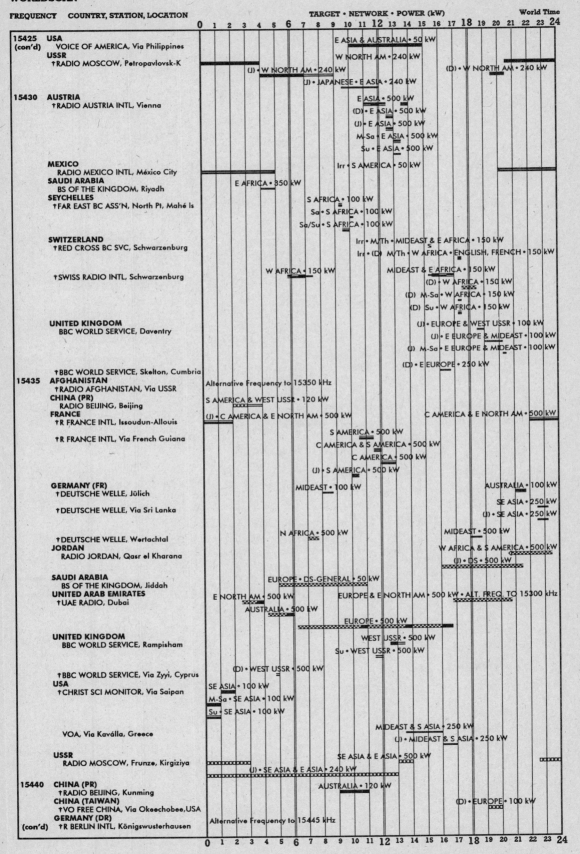

WORLDSCAN

15425–15440 kHz

FREQUENCY   COUNTRY, STATION, LOCATION

TARGET • NETWORK • POWER (kW)

World Time

0 1 2 3 4 5 6 7 8 9 10 11 12 13 14 15 16 17 18 19 20 21 22 23 24

15425 **USA**
(con'd) VOICE OF AMERICA, Via Philippines — E ASIA & AUSTRALIA • 50 kW
USSR — W NORTH AM • 240 kW
†RADIO MOSCOW, Petropavlovsk-K — (J) • W NORTH AM • 240 kW ; (D) • W NORTH AM • 240 kW
— (J) • JAPANESE • E ASIA • 240 kW

15430 **AUSTRIA**
†RADIO AUSTRIA INTL, Vienna — E ASIA • 500 kW
— (D) • E ASIA • 500 kW
— (J) • E ASIA • 500 kW
— M-Sa • E ASIA • 500 kW
— Su • E ASIA • 500 kW

MEXICO
RADIO MEXICO INTL, México City — Irr • S AMERICA • 50 kW
SAUDI ARABIA
BS OF THE KINGDOM, Riyadh — E AFRICA • 350 kW
SEYCHELLES
†FAR EAST BC ASS'N, North Pt, Mahé Is — S AFRICA • 100 kW
— Sa • S AFRICA • 100 kW
— Sa/Su • S AFRICA • 100 kW

SWITZERLAND
†RED CROSS BC SVC, Schwarzenburg — Irr • M/Th • MIDEAST & E AFRICA • 150 kW
— Irr • (D) M/Th • W AFRICA • ENGLISH, FRENCH • 150 kW

†SWISS RADIO INTL, Schwarzenburg — W AFRICA • 150 kW ; MIDEAST & E AFRICA • 150 kW
— (D) • W AFRICA • 150 kW
— (D) M-Sa • W AFRICA • 150 kW
— (D) Su • W AFRICA • 150 kW

UNITED KINGDOM
BBC WORLD SERVICE, Daventry — (J) • EUROPE & WEST USSR • 100 kW
— (J) • E EUROPE & MIDEAST • 100 kW
— (J) M-Sa • E EUROPE & MIDEAST • 100 kW

†BBC WORLD SERVICE, Skelton, Cumbria — (D) • E EUROPE • 250 kW

15435 **AFGHANISTAN**
†RADIO AFGHANISTAN, Via USSR — Alternative Frequency to 15350 kHz
CHINA (PR)
RADIO BEIJING, Beijing — S AMERICA & WEST USSR • 120 kW
FRANCE
†R FRANCE INTL, Issoudun-Allouis — (J) • C AMERICA & E NORTH AM • 500 kW ; C AMERICA & E NORTH AM • 500 kW

†R FRANCE INTL, Via French Guiana — S AMERICA • 500 kW
— C AMERICA & S AMERICA • 500 kW
— C AMERICA • 500 kW
— (J) • S AMERICA • 500 kW

GERMANY (FR)
†DEUTSCHE WELLE, Jülich — MIDEAST • 100 kW ; AUSTRALIA • 100 kW
†DEUTSCHE WELLE, Via Sri Lanka — SE ASIA • 250 kW
— (J) • SE ASIA • 250 kW

†DEUTSCHE WELLE, Wertachtal — N AFRICA • 500 kW ; MIDEAST • 500 kW
JORDAN
RADIO JORDAN, Qasr el Kharana — W AFRICA & S AMERICA • 500 kW
— (J) • DS • 500 kW

SAUDI ARABIA
BS OF THE KINGDOM, Jiddah — EUROPE • DS-GENERAL • 50 kW
UNITED ARAB EMIRATES
†UAE RADIO, Dubai — E NORTH AM • 500 kW ; EUROPE & E NORTH AM • 500 kW • ALT. FREQ. TO 15300 kHz
— AUSTRALIA • 500 kW
— EUROPE • 500 kW

UNITED KINGDOM
BBC WORLD SERVICE, Rampisham — WEST USSR • 500 kW
— Su • WEST USSR • 500 kW

†BBC WORLD SERVICE, Via Zyyi, Cyprus — (D) • WEST USSR • 500 kW
USA
†CHRIST SCI MONITOR, Via Saipan — SE ASIA • 100 kW
— M-Sa • SE ASIA • 100 kW
— Su • SE ASIA • 100 kW

VOA, Via Kaválla, Greece — MIDEAST & S ASIA • 250 kW
— (J) • MIDEAST & S ASIA • 250 kW

USSR
RADIO MOSCOW, Frunze, Kirgiziya — SE ASIA & E ASIA • 500 kW
— (J) • SE ASIA & E ASIA • 240 kW

15440 **CHINA (PR)**
†RADIO BEIJING, Kunming — AUSTRALIA • 120 kW
CHINA (TAIWAN)
†VO FREE CHINA, Via Okeechobee, USA — (D) • EUROPE • 100 kW
GERMANY (DR)
(con'd) †R BERLIN INTL, Königswusterhausen — Alternative Frequency to 15445 kHz

0 1 2 3 4 5 6 7 8 9 10 11 12 13 14 15 16 17 18 19 20 21 22 23 24

ENGLISH ▬   ARABIC ⬚⬚⬚   CHINESE ∘∘∘   FRENCH ═══   GERMAN ▭▭   RUSSIAN ══   SPANISH ▬▬   OTHER ▬

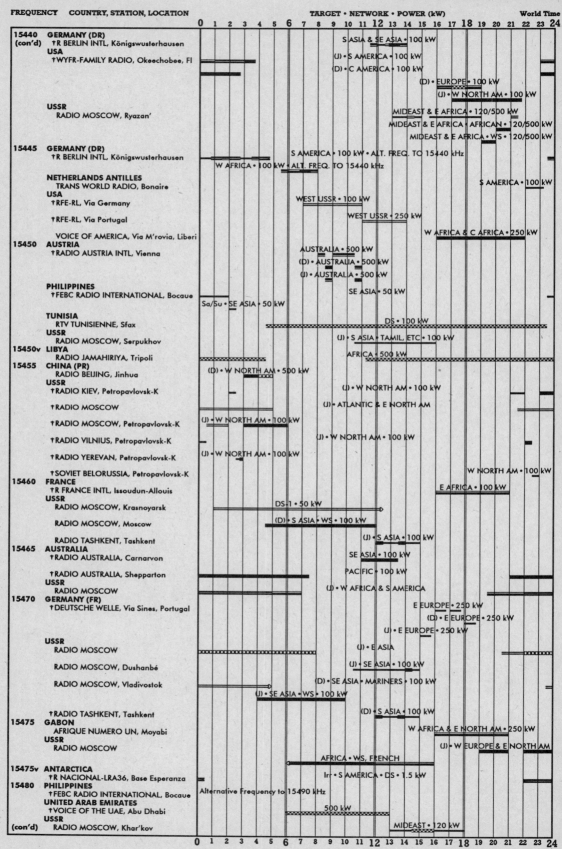

FREQUENCY	COUNTRY, STATION, LOCATION	TARGET • NETWORK • POWER (kW) — World Time
15440 (con'd)	**GERMANY (DR)** †R BERLIN INTL, Königswusterhausen	S ASIA & SE ASIA • 100 kW
	USA †WYFR-FAMILY RADIO, Okeechobee, Fl	(J) • S AMERICA • 100 kW
		(D) • C AMERICA • 100 kW
		(D) • EUROPE • 100 kW
		(J) • W NORTH AM • 100 kW
	USSR RADIO MOSCOW, Ryazan'	MIDEAST & E AFRICA • 120/500 kW
		MIDEAST & E AFRICA • AFRICAN • 120/500 kW
		MIDEAST & E AFRICA • WS • 120/500 kW
15445	**GERMANY (DR)** †R BERLIN INTL, Königswusterhausen	S AMERICA • 100 kW • ALT. FREQ. TO 15440 kHz
		W AFRICA • 100 kW • ALT. FREQ. TO 15440 kHz
	NETHERLANDS ANTILLES TRANS WORLD RADIO, Bonaire	S AMERICA • 100 kW
	USA †RFE-RL, Via Germany	WEST USSR • 100 kW
	†RFE-RL, Via Portugal	WEST USSR • 250 kW
	VOICE OF AMERICA, Via M'rovia, Liberi	W AFRICA & C AFRICA • 250 kW
15450	**AUSTRIA** †RADIO AUSTRIA INTL, Vienna	AUSTRALIA • 500 kW
		(D) • AUSTRALIA • 500 kW
		(J) • AUSTRALIA • 500 kW
	PHILIPPINES †FEBC RADIO INTERNATIONAL, Bocaue	SE ASIA • 50 kW
		Sa/Su • SE ASIA • 50 kW
	TUNISIA RTV TUNISIENNE, Sfax	DS • 100 kW
	USSR RADIO MOSCOW, Serpukhov	(J) • S ASIA • TAMIL, ETC • 100 kW
15450v	**LIBYA** RADIO JAMAHIRIYA, Tripoli	AFRICA • 500 kW
15455	**CHINA (PR)** RADIO BEIJING, Jinhua	(D) • W NORTH AM • 500 kW
	USSR †RADIO KIEV, Petropavlovsk-K	(J) • W NORTH AM • 100 kW
	†RADIO MOSCOW	(J) • ATLANTIC & E NORTH AM
	†RADIO MOSCOW, Petropavlovsk-K	(J) • W NORTH AM • 100 kW
	†RADIO VILNIUS, Petropavlovsk-K	(J) • W NORTH AM • 100 kW
	†RADIO YEREVAN, Petropavlovsk-K	(J) • W NORTH AM • 100 kW
	†SOVIET BELORUSSIA, Petropavlovsk-K	W NORTH AM • 100 kW
15460	**FRANCE** †R FRANCE INTL, Issoudun-Allouis	E AFRICA • 100 kW
	USSR RADIO MOSCOW, Krasnoyarsk	DS-1 • 50 kW
	RADIO MOSCOW, Moscow	(D) • S ASIA • WS • 100 kW
		(J) • S ASIA • 100 kW
	RADIO TASHKENT, Tashkent	
15465	**AUSTRALIA** †RADIO AUSTRALIA, Carnarvon	SE ASIA • 100 kW
	†RADIO AUSTRALIA, Shepparton	PACIFIC • 100 kW
	USSR RADIO MOSCOW	(J) • W AFRICA & S AMERICA
15470	**GERMANY (FR)** †DEUTSCHE WELLE, Via Sines, Portugal	E EUROPE • 250 kW
		(D) • E EUROPE • 250 kW
		(J) • E EUROPE • 250 kW
	USSR RADIO MOSCOW	(J) • E ASIA
	RADIO MOSCOW, Dushanbé	(J) • SE ASIA • 100 kW
	RADIO MOSCOW, Vladivostok	(D) • SE ASIA • MARINERS • 100 kW
		(J) • SE ASIA • WS • 100 kW
	†RADIO TASHKENT, Tashkent	(D) • S ASIA • 100 kW
15475	**GABON** AFRIQUE NUMERO UN, Moyabi	W AFRICA & E NORTH AM • 250 kW
	USSR RADIO MOSCOW	(J) • W EUROPE & E NORTH AM
		AFRICA • WS, FRENCH
15475v	**ANTARCTICA** †R NACIONAL-LRA36, Base Esperanza	Irr • S AMERICA • DS • 1.5 kW
15480	**PHILIPPINES** †FEBC RADIO INTERNATIONAL, Bocaue	Alternative Frequency to 15490 kHz
	UNITED ARAB EMIRATES †VOICE OF THE UAE, Abu Dhabi	500 kW
(con'd)	**USSR** RADIO MOSCOW, Khar'kov	MIDEAST • 120 kW

SUMMER ONLY (J)   WINTER ONLY (D)   JAMMING / OR ∧   EARLIEST HEARD ◁   LATEST HEARD ▷   NEW OR CHANGED FOR 1991 †

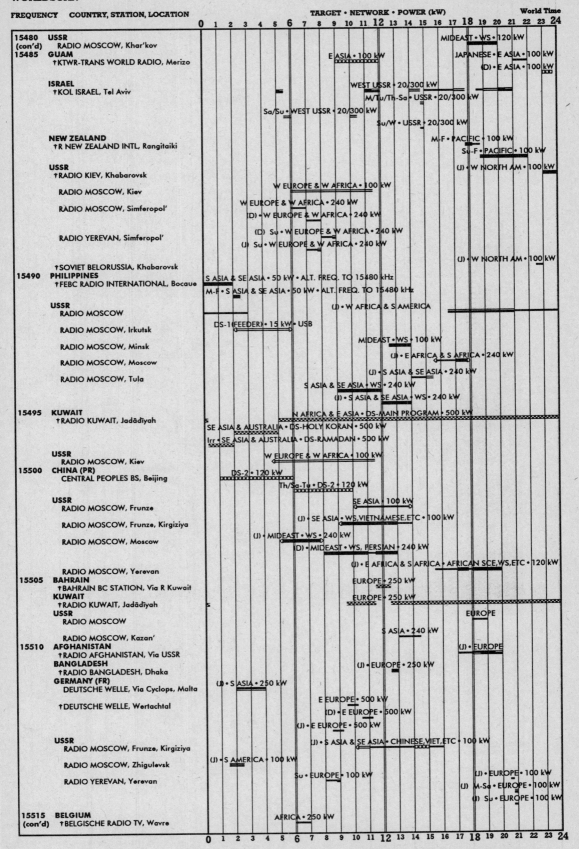

FREQUENCY   COUNTRY, STATION, LOCATION   TARGET • NETWORK • POWER (kW)   World Time

ENGLISH ▬   ARABIC ▨   CHINESE ▦   FRENCH ▭   GERMAN ▤   RUSSIAN ═   SPANISH ▭   OTHER ▬

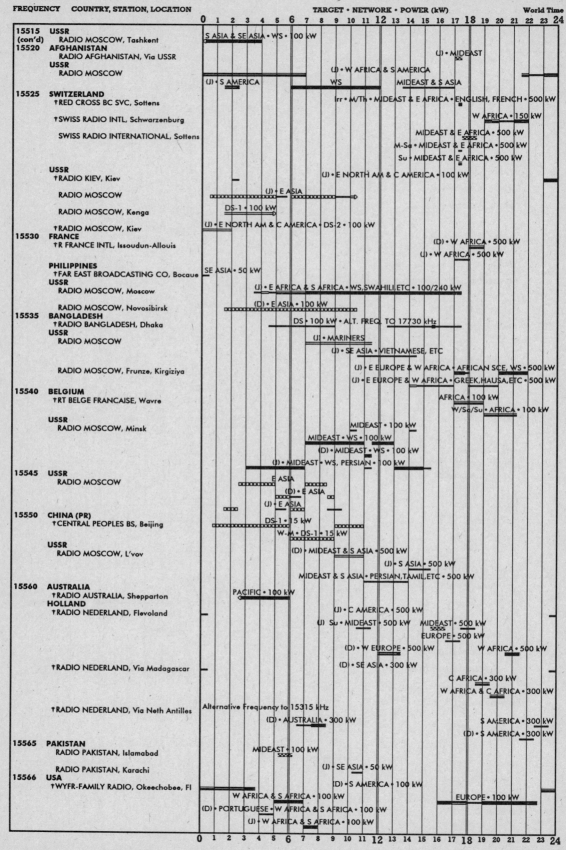

FREQUENCY	COUNTRY, STATION, LOCATION	TARGET • NETWORK • POWER (kW)	World Time

15515 USSR
(con'd)   RADIO MOSCOW, Tashkent — S ASIA & SE ASIA • WS • 100 kW

15520 AFGHANISTAN
  RADIO AFGHANISTAN, Via USSR — (J) • MIDEAST
USSR
  RADIO MOSCOW — (J) • W AFRICA & S AMERICA — (J) • S AMERICA — WS — MIDEAST & S ASIA

15525 SWITZERLAND
  †RED CROSS BC SVC, Sottens — Irr • M/Th • MIDEAST & E AFRICA • ENGLISH, FRENCH • 500 kW
  †SWISS RADIO INTL, Schwarzenburg — W AFRICA • 150 kW
  SWISS RADIO INTERNATIONAL, Sottens — MIDEAST & E AFRICA • 500 kW — M-Sa • MIDEAST & E AFRICA • 500 kW — Su • MIDEAST & E AFRICA • 500 kW
USSR
  †RADIO KIEV, Kiev — (J) • E NORTH AM & C AMERICA • 100 kW
  RADIO MOSCOW — (J) • E ASIA
  RADIO MOSCOW, Kenga — DS-1 • 100 kW
  †RADIO MOSCOW, Kiev — (J) • E NORTH AM & C AMERICA • DS-2 • 100 kW

15530 FRANCE
  †R FRANCE INTL, Issoudun-Allouis — (D) • W AFRICA • 500 kW — (J) • W AFRICA • 500 kW
PHILIPPINES
  †FAR EAST BROADCASTING CO, Bocaue — SE ASIA • 50 kW
USSR
  RADIO MOSCOW, Moscow — (J) • E AFRICA & S AFRICA • WS, SWAHILI, ETC • 100/240 kW
  RADIO MOSCOW, Novosibirsk — (D) • E ASIA • 100 kW

15535 BANGLADESH
  †RADIO BANGLADESH, Dhaka — DS • 100 kW • ALT. FREQ. TO 17730 kHz
USSR
  RADIO MOSCOW — (J) • MARINERS — (J) • SE ASIA • VIETNAMESE, ETC
  RADIO MOSCOW, Frunze, Kirgiziya — (J) • E EUROPE & W AFRICA • AFRICAN SCE, WS • 500 kW — (J) • E EUROPE & W AFRICA • GREEK, HAUSA, ETC • 500 kW

15540 BELGIUM
  †RT BELGE FRANCAISE, Wavre — AFRICA • 100 kW — W/Sa/Su • AFRICA • 100 kW
USSR
  RADIO MOSCOW, Minsk — MIDEAST • 100 kW — MIDEAST • WS • 100 kW — (D) • MIDEAST • WS • 100 kW — (J) • MIDEAST • WS, PERSIAN • 100 kW

15545 USSR
  RADIO MOSCOW — E ASIA — (D) • E ASIA — (J) • E ASIA

15550 CHINA (PR)
  †CENTRAL PEOPLES BS, Beijing — DS-1 • 15 kW — W-M • DS-1 • 15 kW
USSR
  RADIO MOSCOW, L'vov — (D) • MIDEAST & S ASIA • 500 kW — (J) • S ASIA • 500 kW — MIDEAST & S ASIA • PERSIAN, TAMIL, ETC • 500 kW

15560 AUSTRALIA
  †RADIO AUSTRALIA, Shepparton — PACIFIC • 100 kW
HOLLAND
  †RADIO NEDERLAND, Flevoland — (J) • C AMERICA • 500 kW — (J) Su • MIDEAST • 500 kW — MIDEAST • 500 kW — EUROPE • 500 kW — (D) • W EUROPE • 500 kW — W AFRICA • 500 kW
  †RADIO NEDERLAND, Via Madagascar — (D) • SE ASIA • 300 kW — C AFRICA • 300 kW — W AFRICA & C AFRICA • 300 kW
  †RADIO NEDERLAND, Via Neth Antilles — Alternative Frequency to 15315 kHz — (D) • AUSTRALIA • 300 kW — S AMERICA • 300 kW — (D) • S AMERICA • 300 kW

15565 PAKISTAN
  RADIO PAKISTAN, Islamabad — MIDEAST • 100 kW
  RADIO PAKISTAN, Karachi — (J) • SE ASIA • 50 kW
15566 USA
  †WYFR-FAMILY RADIO, Okeechobee, Fl — (D) • S AMERICA • 100 kW — W AFRICA & S AFRICA • 100 kW — EUROPE • 100 kW — (D) • PORTUGUESE • W AFRICA & S AFRICA • 100 kW — (J) • W AFRICA & S AFRICA • 100 kW

SUMMER ONLY (J)   WINTER ONLY (D)   JAMMING / OR ∧   EARLIEST HEARD ◁   LATEST HEARD ▷   NEW OR CHANGED FOR 1991 †

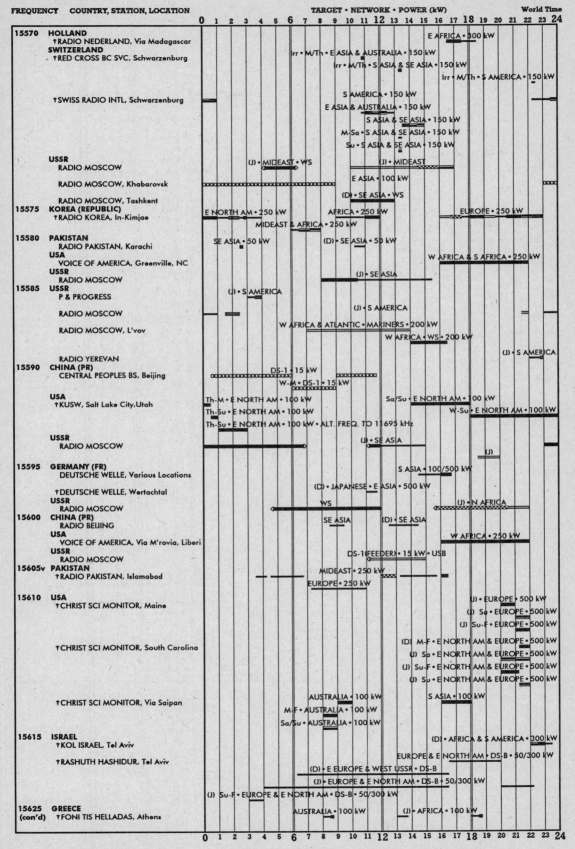

FREQUENCY	COUNTRY, STATION, LOCATION	TARGET • NETWORK • POWER (kW)	World Time

15570 HOLLAND
†RADIO NEDERLAND, Via Madagascar — E AFRICA • 300 kW
SWITZERLAND
†RED CROSS BC SVC, Schwarzenburg — Irr • M/Th • E ASIA & AUSTRALIA • 150 kW
Irr • M/Th • S ASIA & SE ASIA • 150 kW
Irr • M/Th • S AMERICA • 150 kW

†SWISS RADIO INTL, Schwarzenburg
S AMERICA • 150 kW
E ASIA & AUSTRALIA • 150 kW
S ASIA & SE ASIA • 150 kW
M-Sa • S ASIA & SE ASIA • 150 kW
Su • S ASIA & SE ASIA • 150 kW

USSR
RADIO MOSCOW — (J) • MIDEAST • WS ; (J) • MIDEAST
RADIO MOSCOW, Khabarovsk — E ASIA • 100 kW
RADIO MOSCOW, Tashkent — (D) • SE ASIA • WS

15575 KOREA (REPUBLIC)
†RADIO KOREA, In-Kimjae — E NORTH AM • 250 kW ; AFRICA • 250 kW ; EUROPE • 250 kW
MIDEAST & AFRICA • 250 kW

15580 PAKISTAN
RADIO PAKISTAN, Karachi — SE ASIA • 50 kW ; (D) • SE ASIA • 50 kW
USA
VOICE OF AMERICA, Greenville, NC — W AFRICA & S AFRICA • 250 kW
USSR
RADIO MOSCOW — (J) • SE ASIA

15585 USSR
P & PROGRESS — (J) • S AMERICA
RADIO MOSCOW — (J) • S AMERICA
RADIO MOSCOW, L'vov — W AFRICA & ATLANTIC • MARINERS • 200 kW ; W AFRICA • WS • 200 kW
RADIO YEREVAN — (J) • S AMERICA

15590 CHINA (PR)
CENTRAL PEOPLES BS, Beijing — DS-1 • 15 kW ; W-M • DS-1 • 15 kW
USA
†KUSW, Salt Lake City, Utah — Th-M • E NORTH AM • 100 kW ; Sa/Su • E NORTH AM • 100 kW ; Th-Su • E NORTH AM • 100 kW ; W-Su • E NORTH AM • 100 kW ; Th-Su • E NORTH AM • 100 kW • ALT. FREQ. TO 11695 kHz
USSR
RADIO MOSCOW — (J) • SE ASIA ; (J)

15595 GERMANY (FR)
DEUTSCHE WELLE, Various Locations — S ASIA • 100/500 kW
†DEUTSCHE WELLE, Wertachtal — (D) • JAPANESE • E ASIA • 500 kW
USSR
RADIO MOSCOW — WS ; (J) • N AFRICA

15600 CHINA (PR)
RADIO BEIJING — SE ASIA ; (D) • SE ASIA
USA
VOICE OF AMERICA, Via M'rovia, Liberi — W AFRICA • 250 kW
USSR
RADIO MOSCOW — DS-1 (FEEDER) • 15 kW • USB

15605v PAKISTAN
†RADIO PAKISTAN, Islamabad — MIDEAST • 250 kW ; EUROPE • 250 kW

15610 USA
†CHRIST SCI MONITOR, Maine — (J) • EUROPE • 500 kW ; (J) Sa • EUROPE • 500 kW ; (J) Su-F • EUROPE • 500 kW
†CHRIST SCI MONITOR, South Carolina — (D) M-F • E NORTH AM & EUROPE • 500 kW ; (J) Sa • E NORTH AM & EUROPE • 500 kW ; (J) Su-F • E NORTH AM & EUROPE • 500 kW ; (J) Su • E NORTH AM & EUROPE • 500 kW
†CHRIST SCI MONITOR, Via Saipan — AUSTRALIA • 100 kW ; S ASIA • 100 kW ; M-F • AUSTRALIA • 100 kW ; Sa/Su • AUSTRALIA • 100 kW

15615 ISRAEL
†KOL ISRAEL, Tel Aviv — (D) • AFRICA & S AMERICA • 300 kW ; EUROPE & E NORTH AM • DS-B • 50/300 kW
†RASHUTH HASHIDUR, Tel Aviv — (D) • E EUROPE & WEST USSR • DS-B ; (J) • EUROPE & E NORTH AM • DS-B • 50/300 kW ; (J) Su-F • EUROPE & E NORTH AM • DS-B • 50/300 kW

15625 GREECE
(con'd) †FONI TIS HELLADAS, Athens — AUSTRALIA • 100 kW ; (J) • AFRICA • 100 kW

ENGLISH ▬ ARABIC ﹋ CHINESE ▭▭ FRENCH ▬▬ GERMAN ▬▬ RUSSIAN ▬▬ SPANISH ▬▬ OTHER ▬

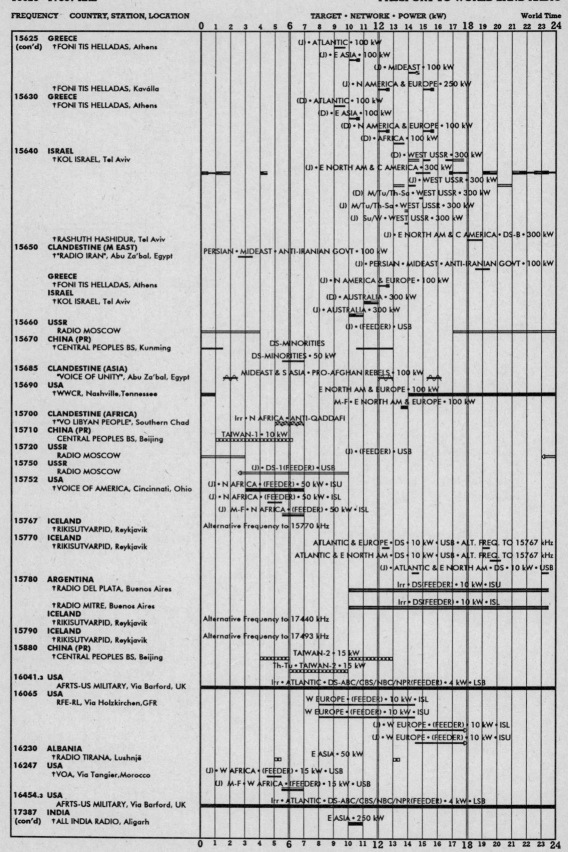

FREQUENCY	COUNTRY, STATION, LOCATION	TARGET • NETWORK • POWER (kW)	World Time

15625 (con'd) GREECE †FONI TIS HELLADAS, Athens
- (J) • ATLANTIC • 100 kW
- (J) • E ASIA • 100 kW
- (J) • MIDEAST • 100 kW

†FONI TIS HELLADAS, Kaválla
- (J) • N AMERICA & EUROPE • 250 kW

15630 GREECE †FONI TIS HELLADAS, Athens
- (D) • ATLANTIC • 100 kW
- (D) • E ASIA • 100 kW
- (D) • N AMERICA & EUROPE • 100 kW
- (D) • AFRICA • 100 kW

15640 ISRAEL †KOL ISRAEL, Tel Aviv
- (D) • WEST USSR • 300 kW
- (J) • E NORTH AM & C AMERICA • 300 kW
- (J) • WEST USSR • 300 kW
- (D) • M/Tu/Th-Sa • WEST USSR • 300 kW
- (J) • M/Tu/Th-Sa • WEST USSR • 300 kW
- (J) • Su/W • WEST USSR • 300 kW
- (J) • E NORTH AM & C AMERICA • DS-B • 300 kW

†RASHUTH HASHIDUR, Tel Aviv

15650 CLANDESTINE (M EAST) †"RADIO IRAN", Abu Za'bal, Egypt
- PERSIAN • MIDEAST • ANTI-IRANIAN GOVT • 100 kW
- (J) • PERSIAN • MIDEAST • ANTI-IRANIAN GOVT • 100 kW

GREECE †FONI TIS HELLADAS, Athens
- (J) • N AMERICA & EUROPE • 100 kW

ISRAEL †KOL ISRAEL, Tel Aviv
- (D) • AUSTRALIA • 300 kW
- (J) • AUSTRALIA • 300 kW

15660 USSR RADIO MOSCOW
- (J) • (FEEDER) • USB

15670 CHINA (PR) †CENTRAL PEOPLES BS, Kunming
- DS-MINORITIES
- DS-MINORITIES • 50 kW

15685 CLANDESTINE (ASIA) "VOICE OF UNITY", Abu Za'bal, Egypt
- MIDEAST & S ASIA • PRO-AFGHAN REBELS • 100 kW

15690 USA †WWCR, Nashville, Tennessee
- E NORTH AM & EUROPE • 100 kW
- M-F • E NORTH AM & EUROPE • 100 kW

15700 CLANDESTINE (AFRICA) †"VO LIBYAN PEOPLE", Southern Chad
- Irr • N AFRICA • ANTI-QADDAFI

15710 CHINA (PR) CENTRAL PEOPLES BS, Beijing
- TAIWAN-1 • 10 kW

15720 USSR RADIO MOSCOW
- (J) • (FEEDER) • USB

15750 USSR RADIO MOSCOW
- (J) • DS-1(FEEDER) • USB

15752 USA †VOICE OF AMERICA, Cincinnati, Ohio
- (J) • N AFRICA • (FEEDER) • 50 kW • ISU
- (J) • N AFRICA • (FEEDER) • 50 kW • ISL
- (J) M-F • N AFRICA • (FEEDER) • 50 kW • ISL

15767 ICELAND †RIKISUTVARPID, Reykjavik
- Alternative Frequency to 15770 kHz

15770 ICELAND †RIKISUTVARPID, Reykjavik
- ATLANTIC & EUROPE • DS • 10 kW • USB • ALT. FREQ. TO 15767 kHz
- ATLANTIC & E NORTH AM • DS • 10 kW • USB • ALT. FREQ. TO 15767 kHz
- (J) • ATLANTIC & E NORTH AM • DS • 10 kW • USB

15780 ARGENTINA †RADIO DEL PLATA, Buenos Aires
- Irr • DS(FEEDER) • 10 kW • ISU

†RADIO MITRE, Buenos Aires
- Irr • DS(FEEDER) • 10 kW • ISL

ICELAND †RIKISUTVARPID, Reykjavik
- Alternative Frequency to 17440 kHz

15790 ICELAND †RIKISUTVARPID, Reykjavik
- Alternative Frequency to 17493 kHz

15880 CHINA (PR) †CENTRAL PEOPLES BS, Beijing
- TAIWAN-2 • 15 kW
- Th-Tu • TAIWAN-2 • 15 kW

16041.3 USA AFRTS-US MILITARY, Via Barford, UK
- Irr • ATLANTIC • DS-ABC/CBS/NBC/NPR(FEEDER) • 4 kW • LSB

16065 USA RFE-RL, Via Holzkirchen, GFR
- W EUROPE • (FEEDER) • 10 kW • ISL
- W EUROPE • (FEEDER) • 10 kW • ISU
- (J) • W EUROPE • (FEEDER) • 10 kW • ISL
- (J) • W EUROPE • (FEEDER) • 10 kW • ISU

16230 ALBANIA †RADIO TIRANA, Lushnjë
- E ASIA • 50 kW

16247 USA †VOA, Via Tangier, Morocco
- (J) • W AFRICA • (FEEDER) • 15 kW • USB
- (J) M-F • W AFRICA • (FEEDER) • 15 kW • USB

16454.3 USA AFRTS-US MILITARY, Via Barford, UK
- Irr • ATLANTIC • DS-ABC/CBS/NBC/NPR(FEEDER) • 4 kW • LSB

17387 (con'd) INDIA †ALL INDIA RADIO, Aligarh
- E ASIA • 250 kW

SUMMER ONLY (J)   WINTER ONLY (D)   JAMMING / OR ⋀   EARLIEST HEARD ◁   LATEST HEARD ▷   NEW OR CHANGED FOR 1991 †

FREQUENCY	COUNTRY, STATION, LOCATION	TARGET • NETWORK • POWER (kW)

World Time

0 1 2 3 4 5 6 7 8 9 10 11 12 13 14 15 16 17 18 19 20 21 22 23 24

17387 **INDIA**
(con'd) †ALL INDIA RADIO, Aligarh — SE ASIA • 250 kW

17440 **ICELAND**
†RIKISUTVARPID, Reykjavik — ATLANTIC & E NORTH AM • DS • 10 kW • USB • ALT. FREQ. TO 15780 kHz
(J) • ATLANTIC & E NORTH AM • DS • 10 kW • USB

17493 **ICELAND**
†RIKISUTVARPID, Reykjavik — ATLANTIC & EUROPE • DS • 10 kW • USB • ALT. FREQ. TO 15790 kHz

17533 **CHINA (PR)**
RADIO BEIJING, Kunming — (D) • S AMERICA • CHINESE, CANTONESE • 120 kW

CLANDESTINE (ASIA)
"DEM KAMPUCHEA", Kunming, China — (J) • SE ASIA • PRO-KHMER ROUGE • 50 kW

17535 **GREECE**
†FONI TIS HELLADAS, Athens — (D) • N AMERICA & EUROPE • 100 kW
(J) • AUSTRALIA • 100 kW
(J) • E ASIA • 100 kW
(J) • N AMERICA & EUROPE • 100 kW

17540 **CLANDESTINE (ASIA)**
"VOICE OF UNITY", Abu Za'bal, Egypt — (J) • MIDEAST & S ASIA • PRO-AFGHAN REBELS • 100 kW

17545 **ISRAEL**
†RASHUTH HASHIDUR, Tel Aviv — W EUROPE & E NORTH AM • DS-B • 50/300 kW
(J) • W EUROPE & E NORTH AM • DS-B • 50/300 kW
Su-F • W EUROPE & E NORTH AM • DS-B • 50/300 kW

17550 **GREECE**
†FONI TIS HELLADAS, Athens — (D) • AUSTRALIA • 100 kW
(D) • N AMERICA & EUROPE • 100 kW

17555 **BELGIUM**
†BELGISCHE RADIO TV, Wavre — (J) • E NORTH AM & C AMERICA • 250 kW
(J) • M-Sa • E NORTH AM & C AMERICA • 250 kW
(J) • Su • E NORTH AM & C AMERICA • 250 kW

USA
†CHRIST SCI MONITOR, South Carolina — C AMERICA • 500 kW • ALT. FREQ. TO 13760 kHz
S AMERICA • 500 kW
M-F • C AMERICA • 500 kW • ALT. FREQ. TO 13760 kHz
M-Sa • S AMERICA • 500 kW
Sa • S AMERICA • 500 kW
Sa/Su • C AMERICA • 500 kW • ALT. FREQ. TO 13760 kHz
Su • S AMERICA • 500 kW
Su-F • S AMERICA • 500 kW

†CHRIST SCI MONITOR, Via Saipan — (J) • E ASIA • 100 kW
(J) M-Sa • E ASIA • 100 kW
(J) Sa • E ASIA • 100 kW
(J) Su-F • E ASIA • 100 kW
(J) Su • E ASIA • 100 kW

17560 **BELGIUM**
†BELGISCHE RADIO TV, Wavre — Alternative Frequency to 17580 kHz

USSR
RADIO MOSCOW — (J) • SOVIETS ABROAD

17570 **SWITZERLAND**
SWISS RADIO INTERNATIONAL, Sottens — AFRICA • 500 kW

USSR
RADIO MOSCOW — (J) • WS

17575 **HOLLAND**
†RADIO NEDERLAND, Flevoland — C AFRICA • 500 kW
(J) • S AMERICA • 500 kW
S ASIA • 300 kW
(D) • SE ASIA • 300 kW

†RADIO NEDERLAND, Via Madagascar — SE ASIA • 300 kW
E ASIA • 300 kW

ISRAEL
†KOL ISRAEL, Tel Aviv — (D) • W EUROPE & E NORTH AM • 300 kW
(J) • S AMERICA • 300 kW
(J) Sa/Su • WEST USSR • 300 kW
(D) • WEST USSR • 300 kW
(J) • W EUROPE & E NORTH AM • 300 kW
(D) Sa/Su • WEST USSR • 300 kW
(J) • WEST USSR • 300 kW
(J) • MIDEAST • 300 kW
(D) M/Tu/Th-Sa • WEST USSR • 300 kW
(J) M/Tu/Th-Sa • W EUROPE & E NORTH AM • 300 kW
(J) Su/W • WEST USSR • 300 kW
(J) Su/W • W EUROPE & E NORTH AM • 300 kW
(D) Tu/Th • MIDEAST • 300 kW
(J) Tu/Th • MIDEAST • 300 kW

17580 **BELGIUM**
†BELGISCHE RADIO TV, Wavre — (D) • AFRICA • 100/250 kW
(D) • AFRICA • 100/250 kW • ALT. FREQ. TO 17560 kHz
(J) • AFRICA • 100/250 kW
(J) • AFRICA • 100/250 kW • ALT. FREQ. TO 21810 kHz
(D) M-Sa • AFRICA • 100/250 kW

(con'd)

0 1 2 3 4 5 6 7 8 9 10 11 12 13 14 15 16 17 18 19 20 21 22 23 24

ENGLISH ▬ ARABIC ▨ CHINESE ▥ FRENCH ▤ GERMAN ▬ RUSSIAN ▬ SPANISH ▬ OTHER —

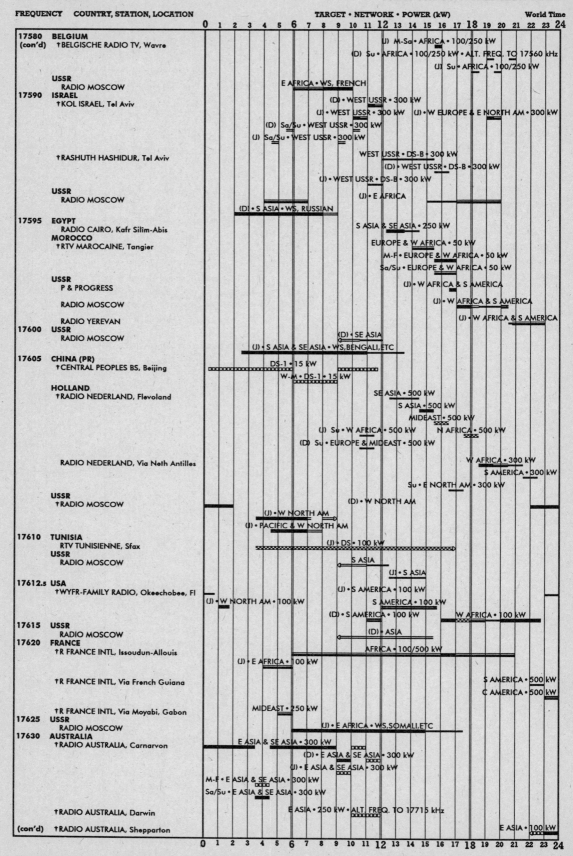

FREQUENCY　　COUNTRY, STATION, LOCATION　　　　　　　TARGET • NETWORK • POWER (kW)　　　　World Time

17580 **BELGIUM**
(con'd)　†BELGISCHE RADIO TV, Wavre
　　　　(J) M-Sa • AFRICA • 100/250 kW
　　　　(D) Su • AFRICA • 100/250 kW • ALT. FREQ. TO 17560 kHz
　　　　(J) Su • AFRICA • 100/250 kW

　　　　USSR
　　　　RADIO MOSCOW
　　　　E AFRICA • WS, FRENCH
17590 **ISRAEL**
　　　　†KOL ISRAEL, Tel Aviv
　　　　(D) • WEST USSR • 300 kW
　　　　(J) • WEST USSR • 300 kW　　(J) • W EUROPE & E NORTH AM • 300 kW
　　　　(D) Sa/Su • WEST USSR • 300 kW
　　　　(J) Sa/Su • WEST USSR • 300 kW

　　　　†RASHUTH HASHIDUR, Tel Aviv
　　　　WEST USSR • DS-B • 300 kW
　　　　(D) • WEST USSR • DS-B • 300 kW
　　　　(J) • WEST USSR • DS-B • 300 kW

　　　　USSR
　　　　RADIO MOSCOW
　　　　(J) • E AFRICA
　　　　(D) • S ASIA • WS, RUSSIAN
17595 **EGYPT**
　　　　RADIO CAIRO, Kafr Silim-Abis
　　　　S ASIA & SE ASIA • 250 kW
　　　　MOROCCO
　　　　†RTV MAROCAINE, Tangier
　　　　EUROPE & W AFRICA • 50 kW
　　　　M-F • EUROPE & W AFRICA • 50 kW
　　　　Sa/Su • EUROPE & W AFRICA • 50 kW

　　　　USSR
　　　　P & PROGRESS
　　　　(J) • W AFRICA & S AMERICA

　　　　RADIO MOSCOW
　　　　(J) • W AFRICA & S AMERICA

　　　　RADIO YEREVAN
　　　　(J) • W AFRICA & S AMERICA
17600 **USSR**
　　　　RADIO MOSCOW
　　　　(D) • SE ASIA
　　　　(J) • S ASIA & SE ASIA • WS, BENGALI, ETC

17605 **CHINA (PR)**
　　　　†CENTRAL PEOPLES BS, Beijing
　　　　DS-1 • 15 kW
　　　　W-M • DS-1 • 15 kW

　　　　HOLLAND
　　　　†RADIO NEDERLAND, Flevoland
　　　　SE ASIA • 500 kW
　　　　S ASIA • 500 kW
　　　　MIDEAST • 500 kW
　　　　(J) Su • W AFRICA • 500 kW　　N AFRICA • 500 kW
　　　　(D) Su • EUROPE & MIDEAST • 500 kW

　　　　RADIO NEDERLAND, Via Neth Antilles
　　　　W AFRICA • 300 kW
　　　　S AMERICA • 300 kW
　　　　Su • E NORTH AM • 300 kW

　　　　USSR
　　　　†RADIO MOSCOW
　　　　(D) • W NORTH AM
　　　　(J) • W NORTH AM
　　　　(J) • PACIFIC & W NORTH AM

17610 **TUNISIA**
　　　　RTV TUNISIENNE, Sfax
　　　　(J) • DS • 100 kW
　　　　USSR
　　　　RADIO MOSCOW
　　　　S ASIA
　　　　(J) • S ASIA

17612.5 **USA**
　　　　†WYFR-FAMILY RADIO, Okeechobee, Fl
　　　　(J) • S AMERICA • 100 kW
　　　　(J) • W NORTH AM • 100 kW
　　　　S AMERICA • 100 kW
　　　　(D) • S AMERICA • 100 kW　　W AFRICA • 100 kW

17615 **USSR**
　　　　RADIO MOSCOW
　　　　(D) • ASIA
17620 **FRANCE**
　　　　†R FRANCE INTL, Issoudun-Allouis
　　　　AFRICA • 100/500 kW
　　　　(J) • E AFRICA • 100 kW

　　　　†R FRANCE INTL, Via French Guiana
　　　　S AMERICA • 500 kW
　　　　C AMERICA • 500 kW

　　　　†R FRANCE INTL, Via Moyabi, Gabon
　　　　MIDEAST • 250 kW
17625 **USSR**
　　　　RADIO MOSCOW
　　　　(J) • E AFRICA • WS, SOMALI, ETC
17630 **AUSTRALIA**
　　　　†RADIO AUSTRALIA, Carnarvon
　　　　E ASIA & SE ASIA • 300 kW
　　　　(D) • E ASIA & SE ASIA • 300 kW
　　　　(J) • E ASIA & SE ASIA • 300 kW
　　　　M-F • E ASIA & SE ASIA • 300 kW
　　　　Sa/Su • E ASIA & SE ASIA • 300 kW

　　　　†RADIO AUSTRALIA, Darwin
　　　　E ASIA • 250 kW • ALT. FREQ. TO 17715 kHz

(con'd)　†RADIO AUSTRALIA, Shepparton
　　　　E ASIA • 100 kW

FREQUENCY   COUNTRY, STATION, LOCATION

TARGET • NETWORK • POWER (kW)

World Time

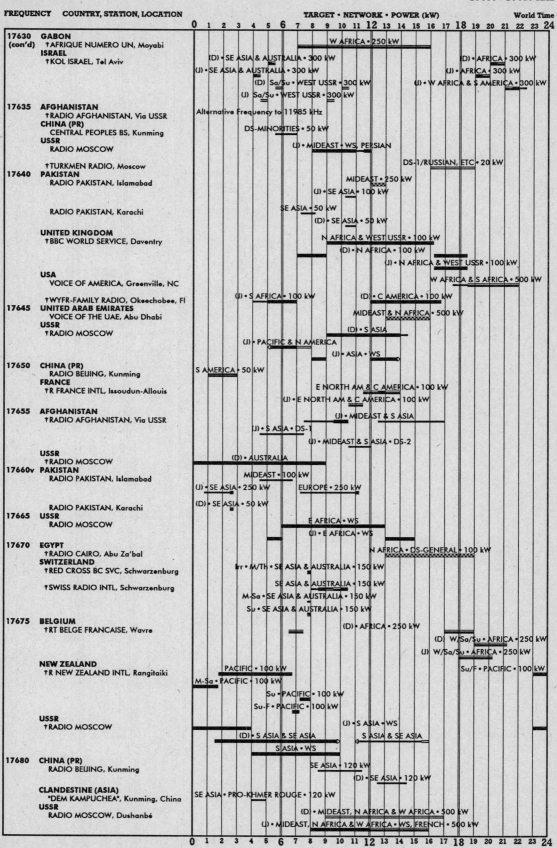

17630	GABON	
(con'd)	†AFRIQUE NUMERO UN, Moyabi	W AFRICA • 250 kW
	ISRAEL	
	†KOL ISRAEL, Tel Aviv	(D) • SE ASIA & AUSTRALIA • 300 kW (D) • AFRICA • 300 kW
		(J) • SE ASIA & AUSTRALIA • 300 kW (J) • AFRICA • 300 kW
		(D) Sa/Su • WEST USSR • 300 kW (J) • W AFRICA & S AMERICA • 300 kW
		(J) Sa/Su • WEST USSR • 300 kW
17635	AFGHANISTAN	
	†RADIO AFGHANISTAN, Via USSR	Alternative Frequency to 11985 kHz
	CHINA (PR)	
	CENTRAL PEOPLES BS, Kunming	DS-MINORITIES • 50 kW
	USSR	
	RADIO MOSCOW	(J) • MIDEAST • WS, PERSIAN
	†TURKMEN RADIO, Moscow	DS-1/RUSSIAN, ETC • 20 kW
17640	PAKISTAN	
	RADIO PAKISTAN, Islamabad	MIDEAST • 250 kW
		(J) • SE ASIA • 100 kW
	RADIO PAKISTAN, Karachi	SE ASIA • 50 kW
		(D) • SE ASIA • 50 kW
	UNITED KINGDOM	
	†BBC WORLD SERVICE, Daventry	N AFRICA & WEST USSR • 100 kW
		(D) • N AFRICA • 100 kW
		(J) • N AFRICA & WEST USSR • 100 kW
	USA	
	VOICE OF AMERICA, Greenville, NC	W AFRICA & S AFRICA • 500 kW
	†WYFR-FAMILY RADIO, Okeechobee, Fl	(J) • S AFRICA • 100 kW (D) • C AMERICA • 100 kW
17645	UNITED ARAB EMIRATES	
	VOICE OF THE UAE, Abu Dhabi	MIDEAST & N AFRICA • 500 kW
	USSR	
	†RADIO MOSCOW	(D) • S ASIA
		(J) • PACIFIC & N AMERICA
		(J) • ASIA • WS
17650	CHINA (PR)	
	RADIO BEIJING, Kunming	S AMERICA • 50 kW
	FRANCE	
	†R FRANCE INTL, Issoudun-Allouis	E NORTH AM & C AMERICA • 100 kW
		(J) • E NORTH AM & C AMERICA • 100 kW
17655	AFGHANISTAN	
	†RADIO AFGHANISTAN, Via USSR	(J) • MIDEAST & S ASIA
		(J) • S ASIA • DS-1
		(J) • MIDEAST & S ASIA • DS-2
	USSR	
	†RADIO MOSCOW	(D) • AUSTRALIA
17660v	PAKISTAN	
	RADIO PAKISTAN, Islamabad	MIDEAST • 100 kW
		(J) • SE ASIA • 250 kW EUROPE • 250 kW
	RADIO PAKISTAN, Karachi	(D) • SE ASIA • 50 kW
17665	USSR	
	RADIO MOSCOW	E AFRICA • WS
		(J) • E AFRICA • WS
17670	EGYPT	
	†RADIO CAIRO, Abu Za'bal	N AFRICA • DS-GENERAL • 100 kW
	SWITZERLAND	
	†RED CROSS BC SVC, Schwarzenburg	Irr • M/Th • SE ASIA & AUSTRALIA • 150 kW
	†SWISS RADIO INTL, Schwarzenburg	SE ASIA & AUSTRALIA • 150 kW
		M-Sa • SE ASIA & AUSTRALIA • 150 kW
		Su • SE ASIA & AUSTRALIA • 150 kW
17675	BELGIUM	
	†RT BELGE FRANCAISE, Wavre	(D) • AFRICA • 250 kW
		(D) W/Sa/Su • AFRICA • 250 kW
		(J) W/Sa/Su • AFRICA • 250 kW
	NEW ZEALAND	
	†R NEW ZEALAND INTL, Rangitaiki	PACIFIC • 100 kW Su/F • PACIFIC • 100 kW
		M-Sa • PACIFIC • 100 kW
		Su • PACIFIC • 100 kW
		Su-F • PACIFIC • 100 kW
	USSR	
	†RADIO MOSCOW	(J) • S ASIA • WS
		(D) • S ASIA & SE ASIA S ASIA & SE ASIA
		S ASIA • WS
17680	CHINA (PR)	
	RADIO BEIJING, Kunming	SE ASIA • 120 kW
		(D) • SE ASIA • 120 kW
	CLANDESTINE (ASIA)	
	"DEM KAMPUCHEA", Kunming, China	SE ASIA • PRO-KHMER ROUGE • 120 kW
	USSR	
	RADIO MOSCOW, Dushanbé	(D) • MIDEAST, N AFRICA & W AFRICA • 500 kW
		(J) • MIDEAST, N AFRICA & W AFRICA • WS, FRENCH • 500 kW

ENGLISH ▬▬   ARABIC ░░░   CHINESE ▫▫▫   FRENCH ▬▬   GERMAN ▬▬   RUSSIAN ═══   SPANISH ▬▬   OTHER ▬▬

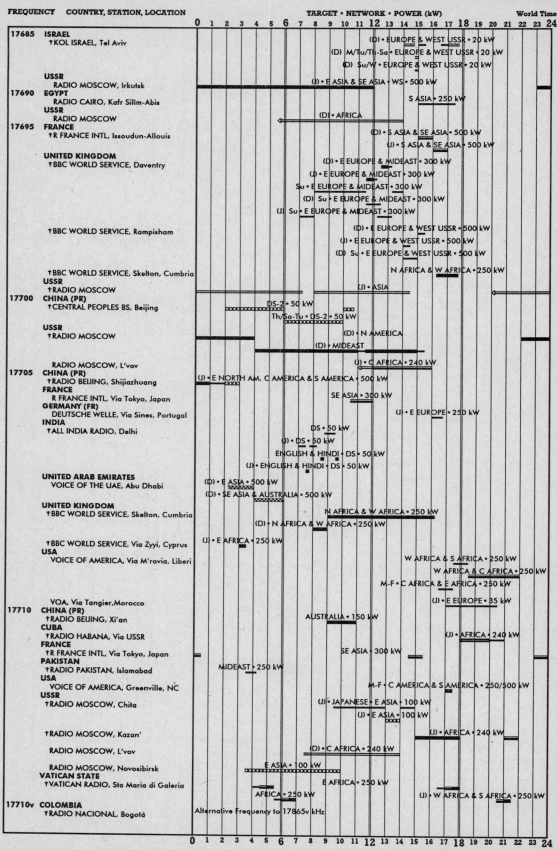

FREQUENCY   COUNTRY, STATION, LOCATION

TARGET • NETWORK • POWER (kW)   World Time

FREQUENCY	COUNTRY, STATION, LOCATION	Details
17685	**ISRAEL** †KOL ISRAEL, Tel Aviv	(D) • EUROPE & WEST USSR • 20 kW / (D) M/Tu/Th-Sa • EUROPE & WEST USSR • 20 kW / (D) Su/W • EUROPE & WEST USSR • 20 kW
	USSR RADIO MOSCOW, Irkutsk	(J) • E ASIA & SE ASIA • WS • 500 kW
17690	**EGYPT** RADIO CAIRO, Kafr Silim-Abis	S ASIA • 250 kW
	USSR RADIO MOSCOW	(D) • AFRICA
17695	**FRANCE** †R FRANCE INTL, Issoudun-Allouis	(D) • S ASIA & SE ASIA • 500 kW / (J) • S ASIA & SE ASIA • 500 kW
	UNITED KINGDOM †BBC WORLD SERVICE, Daventry	(D) • E EUROPE & MIDEAST • 300 kW / • E EUROPE & MIDEAST • 300 kW / Su • E EUROPE & MIDEAST • 300 kW / (D) Su • E EUROPE & MIDEAST • 300 kW / (J) Su • E EUROPE & MIDEAST • 300 kW
	†BBC WORLD SERVICE, Rampisham	(D) • E EUROPE & WEST USSR • 500 kW / (J) • E EUROPE & WEST USSR • 500 kW / (D) Su • E EUROPE & WEST USSR • 500 kW
	†BBC WORLD SERVICE, Skelton, Cumbria	N AFRICA & W AFRICA • 250 kW
	USSR †RADIO MOSCOW	(J) • ASIA
17700	**CHINA (PR)** †CENTRAL PEOPLES BS, Beijing	DS-2 • 50 kW / Th/Sa-Tu • DS-2 • 50 kW
	USSR †RADIO MOSCOW	(D) • N AMERICA / (D) • MIDEAST
	RADIO MOSCOW, L'vov	(J) • C AFRICA • 240 kW
17705	**CHINA (PR)** †RADIO BEIJING, Shijiazhuang	(J) • E NORTH AM, C AMERICA & S AMERICA • 500 kW
	FRANCE R FRANCE INTL, Via Tokyo, Japan	SE ASIA • 300 kW
	GERMANY (FR) DEUTSCHE WELLE, Via Sines, Portugal	(J) • E EUROPE • 250 kW
	INDIA †ALL INDIA RADIO, Delhi	DS • 50 kW / (J) • DS • 50 kW / ENGLISH & HINDI • DS • 50 kW / (J) • ENGLISH & HINDI • DS • 50 kW
	UNITED ARAB EMIRATES VOICE OF THE UAE, Abu Dhabi	(D) • E ASIA • 500 kW / (D) • SE ASIA & AUSTRALIA • 500 kW
	UNITED KINGDOM †BBC WORLD SERVICE, Skelton, Cumbria	N AFRICA & W AFRICA • 250 kW / (D) • N AFRICA & W AFRICA • 250 kW
	†BBC WORLD SERVICE, Via Zyyi, Cyprus	(J) • E AFRICA • 250 kW
	USA VOICE OF AMERICA, Via M'rovia, Liberi	W AFRICA & S AFRICA • 250 kW / W AFRICA & C AFRICA • 250 kW / M-F • C AFRICA & E AFRICA • 250 kW
	VOA, Via Tangier, Morocco	(J) • E EUROPE • 35 kW
17710	**CHINA (PR)** †RADIO BEIJING, Xi'an	AUSTRALIA • 150 kW
	CUBA †RADIO HABANA, Via USSR	(J) • AFRICA • 240 kW
	FRANCE †R FRANCE INTL, Via Tokyo, Japan	SE ASIA • 300 kW
	PAKISTAN †RADIO PAKISTAN, Islamabad	MIDEAST • 250 kW
	USA VOICE OF AMERICA, Greenville, NC	M-F • C AMERICA & S AMERICA • 250/500 kW
	USSR †RADIO MOSCOW, Chita	(J) • JAPANESE • E ASIA • 100 kW / (J) • E ASIA • 100 kW
	†RADIO MOSCOW, Kazan'	(J) • AFRICA • 240 kW
	RADIO MOSCOW, L'vov	(D) • C AFRICA • 240 kW
	RADIO MOSCOW, Novosibirsk	E ASIA • 100 kW
	VATICAN STATE †VATICAN RADIO, Sta Maria di Galeria	E AFRICA • 250 kW / AFRICA • 250 kW / (J) • W AFRICA & S AFRICA • 250 kW
17710v	**COLOMBIA** †RADIO NACIONAL, Bogotá	Alternative Frequency to 17865v kHz

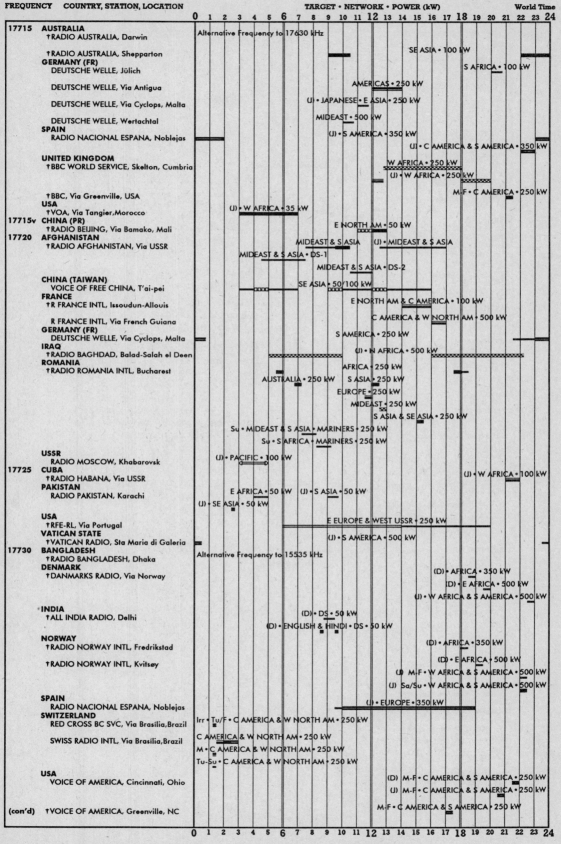

FREQUENCY	COUNTRY, STATION, LOCATION	TARGET • NETWORK • POWER (kW)	World Time

17715   AUSTRALIA
         †RADIO AUSTRALIA, Darwin — Alternative Frequency to 17630 kHz

         †RADIO AUSTRALIA, Shepparton — SE ASIA • 100 kW
         GERMANY (FR)
         DEUTSCHE WELLE, Jülich — S AFRICA • 100 kW

         DEUTSCHE WELLE, Via Antigua — AMERICAS • 250 kW

         DEUTSCHE WELLE, Via Cyclops, Malta — (J) • JAPANESE • E ASIA • 250 kW

         DEUTSCHE WELLE, Wertachtal — MIDEAST • 500 kW
         SPAIN
         RADIO NACIONAL ESPANA, Noblejas — (J) • S AMERICA • 350 kW   (J) • C AMERICA & S AMERICA • 350 kW

         UNITED KINGDOM
         †BBC WORLD SERVICE, Skelton, Cumbria — W AFRICA • 250 kW   (J) • W AFRICA • 250 kW

         †BBC, Via Greenville, USA — M-F • C AMERICA • 250 kW
         USA
         †VOA, Via Tangier, Morocco — (J) • W AFRICA • 35 kW
17715v CHINA (PR)
         †RADIO BEIJING, Via Bamako, Mali — E NORTH AM • 50 kW
17720   AFGHANISTAN
         †RADIO AFGHANISTAN, Via USSR — MIDEAST & S ASIA   (J) • MIDEAST & S ASIA
                                        MIDEAST & S ASIA • DS-1
                                        MIDEAST & S ASIA • DS-2

         CHINA (TAIWAN)
         VOICE OF FREE CHINA, T'ai-pei — SE ASIA • 50/100 kW
         FRANCE
         †R FRANCE INTL, Issoudun-Allouis — E NORTH AM & C AMERICA • 100 kW

         R FRANCE INTL, Via French Guiana — C AMERICA & W NORTH AM • 500 kW
         GERMANY (FR)
         DEUTSCHE WELLE, Via Cyclops, Malta — S AMERICA • 250 kW
         IRAQ
         †RADIO BAGHDAD, Balad-Salah el Deen — (J) • N AFRICA • 500 kW
         ROMANIA
         †RADIO ROMANIA INTL, Bucharest — AFRICA • 250 kW
                                          AUSTRALIA • 250 kW   S ASIA • 250 kW
                                          EUROPE • 250 kW
                                          MIDEAST • 250 kW
                                                   S ASIA & SE ASIA • 250 kW
                                          Su • MIDEAST & S ASIA • MARINERS • 250 kW
                                          Su • S AFRICA • MARINERS • 250 kW
         USSR
         RADIO MOSCOW, Khabarovsk — (J) • PACIFIC • 100 kW
17725   CUBA
         †RADIO HABANA, Via USSR — (J) • W AFRICA • 100 kW
         PAKISTAN
         RADIO PAKISTAN, Karachi — E AFRICA • 50 kW   (J) • S ASIA • 50 kW
                                   (J) • SE ASIA • 50 kW

         USA
         †RFE-RL, Via Portugal — E EUROPE & WEST USSR • 250 kW
         VATICAN STATE
         †VATICAN RADIO, Sta Maria di Galeria — (J) • S AMERICA • 500 kW
17730   BANGLADESH
         †RADIO BANGLADESH, Dhaka — Alternative Frequency to 15535 kHz
         DENMARK
         †DANMARKS RADIO, Via Norway — (D) • AFRICA • 350 kW
                                        (D) • E AFRICA • 500 kW
                                        (J) • W AFRICA & S AMERICA • 500 kW

         INDIA
         †ALL INDIA RADIO, Delhi — (D) • DS • 50 kW
                                   (D) • ENGLISH & HINDI • DS • 50 kW

         NORWAY
         †RADIO NORWAY INTL, Fredrikstad — (D) • AFRICA • 350 kW

         †RADIO NORWAY INTL, Kvitsøy — (D) • E AFRICA • 500 kW
                                        (J) • M-F • W AFRICA & S AMERICA • 500 kW
                                        (J) • Sa/Su • W AFRICA & S AMERICA • 500 kW

         SPAIN
         RADIO NACIONAL ESPANA, Noblejas — (J) • EUROPE • 350 kW
         SWITZERLAND
         RED CROSS BC SVC, Via Brasília, Brazil — Irr • Tu/F • C AMERICA & W NORTH AM • 250 kW

         SWISS RADIO INTL, Via Brasília, Brazil — C AMERICA & W NORTH AM • 250 kW
                                                  M • C AMERICA & W NORTH AM • 250 kW
                                                  Tu-Su • C AMERICA & W NORTH AM • 250 kW

         USA
         VOICE OF AMERICA, Cincinnati, Ohio — (D) • M-F • C AMERICA & S AMERICA • 250 kW
                                              (J) • M-F • C AMERICA & S AMERICA • 250 kW

(con'd) †VOICE OF AMERICA, Greenville, NC — M-F • C AMERICA & S AMERICA • 250 kW

ENGLISH ▬ ARABIC ▨ CHINESE ▱▱▱ FRENCH ▬ GERMAN ▬ RUSSIAN ═ SPANISH ▬ OTHER ▬

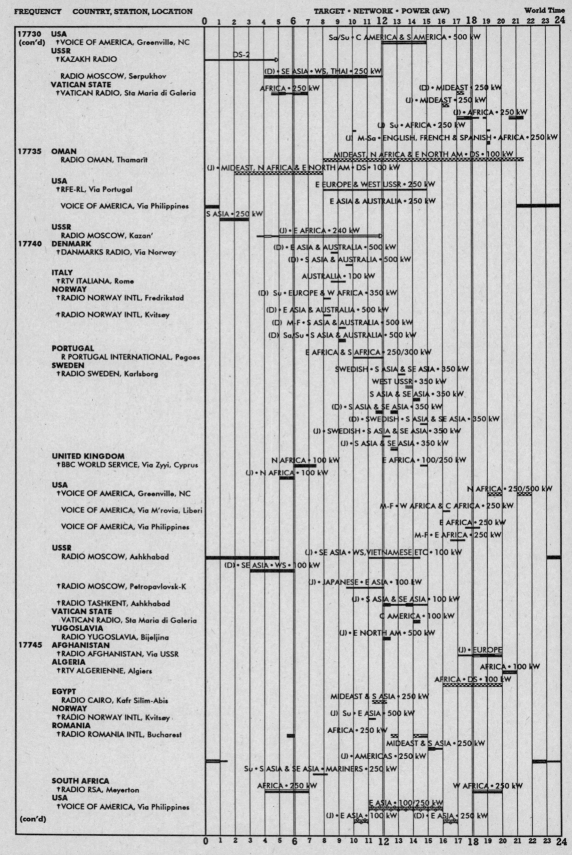

17730 **USA**
(con'd) †VOICE OF AMERICA, Greenville, NC   Sa/Su • C AMERICA & S AMERICA • 500 kW
     USSR
     †KAZAKH RADIO   DS-2

     RADIO MOSCOW, Serpukhov   (D) • SE ASIA • WS, THAI • 250 kW
     VATICAN STATE
     †VATICAN RADIO, Sta Maria di Galeria   AFRICA • 250 kW   (D) • MIDEAST • 250 kW
     (J) • MIDEAST • 250 kW
     (J) • AFRICA • 250 kW
     (J) Su • AFRICA • 250 kW
     (J) M-Sa • ENGLISH, FRENCH & SPANISH • AFRICA • 250 kW

17735 **OMAN**
     RADIO OMAN, Thamarīt   MIDEAST, N AFRICA & E NORTH AM • DS • 100 kW
     (J) • MIDEAST, N AFRICA & E NORTH AM • DS • 100 kW

     USA
     †RFE-RL, Via Portugal   E EUROPE & WEST USSR • 250 kW

     VOICE OF AMERICA, Via Philippines   E ASIA & AUSTRALIA • 250 kW
     S ASIA • 250 kW

     USSR
     RADIO MOSCOW, Kazan'   (J) • E AFRICA • 240 kW
17740 **DENMARK**
     †DANMARKS RADIO, Via Norway   (D) • E ASIA & AUSTRALIA • 500 kW
     (D) • S ASIA & AUSTRALIA • 500 kW

     ITALY
     †RTV ITALIANA, Rome   AUSTRALIA • 100 kW
     NORWAY
     †RADIO NORWAY INTL, Fredrikstad   (D) Su • EUROPE & W AFRICA • 350 kW
     †RADIO NORWAY INTL, Kvitsøy   (D) • E ASIA & AUSTRALIA • 500 kW
     (D) M-F • S ASIA & AUSTRALIA • 500 kW
     (D) Sa/Su • S ASIA & AUSTRALIA • 500 kW

     PORTUGAL
     R PORTUGAL INTERNATIONAL, Pegoes   E AFRICA & S AFRICA • 250/300 kW
     SWEDEN
     †RADIO SWEDEN, Karlsborg   SWEDISH • S ASIA & SE ASIA • 350 kW
     WEST USSR • 350 kW
     S ASIA & SE ASIA • 350 kW
     (D) • S ASIA & SE ASIA • 350 kW
     (D) • SWEDISH • S ASIA & SE ASIA • 350 kW
     (J) • SWEDISH • S ASIA & SE ASIA • 350 kW
     (J) • S ASIA & SE ASIA • 350 kW

     UNITED KINGDOM
     †BBC WORLD SERVICE, Via Zyyi, Cyprus   N AFRICA • 100 kW   E AFRICA • 100/250 kW
     (J) • N AFRICA • 100 kW

     USA
     †VOICE OF AMERICA, Greenville, NC   N AFRICA • 250/500 kW
     VOICE OF AMERICA, Via M'rovia, Liberi   M-F • W AFRICA & C AFRICA • 250 kW
     VOICE OF AMERICA, Via Philippines   E AFRICA • 250 kW
     M-F • E AFRICA • 250 kW

     USSR
     RADIO MOSCOW, Ashkhabad   (J) • SE ASIA • WS, VIETNAMESE ETC • 100 kW
     (D) • SE ASIA • WS • 100 kW

     †RADIO MOSCOW, Petropavlovsk-K   (J) • JAPANESE • E ASIA • 100 kW

     †RADIO TASHKENT, Ashkhabad   (J) • S ASIA & SE ASIA • 100 kW
     VATICAN STATE
     †VATICAN RADIO, Sta Maria di Galeria   C AMERICA • 100 kW
     YUGOSLAVIA
     RADIO YUGOSLAVIA, Bijeljina   (J) • E NORTH AM • 500 kW
17745 **AFGHANISTAN**
     †RADIO AFGHANISTAN, Via USSR   (J) • EUROPE
     ALGERIA
     †RTV ALGERIENNE, Algiers   AFRICA • 100 kW
     AFRICA • DS • 100 kW

     EGYPT
     RADIO CAIRO, Kafr Silim-Abis   MIDEAST & S ASIA • 250 kW
     NORWAY
     †RADIO NORWAY INTL, Kvitsøy   (J) Su • E ASIA • 500 kW
     ROMANIA
     †RADIO ROMANIA INTL, Bucharest   AFRICA • 250 kW
     MIDEAST & S ASIA • 250 kW
     (J) • AMERICAS • 250 kW
     Su • S ASIA & SE ASIA • MARINERS • 250 kW

     SOUTH AFRICA
     †RADIO RSA, Meyerton   AFRICA • 250 kW   W AFRICA • 250 kW
     USA
     †VOICE OF AMERICA, Via Philippines   E ASIA • 100/250 kW
(con'd)   (J) • E ASIA • 100 kW   (D) • E ASIA • 250 kW

FREQUENCY   COUNTRY, STATION, LOCATION   TARGET • NETWORK • POWER (kW)   World Time

0 1 2 3 4 5 6 7 8 9 10 11 12 13 14 15 16 17 18 19 20 21 22 23 24

Freq	Country / Station / Location	Notes
17745 (con'd)	**USSR** — RADIO MOSCOW, Frunze, Kirgiziya	(D) • SE ASIA • MARINERS • 100 kW
17750	**AUSTRALIA** — †RADIO AUSTRALIA, Darwin	E ASIA • 250 kW; SE ASIA • 250 kW; M-F • E ASIA • 250 kW; Sa/Su • E ASIA • 250 kW
	GUAM — †KTWR-TRANS WORLD RADIO, Merizo	(J) • E ASIA • 100 kW
	SURINAME — †R SURINAME INTL, Via Brasília, Brazil	Alternative Frequency to 17755 kHz
	USA — †RFE-RL, Via Germany	WEST USSR • 100/250 kW
	†WYFR-FAMILY RADIO, Okeechobee, Fl	(J) • S AMERICA • 100 kW; EUROPE • 100 kW; (J) • C AMERICA • 100 kW; (J) • EUROPE • 100 kW
17755	**SAUDI ARABIA** — †BS OF THE KINGDOM, Riyadh	E AFRICA • 350 kW
	SURINAME — †R SURINAME INTL, Via Brasília, Brazil	M-F • EUROPE • 250 kW • ALT. FREQ. TO 17750 kHz; M-F • EUROPE • 250 kW
	UNITED KINGDOM — †BBC WORLD SERVICE, Via Zyyi, Cyprus	(J) • N AFRICA • 250 kW
	USA — VOICE OF AMERICA, Via Philippines	E AFRICA • 250 kW
17760	**UNITED KINGDOM** — BBC WORLD SERVICE, Via Antigua	S AMERICA • 250 kW
	USA — †RFE-RL, Via Germany	WEST USSR • 100 kW
17765	**DENMARK** — †DANMARKS RADIO, Via Norway	(D) • MIDEAST & E AFRICA • 500 kW; (J) • W NORTH AM • 350 kW; (J) • N AMERICA • 500 kW; (J) • W NORTH AM • 500 kW
	GERMANY (FR) — †DEUTSCHE WELLE, Via Sri Lanka	(D) • SE ASIA & AUSTRALIA • 250 kW; S AFRICA • 250 kW
	†DEUTSCHE WELLE, Wertachtal	W AFRICA • 500 kW; E AFRICA • 500 kW; (D) • S AFRICA • 500 kW; S AFRICA • 500 kW
	JAPAN — †RADIO JAPAN/NHK, Tokyo-Yamata	E ASIA • 300 kW; JAPANESE • E ASIA • GENERAL • 300 kW; E ASIA • GENERAL • 300 kW; (J) • E ASIA • GENERAL • 100/300 kW; (J) • JAPANESE • E ASIA • GENERAL • 100/300 kW
	KOREA (DPR) — †RADIO PYONGYANG, Pyongyang	SE ASIA • 200 kW; (J) • E AFRICA • 200 kW
	NORWAY — †RADIO NORWAY INTL, Fredrikstad	(J) • W NORTH AM • 350 kW
	†RADIO NORWAY INTL, Kvitsøy	(D) • MIDEAST & E AFRICA • 500 kW
	†RADIO NORWAY INTL, Sveio	(J) • N AMERICA • 500 kW; (J) • M-F • N AMERICA • 500 kW; (J) • M-F • W NORTH AM • 500 kW; (J) • Sa/Su • N AMERICA • 500 kW; (J) • Sa/Su • W NORTH AM • 500 kW
	SOUTH AFRICA — †RADIO RSA, Meyerton	C AFRICA • 250 kW
	USA — †VOICE OF AMERICA, Via Philippines	E ASIA • 250 kW; (D) • E ASIA • 250 kW; (J) • E ASIA • 250 kW
	USSR — RADIO MOSCOW, Armavir	(J) • S ASIA & SE ASIA • WS, HINDI, URDU, ETC • 500 kW
	RADIO MOSCOW, Tula	(D) • S ASIA & SE ASIA • WS, HINDI, URDU • 240 kW
17765v	**MEXICO** — RADIO MEXICO INTL, México City	Irr • W NORTH AM • 10 kW
17770	**EGYPT** — †RADIO CAIRO, Kafr Silim-Abis	S AMERICA • 250 kW; SE ASIA • 250 kW
	GERMANY (FR) — DEUTSCHE WELLE, Jülich	(J) • S ASIA • 100 kW
	QATAR — †QATAR BC SERVICE, Doha-Al Khaisah	(J) • EUROPE • 100/250 kW
	SPAIN — RADIO NACIONAL ESPANA, Noblejas	M Sa • MIDEAST • 350 kW; Th • MIDEAST • LADINO • 350 kW
	UNITED KINGDOM — BBC WORLD SERVICE, Daventry	(J) • WEST USSR • 300 kW; (J) Su • WEST USSR • 300 kW
	USA — †RFE-RL, Via Pals, Spain	WEST USSR • 250 kW

0 1 2 3 4 5 6 7 8 9 10 11 12 13 14 15 16 17 18 19 20 21 22 23 24

ENGLISH ▬▬   ARABIC ░░░   CHINESE ▫▫▫   FRENCH ▬▬   GERMAN ▬▬   RUSSIAN ═══   SPANISH ▬▬   OTHER ▬

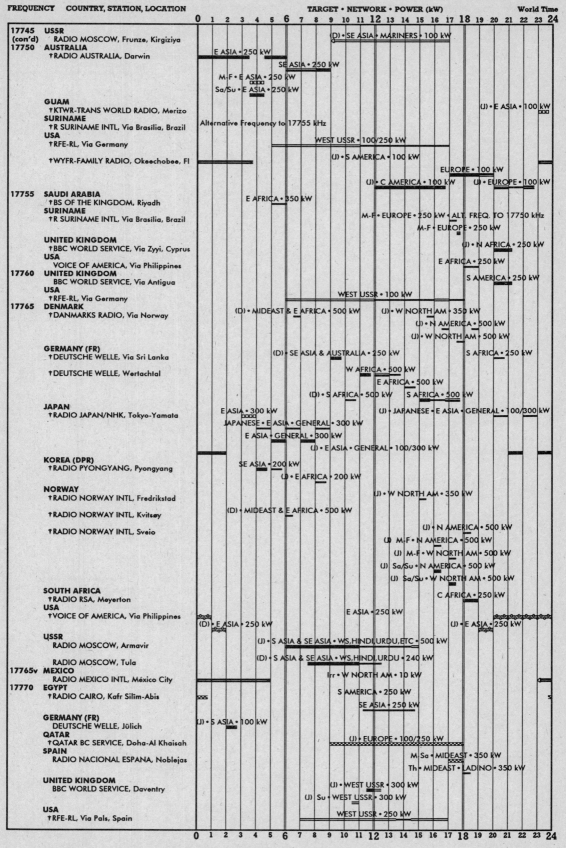

FREQUENCY   COUNTRY, STATION, LOCATION   TARGET • NETWORK • POWER (kW)   World Time

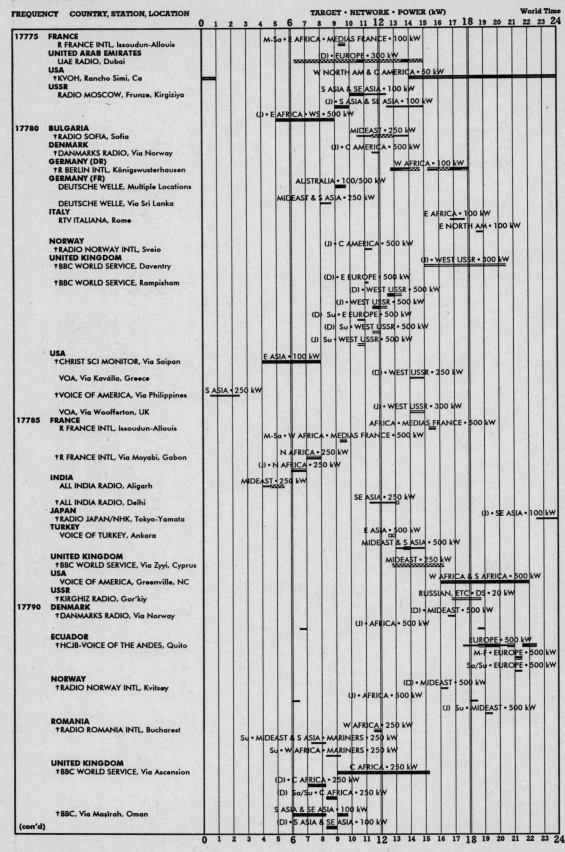

17775	**FRANCE**
	R FRANCE INTL, Issoudun-Allouis — M-Sa • E AFRICA • MEDIAS FRANCE • 100 kW
	UNITED ARAB EMIRATES
	UAE RADIO, Dubai — (D) • EUROPE • 300 kW
	USA
	†KVOH, Rancho Simi, Ca — W NORTH AM & C AMERICA • 50 kW
	USSR
	RADIO MOSCOW, Frunze, Kirgiziya — S ASIA & SE ASIA • 100 kW
	(J) • S ASIA & SE ASIA • 100 kW
	(J) • E AFRICA • WS • 500 kW
17780	**BULGARIA**
	†RADIO SOFIA, Sofia — MIDEAST • 250 kW
	DENMARK
	†DANMARKS RADIO, Via Norway — (J) • C AMERICA • 500 kW
	GERMANY (DR)
	†R BERLIN INTL, Königswusterhausen — W AFRICA • 100 kW
	GERMANY (FR)
	DEUTSCHE WELLE, Multiple Locations — AUSTRALIA • 100/500 kW
	DEUTSCHE WELLE, Via Sri Lanka — MIDEAST & S ASIA • 250 kW
	ITALY
	RTV ITALIANA, Rome — E AFRICA • 100 kW
	E NORTH AM • 100 kW
	NORWAY
	†RADIO NORWAY INTL, Sveio — (J) • C AMERICA • 500 kW
	UNITED KINGDOM
	†BBC WORLD SERVICE, Daventry — (J) • WEST USSR • 300 kW
	†BBC WORLD SERVICE, Rampisham — (D) • E EUROPE • 500 kW
	(D) • WEST USSR • 500 kW
	(J) • WEST USSR • 500 kW
	(D) Su • E EUROPE • 500 kW
	(D) Su • WEST USSR • 500 kW
	(J) Su • WEST USSR • 500 kW
	USA
	†CHRIST SCI MONITOR, Via Saipan — E ASIA • 100 kW
	VOA, Via Kaválla, Greece — (D) • WEST USSR • 250 kW
	†VOICE OF AMERICA, Via Philippines — S ASIA • 250 kW
	VOA, Via Woofferton, UK — (J) • WEST USSR • 300 kW
17785	**FRANCE**
	R FRANCE INTL, Issoudun-Allouis — AFRICA • MEDIAS FRANCE • 500 kW
	M-Sa • W AFRICA • MEDIAS FRANCE • 500 kW
	†R FRANCE INTL, Via Moyabi, Gabon — N AFRICA • 250 kW
	(J) • N AFRICA • 250 kW
	INDIA
	ALL INDIA RADIO, Aligarh — MIDEAST • 250 kW
	†ALL INDIA RADIO, Delhi — SE ASIA • 250 kW
	JAPAN
	†RADIO JAPAN/NHK, Tokyo-Yamata — (J) • SE ASIA • 100 kW
	TURKEY
	VOICE OF TURKEY, Ankara — E ASIA • 500 kW
	MIDEAST & S ASIA • 500 kW
	UNITED KINGDOM
	†BBC WORLD SERVICE, Via Zyyi, Cyprus — MIDEAST • 250 kW
	USA
	VOICE OF AMERICA, Greenville, NC — W AFRICA & S AFRICA • 500 kW
	USSR
	†KIRGHIZ RADIO, Gor'kiy — RUSSIAN, ETC • DS • 20 kW
17790	**DENMARK**
	†DANMARKS RADIO, Via Norway — (D) • MIDEAST • 500 kW
	(J) • AFRICA • 500 kW
	ECUADOR
	†HCJB-VOICE OF THE ANDES, Quito — EUROPE • 500 kW
	M-F • EUROPE • 500 kW
	Sa/Su • EUROPE • 500 kW
	NORWAY
	†RADIO NORWAY INTL, Kvitsøy — (D) • MIDEAST • 500 kW
	(J) • AFRICA • 500 kW
	(J) Su • MIDEAST • 500 kW
	ROMANIA
	†RADIO ROMANIA INTL, Bucharest — W AFRICA • 250 kW
	Su • MIDEAST & S ASIA • MARINERS • 250 kW
	Su • W AFRICA • MARINERS • 250 kW
	UNITED KINGDOM
	†BBC WORLD SERVICE, Via Ascension — C AFRICA • 250 kW
	(D) • C AFRICA • 250 kW
	(D) Sa/Su • C AFRICA • 250 kW
	†BBC, Via Maşīrah, Oman — S ASIA & SE ASIA • 100 kW
	(D) • S ASIA & SE ASIA • 100 kW

(con'd)

FREQUENCY   COUNTRY, STATION, LOCATION

TARGET • NETWORK • POWER (kW)   World Time

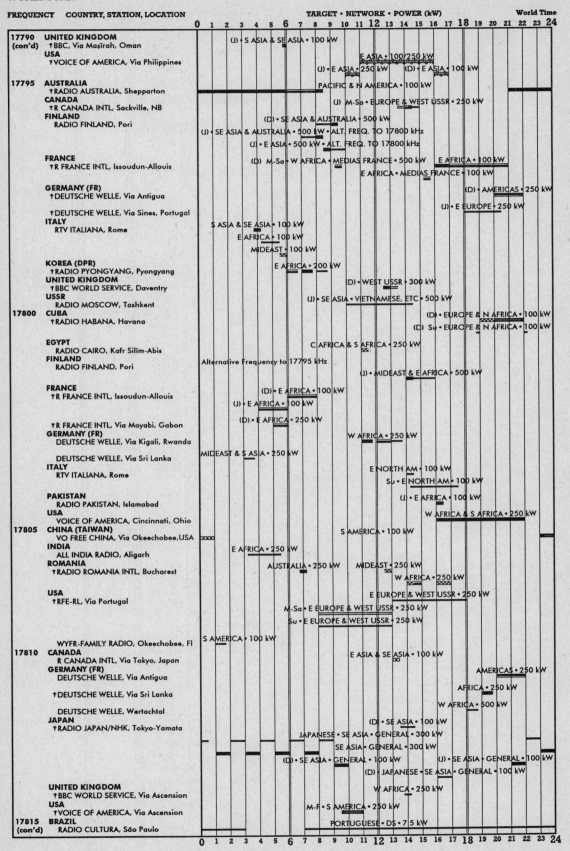

17790 (con'd)	**UNITED KINGDOM** †BBC, Via Maṣīrah, Oman	(J) • S ASIA & SE ASIA • 100 kW
	USA †VOICE OF AMERICA, Via Philippines	E ASIA • 100/250 kW; (J) • E ASIA • 250 kW; (D) • E ASIA • 100 kW
17795	**AUSTRALIA** †RADIO AUSTRALIA, Shepparton	PACIFIC & N AMERICA • 100 kW
	CANADA †R CANADA INTL, Sackville, NB	(J) • M-Sa • EUROPE & WEST USSR • 250 kW
	FINLAND RADIO FINLAND, Pori	(D) • SE ASIA & AUSTRALIA • 500 kW; (J) • SE ASIA & AUSTRALIA • 500 kW • ALT. FREQ. TO 17800 kHz; (J) • E ASIA • 500 kW • ALT. FREQ. TO 17800 kHz
	FRANCE †R FRANCE INTL, Issoudun-Allouis	(D) M-Sa • W AFRICA • MEDIAS FRANCE • 500 kW; E AFRICA • 100 kW; E AFRICA • MEDIAS FRANCE • 100 kW
	GERMANY (FR) †DEUTSCHE WELLE, Via Antigua	(D) • AMERICAS • 250 kW
	†DEUTSCHE WELLE, Via Sines, Portugal	(J) • E EUROPE • 250 kW
	ITALY RTV ITALIANA, Rome	S ASIA & SE ASIA • 100 kW; E AFRICA • 100 kW; MIDEAST • 100 kW
	KOREA (DPR) †RADIO PYONGYANG, Pyongyang	E AFRICA • 200 kW
	UNITED KINGDOM †BBC WORLD SERVICE, Daventry	(D) • WEST USSR • 300 kW
	USSR RADIO MOSCOW, Tashkent	(J) • SE ASIA • VIETNAMESE, ETC • 500 kW
17800	**CUBA** †RADIO HABANA, Havana	(D) • EUROPE & N AFRICA • 100 kW; (D) Su • EUROPE & N AFRICA • 100 kW
	EGYPT RADIO CAIRO, Kafr Silim-Abis	C AFRICA & S AFRICA • 250 kW
	FINLAND RADIO FINLAND, Pori	Alternative Frequency to 17795 kHz; (J) • MIDEAST & E AFRICA • 500 kW
	FRANCE †R FRANCE INTL, Issoudun-Allouis	(D) • E AFRICA • 100 kW; (J) • E AFRICA • 100 kW; (D) • E AFRICA • 250 kW
	†R FRANCE INTL, Via Moyabi, Gabon	
	GERMANY (FR) DEUTSCHE WELLE, Via Kigali, Rwanda	W AFRICA • 250 kW
	DEUTSCHE WELLE, Via Sri Lanka	MIDEAST & S ASIA • 250 kW
	ITALY RTV ITALIANA, Rome	E NORTH AM • 100 kW; Su • E NORTH AM • 100 kW
	PAKISTAN RADIO PAKISTAN, Islamabad	(J) • E AFRICA • 100 kW
	USA VOICE OF AMERICA, Cincinnati, Ohio	W AFRICA & S AFRICA • 250 kW
17805	**CHINA (TAIWAN)** VO FREE CHINA, Via Okeechobee, USA	S AMERICA • 100 kW
	INDIA ALL INDIA RADIO, Aligarh	E AFRICA • 250 kW
	ROMANIA †RADIO ROMANIA INTL, Bucharest	AUSTRALIA • 250 kW; MIDEAST • 250 kW; W AFRICA • 250 kW
	USA †RFE-RL, Via Portugal	E EUROPE & WEST USSR • 250 kW; M-Sa • E EUROPE & WEST USSR • 250 kW; Su • E EUROPE & WEST USSR • 250 kW
	WYFR-FAMILY RADIO, Okeechobee, Fl	S AMERICA • 100 kW
17810	**CANADA** R CANADA INTL, Via Tokyo, Japan	E ASIA & SE ASIA • 100 kW
	GERMANY (FR) DEUTSCHE WELLE, Via Antigua	AMERICAS • 250 kW
	†DEUTSCHE WELLE, Via Sri Lanka	AFRICA • 250 kW
	DEUTSCHE WELLE, Wertachtal	W AFRICA • 500 kW
	JAPAN †RADIO JAPAN/NHK, Tokyo-Yamata	(D) • SE ASIA • 100 kW; JAPANESE • SE ASIA • GENERAL • 300 kW; SE ASIA • GENERAL • 300 kW; (D) • SE ASIA • GENERAL • 100 kW; (J) • SE ASIA • GENERAL • 100 kW; (D) • JAPANESE • SE ASIA • GENERAL • 100 kW
	UNITED KINGDOM †BBC WORLD SERVICE, Via Ascension	W AFRICA • 250 kW
	USA †VOICE OF AMERICA, Via Ascension	M-F • S AMERICA • 250 kW
17815 (con'd)	**BRAZIL** RADIO CULTURA, São Paulo	PORTUGUESE • DS • 7.5 kW

ENGLISH ▬ **ARABIC** ░ **CHINESE** ▭▭ **FRENCH** ▬▬ **GERMAN** ▬ **RUSSIAN** ═══ **SPANISH** ▬ **OTHER** ▬

FREQUENCY   COUNTRY, STATION, LOCATION   TARGET • NETWORK • POWER (kW)   World Time

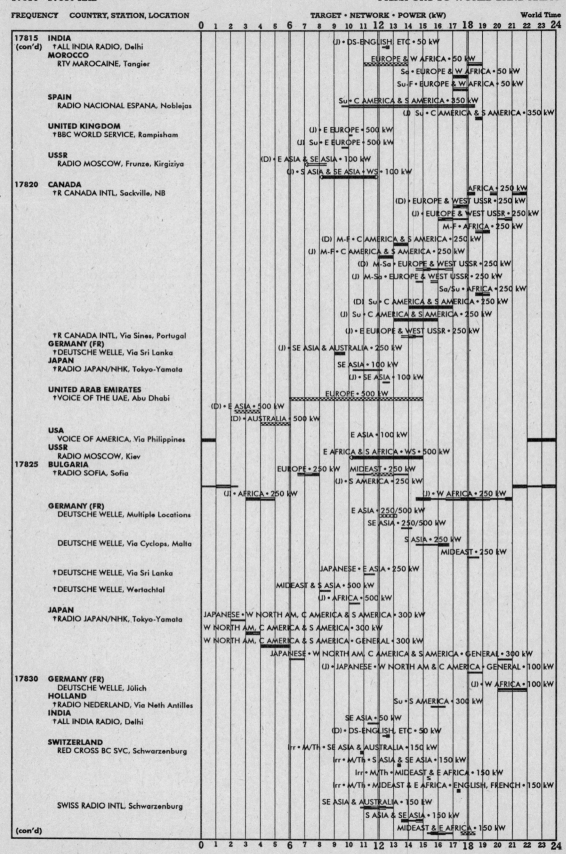

	0 1 2 3 4 5 6 7 8 9 10 11 12 13 14 15 16 17 18 19 20 21 22 23 24
17815 INDIA	
(con'd) †ALL INDIA RADIO, Delhi	(J) • DS-ENGLISH, ETC • 50 kW
MOROCCO	
RTV MAROCAINE, Tangier	EUROPE & W AFRICA • 50 kW
	Sa • EUROPE & W AFRICA • 50 kW
	Su-F • EUROPE & W AFRICA • 50 kW
SPAIN	
RADIO NACIONAL ESPANA, Noblejas	Su • C AMERICA & S AMERICA • 350 kW
	(J) Su • C AMERICA & S AMERICA • 350 kW
UNITED KINGDOM	
†BBC WORLD SERVICE, Rampisham	(J) • E EUROPE • 500 kW
	(J) Su • E EUROPE • 500 kW
USSR	
RADIO MOSCOW, Frunze, Kirgiziya	(D) • E ASIA & SE ASIA • 100 kW
	(J) • S ASIA & SE ASIA • WS • 100 kW
17820 CANADA	
†R CANADA INTL, Sackville, NB	AFRICA • 250 kW
	(D) • EUROPE & WEST USSR • 250 kW
	(J) • EUROPE & WEST USSR • 250 kW
	M-F • AFRICA • 250 kW
	(D) M-F • C AMERICA & S AMERICA • 250 kW
	(J) M-F • C AMERICA & S AMERICA • 250 kW
	(D) M-Sa • EUROPE & WEST USSR • 250 kW
	(J) M-Sa • EUROPE & WEST USSR • 250 kW
	Sa/Su • AFRICA • 250 kW
	(D) Su • C AMERICA & S AMERICA • 250 kW
	(J) Su • C AMERICA & S AMERICA • 250 kW
†R CANADA INTL, Via Sines, Portugal	(J) • E EUROPE & WEST USSR • 250 kW
GERMANY (FR)	
†DEUTSCHE WELLE, Via Sri Lanka	(J) • SE ASIA & AUSTRALIA • 250 kW
JAPAN	
†RADIO JAPAN/NHK, Tokyo-Yamata	SE ASIA • 100 kW
	(J) • SE ASIA • 100 kW
UNITED ARAB EMIRATES	
†VOICE OF THE UAE, Abu Dhabi	EUROPE • 500 kW
	(D) • E ASIA • 500 kW
	(D) • AUSTRALIA • 500 kW
USA	
VOICE OF AMERICA, Via Philippines	E ASIA • 100 kW
USSR	
RADIO MOSCOW, Kiev	E AFRICA & S AFRICA • WS • 500 kW
17825 BULGARIA	
†RADIO SOFIA, Sofia	EUROPE • 250 kW MIDEAST • 250 kW
	(J) • S AMERICA • 250 kW
	(J) • AFRICA • 250 kW (J) • W AFRICA • 250 kW
GERMANY (FR)	
DEUTSCHE WELLE, Multiple Locations	E ASIA • 250/500 kW
	SE ASIA • 250/500 kW
DEUTSCHE WELLE, Via Cyclops, Malta	S ASIA • 250 kW
	MIDEAST • 250 kW
†DEUTSCHE WELLE, Via Sri Lanka	JAPANESE • E ASIA • 250 kW
†DEUTSCHE WELLE, Wertachtal	MIDEAST & S ASIA • 500 kW
	(J) • AFRICA • 500 kW
JAPAN	
†RADIO JAPAN/NHK, Tokyo-Yamata	JAPANESE • W NORTH AM, C AMERICA & S AMERICA • 300 kW
	W NORTH AM, C AMERICA & S AMERICA • 300 kW
	W NORTH AM, C AMERICA & S AMERICA • GENERAL • 300 kW
	JAPANESE • W NORTH AM, C AMERICA & S AMERICA • GENERAL • 300 kW
	(J) • JAPANESE • W NORTH AM & C AMERICA • GENERAL • 100 kW
17830 GERMANY (FR)	
DEUTSCHE WELLE, Jülich	(J) • W AFRICA • 100 kW
HOLLAND	
†RADIO NEDERLAND, Via Neth Antilles	Su • S AMERICA • 300 kW
INDIA	
†ALL INDIA RADIO, Delhi	SE ASIA • 50 kW
	(D) • DS-ENGLISH, ETC • 50 kW
SWITZERLAND	
RED CROSS BC SVC, Schwarzenburg	Irr • M/Th • SE ASIA & AUSTRALIA • 150 kW
	Irr • M/Th • S ASIA & SE ASIA • 150 kW
	Irr • M/Th • MIDEAST & E AFRICA • 150 kW
	Irr • M/Th • MIDEAST & E AFRICA • ENGLISH, FRENCH • 150 kW
SWISS RADIO INTL, Schwarzenburg	SE ASIA & AUSTRALIA • 150 kW
	S ASIA & SE ASIA • 150 kW
	MIDEAST & E AFRICA • 150 kW
(con'd)	0 1 2 3 4 5 6 7 8 9 10 11 12 13 14 15 16 17 18 19 20 21 22 23 24

SUMMER ONLY (J)   WINTER ONLY (D)   JAMMING / OR ∧   EARLIEST HEARD ◁   LATEST HEARD ▷   NEW OR CHANGED FOR 1991 †

FREQUENCY   COUNTRY, STATION, LOCATION   TARGET • NETWORK • POWER (kW)   World Time

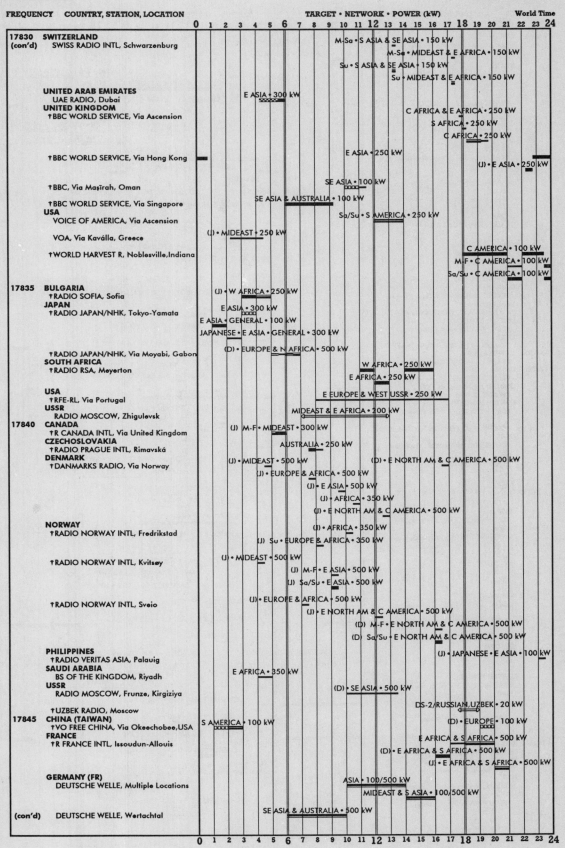

17830 SWITZERLAND
(con'd)   SWISS RADIO INTL, Schwarzenburg — M-Sa • S ASIA & SE ASIA • 150 kW; M-Sa • MIDEAST & E AFRICA • 150 kW; Su • S ASIA & SE ASIA • 150 kW; Su • MIDEAST & E AFRICA • 150 kW

UNITED ARAB EMIRATES
UAE RADIO, Dubai — E ASIA • 300 kW
UNITED KINGDOM
†BBC WORLD SERVICE, Via Ascension — C AFRICA & E AFRICA • 250 kW; S AFRICA • 250 kW; C AFRICA • 250 kW
†BBC WORLD SERVICE, Via Hong Kong — E ASIA • 250 kW; (J) • E ASIA • 250 kW
†BBC, Via Maşīrah, Oman — SE ASIA • 100 kW
†BBC WORLD SERVICE, Via Singapore — SE ASIA & AUSTRALIA • 100 kW
USA
VOICE OF AMERICA, Via Ascension — Sa/Su • S AMERICA • 250 kW
VOA, Via Kaválla, Greece — (J) • MIDEAST • 250 kW
†WORLD HARVEST R, Noblesville, Indiana — C AMERICA • 100 kW; M-F • C AMERICA • 100 kW; Sa/Su • C AMERICA • 100 kW

17835 BULGARIA
†RADIO SOFIA, Sofia — (J) • W AFRICA • 250 kW
JAPAN
†RADIO JAPAN/NHK, Tokyo-Yamata — E ASIA • 300 kW; E ASIA • GENERAL • 100 kW; JAPANESE • E ASIA • GENERAL • 300 kW
†RADIO JAPAN/NHK, Via Moyabi, Gabon — (D) • EUROPE & N AFRICA • 500 kW
SOUTH AFRICA
†RADIO RSA, Meyerton — W AFRICA • 250 kW; E AFRICA • 250 kW
USA
†RFE-RL, Via Portugal — E EUROPE & WEST USSR • 250 kW
USSR
RADIO MOSCOW, Zhigulevsk — MIDEAST & E AFRICA • 200 kW

17840 CANADA
†R CANADA INTL, Via United Kingdom — (J) M-F • MIDEAST • 300 kW
CZECHOSLOVAKIA
†RADIO PRAGUE INTL, Rimavská — AUSTRALIA • 250 kW
DENMARK
†DANMARKS RADIO, Via Norway — (J) • MIDEAST • 500 kW; (D) • E NORTH AM & C AMERICA • 500 kW; (J) • EUROPE & AFRICA • 500 kW; (J) • E ASIA • 500 kW; (J) • AFRICA • 350 kW; (J) • E NORTH AM & C AMERICA • 500 kW

NORWAY
†RADIO NORWAY INTL, Fredrikstad — (J) • AFRICA • 350 kW; (J) Su • EUROPE & AFRICA • 350 kW
†RADIO NORWAY INTL, Kvitsøy — (J) • MIDEAST • 500 kW; (J) M-F • E ASIA • 500 kW; (J) Sa/Su • E ASIA • 500 kW
†RADIO NORWAY INTL, Sveio — (J) • EUROPE & AFRICA • 500 kW; (J) • E NORTH AM & C AMERICA • 500 kW; (D) M-F • E NORTH AM & C AMERICA • 500 kW; (D) Sa/Su • E NORTH AM & C AMERICA • 500 kW

PHILIPPINES
†RADIO VERITAS ASIA, Palauig — (J) • JAPANESE • E ASIA • 100 kW
SAUDI ARABIA
BS OF THE KINGDOM, Riyadh — E AFRICA • 350 kW
USSR
RADIO MOSCOW, Frunze, Kirgiziya — (D) • SE ASIA • 500 kW
†UZBEK RADIO, Moscow — DS-2/RUSSIAN,UZBEK • 20 kW

17845 CHINA (TAIWAN)
†VO FREE CHINA, Via Okeechobee, USA — S AMERICA • 100 kW; (D) • EUROPE • 100 kW
FRANCE
†R FRANCE INTL, Issoudun-Allouis — E AFRICA & S AFRICA • 500 kW; (D) • E AFRICA & S AFRICA • 500 kW; (J) • E AFRICA & S AFRICA • 500 kW

GERMANY (FR)
DEUTSCHE WELLE, Multiple Locations — ASIA • 100/500 kW; MIDEAST & S ASIA • 100/500 kW
(con'd)   DEUTSCHE WELLE, Wertachtal — SE ASIA & AUSTRALIA • 500 kW

ENGLISH ▬   ARABIC ⬚⬚⬚   CHINESE ⬚⬚⬚   FRENCH ▬▬   GERMAN ▬   RUSSIAN ▭▭   SPANISH ▬   OTHER ▬

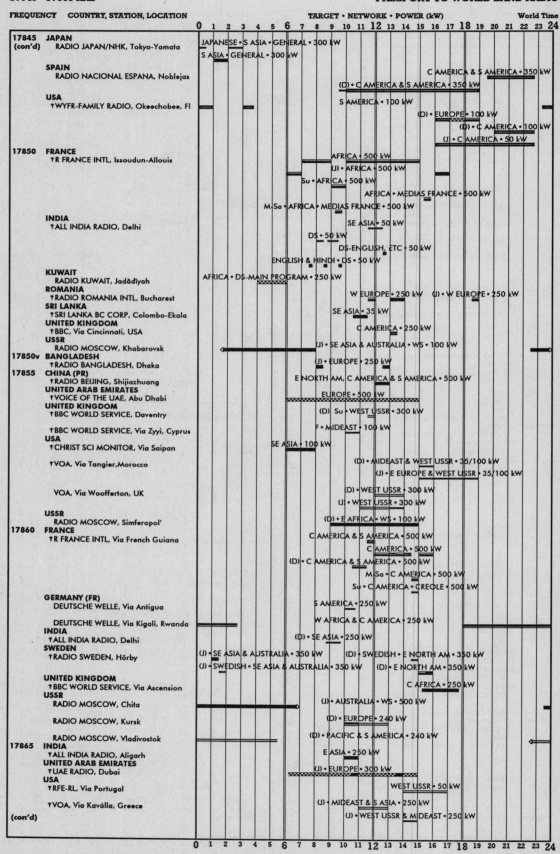

FREQUENCY   COUNTRY, STATION, LOCATION   TARGET • NETWORK • POWER (kW)   World Time

17845   JAPAN
(con'd)   RADIO JAPAN/NHK, Tokyo-Yamata   JAPANESE • S ASIA • GENERAL • 300 kW
                                                    S ASIA • GENERAL • 300 kW

        SPAIN
            RADIO NACIONAL ESPANA, Noblejas   C AMERICA & S AMERICA • 350 kW
                                                    (D) • C AMERICA & S AMERICA • 350 kW
        USA
            †WYFR-FAMILY RADIO, Okeechobee, Fl   S AMERICA • 100 kW
                                                              (D) • EUROPE • 100 kW
                                                                   (D) • C AMERICA • 100 kW
                                                                   (J) • C AMERICA • 50 kW

17850   FRANCE
            †R FRANCE INTL, Issoudun-Allouis   AFRICA • 500 kW
                                                    (J) • AFRICA • 500 kW
                                                    Su • AFRICA • 500 kW
                                                              AFRICA • MEDIAS FRANCE • 500 kW
                                                    M-Sa • AFRICA • MEDIAS FRANCE • 500 kW
        INDIA
            †ALL INDIA RADIO, Delhi   SE ASIA • 50 kW
                                                    DS • 50 kW
                                                          DS-ENGLISH, ETC • 50 kW
                                                    ENGLISH & HINDI • DS • 50 kW
        KUWAIT
            RADIO KUWAIT, Jadādīyah   AFRICA • DS-MAIN PROGRAM • 250 kW
        ROMANIA
            †RADIO ROMANIA INTL, Bucharest   W EUROPE • 250 kW   (J) • W EUROPE • 250 kW
        SRI LANKA
            †SRI LANKA BC CORP, Colombo-Ekala   SE ASIA • 35 kW
        UNITED KINGDOM
            †BBC, Via Cincinnati, USA   C AMERICA • 250 kW
        USSR
            RADIO MOSCOW, Khabarovsk   (J) • SE ASIA & AUSTRALIA • WS • 100 kW
17850v BANGLADESH
            †RADIO BANGLADESH, Dhaka   (J) • EUROPE • 250 kW
17855   CHINA (PR)
            †RADIO BEIJING, Shijiazhuang   E NORTH AM, C AMERICA & S AMERICA • 500 kW
        UNITED ARAB EMIRATES
            †VOICE OF THE UAE, Abu Dhabi   EUROPE • 500 kW
        UNITED KINGDOM
            †BBC WORLD SERVICE, Daventry   (D) Su • WEST USSR • 300 kW

            †BBC WORLD SERVICE, Via Zyyi, Cyprus   F • MIDEAST • 100 kW
        USA
            †CHRIST SCI MONITOR, Via Saipan   SE ASIA • 100 kW

            †VOA, Via Tangier, Morocco   (D) • MIDEAST & WEST USSR • 35/100 kW
                                                              (J) • E EUROPE & WEST USSR • 35/100 kW

            VOA, Via Woofferton, UK   (D) • WEST USSR • 300 kW
                                                         (J) • WEST USSR • 300 kW
        USSR
            RADIO MOSCOW, Simferopol'   (D) • E AFRICA • WS • 100 kW
17860   FRANCE
            †R FRANCE INTL, Via French Guiana   C AMERICA & S AMERICA • 500 kW
                                                         C AMERICA • 500 kW
                                                    (D) • C AMERICA & S AMERICA • 500 kW
                                                         M-Sa • C AMERICA • 500 kW
                                                         Su • C AMERICA • CREOLE • 500 kW
        GERMANY (FR)
            DEUTSCHE WELLE, Via Antigua   S AMERICA • 250 kW

            DEUTSCHE WELLE, Via Kigali, Rwanda   W AFRICA & C AMERICA • 250 kW
        INDIA
            †ALL INDIA RADIO, Delhi   (D) • SE ASIA • 250 kW
        SWEDEN
            †RADIO SWEDEN, Hörby   (J) • SE ASIA & AUSTRALIA • 350 kW   (D) • SWEDISH • E NORTH AM • 350 kW
                                             (J) • SWEDISH • SE ASIA & AUSTRALIA • 350 kW   (D) • E NORTH AM • 350 kW
        UNITED KINGDOM
            †BBC WORLD SERVICE, Via Ascension   C AFRICA • 250 kW
        USSR
            RADIO MOSCOW, Chita   (J) • AUSTRALIA • WS • 500 kW

            RADIO MOSCOW, Kursk   (D) • EUROPE • 240 kW

            RADIO MOSCOW, Vladivostok   (D) • PACIFIC & S AMERICA • 240 kW
17865   INDIA
            †ALL INDIA RADIO, Aligarh   E ASIA • 250 kW
        UNITED ARAB EMIRATES
            †UAE RADIO, Dubai   (J) • EUROPE • 300 kW
        USA
            †RFE-RL, Via Portugal   WEST USSR • 50 kW

            †VOA, Via Kaválla, Greece   (J) • MIDEAST & S ASIA • 250 kW
(con'd)   (J) • WEST USSR & MIDEAST • 250 kW

FREQUENCY   COUNTRY, STATION, LOCATION   TARGET · NETWORK · POWER (kW)   World Time

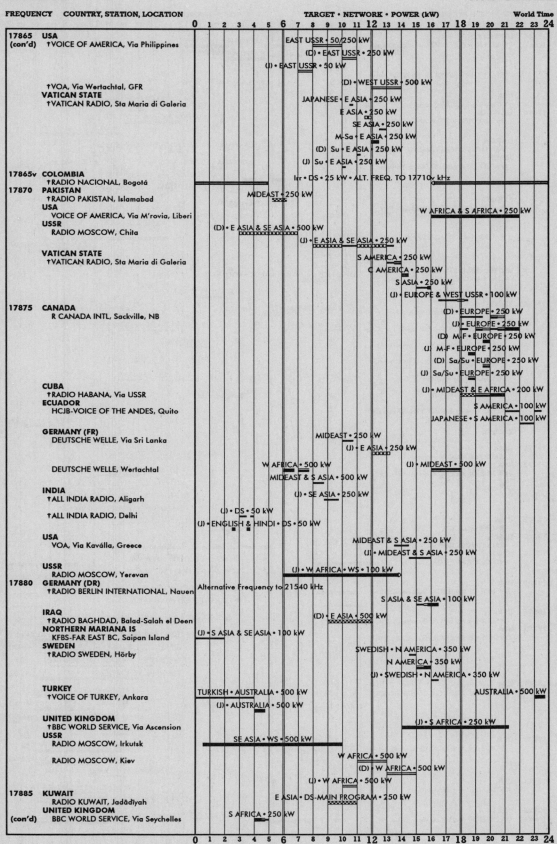

Frequency	Country / Station / Location	Target · Network · Power
17865 (con'd)	**USA** †VOICE OF AMERICA, Via Philippines	EAST USSR · 50/250 kW
		(D) · EAST USSR · 250 kW
		(J) · EAST USSR · 50 kW
	†VOA, Via Wertachtal, GFR	(D) · WEST USSR · 500 kW
	VATICAN STATE †VATICAN RADIO, Sta Maria di Galeria	JAPANESE · E ASIA · 250 kW
		E ASIA · 250 kW
		SE ASIA · 250 kW
		M-Sa · E ASIA · 250 kW
		(D) Su · E ASIA · 250 kW
		(J) Su · E ASIA · 250 kW
17865v	**COLOMBIA** †RADIO NACIONAL, Bogotá	Irr · DS · 25 kW · ALT. FREQ. TO 17710v kHz
17870	**PAKISTAN** †RADIO PAKISTAN, Islamabad	MIDEAST · 250 kW
	USA VOICE OF AMERICA, Via M'rovia, Liberi	W AFRICA & S AFRICA · 250 kW
	USSR RADIO MOSCOW, Chita	(D) · E ASIA & SE ASIA · 500 kW
		(J) · E ASIA & SE ASIA · 250 kW
	VATICAN STATE †VATICAN RADIO, Sta Maria di Galeria	S AMERICA · 250 kW
		C AMERICA · 250 kW
		S ASIA · 250 kW
		(J) · EUROPE & WEST USSR · 100 kW
17875	**CANADA** R CANADA INTL, Sackville, NB	(D) · EUROPE · 250 kW
		(J) · EUROPE · 250 kW
		(D) M-F · EUROPE · 250 kW
		(J) M-F · EUROPE · 250 kW
		(D) Sa/Su · EUROPE · 250 kW
		(J) Sa/Su · EUROPE · 250 kW
	CUBA †RADIO HABANA, Via USSR	(J) · MIDEAST & E AFRICA · 200 kW
	ECUADOR HCJB-VOICE OF THE ANDES, Quito	S AMERICA · 100 kW
		JAPANESE · S AMERICA · 100 kW
	GERMANY (FR) DEUTSCHE WELLE, Via Sri Lanka	MIDEAST · 250 kW
		(J) · E ASIA · 250 kW
	DEUTSCHE WELLE, Wertachtal	W AFRICA · 500 kW
		(J) · MIDEAST · 500 kW
		MIDEAST & S ASIA · 500 kW
	INDIA †ALL INDIA RADIO, Aligarh	(J) · SE ASIA · 250 kW
	†ALL INDIA RADIO, Delhi	(J) · DS · 50 kW
		(J) · ENGLISH & HINDI · DS · 50 kW
	USA VOA, Via Kaválla, Greece	MIDEAST & S ASIA · 250 kW
		(J) · MIDEAST & S ASIA · 250 kW
	USSR RADIO MOSCOW, Yerevan	(J) · W AFRICA · WS · 100 kW
17880	**GERMANY (DR)** †RADIO BERLIN INTERNATIONAL, Nauen	Alternative Frequency to 21540 kHz
		S ASIA & SE ASIA · 100 kW
	IRAQ †RADIO BAGHDAD, Balad-Salah el Deen	(D) · E ASIA · 500 kW
	NORTHERN MARIANA IS KFBS-FAR EAST BC, Saipan Island	(J) · S ASIA & SE ASIA · 100 kW
	SWEDEN †RADIO SWEDEN, Hörby	SWEDISH · N AMERICA · 350 kW
		N AMERICA · 350 kW
		(J) · SWEDISH · N AMERICA · 350 kW
	TURKEY †VOICE OF TURKEY, Ankara	TURKISH · AUSTRALIA · 500 kW
		(J) · AUSTRALIA · 500 kW
		AUSTRALIA · 500 kW
	UNITED KINGDOM †BBC WORLD SERVICE, Via Ascension	(J) · S AFRICA · 250 kW
	USSR RADIO MOSCOW, Irkutsk	SE ASIA · WS · 500 kW
	RADIO MOSCOW, Kiev	W AFRICA · 500 kW
		(D) · W AFRICA · 500 kW
		(J) · W AFRICA · 500 kW
17885	**KUWAIT** RADIO KUWAIT, Jadādīyah	E ASIA · DS-MAIN PROGRAM · 250 kW
	UNITED KINGDOM BBC WORLD SERVICE, Via Seychelles	S AFRICA · 250 kW
(con'd)		

ENGLISH ▬   ARABIC ⚒   CHINESE ᴑᴑ   FRENCH ▬   GERMAN ▬   RUSSIAN ═   SPANISH ▬   OTHER ▬

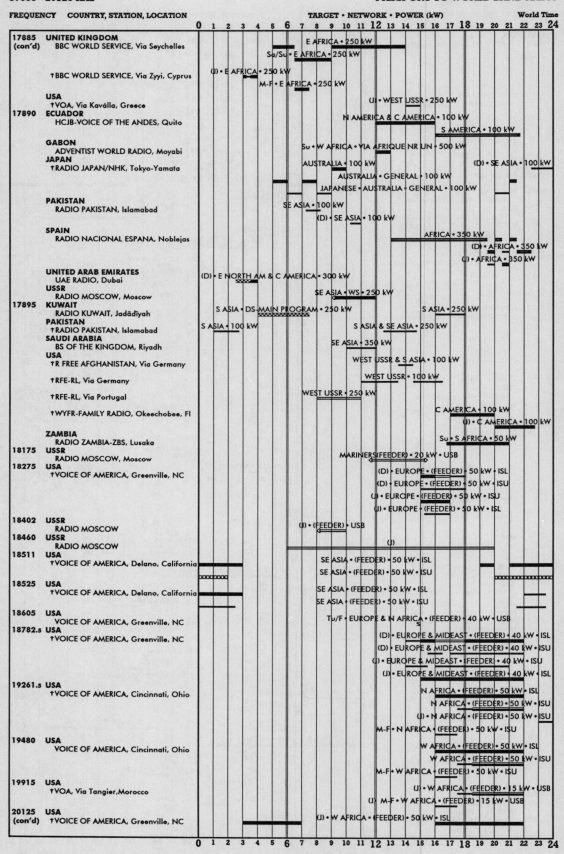

17885 **UNITED KINGDOM**
(con'd)   BBC WORLD SERVICE, Via Seychelles — E AFRICA • 250 kW
                Sa/Su • E AFRICA • 250 kW
                †BBC WORLD SERVICE, Via Zyyi, Cyprus — (J) • E AFRICA • 250 kW
                M-F • E AFRICA • 250 kW
         USA
                †VOA, Via Kaválla, Greece — (J) • WEST USSR • 250 kW
17890 **ECUADOR**
                HCJB-VOICE OF THE ANDES, Quito — N AMERICA & C AMERICA • 100 kW
                S AMERICA • 100 kW
         GABON
                ADVENTIST WORLD RADIO, Moyabi — Su • W AFRICA • VIA AFRIQUE NR UN • 500 kW
         JAPAN
                †RADIO JAPAN/NHK, Tokyo-Yamata — AUSTRALIA • 100 kW
                (D) • SE ASIA • 100 kW
                AUSTRALIA • GENERAL • 100 kW
                JAPANESE • AUSTRALIA • GENERAL • 100 kW
         PAKISTAN
                RADIO PAKISTAN, Islamabad — SE ASIA • 100 kW
                (D) • SE ASIA • 100 kW
         SPAIN
                RADIO NACIONAL ESPANA, Noblejas — AFRICA • 350 kW
                (D) • AFRICA • 350 kW
                (J) • AFRICA • 350 kW
         UNITED ARAB EMIRATES
                UAE RADIO, Dubai — (D) • E NORTH AM & C AMERICA • 300 kW
         USSR
                RADIO MOSCOW, Moscow — SE ASIA • WS • 250 kW
17895 **KUWAIT**
                RADIO KUWAIT, Jadādīyah — S ASIA • DS-MAIN PROGRAM • 250 kW   S ASIA • 250 kW
         PAKISTAN
                †RADIO PAKISTAN, Islamabad — S ASIA • 100 kW   S ASIA & SE ASIA • 250 kW
         SAUDI ARABIA
                BS OF THE KINGDOM, Riyadh — SE ASIA • 350 kW
         USA
                †R FREE AFGHANISTAN, Via Germany — WEST USSR & S ASIA • 100 kW
                †RFE-RL, Via Germany — WEST USSR • 100 kW
                †RFE-RL, Via Portugal — WEST USSR • 250 kW
                †WYFR-FAMILY RADIO, Okeechobee, Fl — C AMERICA • 100 kW
                (J) • C AMERICA • 100 kW
         ZAMBIA
                RADIO ZAMBIA-ZBS, Lusaka — Su • S AFRICA • 50 kW
18175 **USSR**
                RADIO MOSCOW, Moscow — MARINERS (FEEDER) • 20 kW • USB
18275 **USA**
                †VOICE OF AMERICA, Greenville, NC — (D) • EUROPE • (FEEDER) • 50 kW • ISL
                (D) • EUROPE • (FEEDER) • 50 kW • ISU
                (J) • EUROPE • (FEEDER) • 50 kW • ISU
                (J) • EUROPE • (FEEDER) • 50 kW • ISL
18402 **USSR**
                RADIO MOSCOW — (J) • (FEEDER) • USB
18460 **USSR**
                RADIO MOSCOW — (J)
18511 **USA**
                †VOICE OF AMERICA, Delano, California — SE ASIA • (FEEDER) • 50 kW • ISL
                SE ASIA • (FEEDER) • 50 kW • ISU
18525 **USA**
                †VOICE OF AMERICA, Delano, California — SE ASIA • (FEEDER) • 50 kW • ISL
                SE ASIA • (FEEDER) • 50 kW • ISU
18605 **USA**
                VOICE OF AMERICA, Greenville, NC — Tu/F • EUROPE & N AFRICA • (FEEDER) • 40 kW • USB
18782.5 **USA**
                †VOICE OF AMERICA, Greenville, NC — (D) • EUROPE & MIDEAST • (FEEDER) • 40 kW • ISL
                (D) • EUROPE & MIDEAST • (FEEDER) • 40 kW • ISU
                (J) • EUROPE & MIDEAST • (FEEDER) • 40 kW • ISU
                (J) • EUROPE & MIDEAST • (FEEDER) • 40 kW • ISL
19261.5 **USA**
                †VOICE OF AMERICA, Cincinnati, Ohio — N AFRICA • (FEEDER) • 50 kW • ISL
                N AFRICA • (FEEDER) • 50 kW • ISU
                (J) • N AFRICA • (FEEDER) • 50 kW • ISU
                M-F • N AFRICA • (FEEDER) • 50 kW • ISU
19480 **USA**
                VOICE OF AMERICA, Cincinnati, Ohio — W AFRICA • (FEEDER) • 50 kW • ISL
                W AFRICA • (FEEDER) • 50 kW • ISU
                M-F • W AFRICA • (FEEDER) • 50 kW • ISU
19915 **USA**
                †VOA, Via Tangier, Morocco — (J) • W AFRICA • (FEEDER) • 15 kW • USB
                (J) M-F • W AFRICA • (FEEDER) • 15 kW • USB
20125 **USA**
(con'd)   †VOICE OF AMERICA, Greenville, NC — (J) • W AFRICA • (FEEDER) • 50 kW • ISL

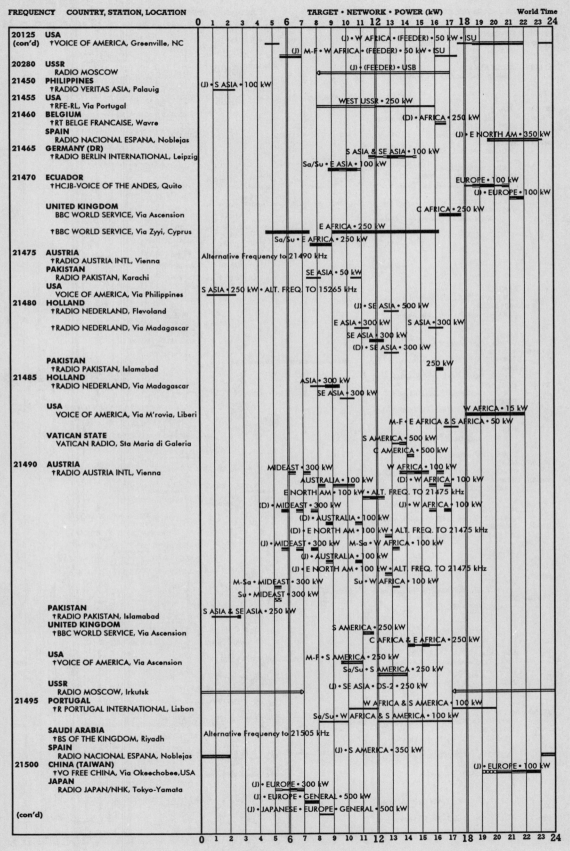

FREQUENCY	COUNTRY, STATION, LOCATION
20125 (con'd)	**USA** †VOICE OF AMERICA, Greenville, NC
20280	**USSR** RADIO MOSCOW
21450	**PHILIPPINES** †RADIO VERITAS ASIA, Palauig
21455	**USA** †RFE-RL, Via Portugal
21460	**BELGIUM** †RT BELGE FRANCAISE, Wavre
	SPAIN RADIO NACIONAL ESPANA, Noblejas
21465	**GERMANY (DR)** †RADIO BERLIN INTERNATIONAL, Leipzig
21470	**ECUADOR** †HCJB-VOICE OF THE ANDES, Quito
	UNITED KINGDOM BBC WORLD SERVICE, Via Ascension
	†BBC WORLD SERVICE, Via Zyyi, Cyprus
21475	**AUSTRIA** †RADIO AUSTRIA INTL, Vienna
	PAKISTAN RADIO PAKISTAN, Karachi
	USA VOICE OF AMERICA, Via Philippines
21480	**HOLLAND** †RADIO NEDERLAND, Flevoland
	†RADIO NEDERLAND, Via Madagascar
	PAKISTAN †RADIO PAKISTAN, Islamabad
21485	**HOLLAND** †RADIO NEDERLAND, Via Madagascar
	USA VOICE OF AMERICA, Via M'rovia, Liberi
	VATICAN STATE VATICAN RADIO, Sta Maria di Galeria
21490	**AUSTRIA** †RADIO AUSTRIA INTL, Vienna
	PAKISTAN †RADIO PAKISTAN, Islamabad
	UNITED KINGDOM †BBC WORLD SERVICE, Via Ascension
	USA †VOICE OF AMERICA, Via Ascension
	USSR RADIO MOSCOW, Irkutsk
21495	**PORTUGAL** †R PORTUGAL INTERNATIONAL, Lisbon
	SAUDI ARABIA †BS OF THE KINGDOM, Riyadh
	SPAIN RADIO NACIONAL ESPANA, Noblejas
21500	**CHINA (TAIWAN)** †VO FREE CHINA, Via Okeechobee,USA
	JAPAN RADIO JAPAN/NHK, Tokyo-Yamata
(con'd)	

TARGET • NETWORK • POWER (kW)　　　　World Time

20125 USA: (J) • W AFRICA • (FEEDER) • 50 kW • ISU; (J) M-F • W AFRICA • (FEEDER) • 50 kW • ISU

20280 USSR: (J) • (FEEDER) • USB

21450 PHILIPPINES: (J) • S ASIA • 100 kW

21455 USA: WEST USSR • 250 kW

21460 BELGIUM: (D) • AFRICA • 250 kW
SPAIN: (J) • E NORTH AM • 350 kW

21465 GERMANY (DR): S ASIA & SE ASIA • 100 kW; Sa/Su • E ASIA • 100 kW

21470 ECUADOR: EUROPE • 100 kW; (J) • EUROPE • 100 kW
UNITED KINGDOM: C AFRICA • 250 kW; E AFRICA • 250 kW; Sa/Su • E AFRICA • 250 kW

21475 AUSTRIA: Alternative Frequency to 21490 kHz
PAKISTAN: SE ASIA • 50 kW
USA: S ASIA • 250 kW • ALT. FREQ. TO 15265 kHz

21480 HOLLAND: (J) • SE ASIA • 500 kW; E ASIA • 300 kW; S ASIA • 300 kW; SE ASIA • 300 kW; (D) • SE ASIA • 300 kW; 250 kW

21485 HOLLAND: ASIA • 300 kW; SE ASIA • 300 kW
USA: W AFRICA • 15 kW; M-F • E AFRICA & S AFRICA • 50 kW
VATICAN STATE: S AMERICA • 500 kW; C AMERICA • 500 kW

21490 AUSTRIA: MIDEAST • 300 kW; W AFRICA • 100 kW; AUSTRALIA • 100 kW; (D) • W AFRICA • 100 kW; E NORTH AM • 100 kW • ALT. FREQ. TO 21475 kHz; (D) • MIDEAST • 300 kW; (J) • W AFRICA • 100 kW; (D) • AUSTRALIA • 100 kW; (D) • E NORTH AM • 100 kW • ALT. FREQ. TO 21475 kHz; (J) • MIDEAST • 300 kW; M-Sa • W AFRICA • 100 kW; (J) • AUSTRALIA • 100 kW; (J) • E NORTH AM • 100 kW • ALT. FREQ. TO 21475 kHz; M-Sa • MIDEAST • 300 kW; Su • W AFRICA • 100 kW; Su • MIDEAST • 300 kW
PAKISTAN: S ASIA & SE ASIA • 250 kW
UNITED KINGDOM: S AMERICA • 250 kW; C AFRICA & E AFRICA • 250 kW
USA: M-F • S AMERICA • 250 kW; Sa/Su • S AMERICA • 250 kW
USSR: (J) • SE ASIA • DS-2 • 250 kW

21495 PORTUGAL: W AFRICA & S AMERICA • 100 kW; Sa/Su • W AFRICA & S AMERICA • 100 kW
SAUDI ARABIA: Alternative Frequency to 21505 kHz
SPAIN: (J) • S AMERICA • 350 kW

21500 CHINA (TAIWAN): (J) • EUROPE • 100 kW
JAPAN: (J) • EUROPE • 300 kW; (J) • EUROPE • GENERAL • 500 kW; (J) • JAPANESE • EUROPE • GENERAL • 500 kW

ENGLISH ■■■　ARABIC ≋≋≋　CHINESE □□□　FRENCH ══　GERMAN ━━━　RUSSIAN ═══　SPANISH ▬▬　OTHER ──

FREQUENCY   COUNTRY, STATION, LOCATION   TARGET • NETWORK • POWER (kW)   World Time

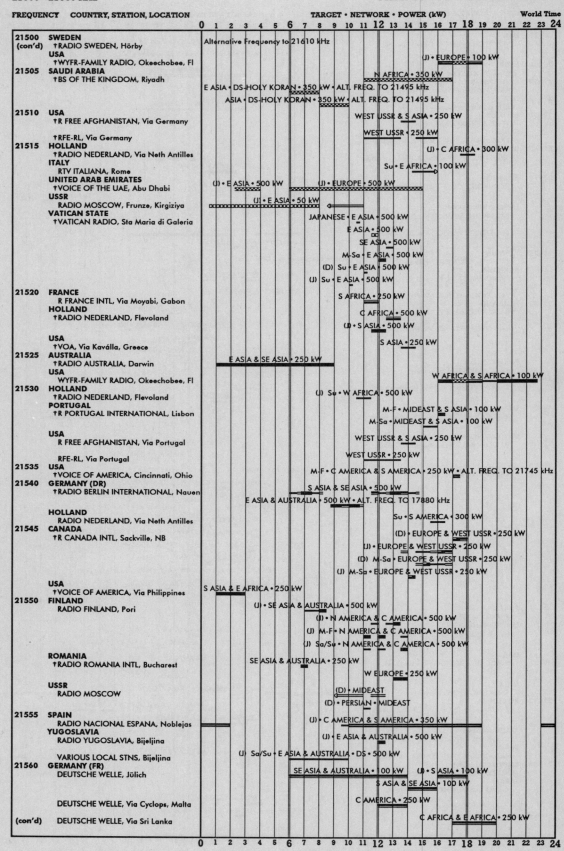

FREQUENCY	COUNTRY, STATION, LOCATION	TARGET • NETWORK • POWER (kW)
21500 (con'd)	SWEDEN †RADIO SWEDEN, Hörby	Alternative Frequency to 21610 kHz
	USA †WYFR-FAMILY RADIO, Okeechobee, Fl	(J) • EUROPE • 100 kW
21505	SAUDI ARABIA †BS OF THE KINGDOM, Riyadh	N AFRICA • 350 kW; E ASIA • DS-HOLY KORAN • 350 kW • ALT. FREQ. TO 21495 kHz; ASIA • DS-HOLY KORAN • 350 kW • ALT. FREQ. TO 21495 kHz
21510	USA †R FREE AFGHANISTAN, Via Germany	WEST USSR & S ASIA • 250 kW
	†RFE-RL, Via Germany	WEST USSR • 250 kW
21515	HOLLAND †RADIO NEDERLAND, Via Neth Antilles	(J) • C AFRICA • 300 kW
	ITALY RTV ITALIANA, Rome	Su • E AFRICA • 100 kW
	UNITED ARAB EMIRATES †VOICE OF THE UAE, Abu Dhabi	(J) • E ASIA • 500 kW; (J) • EUROPE • 500 kW
	USSR RADIO MOSCOW, Frunze, Kirgiziya	(J) • E ASIA • 50 kW
	VATICAN STATE †VATICAN RADIO, Sta Maria di Galeria	JAPANESE • E ASIA • 500 kW; E ASIA • 500 kW; SE ASIA • 500 kW; M-Sa • E ASIA • 500 kW; (D) Su • E ASIA • 500 kW; (J) Su • E ASIA • 500 kW
21520	FRANCE R FRANCE INTL, Via Moyabi, Gabon	S AFRICA • 250 kW
	HOLLAND †RADIO NEDERLAND, Flevoland	C AFRICA • 500 kW; (J) • S ASIA • 500 kW
	USA †VOA, Via Kaválla, Greece	S ASIA • 250 kW
21525	AUSTRALIA †RADIO AUSTRALIA, Darwin	E ASIA & SE ASIA • 250 kW
	USA WYFR-FAMILY RADIO, Okeechobee, Fl	W AFRICA & S AFRICA • 100 kW
21530	HOLLAND †RADIO NEDERLAND, Flevoland	(J) • Su • W AFRICA • 500 kW
	PORTUGAL †R PORTUGAL INTERNATIONAL, Lisbon	M-F • MIDEAST & S ASIA • 100 kW; M-Sa • MIDEAST & S ASIA • 100 kW
	USA R FREE AFGHANISTAN, Via Portugal	WEST USSR & S ASIA • 250 kW
	RFE-RL, Via Portugal	WEST USSR • 250 kW
21535	USA †VOICE OF AMERICA, Cincinnati, Ohio	M-F • C AMERICA & S AMERICA • 250 kW • ALT. FREQ. TO 21745 kHz
21540	GERMANY (DR) †RADIO BERLIN INTERNATIONAL, Nauen	S ASIA & SE ASIA • 500 kW; E ASIA & AUSTRALIA • 500 kW • ALT. FREQ. TO 17880 kHz
	HOLLAND RADIO NEDERLAND, Via Neth Antilles	Su • S AMERICA • 300 kW
21545	CANADA †R CANADA INTL, Sackville, NB	(D) • EUROPE & WEST USSR • 250 kW; (J) • EUROPE & WEST USSR • 250 kW; (D) M-Sa • EUROPE & WEST USSR • 250 kW; (J) M-Sa • EUROPE & WEST USSR • 250 kW
	USA †VOICE OF AMERICA, Via Philippines	S ASIA & E AFRICA • 250 kW
21550	FINLAND RADIO FINLAND, Pori	(J) • SE ASIA & AUSTRALIA • 500 kW; (J) • N AMERICA & C AMERICA • 500 kW; (J) M-F • N AMERICA & C AMERICA • 500 kW; (J) Sa/Su • N AMERICA & C AMERICA • 500 kW
	ROMANIA †RADIO ROMANIA INTL, Bucharest	SE ASIA & AUSTRALIA • 250 kW; W EUROPE • 250 kW
	USSR RADIO MOSCOW	(D) • MIDEAST; (D) • PERSIAN • MIDEAST
21555	SPAIN RADIO NACIONAL ESPANA, Noblejas	(J) • C AMERICA & S AMERICA • 350 kW
	YUGOSLAVIA RADIO YUGOSLAVIA, Bijeljina	(J) • E ASIA & AUSTRALIA • 500 kW
	VARIOUS LOCAL STNS, Bijeljina	(J) Sa/Su • E ASIA & AUSTRALIA • DS • 500 kW
21560	GERMANY (FR) DEUTSCHE WELLE, Jülich	SE ASIA & AUSTRALIA • 100 kW; (J) • S ASIA • 100 kW; S ASIA & SE ASIA • 100 kW
	DEUTSCHE WELLE, Via Cyclops, Malta	C AMERICA • 250 kW
(con'd)	DEUTSCHE WELLE, Via Sri Lanka	C AFRICA & E AFRICA • 250 kW

SUMMER ONLY (J)   WINTER ONLY (D)   JAMMING / OR ∧   EARLIEST HEARD ◁   LATEST HEARD ▷   NEW OR CHANGED FOR 1991 †

FREQUENCY   COUNTRY, STATION, LOCATION

TARGET • NETWORK • POWER (kW)

World Time

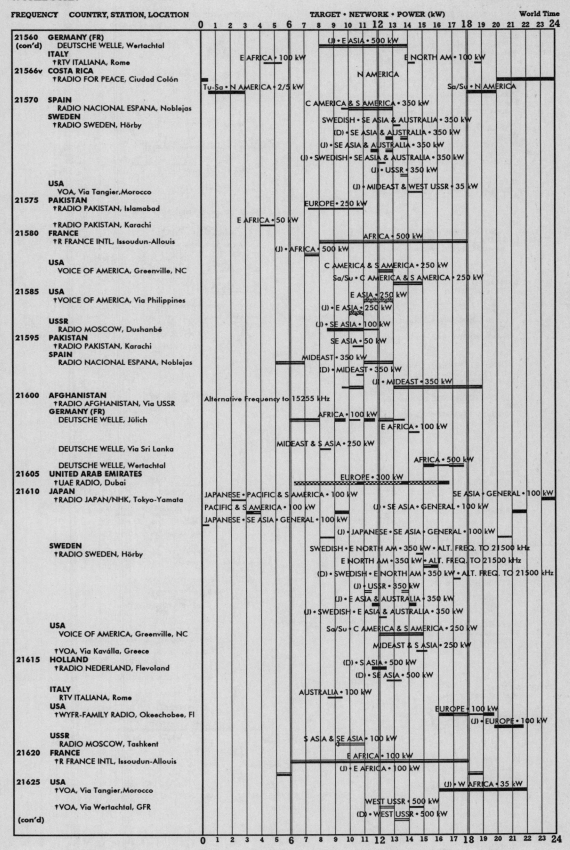

21560 (con'd)	**GERMANY (FR)** DEUTSCHE WELLE, Wertachtal	(J) • E ASIA • 500 kW	
	ITALY ↑RTV ITALIANA, Rome	E AFRICA • 100 kW E NORTH AM • 100 kW	
21566v	**COSTA RICA** ↑RADIO FOR PEACE, Ciudad Colón	N AMERICA Tu-Sa • N AMERICA • 2/5 kW Sa/Su • N AMERICA	
21570	**SPAIN** RADIO NACIONAL ESPANA, Noblejas	C AMERICA & S AMERICA • 350 kW	
	SWEDEN ↑RADIO SWEDEN, Hörby	SWEDISH • SE ASIA & AUSTRALIA • 350 kW (D) • SE ASIA & AUSTRALIA • 350 kW (J) • SE ASIA & AUSTRALIA • 350 kW (J) • SWEDISH • SE ASIA & AUSTRALIA • 350 kW (J) • USSR • 350 kW	
	USA VOA, Via Tangier, Morocco	(J) • MIDEAST & WEST USSR • 35 kW	
21575	**PAKISTAN** ↑RADIO PAKISTAN, Islamabad	EUROPE • 250 kW	
	↑RADIO PAKISTAN, Karachi	E AFRICA • 50 kW	
21580	**FRANCE** ↑R FRANCE INTL, Issoudun-Allouis	AFRICA • 500 kW (J) • AFRICA • 500 kW	
	USA VOICE OF AMERICA, Greenville, NC	C AMERICA & S AMERICA • 250 kW Sa/Su • C AMERICA & S AMERICA • 250 kW	
21585	**USA** ↑VOICE OF AMERICA, Via Philippines	E ASIA • 250 kW (J) • E ASIA • 250 kW	
	USSR RADIO MOSCOW, Dushanbé	(J) • SE ASIA • 100 kW	
21595	**PAKISTAN** ↑RADIO PAKISTAN, Karachi	SE ASIA • 50 kW	
	SPAIN RADIO NACIONAL ESPANA, Noblejas	MIDEAST • 350 kW (D) • MIDEAST • 350 kW (J) • MIDEAST • 350 kW	
21600	**AFGHANISTAN** ↑RADIO AFGHANISTAN, Via USSR	Alternative Frequency to 15255 kHz	
	GERMANY (FR) DEUTSCHE WELLE, Jülich	AFRICA • 100 kW E AFRICA • 100 kW	
	DEUTSCHE WELLE, Via Sri Lanka	MIDEAST & S ASIA • 250 kW	
	DEUTSCHE WELLE, Wertachtal	AFRICA • 500 kW	
21605	**UNITED ARAB EMIRATES** ↑UAE RADIO, Dubai	EUROPE • 300 kW	
21610	**JAPAN** ↑RADIO JAPAN/NHK, Tokyo-Yamata	JAPANESE • PACIFIC & S AMERICA • 100 kW SE ASIA • GENERAL • 100 kW PACIFIC & S AMERICA • 100 kW (J) • SE ASIA • GENERAL • 100 kW JAPANESE • SE ASIA • GENERAL • 100 kW (J) • JAPANESE • SE ASIA • GENERAL • 100 kW	
	SWEDEN ↑RADIO SWEDEN, Hörby	SWEDISH • E NORTH AM • 350 kW • ALT. FREQ. TO 21500 kHz E NORTH AM • 350 kW • ALT. FREQ. TO 21500 kHz (D) • SWEDISH • E NORTH AM • 350 kW • ALT. FREQ. TO 21500 kHz (J) • USSR • 350 kW (J) • E ASIA & AUSTRALIA • 350 kW (J) • SWEDISH • E ASIA & AUSTRALIA • 350 kW	
	USA VOICE OF AMERICA, Greenville, NC	Sa/Su • C AMERICA & S AMERICA • 250 kW MIDEAST & S ASIA • 250 kW	
	↑VOA, Via Kaválla, Greece		
21615	**HOLLAND** ↑RADIO NEDERLAND, Flevoland	(D) • S ASIA • 500 kW (D) • SE ASIA • 500 kW	
	ITALY RTV ITALIANA, Rome	AUSTRALIA • 100 kW	
	USA ↑WYFR-FAMILY RADIO, Okeechobee, Fl	EUROPE • 100 kW (J) • EUROPE • 100 kW	
	USSR RADIO MOSCOW, Tashkent	S ASIA & SE ASIA • 100 kW	
21620	**FRANCE** ↑R FRANCE INTL, Issoudun-Allouis	E AFRICA • 100 kW (J) • E AFRICA • 100 kW	
21625	**USA** ↑VOA, Via Tangier, Morocco	(J) • W AFRICA • 35 kW	
	↑VOA, Via Wertachtal, GFR	WEST USSR • 500 kW (D) • WEST USSR • 500 kW	
(con'd)			

ENGLISH ▬   ARABIC ▨▨▨   CHINESE ▭▭▭   FRENCH ▬▬   GERMAN ▬   RUSSIAN ═══   SPANISH ▬   OTHER ▬

FREQUENCY	COUNTRY, STATION, LOCATION	TARGET • NETWORK • POWER (kW) World Time

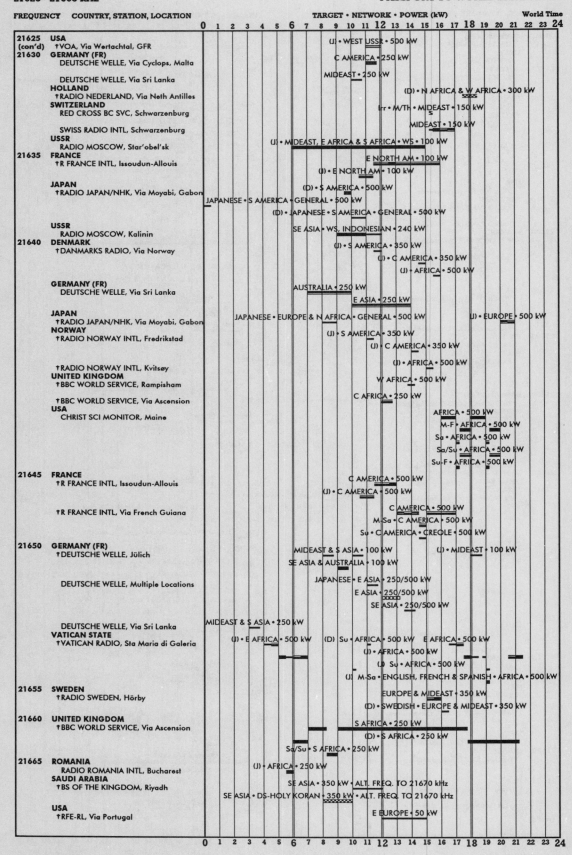

FREQUENCY	COUNTRY, STATION, LOCATION	TARGET • NETWORK • POWER (kW)
21625 (con'd)	USA †VOA, Via Wertachtal, GFR	(J) • WEST USSR • 500 kW
21630	GERMANY (FR) DEUTSCHE WELLE, Via Cyclops, Malta	C AMERICA • 250 kW
	DEUTSCHE WELLE, Via Sri Lanka	MIDEAST • 250 kW
	HOLLAND †RADIO NEDERLAND, Via Neth Antilles	(D) • N AFRICA & W AFRICA • 300 kW
	SWITZERLAND RED CROSS BC SVC, Schwarzenburg	Irr • M/TH • MIDEAST • 150 kW
	SWISS RADIO INTL, Schwarzenburg	MIDEAST • 150 kW
	USSR RADIO MOSCOW, Star'obel'sk	(J) • MIDEAST, E AFRICA & S AFRICA • WS • 100 kW
21635	FRANCE †R FRANCE INTL, Issoudun-Allouis	E NORTH AM • 100 kW
		(J) • E NORTH AM • 100 kW
	JAPAN †RADIO JAPAN/NHK, Via Moyabi, Gabon	(D) • S AMERICA • 500 kW
		JAPANESE • S AMERICA • GENERAL • 500 kW
		(D) • JAPANESE • S AMERICA • GENERAL • 500 kW
	USSR RADIO MOSCOW, Kalinin	SE ASIA • WS, INDONESIAN • 240 kW
21640	DENMARK †DANMARKS RADIO, Via Norway	(J) • S AMERICA • 350 kW
		(J) • C AMERICA • 350 kW
		(J) • AFRICA • 500 kW
	GERMANY (FR) DEUTSCHE WELLE, Via Sri Lanka	AUSTRALIA • 250 kW
		E ASIA • 250 kW
	JAPAN †RADIO JAPAN/NHK, Via Moyabi, Gabon	JAPANESE • EUROPE & N AFRICA • GENERAL • 500 kW (J) • EUROPE • 500 kW
	NORWAY †RADIO NORWAY INTL, Fredrikstad	(J) • S AMERICA • 350 kW
		(J) • C AMERICA • 350 kW
	†RADIO NORWAY INTL, Kvitsøy	(J) • AFRICA • 500 kW
	UNITED KINGDOM †BBC WORLD SERVICE, Rampisham	W AFRICA • 500 kW
	†BBC WORLD SERVICE, Via Ascension	C AFRICA • 250 kW
	USA CHRIST SCI MONITOR, Maine	AFRICA • 500 kW
		M-F • AFRICA • 500 kW
		Sa • AFRICA • 500 kW
		Sa/Su • AFRICA • 500 kW
		Su-F • AFRICA • 500 kW
21645	FRANCE †R FRANCE INTL, Issoudun-Allouis	C AMERICA • 500 kW
		(J) • C AMERICA • 500 kW
	†R FRANCE INTL, Via French Guiana	C AMERICA • 500 kW
		M-Sa • C AMERICA • 500 kW
		Su • C AMERICA • CREOLE • 500 kW
21650	GERMANY (FR) †DEUTSCHE WELLE, Jülich	MIDEAST & S ASIA • 100 kW (J) • MIDEAST • 100 kW
		SE ASIA & AUSTRALIA • 100 kW
	DEUTSCHE WELLE, Multiple Locations	JAPANESE • E ASIA • 250/500 kW
		E ASIA • 250/500 kW
		SE ASIA • 250/500 kW
	DEUTSCHE WELLE, Via Sri Lanka	MIDEAST & S ASIA • 250 kW
	VATICAN STATE †VATICAN RADIO, Sta Maria di Galeria	(J) • E AFRICA • 500 kW (D) Su • AFRICA • 500 kW E AFRICA • 500 kW
		(J) • AFRICA • 500 kW
		(J) Su • AFRICA • 500 kW
		(J) M-Sa • ENGLISH, FRENCH & SPANISH • AFRICA • 500 kW
21655	SWEDEN †RADIO SWEDEN, Hörby	EUROPE & MIDEAST • 350 kW
		(D) • SWEDISH • EUROPE & MIDEAST • 350 kW
21660	UNITED KINGDOM †BBC WORLD SERVICE, Via Ascension	S AFRICA • 250 kW
		(D) • S AFRICA • 250 kW
		Sa/Su • S AFRICA • 250 kW
21665	ROMANIA RADIO ROMANIA INTL, Bucharest	(J) • AFRICA • 250 kW
	SAUDI ARABIA †BS OF THE KINGDOM, Riyadh	SE ASIA • 350 kW • ALT. FREQ. TO 21670 kHz
		SE ASIA • DS-HOLY KORAN • 350 kW • ALT. FREQ. TO 21670 kHz
	USA †RFE-RL, Via Portugal	E EUROPE • 50 kW

SUMMER ONLY (J)   WINTER ONLY (D)   JAMMING / OR ∧   EARLIEST HEARD ◁   LATEST HEARD ▷   NEW OR CHANGED FOR 1991 †

FREQUENCY	COUNTRY, STATION, LOCATION	TARGET • NETWORK • POWER (kW)	World Time

Time scale: 0 1 2 3 4 5 6 7 8 9 10 11 12 13 14 15 16 17 18 19 20 21 22 23 24

21670 CUBA
 †RADIO HABANA, Via USSR — (J) • AFRICA • 100 kW

SAUDI ARABIA
 †BS OF THE KINGDOM, Riyadh — Alternative Frequency to 21665 kHz

USSR
 †RADIO MOSCOW, Armavir — (J) • AFRICA • 100 kW

21675 CANADA
 R CANADA INTL, Sackville, NB
 — (J) • EUROPE & WEST USSR • 250 kW
 — (J) M-F • EUROPE & WEST USSR • 250 kW
 — (J) Sa/Su • EUROPE & WEST USSR • 250 kW

KUWAIT
 RADIO KUWAIT, Jadādīyah — EUROPE & E NORTH AM • 250 kW

UNITED ARAB EMIRATES
 †UAE RADIO, Dubai — (J) • E NORTH AM • 300 kW

21680 GERMANY (FR)
 DEUTSCHE WELLE, Jülich — MIDEAST & S ASIA • 100 kW

 DEUTSCHE WELLE, Multiple Locations — S ASIA & SE ASIA • 100/250 kW

 DEUTSCHE WELLE, Via Cyclops, Malta — S ASIA • 250 kW

 DEUTSCHE WELLE, Wertachtal — SE ASIA & AUSTRALIA • 500 kW

HOLLAND
 †RADIO NEDERLAND, Via Neth Antilles — (D) • C AFRICA • 300 kW

21685 FRANCE
 †R FRANCE INTL, Issoudun-Allouis
 — W AFRICA • 500 kW
 — (J) • W AFRICA • 500 kW
 — Su • W AFRICA • 500 kW
 — W AFRICA • MEDIAS FRANCE • 500 kW
 — M-Sa • W AFRICA • MEDIAS FRANCE • 500 kW

HOLLAND
 RADIO NEDERLAND, Via Neth Antilles — W AFRICA & C AFRICA • 300 kW

21690 ITALY
 RTV ITALIANA, Rome
 — E AFRICA • 100 kW
 — AFRICA • 100 kW
 — Su • AFRICA & S AMERICA • 50 kW

JAPAN
 †RADIO JAPAN/NHK, Via Moyabi, Gabon
 — (J) • EUROPE & N AFRICA • 500 kW
 — (J) • EUROPE & N AFRICA • GENERAL • 500 kW
 — (J) • JAPANESE • EUROPE & N AFRICA • GENERAL • 500 kW

SWEDEN
 †RADIO SWEDEN, Hörby
 — SWEDISH • EUROPE & MIDEAST • 350 kW
 — (D) • EUROPE & MIDEAST • 350 kW
 — (D) • SWEDISH • EUROPE & MIDEAST • 350 kW
 — (J) • SWEDISH • EUROPE & MIDEAST • 350 kW
 — (J) • EUROPE & MIDEAST • 350 kW

USSR
 RADIO MOSCOW, Irkutsk — (J) • S ASIA • 100 kW

21695 SWITZERLAND
 RED CROSS BC SVC, Schwarzenburg
 — Irr • M/Th • AUSTRALIA • 150 kW
 — Irr • M/Th • S ASIA & SE ASIA • 150 kW

 SWISS RADIO INTL, Schwarzenburg
 — AUSTRALIA • 150 kW
 — S ASIA & SE ASIA • 150 kW
 — M-Sa • AUSTRALIA • 150 kW
 — M-Sa • S ASIA & SE ASIA • 150 kW
 — Su • AUSTRALIA • 150 kW
 — Su • S ASIA & SE ASIA • 150 kW

21700 JAPAN
 RADIO JAPAN/NHK, Via Moyabi, Gabon
 — EUROPE • GENERAL • 500 kW
 — JAPANESE • EUROPE • GENERAL • 500 kW

NORWAY
 †RADIO NORWAY INTL, Kvitsøy — (D) Su • S ASIA & AUSTRALIA • 500 kW

PORTUGAL
 †R PORTUGAL INTERNATIONAL, Lisbon
 — E AFRICA & S AFRICA • 100 kW
 — Sa/Su • E AFRICA & S AFRICA • 100 kW

UNITED ARAB EMIRATES
 UAE RADIO, Dubai — AUSTRALIA • 300 kW

21705 CZECHOSLOVAKIA
 †RADIO PRAGUE INTL, Rimavská — AUSTRALIA • 250 kW

DENMARK
 †DANMARKS RADIO, Via Norway
 — AUSTRALIA • 500 kW
 — (J) • W AFRICA & S AMERICA • 500 kW
 — E NORTH AM & C AMERICA • 500 kW
 — (D) • E ASIA • 500 kW
 — (D) • C AMERICA • 500 kW
 — (D) • N AMERICA & C AMERICA • 500 kW
 — (J) • E NORTH AM & C AMERICA • 500 kW

NORWAY
 †RADIO NORWAY INTL, Kvitsøy
 — E ASIA • 500 kW
 — (J) • W AFRICA & S AMERICA • 500 kW
 — (J) Su • S ASIA & AUSTRALIA • 500 kW

(con'd)

Time scale: 0 1 2 3 4 5 6 7 8 9 10 11 12 13 14 15 16 17 18 19 20 21 22 23 24

ENGLISH ▬ ARABIC ≋ CHINESE ▭▭▭ FRENCH ═ GERMAN ▬ RUSSIAN ══ SPANISH ▬ OTHER ▬

FREQUENCY   COUNTRY, STATION, LOCATION

TARGET • NETWORK • POWER (kW)   World Time

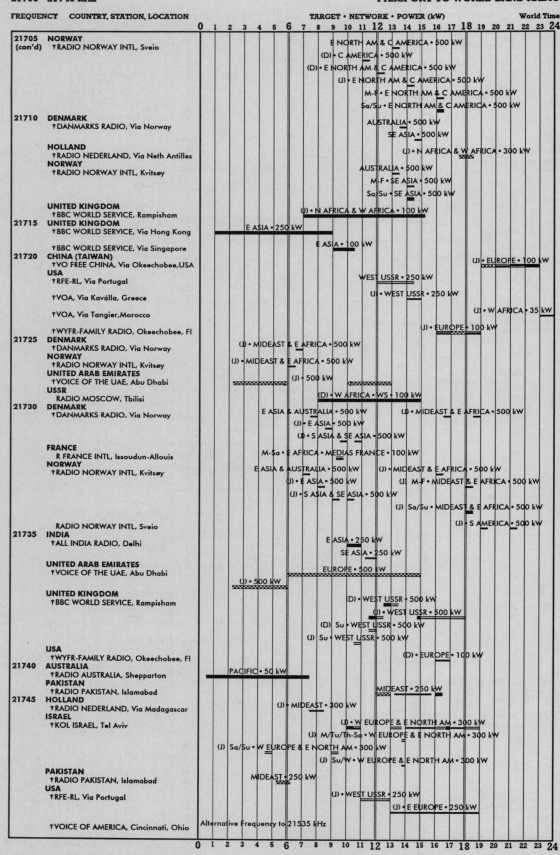

FREQUENCY   COUNTRY, STATION, LOCATION   TARGET • NETWORK • POWER (kW)   World Time

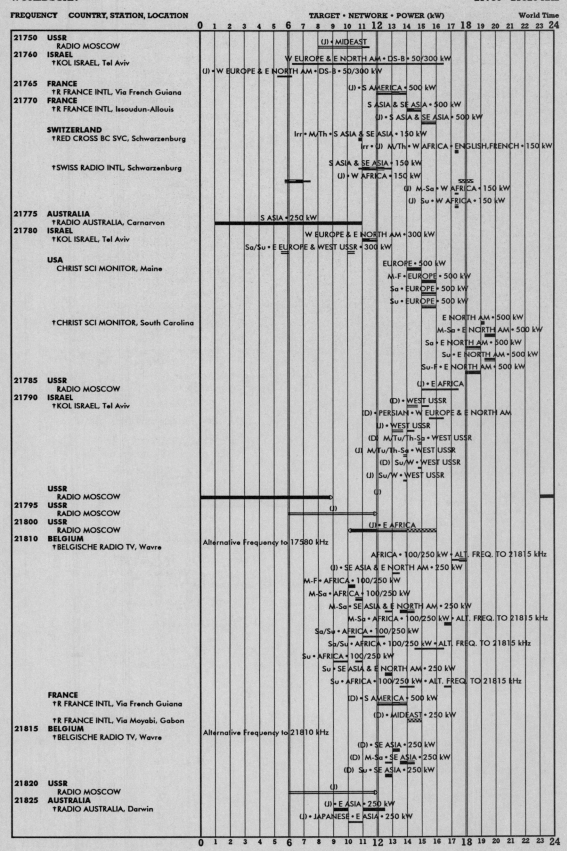

21750 USSR
          RADIO MOSCOW
                                        (J) • MIDEAST
21760 ISRAEL
          ↑KOL ISRAEL, Tel Aviv
                                        W EUROPE & E NORTH AM • DS-B • 50/300 kW
                                        (J) • W EUROPE & E NORTH AM • DS-B • 50/300 kW

21765 FRANCE
          ↑R FRANCE INTL, Via French Guiana
                                        (J) • S AMERICA • 500 kW
21770 FRANCE
          ↑R FRANCE INTL, Issoudun-Allouis
                                        S ASIA & SE ASIA • 500 kW
                                        (J) • S ASIA & SE ASIA • 500 kW

          SWITZERLAND
          ↑RED CROSS BC SVC, Schwarzenburg
                                        Irr • M/Th • S ASIA & SE ASIA • 150 kW
                                        Irr • (J) M/Th • W AFRICA • ENGLISH, FRENCH • 150 kW

          ↑SWISS RADIO INTL, Schwarzenburg
                                        S ASIA & SE ASIA • 150 kW
                                        (J) • W AFRICA • 150 kW
                                        (J) M-Sa • W AFRICA • 150 kW
                                        (J) Su • W AFRICA • 150 kW

21775 AUSTRALIA
          ↑RADIO AUSTRALIA, Carnarvon
                                        S ASIA • 250 kW
21780 ISRAEL
          ↑KOL ISRAEL, Tel Aviv
                                        W EUROPE & E NORTH AM • 300 kW
                                        Sa/Su • E EUROPE & WEST USSR • 300 kW

          USA
          CHRIST SCI MONITOR, Maine
                                        EUROPE • 500 kW
                                        M-F • EUROPE • 500 kW
                                        Sa • EUROPE • 500 kW
                                        Su • EUROPE • 500 kW

          ↑CHRIST SCI MONITOR, South Carolina
                                        E NORTH AM • 500 kW
                                        M-Sa • E NORTH AM • 500 kW
                                        Sa • E NORTH AM • 500 kW
                                        Su • E NORTH AM • 500 kW
                                        Su-F • E NORTH AM • 500 kW

21785 USSR
          RADIO MOSCOW
                                        (J) • E AFRICA
21790 ISRAEL
          ↑KOL ISRAEL, Tel Aviv
                                        (D) • WEST USSR
                                        (D) • PERSIAN • W EUROPE & E NORTH AM
                                        (J) • WEST USSR
                                        (D) M/Tu/Th-Sa • WEST USSR
                                        (J) M/Tu/Th-Sa • WEST USSR
                                        (D) Su/W • WEST USSR
                                        (J) Su/W • WEST USSR

          USSR
          RADIO MOSCOW
                                        (J)
21795 USSR
          RADIO MOSCOW
                                        (J)
21800 USSR
          RADIO MOSCOW
                                        (J) • E AFRICA
21810 BELGIUM
          ↑BELGISCHE RADIO TV, Wavre
                                        Alternative Frequency to 17580 kHz
                                        AFRICA • 100/250 kW • ALT. FREQ. TO 21815 kHz
                                        (J) • SE ASIA & E NORTH AM • 250 kW
                                        M-F • AFRICA • 100/250 kW
                                        M-Sa • AFRICA • 100/250 kW
                                        M-Sa • SE ASIA & E NORTH AM • 250 kW
                                        M-Sa • AFRICA • 100/250 kW • ALT. FREQ. TO 21815 kHz
                                        Sa/Su • AFRICA • 100/250 kW
                                        Sa/Su • AFRICA • 100/250 kW • ALT. FREQ. TO 21815 kHz
                                        Su • AFRICA • 100/250 kW
                                        Su • SE ASIA & E NORTH AM • 250 kW
                                        Su • AFRICA • 100/250 kW • ALT. FREQ. TO 21815 kHz

          FRANCE
          ↑R FRANCE INTL, Via French Guiana
                                        (D) • S AMERICA • 500 kW

          ↑R FRANCE INTL, Via Moyabi, Gabon
                                        (D) • MIDEAST • 250 kW
21815 BELGIUM
          ↑BELGISCHE RADIO TV, Wavre
                                        Alternative Frequency to 21810 kHz
                                        (D) • SE ASIA • 250 kW
                                        (D) M-Sa • SE ASIA • 250 kW
                                        (D) Su • SE ASIA • 250 kW

21820 USSR
          RADIO MOSCOW
                                        (J)
21825 AUSTRALIA
          ↑RADIO AUSTRALIA, Darwin
                                        (J) • E ASIA • 250 kW
                                        (J) • JAPANESE • E ASIA • 250 kW

ENGLISH ▬▬   ARABIC ⧰⧰⧰   CHINESE ▫▫▫   FRENCH ▬▬   GERMAN ▬▬   RUSSIAN ══   SPANISH ▬▬   OTHER ──

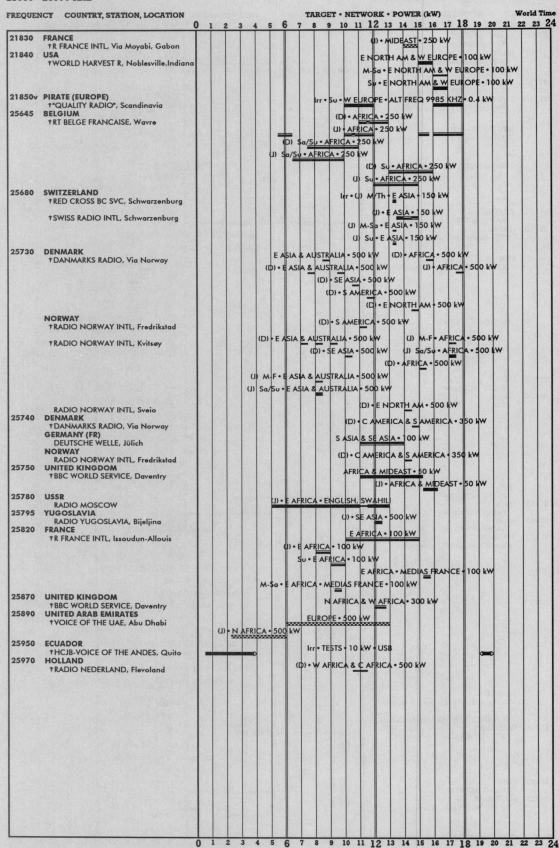

FREQUENCY   COUNTRY, STATION, LOCATION   TARGET • NETWORK • POWER (kW)   World Time

0 1 2 3 4 5 6 7 8 9 10 11 12 13 14 15 16 17 18 19 20 21 22 23 24

21830 FRANCE
    †R FRANCE INTL, Via Moyabi, Gabon   (J) • MIDEAST • 250 kW
21840 USA
    †WORLD HARVEST R, Noblesville, Indiana   E NORTH AM & W EUROPE • 100 kW
                                                                        M-Sa • E NORTH AM & W EUROPE • 100 kW
                                                                        Su • E NORTH AM & W EUROPE • 100 kW

21850v PIRATE (EUROPE)
    †"QUALITY RADIO", Scandinavia   Irr • Su • W EUROPE • ALT FREQ 9985 KHZ • 0.4 kW
25645 BELGIUM
    †RT BELGE FRANCAISE, Wavre   (D) • AFRICA • 250 kW
                                                                        (J) • AFRICA • 250 kW
                                                          (D) Sa/Su • AFRICA • 250 kW
                                                          (J) Sa/Su • AFRICA • 250 kW
                                                                        (D) Su • AFRICA • 250 kW
                                                                        (J) Su • AFRICA • 250 kW

25680 SWITZERLAND
    †RED CROSS BC SVC, Schwarzenburg   Irr • (J) • M/Th • E ASIA • 150 kW

    †SWISS RADIO INTL, Schwarzenburg   (J) • E ASIA • 150 kW
                                                                        (J) M-Sa • E ASIA • 150 kW
                                                                        (J) Su • E ASIA • 150 kW

25730 DENMARK
    †DANMARKS RADIO, Via Norway   E ASIA & AUSTRALIA • 500 kW   (D) • AFRICA • 500 kW
                                          (D) • E ASIA & AUSTRALIA • 500 kW   (J) • AFRICA • 500 kW
                                                (D) • SE ASIA • 500 kW
                                                (D) • S AMERICA • 500 kW
                                                                        (D) • E NORTH AM • 500 kW

    NORWAY
    †RADIO NORWAY INTL, Fredrikstad   (D) • S AMERICA • 500 kW

    †RADIO NORWAY INTL, Kvitsøy   (D) • E ASIA & AUSTRALIA • 500 kW   (J) M-F • AFRICA • 500 kW
                                                (D) • SE ASIA • 500 kW   (J) Sa/Su • AFRICA • 500 kW
                                                                        (D) • AFRICA • 500 kW

                                          (J) M-F • E ASIA & AUSTRALIA • 500 kW
                                          (J) Sa/Su • E ASIA & AUSTRALIA • 500 kW

        RADIO NORWAY INTL, Sveio   (D) • E NORTH AM • 500 kW
25740 DENMARK
    †DANMARKS RADIO, Via Norway   (D) • C AMERICA & S AMERICA • 350 kW
    GERMANY (FR)
        DEUTSCHE WELLE, Jülich   S ASIA & SE ASIA • 100 kW
    NORWAY
        RADIO NORWAY INTL, Fredrikstad   (D) • C AMERICA & S AMERICA • 350 kW
25750 UNITED KINGDOM
    †BBC WORLD SERVICE, Daventry   AFRICA & MIDEAST • 50 kW
                                                                    (J) • AFRICA & MIDEAST • 50 kW

25780 USSR
        RADIO MOSCOW   (J) • E AFRICA • ENGLISH, SWAHILI
25795 YUGOSLAVIA
        RADIO YUGOSLAVIA, Bijeljina   (J) • SE ASIA • 500 kW
25820 FRANCE
    †R FRANCE INTL, Issoudun-Allouis   E AFRICA • 100 kW

                                          (J) • E AFRICA • 100 kW
                                          Su • E AFRICA • 100 kW
                                                E AFRICA • MEDIAS FRANCE • 100 kW
                                          M-Sa • E AFRICA • MEDIAS FRANCE • 100 kW

25870 UNITED KINGDOM
    †BBC WORLD SERVICE, Daventry   N AFRICA & W AFRICA • 300 kW
25890 UNITED ARAB EMIRATES
    †VOICE OF THE UAE, Abu Dhabi   EUROPE • 500 kW
                                          (J) • N AFRICA • 500 kW

25950 ECUADOR
    †HCJB-VOICE OF THE ANDES, Quito   Irr • TESTS • 10 kW • USB
25970 HOLLAND
    †RADIO NEDERLAND, Flevoland   (D) • W AFRICA & C AFRICA • 500 kW

0 1 2 3 4 5 6 7 8 9 10 11 12 13 14 15 16 17 18 19 20 21 22 23 24

SUMMER ONLY (J)   WINTER ONLY (D)   JAMMING / OR ∧   EARLIEST HEARD ◁   LATEST HEARD ▷   NEW OR CHANGED FOR 1991 †

GLOSSARIES AND GUIDES

Terms and Abbreviations Used in World Band Radio

A wide variety of terms and abbreviations is used in world band radio. Some are specialized and need explanation; a few are foreign words that need translation; and yet others are simply adaptations of common usage. Here, then, is *Passport's* guide to what's what in world band terminology and abbreviations—including what each one means. For a thorough writeup on what determines how well a world band radio performs, please see the *RDI White Paper*, "How to Interpret Receiver Specifications and Lab Tests."

Adjacent-Channel Rejection. *See* Selectivity.

AGC. *See* Automatic Gain Control.

Alt. Alternative frequency or channel. Frequency or channel that may be used irregularly or unexpectedly in place of the regularly scheduled frequency or channel.

Amateur Radio. *See* Hams.

AM Band. The local radio band, which currently runs from 520 to 1,611 kHz (530–1700 kHz in North America as of mid-1990), within the Medium Frequency (MF) range. In many countries it is called the mediumwave (MW) band.

Artificial Intelligence. The ability of a computer to operate similarly to the human brain.

Audio Quality, Audio Fidelity. *See* High Fidelity.

Automatic Gain Control. Smoothes out the fluctuations in signal strength brought about by fading, a common occurrence with world band signals.

AV. A Voz—Portuguese for Voice of.

Bandwidth. One of the variables that determines selectivity (*see*), bandwidth is the amount of radio signal a set will let pass through. With world band channel spacing at 5 kHz, the best single bandwidths are usually in the vicinity of 3–6 kHz. Better radios offer two or more selectable bandwidths: one of 5–7 kHz or so for when a station is "in the clear," and one or more others between 2–4 kHz for when a station is hemmed in by other stations next to it.

BC, BS. Broadcasting, Broadcasting Company, Broadcasting Corporation, Broadcasting Station, Broadcasting Service.

Broadcast. A radio or TV transmission meant for the general public. *Compare* Utility Stations.

Cd. Ciudad—Spanish for City.

Channel. An everyday term to indicate where a station is supposed to be located on the dial. World band channels are exactly 5 kHz apart. Stations operating outside this norm are "off channel" (for these, *Passport* provides resolution to better than one kHz to aid in station identification). Measured in units of 5 kHz; that is, world band channels, unlike some other radio/TV channels, aren't assigned sequentially, like street numbers, in an *n + 1* fashion.

Cl. Club, Clube.

Cu, Cult. Cultura, Cultural, Culture.

(D). Frequency operates at this time winters only. Not heard summers.

Digital Channel Display, Digital Frequency Display, Digital Tuning Display. *See* Synthesizer.

DS. Domestic Service—Broadcasting intended for audiences in the broadcaster's home country. *Compare* ES.

DXers. From an old telegraph term "to DX"; that is, to communicate over a great distance. Thus, "DXers" are those who specialize in finding distant or exotic stations.

Dynamic Range. The ability of a set to handle weak signals in the presence of strong competing signals within the same world band segment (*see* World Band Spectrum). Sets with inferior dynamic range sometimes "overload," causing a mishmash of false signals mixed together up and down—and even beyond—the band segment being received.

Earliest Heard (or **Latest Heard**). See the key at the bottom of each "Blue Page." If the *Passport* monitoring team cannot establish the definite sign-on (or sign-off) time of a station, the earliest (or latest) time the station could be traced is indicated, instead, by a triangular "flag." This means that the station almost certainly operates beyond the time shown by that "flag." It also means that, unless you live relatively close to the station, you're unlikely to be able to hear it beyond that "flagged" time.

Ed, Educ. Educational, Educação, Educadora.

Em. Emissora, Emisora, Emissor, Emetteur—In effect, station in various languages.

EP. Emissor Provincial—Portuguese for Provincial Station.

ER. Emissor Regional—Portuguese for Regional Station.

Ergonomics. How handy and comfortable a set is to operate, especially hour after hour.

ES. External Service—Broadcasting intended for foreign audiences. *Compare* DS.

F. Friday.

Feeder. A "utility" station that transmits programs from the broadcaster's home country to a relay site abroad. Although these stations are not intended to be received by the general public, many world band radios can handle these quasi-broadcasts anyway. Feeders operate in lower sideband (LSB), upper sideband (USB) or independent sideband (termed ISL if heard on the lower side, ISU if heard on the upper side) modes. See Single Sideband.

FR. Federal Republic.

Frequency. The standard term to indicate where a station is located on the dial—regardless whether it's "on-channel" or "off-channel" (*see* channel). Measured in kilohertz (kHz) or Megahertz (MHz).

GMT. Greenwich Mean Time—*See* UTC.

Hams. Government-licensed amateur radio hobbyists that communicate with each other by radio for pleasure within special "amateur bands."

High Fidelity, Enhanced Fidelity. World band reception is ordinarily of only fair audio quality, or fidelity, with some stations sounding even worse. Advanced radios with good audio performance and certain high-tech circuits already can improve on this, and radios of the 21st century are expected to provide genuine high fidelity; i.e., smooth wideband audio and freedom from distortion.

Independent Sideband. *See* Single Sideband.

Interference. Sounds from other stations that are disturbing the station you're trying to hear.

Ionosphere. *See* Propagation.

Irr. Irregular operation or hours of operation; i.e., schedule tends to be unpredictable.

(J). Frequency operates at this time summers only. Not heard winters.

Jamming. Deliberate interference to a transmission with the intent of making reception impossible.

kHz. Kilohertz, the most common unit for measuring where a station is on the dial. Formerly known as "kilocycles/second." 1,000 kilohertz equals one Megahertz.

kW. Kilowatt(s), the most common unit of measurement for transmitter power (*see*).

Loc. Local.

Location. The physical location of the station's transmitter, which may be different from the studio location. Transmitter location is useful as a guide to reception quality. For example, if you're in Eastern North America and wish to listen to Radio Moscow, a transmitter located in the Western USSR will almost certainly provide better reception than one located in Siberia, and one located in Cuba will probably be better yet.

LV. La Voix, La Voz—French and Spanish for The Voice.

M. Monday.

Mediumwave Band. *See* AM Band.

Meters. The unit of measurement used for individual world band segments of the shortwave spectrum. The frequency range covered by a given meters designation—also known as "wavelength"—can be gleaned from the following formula: frequency (kHz) = 299,792/meters. Thus, 49 meters comes out to a frequency of 6118 kHz—well within the range of frequencies included in that segment (*see* World Band Spectrum). Inversely, meters can be derived from the following: meters = 299,792/frequency (kHz).

MHz. Megahertz, a common unit to measure where a station is on the dial. Formerly known as "Megacycles/second." One Megahertz equals 1,000 kilohertz.

N. New, Nueva, Nuevo, Nouvelle, Nacional, National.

Nac. Nacional.

Narrow-Band Facsimile Video. A technique in which pictures can be transmitted without taking up a great deal of radio spectrum space.

Nat, Natl. National, Nationale.

Other. Programs are in a language *other* than one of the world's primary languages.

Overloading. *See* Dynamic Range.

PBS. People's Broadcasting Station.

Power. Transmitter power *before* amplification by the antenna, expressed in kilowatts (kW). The present range of world band powers is 0.01 to 600 kW.

PR. People's Republic.

Programmable Channel Memory. Allows you to push one button, as on a car radio, to select a station.

Propagation. World band signals travel, like a basketball, up and down from the station to your radio. The "floor" below is the earth's surface, whereas the "player's hand" on high is the *ionosphere*, a gaseous layer that envelops the earth. While the earth's surface remains pretty much the same from day-to-day, the ionosphere—nature's own satellite—varies in how it propagates radio signals, depending on how much sunlight hits the "bounce points."

This is why some world band segments do well mainly by day, whereas others are best by night. During winter there's less sunlight, so the "night bands" become unusually active, while the "day bands" become correspondingly less useful (*see* World Band Spectrum). Day-to-day changes in the sun's weather also cause short-term changes in world band radio reception; this explains why some days you hear rare signals. Additionally, the 11-year sunspot cycle has a long-term effect on propagation. It's now peaking, so the high bands should be even better than usual through about 1993.

PS. Provincial Station, Pangsong.

Pto. Puerto, Pôrto.

QSL. A card or letter from a station verifying that a listener indeed heard that particular station.

R. Radio, Radiodiffusion, Radiodifusora, Radiodifusão,

Radiofonikos, Radiostansiya, Radyo, Radyosu, and so forth.

Receiver. Synonym for a radio. In practice, "receiver" is often used to designate a set—usually a tabletop model—with superior ability to ferret out weak, hard-to-hear signals.

Reg. Regional.

Relay. A retransmission facility—shown in **bold** in "Worldwide Broadcasts"—located outside the broadcaster's country. Relay signals, being closer to the target audience, usually provide superior reception. *See* Feeder.

Rep. Republic, République, República.

RN. *See* R and N.

RS. Radio Station, Radiostantsiya, Radiofonikos Stathmos.

RT, RTV. Radiodiffusion Télévision, Radio Télévision, and so forth.

S. San, Santa, Santo, São, Saint.

Sa. Saturday.

Selectivity. The ability of a set to ignore strong signals next to the one being heard. *See* Bandwidth.

Sensitivity. The ability of a set to receive weak signals.

Shortwave Spectrum. The shortwave spectrum—also known as the High Frequency (HF) spectrum—is, strictly speaking, that portion of the radio spectrum from 3–30 MHz (3,000–30,000 kHz). However, common usage places it between 2–30 MHz (2,000–30,000 kHz). It includes not only world band stations, but also "utility" stations and "hams." *See* World Band Spectrum, Utility Stations and Hams.

Single Sideband, Independent Sideband. Spectrum-conserving modes of transmission commonly used by "utility" stations and "hams." Very few broadcasters—world band or other—use these modes, but this is expected to change early in the 21st century. Many world band radios are already capable of receiving single sideband transmissions, and some can even receive independent sideband transmissions. *See* Feeder.

St, Sta, Sto. Saint.

Su. Sunday.

Synchronous Detector. World band radios are increasingly coming equipped with this hightech circuit that improves adjacent-channel rejection (*see*).

Synthesizer. Simple radios use ordinary needle-and-dial tuning that makes it difficult to find a desired channel, or to tell what you are hearing, except by ear. Advanced models utilize a digital frequency *synthesizer* to tune in signals without your having to "hunt and peck." Among other things, synthesizers allow for pushbutton tuning and display the exact frequency digitally—two plusses that make tuning in the world much easier.

Target. Where a transmission is beamed if it is intended to be heard outside the country.

Th. Thursday.

Tu. Tuesday.

Universal Time. *See* UTC.

UTC. Coordinated Universal Time, also known as World Time, Greenwich Mean Time and Zulu. With 161 countries on world band radio, if each announced its own local time you would need a calculator to figure it all out. To get around this, a single international time—UTC—is used. The difference between UTC and local time is determined simply by listening to UTC time checks given on the hour by world band broadcasters. A 24-hour clock is used, so "1800 UTC" means 6:00 PM UTC. If you're in North America, Eastern Time is five hours behind UTC winters and four hours behind UTC summers, so 1800 UTC would be 1:00 PM EST or 2:00 PM EDT. The easiest solution is to use a 24-hour clock set to UTC. Many radios already have these built in, and UTC clocks are also available as accessories.

"Utility" Stations. Most signals within the shortwave spectrum are not world band stations. Rather, they are professional "utility" stations—radio telephones, ships at sea, aircraft and the like—that transmit point-to-point and are not intended to be heard by the general public. *Compare* Broadcast, Hams and Feeders.

v. Variable frequency; i.e., one that is unstable or drifting

because of a transmitter malfunction.
Vo. Voice of.
W. Wednesday.
Wavelength. *See* Meters.
World Band Radio. Similar to regular AM band and FM band radio, except that world band broadcasts can be heard for enormous distances and thus often carry programs created especially for audiences abroad. Hundreds of millions of people on every continent now listen to world band radio.
World Band Spectrum. The collected segments of the shortwave spectrum set aside by the International Telecommunication Union (ITU) for broadcasting. The ITU also allows some world band broadcasting to take place outside these segments. The official world band segments—along with, when appropriate, the "real world" segments [in brackets]— follow, with general guides as to when reception may be best. Remember, these are only *general* guides—actual reception will vary according to your location, the station's location, the time of year, and other factors (*see* Propagation).

Weak Reception Winter Nights

*120 Meters:
2300–2498 kHz (Tropical Domestic Stations)
*90 Meters:
3200–3400 kHz (Tropical Domestic Stations)

Fair Reception Winter Nights

*75 Meters:
3900–3950 kHz (Asia & Pacific only)
3950–4000 kHz
*60 Meters:
4750–5060 kHz [4600–5100 kHz] (Tropical Domestic Stations)

Strong Nighttime Reception

49 Meters:
5950–6200 kHz [5850–6250 kHz]
*41 Meters:
7100–7300 kHz [7100–7600 kHz]

Strong Night and Day Reception

31 Meters:
9500–9775 kHz [9300–9995 kHz]
25 Meters:
11700–11975 kHz [11500–12100 kHz]

Strong Daytime Reception

*22 Meters:
[13600–13800 kHz]
19 Meters:
15100–15450 kHz [15005–15700 kHz]
16 Meters:
17700–17900 kHz [17500–17900 kHz]
13 Meters:
21450–21750 kHz [21450–21850 kHz]

Fair Daytime Reception

11 Meters:
25670–26100 kHz**
World Time. *See* UTC.
WS. World Service.

---

*Shared with other radio services, such as "utility" stations and "hams."
**Provides interference-free reception briefly many days.

Directory of Advertisers